The Literatures of the World
in English Translation

THE LITERATURES OF THE WORLD
IN ENGLISH TRANSLATION
A Bibliography

VOLUME I   THE GREEK AND LATIN LITERATURES
Edited by George B. Parks and Ruth Z. Temple

VOLUME II   THE SLAVIC LITERATURES
Compiled by Richard C. Lewanski
assisted by Lucia G. Lewanski and Maya Deriugin

VOLUME III THE ROMANCE LITERATURES
Edited by George B. Parks and Ruth Z. Temple

PART 1   CATALAN, ITALIAN, PORTUGUESE AND BRAZILIAN, PROVENÇAL,
RUMANIAN, SPANISH AND SPANISH AMERICAN LITERATURES

PART 2   FRENCH LITERATURE

VOLUME IV THE CELTIC, GERMANIC,
AND OTHER LITERATURES OF EUROPE

VOLUME V   THE LITERATURES OF ASIA AND AFRICA

The Literatures of the World in English Translation

A Bibliography

Editors

GEORGE B. PARKS *and* **RUTH Z. TEMPLE**

Volume III

THE ROMANCE
LITERATURES

PART 1   CATALAN,

ITALIAN,

PORTUGUESE AND BRAZILIAN,

PROVENÇAL,

RUMANIAN,

SPANISH AND SPANISH AMERICAN

FREDERICK UNGAR PUBLISHING CO.

New York

Copyright © 1970 by Frederick Ungar Publishing Co., Inc.
Printed in the United States of America
Library of Congress Card Catalog Number: 70-98341
ISBN 0-8044-3239-2

CONTENTS

CONTRIBUTORS

THEODORE ANDRICA   RUMANIAN
    The Cleveland Press

VICTOR ANGELESCU   RUMANIAN
    Professor and Chairman of Language and Literature
    Lawrence Institute of Technology, Southfield, Michigan

WILLIAM BERRIEN   PORTUGUESE AND BRAZILIAN
    Late Professor of Romance Languages and Literatures
    University of Southern California

ANNA E. DOUGHERTY   BIBLIOGRAPHIES OF TRANSLATIONS
    Assistant Librarian
    National Institutes of Health Library, Washington

JOHN MORTON FEIN   BRAZILIAN
    Professor of Romance Languages
    Duke University

JOSEPH GUERIN FUCILLA   ITALIAN
    Professor of Romance Languages
    Northwestern University
    Editor of *Italica*

ALFRED HOWER   PORTUGUESE
    Professor of Spanish and Portuguese
    University of Florida

MURIEL J. HUGHES   COLLECTIONS OF TRANSLATIONS
    Professor of English
    University of Vermont

WILLIS KNAPP JONES   SPANISH AMERICAN
     Professor Emeritus of Romance Languages
     Miami University, Ohio

CHARLTON GRANT LAIRD   HISTORY AND THEORY OF TRANSLATION,
                        COLLECTIVE HISTORIES OF LITERATURE
     Professor of English
     University of Nevada

GERALD M. MOSER   PORTUGUESE
     Professor of Spanish and Portuguese
     Pennsylvanian State University

REMIGIO UGO PANE   SPANISH
     Professor and Chairman of Romance Languages
     Rutgers, The State University of New Jersey

THOMAS A. PERRY   RUMANIAN
     Professor of English
     East Texas State University
     sometime Fulbright Lecturer, *University of Bucarest*

ALPHONSE VICTOR ROCHE   PROVENÇAL (CONSULTANT)
     Professor of Romance Languages
     Northwestern University and University of Arizona

RUTH ZABRISKIE TEMPLE   BIBLIOGRAPHIES OF TRANSLATIONS,
                        COLLECTIONS OF TRANSLATIONS
     Professor of English
     Brooklyn College of the City University of New York

BENJAMIN M. WOODBRIDGE, JR.   PORTUGUESE AND BRAZILIAN
     Associate Professor of Spanish and Portuguese
     University of California, Berkeley

MARION ALBERT ZEITLIN   PORTUGUESE
     Professor Emeritus of Spanish and Portuguese
     University of California, Los Angeles

PREFACE

We remind our readers that this bibliography was originated by a committee of the National Council of Teachers of English, and was and is intended especially for the use of professors and students of literature. It adds therefore to the translations from each literature a number of selected background works, especially histories and other useful studies of the people and their literature. Since teachers and students usually approach literature in terms of chronological periods, we group the translations and the ancillary studies by periods, believing that the index of authors at the end of each part will sufficiently locate a given author.

In a cooperative work of this kind some parts are more detailed than others. Among the Romance literatures, translations from Spanish have been, for example, given special attention in the past, and we are fortunate in having the continuing aid of Professor Pane, whose earlier bibliography was published in 1944. We have also derived great help from the several bibliographies of translations from Spanish American literature which go back to the early days of the Pan American Union, and which the veteran competence of Professor Jones has drawn upon. Our bibliographies of translations from the other languages have generally been done virtually *de novo*, except for the medieval portions, for which we can draw upon the help of the indispensable Farrar and Evans. While we have aimed at completeness, we have not always been able to list brief items from collections and periodicals.

To all our friends and helpers in this volume dealing with the Romance literatures the editors express their gratitude.

In Part 1, Professor Fucilla has throughout had charge of Italian, and Professor Pane of Spanish. Other contributors have been obliged to withdraw, and we have been fortunate in finding scholars to replace them. We list the original contributors to Portuguese and Brazilian, and now give our thanks to them, as we do to Professor Woodbridge for taking over. We give like thanks for Rumanian to Mr. Andrica, who began it, and now to Professors Angelescu and Perry. Our original contributor to Spanish American was the late Madaline W. Nichols, and we are grateful to Professor Jones for his full-scale renovation.

Provençal has further profited by the aid of Professor Roche. In our gratitude to all these friends, we still wish it understood that the editors take complete responsibility for the inevitable inadequacies of the volume, so much of which has not been done or even tried before.

The French section was originally designed, upon our much smaller initial scale, by Professors Henri Peyre of Yale University and Douglas M. Knight, then also of Yale; it was greatly enlarged by Professor Temple, and benefited by an addition made by Professor James R. Kreuzer, now of Lehman College of the City University of New York. It has now been fully redone by the editors in order to make it comprehensive, and our efforts have been supplemented by the contributions of Professor Friederich for Switzerland, M. Brucher for Belgium, and Professors Leland and Hare for Canada. We are grateful to our collaborators, and we give thanks also to Mr. E. Clark Stillman, former president of the Belgian-American Educational Foundation, for introducing M. Brucher to our company.

We may not omit our great indebtedness to our main printed sources of information: first the great British Museum Catalogue, which was completed just in time for our use; then the Library of Congress Catalogue, the United States Catalogue and the Cumulative Book Index, and the National Union Catalogue, all of which are needed to trace American publication; and the impressive annual Index Translationum published by UNESCO. Like the last work, we try always to note both British and American publication of each item.

We reprint the General Reference section from Volume I, somewhat expanded and updated, and thank its authors Professors Hughes and Laird and Miss Dougherty. We refer to Volume I of this series for a statement of the scope and plan of our work. In Volume III we have endeavored to bring the entries down to and including 1968.

George B. Parks
Ruth Z. Temple

ABBREVIATIONS

GENERAL

abr., abgd.	abridged
Amer.	American, America
assn	association
bibliog.	bibliography, bibliographical
bk	book
c.	century (with an ordinal numeral); *circa* (with a date)
ch., chapt.	chapter
comp.	compiled
cont.	continued, continuation
ed.	editor, edited by
edn	edition
enl.	enlarged
et al.	and others
et seq.	and following
facs.	facsimile
lib. or Lib.	library
LC	Library of Congress
fl.	flourished (with a date, fixing an author's lifetime)
incl.	includes, including
intro.	introduction (by)
ms, mss	manuscript, manuscripts
n.d.	no date (given)
n.p.	no place (given)
no., nr.	number
n.s.	new series
p., pp.	page, pages
Pr.	press
pr.	printed
pr. pr.	privately printed

pref.	preface by
pt.	part
pub.	published, publisher, publication
q.v., qq.v.	see the indicated item or items
repr.	reprinted: used for a new impression, a new issue, a new edition
retr.	re-translated
rev.	revised (by)
sec.	section
sel.	selected, selections
ser. or Ser.	series
s.v.	*sub verbo:* look under the word or name
tr.	translated by, translation, translator
Univ.	University
vol., vols.	volume, volumes

Note: An asterisk preceding a translation indicates that the translation is recommended.

A date within [ ] immediately following a title indicates date of publication of the original.

PUBLICATIONS, SERIES, SOCIETIES

BMC	British Museum Catalogue
BSL	Bohn's Standard Library
Bull.	Bulletin
CBEL	Cambridge Bibliography of English Literature (Cambridge Univ. Pr., 1940, and N.Y., Macmillan, 1941, 4 v. V. 1, 600–1660; v. 2, 1660–1800; v. 3, 1800–1900; v. 4, Index. Supplement, v. 5, 1957. Bibliographies of translations into English, v. 1, p. 799–822 [1500–1660]; v. 2, p. 757–814 [1660–1800])
CURC	Columbia University Records of Civilization (English translations of important medieval books)
EETS	Early English Text Society (London, 1864—). Two series of editions: OS, Ordinary Series (eds. of mss.); ES, Extra Series (eds. of books). Recent volumes are numbered in one series.
EL	Everyman's Library (London, Dent, and N.Y., Dutton, 1906—)

Great Books	Great Books of the Western World (Chicago, Encyclopaedia Britannica, 1952, 54 v.)
ML	Modern Library (N.Y., now published by Random House, 1925—)
MLA	Modern Language Association (of America)
NCTE	National Council of Teachers of English
New Amer. Lib.	New American Library (N.Y., 1946—, paperback)
Penguin	Penguin Books (Harmondsworth, England, and Baltimore, Md., 1935—, paperback)
PMLA	Publications of the Modern Language Association (New York, 1884—)
Proc.	Proceedings
S. C. M. Pr.	Student Christian Movement Press (London, 1929—)
S. P. C. K.	Society for Promoting Christian Knowledge (London, 1698—)
STC	Short-Title Catalogue of English Books 1485–1640 (London, 1926; a revision is in preparation)
Trans.	Transactions
WC	World's Classics (London and N.Y., Oxford University Press, 1901—)

GENERAL REFERENCE

History and Theory of Translation
CHARLTON G. LAIRD

Amos, Flora Ross. Early Theories of Translation. (Columbia Univ. diss.) N.Y., Columbia Univ. Pr., 1920. 184 pp.

Traces theories of translation as formulated by English writers through Pope, with emphasis on the 16th century. For the latter, see also W. Schwarz, *Modern Language Review*, vol. 40 (1945), pp. 289–99; and Paul Herbert Larwill, *La Théorie de la traduction au début de la renaissance (d'après les traductions imprimées en France entre 1427 et 1527)*, ([Munich diss.] Munich, C. Wolf, 1934, 64 pp.), especially the bibliography. For other developments, see Samuel K. Workman, *Fifteenth Century Translation as an influence on English Prose* (Princeton, N.J., Princeton Univ. Pr., 1940, 210 pp.); Eric Jacobsen, *Translation: A Traditional Craft* (Copenhagen, Gyldendal, 1958, 219 pp.), with special reference to Marlowe, including bibliography; William Frost, *Dryden and the Art of Translation* (Yale Studies in English 128, New Haven, Conn., Yale Univ. Pr., 1955, 100 pp.), with bibliographical footnotes; John W. Draper, "The Theory of Translation in the 18th Century," *Neophilologus*, vol. 6 (1921), pp. 241–54, with extensive bibliography.

Arrowsmith, William, and **Shattuck, Roger,** eds. The Craft and Context of Translation: A Symposium. Austin, Univ. of Texas Pr. for Humanities Research Center, 1961. 206 pp.
The first ten essays are lectures given at a University of Texas symposium on translation, November 1959.

Babel: International Journal of Translation. Fédération internationale des traducteurs (FIT), Paris. Ed. Bonn, 1955–63, Paris, 1964—, sponsored by UNESCO. A quarterly.
See Pierre-François Caillé, "Rapport sur *Babel*," in *Ten Years of Translation*, 1967, q.v. below, pp. 150–53. Articles in various languages on latest developments in translation as well as on the history of the trans-

lation of specific authors; reports of congresses and of the translation work of UNESCO; book reviews; annotated international bibliography of translation, including articles. See also *Translation Monthly* (vols. 1–4, Chicago, 1955–58: no more pub.); and for articles on and reviews of translations, and (since 1960) an annual bibliography of English translations published in the United States, *The Yearbook of Comparative and General Literature* (Chapel Hill, N.C., 1952–59; Bloomington, Ind., 1960—). The PMLA *Bibliography* from 1957 lists authors and articles on Translation, a sub-topic under General Language and Linguistics, then from 1962 under Themes and Types of Literature; Machine Translation, a sub-topic under Translation, remained under General Linguistics. Useful information is to be found in William W. Bower, *International Manual of Linguistics and Translators* (N.Y., Scarecrow Pr., 1949, 451 pp.) and *First Supplement* (ibid., 1961, 450 pp.).

Bates, E[rnest] S[tuart]. Modern Translation. London, Oxford Univ. Pr., 1936. 162 pp.

Theory and practice, with problems illustrated by citations of translations into English from European languages, mostly in verse. See also the same author's *Intertraffic: Studies in Translation* (London, Cape, 1943, 179 pp.), a survey of translations of poetry done in Italy and the Far and Near East; it has appendices with examples.

Bayerische Akademie der Schönen Künste, Munich. Die Kunst der Übersetzung. Munich, Oldenbourg, 1963. 205 pp. (Gestalt und Gedanke, 8).

Beede, Grace Lucile. Vergil and Aratus: A Study in the Art of Translation. (Univ. of Chicago diss.) Chicago, Univ. of Chicago Pr., 1936. 90 pp.
A study of the *Georgics* translated from the Greek of Aratus, revealing Virgil's techniques and devices for creating poetic effects.

Belloc, Hilaire. On Translation. (Taylorian Lecture, 1931). Oxford, Clarendon Pr., 1931. 44 pp.
Still a useful essay.

Blignières, Auguste le Barbier de. Essai sur Amyot et les traducteurs français au XVIe siècle. Paris, Durand, 1851. 464 pp.
Amyot's translations of the classics studied beside later French versions of the same works.

*Brower, Reuben A., ed. On Translation. (Harvard Studies in Comparative Literature, 23). Cambridge, Mass., Harvard Univ. Pr., 1959. xi, 297 pp.
> Contributions from eighteen distinguished scholars and translators, divided into: I. Translators and Translating; II. Approaches to the Problem; III. Critical Bibliography of Works on Translation. The last, chronological from 46 B.C. to 1958, by Bayard Quincy Morgan, mainly follows the Western cultural tradition, and is especially strong for recent years. Parts I and II deal with translations into English from the Bible, from Greek, Latin, French, German, and Russian, and with period differences in taste.

Cary, Edmond. La Traduction dans le monde moderne. Geneva, Librairie de l'Université, 1956. 196 pp.
> Systematic treatment of the whole subject, including translation of all kinds of material and use of machines.

Cary, Edmond, and Jumpelt, Rudolf Walter, eds. Quality in Translation: Proceedings of the Third Congress of the FIT (International Federation of Translators), Bad Godesberg, 1959. Oxford, Pergamon Pr., and N.Y., Macmillan, 1963. xxiii, 544 pp.

> One section on literary, one on scientific and technical translation. Many contributions, mostly short, by many hands, on theory and practice.

Catford, J[ohn] C[unnison]. A Linguistic Theory of Translation: An Essay in Applied Linguistics. (Language and Learning, 8) London, Oxford Univ. Pr., 1965. viii, 103 pp.

Cohen, J[ohn] M[ichael]. English Translators and Translations. (Bibliographical Series of Supplements to British Book News). London, pub. for British Council by Longmans, Green, 1962. 56 pp., ill.
> Excellent historical intro.; selected list of "best" translations of authors from Aeschylus to Proust.

Cowan, G[eorge] H[amilton]. Latin Translation, Principle to Practice. London, Macmillan, 1964, and N.Y., St. Martin's Pr., 1965. viii, 184 pp.

Etkind, Efim Grigor'evich. Poezia i perevod (Poetry and Translation). Moscow, Soviet Writers, 1963. 428 pp.

Fédération Internationale des Traducteurs. Rome, Associazione italiana dei traduttori ed interpreti, 1956—.

> Transactions of Premier Congrès mondial de la traduction; subsequent reports irregular.

*Fedorov, Andrei Venediktovich. Vvedenie v teoriju perevoda; lingvisticheskie problemy (Introduction to the Theory of Translation; Linguistic Problems). 2d ed. Moscow, Literature Publishing House, 1958. 370 pp.

> Historical sketch of Russian views on problems of translation, both linguistic and artistic, by the chief Russian specialist in translation. See also the report of a meeting (June 1961) at Leningrad University: *Teoriia i kritika perevoda* (Theory and Criticism of Translation), ed. B. A. Larin (Leningrad, Pubns. of Leningrad Univ., 1962, 166 pp.). For other east European studies of translation, see *O sztuce tłumaczenia* (On the Art of Translation), ed. Michal Rusinek (Breslau, Ossolínskich Publishing House, 1955, 559 pp.), containing 24 essays by various authors with English summaries at pp. 534–49; and Olgierd Weytasiewicz, *Wstep do teorii tłumaczenia* (History of the Theory of Translation) (Breslau, Ossolínskich Publishing House, 1957, 135 pp.), also with English summaries; Jiří Levý, *Ceské theorie překladu* (Czech Theories of Translation: Literature, Music, Science) (Prague, State Publishing House, 1957, 946 pp.), a history of Czech translation since the 16th century, with essays by translators and critics, and detailed international bibliography. See also this author's *Uměni překladu* (Art of Translation) (Prague, The Czech Writer, 1963, 283 pp.).

Fränzel, Walter Friedrich Artur. Geschichte des Übersetzens im 18. Jahrhundert. In Beiträge zur Kultur- und Universalgeschichte, ed. Karl Kamprecht, Heft 25. Leipzig, H. Voigtländer, 1914. viii, 233 pp.

Geschichte der Textüberlieferung der Antiken und Mittelalterlichen Literatur. Mit einem Vorwort von Martin Bodmer. Zürich, Atlantis, [1961–64]. 2 vols. ill.

> Vol. 1 by Herbert Hunger et al., ed. M. Meier; vol. 2 by Karl Langosch et al., ed. G. Ineichen et al.

Güttinger, Fritz. Zielsprache: Theorie und Technik des Übersetzens. Zürich, Manesse, 1963. 263 pp.

Haggard, J[ean] Villasana, assisted by **Malcolm Dallas McLean.** Handbook for Translators of Spanish Historical Documents. Austin, Univ. of
Texas, 1941. vii, 198 pp.

> A guide to procedure, with practical helps in special terms and paleo-
> graphical practice; extensive bibliography. For scientific material in
> Spanish, see Justo Garate, *Cultura biologica y arte de traducir* (Buenos
> Aires, Ekin., 1943, 284 pp.). For esthetic and linguistic problems in-
> volving Spanish, see Aron Benvenuto Terracini, *Conflictos de lenguas y de
> cultura* (Buenos Aires, Ediciones Imán, 1951, 229 pp.); Olaf Blixen,
> *La Traducción literaria y sus problemas* (Montevideo, Universidad de la
> República, Facultad de Humanidades y Ciencias, 1954, 72 pp.); Ronald
> M[axwell] Macandrew, *Translation from Spanish* (London, Black, 1936,
> xxii, 239 pp.). Rodolfo Lenz, *El Arte de la traducción* (Santiago, Chile,
> 1914), important but very rare.

Heck, Philip. Übersetzungsprobleme im frühen Mittelalter. Tübingen,
J. C. B. Mohr, 1931. 303 pp.

Italiaander, Rolf, ed. Übersetzen: Vorträge und Beiträge vom Inter-
nationalen Kongress literarischen Übersetzer in Hamburg 1963. Frankfurt,
Athenäum, 1965. 192 pp. paper.

Jacobsen, Eric. Translation: A Traditional Craft: An Introductory Sketch,
with a Study of Marlowe's *Elegies*. Classica et Mediaevalia, Dissertationes 6.
Copenhagen, Gyldendal, 1958. 219 pp.

Knox, R[onald] A[rbuthnot]. On English Translation. (Romanes Lecture,
Oxford University, 1957) Oxford, Clarendon Pr., 1957. 26 pp.

Larbaud, Valéry. Sous l'invocation de Saint Jérôme. Paris, Gallimard, 1946.
341 pp.

> Thorough discussion, including literary, cultural, philological, and tech-
> nical questions; richly illustrated with a wide range of citations.

*Matthiessen, F[rancis] O. Translation, An Elizabethan Art. Cambridge,
Mass., Harvard Univ. Pr., 1931. viii, 232 pp. Repr. N.Y., Octagon Books,
1965.

> The general qualities of the Elizabethan translator as revealed in the work
> of Hoby, North, Florio, and Holland; closely documented, with biblio-
> graphical notes.

Mounin, Georges. Les Problèmes théoriques de la traduction. Paris, Galli-mard, 1963. 296 pp.

> Historical and theoretical. Author calls it with justice a "défense et illustration de l'art de traduire." See also, a classic, the author's *Les Belles infidèles* (Paris, Cahiers du Sud, 1955, 159 pp.), and *La Machine à traduire, histoire des problèmes linguistiques* ([2d thesis, Paris 1963] The Hague, Mouton, 1964, 209 pp., charts).

Nida, Eugene Albert. Toward a Science of Translating, with Special Reference to Principles and Procedures Involved in Bible Translating. Leiden, Brill, 1964. x, 331 pp.

Oettinger, Anthony G. Automatic Language Translation: Lexical and Technical Aspects, with Particular Attention to Russian. (Harvard Monographs in Applied Science, 8). Cambridge, Mass., Harvard Univ. Pr., 1960. 380 pp.

> Perhaps the best general work now available; Joshua Whatmough in the foreword calls it "quite a remarkable baby." Bibliography. For a simpler treatment, see Emile Delavenay, *An Introduction to Machine Translation*, tr. Katharine M. Delavenay and the author from the French (pub. 1959) (N.Y., Praeger, and London, Thames and Hudson, 1960, 144 pp.). For a more technical treatment, see *Linguistic and Engineering Studies in the Automatic Translation of Scientific Russian into English*, Technical Report, Phase 2 (Seattle, Univ. of Washington Pr., 1960, 492 pp.), detailed bibliography by Irwin Reifler, pp. 35–65; see also *National Symposium on Machine Translation, Univ. of California, Los Angeles, 1960: Proceedings*, ed. H. P. Edmundson (Englewood Cliffs, N.J., 1961, xvii, 525 pp.); and *Proceedings of the 1961 International Conference on Machine Translation of Languages and Applied Language Analysis* (London, H.M. Stationery Office, 1962, 2 vols.). A very recent study is I[saak] I[osifovich] Revzin and V. Iu. Rozentsveig, *Osnovy ohshchego i machinnogo perevoda* (Fundamentals of General and Machine Translation) (Moscow, Vysshaia Shkola, 1964, 242 pp.). Books on this phase of translation are subject to early obsolescence, and bibliographies are now available. See Emile and Katharine Delavenay, *Bibliographie de la traduction automatique* (with English tr.), ('s-Gravenhage, Mouton, 1960, 69 pp.); *Literature on Information Retrieval and Machine Translation*, ed. Charles F. Balz and Richard H. Stanwood (White Plains, N.Y., International Business Machines Corporation, 1962, 117 pp.); Josephine L. Walkowitz, *A Bibliography of*

Foreign Developments in Machine Translation and Information Processing (Washington, D.C., U.S. Government Printing Office, 1963, ii, 191 pp.).

P. E. N. (World Association of Writers). Translation and Translations: A Round Table Discussion in Rome, Nov. 1–4, 1961. Reported by Ladislas Gare et al. London, International P. E. N., n.d. 179 pp.
General discussion of translation of various kinds; specific and practical discussion of problems and status of translators.

*Postgate, J[ohn] P[ercival]. Translation and Translations: Theory and Practice. London, Bell, 1922. xii, 206 pp.
Intensive study of problems in translating Greek and Latin verse into English. For the handling of classical hexameters and for general theory, see Matthew Arnold, *On Translating Homer* (1861–62), ed. with intro. and notes by W. H. D. Rouse (London, Murray, 1905, 200 pp.).

Richards, I[vor] A[rmstrong]. Mencius on the Mind: Experiments in Multiple Definition. London, Kegan Paul, 1932. 131, 44 pp.
Chapters 1 and 4 study puzzling linguistic situations of interest outside English-Chinese translation. See also Richards' "Toward a Theory of Translating," in *Studies in Chinese Thought*, ed. A[rthur] F[rederick] Wright et al. (Amer. Anthropological Assn Memoir no. 75, Chicago, 1953, pp. 247–61).

Ritchie, R[obert] L[indsay] Graeme. Translation from French. Cambridge University Pr., 1918. xii, 258 pp.

*Savory, Theodore Horace. The Art of Translation. London, Cape, 1957. 159 pp. Repr. Philadelphia, Dufour, 1960.
Bayard Quincy Morgan has called this "the best book on the subject in English."

Selver, Paul. The Art of Translating Poetry. London, John Baker, and Boston, The Writer, 1966. 122 pp.

Stoerig, Hans Joachim. Das Problem des Übersetzens. Stuttgart, Goverts, 1963. xxviii, 488 pp.

Studies in Communication 2: Aspects of Translation. (The Communications Research Center, University College, London). London, Secker, 1958. viii, 145 pp.

Includes Leonard Foster, "Translation: An Introduction"; L. W. Tancock, "Some Problems of Style in Translations from the French"; D. J. Furley, "Translation from Greek Philosophy"; A. D. Booth, "The History and Recent Progress of Machine Translation"; C. Rabin, "The Linguistics of Translation."

Teele, Roy Earl. Through a Glass Darkly: A Study of English Translations of Chinese Poetry. (Columbia Univ. diss.). Ann Arbor, Mich., n. pub., 1949. xi, 173 pp.

Ten Years of Translation: Proceedings of the Fourth Congress of the International Federation of Translators (FIT), Dubrovnik, 1963, Held in Celebration of the Tenth Anniversary of the Federation. Ed. I. J. Citroen. Oxford and N.Y., Pergamon Pr., 1967. xxi, 398 pp.

Tytler, Alexander (Fraser), [Lord Woodhouselee]. Essays on the Principles of Translation. London, 1791. 3d edn rev. enl., 1813, repr. EL, 1907, xiv, 239 pp.
Still a standard work, largely directed to Greek and Latin, but includes discussion of various genres, languages, and individual works.

Weijnen, Antonius Angelus. De Kunst van het Vertalen. Tilburg, W. Bergmans, 1946. Repr. 1947, 144 pp.
Scholarly consideration of divesre special cases.

Widmer, Walter. Fug and Unfug des Übersetzens. Cologne, Küpenheuer und Witsch, 1959. 167 pp.

Collective Bibliographies of Translation into English[†]

ANNA E. DOUGHERTY
AND RUTH Z. TEMPLE

American Scandinavian Foundation. A List of Books by Scandinavians and about Scandinavia. 4th ed. rev. N.Y. ASF, 1946. 37 pp.
> Includes selected bibliography of Scandinavian literature in translation: alphabetical by author.

Baker, Ernest A[lbert], and **Packman, James.** A Guide to the Best Fiction, English and American, Including Translations from Foreign Languages. [1903]. New enl. ed. N.Y., Macmillan, and London, Routledge, 1932. viii, 634 pp. Repr. N.Y., Barnes and Noble, 1967.
> Lists selected tr. from various languages, by country and by period, with descriptive and analytical annotations of some. Selected critical bibliography for some items.

Block, Andrew. The English Novel, 1740–1850: A Catalogue Including Prose Romances, Short Stories, and Translations of Foreign Fiction. Intro. John Crow and Ernest A. Baker. [1939] 2d ed. rev. London, Dawson's, 1961. xv, 349 pp. Repr. London, Dawson's, and Dobbs Ferry, N.Y., Oceana, 1967.
> Gives all data from title page; alphabetical by author, including foreign authors. Index of titles.

Cambridge Bibliography of English Literature. Ed. F. W. Bateson, Cambridge Univ. Pr., and N.Y., Macmillan, 1941. 4 vols., Supplement, vol. 5, 1957.
> In vol. 1, for the period 1500–1660, and vol. 2, for the period 1660–1800, is a section, Translations into English (vol. 1, pp. 799–822; vol. 2, pp. 757–814). Each vol. has also a section, Literary Relations with the Continent, which lists many trs. (vol. 1, pp. 325–345; vol. 2, pp. 31–71), and vol. 2 includes a section of Translations of Foreign Literary Criticism

---

[†] This list includes only bibliographies which, because they include translations from more than one language, are not listed in a language section or in more than one section.

(pp. 27–30). Each vol. includes also a section, under Prose Fiction, of Translations into English (vol. 1, pp. 732–36; vol. 2, pp. 532–35, 540–43, 551–53).

The work is now being redone as New CBEL, ed. George Watson.

Classics of the Western World. Ed. Alan Willard Brown et al. [1st ed. 1927, ed. J. Bartlett Brebner] 3rd ed. rev. Chicago, American Library Association, 1943. 145 pp.

Recommended and supplementary readings in major authors. Trs. listed in order of availability and excellence, or, in some cases, by names of translators alphabetically. From the Bible and Homer to Proust. Critical works on authors and texts.

*Emeneau, M[urray] B[arnson], comp. A Union List of Printed Indic Texts and Translations in American Libraries. Amer. Oriental Ser. 7. New Haven, Conn., Amer. Oriental Soc., 1935, 540 pp.

Includes all books in Sanskrit, Pali, Prakit, and Apabhramsa, and most of the books in the older stages of the vernacular.

Emrys, Sir William, ed. The Reader's Guide: A Guide and Companion for the General Reader, Penguin, 1960. 351 pp.

I, Introduction includes pp. 97–107, a note on the practice of English translation of the classics from the beginning, by E. V. Rieu (ed. of Penguin Classics from their beginning in 1945, and tr. of *Odyssey* and *Iliad*); II, A Guide to the Reading List (comment on the various translations); III, A Reading List (British publications, including Penguin, of English tr. of classics) by genre.

*Farrar, Clarissa P., and **Evans, Austin P.** Bibliography of English Translations from Medieval Sources. Records of Civilization, 39. N.Y., Columbia Univ. Pr., 1946. xiii, 534 pp.

Comprehensive listing of works to 1500 in English translation. Alphabetical by author. A supplement is in preparation.

The Fiction Catalog: The Standard Catalog Series. [1908] 7th ed. N.Y., Wilson, 1961 and supplements. 650 pp.

Under author translated, a selection of trs. with first as well as later editions listed and excerpts from reviews. Only the most read authors included and, of course, only fiction, but so far useful, and kept up to date.

Grimm, Minerva E[thel], comp. Translations of Foreign Novels: A Selected List. Boston, Boston Book Co., 1917. 84 pp.

> Of very limited usefulness because so selective (e.g., 1 from Flemish, 1 from Greek), but full bibliographical information is provided.

Harris, William J[ames]. The First Printed Translations into English of the Great Foreign Classics: A Supplement to Text-Books of English Literature. N.Y., Dutton, and London, Routledge, 1909. vii, 209 pp.

> Alphabetical by author, from the beginning. Only translator's name and date of translation given. Index of titles.

Hatzfeld, Helmut. A Critical Bibliography of the New Stylistics Applied to the Romance Literatures 1900–1952. See French Literature, General, Bibliographies, and continuation for 1955–60.

Hopper, Vincent F[oster], and **Grebanier, Bernard D.M.** Bibliography of European Literature. N.Y., Barron's Educational Series, 1954. xiii, 158 pp.

> A list of standard translations of European classics from the beginning, with a selected list of standard studies of the works and authors.

***Index Translationum: Repertoire International des Traductions.** Nos. 1–31 (July, 1932–Jan. 1940). Paris, Société des nations, Institut international de coopération intellectuelle; New Series, 1— (1948—). Paris, UNESCO, 1949—.

> All languages covered. Quarterly, 1932–40; annual, 1948—. Suspended Feb. 1940–47. Indispensable.

The Reader's Adviser: An Annotated Guide to the Best in Print in Literature, . . . Translations, . . . Ed. Hester R. Hoffmann. [1921 and through 8th ed. as Bookman's Manual] 10th ed. rev. enl. N.Y., Bowker, 1964. xxii, 1292 pp.

> Annotated bibliography by subject. Includes Classical drama; modern drama; Greek and Roman classics in translation; French: authors, history, and criticism, recent collections; Germanic, Russian; other foreign literatures: Africa to Yugoslavia; books on translation, bibliography, collections, translations. Selective lists but strong on recent paperback editions.

***Smith, F. Seymour.** The Classics in Translation. London and N.Y., Scribner, 1930. 307 pp. Repr. N.Y., B. Franklin, 1968.

Annotated guide to preferred translations, mostly modern, of many Greek and Latin works. Alphabetical by author.

Solberg, Thorvald. Bibliography of Scandinavia: A Catalogue of the Important Books in the English Language Relating to the Scandinavian Countries. In Frederick Winkel Horn, History of the Literature of the Scandinavian North. Chicago, Griggs, 1884, pp. 413–500.
Includes English translations, alphabetically by author and translator.

Tatum, George Marvin. Translations from European Literature Published in One Hundred and Eight American Little Magazines 1909–1959. Chapel Hill, North Carolina, 1960 (Univ. of Kentucky Pr. microcards). 397 leaves.

Translations Currently Available in Inexpensive Editions. Comp. B. Q. Morgan. N.Y., MLA, 1955. 16 leaves.

The Yearbook of Comparative and General Literature. 1952— (1952–1960, Chapel Hill, Univ. of North Carolina Pr.; 1960—, Bloomington, Univ. of Indiana Pr.).
From 1960 this annual has carried a list of English translations for the year published in the U.S.

Collective Histories of Literature†

CHARLTON G. LAIRD

Aarne, Antti. The Types of the Folktale: A Classification and Bibliography. Tr. and enl. Stith Thompson. Finnish Folklore Communications, 184. Helsinki, 1961. 588 pp.

---

† Many so-called histories of world literature merely reduce and combine histories of various particular literatures. As such books are obviously inferior to histories of the several literatures, there is no point in listing them. This list is selective, and notes samples of the various kinds of books useful for a general view of literature, including studies of a movement or period in several literatures, but excluding theory of comparative literature.

For the themes of folktales, this should be used with Thompson's *Motif-Index of Folk-Literature* (Bloomington, Indiana Univ. Pr., rev. ed., 1955–58, 5 vols.).

Algemene Literatur Geschiedenis: Geschiedenis van de belangrijkste Figuren en Stromingen in de Wereldliteratur. Ed. F. de Backer and others. Utrecht, W. De Haan, 1943–55. 5 vols. plus register.
   Strong in Mediterranean and Western European cultures; no east Asian. Selective bibliographies.

Auerbach, Erich. Introduction to Romance Languages and Literature: Latin, French, Spanish, Provençal, Italian. [Original German ed., 1949]. Tr. Guy Daniels from French. N.Y., Capricorn Books, 1961. 291 pp. paper.
   From the Roman colonization to Proust. Necessarily brief; writers considered are relatively few, but treatment of them is critical, and the idea of Romance Literature is pursued throughout. Excellent brief bibliography of linguistics and literature, including periodicals.

Cassell's Encyclopedia of Literature. London, Cassell, 1953, and N.Y., Funk and Wagnalls (as Cassell's Encyclopedia of World Literature), 1954. 2 vols.
   Largely biographical.

Chadwick, H[ector] Munro, and **Kershaw, N[ora].** The Growth of Literature. Cambridge Univ. Pr., 1934–40. 3 vols.
   Vol. 1: The Ancient Literatures of Europe; vol. 2: Russian Oral Literature, Yugoslav Oral Poetry, Early Indian Literature, Early Hebrew Literature; vol. 3: The Oral Literature of the Tatars, The Oral Literature of Polynesia and a Note on the Oral Literature of the Sea Dyaks of North Borneo, Notes on the Oral Literature of Some African Peoples. Pt. 4, A General Survey, examines various types of literature in their rise and development (e.g., heroic, theological, gnomic, and descriptive); connections of written with oral literature; problems of authorship.

*Cohen, J[ohn] M[ichael]. A History of Western Literature. Penguin, 1956. Repr. rev. London, Cassell, 1961, 381 pp.
   From the 12th century to the present, excluding English and American and writings in Latin. A history of western literature as a "single expanding tradition." Highly selective; emphasizing ideas, not facts, and also international relationships.

————Poetry of this Age: 1908–65. [1960] London, Hutchinson Univ. Lib., 1966. 256 pp. cloth and paper.

    Considers connections in theme and technique between poetry of various languages. Includes, besides English and American, Alberti, Aleixandre, Campana, Eluard, George, Guillén, Jiménez, Lorca, Machado, Mayakovsky, Montale, Molinari, Neruda, Pasternak, Paz, Quasimodo, Rilke, Valéry.

The Columbia Dictionary of Modern European Literature. Ed. Horatio Smith. N.Y., Columbia Univ. Pr., 1947. xiv, 899 pp.

    Survey articles and biographies, with bibliography, by a number of specialists. Thirty-one European literatures from 1870.

Commission Internationale d'histoire littéraire moderne. Répertoire chronologique des littératures modernes. Directed by Paul Van Tieghem. Paris, Droz, 1935. 145 pp. (issued in parts, 1935–37).

    A chronological list, giving for each year from 1455 to 1900 the principal literary works of that year in European, English, and American literatures. Less detailed but more nearly comprehensive is Adolf Spemann, *Vergleichende Zeittafel der Weltliteratur von Mittelalter bis Neuzeit (1150–1939)* (Stuttgart, Engelehornverlag, 1951, 160 pp.).

The Concise Encyclopedia of Modern World Literature. Ed. Geoffrey Grigson. London, Hutchinson, 1963. 512 pp. ill.

    Biographical and critical (indeed often dogmatic) articles, with photographs of authors. Articles not signed, though contributors are listed. Limited in scope (160 authors).

Diaz-Plaja, Guillermo. La literatura universal. Pref. Angel Valbuena Prat. Barcelona, Ediciones Danae, 1965. 576 pp.

Dictionnaire de littérature contemporaine, 1960–64. Ed. Pierre de Boisdeffre. 2d edn, Paris, Edns universitaires, 1964. 687 pp.

    Short biographical and critical articles on authors, including their bibliography by genre and date.

Dictionnaire des littératures. Dir. Philippe Van Tieghem, avec la collaboration de Pierre Josserand. Paris, Presses universitaires de France, 1968. 3 vols.

*Dizionario letterario Bompiani degli autori di tutti i tempi e di tutte le letterature. Milan, Bompiani, 1951–57, 9 vols. ill.

Highly factual and relatively comprehensive, treating all periods and literatures, including the Oriental, and thus, in spite of some Romanic and religious bias, perhaps the most satisfactory of the world literary dictionaries. Vol. 9 contains a comparative table and elaborate indexes, with titles in the original languages. Lavish illustrations.

Enciclopedia dello spectacolo. Ed. Salvio D'Amico and others. Rome, Casa Editrice Le Maschere, 1954–62. 9 vols.

Encyclopedic treatment of spectacle, including drama and modern mass media. Western emphasis, but with some attention to Slavic and Oriental drama. Sumptuously illustrated.

Encyclopedia of Literature. Ed. Joseph T. Shipley. N.Y., Philosophical Library, 1946. 2 vols.

Brief articles varying in quality on numerous literatures, from Accadian to Yugoslav.

*Encyclopedia of Poetry and Poetics. Ed. Alex Preminger et al. Princeton, N.J., Princeton Univ. Pr., 1965. 906 pp.

Standard, relatively long, scholarly and philosophical articles, many signed, and some with bibliographies. Treats periods, genres, and schools, but neither individual authors nor works.

*Encyclopedia of World Literature in the 20th Century. Ed. Wolfgang Bernard Fleischmann. N.Y., Ungar, 1965—. Vols. 1, 2—.

Revision of Herder's *Lexikon der Weltliteratur im 20. Jahrhundert*. Promised in three volumes, to include surveys of all national literatures, treatments of representative authors, genres, and movements, and "comprehensive record of English translations."

Eppelsheimer, Hanns W. Handbuch der Weltliteratur, von den Anfängen bis zur Gegenwart. [1947–50]. 3rd ed. rev., Frankfurt-am-Main, Klostermann, 1960. xiv, 808 pp.

Really a bibliography. Studies of men and movements, arranged by literature and by period; two or three sentences on each author. The first ed. includes the literatures of Asia, the later has European only, including English and North American.

Ford, Ford Madox. The March of Literature from Confucius' Day to Our Own. N.Y., Dial Pr., 1938, and London, Allen and Unwin, 1939. vii, 878 pp.

> Emphasis on Europe, and, within that, on England. By a writer, not a scholar. Lacks scholarly apparatus, though it has index of names and titles, and makes no attempt to surmount personal preferences. Never-thelesss, it is readable, and includes many quotations (in translation).

*Friederich, Werner P., and **Malone, David Henry.** Outline of Comparative Literature from Dante Alighieri to Eugene O'Neill. Chapel Hill, University of North Carolina Pr., 1954. 451 pp.

> Excellent within its area and purpose, to trace the "flow of forms and ideas across national borders and the dissemination of cultural values." Arranged by conventional periods and by countries within periods. Brief mention of many works; some broad observations.

*Guérard, Albert. Preface to World Literature. N.Y., Holt, 1940. xv, 536 pp. For students. An excellent introduction to the principles and practice of literary study, with wide-ranging examples. Appendix: bibliography and list of world masterpieces; a critic's glossary.

Hallam, Henry. Introduction to the Literature of Europe in the Fifteenth-Sixteenth, and Seventeenth Centuries. [1842]. 4th ed. rev. N.Y., Arm, strong, 1887. 4 vols. in 2.

> A serious attempt to write world history of literature. The preface (1842) traces the development of writing on world literature, mentioning the most important books.

Handbuch der Literaturwissenschaft. Ed. Oskar Walzel. Berlin (later Potsdam), Akademische Verlagsgesellschaft Athenaion, 1923–36. 23 vols. ill.

> V. 1. Bernard Fehr. Englische Literatur (19th–20th c.). 1923. 524 pp.
> V. 2. Hanns Heiss et al. Romanische Literaturen (19th–20th c.). 1925–36 (3 parts). 834, 273, 158 pp.
> V. 3. Andreas Heusler. Altgermanische Dichtung. 1923. 200 pp.
> V. 4. Oskar Walzel. Gehalt und Gestalt im Kunstwerk des Dichters. 1923. 408 pp.
> V. 5. Erich Bethe. Griechische Dichtung. 1924. 382 pp.
> V. 6. Victor Klemperer. Romanische Literaturen von der Renaissance bis zur französischen Revolution. 1924. 419 pp.

V. 7. Helmuth von Glasenapp. Literaturen Indiens. 1929. 340 pp.

V. 8. Alfred Kappelmacher and Moriz Schuster. Literatur der Römer. 1934. 485 pp. (to Charlemagne).

V. 9. Richard Wilhelm. Chinesische Literatur. 1926. 200 pp.

V. 10. Wilhelm Gundert. Japanische Literatur. 1929. 136 pp.

V. 11. Hans Hecht and L. L. Schücking. Englische Literatur des Mittelalters. 1927. 191 pp.

V. 12. Günther Müller. Deutsche Dichtung von der Renaissance zum Ausgang des Barock. 1927. 262 pp.

V. 13. Max Pieper. Ägyptische Literatur. 1927. 102 pp.

V. 14. Bruno Meissner. Babylonisch-Assyrische Literatur. 1927. 103 pp.

V. 15. Wolfgang Keller and Bernard Fehr. Englische Literatur von der Renaissance zur Aufklärung. 1928. 283 pp.

V. 16. Walther Fischer. Literatur der Vereinigten Staaten. 1929. 133 pp.

V. 17. P. N. Sakulin. Russische Literatur. 1927. 259 pp. Julius Klein. Polnische Literatur. 1929. 114 pp.

V. 18. Arne Novak. Tschechische Literatur. 1930. 114 pp. Gerhard Geseman. Serbo-Kroatische Literatur. 1931. 47 pp.

V. 19. Oskar Walzel. Deutsche Dichtung von Gottsched bis zur Gegenwart. 1927–30 (2 parts). 369, 395 pp.

V. 20. Leonardo Olschki. Romanische Literaturen des Mittelalters. 1928. 260 pp.

V. 21. Johann Hempel. Alt-Hebräische Literatur. 1930. 203 pp.

V. 22. Hilmer Borelius. Nordische Literaturen. 1931. 170 pp.

V. 23. Julius Schwietering. Deutsche Dichtung des Mittelalters. 1932. 311 pp.

In spite of its title, more a series of histories of literature (left uncompleted) than a handbook, treating some bodies of writing by area or traditions (e.g., Romance, Hellenic, Scandinavian), some by language or nation (e.g., England, Germany). Especially valuable for areas often neglected (e.g., eastern and southeastern Europe, Babylonian-Assyrian), but modern Asiatic, African, and Latin American literatures not yet reached. Germanic bias; excellent illustrations.

*Histoire des littératures. Directed by Raymond Queneau. Encyclopédie de la Pléiade. Paris, Gallimard, 1955–58. 3 vols. maps.

As the title indicates, this is a collection of histories of literature. It is, however, extremely thorough and up-to-date, and thus warrants inclusion. Sections are by specialists. The preface to each volume, by Raymond Queneau, discusses principles of organization. Each article includes bibliography; each volume has an index of names (with dates and brief identification) and a glossary of literary genres. Vol. 1: Ancient, Eastern, and Oral Literatures; vol. 2: Western Literatures except French; vol. 3: French Literature, including the literatures of areas of strong French influence or colonization. Also chronological tables of world literary events divided into Orient, Occident, and France; table of literary movements; alphabetical table of literatures.

Hopper, Vincent F., and **Grebanier, Bernard D. M.** Essentials of European Literature. Brooklyn, N.Y., Barron's Educational Series, 1952. 2 vols.
  A guide to great books. Brief historical introduction to periods and movements of European literatures; description and appraisal of selected major authors, analysis of selected great books. Vol. 1: from the early Christian writers through the 18th c.; vol. 2: the 19th c.

Kindlers Literatur Lexikon. Ed. Wolfgang Einsiedel, et al. Zürich, Kindler, 1965— (in progress).

Kroeber, A[rthur] L. Configurations of Culture Growth. Berkeley and Los Angeles, Univ. of California Pr., 1944. 882 pp.
  Literature studied broadly in the context of society: see especially pp. 409–623. Includes areas often neglected.

Moulton, Richard G[reen]. World Literature and Its Place in General Culture. N.Y., Macmillan, 1911. ix, 502 pp.
  Useful introduction, though only a survey. Argues for the unity of literature as a concept. Emphasis on certain great authors, books, and genres.

Prampolini, Giacomo. Storia universale della Letteratura. Turin, U.T.E.T., 1933–38. 3 vols. in 5 (vol. 3 has 3 pts., each a vol.).
  Competent and well-balanced, factual and historical, with emphasis on continuity, though each literature is treated separately. Literature is correlated with art, philosophy, history. A good book to read. From the earliest written Chinese to the present. Alphabetical index of authors and works in each volume. Bibliography for each section includes list of trs. of literary works into the various European languages.

The Reader's Companion to World Literature. Ed. Lillian Herlands Hornstein. General ed. Calvin S. Brown. N.Y., Dryden Pr., 1956. 493 pp.

Like the Oxford ''Companions,'' this has dictionary listing of great and minor authors, titles, literary forms.

The Reader's Encyclopedia: An Encyclopedia of World Literature and the Arts. 2d ed. N.Y., Crowell, 1967. 2 vols.

> Comprehensive collection of brief articles treating writers, titles, literary terms, characters, schools, movements, etc. Strong North American-Western European emphasis of the first edn somewhat reduced. For a briefer but better balanced work, see the preceding item.

Der Romanführer. Ed. Wilhelm Olbrich. Stuttgart, Hiersmann, 1950–56. 6 vols.

> Standard guide to the novel; comprehensive and capable. Includes bibliographies, summaries, some criticism.

Saintsbury, George. A History of Criticism and Literary Taste in Europe from the Earliest Texts to the Present Day. [1901–3] 5th edn Edinburgh and London, Blackwood, 1929–34. 3 vols.

> Vol. 1, Classical and medieval criticism; vol. 2, From the Renaissance to the Decline of Eighteenth Century Orthodoxy; vol. 3, Modern criticism.

Scott-James, R[olfe] A. The Making of Literature: Some Principles of Criticism Examined in the Light of Ancient and Modern Theory. 2d edn N.Y., Holt, 1930. 396 pp.

> Central problems of the art of literature in western Europe from the Greeks to the moderns (e.g., Croce and Pirandello), ''as they have presented themselves to men experienced in the arts.''

Van Tieghem, Paul. Outlines of the Literary History of Europe since the Renaissance. Tr. Aimee Leffingwell McKenzie. N.Y., Century, 1930. xvi, 361 pp.

> French original, 1925. By genre rather than by country. Facts, dates, continuity to about 1900. See also this author's *Précis d'histoire littéraire de l'Europe depuis la Renaissance* (Paris, Alcan, 1925, vii, 352 pp.); his massive and classic works, *Le Préromantisme: études d'histoire littéraire européenne* (Paris, Rieder, 1921, 1930, 1945, 3 vols.) and (vol. 4) *Le Sentiment de la nature dans le préromantisme* (Paris, Nizet, 1960, 275 pp.); also *Le Romantisme dans la littérature européenne* (Paris, Michel, 1948, xxv, 560 pp.).

Wellek, René. A History of Modern Criticism, 1750–1950. New Haven, Conn., and London, Yale Univ. Pr., 1955— (4 vols., 5 projected).

Vol. 1, The Later Eighteenth Century (1955); vol. 2, The Romantic Age (1955); vol. 3, The Age of Transition (1965); vol. 4, The Later Nineteenth Century (1965).

Wilpert, Gero von, ed. Lexikon der Weltliteratur: Biographisch-biblio-graphisches Handwörterbuch nach Autoren und anonymen Werken. Stuttgart, Kröner, 1963. 1471 pp.

Yearbook of Comparative and General Literature. Chapel Hill, N.C., 1952–60; Bloomington, Ind., 1961—.

Articles on general literature; short reviews of works on world literature; annual bibliography since 1960 of trs. published in the United States; annual bibliography: "Literary Currents"; "Literary and Semi-literary Genres and Forms," which brings up to date Fernand Baldensperger and Werner P. Friederich, *Bibliography of Comparative Literature* (Chapel Hill, Univ. of North Carolina Studies in Comparative Literature, 1950, xxiv, 701 pp.).

See also *Books Abroad, An International Literary Quarterly* (Norman, Okla., Univ. of Oklahoma, 1927—), for surveys of various literatures (including since 1961 Asian, African, and Slavic) for recent years; for short reviews of important books in all languages; for annual lists of the outstanding books of the year by country (annual index with—not in—winter issue).
See also *Helicon: Revue internationale des problèmes généraux de la littérature*, directed by Janós Hankiss (Amsterdam, *Eds. académiques Panthéon*, 1938–43, vols. 1–5, no more pub.), for articles in five European languages.

Collections of translations
from several languages†

MURIEL J. HUGHES
AND RUTH Z. TEMPLE

Adventures in World Literature. Ed. R[ewey] B[elle] Inglis and M. K. Stewart. [1936] N.Y., Harcourt, Brace, 1946. xix, 1268 pp. ill.
> Pt. 1, European literature; pt. 2, Greek and Roman classic literature; pt. 3, Oriental literature. Biographies of authors.

*An Anthology of Medieval Lyrics. Ed. Angel Flores. ML, 1962. 472 pp.
> Poems from Provence, Northern France, Italy, Germany, the Iberian Peninsula. An excellent collection, with notes and biographical sketches.

An Anthology of World Literature. Ed. Philo M[elvin] Buck, Jr. and Hazel Stewart Alberson. [1934] Rev. ed. N.Y., Macmillan, 1940. xiii, 1146 pp.
> European literature from Homer through the 19th c.; Oriental literature from India, Egypt, Arabia, Persia and Palestine.

*An Anthology of World Poetry. Ed. Mark Van Doren. [1928] Rev. enl. N.Y., Halcyon, 1939. lxii, 1467 pp.
> World poetry, including Oriental, from 35 B.C. to the present day; notable among one-volume anthologies for its critical discrimination in selections and translations, the latter by, for example, Chaucer, Herrick, Pope, Swinburne, Rossetti, Symons, Dowson. Index of translators. *The World's Best Poems*, ed. Mark Van Doren and Garibaldi M. Lapolla ([1929] Cleveland, Ohio, and N.Y., World, 1946, xv, xxi–xlv, 672 pp.) is a smaller collection taken from this. It includes 750 poems from the same 19 languages including Gaelic, Old Norse, Sanskrit.

---

† Collections of translations from one language only will appear in the appropriate language section. Included in this section are various kinds of collections for the general reader and the small library as well as for the student, but only those which have some merit and, with a very few exceptions, only those published in the twentieth century.

An Anthology of World Prose. Ed. Carl Van Doren. [1935] N.Y., Halcyon, 1939. vii–xxvi, 1582 pp.

    Contains material not available in other common anthologies, notably for the Orient. Translators such as Dryden, Shelley, Carlyle.

Baring, Maurice. Have You Anything to Declare? A Note Book with Commentaries. N.Y., Knopf, 1937. 326 pp.

    Short annotated quotations that have pleased the author, from Greek, Latin, German, Italian, French, and Russian, as well as English. Translations are supplied, some standard, some by Baring or friends of his, for all but most of the French.

The Best of the World's Classics, Restricted to Prose. Ed. Henry Cabot Lodge; assoc. ed. F[rancis] W. Halsey. N.Y. and London, Funk and Wagnalls, 1909. 10 vols.

    Six of the small vols. denoted to English and American literature; the other four include Greece, Rome, and Continental Europe: very short selections.

The Book of Oriental Literature. Ed. Ikbāl ʿAlī Shāh. N.Y., Garden City Pub., 1938, and London, Low, Marston, 1937 (as The Coronation Book of Oriental Literature). xii, 404 pp.

    Arranged by countries: Afghanistan to Turkey.

*Century Readings in Ancient Classical and Modern European Literature. Ed. John W[illiam] Cunliffe and Grant Showerman. N.Y., Century, 1925, 2 vols in 1. xx, 614; v, 543 pp.

    Wide range of important authors represented by whole works or long selections in "classic" translations (e.g., Chaucer's of Boethius's *Consolation*, Pope's *Iliad*, 1683 tr. of *Praise of Folly*). Explanatory notes. Vol. 2 is published separately as *Century Readings in European Literature, From the Medieval Period through Croce*, ed. John W. Cunliffe (N.Y., Century, 1925, xi, 542 pp.). The modern works, more briefly excerpted, extend from Romance and Saga to 19th c. French (especially), Russian and, for Italian, Croce.

*Chief Contemporary Dramatists. Ed. Thomas H[erbert] Dickinson. Boston and N.Y., Houghton Mifflin, 1915, 1921, 1930. 1st series, ix, 676; 2nd series, vi, 734; 3d series, ix, 698 pp.

Series 1, 8 Continental plays; 2, 9 Continental; 3, 15 Continental. Reading lists, notes on authors, plays, and productions.

The Chief European Dramatists. Ed. Brander Matthews. Boston and N.Y., Houghton Mifflin, 1916. xi, 786 pp.
> Twenty-one plays, 500 B.C. to A.D. 1879. Standard translations. Biography, notes, bibliography.

The Classic Theatre. Ed. Eric R[ussell] Bentley. Garden City, N.Y., Doubleday, 1958–59. 3 vols. Anchor, paper.
> Vol. 1, Six Italian Plays (Machiavelli to Gozzi); vol. 2, Five German Plays (Goethe, Schiller, Kleist); vol. 3, Six Spanish Plays (the *Celestina* to Calderón). An important collection.

Columbia University Course in Literature. Ed. John W[illiam] Cunliffe et al. N.Y., Columbia Univ. Pr., 1928–29, and London, J. A. Richards, 1945. 18 vols.
> Each pt. edited by a specialist. A representative selection of the literature of different epochs, languages, and civilizations, chronologically arranged, designed for use in Columbia College. Vol. 1, the East; 2, Greece; 3, Rome; 4, medieval Europe including Middle English; 5, Italy; 6, France through the Revolution; 7, Modern France; 8, the small nations; 9, Germany; 10, Scandinavian and Slavonic; remaining vols., English and Amer.

Confucius to Cummings: An Anthology of Poetry. Ed. Ezra Pound and Marcella Spann. [1926] N.Y., New Directions, 1964. xxii, 353 pp. (also paper).
> Brief selections, usually one per poet. Well over half English and Amer. but some Provençal, Italian, medieval and Renaissance French.

Continental Plays. Ed. Thomas H. Dickinson. Boston and N.Y., Houghton Mifflin, 1935. 2 vols.
> Types of contemporary drama. Bibliography.

The Copeland Translations. Chosen, arranged, with intro., by Charles Townsend Copeland. N.Y. and London, Scribner, 1934. xxiii, 1080 pp.
> Mainly in prose, from French, German (slight), Italian, Russian, Irish. Some unusual not to say idiosyncratic selections; some popular writers.

Criticism: Twenty Major Statements. Sel. and ed. Charles Kaplan. San
  Francisco, Chandler, 1964. 482 pp., paper.
  Plato, Aristotle, Longinus, Horace, Tolstoy, in standard trs., and 15
  English and American authors.

Documents of Modern Literary Realism. Ed. George J. Becker. Princeton,
  N.J., Princeton Univ. Pr., 1963. 609 pp.
  Very short selections, only two or three pages each, from Strindberg,
  Paul Alexis, Tolstoy, Léon Lemonnier, Brasil, Engels, Gorky, Proust,
  Agosti, Belinsky, Chernishevsky; Desnoyers, Flaubert, Duranty, and
  Sainte-Beuve on *Madame Bovary*; Taine, the Goncourts, Galdós, Zola,
  Huysmans, Bazán, de Vogüé, Maupassant, Heinrich and Julius Hart, and
  English and American authors.

Drama of the East and West: A Critical Anthology of Plays. with Special
  Sections on Oriental and Philippine Drama. Ed. Jean Edades and Carolyn
  Fosdick. Manila, Bookman, 1956. vii, 658 pp.
  Plays from India, China, Japan; 5 short Philippine plays. The standard
  Western plays from Euripides to Chekov. Collection interesting only for
  the Philippine plays. Notes on history of drama.

The Drama: Its History, Literature, and Influence in Civilization. Ed.
  Alfred Bates et al. London, [Athenian Soc.] Stuart and Stanley, and N.Y.,
  Smart and Stanley. 1903. 20 vols. ill.
  For the general reader. Translators not named. Largely discussion, with
  excerpts for illustration from plays standard to ephemeral. Addenda,
  1904, vols. 21–22: "Classic Curiosities of Dramatic Literature."

*Dramatic Essays of the Neoclassic Age. Ed. Henry Hitchcock Adams and
  Baxter Hathaway. N.Y. and London, Oxford Univ. Pr., 1950. 412 pp.
  Sel. from Lessing's correspondence with Nicolai and Mendelssohn;
  many English authors, and, from French, Corneille, Saint-Évremond,
  Rapin, Le Bossu, Dacier, Houdar de la Motte, Du Bos, Fontenelle,
  Levesque de Pouilly, Voltaire, Diderot, Beaumarchais, Mercier. Some
  contemporary, some new trs. The selections are well chosen and of
  some length. Very valuable collection.

Eight European Plays. Sel. and tr. Winifred Katzin, pref. Barrett H. Clark.
  N.Y., Brentano's, 1927. 426 pp.
  Unusual selection of plays: German plays by Sternheim, Kaiser, Veit

Harlan, Heinrich Mann, Vollmüller; French: 2 plays by J.-J. Bernard; Italian: Rosso di San Secondo.

*European and Asiatic Plays from Euripides to Shirley, 431 B.C. to 1642 A.D. Ed. Joseph Richard Taylor. Boston, Expression Co., 1936. 730 pp.
Euripides, *Medea*, tr. Joseph R. Taylor; Aristophanes, *Frogs*, tr. J. H. Frere; Plautus, *Menaechmi*, tr. Taylor; Seneca, *Medea*, tr. Taylor; Kalidasa, *Shakuntala*, tr. Sir William Jones (1789); *The Sorrows of Hān*, tr. John Francis Davis (1829); 3 No plays: Seami, *Atsumari*, tr. Arthur Waley, Enami no Seyemon, *The Cormorant Fisher*, tr. not named, *The Bird-Catcher in Hell* (parody of a No play); Hroswitha, *Dulcitius*, tr. Taylor; Calderón, *Life is a Dream*, tr. Denis Florence MacCarthy; Corneille, *Cid*, tr. Florence Kendrick Cooper (poor tr. in blank verse); *The Second Shepherds' Play*; *Everyman*; John Heywood, *The Four PP*; Sackville and Norton, *Gorboduc*; Nicholas Udall, *Ralph Roister Doister*; Dekker, *The Shoemaker's Holiday*; Massinger, *A New Way to Pay Old Debts*; Shakespeare, *Comedy of Errors*.

*European Theories of the Drama. Ed. Barrett H. Clark. [1918] Rev. Henry Popkin. N.Y., Crown Pub., 1965. xiv, 628 pp.
Subtitle: "An Anthology of Dramatic Theory and Criticism from Aristotle to the Present Day, in a Series of Selected Texts . . . Including Commentary, Biography and Bibliography." The book was rev. 1929 and 1947, and in the latter year a supplement on the American drama was added. Substantial sel. from: Aristotle, Horace, Donatus, Dante, Daniello, Minturno, Scaliger, Castelvetro, Sebillet, De la Taille, Cervantes, Lope de Vega, Ogier, Schélandre, Chapelain, Odebrecht, D'Aubignac, Corneille, Racine, boileau, Saint-Évremond, Molière, Goldoni, Lessing, Voltaire, Diderot, Beaumarchais, Schiller, Goethe, Schlegel, Wagner, Freytag, Hugo, Dumas fils, Sarcey, Zola, Brunetière, Maeterlinck, and English authors.

*From the Modern Repertoire. Ed. Eric R[ussell] Bentley. Denver, Univ. of Colorado Pr., 1949. 1st series, xiv, 406 pp.
Rather unusual selections, including Musset, Büchner, Becque, Schnitzler, Sternheim, Brecht, Lorca, Cocteau.

————2nd series, ibid., 1952. 511 pp.
Inter alia: Grabbe, Ostrovsky, Mirbeau, Wedekind, Obey, Giraudoux, Brecht.

————3d series, Bloomington, Indiana Univ. Pr., 1956. 527 pp.
> *Inter alia*: Büchner, Musset, Zola, Schnitzler, Romains, Brecht, Cocteau, Anouilh.

The Genius of the Oriental Theatre. Ed. George Lincoln Anderson. N.Y., New Amer. Lib., 1966. 416 pp. (Mentor).
> Includes bibliography.

The Golden Treasury of Indian Literature. Ed. Ikbāl ʿAlī Shāh. London, Low, Marston, 1938, 294 pp.
> Poetry and prose from "most Indian languages" (Preface). No translators named, no critical apparatus. Mostly short poems.

*Great Books of the Western World. Ed. Robert Maynard Hutchins; assoc. ed. Mortimer Adler. Chicago, Encyclopaedia Britannica, 1952. 54 vols.
> Vol. 1, the great conversations, the substance of a liberal education; 2, 3, the great ideas: a synopticon of great books of the western world; each of remaining vols. devoted to one or two authors, usually with complete books, chronologically from Homer to 20th c., including English and Amer. and documents in the history of thought (e.g., 38, Montesquieu and Rousseau; 46, Hegel; 50, Marx; 53, William James).

Great Short Biographies of Ancient Times, the Middle Ages and the Renaissance: A Collection of Short Biographies, Literary Portraits, and Memoirs. Chosen by Barrett H[arper] Clark. N.Y., Boni, 1935. xi, 615 pp.
> Chronological arrangement, excluding Oriental; strong in English and Amer. Completed by *Great Short Biographies of Modern Times: The Seventeenth, Eighteenth, and Nineteenth Centuries*, ed. Clark, N.Y., Boni, 1934, xii, 615–1406 pp. The two parts originally pub. together 1928 as *Great Short Biographies of the World*.

Great Short Novels of the World. Ed. Barrett H. Clark. N.Y., McBride, and London, Heinemann, 1927. xi. 1304 pp. Repr. N.Y., Boni. 1932. 2 vols.
> From the Bible and ancient Greece to the U.S., most countries represented by 1 or 2 selections. India, Arabia, China and Japan as well as Europe. Intro. to each country.

Great Short Stories of All Nations. Ed. Maxim Lieber and Blanche Colton Williams. N.Y., Brentano's, 1932. xii, 1121 pp.
> One hundred sixty stories of all periods and nations.

Great Short Stories of the World. Ed. Barrett H. Clark and Maxim Lieber. N.Y., McBride, 1926. xv, 1072 pp.
> Stories from 28 countries or regions, for the general reader; introduction and bibliographical comments for each section.

*The Harvard Classics. Ed. Charles W[illiam] Eliot. N.Y., Collier, 1909–10. 50 vols.
> The classics of Western literature (East represented only by *The Thousand and One Nights* in Lane's translation, rev. Stanley Lane-Poole) in volumes by genre, with short critical and biographical introductions. Vol. 12, Plutarch's *Lives* (9), tr. "called Dryden's," rev. Arthur Hugh Clough; 14, *Don Quixote*, tr. Thomas Shelton; 17, Aesop, Grimm, Anderson; 33, voyages and travels; 35, Froissart's *Chronicles*, tr. Lord Berners; 49, epic and saga. Completed by *Lectures on the Harvard Classics*, ed. William Allan Neilson (N.Y., Collier, 1914, 400 pp.).

Heath Readings in the Literature of Europe. Ed. Tom Peete Cross and Clark H. Slover. [1927] Boston and N.Y., Heath, 1933. xv, 1194 pp.
> ". . . characteristic examples of the major streams of ancient, medieval and modern European literature" together with readings to illustrate "the literary, philosophical and critical backgrounds of the English-speaking peoples." (Preface) By period and genre, from the *Iliad* to Keller and Sudermann; European except for the Book of Job and Ecclesiastes and some psalms. Many genres and authors, some unusual; translations standard. Scholarly notes on each selection.

The Heritage of European Literature. Ed. Edward H[owell] Weatherly et al. Boston, Ginn, 1948–49. 2 vols.
> Fairly liberal selections from major works. Vol. 1, Greece, Rome, the Middle Ages, the Renaissance; vol. 2, the Age of Reason, the 19th c., Russian literature before the Soviet Era, 20th c. including Soviet literature. Modern portion less satisfactory: merely chapters from novels, etc. Chronological chart, index of authors and titles, critical introductions.

Library of the World's Best Literature. See **Warner Library.**

The Limits of Art, Poetry and Prose Chosen by Ancient and Modern Critics. Ed. Huntington Cairns. N.Y., Pantheon Books, 1948. xliv, 1473 pp. Bollingen Series, 12.

Parallel texts; critic's estimate of each. Brief passages, chosen by named critics as greatest, from authors Homer to Joyce. Standard translations used.

*Literary Criticism: Plato to Dryden. Ed. Allan H. Gilbert. N.Y., Amer. Book, 1940. ix, 704 pp.
The best available collection of criticism. Notes.

*Literary Criticism: Pope to Croce. Ed. Gay Wilson Allen and Harry H. Clark. N.Y., Amer. Book, 1941. 659 pp.
See above comment. Modern selections somewhat too brief.

Literature of Western Civilization. Sel. and ed. Louis G[lenn] Locke, John Pendy Kirby, and M. E. Porter. N.Y., Ronald Pr., 1952. 2 vols. ill.
Not useful by reason of shortness of selections and inferiority of translations.

*A Little Treasury of World Poetry. Ed. Hubert Creekmore. N.Y., Scribner, 1952. xl, 904 pp.
From the great poets of other languages, 2600 B.C. to A.D. 1950. By language and then by poets chronologically. Indexes of authors, titles, translators, languages. Standard translations, many 20th c. and some by editor. Egyptian, Babylonian, Sanskrit (liberal selection), Hebrew, Yiddish, Persian, Arabian, Arakanese, Chinese, Japanese. European includes: Anglo-Saxon, Gaelic, Welsh, Old Norse, Icelandic, Provençal, Latin American, besides the modern Continental.

The Living Theatre: An Anthology of Great Plays. Ed. Alice Venezky Griffin. N.Y., Twayne, 1953. 510 pp.
Aeschylus, Plautus, Molière, Ibsen, Chekhov, Hebbel, Giraudoux, English and American. Tr. various hands.

Lyrics of the Middle Ages. Ed. Hubert Creekmore. N.Y., Grove, 1959. 278 pp.
167 poems translated from 14 languages including Scandinavian but not those of eastern Europe.

Makers of the Modern Theater. Ed. Barry Ulanov. N.Y., Toronto and London, McGraw-Hill, 1961. viii, 743 pp.

Plays by Ibsen, Strindberg, Chekhov, Hauptmann, Shaw, Yeats, Synge, O'Casey, Toller, Pirandello, Betti, Giraudoux, Anouilh, Montherlant, Marcel, Ionesco, Lorca, O'Neill, Williams, Miller. Trs. various hands.

Masterpieces of Foreign Literature. London, C. Griffin, 1866. 339 pp.
Schiller's tragedies, tr. Coleridge; Goethe's *Faust*, tr. L. Filmore; La Fontaine's *Fables*, tr. Elizur Wright; Saintine's *Picciola*, tr. not named.

Masterpieces of the Drama. Ed. Alexander W. Allison et al. 2nd ed. N.Y., Macmillan, 1966. 814 pp.
Sophocles, *Oedipus Rex*; Euripides, *The Bacchae*; Ibsen, *Hedda Gabler*; Chekhov, *The Cherry Orchard*; Lorca, *The House of Bernarda Alba*; Giraudoux, *The Madwoman of Chaillot*; Brecht, *The Chalk Circle*; Beckett, *All That Falls* and *Act Without Words*. Standard trs.

Masterpieces of the Orient. Ed. George L. Anderson. N.Y., Norton, 1961. xiii, 396 pp. paper.
For students. Complete or long selections of fiction, poetry, drama, essays, philosophical and religious documents. Near East, China, India, Japan.

Masters of the Modern Drama. Ed. Haskell M. Block and Robert G. Shedd. N.Y., Random House, 1962. xii, 1198 pp.
Forty-five plays by thirty-five authors from Ibsen to Frisch: a good selection.

Masterworks of World Literature. Ed. Edwin M[allard] Everett, Calvin S. Brown, and John C. Wade. [1947] N.Y., Dryden, 1955. 2 vols.
Vol. 1, Homer to Cervantes; 2, Shakespeare to Mann. European only, except for Bible; English amply represented. More extensive selections from fewer works than in most anthologies, though in vol. 2 one poem each for many authors. "Method of abridgement varies," but attempt made to convey unity of work.

The Medieval Age: Specimens of European Poetry from the Ninth to the Fifteenth Century. Ed. with intro. Angel Flores. N.Y., Dell, 1963. 606 pp. paper, and London, Phoenix House, 1965, xviii, 457 pp.
Epic and heroic poems from Old English, Old Irish, Byzantine Greek, Old French, Old Basque, Spanish, Russian, German Icelandic. Lyric: Old English, Old Irish, Old German, Latin, Byzantine Greek, the

Troubadours and after, Italian 13th c., Portuguese 13th–14th c. Samples of bestiary, lives of the saints, fiction, Dante, etc.

*Medieval Literature in Translation. Ed. Charles W[illiam] Jones. [1950] N.Y. and London, Longmans Green, 1957. xx, 1004 pp. Maps.

Tries to represent all genres, so short selections, but wide range of literatures and good choice of material.

Medieval Narrative: A Book of Translations. See Schlauch, below.

Merwin, W. S. Selected Translations, 1948–1968. N.Y., Atheneum, 1968. 176 pp.

Anon. poems from Egypt, China, Vietnam, Kabylia, Tatary, Rumania, Eskimo, Amazon, Peru, India, Wales, Greece, Rome. Generally one or two poems each by a wide range of poets from Catullus to Brodsky (4).

Modern Continental Dramas. Ed. Harlan Hatcher. N.Y., Harcourt Brace, 1941. viii, 747 pp. Repr. 1961.

Late 19th c. to the present. Biography and bibliography. Plays by Ibsen, Strindberg, Hauptmann, Chekhov, Gorky, Rostand, Maeterlinck, Claudel, Sierra, Molnar, Pirandello, Lenormand, Čapek, Toller, Katayev.

Modern Continental Plays. Ed. S[amuel] Marion Tucker. N.Y. and London, Harper, 1929. xi, 836 pp.

Late 19th, early 20th c. plays by Andreyev, Benavente, Björnson, Bracco, Brieux, Čapek, Chekhov, Claudel, D'Annunzio, Galdós, Gorki, Hauptmann, Kaiser (2), Maeterlinck, Molnar, Rostand, Schnitzler, Strindberg, Vildrac, Wedekind.

See also *Twenty-five Modern Plays*, ed. S. Marion Tucker [1931], rev. 3d ed., Alan S. Downer (N.Y., Harper, 1953, xx, 1008 pp.), which includes most of the continental plays above with some English and American.

*Modern European Poetry. Ed. Willis Barnstone et al. N.Y., Bantam, 1966. xxiii, 605 pp., paper.

Short intro. to each language section: German, French, Greek, Italian, Russian, Spanish. Wide selection, translators various.

Modern European Verse. Sel. Dannie Abse. London, Vista Books, 1964. 48 pp. (The Pocket Poets).

Trs. various, mostly standard. 20th c. verse.

Modern Stories from Many Lands. Ed. Clarence R[aymond] Decker and Charles Angoff. N.Y., Manyland Books, [1963]. 316 pp.
Twenty-four stories from thirteen countries, including Indonesia, Philippines, Turkey.

The Modern Theatre. Ed. Robert W. Corrigan. N.Y., Macmillan, 1966. 1280 pp.
Forty plays by thirty-five playwrights, with letters on the theatre by playwrights.

The Modern Theatre: Plays. Ed. Eric Russell Bentley. Garden City, N.Y., Doubleday, 1955–60. (also Anchor) 6 vols.
From late 19th c. to the present. Modern translations, many by the editor. Each vol. has an assortment of continental plays except vol. 4, American.

The New Theatre of Europe: Five Contemporary Plays from the European Stage. Ed. Robert W. Corrigan. N.Y., Dell, 1963. 399 pp., paper.
Plays by Bolt, Sastre, Peryalis, Ghelderode, Betti. Tr. various hands.

Nicholson, R[eynold] A[lleyne] [translator]. Translations of Eastern Poetry and Prose. Cambridge Univ. Pr., 1922, xi, 200 pp.
About 50 authors, 6th to 15th c. A.D., chronologically by authors. Translations prose into prose, verse into verse. Brief notes on authors. Selections deal with history, morals, religion, culture and character.

Our Heritage of World Literature. Ed. Stith Thompson and John Gassner. [1938] Rev. ed. N.Y., Dryden, 1942. 2 vols.
Little Eastern, many selections short, undistinguished translations, many genres. Aeschylus through Ibsen and Chekhov.

One Thousand and One Poems of Mankind: Memorable Short Poems from the World's Chief Literatures. Comp. Henry Willis Wells. N.Y., McKay, 1953. 448 pp.
Chronological under theme. All periods; "classic" translations. Good representation of Chinese, Japanese, Sanskrit. English and Amer. included.

The Oriental Caravan: A Revelation of the Soul and Mind of Asia.
Ed. Iḳbāl 'Alī Shāh. N.Y., Kendall, and London, Archer, 1933. 331 pp.

Many genres, translators, and countries. Selections from the great religious works.

Painter, William. The Palace of Pleasure [1566]. Ed. Joseph Jacobs. London, Joseph Jacobs, 1890. 3 vols. Repr. Magnolia, Mass., P. Smith, 1967.
Elizabethan versions of 101 classical, French and Italian novellas. Authors include Boccaccio, Bandello, Cinthio, Straparola, Queen Margaret of Navarre.

The Penguin Book of Modern Verse. Ed. with intro. George Steiner. 1966. 332 pp.
Sappho, Horace, Gautier, Ronsard, Montanari, La Fontaine, Saint-John Perse, Li-Po, Rimbaud, Éluard, Lorca, Akmadulina, Heine, Quasimodo, Hakashu, Aristophanes, Neruda, Milosz, many English. Standard trs.

The Play: A Critical Anthology. Ed. Eric R. Bentley. N.Y., Prentice-Hall, 1951. xii, 774 pp.
Plays by Rostand, Wilde, Molière, Shakespeare (2), Sophocles, Ibsen, Strindberg, Miller. Trs. various hands.

The Poem Itself: 45 Modern Foreign Poets in a New Presentation. Ed. Stanley Burnshaw. N.Y., Holt, 1960. Repr. Cleveland, World (Meridian), 1962. 377 pp.
Original poem, literal translation and analysis by a critic. Over 150 poems in French, Spanish, German, Italian, and Portuguese.

*Poetic Drama: An Anthology of Plays in Verse from the Ancient Greek to the Modern American. Ed. Alfred Kreymborg. N.Y., Modern Age Books, 1941. viii, 855 pp.
Translations of varying excellence. Aeschylus, *Agamemnon*, tr. Edith Hamilton; Sophocles, *Oedipus Coloneus*, tr. Sir George Young; Euripides, *Ion*, tr. H. D.; Aristophanes, *The Acharnians*, tr. J. H. Frere; anon. Chinese, *The Chalk Circle*, tr. Ethel Van Der Veer; Seami, *Nakamitsu*, tr. B. H. Chamberlin; *Adam*, tr. Edward Noble Stone; Hans Sachs, *The Wandering Scholar from Paradise*, tr. Samuel A. Eliot, Jr.; Lope de Vega, *The Sheep Well*, tr. John Garrett Underhill; Corneille, *Cinna*, tr. Paul Landis; Racine, *Athaliah*, tr. Robert Bruce Boswell; Molière, *The Misanthrope*, tr. Curtis Hidden Page; Goethe, *Torquato Tasso*, tr. Anna Swanwick; Schiller, *The Death of Wallenstein*, tr. S. T. Coleridge; Hauptmann, *The White Savior*, tr. Willa and Edwin Muir; Rostand,

The Last Night of Don Juan, tr. Lawrason Riggs. All trs. verse or verse
and prose. Distinguished collection.

**The Poetry of the Orient: An Anthology of the Classic Secular Poetry
of the Major Eastern Nations.** Ed. Eunice Tietjens. N.Y. and London,
Knopf, 1928. xxv, 328, xli pp.
> Various translators, mostly well known. Arabia, China, India, Japan,
> Persia.

The Poets and Poetry of Europe. Ed. Henry W[adsworth] Longfellow.
[1845] Rev. enl. Boston, Houghton, 1896. xxi, 921 pp.
> Selections from 10 languages, not including Celtic, Slavonic, or Romaic.
> Translations by Longfellow and others. Biographical notices mostly by
> C. C. Felton.

Pound, Ezra. *See* The Translations of Ezra Pound.

Prose and Poetry of the Continental Renaissance in Translation. Ed.
Harold Hooper Blanchard. [1949] 2nd ed. N.Y. and London, Longmans,
Green, 1955, Repr. 1959. xix, 1084 pp.
> Excellent for quality and range of selections and choice of translation.
> Introduction to each author, including bibliography of his works and
> translations of them, standard biographical and critical works on him.
> Lyric poetry (e.g. Ronsard, Petrarch), *The Praise of Folly* (entire) tr. John
> Wilson 1668 (rev. Mrs. P. S. Allen), Ariosto, 13 cantos, *inter alia*.

Renaissance and Baroque Lyrics: An Anthology. Ed. Harold M[artin]
Priest. Evanston, Ill., Northwestern Univ. Pr., 1962. 288 pp.
> Tr. Priest and others. Important collection of poems rarely found in tr.
> and never before together. French, Italian, Spanish poets, some repre-
> sented by many poems (e.g. Petrarch 20, Michelangelo 27). Long and
> valuable intro. by Priest on Renaissance, Mannerism and Baroque, and
> "On Translating Poetry."

Representative Continental Dramas: Revolutionary and Transitional.
Ed. with intro. Montrose J. Moses. Boston, Little, Brown, 1924. xiv, 688
pp.
> Ibsen, Schnitzler, Hauptmann, Sudermann, Chekhov, Andreyev,
> D'Annunzio, Giacosa, Nördlinger, Benavente, Rostand, Becque, Donnay,
> Maeterlinck, Verhaeren. Some standard, some new trs.

Representative One-Act Plays by Continental Authors. Sel. with Biographical Notes Montrose J. Moses. Boston, Little, Brown, 1922. xvi, 463 pp. Repr. 1926.

    Schnitzler, von Hofmannsthal, Maeterlinck, Bergström, A. de Lorde, Lavedan, Porto-Riche, Sudermann, Wedekind, Giacosa, Andreyev, Evrémov, Quintero, Sierra, Strindberg.

The Sacred Books of the East. Ed. F[riedrich] Max Müller. [1879–1910] Oxford, Oxford Univ. Pr., 1926—. 50 vols. Repr. Mystic, Conn., Verry, 1965–6, 50 vols.

    Indispensable. Vol. 50 General Index. Translators all Oriental scholars. For individual vols. see under Arabic, Chinese, Indic, Persian, etc.

The Sacred Books of the East, with Critical and Biographical Sketches by Epiphanius Wilson. [1900] Rev. ed. N.Y., Willey, 1945. 480 pp.

    Vedic hymns, *Zend-Avesta* (sel), The *Dhamnapada*, The *Upanishads*, The *Koran* (sel.), Life of Buddha by Bodhisattva A.D. 420.

The Sacred Books and Early Literature of the East. Dir. Charles F. Horne. N.Y. and London, Parke, Austin and Lipscomb, 1917. 14 vols.

    With historical surveys of the chief writings of each nation. Bibliography. Vol. 1, Babylonia and Assyria; 2, Egypt; 3, Ancient Hebrew; 4, Medieval Hebrew; 5, Ancient Arabia; 6, Medieval Arabia, Moorish and Turkish; 7, Ancient Persia; 8, Medieval Persia; 9, India and Brahminism; 10, India and Buddhism; 11, Ancient China; 12, Medieval China; 13, Japan; 14, the great rejected books of the Biblica Apocrypha.

*Schlauch Margaret. Medieval Narrative: A Book of Translations. N.Y., Prentice-Hall, 1928. viii, 456 pp.

    Teacher's and scholar's selection; all translations by Schlauch. Icelandic saga, chansons de geste, Tristan legend, legends of Holy Grail, Nibelung cycle, Tale of Troy, Legend of Alexander the Great, pious tales and miracle stories, Saints' lives, fabliaux; introduction to each.

A Select Collection of Novels and Histories in Six Volumes Written by the Most Celebrated Authors in Several Languages. Ed. Samuel Croxall. London, pr. for John Watts, 1720–22. Repr. 1729, 1736, 1740. 5 vols.

". . . all new translations . . . by several eminent hands." Trs. not named. Principally from Cervantes, St. Real, Machiavelli, Madame de Lafayette, Flamiani, Brémond, Scarron.

Sixteen Famous European Plays. Ed. Bennett A. Cerf and Van H. Cartmell. ML, 1943. xxv, 1025 pp.

Tr. various hands. Plays by Ibsen, Hauptmann, Chekhov, Gorky, Ansky, Rostand, Deval, Giraudoux, Sierra, Pirandello, Schnitzler, Čapek, Molnar, Baum, and Irish.

Tellers of Tales. Sel. and with intro. by W. Somerset Maugham. N.Y., Doubleday, Doran, 1939. xxxix, 1526 pp.

100 short stories from U.S., England, France, Russia, Germany. Good selection including some authors not usually collected (e.g., Villiers de l'Isle Adam). Standard translations.

Ten Modern Short Novels. Ed. with commentaries Leo Hamalian and Edmond L. Volpe. N.Y., Putnam, 1958. 718 pp.

Gide, Mann, Faulkner, Unamuno, Tolstoy, Andreyev, Camus, Moravia, Henry James, Conrad. Tr. various hands.

*Translations of Christian Literature. General eds. W. J. Sparrow Simpson and W. K. L. Clarke. London, SPCK, and N.Y., Macmillan 1898–1940.

For the several series and many volumes of this indispensable work, see Greek and Roman Literature, in our Vol. 1.

The Translations of Ezra Pound. N.Y., New Directions, and London, Faber and Faber, 1933. 408 pp.

Introduction by Hugh Kenner. Poets: Arclamon, Catullus, Cavalcanti, Arnaut Daniel, du Bellay, Charles d'Orléans, Leopardi, Remy de Gourmont, Jules Laforgue. Also Noh plays.

A Treasury of Asian Literature. Ed. John D. Yohannen. [1956] N.Y., New Amer. Lib. (Mentor), 1961. 432 pp.

Mostly short selections. Introduction and commentaries. Prose, poetry, drama, scriptures.

A Treasury of Modern Asian Stories. Ed. William Clifford and Daniel L. Milton. N.Y., New Amer. Lib. (Mentor), 1961. 237 pp.

*A Treasury of the Theatre. Ed. John Gassner. Rev. enl., N.Y. Simon and Schuster, 1963. 3 vols.

    Vol. 1, Aeschylus to Turgenev; 2, Modern European from Ibsen to Sartre; 3, Modern British and Amer. A standard text since its appearance in 1935, ed. Burns Mantle and Gassner (2 vols.). Rev. and adapted for colleges 1940 by Philo M. Buck, Gassner, and H. S. Alberson (2 vols.) with apparatus; rev. by Gassner, 1950 (2 vols.).

A Treasury of the World's Great Letters, from Ancient Days to Our Own Time. Ed. M. Lincoln Schuster. N.Y., Simon and Schuster, 1940. xlvii, 563 pp.

    From Greece to Thomas Mann on Hitler. Interesting selection precisely documented.

Tudor Translations. Ed. W. E. Henley. London, Nutt, 1892–1909. 44 vols.

————Second Series. Ed. Charles Whibley. London, Constable, and N.Y., Knopf, 1924–27. 12 vols. Both series repr. N.Y., AMS Pr., 1967.

    Re-eds. of classic trs. made in the Tudor century from Greek (Heliodorus, Herodotus, Plutarch); Latin (Apuleius, Sallust, Seneca, Suetonius); French (Commines, Froissart, Montaigne); Italian (Bandello, Boccaccio, Castiglione, Guazzo, Machiavelli); Spanish (Alemán, Cervantes). A sampling of Tudor trs. was given in *Tudor Translations: An Anthology*, ed. Arthur F. Clements (Oxford, Blackwell and N.Y., Salloch, 1940, xv, 214 pp.), with intro. on major translators, biographical notes on minor.

The Twenty Best European Plays on the American Stage. Ed. John Gassner. [1957] N.Y., Crown 1960. 733 pp.

    Modern. Including Anouilh, S. Ansky, Benavente, Čapek, Chekhov, R. Fauchois, Giraudoux (4), Heijermans, Albert Husson, Molnar, Obey, Pirandello, Sartre, Tolstoy, Turgenev, Werfel.

Types of World Literature. Ed. Percy Hazen Houston and Robert Metcalf Smith. N.Y., Odyssey, 1930. xviii, 1200 pp.

    Masterpieces excerpted for students of comparative literature. Many genres (history, philosophy, letters, satire, biography, politics). From *Iliad* (tr. Edward, Earl of Derby) to Croce. Arranged by genre.

Types of World Tragedy. Ed. Robert Metcalf Smith, N.Y., Prentice-Hall, 1928. viii, 667 pp.

Oedipus, Medea, Phaedra, Othello, The Cenci, Ghosts, The Weavers, The Lower Depths. Mostly anon. trs.

The Warner Library of the World's Best Literature, Ancient and Modern. Ed. Charles Dudley Warner et al. N.Y., International Soc., 1896–98. 30 vols.

Several editions in varying number of vols. to 1928–29, ed. John W. Cunliffe and Ashley Thorndike. ''The selections are made for household and general reading.'' Very short selections but wide variety of literatures. Each vol. a pot-pourri, since listing is alphabetical by author.

Warnke, Frank J. European Metaphysical Poetry. New Haven. Yale Univ. Pr., 1961. xi, 317 pp.

Anthology in parallel texts of late 16th and 17th c. poetry, French, German, Dutch, Spanish, Italian, all translated by Warnke. Long, important historical and critical introduction.

Western World Literature. Ed. Harry Wolcott Robbins and William Harold Coleman. N.Y., Macmillan, 1938. xix, 1422 pp. Maps.

A teaching book, with apparatus. Wide range but generally short selections; mostly old translations (e.g., *Misanthrope*, 1739). Emphasis on English literature.

The Wisdom of the East Series. Original eds., L. Cranmer-Byng and S. A. Kapadia, later L. Cranmer-Byng and Alan W. Watts. London, Orient Pr. (for first item), then John Murray, 1904— (in progress). Some 125 vols. to 1962, the vols. not numbered.

Trs. of Oriental books or selections, or discussions, from Egyptian to Japanese.

World Drama. Ed. Barrett H[arper] Clark [1933] N.Y., Appleton, 1956. 2 vols. Vol. 2 also N.Y., Dover, 1956.

Vol. 1, Ancient Greece, Rome, India, China, Japan, Medieval Europe. Vol. 2, Italy, Spain, France, Germany, Denmark, Russia, Norway. From earliest times to Ibsen.

A World of Great Stories. Ed. Hiram Haydn and John Cournos. N.Y., Crown, 1947. x, 950 pp.

Aim was ''to choose at least one first-rate story from every country in the world with any appreciable literature.'' (Preface) All 20th c. Almost one-third of book English and Amer. Oriental included, also Latin American.

*The World in Literature. Ed. George K. Anderson and Robert Warnock. [1950–51] Rev. ed. Chicago. Scott, Foresman, 1967. 2 or 4 vols. ill.

One-vol. ed. 1959 omits English and Amer. Literary classics and other writings chosen judiciously to illuminate the history of thought. Long introductory sections on movements, works, etc.; author biographies. Selections are whole units. Vol. 1, The Ancient Foundations (China, India, Hebrew Bible, *Iliad*, *Odyssey* [both in Rouse tr.], Aeschylus, Sophocles, Euripides, etc., Rome). Vol. 2, Centuries of Transition (from *Koran*, *Arabian Nights*, Omar, Hafiz, etc.). Vol. 3, Tradition and Revolt, The Literature of the Age of Reason and of the Romantic Era. Vol. 4, Science and Uncertainty (1850—, including Schopenhauer, Rilke, Sartre, Kafka, Gide, Mann, etc.). An epitome of world literature.

World Literature. Ed. E[than] A[llen] Cross. N.Y., Amer. Book, 1935. xv, 1396 pp.

Chronological arrangement. Sketch of literature of each country with short (except for modern plays) illustrative selections, Egypt through 20th c. Europe. Contemporary translations used where possible (e.g., Smollett's *Gil Blas*).

World Literature: An Anthology of Human Experience. Ed. Arthur E. Christy and Henry W. Wells. N.Y., Amer. Book Co., 1947. xxiii, 1118 pp.

By themes, as subtitle indicates (e.g., travel, the unfolding universe, the critical intellect) and chronological under these. Selections mostly very short. Wide range of nations. Author biographies. A teaching book (questions included) to illustrate the unity of human experience. Less useful as introduction to world literature.

*World Masterpieces. General ed. Maynard Mack. [1956] Rev. N.Y., Norton, 1965. 2 vols. (The Continental Edition of World Masterpieces, pub. 1962 in one vol. excluded English and Amer.)

This is now (1966) enlarged to 2 vols. but does not include revisions as in 1965 *World Masterpieces*, of which vol. 1 is The Literature of Western Culture through the Renaissance; vol. 2, The Literature of Western Culture since the Renaissance. Good introductions; modern translations (e.g., Louis MacNeice of *Agamemnon*, Yeats of Sophocles' *Oedipus*, Rex Warner of *Medea*). Policy is to use the whole work wherever possible. For variety, wise selection and length of selections a superior anthology,— of European, not world, literature.

The World's Best Essays from Confucius to Mencken. Ed. F[rancis] H[enry] Pritchard. [1929] N.Y., Halcyon, 1939. 6,1012 pp.
229 essays from English and foreign literature.

The World's Best Humor, Being a True Chronicle from Prehistoric Ages to the Twentieth Century. Ed. Carolyn Wells, N.Y., Boni. 1933. x, 782 pp.
Chronological outline of humor with illustrations, from Ancient Egypt to Wilde and Bret Harte. Index.

The World's Best Orations, from the Earliest Period to the Present Time. Ed. David J. Brewer. St. Louis, Mo., Kaiser, 1900. 10 vols.
Alphabetical. A great deal of English and Amer. but all interesting selections, with indication of source, translator, etc.

*The World's Great Classics.** Ed. Julian Hawthorne. N.Y., Colonial Pr., and London, M. Walter Dunne, 1899–1902. 61 vols.
Inclusive: Babylonian, Assyrian, Armenian, Egyptian, Hebrew, Moorish, Malaysian, Turkish, Persian, Arabian, Indian, Chinese, Japanese (vol. 57 is Sacred Books of the East) as well as European from Greek to de Tocqueville and Taine (*History of English Literature*, vols. 24–26). Also memoirs, orations, decisive battles, essays, ideal commonwealths, Froissart's *Chronicles*, Montesquieu, Voltaire's *History of Charles XII*, Kant, Hegel, Dante, Tasso.

The World's Great Plays. With intro. George Jean Nathan. Cleveland, Ohio, and N.Y., World, 1944. 491 pp.
Aristophanes, *Lysistrata*; Goethe, *Faust*; Ibsen, *The Master Builder*; Rostand, *Cyrano* (in an excellent tr. by Harold Whitehall); Chekhov, *The Cherry Orchard*; O'Neill, *The Emperor Jones*; O'Casey, *The Plough and the Stars*.

CATALAN LITERATURE

Literature in Catalan, the language of northeastern Spain centering in Barcelona, is usually studied in the histories of Spanish literature, and the works on that literature which we list below under Spanish will serve as general reference also for Catalan. The strongly regional spirit of Catalonia calls, however, for the separate mention here of Catalan, with the reminder that the language is closer to Provençal than to Castilian Spanish.

Literary Studies

Bach-y-Rita, P. "Catalan," in Encyclopedia of Literature, ed. Joseph T. Shipley. N.Y., Philosophical Lib., 1946, vol. 1, 138–42.

Fitzmaurice-Kelly, James, and Morel-Fatio, Alfred, and Trend, J. B. "Catalan Literature," in the article "Spanish Literature." Encyclopaedia Britannica, 14th edn., 1929 et seq., vol. 21, 161–63.

García Silvestre, Manuel. *Historia sumaria de la literatura catalana*. Barcelona, Editorial Balmes, 1932. xvii, 424 pp.

Triadú, Joan. "Introduction" to Anthology of Catalan Poetry, ed. Joan Gili. Oxford, Dolphin Book Co., 1953. lxxx, 395 pp.
   The poems are not tr.

Medieval Period

For recent scholarly studies of Catalan literature, see Joan Ruiz i Calonja and Josep Roca i Pons, "Medieval Catalan Literature," in *The Medieval Literature of Western Europe, a Review of Research* (N.Y., New York Univ. Pr. for Modern Language Association, 1966, pp. 365–69).

INDIVIDUAL AUTHORS

See under Spanish Literature, Medieval, below, **Bernat Desclot, Jaime I of Aragon, Ramón Lull, Ramón Muntaner, Mystery of Elche.** We add reference here to **Arnaldus de Villanova** (d. 1313?), whose medical works have received scattered trs. into English: see Clarissa P. Farrar and Austin P. Evans, *English Translations from Medieval Sources* (N.Y., Columbia Univ. Pr., 1946, nos. 373–75); **Joan Martorell,** *Tirant lo Blanch,* an important novel (1460), which may be read in the French adaptation by Anne-Claude-Philippe de Caylus (London, 1740, 2 vols., repr. 1775, repr. Amsterdam 1786); and **St. Vincent Ferrer (1350–1419),** whose sermons in Catalan and/or Latin may be approached in *A Christology from the Sermons,* ed. and tr. Sister Mary Catherine, O.P. (London, Blackfriars Pubns, 1954, viii, 211 pp.).

Modern Period (19th–20th Centuries)

Literary Studies

Amade, Jean.   *Origines et premières manifestations de la renaissance littéraire en Catalogne aux XIXe siècle.* Toulouse, E. Privat, 1924. 568 pp.

Bertrand, Jean-Jacques-Achille.   *La Littérature catalane contemporaine* 1833–1933. Paris, Les Belles Lettres, 1933. 191 pp.

Sales, Joan.   "Catalonian Literature [since 1815]," in Columbia Dictionary of Modern European Literature, 1947, q.v. in General Reference, above.

INDIVIDUAL AUTHORS

19th century, **Victor Balaguer, Jacint Verdaguer** have not been tr. into English. 20th century, **Ángel Guimerá, Carlos Riba Bracons, Merce Rodoreda, Santiago Rusiñol:** See under Spanish Literature, below.

ITALIAN LITERATURE

JOSEPH G. FUCILLA

Background

Italy: A Companion to Italian Studies. Ed. Edmund G. Gardner. London, Methuen, [1934]. x, 274 pp.

Olschki, Leonardo. The Genius of Italy. N.Y., Oxford, 1949, and London, Gollancz, 1950. vii, 481 pp. Repr. Ithaca, N.Y., Cornell Univ. Pr., 1954.
A fine, sympathetic, yet unsentimental account of Italian cultural and intellectual life from the Middle Ages to the present.

Salvatorelli, Luigi. A Concise History of Italy from Prehistoric Times to Our Own Day (*Sommario della storia d'Italia*). Tr. Bernard Miall. London, Allen and Unwin, and N.Y., Oxford, 1940. 688 pp.

Countless histories and studies of Italy and the Italians could be mentioned, but the Gardner book (above) should provide adequate references up to 1934.

Bibliography

"Bibliography of Italian Studies in America." In Italica, vol. 1— (1924—).
The most comprehensive current analytical bibliography.

Fucilla, Joseph G. Universal Author Repertory of Italian Essay Literature. N.Y., Vanni, 1941. 534 pp.
An index of the contents of 1697 volumes of collected Italian literary studies of Italian and foreign writers published from 1821 to 1938. Continued in the following:

————*Saggistica letteraria italiana: Bibliografia per soggetti: 1938-1952.* Firenze, Sansoni antiquariato, 1956. 281 pp.
533 more volumes are covered here.

Modern Language Association. International Bibliography of Books and Articles on the Modern Languages and Literatures. PMLA, vol. 72— (1957—).
> Exhaustive current bibliography of scholarship, which, of course, includes Italian.

Palfrey, Thomas R., Fucilla, Joseph G., and Holbrook, William C. A Bibliographical Guide to the Romance Languages and Literatures. 5th ed. Evanston, Ill., Chandler's, 1963. iv, 121 pp.
> Italian section, pp. 65–85; lists works of reference, periodicals, etc.

Prezzolini, Giuseppe. *Repertorio Bibliografico della storia e della critica della letteratura italiana dal 1902 al 1932.* Roma, Edizioni Roma, 1935. 2 vols.

————(The same) *dal 1932 al 1942.* N.Y., Vanni, 1946. 331 pp.
> An absolutely indispensable listing of scholarly books and articles, especially those written on individual authors.

Shields, Nancy Catching. Italian Translations in America. N.Y., Institute of French Studies, Columbia University [1931]. 410 pp.
> Not always complete or reliable, but registering most of the translations (omitting Dante) which appeared in the U.S. to 1930.

Literary Studies

De Sanctis, Francesco. History of Italian Literature. Tr. Joan Redfern. N.Y., Harcourt, 1931, and London, Oxford Univ. Pr., 1932. 2 vols. Repr. N.Y, Basic Books, 1960; N.Y., Barnes & Noble, 1968.
> Written 1870–72 by the greatest of Italian critics. The work is stimulating but requires some background in order to be appreciated.

Dole, Nathan Haskell. A Teacher of Dante and Other Studies in Italian Literature. N.Y., Moffat, Yard, 1908. 341 pp. Repr. Freeport, N.Y., Books for Libraries, 1967.
> Informative essays by a dilettante on Dante, Petrarch, Boccaccio, Goldoni, Alfieri, and Italian theatre.

Flamini, Francesco. A History of Italian Literature 1265–1907. Tr. Evangeline O'Connor, intro. William M. Rossetti. [N.Y.], National Alumni [1907]. xxx, 370 pp.
> Good criticism of the older school.

Foligno, Cesare. Epochs of Italian Literature. Oxford, Clarendon Pr., 1920. 84 pp.
　　Stimulating and useful summary.

Garnett, Richard. A History of Italian Literature. London, Heinemann, 1898, and N.Y., Appleton, 1900. 431 pp. Repr. N.Y., 1928.
　　Superseded but still of some use.

Hall, Robert A. Jr. A Short History of Italian Literature. Ithaca, N.Y., Linguistica, 1951. 429 pp.
　　Presents literary aspects in the light of their historical background.

Italian Studies Presented to E. R. Vincent. Eds. C. P. Brand, K. Foster, U. Limentani. Cambridge, Eng., Heffer, 1962. x, 316 pp.
　　Scholarly contributions on Dante, Petrarch, Ansius of Viterbo, Antonio Pucci, A. Piccolomini, Tasso, and Manzoni.

Kennard, Joseph Spencer. A Literary History of the Italian People. N.Y., Macmillan, 1941. 418 pp.
　　Draws extensively on the ideas of Carducci, De Sanctis, and Vittorio Rossi.

Kuhns, Oscar. Studies in the Poetry of Italy. II. Italian. N.Y., Chautauqua Pr., 1913. pp. 169–348.
　　On Dante, Petrarch, Boccaccio, Ariosto, Tasso, the origins of Italian literature, the period of decadence, and the revival. Popular presentation.

Luciani, Vincent. A Brief History of Italian Literature. N.Y., Vanni, 1967. 300 pp.
　　Useful manual for students.

————A Concise History of the Italian Theatre. N.Y., Vanni, 1961. 81 pp.
　　Concentrates mainly on the modern period. Original in evaluation.

Prezzolini, Giuseppe. The Legacy of Italy. N.Y., Vanni, 1948. 340 pp.
　　Thirty chapters, including chapters on St. Francis, Dante, Castiglione, Della Casa, Machiavelli, Vasari, G. C. Croce, Galileo, Vico, Humanism, Renaissance, *Commedia dell'arte*, and Romanticism. Stimulating and provocative.

Vittorini, Domenico. High Points in the History of Italian Literature. N.Y., McKay, 1958. 307 pp.
> Essays on special topics relating to authors from Dante to Pirandello and Croce, plus discussions of Romanticism, Realism, and *Verismo.*

Whitfield, John Humphries. A Short History of Italian Literature. Penguin, 1960. 303 pp. Repr. London, Cassell, 1962; N.Y., Barnes & Noble, 1964.
> Sees literature as a continuity of forms. Perceptive and worthwhile.

Wilkins, Ernest Hatch. A History of Italian Literature. Cambridge, Mass., Harvard Univ. Pr., and London, Oxford Univ. Pr., 1954. ix, 523 pp.
> Authoritative, clear. Emphasis on topics of natural interest to American and English readers; stresses literary relations between Italian- and English-speaking countries.

——————The Invention of the Sonnet and Other Studies in Italian Literature. Rome, Edizioni di Storia e Letteratura, 1959. 354 pp.
> Brilliant essays on special topics relating to Dante, Guinizelli, Boccaccio, Pulci, Lorenzo De' Medici, Boiardo, Alfieri, Foscolo, etc.

For supplementary reading see also Edward Armstrong, *Italian Studies,* ed. Cecilia M. Ady (London and N.Y., Macmillan, 1934, xx, 344 pp.), with chs. on Dante, A. E. Piccolomini, and Machiavelli; Erich Auerbach, *Mimesis,* tr. Willard Trask from the German (Princeton, N.J., Princeton Univ. Pr., 1953, and London, Oxford Univ. Pr., 1954, 563 pp.; repr. N.Y., Doubleday, Anchor Books, 1957), with chs. on Dante and Boccaccio; Huntington Cairns, Allen Tate, Mark Van Doren, *Invitation to Learning* (N.Y., Random House, 1941, xix, 431 pp.; repr. New Home Library, 1942), with chs. on Machiavelli, Dante, and Da Vinci; Gilbert Highet, *The Classical Tradition: Greek and Roman Influences in Western Literature* (London and N.Y., Oxford Univ. Pr., 1949, xxxviii, 763 pp.; repr. 1953), with chs. on Dante, Petrarch, Boccaccio, and numerous references to other Italian writers; Giovanni Papini, *Four and Twenty Minds: Essays,* tr. Ernest Hatch Wilkins (N.Y., Crowell, 1922, and London, Harrap, 1923, vii, 324 pp.), with chs on Dante, Da Vinci, L. B. Alberti, Croce, Spadini, Soffici, Oriani, Papini; idem, *Labourers in the Vineyard,* tr. Alice Curtayne (London, Sheed and Ward, and N.Y., Longmans, 1930, ix, 262 pp.), with chs. on Petrarch, Michelangelo, Jacopone da Todi, Manzoni, Giuliotti; George Santayana, *Essays in Literary Criticism,* selected and ed. with intro. Irving Singer (N.Y.,

Scribner, 1956, xxviii, 414 pp.), with chs. on Dante and Leopardi; William Roscoe Thayer, *Italica*: *Studies in Italian Life and Letters* (Boston, Mass., Houghton Mifflin, and London, Constable, 1908, viii, 364 pp.; repr. 1915), with chs. on Dante, Bruno, Leopardi, and Carducci. For special topics which include discussion of Dante, Tasso, D'Annunzio, etc., see Rudolph Altrocchi, *Sleuthing in the Stacks* (Cambridge, Mass., Harvard Univ. Pr., 1944, xiii, 279 pp.).

Collections

An Anthology of Italian Authors from Cavalcanti to Fogazzaro (1270–1907).   Ed. Rossiter Johnson. N.Y., National Alumni, 1907. ix, 388 pp.
Brief selections from twenty-six authors, the longest being by Giordano Bruno, from *Causes and Principle*, tr. John Toland, pp. 99–128; by Metastasio, the play *Achilles in Scyros*, tr. John Hoole, pp. 141–229; and by Gionanni Verga, the two stories "Rustic Chivalry" and "The Wolf," tr. Dora Knowlton Ranous.

The Classic Theatre.   Vol. 1. Six Italian Plays. Ed. Eric Bentley, trs. various. Garden City, N.Y., Doubleday (Anchor Books), 1958. 375 pp.
Machiavelli, *The Mandrake*, tr. Frederick May and Eric Bentley; Angelo Beolco, *Rozzante Returns from the Wars*, tr. Angela Ingold and Theodore Hoffman; anon., *The Three Cuckolds*, tr. Leo Katz; Goldoni, *The Servant of Two Masters*, tr. Edward J. Dent, and *Mirandolina (La Locandiera)*, tr. Lady Augusta Gregory; Gozzi, *The King Stag*, tr. Carl Wildman.

Crane, Thomas Frederick, ed. and tr.   Italian Popular Tales. N.Y., Houghton Mifflin, 1885. 389 pp.
Rich repertoire.

De'Lucchi, Lorna, ed. and tr.   An Anthology of Italian Poems, 13th–19th Century. Pref. Cesare Foligno. London, Heinemann, and N.Y., Knopf, 1922. xxiii, 159 pp., parallel texts. Repr. N.Y., Biblo and Tannen, 1966.
Readable versions of poems by Dante, St. Francis, Boccaccio, Machiavelli, Michelangelo, Manzoni, Carducci.

European Theories of the Drama.   Ed. Barrett H. Clark. Rev. N.Y., Crown, 1947. 576 pp.
Includes selections from Dante, Daniello, Minturno, Scaliger, Castel-

vetro, Goldoni, and a bibliography of Italian dramatic criticism from the Renaissance to the present.

Everett, William.   The Italian Poets since Dante: Accompanied by Verse Translations. N.Y., Scribner, 1904, and London, Duckworth, 1905. xi, 251 pp.

The Folksongs of Italy.   Ed. R[achel] H[arriette] Busk. London, Sonnenschein, 1887. 290 pp.
Specimens from each province, with trs. and notes.

The Genius of the Italian Theatre.   Ed. Eric Bentley, trs. various. N.Y., New Amer. Lib., 1964. 584 pp.
Bibbiena, *The Follies of Calandro*; Bruno, *The Candle Bearer*; Tasso, *Aminta*; Gozzi, *Turandot*; De Filippo, *Filumena Marturano*; Pirandello, *The Emperor* (Henry IV).

Great Italian Short Stories.   Ed. Decio Pettoello. London, Bonn, 1930. 923 pp.
From the Renaissance to our time, but mainly contemporary.

Hall, Robert A., Jr., ed. and tr.   Italian Stories/*Novelle Italiane*. N.Y., Bantam, [1926]. 1961. xii, 351 pp.
Stories from Bandello, Boccaccio, Machiavelli, Fogazzaro, Fucini, Verga, Alvaro, D'Annunzio, Moravia, Palazzeschi, Pirandello.

An Italian Anthology.   Selected and ed. Florence Trail. Boston, Badger, [1926]. 208 pp.
One hundred and eighty selections, trs. various.

Kay, George R., tr.   The Penguin Book of Italian Verse. Penguin, 1958. xxxv, 424 pp., parallel texts. Repr. enl. 1965, xxxv, 438 pp.
Selections from St. Francis to Quasimodo, with literal prose trs.

The Literature of Italy, 1265–1907.   Ed. Rossiter Johnson. N.Y., National Alumni, 1907. xiv, 344 pp.
Dante, *The New Life*, tr. Rossetti; Petrarch, one hundred sonnets, trs. various; Boccaccio, *La Fiammetta*, tr. James C. Brogan; Michelangelo, poems, tr. J. A. Symonds.

Longfellow, Henry Wadsworth, tr.   The Poets and Poetry of Europe. Rev. enl. Boston, Houghton Mifflin, 1896. xxi, 921 pp.
> Original, 1845. Among the ten languages represented is, of course, Italian.

Pasinetti, P. M., ed. and tr.   Great Italian Short Stories. N.Y., Dell, 1959. 412 pp.
> From Boccaccio and Sacchetti to Moravia and Vittorini.

Penguin Book of Italian Short Stories.   Ed. Guido Waldman, trs. various. Penguin, 1969. 335 pp.
> Twenty-five stories from eight medieval and renaissance collections, and fifteen stories by recent writers from Verga to Calvino.

Rendel, Romilda, ed. and tr.   An Anthology of Italian Lyrics from the Thirteenth Century to the Present. London, Lane, 1923. 265 pp.
> Good verse trs.

Roscoe, Thomas, tr.   The Italian Novelists. London, Prowett, 1825. 4 vols. Repr. 1836, 1880.
> A large number of Italian *novelle* (short stories) by some thirty authors from the earliest times. For names of authors, see the Library of Congress Catalogue.

Whitmore, Frederick, tr.   Sonnets After the Italian and Other Sonnets. Springfield, Mass., Ridgewood Pr., 1902. 44 pp.
> Trs. from Petrarch, Dante, Della Casa, Michelangelo, Vittoria Colonna, Filicaia, Zappi, Frugoni, Cassiani, Parini, Carducci.

Medieval Period

Literary Studies

Gaspary, Adolph.   The History of Italian Literature to the Death of Dante, Together with the Author's Additions to the Italian Translation [1887].

Tr. Herman Oelsner from German. London, Bell, 1901. 414 pp.
Somewhat outmoded, but still reliable.

Luciani, Vincent. "Medieval Italian Literature," in The Medieval Literature of Western Europe: A Review of Research, Mainly 1930–1960. N.Y., N.Y. Univ. Pr. for Modern Language Association, 1966, pp. 281–327.

Ozanam, Frederick [i.e., Antoine-Frédéric Ozanam]. The Franciscan Poets in Italy of the Thirteenth Century. Tr. A. E. Nellen and N. C. Craig from French (1852). London, Nutt, 1914. 329 pp.
Convincing presentation of the spirit of the Franciscan movement.

Vittorini, Domenico. The Age of Dante: A Concise History of Italian Culture in the Years of the Early Renaissance. Illus. Fred Haucke. Syracuse, N.Y., Syracuse Univ. Pr., 1957. xv, 188 pp.
Main topics are Dante, Popular Poetry, Courtly Poetry, Prose Writings of the 13th Century.

**Vossler, Karl. Mediaeval Culture: An Introduction to Dante and His Times. Tr. William Cranston Lawton from German. N.Y., Harcourt, and London, Constable, [1929]. 2 vols. Repr. N.Y., Ungar, 1958.
One of the most important studies of the literary background; the tr. adds an extensive bibliog. by J. E. Spingarn.

Collections

The Early Italian Poets, with Dante's Vita Nuova. Tr. Dante Gabriel Rossetti. London, Smith Elder, 1861. xxxvi, 464 pp. Repr. enl. as Dante and His Circle, 1874. Many reprs. under either title, notably in The Muses' Library: London, Routledge, and N.Y., Dutton, 1905; and EL (in the vol. Poems and Translations by Rossetti), 1912 et seq.
Poetical trs., Pre-Raphaelite in wording, not always literal.

INDIVIDUAL AUTHORS

Dante Alighieri (1265–1321). The Portable Dante: The Divine Comedy: La Vita Nuova: Excerpts from the Latin Prose Works. Ed. with intro. Paolo Milano. N.Y., Viking Pr., 1947. xlii, 662 pp. Repr. 1955, 1963.

The *Divine Comedy* is tr. Laurence Binyon, q.v. below; the *Vita Nuova* by Rossetti, see Collections, Medieval, above.

————The Divine Comedy. Tr. Henry Boyd in blank verse as The Divina Commedia. London, Cadell and Davies, 1802. 3 vols.
The first complete English tr.

Tr. Henry Francis Cary in blank verse as The Vision. London, Barfield, 1814. 3 vols. Repr. 1814, etc., to 1844 (the last ed. during the translator's lifetime). Numerous reprs., especially in Bohn's Library, and in EL (1908 et seq.); the famous illustrations of Gustave Doré first appeared in the 1866 ed.; the Botticelli drawings and the Italian text were included in the repr. Florence, Fattorusso, 1930, etc.
The classic English tr.

Eighteen other trs. are recorded in the 19th century, including that in blank verse by Henry Wadsworth Longfellow (Boston, Ticknor and Fields, and London, Routledge, 1867, 3 vols., often repr., e.g., The Inferno, N.Y., Collier Books, 1962); and that in prose by his successor Charles Eliot Norton (Boston, Houghton Mifflin, 1891–92, 3 vols.), which tries to render Dante's own words in words that closely correspond to them: often repr., notably with useful appendix by Ernest H. Wilkins (1941, 3 vols in 1), and again in Great Books, vol. 21 (1952, x, 163 pp.).

The 20th century counts so far 32 complete trs., of which the following earlier ones may be noted.
Tr. prose John A. Carlyle (*Inferno*), Thomas Okey (*Purgatorio*), and P. H. Wicksteed (*Paradiso*). Temple Classics. London, Dent, 1899–1901. 3 vols. Repr. with intro. C. H. Grandgent, ML, 1932 et seq. xv, 601 pp.
One of the best of the literal trs., with adequate notes.

Tr. terza rima Melville Best Anderson. Yonkers, N.Y., World Book, and London, Oxford Univ. Pr., 1921. xiii, 449 pp. Repr. San Francisco, 1929, 3 vols.; in parallel texts, London [1932], 3 vols.; London [1933]; N.Y., Heritage Pr., 1944, with the Blake illustrations; N.Y., Dial Pr., 1959.

Tr. unlinked tercets Jefferson B. Fletcher. N.Y., Macmillan, 1931. xxii, 471 pp. Repr. N.Y., Columbia Univ. Pr., 1951.

Tr. terza rima Lacy Lockert. Princeton, N.J., Princeton Univ. Pr., 1931–34. 3 vols.

Tr. terza rima Laurence Binyon. London, Macmillan, 1933–43. 2 vols. Repr. in The Portable Dante, 1947, see above.

The following translations have been published since 1945.

Tr. prose John D. Sinclair. London, Lane, 1939–46. 3 vols. Rev. 1948; repr. N.Y., Oxford, 1961.

Tr. blank verse Lawrence Grant White. N.Y., Pantheon, 1948. 202 pp.

Tr. prose Harry Morgan Ayres. N.Y., Vanni, 1949–53. 3 vols.

Tr. blank verse Thomas G. Bergin. N.Y., Appleton, 1948–54. 3 vols. Repr. 1955.

> Occasional passages are summarized in prose. The tr. gives a satisfying presentation of the substance of Dante's poem.

Tr. blank verse John Ciardi. Brunswick, N.J., Rutgers Univ. Pr., 1954. 3 vols. Repr. N.Y., New Amer. Lib., 1954, 1961.

> An excellent attempt to preserve "Dante's vulgate" and "Dante's pace." Well annotated.

Tr. prose Howard Russell Huse. N.Y., Rinehart, 1954. 492 pp.

Tr. triple rhyme Geoffrey L. Bickersteth. Aberdeen, Aberdeen Univ. Pr., 1955. xv, 239 pp. Repr. Oxford, Shakespeare Head Pr., and Cambridge, Mass., Harvard Univ. Pr., 1965. xliii, 795 pp., parallel texts.

> The tr. of Paradiso was pub. Cambridge Univ. Pr., 1932.

Tr. terza rima Glen Levin Swiggett. Sewanee, Tenn., Univ. Pr. of the Univ. of the South, 1956. xiv, 567 pp.

Tr. blank hendecasyllabic verse Mary Prentice Lillie as The Comedy. San Francisco, Grabhorn Pr., 1958. 3 vols.

Tr. blank verse and terza rima Dorothy Leigh Sayers and Barbara Reynolds. Penguin, 1955–62. 3 vols. Repr. with selected Blake drawings, N.Y., Basic Books, 1962. 3 vols.

> Completed by Miss Reynolds after the death of Miss Sayers. A good colloquial tr., which succeeds in capturing Dante's humor better than other trs. Ample notes.

Tr. Clara S. Reed as The Divine Poem. Wilbraham, Mass., Stinehour Pr., 1962. vi, 312 pp.

Tr. blank verse Louis Biancolli. N.Y., Washington Square Pr., 1966. 3 vols., parallel texts. Repr. 1968, 466 pp. paper.

> An interesting new verse tr. of the Inferno is that of Aldo Maugeri as Dante's Hell (Messina, La Sicilia, 1965, 208 pp.).

The bibliographical authority on the trs. is Paget Toynbee, *Britain's Tribute to Dante* . . . [c. 1380–1920] (London, British Academy [1921]); this is supplemented and summarized for the *Divine Comedy* by Farrar and Evans, *English Trs. from Medieval Sources* (1946), nos. 1187–1223. For an evaluation of the American trs., see Angelina La Piana, *Dante's American Pilgrimage* (*1800–1944*) (Cambridge, Mass., Harvard Univ. Pr., 1948). For a valuable analysis of a number of trs., see William J. De Sua, *Dante into English* (Univ. North Carolina Studies Comparative Literature 32, Univ. North Carolina Pr., 1964): pp. 127–32 gives a complete "Chronological List of Translations." See also Gilbert F. Cunningham, *The Divine Comedy in English: A Critical Bibliography*, *1782–1900* (Edinburgh and London, Oliver and Boyd, and N.Y., Barnes and Noble, 1967, xii, 206 pp.).

————Dante's Lyric Poetry. Ed. and tr. Kenelm Foster and Patrick Boyde. Oxford, Clarendon Pr., and N.Y., Oxford Univ. Pr., 1967. 2 vols., parallel texts. (Vol. 2 contains commentary.)

Tr. Lorna de' Lucchi as The Minor Poems. London, Milford, 1926. ix, 172 pp.

————The Odes (*Canzoni*). Tr. H. S. Vere-Hodge. Oxford, Clarendon Pr., 1963. x, 269 pp.

————The New Life (*Vita Nuova*). Tr. Dante Gabriel Rossetti: see The Early Italian Poets, in Collections, Medieval Period, above.

Tr. Ralph Waldo Emerson. Ed. and annotated J. Chesley Matthews. Harvard Library Bulletin, vol. 11 (1957), 346–62. Repr. rev. Chapel Hill, Univ. of North Carolina Pr., 1960, xiii, 145 pp.

Tr. Charles Eliot Norton. Boston, Ticknor and Fields, 1867. 149 pp. Many reprs. to 1920.

Tr. Mark Musa. New Brunswick, N.J., Rutgers Univ. Pr., and London, Paterson, 1957. ix, 86 pp., parallel texts. Rev. Bloomington, Indiana Univ. Pr., 1962; repr. Gloucester, Mass., P. Smith, 1966. Faithful, harmonious, and verbally beautiful version.

Tr. William S. Anderson. Penguin, 1964. 110 pp.

Tr. Barbara Reynolds as *La vita nuova* (*Poems of Youth*). Penguin, 1969. 123 pp. Farrar and Evans, *English Translations from Medieval Sources*, lists six other trs. (nos. 1235–42), besides two other trs. of the complete *Canzoniere* (nos. 1175–76).

ITALIAN PROSE WORKS

————The Banquet (*Il convivio*). Tr. Philip H. Wicksteed. Temple Classics. London, Dent, 1903. ii, 447 pp. Repr. 1908, 1909, 1912.

Tr. William Walrond Jackson as Dante's Convivio. Oxford, Clarendon Pr., 1909. 318 pp.

Two other trs. are listed by Farrar and Evans (nos. 1178–79).

LATIN WORKS

————The Latin Works. Tr. A. G. Ferrers Howell and Philip H. Wicksteed. Temple Classics. London, Dent, 1904. viii, 428 pp.
De monarchia; *De vulgari eloquentia* (originally pub. separately by A. G. Ferrers Howell, London 1890); *Quaestio de aqua et terra*; *Epistolae*; *Eclogae* (also pub. separately in a prose version by Philip H. Wicksteed with the Latin text, Westminster, Constable, 1902. x, 340 pp.). See Farrar and Evans, nos. 1174, 1183–86, 1224–34. Other versions of individual works should be mentioned.

————The *De Monarchia*. Tr. Aurelia Henry. Boston and N.Y., Houghton Mifflin, 1904. li, 216 pp.

Tr. Donald Nicholl as Monarchy and Three Political Letters (the Letters tr. Colin Hardie). London, Weidenfeld, and N.Y., Noonday Pr., 1954. xxi, 121 pp. Repr. N.Y., Hillary House, 1965.

Tr. Herbert W. Schneider as On World-Government. N.Y., Liberal Arts Pr., 1957. 80 pp.

————*Epistolae*: The Letters of Dante. Tr. Paget Toynbee. Oxford, Clarendon Pr., 1920. liv, 305 pp., parallel texts. Repr. ed. C. G. Hardie, London and N.Y., Oxford Univ. Pr., 1967.

The greatest collection of Danteiana is described in the Cornell Univ. Library *Catalogue of the Dante Collection*, ed. Theodore W. Koch (Ithaca, N.Y., 1898–1900, 2 vols.) and *Additions 1898–1920* (vol. 3, 1921). For other bibliographies, see N. D. Evola, *Bibliografia dantesca: 1920–30*

(Florence, Olschki, 1932). From 1955 the indispensable bibliography is Anthony L. Pellegrini, "American Dante Bibliography" in *Annual Report of the Dante Society*. See also Daniel J. Donno, "Recent Scholarship on Dante," in *Renaissance Quarterly*, vol. 20 (1967), pp. 273–78.

Among the many fine books in English on Dante, the following are most useful: Erich Auerbach, *Dante: Poet of the Secular World*, tr. Ralph Manheim from German (Chicago, Ill., Univ. of Chicago Pr., 1961, viii, 194 pp.); Michele Barbi, *Life of Dante*, tr. and ed. P. G. Ruggiers (Berkeley, Univ. of California Pr., 1954, x, 132 pp.); Thomas G. Bergin, *Dante* (Boston, Mass., Houghton Mifflin, and London, Bodley Head [as An Approach to Dante], 1965, 326 pp.); Thomas Caldecot Chubb, *Dante and His World* (Boston, Mass., Little Brown, 1967, 831 pp.); Umberto Cosmo, *A Handbook to Dante Studies*, tr. David Moore from Italian (Oxford, Blackwell, and N.Y., Barnes and Noble, 1950, vi, 194 pp.); Benedetto Croce, *The Poetry of Dante*, tr. Douglas Ainslie from Italian (London, Allen and Unwin, and N.Y., Holt, 1922, vi, 313 pp.); Francesco De Sanctis, *De Sanctis on Dante*, eds. Joseph Rossi and Alfred Galpin (Madison, Univ. of Wisconsin Pr., 1957, 192 pp.); Werner Paul Friederich, *Dante's Fame Abroad: 1350–1800: The Influence of Dante on the Poets and Scholars of Spain, France, England, Germany, Switzerland, and the United States* (Rome, Edizioni di Storia e Letteratura, and Chapel Hill, Univ. of North Carolina Pr., 1950, 583 pp.); Charles S. Singleton, *Dante Studies I and II* (Cambridge, Mass., Harvard Univ. Pr., for the Dante Society, 1949, 168 pp.); Paget Toynbee, *Concise Dictionary of Proper Names and Notable Matters in the Works of Dante* (Oxford, Clarendon Pr., 1914, viii, 568 pp.; rev. Charles S. Singleton, ibid., and N.Y., Oxford Univ. Pr., 1967); Karl Vossler, *Mediaeval Culture* (see Literary Studies, Medieval Period, above). For the earliest biographies, see Boccaccio, below.

Angela of Foligno, The Blessed (1248–1309). The Book of Visions and Instructions as Taken Down from Her Own Lips by Brother Arnold. Tr. A. P. J. Cruikshank from Latin. London, etc., Thomas Richardson, 1871. xxiv, 349 pp.

————The Book of Divine Consolation. Tr. Mary G. Steegmann from Italian. London, Chatto, and N.Y., Duffield, 1909. xliv, 265 pp. Repr. N.Y., Cooper Square, 1966.

Cavalcanti, Guido (c. 1250–1300). The Sonnets and Ballate. Tr. Ezra Pound. Boston, Mass., Small, Maynard, and London, Swift, 1912. xxiv, 119 pp.

See also *The Early Italian Poets*, in Collections, Medieval Period, above, for Rossetti's tr. of twenty-nine of the poems. On Cavalcanti, see James Eustace Shaw, *Guido Cavalcanti's Theory of Love and the "Canzone d'Amore" and Other Related Problems* (Toronto, Univ. of Toronto Pr., 1949, 228 pp.).

Compagni, Dino (c. 1260–1324).   The Chronicles of Dino Compagni. Trs. Else C. M. Benecke and A. G. Ferrers Howell. Temple Classics. London, Dent, 1906. vii, 284 pp.

Folgore da San Gimignano (13th c.).   The Months of the Year, Twelve Sonnets (*Sonetti de' mesi*). Tr. Thomas Caldecot Chubb. Sanbornville, N.H., Wake-Brook House, 1960. 63 pp.

*———A Wreath for San Gemignano. Tr. Richard Aldington. N.Y., Duell Sloan, 1945, and London, Heinemann, 1946. 30 pp.
    A beautiful prose rendering.

Francis of Assisi, St. (1182–1226).   The [Latin] Writings of St. Francis of Assisi. Tr. Father Paschal Robinson. Philadelphia, Pa., Dolphin Pr., 1906. xxxii, 208 pp.

   Tr. Benen Fahy, O.F.M., with intro. Placid Hermann, O.F.M. Chicago, Ill., Franciscan Herald Pr., 1964. 200 pp.
      Tr. from the approved Quaracchi ed. of the *Opuscula*, 1904, repr. 1949.

———The Little Flowers (*Fioretti*). Tr. anon. and ed. Rev. H. E. Manning (later Cardinal). London, Burns and Lambert [1864]. xv, 260 pp. Repr. London and N.Y., 1887; London, 1915; rev. Dom Roger Hudleston, 1926, and with intro. Arthur Livingston, N.Y., Limited Eds., 1930; repr. Westminster, Md., Newman Pr., and London, Burns Oates, 1953, xxii, 245 pp.; repr. N.Y., Heritage Pr., 1965, 261 pp.

   Tr. T. W. Arnold. Temple Classics. London, Dent, 1898. xiii, 320 pp. Repr. 1900, 1903, 1908, 1909, 1925.

   Tr. verse James Rhoades. London, Chapman and Hall, 1904. xv, 302 pp. Repr. WC, [1925], [1934], 1950.

   Tr. William Heywood. London, Methuen, [1906]. xxviii, 202 pp. Repr. [1924], 1950.

Tr. Thomas Okey, with The Life by St. Bonaventura, and The Mirror of Perfection by Brother Leo. EL, [1910]. xxii, 397 pp. Repr. 1912, 1917, 1927, 1934, 1951, 1963.

Possibly the best tr. *The Mirror* is tr. by Robert Steele, originally pub. 1903.

Tr. Rev. Valentine Long. N.Y., Catholic Book Pub Co., 1946. 384 pp.

Tr. Raphael Brown. Garden City, N.Y., Hanover House, also Image Books, 1958. 357 pp.

Tr. Leo Sherley-Price. Penguin, 1959. 205 pp.

Tr. Serge Hughes as The Little Flowers and Other Franciscan Writings. N.Y., New Amer. Lib., 1964. 222 pp.

Tr. Hilda Noel Schroetter. N.Y., Golden Pr., 1967. 62 pp.

The biographies and legends of St. Francis are conveniently surveyed in the *Encyclopaedia Britannica* article on the saint by Dom E. C. Butler. The works translated (from the original Latin) are as follows.

————The Lady Poverty: A XIII Century Allegory (*Sacrum commercium beati Francisci cum Domina Paupertate*). Tr. and ed. Montgomery Carmichael. London, Murray, also Burns and Oates, 1901. xlviii, 209 pp. Repr. 1902, also N.Y., Tennant and Ward, 1902.

Tr. Canon H. D. Rawnsley as The Converse of Francis and His Sons with Holy Poverty. Temple Classics. London, Dent, 1904. xxvii, 118 pp.

A poem by a disciple.

————The Legend of St. Francis by the Three Companions (*Legenda trium sociorum*). Tr. E. Gurney Salter. Temple Classics. London, Dent, 1902. 136 pp. Repr. 1904, 1905.

————The Life of St. Francis (*Legenda Sancti Francisci*), by St. Bonaventura (1221–1274). Tr. E. Gurney Salter as The Life and Miracles. Temple Classics. London, Dent, 1904. vi, 219 pp. The Life (only) repr. EL, 1910 et seq., with The Little Flowers of St. Francis, see above.
For earlier trs., see Farrar and Evans, *English Translations from Medieval Sources*, nos. 726–28.

————The Lives of St. Francis, by Brother Thomas of Celano (13th c.). Tr. A. G. Ferrers Howell. London, Methuen, and N.Y., Dutton, 1908. xxiv, 360 pp.

> Tr. and ed. Placid Hermann, O.F.M., as The First and Second Lives of St. Francis. Chicago, Franciscan Herald, 1963. xxx, 245 pp.

————The Mirror of Perfection (*Speculum perfectionis*). Tr. Sebastian Evans. London, Nutt, 1898. xvi, 231 pp. Repr. 1899, 1900, and Boston, Page, 1900.

> Once ascribed to Brother Leo.

> Tr. Constance Countess de la Warr. London, Burns and Oates, 1902. xvi, 185 pp.

> Tr. Robert Steele from Manuscript. Temple Classics. London, Dent, 1903. 197 pp. Repr. EL, 1910 et seq., with The Little Flowers.

> Tr. Leo Sherley-Price. London, Mowbray, 1959, and N.Y., Harper, 1960. 234 pp.

On St. Francis, see the Danish biographer Johannes Jørgensen (English tr., 1912) and the French biographer Paul Sabatier (English tr., 1901); the latest biography is by Thomas S. Boase, *Francis of Assisi* (Bloomington, Indiana Univ. Pr., 1968, ill., 120 pp.). For the early chronicles of the Franciscans, see in vol. 1, Medieval Latin Literature, Thomas of Celano (*Life of St. Clare*) and Thomas of Eccleston.

Il Novellino: The Hundred Old Tales.   Tr. Edward Storer. Broadway Trs. London, Routledge, and N.Y., Dutton, 1928. 211 pp.
> A pleasing tr. of the anon. work (c. 1200 A.D.), with a good introduction.

Jacopone da Todi (1228–1306).   A Selection from the Spiritual Songs. Tr. Mrs. Theodore Beck, in Evelyn Underhill, Jacopone da Todi: Poet and Mystic. London, Dent, and N.Y., Dutton, 1919, pp. 241–501.

Odorico da Pordenone (1286–1331).   For the account of his journey to China, see vol. 1, Medieval Latin Literature, s.v.

Polo, Marco (1245–1325).   The Book of Ser Marco Polo. Tr. Sir Henry Yule. 3d ed. rev. by Henri Cordier. London, Murray, and N.Y., Scribner, 1903. 2 vols.
> A classic tr. of Polo's *Travels* (1st ed., 1871) from the original French,

plus the expansions of the Ramusio Italian version. The text is now superseded by changes embodied in later eds. of the original, but the notes make this tr. indispensable. The Yule tr., without the extensive Yule notes, was rev. and ed. George B. Parks (N.Y., Macmillan, 1927, xxxiii, 392 pp.).

Tr. Aldo Ricci as The Travels of Marco Polo. Broadway Trs. London, Routledge, and N.Y., Viking, 1931. 329 pp. Repr. 1951.
From the modern Italian version by L. F. Benedetto, editor of the authoritative text (1928) of the original French (*Il Milione*).

Tr. A. C. Moule and Paul Pelliot as The Description of the World. London, Routledge, 1938. 2 vols.
Vol. 1 is a new tr. of a composite original, making use of the expanded Latin version of the original recently discovered at Toledo. Vol. 2 is an ed. of that version.

Tr. Ronald Latham as The Travels. Penguin, 1958. xxxi, 351 pp. Repr. London, Folio Soc., 1968.
The 1579 English tr. by John Frampton, done from the Spanish version, was repr. with valuable notes by N. M. Penzer (London, Argonaut Pr., 1929, lx, 381 pp.; repr. London, Black, 1937). The rather stiff tr. by William Marsden (1818) from Ramusio's Italian version (which contains much material now known to be derived from the Toledo ms.) has been the one most repr., notably by EL 1908 et seq., and recently, with intro. by Milton Rugoff, in the New Amer. Lib. (N.Y., 1961, 302 pp. paper), and again (N.Y., AMS Pr., 1968). On Marco Polo's book, see Leonardo Olschki, *Marco Polo's Asia: An Introduction to His Description of the World Called Il Milione*, tr. from Italian by John A. Scott and rev. by the author (Berkeley, Univ. of California Pr., 1960, ix, 459 pp.); and Henry Hersch Hart, *Marco Polo, Venetian Adventurer* (Norman, Univ. of Oklahoma Pr., 1968, xxii, 306 pp.).

Villani, Giovanni (d. 1348).   Selections from the First Nine Books of the *Croniche Fiorentine*. Tr. Rose E. Selfe, ed. Philip H. Wicksteed. Westminster, Constable, 1896. xlviii, 461 pp. Repr. London, 1906, and N.Y., Dutton, 1907.

The Renaissance

Bibliography

"Recent Literature of the Renaissance: Italian."   Studies in Philology, vols. 36–69 (1931–69).
> An annual listing.

Scott, Mary Augusta.   Elizabethan Translations from the Italian [to 1660]. Boston, Houghton Mifflin, 1916. xxxi, 558 pp.

> See also Fucilla, PMLA, Prezzolini, in Italian Literature, Bibliographies, above.

Literary Studies

Art, Science, and History in the Renaissance.   Ed. Charles Singleton. Baltimore, Johns Hopkins Pr., 1968. 448 pp.
> Contains studies of Lorenzo de'Medici, Bruno, Galileo, and Machiavelli.

*Baron, Hans.   The Crisis of the Early Renaissance: Civic Humanism and Republican Liberty in an Age of Classicism and Tyranny. Princeton, N.J., Princeton Univ. Pr., 1955. 2 vols. Repr. rev. 1966, xxviii, 582 pp. paper.
> Keen analyses of individual writings or group of writings including discussions of Bruni, Salutati, Vergerio, and Dati.

——————From Petrarch to Leonardo Bruni: Studies in Humanistic and Political Literature. Chicago, Univ. of Chicago Pr., 1968. 269 pp.

——————Humanistic and Political Literature in Florence and Venice at the Beginning of the Quattrocento. Cambridge, Mass., Harvard Univ. Pr., 1954. x, 222 pp.
> Painstaking and exhaustive scholarship. Includes G. Da Prato, G. Dati, and L. Bruni.

Burckhardt, Jakob Christoph.   The Civilization of the Renaissance in Italy. Tr. S. G. C. Middelmore from the German (3d ed.). London, 1878. Tr. the same (from the 15th ed.), London, Harrap, and N.Y., Harper, 1929,

526 pp. Repr. Vienna, Phaidon Pr., and London, Allen and Unwin, 1937, xxiii, 642 pp., reprs. to 6th printing, London, Phaidon Pr., 1960, and N.Y., Oxford Univ. Pr., 1962. Rev. Irene Gordon, N.Y., New Amer. Lib., 1961, 392 pp. paper.

Crane, Thomas Frederick.   Italian Social Customs of the Sixteenth Century and Their Influence on the Literature of Europe. New Haven, Conn., Yale Univ. Pr., 1920. 689 pp.
   A study of the tradition of courtly love; invaluable background for comparative literature.

Duchartre, Pierre Louis.   The Italian Comedy: The Improvisation, Scenarios, Lives, Attributes, Portraits and Masks of Illustrious Characters of the Commedia dell'Arte. Tr. Randolph T. Weaver from French. London, Harrap, and N.Y., Day, 1929. 331 pp. Repr. N.Y., Dover, 1966.
   Fine study, profusely illustrated.

**Einstein, Alfred.   The Italian Madrigal. Tr. A. H. Krappe, R. H. Sessions, and Oliver Strunk. Princeton, N.J., Princeton Univ. Pr., 1950. xvi, 1266 pp. (3 vols.).
   Thorough, detailed, critically important.

Ferguson, Wallace K.   The Renaissance in Historical Thought: Five Centuries of Interpretation. Boston, Houghton Mifflin, 1948. xiv, 429 pp.
   Solid; academic in treatment.

Fletcher, Jefferson Butler.   Literature of the Italian Renaissance. N.Y. and London, Macmillan, 1934. 347 pp. Repr. Port Washington, N.Y., Kennikat Pr., 1964.
   Attractive introduction to Renaissance literature, of particular interest to laymen rather than specialists.

*Gardner, Edmund G.   Dukes and Poets of Ferrara: A Study in the Religion and Politics of the Fifteenth and Early Sixteenth Century. London, Constable, and N.Y., Dutton, 1904. 578 pp.
   Admirable background material.

Garin, Eugenio.   Italian Humanism. Tr. Peter Munz from the rev. Italian ed. N.Y., Harper, 1965, and Oxford, Blackwell, 1966. xxiv, 227 pp.

Greg, Walter W. Pastoral Poetry and Pastoral Drama: A Literary Inquiry with Special Reference to the Pre-Restoration Stage in England. London, Bullen, 1907. 464 pp. Repr. N.Y., Russell, 1959.
Informative.

Grillo, Giacomo. Poets of the Court of Ferrara: Ariosto, Tasso, and Guarini, with a Chapter on Michelangelo. Boston, Excelsior Pr., 1943. 139 pp.
May serve for an introductory orientation.

Hall, Vernon, Jr. Renaissance Literary Criticism: A Study of Its Social Content. N.Y., Columbua Univ. Pr., 1945. 260 pp.

Hathaway, Baxter. The Age of Criticism: The Late Renaissance in Italy. Ithaca, N.Y., Cornell Univ. Pr., 1962. 473 pp.
Discusses concepts of literary criticism at the time, with special chapters on Patrizi, Tasso, Robortello and Maggi, Speroni and Tomitano, Fracastoro, and Mazzoni.

————Marvels and Commonplaces: Renaissance Literary Criticism. N.Y., Random House, 1968. 224 pp. paper.

Hay, Denys. The Italian Renaissance in Its Historical Background. Cambridge, Cambridge Univ. Pr., 1961. xii, 218 pp.
An unbiased, fresh appraisal which is provocative and valuable.

Herrick, Marvin T. The Fusion of Horatian and Aristotelian Criticism, 1551–1555. Urbana, Ill., Univ. of Illinois Pr., 1946. 117 pp.
Discussion of critical theories of Castelvetro, De Nores, Maggi, Minturno, Philippus, Robortello, Scaliger, Landino, etc.

————Italian Comedy in the Renaissance. Urbana, Ill., Univ. of Illinois Pr., 1960. 338 pp.
With summaries and interesting observations; aimed mainly at readers not familiar with Italian.

————Italian Tragedy in the Renaissance. Urbana, Univ. of Illinois Pr., 1964. 320 pp.

Italian Renaissance Studies: A Tribute to the Late Cecilia M. Ady. Ed. E. F. Jacob. London, Faber, and N.Y., Barnes and Noble, 1960. 507 pp.
Distinguished essays by well-known English scholars.

Kristeller, Paul Oskar. The Classics and Renaissance Thought. Martin Classical Lectures, XV. Pub. for Oberlin College by Harvard Univ. Pr., 1955. xiv, 106 pp.
> Lectures on Humanism, Aristotelism, Platonism, Paganism, and Christianity.

——————Eight Philosophers of the Italian Renaissance. Stanford, Calif., Stanford Univ. Pr., 1964. 193 pp.
> Includes lectures on Petrarch, Valla, Ficino, Pico, Pomponazzi, Telesio, Patrizi, and Bruno. From a discussion of these pivotal figures we can acquire an excellent unified interpretation of Italian Renaissance thought.

——————Renaissance Philosophy and Mediaeval Tradition. Latrobe, Pa., Archabbey Pr., 1966. 120 pp.

——————Studies in Renaissance Thought and Letters. Roma, Edizioni di Storia e Letteratura, 1956. xvi, 690 pp.
> A series of penetrating chapters: nine on Ficino and his circle, ten on problems and aspects of the Renaissance, and three on the topic "From the Middle Ages to the Renaissance."

Lea, Kathleen M. Italian Popular Comedy: A Study in the Commedia dell'Arte, 1560–1620, with Special Reference to the English Stage. Oxford, Clarendon Pr., and N.Y., Oxford Univ. Pr., 1934. 697 pp.
> Rich in materials, although somewhat badly arranged.

Martines, Lauro. The Social World of the Florentine Humanists, 1390–1460. Princeton, N.J., Princeton Univ. Pr., 1963. 419 pp.
> The humanists treated are Salutati, R. de'Rossi, Niccoli, L. Bruni, Bracciolini, Manetti, Marsuppino, M. Palmieri, C. Rinuccini, L. B. Alberti, and F. di Ser Ugolino Peruzzi. Accomplishes objective fairly well.

Nicoll, Allardyce. The World of Harlequin: A Critical Study of the Commedia dell'Arte. Cambridge, Eng., Cambridge Univ. Pr., 1963. 243 pp.
> Full and clear documentation; now the best work on the subject.

Oreglia, Giacomo. The Commedia dell'Arte. Tr. Lovett F. Edwards, intro. Evert Sprinchorn. N.Y., Hill and Wang, 1968. xvi, 168 pp.

Radcliff-Umstead, Douglas. The Birth of Modern Comedy in Renaissance Italy. Chicago, Univ. of Chicago Pr., 1969. 312 pp.

Robb, Nesca A.   Neoplatonism of the Italian Renaissance. London, Allen and Unwin, 1935. 315 pp.

> Imperfect study; deals best with Ficino, the Medici circle, and the *trattato d'amore*.

Roeder, Ralph.   The Man of the Renaissance. N.Y., Viking, 1933, and London, Routledge, 1934. 307 pp. Repr. N.Y., Meridian Books, and London, Mayflower, 1960.

> Savonarola, Aretino, Machiavelli, and Castiglione taken as typical.

Rotunda, Dominic P.   Motif Index of the Italian Novella in Prose. Bloomington, Indiana Univ. Pr., 1942. 216 pp.

> Invaluable for the study of folklore motifs.

Smith, Winifred.   The Commedia dell'Arte: A Study in Italian Popular Comedy. N.Y., Columbia Univ. Pr., 1912. 289 pp.

> A good survey in English.

Spingarn, Joel E.   A History of Literary Criticism in the Renaissance. N.Y., Macmillan, 1899. ix, 350 pp. Repr. N.Y., Columbia Univ. Pr., 1908 et seq.

> Superseded by Weinberg, below.

**Symonds, John Addington.   The Renaissance in Italy. London, Smith Elder, 1875–86. 7 vols. Repr. 1897–98; ML, 1935, 2 vols.; vol. 3 (The Fine Arts) repr. Gloucester, Mass., 1967, xii, 304 pp.

> The best English discussion of the period as a whole, especially of its art, learning, and literature.

Toffanin, Giuseppe.   History of Humanism. Tr. Elio Gianturco. N.Y., Las Americas Pub. Co., 1954. xxxvi, 356 pp.

> In opposition to Burckhardt, Professor Toffanin maintains that humanism of the Renaissance is to be identified with Catholic orthodoxy.

Ullman, Berthold L.   Studies in the Italian Renaissance. Rome, Edizioni di Storia e Letteratura, 1955. 393 pp.

> Deals with Petrarch, Salutati, Bruni, Poggio, etc.; unbiased handling of sources; convincing solution of a number of problems.

Vaughan, Herbert M.   Studies in the Italian Renaissance. London, Methuen,

and N.Y., Dutton, 1930. x, 264 pp.
  Informative lectures on leading figures.

Weinberg, Bernard. A History of Literary Criticism in the Italian Renaissance. Chicago, Ill., Univ. of Chicago Pr., 1961. 2 vols.
  A monumental study. Part 1 is devoted to critical theory, part 2 to
  critical practice.

Collections

Elizabethan Love Stories. Ed. T. J. B. Spencer, trs. mostly Elizabethan.
  Penguin, 1968. 215 pp.
  Eight stories which Shakespeare dramatized, all but one from the Italian.
  Two stories of which no Elizabethan version is known were tr. by the
  editor: the *Merchant of Venice* story, written by Il Pecorone, and the
  Othello story, written by Cinthio Giraldi.

Fallico, Arturo B. L., and Shapiro, Herman, eds. and trs. The Italian
  Philosophers: Selected Readings from Petrarch to Bruno. ML, 1967.
  xx, 425 pp.
  Vol. 1 of *Renaissance Philosophy* (work in progress). Selections from
  Petrarch, Alberti, Ficino, Manetti, Valla, Pico della Mirandola, Leone
  Ebreo, Pomponazzi, Tasso, Telesio, Campanella, and Bruno.

Literary Criticism: Plato to Dryden. Ed. Allen H. Gilbert. N.Y., Amer.
  Book Co., 1940. 704 pp.
  Includes trs. of many important selections from critical treatises by
  Trissino, Giraldi Cinthio, Minturno, Castelvetro, Mazzoni, Torquato
  Tasso, and Guarino.

Literary Sources of Art History: An Anthology of Texts from The-
  ophilus to Goethe. Selected and ed. Elizabeth Gilmore Holt. Princeton,
  N.J., Princeton Univ. Pr., 1947. 555 pp.
  Includes selections from Ghiberti, Cennini, Alberti, Filarete, Piero della
  Francesca, Leonardo, Serlio, Palladio, Lomazzo, and the letters and
  poems of Michelangelo.

Lyric Poetry of the Italian Renaissance: An Anthology with Verse
  Translations. Collected by Levi Robert Lind, with intro. Thomas G.

Bergin. New Haven, Conn., Yale Univ. Pr., and London, Oxford Univ. Pr., 1954. xxvii, 334 pp., parallel texts. Repr. 1964.

Good selections, as well as good critical apparatus.

The Palace of Pleasure, Beautified, Adorned and Well Furnished, with Pleasaunt Histories and Excellent Nouells.   Selected and tr. William Painter. London, Denham and (vol. 2) Bynneman, 1566–67. 2 vols. Repr., vol. 1, 1569, 1575; vol. 2, 1575; 1813, 2 vols.; 1890, ed. Joseph Jacobs, 3 vols.; 1930, ed. H. Miles, 4 vols.; 1967, repr. of Jacobs ed. (Magnolia, Mass., P. Smith, 3 vols.).

One hundred and one stories, largely from the Italian of Bandello, Boccaccio, Masuccio, Il Pecorone, and Straparola.

The Portable Renaissance Reader.   Ed. James Bruce Ross and Mary Martin McLaughlin. N.Y., Viking Pr., 1953. xii, 756 pp.

Prose and Poetry of the Continental Renaissance.   Selected and ed. Harold Hooper Blanchard. N.Y. and London, Longmans, 1949. 1084 pp. Rev. 1955.

Ample selections from Petrarch, Boccaccio, Machiavelli, Ariosto, and Tasso.

Renaissance and Baroque Lyrics: An Anthology of Translations from the Italian, French, and Spanish.   Ed. Harold M. Priest. Evanston, Ill., Northwestern Univ. Pr., 1962. lxix, 288 pp.

Petrarch, Boccaccio, Politian, Lorenzo de'Medici, Ariosto, Guidiccioni, Michelangelo, Tasso, and Marino are well represented by selections.

The Renaissance Philosophy of Man.   Ed. and tr. Ernst Cassirer et al. Chicago, Ill., Univ. of Chicago Pr., 1948. 412 pp. Repr. 1956, paper.

See vol. 1 above, Neo-Latin Literature, for the contents.

A Renaissance Treasury: A Collection of Representative Writings of the Renaissance in the Continent of Europe.   Eds. Hiram Haydn and John Charles Nelson. Garden City, N.Y., Doubleday, 1953. 432 pp.

Scenarios of the Commedia Dell'Arte.   Ed. and tr. Henry F. Salerno. N.Y., N.Y. Univ Pr., 1967. 411 pp.

The original collection by Flaminio Scala (fl. 1600–1612) was entitled

Il Teatro delle favole rappresentative, ovvero la Ricreatione comica, boscareccia, e tragica, divisa in cinquanta giornate (Venice, 1611).

Wit and Wisdom of the Italian Renaissance.   Ed. and tr. Charles Speroni. Berkeley, Univ. of California Pr., and London, Cambridge Univ. Pr., 1964. 317 pp.

Works of the English Poets.   Ed. Alexander Chalmers. Edinburgh, 1810. 21 vols.
> Vol. 19 includes Christopher Pitt's tr. of Vida; vol. 21 includes John Hoole's trs. of Ariosto and of Tasso.

INDIVIDUAL AUTHORS

Alberti, Leon Battista (1404–1472).   The Architecture in Ten Books, of Painting in Three Books, and of Statuary in One Book. Tr. James Leoni from the Italian version of the original Latin. London, Edlin, 1726. 3 vols. in 1. Repr. 1739, 1755; The Architecture repr. London, Tiranti, 1955, xx, 256 pp., repr. N.Y., Transatlantic Arts, 1966, 322 pp.

————The Family in Renaissance Florence (*I libri della famiglia*). Tr. Renée Neu Watkins. Columbia, Univ. of South Carolina Pr., 1969, 322 pp.

————Hecatonphila: The Arte of Love. Tr. anon. from the French version. London, Leake, 1598. 40 fols.

————The Painting. Tr. John R. Spencer. New Haven, Conn., Yale Univ. Pr., 1956. 141 pp. Rev. 1966.
> On Alberti see Silvio George Santayana, *Two Renaissance Educators: Alberti and Piccolomini* (N.Y., Meador, 1930, 125 pp.); and Joan Gadol, *Leon Battista Alberti, Universal Man of the Early Renaissance* (Chicago, Univ. of Chicago Pr., 1969, 320 pp.).

Anonymous. La venexiana: A Sixteenth Century Comedy.   Tr. Matilde Valenti Pfeifer. N.Y., Vanni, 1950. 163 pp., parallel texts.

Aretino, Pietro (1492–1566).   The Works of Aretino. Tr. Samuel Putnam. Chicago, Pascal Covici, 1926. 2 vols. Repr. N.Y., Covici-Friede, 1933.
> Good tr., intro. breezy but valuable. Vol. 1 contains the six *Ragiona-*

menti (*Dialogues*) and the play (*The Courtesan*); vol. 2 contains a number of letters, and the sonnets (*Lussuriosi*).

————————The Letters (selections). Ed. and tr. Thomas Caldecot Chubb. N.Y., Archon Books, 1967. 362 pp.

————————*Ragionamenti*: The Harlots' Dialogue. Tr. unnamed. North Hollywood, Calif., Brandon House, 1967. 100 pp.

On Aretino, see Thomas Caldecot Chubb, *Aretino the Scourge of Princes* (N.Y., Reynal and Hitchcock, 1940, 478 pp.): overenthusiastic, gossipy, but a good sympathetic presentation. For a different view, see James Cleugh, *The Divine Aretino* (N.Y., Stein and Day, 1966, 256 pp.).

Ariosto, Ludovico (1474–1533). *La Lena.* Tr. Roberta Simone Chamberlain, with intro. on the comedies of Ariosto. Urbana, Univ. of Illinois dissertation, 1965. 188 pp.

————————The *Orlando Furioso*. Tr. Sir John Harington in ottava rima. London, 1591. Repr. 1607; 1634; ed. Graham Hough, London, Centaur Pr., and Carbondale, Southern Illinois Univ. Pr., 1963, 563 pp.
   A vol. of *Selections* from this tr., ed. Rudolf Gottfried (Bloomington, Indiana Univ. Pr., 1962, 351 pp.) includes cantos 1–7, 33–35, and selections from seven further cantos of the 46.

   *Tr. William Stewart Rose in ottava rima. London, Murray, 1823–31. 9 vols. Repr. London, Bohn, 1858, et seq., 2 vols.; repr. Indianapolis, Ind., Bobbs-Merrill, 1968, xlviii, 524 pp.
   A graceful and flowing tr., as literal as the differences between the two languages and the exigencies of verse permit.

   Tr. prose Allan H. Gilbert. N.Y., Vanni, 1954. 3 vols.
   Reliable and thoroughly competent tr.

   Two 18th century trs. should be noted: by William Huggins in ottava rima, 1755; by John Hoole in couplets, 1783 et seq., repr. in Chalmers' Works of the English Poets, vol. 21 (1810).

————————Satyres, in Seven Famous Discourses. Tr. Robert Tofte. London, Okes, 1608. 108 pp. Repr. 1618 (adding three elegies in tr.).

   Tr. Rev. Mr. H-rt-n (5 of the 7) and Temple Henry Coker. London, 1759. 135 pp.

————Supposes: A Comedy. Tr. George Gascoigne. London, 1566. Repr. in Supposes and Jocasta, ed. J. W. Cunliffe, Boston and London, Heath, 1906; in Elizabethan and Jacobean Comedy, ed. Robert Ornstein and Hazelton Spencer, N.Y., Heath, 1964.

> On Ariosto, see the fine study of Edmund G. Gardner, *The King of Court Poets: A Study of the Life and Times of Ariosto* (London, Constable, 1906, 395 pp.; repr. N.Y., Haskell House, 1968).

Bandello, Matteo (1480–1562).   The Novels. Tr. John Payne. London, Villon Soc., 1890. 5 vols.

> Part tr. (13 stories) Geoffrey Fenton from the French version as Certain Tragical Discourses. London, Marshe, 1567. 317 leaves. Repr. 1576; 1579; in Tudor Trs., vols. 19, 20, London, Nutt, 1898, repr. N.Y., AMS Pr., 1967; in modern spelling, London, Routledge, and N.Y., Dutton, n.d.

> For many other Elizabethan trs. and adaptations as plays of Bandello *novelle*, see Mary Elizabeth Scott, *Elizabethan Translations from the Italian* (in The Renaissance, Bibliography, above), s.v. Bandello in Index. She notes that the first tr. was Arthur Brooke's verse *Tragicall Historye of Romeus and Juliet* (1562), adapted from the French version; and that the largest number of Bandello stories was tr. in William Painter, *The Palace of Pleasure* (1566–67), for which see The Renaissance, Collections, above.

Basile, Giambattista (1575–1632).   The Pentameron. Tr. N. M. Penzer from the Italian version (by Benedetto Croce) of the original Neapolitan dialect. London, Lane, and N.Y., Dutton, 1932. 2 vols.

> Tr. John Edward Taylor, ill. George Cruikshank. London, Bogue, 1848. xvi, 404 pp. Repr. 1893, 1902.

> Tr. Sir Richard Burton as Il Pentamerone, or the Tale of Tales. London, Henry and Co., 1894. 2 vols. Repr. London, Kimber, 1952.

> Tr. (extracts) Rose L. Mincieli as Old Neapolitan Fairy Tales. N.Y., Knopf, 1963. 123 pp.
> The work appeals chiefly to folklorists and bibliographers.

Bembo, Pietro (1470–1547).   *Gli Asolani*. Tr. Rudolf B. Gottfried. Bloomington, Indiana Univ. Pr., 1954. xx, 200 pp.
> An important document on Platonism.

Bernardino of Siena, St. (1380–1444). Sermons. Selected and ed. Don Nazareno Orlandi, tr. Helen Josephine Robins. Siena, Tipografia sociale, 1920. 248 pp.

> Part tr. Ada Harrison as Examples of St. Bernardino. London, Howell, 1936. 150 pp.

> > For a warm appraisal of the great preacher, see A. G. Ferrers Howell, *San Bernardino of Siena* (with chapter on "St. Bernardino in Art" by Julia Cartwright [Mrs. Ady]: London, Methuen, 1913, xv, 373 pp.); also Iris Origo, *The World of San Bernardino* (N.Y., Harcourt, 1962, and London, Cape, 1963, 302 pp.).

Bibbiena, Bernardo Dovizi da, Cardinal (1471–1520). The Follies of Calandro (*Calandria*). Tr. Oliver Evans, in The Genius of the Italian Theatre: see Collections, above.

Boccaccio, Giovanni (1313–1375). Chamber of Love: A Selection of His Complete Works. Tr. Gertrude Flor, ed. Wolfgang Kraus. N.Y., Philosophical Library, 1958. 158 pp.

——————Amorous Fiammetta (*La Fiammetta*). Tr. Bartholomew Yong. London, Charlewood, 1587. 123 leaves. Repr. rev. with intro. Edward Hutton, London, Navarre Soc., 1926, xl, 356 pp.; and (without intro.) N.Y., Rarity Pr., 1926, 336 pp. Repr. with intro. K. H. Josling, London, Mandrake Pr., 1929. xlix, 160 pp.

> Tr. James C. Brogan as La Fiammetta. In The Literature of Italy, 1265–1907, pp. 121–324: see Collections, above.

——————The Decameron. Tr. anon. London, Jaggard, 1620, 2 vols. Many reprs., especially in Tudor Translations (see General Reference, Collections of Translations, above), London, Nutt, 1909, 4 vols. (with list of trs. of separate stories before 1620).

> Tr. John Payne. London, Villon Soc., 1886. 3 vols. Several reprs., including ML, 1931.

> Tr. J. M. Rigg. London, Bullen, 1903. 2 vols. Repr. EL, 1930, 1960.

> Tr. Richard Aldington. N.Y., Covici Friede, 1930. 2 vols. Repr. Garden City, N.Y., Garden City Pub. Co., 1938, 576 pp.; repr. ibid. 1949, ill. Rockwell Kent; repr. N.Y., Duschnes, 1955, 2 vols.; repr. London,

Elek, 1957, xii, 673 pp., and ibid., 1958–59, 2 vols.; repr. N.Y., Dell, 1962, 640 pp. paper.

Tr. Frances Winwar. N.Y., Limited Eds. Club, 1930. 2 vols.

Other trs. listed by Farrar and Evans: anon. 1702; C. Balguy, 1741; anon., 1873; rev. W. M. Thomson, 1896 (nos. 686–88, 690).

The most useful book on the *Decameron* is A. Collingwood Lee, *The Decameron: Its Sources and Analogues* (London, Nutt, 1909, 363 pp.; repr. N.Y., Haskell, 1967). Consult also Aldo S. Scaglione, *Nature and Love in the Late Middle Ages: An Essay on the Cultural Context of the Decameron* (Berkeley, Univ. of California Pr., 1963, 250 pp.)

————— (*Il Filocolo*). A small part (of pt. 4) tr. H. G. as The Most Pleasant and Delectable Questions of Love (13 questions). London, 1566. Several reprs., and repr. with intro. Edward Hutton, London, 1927; repr. modern spelling, ed. Thomas Bell, N.Y., ill. eds., 1931, 133 pp.; repr. N.Y., Halcyon House, 1950.

—————The Filostrato. Trs. prose Nathaniel Edward Griffin and Arthur Beckwith Myrick. Philadelphia, Pa., Univ. of Pennsylvania Pr., 1929. ix, 505 pp., parallel texts. Repr. N.Y., Biblo and Tannen, 1967.

Tr. verse Hubertis Cummings as Il Filostrato: The Story of the Love of Troilo. Princeton, N.J., Princeton Univ. Pr., 1934. 193 pp.

—————Life of Dante. Tr. Philip H. Wicksteed, in The Early Lives of Dante (with Bruni's Life). Hull, pr. pr., 1898. pp. 11–72. Repr. London, King's Classics, 1904, 1907, 1911, xv, 159 pp.; repr. N.Y., Russell, as The Earliest Lives of Dante, 1968. Repr. separately, Cambridge, Mass., Riverside Pr., 1904. 74 pp.

Tr. G. R. Carpenter. N.Y., Grolier Club, 1900. 186 pp.

Tr. James Robinson Smith (with the Life by Bruni). Yale Studies in English. N.Y., Holt, 1901. 103 pp. Repr. N.Y., Ungar, 1963.

—————The Nymph of Fiesole (*Il Ninfale Fiesolano*). Tr. prose Daniel J. Donno. N.Y., Columbia Univ. Pr., 1960. xvii, 149 pp.
A prose tr. from the French was done by John Gobourne as *Affrican and Mensola* (pub. 1597).

LATIN WORKS

————Concerning Famous Women (*De claris mulieribus*). Tr. Guido A. Guarino. New Brunswick, N.J., Rutgers Univ. Pr., 1963. 257 pp.

————The Fall of Princes (*De casibus virorum illustrium*). Freely tr. verse John Lydgate (from a French version, A.D. 1420). London, Pynson, 1494. Repr. 1527, 1554, 1555? Repr. ed. Henry Bergen, Washington, D.C., and London, EETS ES 121–24, 1923–27; repr. 1967.

Tr. abridged Louis Brewer Hall as The Fates of Illustrious Men. N.Y., Ungar, 1965. xxii, 243 pp., also paper.

————Boccaccio's Olympia (*Egloga XIV*). Ed. and tr. Israel Gollancz. London, Chatto and Windus, 1913. 56 pp. Repr. rev. in Pearl: An English Poem . . . with Boccaccio's Olympia, London, 1921.

————Boccaccio on Poetry, Being the Preface and Fourteenth and Fifteenth Books of Boccaccio's Genealogia deorum gentilium. Tr. Charles G. Osgood. Princeton, N.J., Princeton Univ. Pr., 1930. xlix, 213 pp.

On Boccaccio, see Catherine Carswell, *The Tranquil Heart: Portrait of Giovanni Boccaccio* (N.Y., Harcourt [1937], xi, 346 pp.); Thomas Caldecot Chubb, *The Life of Giovanni Boccaccio* (N.Y., A. and C. Boni, 1940, 286 pp.; repr. Port Washington, N.Y., Kennikat Pr., 1969), which assembles existing knowledge with an attempt to recreate the personality; Edward Hutton, *Giovanni Boccaccio: A Biographical Study* (London, Lane, 1910, 426 pp.), a comprehensive, moderately scholarly approach. Marga Cottini-Jones, *An Anatomy of Boccaccio's Style* (Napoli, Editrice Cymba, 1968), can be useful to those making a more specialized study of Boccaccio.

Boccalini, Trajano (1586–1613). The Works of the Celebrated Trajano Boccalini. Tr. J. G. London, Smith, 1714. 5 vols. in 3.
Considerably adapted. For earlier trs. of single works, see CBEL, I, 811, and II, 808.

Boiardo, Matteo Maria (1440 or 1441–1494). The Orlando Innamorato. Tr. prose W. S. Rose from the Italian revision by Francesco Berni and interspersed with extracts in the same stanza as the original. Edinburgh, Blackwood, 1823. lviii, 279 pp.
The Domenichi revision was tr. verse Robert Tofte, 1598.

Useful comment: Giacomo Grillo, *Two Aspects of Chivalry: Pulci and Boiardo* (Boston, Excelsior Pr., 1942, 50 pp.).

Bruni, Leonardo (1374–1444).   The Historie of . . . the Warres betwene the Imperialles and Gothes for the Possession of Italy. Tr. Arthur Golding from Latin. London, Rouland Hall, 1563. 180 leaves.

——————Life of Dante. Tr. with Boccaccio's Life, q.v. above.

On Bruni, see C. C. Bayley, *War and Society in Renaissance Florence: The De Militia of Leonardo Bruni* (Toronto, Univ. of Toronto Pr., 1961, 440 pp.); and the writings of Hans Baron, Renaissance Period Literary Studies, above.

Bruno, Giordano (1548–1600).   The Candle Bearer. Tr. John R. Hale, in The Genius of the Italian Theatre: see Collections, above.

——————Concerning the Cause, Principle, and One. Tr. Sidney Greenberg in The Infinite in Giordano Bruno. N.Y., King's Crown Pr., 1950. 203 pp.

Tr. Jack Lindsay as Cause, Principle, and Unity. Castle Hedingham, Daimon Pr., and N.Y., International Publishers, 1964. vii, 177 pp.

——————The Expulsion of the Triumphant Beast (*Spaccio della bestia trionfante*). Tr. Arthur D. Imerti. New Brunswick, N.J., Rutgers Univ. Pr., 1964. ix, 324 pp.
Excellent tr. and fine intro. Earlier tr. William Morehead, 1713.

——————The Heroic Frenzies (*De gli eroici furori*). Tr. Paul Eugene Memmo, Jr. Chapel Hill, Univ. of North Carolina Pr., 1964. 274 pp.

See John Charles Nelson, *The Renaissance Theory of Love: The Context of Giordano Bruno's Eroici furori* (N.Y., Columbia Univ. Pr., 1958, 280 pp.).

——————Of the Infinite Universe and Worlds. Tr. Dorothea Waley Singer from the Latin in her Giordano Bruno, His Life and Thought. N.Y., Schuman, 1950, and London, Constable, 1951. 389 pp.

For more general studies, see Irving Louis Horwitz, *The Renaissance Philosophy of Giordano Bruno* (N.Y., Coleman-Rors, 1952, viii, 150 pp.); and Paul Oskar Kristeller, *Eight Philosophers of the Italian Renaissance*, listed in Literary Studies, Renaissance Period, above.

Buonarroti, Michelangelo (1475–1564). Complete Poems and Selected Letters. Tr. Creighton Gilbert. N.Y., Random House, 1963. lvi, 317 pp. Repr. ML, 1965.

————The Complete Poems. Tr. Joseph Tusiani. N.Y., Noonday Pr., 1960, and London, Owen, 1961. 217 pp.

————Sonnets and Madrigals. Tr. William Wells Newell. Boston, Houghton Mifflin, 1890. 109 pp.

————The Sonnets. Tr. John Addington Symonds. London, Smith Elder, 1878. 212 pp. Many reprs. to N.Y., Crown, 1948, 63 pp.; London, Vision Pr., 1950, 199 pp.; N.Y., Irving Ravin, 1950, 199 pp.
  These four trs. of the poems are well done. For numerous other trs., on the whole mediocre, see Creighton Gilbert's bibliography, "Michael Angelo's Poetry in English Verse," *Italica*, vol. 22 (1945), 180–95, and vol. 24 (1947), 45–53; add now The Sonnets, tr. Elizabeth Jennings (London, Folio Soc., 1961, repr. London, Alison and Busby, 1969, 100 pp.). For a study of the poetry, see Robert J. Clements, *The Poetry of Michelangelo* (N.Y., Oxford Univ. Pr., 1965, and London, Owen, 1966, xii, 368 pp.).

————The Letters of Michelangelo. Tr. E. M. Ramsden. Stanford, Calif., Stanford Univ. Pr., 1963. 2 vols.
  Complete and laudably done.

Tr. Charles Speroni as I, Michelangelo Sculptor: An Autobiography Through Letters, eds. Irving and Jean Stone. N.Y., Doubleday, 1962. 283 pp. Repr. London, Collins, 1965.
  Indispensable.

Tr. and ed. Robert J. Clements as Michelangelo: A Self-portrait. Englewood, N.J., Prentice-Hall, 1963. 184 pp.
  Trs. from letters, poetry, and records of conversations, which draw upon the best trs. and to which Clements adds his own versions.

On Michelangelo it is almost needless to mention the masterly novelized biography by Irving Stone, *The Agony and the Ecstasy*: *The Biographical Novel of Michelangelo* (N.Y., Doubleday, 1961, 664 pp.). For literary biographies: John Addington Symonds, *The Life of Michelangelo Buonarroti* (London, Nimmo, 1893, 2 vols., many reprs.); Georg Brandes, *Michelangelo: His Life,*

His Times, His Era, tr. from the German (1921) Heinz Norden (N.Y., Ungar, 1963, xv, 434 pp., 24 pls.); Adolfo Venturi, *Michelangelo*, tr. Joan Redfern (London and N.Y., Warne, 1928, 105 pp.). See also Robert J. Clements, *Michelangelo's Theory of Art* (N.Y., New York Univ. Pr., 1961, xxxvii, 471 pp., 20 pls.).

Campanella, Tommaso (1568–1639).   The City of the Sun. Tr. (with omissions) Thomas W. Halliday from Latin (2d ed., Paris, 1637), in Ideal Commonwealths comprising More's Utopia, Bacon's New Atlantis, Campanella's City of the Sun, and Harrington's Oceana. Ed. Henry Morley. London and N.Y., Routledge, 1886. 284 pp. Repr. 1901; in Famous Utopias, with intro. Charles M. Andrews, N.Y., Tudor, 1901, pp. 273–317; in Famous Utopias of the Renaissance, ed. Frederic R. White, Chicago, Ill., Packard, 1946, pp. 155–264.

Tr. (with omissions) William J. Gilstrap as The City of the Sun or The Idea of a Republic from Latin (1st ed., Frankfurt, 1623), in The Quest for Utopia, eds. Glenn Kegley and J. Max Patrick. N.Y., Schuman [1952], pp. 137–47. Repr. Garden City, N.Y., Doubleday (Anchor), 1962, pp. 311–42.

————Defence of Galileo (*Apologia pro Galileo*). Tr. Grant McColley from Latin original (1622). Northampton, Mass., Smith College Studies in History, 1937. xliv, 98 pp.

For a tr. of Campanella's *Spanish Monarchy*, see Neo-Latin Literature, vol. 1 above.
Francesco Grillo's *Tommaso Campanella in America* (N.Y., Vanni, 1954, 110 pp.), although quite defective, has nevertheless a limited usefulness.

Castiglione, Baldassare (1478–1529).   The Book of the Courtier. Tr. Sir Thomas Hoby. London, 1561, et seq. Repr. London, Nutt, 1900, lxxxvii, 377 pp.; EL, 1923 et seq.; in Three Renaissance Classics, N.Y., Scribner, 1953, pp. 241–618; London, Dent, 1956; N.Y., AMS Pr., 1967.

Tr. Leonard Eckstein Opdycke. N.Y., Scribner, 1901. 439 pp. Repr. 1903; N.Y., Liveright, 1929.
Better than Hoby, but somewhat stilted in its literalness.

Tr., abr., and intro. Friench Simpson. N.Y., Ungar, 1959. x, 99 pp.

*Tr. Charles S. Singleton. Garden City, N.Y., Doubleday, 1959. xii,
387 pp.
Flexible tr., adhering closely to the original.

Tr. George Bull. Penguin, 1967. 361 pp.

> For two 18th century trs., see CBEL, vol. 2, p. 809. For a well-pre-
> sented account of Castiglione, see Julia Cartwright, *The Perfect
> Courtier: Baldassare Castiglione* (London, Murray, and N.Y., Dutton,
> 1908, 2 vols.).

Catherine of Siena, St. (1347–1380).   The Orchard of Syon (*Libro della divine
dottrina*). Tr. Dan [Don] James (early 15th c.) from the Latin version.
Westminster, de Worde, 1519. Repr. eds. Phyllis Hodgson and Gabriel M.
Liegey from Ms. EETS 258 (1966), vol. 1, Text, with notes and intro. to
follow in vol. 2.

Tr. Algar Thorold from Italian as The Dialogue of the Seraphic Virgin,
Dictated by Her while in a State of Ecstasy, 1370. London, Kegan Paul,
1896. vii, 360 pp. Repr. abridged 1907, 1925.

————The Treatise on Purgatory. Tr. with pref. by Rev. (later Cardinal)
H. E. Manning. London, Burns and Lambert, 1858. viii, 28 pp. Reprs. to
4th edn. (1915?).

Tr. J. M. A. from a French version. London, Hodges, 1878. 56 pp.

Tr. W. F. P.   Dublin, Catholic Truth Soc., 1909. 64 pp.

————Saint Catherine of Siena as Seen in Her Letters. Tr. and ed. Vida D.
Scudder. London, Dent, and N.Y., Dutton, 1905. x, 352 pp. Repr. 1927
(selected letters).

The Life and Sayings (extracts), tr. Paul Garvin, was pub. Staten Island, N.Y.,
Alba House, 1964, 139 pp. The biography of the saint by her confessor
Fra Raimondo de Capua was tr. anon. from Latin as *The lyf of saint Katherin
of Senis* (Westminster, de Worde, c. 1493). It was retr. from Italian by John
Fen (Louvain, 1608?); a more recent tr. from the French version by Mother
Regis Hamilton was pub. in 1860 (N.Y., Kenedy, and Philadelphia, Cunning-
ham, 432 pp.). A splendid modern biography is by Sigrid Undset, *Catherine of
Siena*, tr. Kate Austin-Lind from Norwegian (London and N.Y., Sheed and
Ward, 1954, 293 pp.).

Cellini, Benvenuto (1500–1571). The Life (*Vita*). Tr. Thomas Nugen, London, 1771. 2 vols. Many reprs., especially ed. Thomas Roscoe (as The Autobiography), London, 1822; London, Newnes, and N.Y., Scribner, 1904, 571 pp., rev. WC, 1927.

> Tr. John Addington Symonds. London, Nimmo, and N.Y., Scribner, 1888, 2 vols. Many reprs., especially Harvard Classics, vol. 31, 1910; ML, 1927; London, Phaidon Pr., 1949, ill.

> Tr. Anne Macdonell as The Memoirs. London, Dent, and N.Y., Dutton. 1903. 2 vols. Repr. EL [1907] et seq.

> Tr. Robert H. Hobart Cust. London, Bell, 1910. 2 vols., ill. Repr. 1927; 1935; N.Y., Dodd Mead, 1961, 547 pp., ill.

> Tr. George Bull. Penguin, 1956. 396 pp.

──────The Treatises on Goldsmithing and Sculpture. Tr. C. R. Ashbee. London, Edward Arnold, 1898. xiv, 164 pp. Repr. N.Y., Dover, 1967.

Cennini, Cennino (15th c.). The Craftsman's Handbook (*Il Libro dell' Arte*). Ed. and tr. Daniel V. Thompson, Jr. New Haven, Conn., Yale Univ. Pr., and London, Milford, 1932–33. 2 vols., parallel texts. Vol. 2 (the tr.) repr. N.Y., Dover, 1960, xxvii, 142 pp.

> Also tr. Mrs. Merrífield as *A Treatise on Painting* (London, 1844); and tr. Christiana J. Herringham as *The Book of the Art of Cennino Cennini* (London and N.Y., 1899, and reprs.): see Farrar and Evans, *English Translations from Medieval Sources*, nos. 838, 839.

Christophoro Armeno (fl. 1555). The Peregrination of the Three Young Sons of the King of Serendippo. Trs. Augusto G. and Theresa L. Borselli, and ed. Theodore G. Remer, in Serendipity and the Three Princes. Norman, Univ. of Oklahoma Pr., 1965, pp. 50–163.

> Ostensibly a tr. from the Persian. An English version of it pub. 1722 was in fact made from a much altered French tr.; Horace Walpole's invention of the word serendipity was suggested by this version.

Colonna, Francesco (d. 1527). Hypnerotomachia: The Strife of Love in a Dream. Tr. (book 1 only) R. D.   London, 1592. Repr., ed. Andrew Lang, London, Nutt, 1890, xvii, 248 pp.

> An interesting adaptation, *The Dream of Poliphili* (N.Y., Pantheon, 1950, xv, 243 pp.), is not a tr. of the original but a tr. of an abridged para-

phrase in German made by Linda Fierz-David, the English tr. of it by Mary Hottinger. A complete tr. of the work into French is *Le Songe de Poliphile*, tr. Claudius Popelin (Paris, no pub., 1880–83, 2 vols.); also a 16th c. French tr., repr. (Paris, Payot, 1926, 311 pp.).

Croce, Giulio Cesare (d. 1609). Bertoldo. Tr. Palmer Di Giulio. N.Y., Vantage Pr., 1958. 94 pp.

Da Bisticci, Vespasiano (1421–1498). The Vespasiano Memoirs: Lives of Illustrious Men of the Fifteenth Century. Tr. William George and Emily Waters. London, Routledge, and N.Y., Dial Pr., 1926. 475 pp. Repr. as Renaissance Princes, Peoples, and Prelates, with intro. Myron H. Gilmore, N.Y. and London, Harper (Torchbooks), 1963, paper.

Da Porto, Luigi (d. 1529). The Original Story of Romeo and Juliet (*Istoria di due nobili amanti*). Ed. and tr. G. Pace-Sanfelice. Cambridge, Deighton, 1868. lxii, 80 pp.
Edn. of the 1530 Italian text, with English tr.

Tr. Maurice Jonas as Romeo and Juliet. London, Davis and Orioli, 1921. xxxii, 38 leaves, 37 pp. (facs. ed. and tr. of 1535 and 1539 edns).

Many other trs., especially by Thomas Roscoe, *The Italian Novelists*, 1825, vol. 2: see Collections, above. An earlier version of the story, although with different names, was written by Masuccio Salernitano in his *Novellino* (story 33), q.v. below. A later version was written by Matteo Bandello in his *Novelle* (II 9, 1555), q.v. above, The Bandello version was paraphrased in prose from a French intermediary by William Painter in his *Palace of Pleasure* (II 25, 1567), q.v. in Collections, above; and was paraphrased at length in verse, again from the French, by Arthur Brooke as *The Tragicall Historye of Romeus and Juliet* (London, 1562), which in turn was the source of Shakespeare's play (c. 1595).

The Deceived (*Gl'Ingannati*, anon., 1531). Tr. and abr. Thomas Love Peacock. London, 1862. Repr. in the Works, Halliford ed., London, Constable, and N.Y., G. Wells, vol. 10, 1934.

Tr. Geoffrey Bullough in his Narrative and Dramatic Sources of Shakespeare. London, Routledge, and N.Y., Columbia Univ. Pr., vol. 2, 1958, pp. 286–339.
A parallel to the Viola story in *Twelfth Night*.

Della Casa, Giovanni (1503–1556).   Galateo. Tr. Robert Peterson. London, 1576. Repr., ed. H. J. Reid, London, 1892. Repr., ed. J. E. Spingarn, as Galateo, Of Manners and Behaviours, Boston, Merrymount Pr., 1914, 122 pp.

Tr. R. S. Pine-Coffin as Galateo, or The Book of Manners. Penguin, 1958. 131 pp.

Della Porta, Giambattista (1535–1615).   The finest comic playwright in Renaissance Italy. No trs. known of his plays, but for a detailed analysis of his plays and influence outside Italy, consult Louise George Clubb, *Giambattista Della Porta* (Princeton, N.J., Princeton Univ. Pr., 1964, 420 pp.). Of his scientific works, the following has been tr.:

————Natural Magick . . . in twenty books. Tr. anon. from the original Latin. London, 1658. 409 pp. Repr. as Natural Magic, N.Y., Basic Books, 1957, 418 pp.

Dolce, Ludovico (1508–1568).   Aretin, A Dialogue on Painting. Tr. W. Brown. London, 1770. xviii, 262 pp. Repr. Glasgow, 1870 [sic for 1770].

————Jocasta. Tr. George Gascoigne and Francis Kinwelmershe, in George Gascoigne, A Hundreth Sundrie Flowers. London, 1573. Repr. 1575 in The Posies, and in The Whole Woorkes, 1587. Repr. separately with the original Italian, ed. J. W. Cunliffe, in Supposes and Jocasta, Boston, Heath, 1906, xxx, 411 pp.

Ficino, Marsilio (1439–1499).   See Neo-Latin Literature, in vol. 1, above.

Filarete (Antonio Averlino, c. 1400–1469?).   Treatise on Architecture. Tr. John R. Spencer. New Haven, Conn., Yale Univ. Pr., 1966. 2 vols. (vol. 1, the tr.; vol. 2, facs. of original).

Firenzuola, Agnolo (1493–1545).   Tales of Firenzuola, Benedictine Monk of Vallombrosa. Tr. anon. Paris, Liseux, 1889. 136 pp. Repr. n.p., n.d., 178 pp.

Fracastoro, Girolamo (1483–1553).   See Neo-Latin Literature, in vol. 1 above.

Galilei, Galileo (1564–1642).   The Systems of the World, in Four Dialogues. The Ancient and Modern Doctrine of the Holy Fathers . . . Concerning the Rash Citation of . . . Scripture in Conclusions Merely Natural. Mathematical Discourses . . . Touching Two New Sciences . . . Mechanicks and Local Motion. A Discourse Concerning the Natation of Bodies upon the Water. All in Thomas Salusbury, Mathematical Collections. London, Leybourne, 1661, vol. 1, pt. 1. Repr. London, Dawsons, 1967. Reprs. of separate works are given below.

———————The Achievement of Galileo. Ed. with notes, James Brophy and Henry Paolucci. N.Y., Twayne, 1962. 256 pp.
   Selections by and about Galileo.

———————Discoveries and Opinions of Galileo. Tr. Stillman Drake. Garden City., N.Y., Doubleday, 1957. vii, 302 pp.
   Trs. from *Sidereus Nuncius*; *Nova-antiqua . . . doctrina de sacrae scripturae testimoniis*, etc.; *Istoria e dimostrazioni intorno alle macchie solari.*

———————Dialogue on the Great World Systems. Repr. of Salusbury tr. above, rev. Giorgio di Santillana. Chicago, Ill., Univ. of Chicago Pr., and London, Cambridge Univ. Pr., 1953. lviii, 506 pp. Repr. 1964.

   Tr. Stillman Drake as Dialogue Concerning the Two Chief World Systems, Ptolemaic and Copernican, with foreword by Albert Einstein. Berkeley, Univ. of California Pr., 1953. xxvii, 496 pp. Repr. 1967.

———————Dialogues Concerning Two New Sciences. Tr. Henry Crew and Alfonso De Salvio. N.Y., Macmillan, 1914. xxi, 300 pp.
   Successful tr. by a well-known scientist and a literary man. An earlier tr., following Salusbury's, was by Thomas Weston (1730).

———————Discourse on Bodies in Water. Salusbury tr. repr. with intro. Stillman Drake. Urbana, Univ. of Illinois Pr., 1960. xxvi, 89 pp.

———————On Motion. On Mechanics. Tr. I. E. Drabkin and Stillman Drake. Madison, Univ. of Wisconsin Pr., 1960. viii, 193 pp.

———————The Sidereal Messenger. Tr. Edward S. Carlos. Edinburgh, Univ. Pr., and London, Rivingtons, 1880. xi, 111 pp.

On Galileo consult the five readable essays in *Galileo Reappraised*, ed. Carlo I. Golino (Berkeley, Univ. of California Pr., 1966, 110 pp.).

Gelli, Giovanni Battista (1498–1563). The Circe of Signior Giovanni Battista Gelli. Tr. Thomas Brown. London [1702]. Rev. with intro. Robert M. Adams, Ithaca, N.Y., Cornell Univ. Pr., 1963, xlix, 179 pp.
First tr. Henry Iden, 1557; also tr. Henry Laynge, 1744.

————The Fearful Fansies of the Florentine Couper (*I capricci del bottaio*). Tr. William Barker. London, 1568. 138 leaves. Repr. 1569.

Giovio, Paolo (Jovius, 1483–1552).   See Neo-Latin Literature, vol. 1 above.

Giraldi, Giambattista Cinthio (1503–1573).   *Epitia*. Summarized in English, scene by scene, by Geoffrey Bullough, in his Narrative and Dramatic Sources of Shakespeare. London, Routledge, and N.Y., Columbia Univ. Pr., vol. 2, 1958, pp. 430–32.
The play is a dramatization by its author of "The Story of Epitia," below.

————"The Moor of Venice" (*Hecatommithi*, Decade III, novella 7). Tr. in Shakespeare's Library, ed. John Payne Collier (1843), rev. William C. Hazlitt. London, 1875, vol. 2, pp. 285–308, parallel texts.

Tr. T. J. B. Spencer as The Story of Disdemona of Venice and The Moorish Captain, in Elizabethan Love Stories. Penguin, 1968, pp. 197–210.
The source of Shakespeare's *Othello*. Like the sources of other Shakespeare plays, it is also tr. in the Variorum ed. of Shakespeare's play, and it will probably be tr. also in Bullough, op. cit.

————On Romances (*Discorso intorno al comporre dei romanzi*). Tr. Henry L. Snuggs. Lexington, Univ. of Kentucky Pr., 1968. 216 pp.

Giraldi's other critical writings have not been completely tr., but the topics discussed are treated at length in Weinberg (see The Renaissance, Literary Studies, above) and many passages are tr. in Gilbert (see Italian Literature, Collections, above).

————"The Story of Epitia" (*Hecatommithi*, Decade X, novella 5). Tr. Geoffrey Bullough, in his Narrative and Dramatic Sources of Shakespeare, vol. 2, 1958, pp. 420–30.

The ultimate source of Shakespeare's *Measure for Measure*. It was paraphrased in English by George Whetstone as *Promos and Cassandra*, first
in prose narrative and then as a double (ten-act) play, before Shakespeare made use of the story, probably with recourse to the Italian
original.

For Giraldi's plays, not tr., consult P. H. Horne, *The Tragedies of
Giambattista Cinthio Giraldi* (London and N.Y., Oxford Univ. Pr.,
1962, ix, 174 pp.).

Guarini, Giambattista (1538–1612). Il Pastor Fido or The Faithfull Shep-
heard. Tr. [Edward Dymock]. London, 1602. Repr. 1633.

Tr. Sir Richard Fanshawe. London, 1647. Rev. Elkanah Settle, 1677,
1689, 1694; repr. in Nicoletta Neri, *Il Pastor Fido in Inghilterra*, Torino,
Giappichelli, 1963; repr., ed. Walter F. Staton, Jr., and William E.
Simeone, London and N.Y., Oxford Univ. Pr., 1964, 191 pp.

Tr. William Grove. London, Blyth, 1782. 241 pp.
Deserves to be reprinted.

Guazzo, Stefano (16th c.). The Civile Conversation (*La civil Conversatione*).
Tr. George Pettie [3 books] and Bartholomew Yong [book 4]. London, East,
1581–86. Repr. Tudor Trs., London, Constable, and N.Y., Knopf, 1925,
2 vols.

Tr. anon. as The Art of Conversation. London, 1738. 278 pp.

On the influence of Guazzo in England, see John Leon Lievsay, *Stefano
Guazzo and the English Renaissance*, 1575–1675 (Chapel Hill, Univ. of North
Carolina Pr., 1960, 356 pp.).

Guicciardini, Francesco (1483–1540). The Historie of Guicciardin, Containing the Warres of Italie (*L'historia d' Italia*). Tr. Geoffrey Fenton.
London, Vautrollier, 1579. 1184 pp. Repr. London, Field, 1609, 943 pp.;
1618, 821 pp.

Tr. Austin Parke Goddard as The History of Italy. London, 1753–56.
10 vols. Repr. to 3rd ed., 1763.

Tr. Cecil Grayson abridged (with The History of Florence). N.Y.,
Washington Square Pr., 1964, and Twayne, 1965, and London, New
English Library, 1966. lii, 378 pp.

Tr. Sidney Alexander abr. N.Y., Macmillan, 1969. xxx, 457 pp.

—————The Maxims (*Ricordi politici*). Tr. Emma Martin, with parallel passages from Machiavelli, Bacon, Pascal, La Rochefoucauld, Montesquieu, Burke, Talleyrand, and others. London, Longmans, 1845. 156 pp.

Tr. Ninian Hill Thomson as Counsels and Reflections. London, Kegan Paul, 1890. xxxi, 206 pp. Repr. N.Y., Vanni, 1949, 291 pp., parallel texts.

Tr. Mario Domandi as Maxims and Reflections of a Renaissance Statesman. N.Y., Harper Torchbooks, 1965. xxxii, 107 pp.

—————Selected Writings. Tr. Margaret Grayson, ed. and intro. Cecil Grayson. London and N.Y., Oxford Univ. Pr., 1965. 170 pp.

On Guicciardini, see Vincent Luciani, *Francesco Guicciardini and His European Reputation* (N.Y., Otto, 1936, 438 pp.), a thoroughgoing account; and Roberto Ridolfi, *The Life of Francesco Guicciardini* (London, Routledge, 1927. and N.Y., Knopf, 1968, 338 pp.).

Landucci, Luca (1463?–1516). A Florentine Diary from 1450 to 1516, Continued by an Anonymous Writer till 1542. Tr. Alice de Rosen Jervis, with notes by Iodoco della Badia. London, Dent, and N.Y., Dutton, 1927. 308 pp.

Leo Africanus (16th c.). A Geographical Historie of [North] Africa. Tr. John Pory, with additions, from a Latin version of the Italian. London, Bishop, 1600. 420 pp. Repr. ed. Robert Brown, Hakluyt Society Works, nos. 92–94, 1896. 3 vols., which repr. N.Y., Burt Franklin, 1963.
A geographical classic, presumably written originally in Arabic, although no text survives, and first ed. in Italian by G. B. Ramusio, *Navigationi et viaggi* (Venice, vol. 1, 1550).

**Leonardo da Vinci (1452–1519). The Literary Works. Compiled and ed. Jean Paul Richter. 2d ed. rev. and enl. by the ed. and by Irma A. Richter. London, Oxford Univ. Pr., 1939. 2 vols.
A superb achievement. The *Paragone* (Book 1 of the *Trattato della Pittura*) was repr. separately (London and N.Y., Oxford Univ. Pr., 1949).

————The Notebooks (*I Manoscritti*). Ed. and tr. with intro. Edward McCurdy. London, Duckworth, and N.Y., Scribner, 1906. 289 pp. Repr. 1908; 1923; 1935; 1938; 1939; 1958. Selections containing most of the material were repr. London, Cape, and N.Y., Reynal and Hitchcock, 1938, 2 vols., and 1939; WC, 1952 et seq.; N.Y., George Braziller, 1954, 1247 pp.; ML, 1957, 455 pp.; N.Y., New Amer. Lib., 1960.

————On Painting: A Lost Book Reassembled from Manuscripts. Ed. Carlo Pedretti with English tr. London, Owen, and Berkeley, Univ. of California Pr., 1964. 301 pp., parallel texts.

————Thoughts on Art and Life. Tr. Maurice Baring. Humanists' Lib. Boston, Merrymount Pr., 1906. xxiv, 200 pp.

————A Treatise on Painting (*Libro di pittura*). Tr. anon. London, Printed for J. Senex, 1721. 189 pp. Repr. 1796.

    Tr. John Francis Rigaud. London, 1802. Many reprs., esp. Bohn Standard Lib., London, Bell, 1877, lxvii, 238 pp., and 1892; also (as The Art of Painting) N.Y., Philosophical Lib., 1957, 224 pp.

    Tr. A. Philip McMahon as Treatise on Painting. Princeton, N.J., Princeton Univ. Pr., 1956. 2 vols., parallel texts.

The standard bibliog. is Ettore Verga, *Bibliografia vinciana, 1493–1930* (Bologna, Zanichelli, 1931, 2 vols.). On Leonardo, see Rachel Annand Taylor, *Leonardo the Florentine: A Study in Personality* (N.Y. and London, Harper, 1928, xxv, 580 pp.); and V. P. Zubov, *Leonardo da Vinci*, tr. David Kraus from Russian (Cambridge, Mass., Harvard Univ. Pr., and London, Oxford Univ. Pr., 1968, xx, 335 pp.).

Leone Ebreo (d. 1535).   The Philosophy of Love (*Dialoghi d'amore*). Tr. F. Friedberg-Seeley and J. H. Barnes with intro. Cecil Roth. London, Soncino Pr., 1937. xv, 468 pp.

Machiavelli, Niccolò (1496–1527).

COLLECTED WORKS

————The Works. Tr. Henry Nevile. London, 1675. 529 pp. Repr. 1680, 1694, 1720.

Tr. Ellis Farneworth. London, Davies, 1762. 2 vols. Repr. 1775, 4 vols.

Tr. Christian E. Detmold as The Historical, Political, and Diplomatic Writings. Boston, Osgood, 1882. 4 vols.
> Vol. 1, The Florentine History; vol. 2, The Prince, and The Discourses; vols. 3, 4, The Missions (diplomatic). The Discourses repr. ML, 1950; The Prince repr. N.Y., Washington Square Pr., 1963, 119 pp.

Tr. Allan H. Gilbert as The Chief Works and Others. Durham, N.C., Duke Univ. Pr., 1965. 3 vols.

Tr. John R. Hale as The Literary Works. London and N.Y., Oxford Univ. Pr., 1961. xxvi, 202 pp.
> *Mandragola*; *Clizia*; *A Dialogue on Language*; *Belfagor*; selected letters.

INDIVIDUAL WORKS

————The Art of War. In Nevile, Farneworth, Gilbert, above; the Farneworth version repr. Indianapolis, Ind., Bobbs-Merrill, 1965, 247 pp.

Tr. Peter Whitehorne. London, 1560–62. Repr. 1574, 1588; in Tudor Trs. (with the Bedingfield tr. of the History, and the Dacres tr. of The Prince and The Discourses), London, Nutt, 1905, 2 vols., which repr. N.Y., AMS Pr., 1967.

————Belfagor. Tr. Thomas Roscoe, in The Italian Novelists. London, 1825, vol. 2, pp. 267–89.

Tr. John R. Hale, in The Literary Works, 1961 (see above).

For 18th c. trs., see CBEL, vol. 2, p. 811.

————Clizia. Tr. John R. Hale, in The Literary Works (see above).

Tr. Oliver Evans. Great Neck, N.Y., Barron, 1962. 85 pp.

————The Discourses on Livy. Tr. in Nevile, Farneworth, Detmold, Gilbert (see above).

Tr. Edward Dacres. London, 1636. 646 pp. Repr. Tudor Trs., 1905.

Tr. Ninian Hill Thomson. London, Kegan Paul, 1883. xvi, 187 pp.

Tr. Leslie J. Walker. London, Routledge, 1950. 2 vols., and New Haven, Conn., Yale Univ. Pr., 1950, 698 pp.

————The Florentine History. In Nevile, Farneworth, Detmold, Gilbert (see above).

Tr. Thomas Bedingfield. London, 1595. Repr. Tudor Trs., 1905, 2 vols.

Tr. M. K. London, 1674. Repr. 1761.

Tr. S. Edwards Lester. N.Y., Paine and Burgess, 1845. 2 vols.

Tr. anon. (with The Prince, and some historical tracts). London, Bohn, 1847. xx, 522 pp. Repr. 1851, 1854, 1901.

Tr. anon. N.Y., Colonial Pr., 1901. xvii, 444 pp. Repr. with intro. Felix Gilbert, N.Y., Harper (Torchbooks), 1960, paper.

Tr. anon. Washington, D.C., Dunne, 1901. xvii, 417 pp.

Tr. Ninian Hill Thomson. London, Constable, 1906. 2 vols.

Tr. W. K. Marriott. EL, 1909 et seq. xvi, 363 pp.

————The Letters: A Selection. Tr. Allan H. Gilbert. N.Y., Capricorn Books, 1961. 252 pp.
With a substantial introduction.

————Lust and Liberty: The Poems of Machiavelli. Tr. Joseph Tusiani. N.Y., Obolensky, 1963. xxiv, 196 pp.

————Mandragola. Tr. Ashley Dukes. London, Bloomsbury Pub., 1940. 86 pp.
First pr. 1930. Parts are adapted.

Tr. Stark Young. N.Y., Macaulay, 1927. 198 pp.
With Lord Macaulay's essay on Machiavelli.

Tr. Anne and Henry Paolucci. N.Y., Liberal Arts Pr., 1951. 61 pp.

Tr. John R. Hale. Swinford, Fantasy Pr., 1956. iv, 52 pp. Repr. in The Literary Works (see above).

Tr. Frederick May and Eric Bentley, in The Classic Theatre, vol. 1, 1958: see Collections, above.

————The Prince. Tr. in the Collected Works, above.

Tr. anon., c. 1560. Ed. Hardin Craig. Chapel Hill, Univ. of North Carolina Pr., 1944. xli, 177 pp.

Tr. Edward Dacres. London, 1640. Repr. Tudor Trs., 1905, vol. 1, pp. 252–356, repr. N.Y., AMS Pr., 1967; in Three Renaissance Classics, N.Y., Scribner, 1952.

Tr. Ninian Hill Thomson. London, Kegan Paul, 1882. xi, 118 pp. Rev. Oxford, 1897; in Harvard Classics, 1910; Oxford, 1913; N.Y., Limited Eds. Club, 1954.

Tr. Luigi Ricci. WC, 1903. viii, 107 pp. Rev. E. R. P. Vincent, WC, 1935. Repr. (with The Discourses), ML, 1940; with intro. Christian Gauss, N.Y., New Amer. Lib., 1952, 139 pp.

Tr. William K. Marriott. EL, 1908 et seq. xxvi, 209 pp. Repr. (with Thomas Hobbes' Leviathan) Great Books, vol. 23, 1952.

Tr. Allan H. Gilbert in The Prince and Other Works. Chicago, Ill., Packard, 1941. ix, 322 pp.

Tr. Peter Rodd as The Ruler. London, Lane, 1954. 125 pp. Repr. with intro. A. Robert Caponigri, Chicago, Ill., Regnery, 1955.

Tr. A. Robert Caponigri. Chicago, Regnery, 1963. x, 148 pp.

Tr. Mark Musa. N.Y., St. Martin's Pr., 1964. 225 pp., parallel texts.

Tr. Daniel Donno (with selected Discourses). N.Y., Bantam, 1966. 146 pp.

On the masterpiece see Allan H. Gilbert, *Machiavelli's Prince and Its Fore-runners* (Durham, N.C., Duke Univ. Pr., 1938, 266 pp., repr. N.Y., Barnes and Noble, 1968), a learned monograph free from common Anglo-Saxon prejudices. On Machiavelli, see Pasquale Villari, *The Life and Times of Niccolò Machiavelli*, tr. Linda Villari (London, Unwin, 1878, 2 vols., reprs. to 1898); Herbert Butterfield, *The Statecraft of Machiavelli* (London, Bell, 1940, 167 pp., repr. ibid. and N.Y., Macmillan, 1956); Federico Chabod, *Machiavelli and the Renaissance*, tr. David Moore (London, Bowes, and Cambridge, Mass., Harvard Univ. Pr., 1958, xviii, 258 pp.); John R. Hale, *Machiavelli and Renaissance Italy* (London, Hodder, and N.Y., Macmillan, 1960, xii, 244 pp.); Giuseppe Prezzolini, *Machiavelli*, tr. Gioconda Savini (N.Y., Farrar Straus, 1967, 372 pp.); Felix Raab, *The English Face of Machiavelli: A Changing Interpretation 1500–1700* (London, Routledge, and Toronto, Ont., Univ. of Toronto Pr., 1964, xii, 306 pp.); Roberto Ridolfi, *The Life of Niccolò Machiavelli*, tr. Cecil Grayson (London, Routledge, and Chicago, Ill., Univ. of Chicago Pr., 1963, 352 pp.); Leo Strauss, *Thoughts on Machiavelli* (Glencoe, Ill., Free Pr., 1958, 348 pp.).

Marino, Giambattista (1569–1625).   Adonis (selections from *L'Adone*). Ed. and tr. Harold Martin Priest. Ithaca, N.Y., Cornell Univ. Pr., 1967. lvii, 275 pp.

> Important passages (about one fifth of the poem) tr. in unrhymed verse stanzas.

————The Slaughter of the Innocents by Herod. Tr. verse R. T.   London, 1675.

> Tr. freely in verse (canto 1 only) Richard Crashaw, in Steps to the Temple: Sacred Poems. London, 1646. Repr. 1648, 1670, and in later eds. of Crashaw's Poems.

> See James V. Mirollo, *The Poet of the Marvelous: Giambattista Marino* (N.Y., Columbia Univ. Pr., 1963, 339 pp.) for texts and trs. (pp. 280–301) of *La canzone dei baci*, *La maddalena di Tiziano*, and *La Pastorella* (extracts).

Masuccio Salernitano (Tommaso Guardati, ?1420–?1500). The Novellino. Tr. William George Waters. London, Lawrence and Bullen, 1895. 2 vols. Repr. London, Aldus Society, 1903.

> Story 14 was repr. ed. by Geoffrey Bullough in *The Narrative and Dramatic Sources of Shakespeare*, vol. 1 (1957), pp. 497–505 (the Jessica story of *The Merchant of Venice*).

Matarazzo, Francesco (d. 1518).   Chronicles of the City of Perugia, 1492–1503. Tr. Edward Strachan Morgan. London, Dent, and N.Y., Dutton, 1905. xviii, 286 pp.

Medici, House of.   Lives of the Early Medici, as Told in Their Correspondence. Tr. Janet Ross. London, Chatto, 1910. xix, 351 pp.

De' Medici, Lorenzo (1449–1492).

> Only a few scattered poems have appeared in trs., notably the *Nencia*, in Edwin Arnold, The Secret of Death (London and Boston, 1885, pp. 66–88).

Palladio, Andrea (1518–1580).   The Architecture in Four Books. Rev. James Leoni, tr. N. DuBois. London, Leoni, 1715. Repr. 1721, 1742, 2 vols.

> Tr. Isaac Ware. London, 1738. Repr. N.Y., Dover, 1965, vii, 110 pp.

Petrarch, Francesco (1304–1374).

ITALIAN WORKS

————Sonnets, Triumphs, and Other Poems. Tr. various hands; complete. London, Bohn (Standard Library), 1859 et seq. to 1916. cxl, 416 pp.

The one complete tr. of all the Italian verse; the Latin verse has not been tr. Since no one person has tr. all the Petrarch poems, the anon. editor has chosen "from all the known versions those most distinguished for fidelity and rhythm" and regularly gives two versions of the same poem. He includes some thirty translators, beginning with Chaucer (sonnet 102), and including Wyatt, Surrey, Harington, and Drummond from the Tudor period; Spenser is mentioned but does not appear. We count the largest number (266 of the 367) of the *Rime* (lyric poems) translated by the very recent "Major Macgregor"; the "Rev. Dr. Nott" is next with 57; "Miss Wollaston" is third; the "Rev. Francis Wrangham" is fourth; "Lady Dacre" is fifth. Since the editor does not identify these translators otherwise, we list them in the order of their original publication: John Nott (1777, 1795). Barbarina Lady Dacre (1815 et seq.). Francis Wrangham (1817). Susan Wollaston (1841). Robert G. Macgregor (1851, 1854).

For the narrative poems in terza rima, the six Triumphs, the Bohn ed. is content with five in the Henry Boyd tr.: see below, under Triumphs. One Triumph, that of Death, is divided between MacGregor and Miss Hume (Anna Hume, Edinburgh, 1644).

————(The complete *Rime*). Tr. Robert G. Macgregor. (1) Odes of Petrarch· London, Smith Elder, 1851. viii, 230 pp. (2) Petrarch, in Indian Leisure. Ibid., 1854. 580 pp.

————The Sonnets and Stanzas [canzoni]. Tr. C. B. Cayley. London, Longmans, 1879. 474 pp.

————Sonnets and Songs. Tr. Anna Maria Armi, with intro. Theodor E. Mommsen. N.Y., Pantheon, 1946. 521 pp., parallel texts.

Excellent trs. mixed with unsuccessful efforts.

————The Sonnets. Tr. Joseph Auslander. N.Y. and London, Longmans, 1931. 336 pp.

Felicitous in only a few instances.

Numerous part trs. have been published of the sonnets and canzoni: see the British Museum Catalogue, and also Farrar and Evans, *English Trs. from Medieval Sources*. Some recent ones may be noted:

Tr. Albert Crompton as One Hundred Sonnets. London, Kegan Paul, 1898. 228 pp., parallel texts.

Tr. various as One Hundred Sonnets, in The Literature of Italy, 1265–1907: see Collections, above.

Tr. William Dudley Foulke as Some Love Songs of Petrarch. London, Oxford Univ. Pr., 1915. 244 pp.
   A number of good trs.

Tr. Morris Bishop as Love Rhymes of Petrarch. Ithaca, N.Y., Dragon Pr., 1932. 62 pp.
   Readable, and frequently excellent.

Ed. Thomas G. Bergin as The Rhymes: Selections of Trs. Edinburgh and London, Oliver and Boyd, 1955. xi, 61 pp.
   Excellent choices.

Ed. Thomas G. Bergin as The Sonnets in Italian with English trs. Verona, Limited Editions Club, 1965, and N.Y., Heritage Pr., 1966. xviii, 369 pp.

For a bibliog. of English trs. from the *Canzoniere* and an alphabetical list of versions from it, see George Watson, *A Critical Bibliography of the Canzoniere* (London, Warburg Institute Surveys 3, 1967, 47 pp.).

————The Triumphs (*Trionfi*). Tr. verse Henry Parker, Lord Morley. London, 1554? Repr. Roxburghe Club, 1887.

Tr. verse Henry Boyd. London, Longmans, 1807. lxviii, 216 pp. Repr. (5 out of the 6) in Sonnets, Triumphs, etc., 1859, see above. Repr. London, Murray, and Boston, Mass., Little Brown, 1906, 181 pp.; repr. San Francisco, 1927.

Tr. Ernest Hatch Wilkins. Chicago, Ill., Univ. of Chicago Pr., 1962. ix, 313 pp.
   Most elegant.

Part tr. Anna Hume (3 Triumphs). Edinburgh, 1644. 98 pp.

LATIN WORKS

—————The Letters. (No complete tr. has been made of the several volumes of letters. The following are important trs. of selections.)

Tr. James Harvey Robinson and Henry W. Rolfe. Petrarch the First Modern Scholar and Man of Letters: A Selection of His Correspondence. N.Y. and London, Putnam, 1898. 436 pp. Repr. 1909, 1914.

Tr. Mario E. Cosenza as Letters to Classical Authors. Chicago, Ill., Univ. of Chicago Pr., 1910. 208 pp.

Tr. Ernest Hatch Wilkins as Petrarch at Vaucluse: Letters in Verse and Prose. Chicago, Ill., Univ. of Chicago Pr., 1958. xi, 217 pp.

Tr. Morris Bishop as Letters from Petrarch. Bloomington, Indiana Univ. Pr., 1967. xi, 306 pp.

For other selections, see Mario E. Cosenza, *Francesco Petrarca and the Revolution of Cola di Rienzo* (Chicago, Ill., Univ. of Chicago Pr., 1913, 330 pp.); and Edward H. R. Tatham, *Francesco Petrarca, the First Modern Man of Letters: His Life and Correspondence* [to 1347] (London, Sheldon, 1925–26, 2 vols.).

—————On His Own Ignorance and That of Many Others (*De sui ipsius et multorum ignorantia*). Tr. Hans Nachod, in Ernst Cassirer, ed., The Renaissance Philosophy of Man, 1948, pp. 47–133. See Collections, above.

—————Physic against Fortune, as Well Prosperous as Adverse (*De remediis utriusque fortunae*). Tr. Thomas Twyne. London, 1579. 324 leaves. Part repr., ed. Mrs. Dobson, 1791, 1797.

Part tr. Conrad H. Rawski as Four Dialogues for Scholars. Cleveland, Ohio, Western Reserve Univ. Pr., 1967. 224 pp.

—————The Praise of Private Life (*De vita solitaria*). Tr. Sir John Harington (c. 1606). Ed. from ms. Norman E. McClure in The Letters and Epigrams of Sir John Harington. Philadelphia, Pa., 1930, pp. 323–78.

Tr. Jacob Zeitlin as The Life of Solitude. Urbana, Univ. of Illinois Pr., 1924. 316 pp.

—————Petrarch's Secret, or the Soul's Conflict with Passion (*Secretum*, also called *De contemptu mundi*). Tr. William H. Draper. London, Chatto and Windus, 1911. 192 pp.

————Seven Penitential Psalms. Tr. George Chapman. London, 1612. Repr. in The Works of George Chapman, vol. 2, London, 1875.

> Petrarch's "Confessional Psalms," doubtfully ascribed to him, were ed. and tr. Allan H. Gilbert, in *Romanic Review*, vol. 2 (1911), pp. 429–43, parallel texts.

————(The Tale of Griselda). Tr. in paraphrase by Geoffrey Chaucer as "The Clerk's Tale," in The Canterbury Tales (c. 1390). In all eds. of the Works of Chaucer.

> Tr. Robert D. French in A Chaucer Handbook. N.Y., Crofts, 1927, pp. 291–311. Repr. 1947, 1955.
>
> This is Petrarch's Latin version of the final story (X, 10) of Boccaccio's *Decameron*, included by Petrarch in his *Epistolae Seniles* (XVII, 3). Chaucer based "The Clerk's Tale" on the Petrarch version, together with an anon. French tr. of the Latin.

————The Testament. Ed. and tr. Theodor E. Mommsen. Ithaca, N.Y., Cornell Univ. Pr., 1957. viii, 93 pp., parallel texts.

For extensive Petrarch bibliography, see Cornell Univ. Lib., *Catalogue of the Petrarch Collection Bequeathed by Willard Fiske* compiled by Mary Fowler (London, Oxford Univ. Pr., 1916, 547 pp.); and for recent scholarship, Vincent Luciani, "Medieval Italian Literature" in *The Medieval Literature of Western Europe: A Review of Research* (N.Y., Modern Language Association, and London, Univ. of London Pr., 1966), Petrarch being discussed on pp. 311–18. On Petrarch, see H. C. Holloway-Calthrop, *Petrarch: His Life and Times* (London, Methuen, 1907, 319 pp.), gracefully written and well informed; Tatham, op. cit. (1925–26), the most extensive discussion of the earlier years; Ernest Hatch Wilkins, *Life of Petrarch* (Chicago, Ill., Univ. of Chicago Pr., 1963, 276 pp.), our most reliable biography. See also John Humphries Whitfield, *Petrarch and the Renaissance* (Oxford, Blackwell, 1943, 170 pp., repr. N.Y., Russell, 1966); Aldo S. Bernardo, *Petrarch, Scipio, and the Africa: The Birth of Humanism's Dream* (Baltimore, Md., Johns Hopkins Univ. Pr., 1962, 288 pp.); Morris Bishop, *Petrarch and His World* (Bloomington, Indiana Univ. Pr., 1963, 399 pp.).

Piccolomini, Alessandro (1508–1578).   Raffaella, Or rather a dialogue of the fair perfecting of Ladies. Tr. J[ohn] N[evinson] [c. 1540]. Glasgow, Glasgow Univ. Pr., 1968. 105 pp.

Pico Della Mirandola, Giovanni (1463–1494).   Dyvers Epistles and Other
Werkes. Tr. Thomas More from Latin original, together with The Lyfe of
Pico [by Pico's nephew, see next author, below]. London, Rastell [1510?].
40 leaves. Repr. London, de Worde [1510?]; in The [English] Workes of
Thomas More, London, 1557, pp. 1–34, which repr. facs. London and N.Y.,
1931, vol. 1. Repr. of the 1510 de Worde edn., ed. J. M. Rigg, London,
Nutt, 1890, xl, 95 pp.

> More tr. *XII Rules of a Man in Spyrituall Batayle*; *The XII Wepens* [of the
> same]; *XII Propertees or Condycyons of a Lover*; *A Prayer unto God*: all ex-
> panded in verse paraphrases. Also in prose three letters of Pico; and his
> *Interpretacion upon the psalme* [16] *Conserva me Domine*.

——————On the Dignity of Man, tr. Charles Glenn Wallis; On Being and the
One, tr. Paul J. W. Miller; Heptaplus, tr. Douglas Carmichael. Indianapolis,
Ind., Bobbs-Merrill [1965]. xxxiii, 174 pp., paper.

All tr. from Latin originals.

——————Of Being and Unity (*De ente et uno*). Tr. Victor M. Hamm. Milwaukee,
Wis., Marquette Univ. Pr., 1943. 34 pp., paper.

> Tr. Paul J. W. Miller, with On the Dignity of Man, etc. [1965], see
> preceding entry.

——————On the Dignity of Man. Tr. Charles Glenn Wallis. Annapolis, Md.,
St. John's Book Store, 1940. 30 leaves. Rev. with On Being and the One,
etc. [1965], see above.

——————Tr. Elizabeth L. Forbes (part) in Journal of the History of Ideas, vol. 3
(1942), 347–54. Repr. in The Renaissance Philosophy of Man, 1948: see
Collections, above.

> Tr. A. Robert Caponigri. Chicago, Regnery, 1956. xii, 40 pp.

——————A Platonick Discourse on Love (*Commento sopra una canzone de amore*).
Tr. Thomas Stanley, in his Poems. London, 1651. Repr. in Thomas
Stanley, The History of Philosophy, part 5, 1656, which repr. 1687, 1701,
1743; repr. ed. Edmund G. Gardner, Boston, Merrymount Pr., 1914,
xxvii, 83 pp.; repr. in Thomas Stanley, Poems and Translations, ed Galbraith
Miller, Oxford, Clarendon Pr., 1962.

——————XII Rules of a Man in Spyrituall Batayle. Tr. Thomas More in verse
paraphrase [1510?]: see Dyvers Epistles, above.

Tr. Sir Thomas Elyot as The Rules of a Christian lyfe. London, 1534 (with his tr. of Cyprian's Sermon on the Mortalitie of Man). Repr. 1539; [Rouen] 1585 (with The Following of Christ), London, 1615 (with the same).

Tr. W. H. as Twelve Rules, and Weapons Concerning the Spirituall Battel. London, 1589. 39 pp.
> Includes also *Twelve Conditions of a Lover*; *The Commentarie upon the Sixteene Psalme*; two letters to the nephew.

Pico Della Mirandola, Giovanni Francesco (1470–1533).　On the Imagination. Ed. and tr. Harry Caplan from Latin. Cornell Studies in English 16. New Haven, Conn., Yale Univ. Pr., 1930. 102 pp.

————The Lyfe of John Picus, Earl of Mirandula. Tr. Thomas More from Latin, with Dyvers Epistles [by the senior Pico] [1510?]. See the preceding author.

Poggio Bracciolini (1380–1449).　See vol. 1, Medieval Latin Literature.

Politian (Angelo Poliziano, 1454–1494).　Orpheo. Tr. John Addington Symonds in Sketches and Studies in Italy. London, Smith Elder, 1879, pp. 226–42. Repr. 1898 (Second Series), 1914, 1929.
> Trs. the larger version, *Orphei Tragoedia*.

Tr. Harry Morgan Ayres as Poliziano's Orfeo. Romanic Review, vol. 20, 1929, pp. 13–24.
> In some respects better than the following. Tr. of the earlier version, *La favola di Orfeo*.

Tr. prose Louis E. Lord in A Translation of the Orpheus of Angelo Politian and the Aminta of Torquato Tasso. London, Oxford Univ. Pr., 1931. 182 pp.
> Trs. both versions.

Pulci, Luigi (1432–1484).　*Il Morgante*. Tr. George Gordon Lord Byron (canto 1 only) in The Liberal, no. 4, July 30, 1823. Repr. in The Works of Lord Byron, London, 1824, and thereafter.
> We should have a complete tr. of this comic masterpiece.

Sacchetti, Franco (c. 1330–c. 1400).　Tales from Sacchetti. Tr. Mary G. Steegman. London, Dent, and N.Y., Dutton, 1908. xxiv, 307 pp.

Salutati, Coluccio (1341–1406).   See vol. 1, Medieval Latin Literature.

Sannazzaro, Jacopo (1458–1530).   Arcadia and Piscatorial Eclogues. Tr. Ralph Nash. Detroit, Mich., Wayne State Univ. Pr., 1966. 180 pp.

Sarpi, Paolo (i.e., Pietro, 1552–1623).   History of Benefices. Tr. with intro. Peter Burke. N.Y., Washington Square Pr., 1967. xlvi, 322 pp., paper. Includes selections from the *Historia del Concilio Tridentino*.

————Historie of the Councel of Trent. Tr. Nathanael Brent. London, Barker, 1620. 825 pp. Repr. enl. 1629, 1640, 1676.

————The History of the Quarrels of Pope Paul V with the State of Venice. Tr. C. P.   London, Bill, 1626. 435 pp.

————The Free Schoole of Warre, of . . . Whether It Be Lawfull to Beare Armes for . . . a Prince That Is of a Divers Religion. Tr. William Bedell. London, Bill, 1625.

————The Letters . . . to the Republic of Venice. Tr. Edward Browne. London, Chiswell, 1693. cxvii, 430 pp.

————The Rights of Sovereigns and Subjects. Tr. S. Whatley. London, Graves, 1722. lxxxviii, 392 pp.

————A Treatise of Matters Beneficiary [of church revenues]. Tr. William Denton. London, 1680.

   Tr. C. Hayes. Westminster, 1727. Repr. 1730.

   Tr. Tobias Jenkins. London, 1736. cv, 260 pp.

Savonarola, Girolamo (1452–1498).   The Triumph of the Cross. Tr. John Procter. London, Sands, and Dublin, Gill, 1901. xxxi, 213 pp.

For other writings, see Neo-Latin Literature, vol. 1 above.

On Savonarola, see Michael de la Bedoyère, *The Meddlesome Friar* (London, Collins, and N.Y., Doubleday, 1958, 256 pp.); Roberto Ridolfi, *The Life of Girolamo Savonarola*, tr. Cecil Grayson (London, Routledge, and N.Y.,

Knopf, 1959, 325 pp.); Pierre Van Paassen, *A Crown of Fire: The Life and Times of Girolamo Savonarola* (London, Hutchinson, 1961, 330 pp.); Pasquale Villari, *Life and Times of Girolamo Savonarola*, tr. Linda Villari (London, Unwin, 1888, 2 vols.; repr. 1927).

Secchi, Niccolò (16th c.).   Self-Interest (*L'Interesse*). Tr. William Reymes. Seattle, Univ. of Washington Pr., 1953. xxix, 136 pp.
　　From an unpublished 17th c. ms. in the Folger Library.

Stampa, Gaspara (d. 1554).   [Selected Sonnets.] Tr. George Fleming in Eugene Benson, Gaspara Stampa. Boston, Mass., Roberts Bros., 1881. 85 pp.
　　Tr. mediocre.

Straparola, Giovanni Francesco (fl. 1540).   The Facetious Nights (*Le piacevoli notti*). Tr. W. G. Waters. London, Soc. of Bibliophiles, 1901. 4 vols.

Tr. anon. as The Most Delectable Nights. Paris, Charles Charrington, 1909. 4 vols.

Tasso, Torquato (1544–1595).   Aminta. Tr. hexameters Abraham Fraunce (nearly complete) as The Affectionate Life and Unfortunate Death of Phillis and Amyntas, in The Countesse of Pembrokes Ivychurch. London, 1591. 48 leaves.

Tr. verse Henry Reynolds as Aminta Englisht. London, 1628. 47 leaves. Repr. as Aminta: A Pastoral Comedy, Oxford, [1650?], parallel texts.

Tr. verse John Dancer as Aminta: The Famous Pastoral. London, 1660. 134 pp.

Tr. John Oldmixon as Amintas: A Pastoral. 1698. 56 pp.

Tr. verse W. Ayre. London, 1737. 96 pp.

Tr. Percival Stockdale. London, 1770. xviii, 170 pp.

Tr. verse Leigh Hunt. London, Allman, 1820. xxxii, 146 pp. Repr. in The Genius of the Italian Theatre, ed. Eric Bentley, see Collections, above.

Tr. verse Frederic Whitmore as Amyntas: A Sylvan Fable. Springfield, Mass., Ridgewood Pr., and Penzance, A. J. George, 1900. 72 pp.
　　Good despite archaisms.

Tr. prose Ernest Grillo. London, Dent, and N.Y., Dutton, 1924. 200 pp., parallel texts.

Tr. prose Louis E. Lord in A Translation of the Orpheus of Angelo Politian and the Aminta of Torquato Tasso. London, Oxford Univ. Pr., 1931. 182 pp.
    A fair tr., less attractive than the Whitmore, above.

——————[Jerusalem Delivered.] Tr. Edward Fairfax as Godfrey of Bulloigne. London, 1600. Many reprs., especially in Morley's Universal Lib., London and N.Y., Routledge, 1890, 446 pp.; rev. N.Y., Colonial, 1901, repr. N.Y., National Alumni, 1907; with intro. Roberto Weiss, London, Centaur Pr., and Carbondale, Southern Illinois Univ. Pr., 1962, xxi, 545 pp.; with intro. John Charles Nelson, N.Y., Putnam, 1963, xxiv, 446 pp., and Capricorn Books, paper.

Other trs., normally with the title Jerusalem Delivered:

Tr. Patrick Doyne in blank verse. Dublin, 1761. 2 vols.

Tr. John Hoole in couplets. London, 1763, 2 vols., et seq. to 1821.

Tr. J. H. Hunt. London, 1818. Repr. 1822.

Tr. J. H. Wiffen in Spenserian stanzas. London, 1824–25, 2 vols. Reprs. to 1854 (Bohn's Lib.).

Tr. verse J. R. Broadhead. London, Evans, 1837. 2 vols.

Tr. verse C. L. Smith. London, Longmans, 1851, 2 vols. Reprs. 1874, 1876, 1878.

Tr. A. C. Robinson. London, Blackwood, 1853. xii, 527 pp.

Tr. H. Bent in octaves. London, Bell and Daldy, 1856. 2 vols.

Tr. verse H. A. Griffith. Belfast, 1863. vi, 497 pp.

Tr. verse Sir J. K. James. London, Longmans, 1865. 2 vols. Repr. 1884.

Tr. James Denis Twinberrow. Bromley, Kent, 1935? (typescript).

    The first English tr., of five cantos in octaves, was done by Richard Carew, pub. 1594 in parallel texts.

A good modern tr. is badly needed.

————Rinaldo. Tr. verse John Hoole. London, Dodsley, 1792. 226 pp. Repr. in A. Chalmers, Works of the English Poets, vol. 21, 1810.

For bibliog. of Tasso studies, see A. Tortoreto and J. G. Fucilla, *Bibliografia analitica tassiana* (Milano, Bolaffio, 1935), and Professor Tortoreto's annual bibliog. from 1952 to date in *Studi tassiani*. On Tasso, consult the full-scale biography by William Boulting, *Tasso and His Times* (London, Methuen, and N.Y., Putnam, 1907, 310 pp.). A more comprehensive treatment is by C. P. Brand, *Torquato Tasso: A Study of the Poet and His Contribution to English Literature* (Cambridge, Eng., Univ. Pr., 1965, 338 pp.).

Varthema, Ludovico (fl. 1502–1510).   The Navigation and Voyages . . . to the . . . East Indies (*Itinerario*). Tr. Richard Eden from a Latin version of the Italian in his History of Travayle, 2d ed., London, 1577.

Tr. John Winter Jones as The Travels. London, Hakluyt Soc., Works no. 32, 1863. 121, 131 pp. Repr. facs. N.Y., Burt Franklin, 1964. Repr. as The Itinerary, with intro. Sir Richard Carnac Temple, London, Argonaut Pr., 1928, lxxxvi, 122 pp.; rev. Lincoln Davis Hammond in Travelers in Disguise, Cambridge, Mass., Harvard Univ. Pr., 1963, pp. 47–233, paper.
A classic of travel narrative.

Vasari, Giorgio (1511–1574).   Lives of the Most Eminent Painters, Sculptors and Architects. Tr. Mrs. Jonathan Foster. Bohn's Standard Lib. London, Bell, 1850–85. 5 vols. Repr. in part as Lives of the Artists, London, Allen and Unwin, 1960, xv, 309 pp.; repr. N.Y., Heritage Pr., 1967, 2 vols.

Tr. A. B. Hinds. Temple Classics. London, Dent, 1900. 8 vols. Repr. EL, 1927 et seq., 4 vols.

Tr. Gaston Du C. De Vere. London, Macmillan and Medici Soc., 1912–15. 10 vols. Repr. in part Medici Soc., 1959, xii, 435 pp., and N.Y., ML, 1959.

Tr. (extracts) George Bull. Penguin, 1965. 478 pp.

————The *Maniera* of Vasari. Tr. Mrs. Jonathan Foster, ed. J. G. Freeman. London, 1867, parallel texts.

————Vasari on Technique: Being the Introduction to the Three Arts Prefixed to The Lives. Tr. Louisa S. Maclehose, ed. with intro. G. Baldwin Brown. London, Dent, and N.Y., Dutton, 1907. xxiv, 328 pp.

For other selections from *The Lives* in tr., see the British Museum Catalogue.

Vida, Marco Girolamo (1470–1556).   See Neo-Latin Literature, in vol. 1 above.

Modern Period (1600–1900)

Literary Studies

Collison-Morley, Lacy.   Modern Italian Literature, London, Pitman, 1911. vii, 356 pp.
> Useful as an initial survey.

**Croce, Benedetto.   European Literature of the Nineteenth Century. Tr. Douglas Ainslie. London, Chapman and Hall, 1904. ix, 373 pp.
> Penetrating aesthetic evaluations of Alfieri, Monti, Foscolo, Leopardi, Manzoni, Berchet, Giusti, and Carducci.

Grillo, Ernesto.   Studies in Modern Italian Literature. Glasgow, Jackson Wylie, 1930. 256 pp.
> Deals, not exhaustively, with Goldoni, Metastasio, Alfieri, Parini, Monti, and Carducci.

*Howells, William Dean.   Modern Italian Poets: Essays and Versions. N.Y., Harper, and Edinburgh, D. Douglas, 1887. 368 pp.
> From Parini to Mercantini: a delightful series.

Kennard, Joseph Spencer.   Italian Romance Writers. N.Y., Brentano, 1922. 472 pp.
> From Manzoni to D'Annunzio: rather superficial.

————The Italian Theatre from the Close of the Seventeenth Century. N.Y., Rudge, 1932. 2 vols. Repr. N.Y., Blom, 1964.
> Most extensive discussion in English, but neither profound nor original.

**Lee, Vernon   (pseud. of Violet Paget).   Studies in the Eighteenth Century in Italy. London, Satchell, 1880. 298 pp. Rev. London, Unwin, 1907, and Chicago, Ill., McClurg, 1908, xlix, 450 pp.
>   Contains "The Arcadian Academy"; "The Musical Life"; "Metastasio and the Opera"; "The Comedy of Mask"; "Goldoni and the Realistic Comedy"; "Carlo Gozzi and the Venetian Fairy Comedy." One of the best studies of the period.

*Robertson, J[ohn] G[eorge].   Studies in the Genesis of the Romantic Theory in the Eighteenth Century. Cambridge, Eng., Univ. Pr., 1923. 298 pp.
>   Includes studies on Gravina, Muratori, Conti, Martelli, Maffei, Calepio, and Vico. Upholds the primacy of Italy in the development of critical theory.

Vittorini, Domenico.   The Modern Italian Novel. Philadelphia, Univ. of Pennsylvania Pr., 1930, 296 pp.
>   Survey from 1827 to 1929. Good analyses of many novels; does not always distinguish between major and minor writers.

Collections

*Ellet, Elizabeth Fries (Lummis).   Poems, Translated and Original. Philadelphia, Pa., Key and Biddle, 1835. 229 pp.
>   Foscolo (*Sepulchres*), Alfieri, Testi, Bettinelli, Grossi, Pindemonte, and Niccolini. Readable versions.

Italian Lyrists of Today.   Tr. George Arthur Greene. London, Matthews and Lane, and N.Y., Macmillan, 1893. 232 pp. Repr. London and N.Y., Lane, 1898.
>   Eighty-two poems from thirty-four authors. Trs. mediocre.

Italian Regional Tales of the Nineteenth Century.   Tr. Bernard Wall and others, with intro. Archibald Colquhoun. London and N.Y., Oxford Univ. Pr., 1961. xv, 268 pp.
>   Stories by D'Annunzio, De Amicis, Deledda, and Serao, and by authors not previously tr.: Boito, Di Giacomo, Fucini, R. Sacchetti, Scarfoglio, and Tarchetti.

INDIVIDUAL AUTHORS

Alfieri, Vittorio (1749–1803).   The Tragedies. Tr. Charles Lloyd. London, Baldwin, 1815. 4 vols. Repr. 1821; enl., ed. E. A. Bowring, London and N.Y., Bell, 1876, 2 vols.

Lloyd tr. 19 plays; Bowring added the three posthumously printed plays for a complete tr. The tr. of *Myrrha* is repr. in *The Drama*, vol. 5 (1903), pp. 285–336; and in *Chief European Dramatists*, 1916: see General Reference, Collections, above. The trs. of three tragedies were repr. with *Three Comedies of Goldoni* (N.Y., National Alumni, 1907), viz. *The Conspiracy of the Pazzi*; *Mary Stuart*; and *Antigone*.

For other trs. of individual plays, see British Museum Catalogue.

————Memoirs. Tr. anon. London, 1810. Rev. E. R. Vincent, London and N.Y., Oxford Univ. Pr., 1961, xix, 310 pp.

Tr. Sir Henry McAnally as The Life of Vittorio Alfieri Written by Himself. Slough, Buckinghamshire, Kenton Pr. (pr. pr.), 1949. Repr. Lawrence, Univ. of Kansas Pr., 1953, 288 pp.

For other trs., see Library of Congress Catalogue.

————Of Tyranny. Tr. Julius A. Molinaro and Beatrice Corrigan. Toronto, Ont., Univ. of Toronto Pr., 1961. xxxvi, 120 pp.

Good presentation.

On Alfieri, see Charles R. D. Miller, *Alfieri: A Biography* (Williamsport, Pa., Bayard Pr., 1936, 262 pp.); Gaudens Megaro, *Vittorio Alfieri: Forerunner of Italian Nationalism* (N.Y., Columbia Univ. Pr., 1930, 175 pp.). For bibliog., consult E. H. Wilkins, "Alfieri in America," in *The Invention of the Sonnet and Other Studies* (Rome, Edizioni di Storia e Letteratura, 1959, pp. 295–513).

Andreini, Giovanni Battista (1578–1650).   Adam: A Sacred Drama. Tr. verse William Cowper and William Hayley in Life and Poetical Works of John Milton, ed. William Hayley. Chichester, 1810, vol. 3. Repr. in The Life and Works of William Cowper, ed. Robert Southey, vol. 10 (1837), pp. 239–87; repr. Bohn ed., vol. 6 (1855), pp. 319–434.

Tr. from the first ed. of the *Adamo* (1613).

Barrili, Anton Giulio (1836–1906).   The Adventures of Captain Dodero. (*Capitan Dodèro*). Tr. H. B. Cotterill. London, Harrap, and N.Y., Brentano, 1920. 63 pp., parallel texts.

————The Devil's Portrait (*Fiordalisa: Il ritratto del diavolo*). Tr. Evelyn Wodehouse. London, Remington, and N.Y., Gottesberger, 1885. 312 pp.

————The Eleventh Commandment. Tr. Clara Bell. London, Remington, and N.Y., Gottesberger, 1882. 377 pp.

————A Noble Kinsman (*Cuor di ferro*). Tr. H. A. Martin. London, T. F. Unwin, 1885. 2 vols.

————The Princess' Private Secretary (*Il lettore della principessa*). Tr. Judge Stephen. London, Digby Long, 1893. viii, 335 pp.

————A Whimsical Wooing. Tr. Clara Bell. London, Remington, and N.Y., Gottesberger, 1882. 88 pp.

Beccaria, Cesare Bonesana (1738–1794).   A Discourse on Public Oeconomy and Commerce. Tr. anon. London, 1769. vi, 47 pp.

————An Essay on Crimes and Punishments. Tr. anon. from the French version, with commentary ascribed to Voltaire. London, Almon, 1767. xii, 179 pp. Reprs. numerous in England to 1809, in America 1777, 1778, 1809.

   Tr. Edward D. Ingraham from the French version. Philadelphia, Pa., 1819. Facs. repr. Stanford, Calif., Academic Reprints, 1953, 239 pp.; rev. abridged Henry Paolucci, N.Y., Bobbs-Merrill, 1963, 99 pp.

   Also tr. J. A. Farrer, London, 1880; and tr. Jane Grigson, with *The Column of Infamy* by Manzoni, 1964 (see Manzoni, below).

*****Belli, Giuseppe Gioachino (1791–1863).**   Roman Sonnets (*Sonetti romaneschi*). Tr. Harold Norse, with preface William Carlos Williams and intro. Alberto Moravia. Highlands, N.C., J. Williams, 1960. Unpaged.
   Forty-five sonnets attractively tr. in American slang.

Capuana, Luigi (1839–1915).   Golden-Feather. Tr. Dorothy Emmrich. N.Y., Dutton, 1930. vii, 265 pp.

————Italian Fairy Tales. Tr. Dorothy Emmrich. N.Y., Dutton, 1929. v, 209 pp.

————Nimble-Legs: A Story for Boys. Tr. Frederick Taber Cooper. N.Y. and London, Longmans, 1927. 191 pp.

————Once Upon a Time: Fairy Tales. Tr. anon. (Children's Lib.). London, Unwin, 1892. 218 pp.

The best of Capuana remains to be tr.

On Capuana, see S. E. Scalia, *Luigi Capuana and his Times* (N.Y., Vanni, 1952, xv, 251 pp.).

Carcano, Giulio (1812–1884).   Damiano: The Story of a Poor Family. Tr. William Shepard Walsh. N.Y., National Alumni, 1907. 387 pp.

Carducci, Giosuè (1836–1907).   Poems of Giosuè Carducci. Tr. verse Frank Sewall. N.Y., Dodd Mead, 1892, and London, Osgood McIlvaine, 1893. v, 135 pp. (41 poems).
  The best of the verse trs. Includes two essays: "Carducci and the Hellenic Reaction in Italy" and "Carducci and the Classic Realism."

Tr. Maud Holland as Poems. N.Y., Scribner, 1907. 175 pp.

Tr. verse C. L. Bickersteth as A Selection of His Poems. London and N.Y., Longmans Green, 1913. xvi, 346 pp., parallel texts.
  Not so good as his tr. of Leopardi, but nevertheless excellent.

Tr. Emily A. Tribe as A Selection from the Poems. London and N.Y., Longmans, 1921. lxxxii, 154 pp. (46 poems).

————The Barbarian Odes of Giosuè Carducci. Tr. prose William Fletcher Smith. Menasha, Wis., Banta, 1939. 50 pp. Rev. Dino Bigongiari and Giuseppe Prezzolini, N.Y., Vanni, 1950, 243 pp., parallel texts.

Tr. Mary W. Arms of six of these as Poems of Italy. N.Y., Grafton Pr., 1906. 43 pp.

————The Lyrics and Rhythms (*Rime e Ritmi*). Tr. prose William Fletcher Smith. Colorado Springs, Colo., pr. pr., 1942. 52 pp.

—————Political and Satiric Verse. Tr. William Fletcher Smith. Ibid., pr. pr., 1942. 63 pp.

All the Smith versions are in prose: only occasionally successful.

—————*Rime Nuove* of Carducci. Tr. Laura Fullerton Gilbert. Boston, Mass., Badger, and Toronto, Copp-Clark, 1916. 186 pp. (93 of the 104 poems).

Tr. William Fletcher Smith as The New Lyrics. Colorado Springs, Colo., pr. pr., 1942. 102 pp.

Tr. Maud Holland as Poems. N.Y., Scribner, 1907. 175 pp.

On Carducci, see Orlo Williams, *Giosuè Carducci* (London, Constable, and Boston, Houghton, 1914, 123 pp.); S. E. Scalia, *Carducci: His Critics and Translators in England and America, 1881–1932* (N.Y., Vanni, 1937, 103 pp.); William Fletcher Smith, *A Bibliography of Critical Material (1858–1940) on Giosuè Carducci* (Colorado Springs, pr. pr., 1942, 312 pp.).

Carletti, Francesco (1573?–1636).   My Voyage Round the World (*Ragionamenti del mio viaggio intorno al mondo*). Tr. Herbert Weinstock. N.Y., Pantheon, 1964, and London, Methuen, 1965. xv, 270 pp.

Casanova di Seingalt, Giacomo Girolamo (1725–1798).   Memoirs. Tr. A. Baillot from the French original (Leipzig, 1826–38, 12 vols.). Brunswick, Neuhoff, 1863. vols. 1–6 (all published).

Tr. Arthur Machen. London, Casanova Soc., 1922. 12 vols. Repr. Edinburgh for Limited Edns Club, 1940, 8 vols.; London, Elek, 1958–60, 6 vols.; N.Y., Putnam, 1959–61, 6 vols. Abridged, London, Routledge, 1930, 2 vols.; London, Joiner and Steele, 1932, 2 vols.; N.Y., Boni, 1932, 2 vols.; N.Y., Regency House, 1938, 2 vols.

Tr. Willard R. Trask from ms. London, Longmans, 1966—, and N.Y., Harcourt, 1967—. Vols. 1–4 (12 vols. planned).

Many part trs. from the *Memoirs*, also abridgements as, e.g., London, Chapman and Hall, 1902, 2 vols., repr. London, Navarre Soc., 1922; also ML, 1929 et seq.; also London, W. H. Allen, 1953, and N.Y., Bantam, 1968, tr. Lowell Bair.

Casti, Giambattista (1724–1803).   The Court and Parliament of Beasts (*Gli animali parlanti*). Freely tr. William Stewart Rose. London, Bulmer, 1816. 110 pp. Repr. London, Murray, 1819.

————The Trè Giuli. Tr. verse Montague Montague. London, Hatchard, 1826
xxxii, 208 pp. Repr. London, H. Starie, 1841.

Collodi, Carlo (pseud. of Carlo Lorenzini, 1831–1890).   The Story of a
Puppet or the Adventures of Pinocchio. Tr. M. A. Murray. London, Unwin,
and N.Y., Cassell, 1892. 232 pp. Frequent reprs., especially EL, 1911 et seq.
Other trs. and other titles are numerous.

Da Ponte, Lorenzo (1749–1838).   *Così fan tutte* (Women Are Like That).
Tr. Ruth and Thomas Martin. N.Y., Schirmer, [1951]. 76 pp.
The libretto for Mozart's opera.

————Don Giovanni. Tr. Adrienne M. Schizzano and Oscar Mandel as The
Punished Libertine, or Don Giovanni, in The Theatre of Don Juan, ed. Oscar
Mandel. Lincoln, Univ. of Nebraska Pr., 1963. 731 pp.

   Tr. Ellen H. Bleiler. N.Y., Dover, and Gloucester, Mass., Peter Smith,
   1964. 209 pp., parallel texts.
   Also a libretto.

————The Marriage of Figaro. Tr. E. J. Dent. London and N.Y., Oxford
Univ. Pr., 1937. xiii, 95 pp.
   Also a libretto.

————Memoirs. Tr. Elisabeth Abbott, ed. Arthur Livingston. Philadelphia,
Lippincott, 1929. 512 pp. Repr. with pref. Thomas G. Bergin, abridged,
N.Y., Orion Pr., 1959, xxi, 277 pp.; repr. N.Y., Dover, 1967, x, 512 pp.

   Tr. L. A. Sheppard. London, Routledge, 1929. 387 pp.

On Da Ponte, see Joseph Louis Russo, *Lorenzo Da Ponte: Poet and Adventurer*
(N.Y., Columbia Univ. Pr., 1922, 166 pp.; repr. N.Y., AMS Pr., 1968).

D'Azeglio, Massimo Tapparelli (1798–1866).   Ettore Fieramosca, or The
Challenge of Barletta: An Historical Romance of the Time of the Medici.
Tr. C. Edwards Lester. N.Y., Paine and Burgess, 1845. 274 pp.
   Also tr. M. H. Rankin as *Hector Fieramosca* (London, 1835), and Lady L.
   Magenis as *The Challenge of Barletta* (London, Allen, 1880, 2 vols.).

————The Maid of Florence, or Niccolò de' Lapi. Tr. W. Felgate. London,
1853. 3 vols.

Tr. by a Lady as Florence Betrayed, or the Last Days of the Republic. Boston, Spencer, 1856. 529 pp. Repr. 1860 as Niccolò de' Lapi.

─────────Recollections (*I miei Ricordi*). Tr. Count Maffei. London, 1862. 2 vols.

Tr. E. R. Vincent as Things I Remember. London and N.Y., Oxford Univ. Pr., 1966. xvii, 349 pp.

For some of his political pamphlets, see British Museum Catalogue.

De Amicis, Edmondo (1846–1908).   The Heart of a Boy (*Il Cuore*). Tr. abridged Sophie Jewett. Chicago, Ill., Rand McNally, 1912. Repr. N.Y., Ungar, 1960, 286 pp.

Other trs. by Isabel F. Hapgood (N.Y., 1887, repr, 1901); G. S. Godkin (London, 1895); Gaetano Mantellini (Chicago, Ill., 1895, repr. 1899); Oscar Durante (Chicago and N.Y., 1901).

─────────Military Life in Italy: Sketches (*La vita militare*). Tr. Wilhelmina W. Cady. N.Y., Putnam, 1882. ix, 440 pp.

─────────The Romance of a Schoolmaster. Tr. Mary A. Craig. London, Osgood, 1892. 3 vols.

─────────Won by a Woman (*La Maestrina degli Operai*). Tr. Gaetano Mantellini. Chicago, Ill., Laird and Lee, 1897. 240 pp.

For his books of travel and studies of foreign countries, see the British Museum Catalogue.

Della Valle, Pietro (1586–1652).   The Travels . . . into East India and Arabia Deserta. Tr. George Havers. London, 1665. Repr. ed. Edward Grey, London, Hakluyt Society, vols. 84–85, 1891, 2 vols., repr. N.Y., 1963.

Fogazzaro, Antonio (1842–1911).   Daniele Cortis, a Novel. Tr. Mrs. I. R. Tilton. N.Y., Holt, 1887. 308 pp.

Tr. S. L. Simeon. London, Remington, 1890. viii, 375 pp.

Tr. Gaetano Mantellini as The Politician. Boston, Mass., Luce, and Toronto, Musson, 1908. 473 pp.

————Leila. Tr. Mary Prichard Agnetti. London, Hodder, 1911. vii, 468 pp.

————Malombra. Tr. F. T. Dickson. London, T. F. Unwin, 1896. viii, 561 pp. Repr. London and Philadelphia, 1907.

————The Man of the World (*Piccolo Mondo moderno*). Tr. Mary Prichard Agnetti. London, Hodder, and N.Y., Putnam (as The Sinner), 1907. xii, 356 pp.

————The Patriot (*Piccolo mondo antico*). Tr. Mary Prichard Agnetti. London, Hodder, and N.Y., Putnam, 1906. xiv, 433 pp.

    Tr. W. J. Strachan as The Little World of the Past. London and N.Y., Oxford Univ. Pr., 1962. xvi, 358 pp.
    Tr. abridged Guido Waldman as A House Divided. London, New English Library, 1962. 282 pp.

————The Poet's Mystery. Tr. Anita McMahon and A. Warren. London, Duckworth, 1903. vii, 332 pp.

————The Saint. Tr. Mary Prichard Agnetti. London and N.Y., Putman, 1906. xx, 400 pp.

————The Sinner. See The Man of the World, above.

On Fogazzaro, see Tommaso Gallarati-Scotti, *The Life of Antonio Fogazzaro*, tr. Mary Prichard Agnetti (London, Hodder, and N.Y., Doran, 1922, 314 pp.).

Foscolo, Ugo (1778–1827). Essays on Petrarch. Tr. anon. London, Bentley, 1821. 211 pp. Repr. 1823.

————Letters of Ortis (*Ultime lettere di Jacopo Cortis*). Tr. F. B. 2d ed. London, H. Colburn, 1818. iv, 233 pp.

    Tr. Dale McAdoo and Anthony Winner as The Last Letters, etc., in Great European Short Novels, vol. 1. N.Y., Harper, 1968.

————Ricciarda, A Tragedy in Five Acts. Tr. J. Atkinson. Calcutta, 1823.

————The Sepulchres (*Carme sui sepolcri*). See Ellet, Collections, above.

Tr. Ernesto Grillo. London, Blackie, 1928. 59 pp.

Tr. Joseph Tusiani. Italian Quarterly, vol. 3, no. 12 (1960), pp. 13–20. Better than the Ellet tr.

Giacosa, Giuseppe (1847–1906). The Stronger, Like Falling Leaves (*Come le foglie*), Sacred Ground (*Diritti dell'anima*). Tr. E. and A. Updegraff. Boston, Little, Brown, 1915. 326 pp. Repr. 1921. *Like Falling Leaves* repr. in *Representative Continental Dramas*, ed. Montrose J. Moses (Boston, Little, Brown, 1924). *Sacred Ground* repr. in *Representative One-Act Plays by Continental Authors*, ed. Montrose J. Moses (ibid., 1922; repr. 1926).

————As the Leaves. Tr. anon. Drama, vol. 1 (1911), pp. 8–97.
Also see above, *Like Falling Leaves*.

————*Fatti Maschi, Parole Feminine*. Tr. G. Gruenbaum, versified Carol Wight. Johns Hopkins Alumni Magazine, vol. 12 (1924), pp. 101–23.

————The Rights of the Soul (*Diritti dell'anima*). Tr. E. and A. Updegraff as Sacred Ground. See above.

Tr. Isaac Goldberg. Stratford Journal, vol. 2 (1918), pp. 26–43.

Tr. Theodore Marcone, in Fifty Contemporary One-Act Plays, ed. Frank Shay and Pierre Loving. Cincinnati, Ohio, Stewart and Kidd [1920], pp. 201–12. Repr. N.Y. and London, Appleton, 1925.

————The Stronger. Tr. anon. Drama, vol. 10 (1913), pp. 32–156.

Tr. E. and A. Updegraff, see above.

————Unhappy Love (*Tristi amori*). Tr. Albert E. Trombly. Poet Lore, vol. 27 (1916), pp. 601–51. Repr. in Poet Lore Plays, Boston, Badger, 1916.

————The Wager (*Una partita a scacchi*). Tr. Barrett H. Clark. N.Y., French, 1914. 16 pp.

Giusti, Giuseppe (1809–1850). No trs.

On Giusti, see Susan Horner. *The Tuscan Poet Giuseppe Giusti and His Times* (London, Macmillan, 1864, 374 pp.), useful for selections from Giusti's correspondence.

Goldoni, Carlo (1707–1793). The Comedies. Tr. with intro. Helen Zimmern. London, Stott, and Chicago, McClurg, 1892. 287 pp.
> *The Beneficent Bear (Il barbaro benefico); The Fan; The Spendthrift Miser (L'avaro fastoso); A Curious Mishap (Un curioso accidente).*

————Four Comedies. Tr. Clifford Bax, M. Tracy, H. and E. Farjeon. London, Palmer, 1922. xiv, 320 pp.
> *Mine Hostess (La locandiera); The Impresario from Smyrna; The Good Girl (La putta onorata); The Fan.*

————Four Comedies. Tr. Frederick Davies. Penguin, 1968. 333 pp.
> *The Venetian Twins; The Artful Widow; Mirandolina (La locandiera); The Superior Residence (La casa nova).*

————Three Comedies. Tr. Charles Lloyd (with Three Tragedies by Alfieri). N.Y., National Alumni, 1907. x, 372 pp.
> *The Fan; An Odd Misunderstanding; The Beneficent Bear.*

————Three Comedies (Mine Hostess, The Boors, The Fan). Tr. Clifford Bax, I. M. Rawson, and E. and H. Farjeon. London and N.Y., Oxford Univ. Pr., 1961. xxvii, 293 pp.
> *The Boors* is a tr. of *I rusteghi.* Trs. are of unequal quality.

————The Beneficent Bear. Tr. Barrett H. Clark. N.Y., French, 1915. 51 pp.

————The Coffee-House (*La bottega del Caffè*). Tr. Henry B. Fuller. N.Y. and London, French, 1925. 94 pp.
> Fairly literal, except for condensation of longer speeches.

————The Comic Theatre. Tr. John W. Miller, intro. Donald Cheney. Lincoln, Univ. of Nebraska Pr., 1969. xxii, 94 pp.

————A Curious Mishap. Tr. and adapted Richard D. T. Hollister. Ann Arbor, Mich., Wahr, 1924. 105 pp.
> Based on the Zimmern tr., smooth and sprightly.

————The Fan. Tr. Kenneth McKenzie. New Haven, Conn., Yale Univ. Dramatic Assn., 1911. xix, 92 pp.

> Tr. Henry B. Fuller. London and N.Y., French, 1925. 123 pp.
> Reproduces the literalness of the original.

Adapted Frederick Davies. London, Heinemann Educational, 1968. xiv, 98 pp.

————The Good-Humoured Ladies. Tr. Richard Aldington, with an essay on Goldoni by Arthur Symons. London, Beaumont, 1922. 76 pp.

————The Liar. Tr. Grace Lovat Fraser. London, Selwyn and Blount, and N.Y., Knopf, 1927. 93 pp.
The tr. uses English country dialect to reproduce dialects spoken by the commedia dell'arte characters.

Tr. adapted Frederick H. Davies for a children's theatre. London, Heinemann, and N.Y., Theatre Arts, 1963. xiv, 73 pp.

————*La Locandiera* (The Mistress of the Inn). Tr. Merle Pierson. Madison, Wis., Dramatic Society, 1912. 100 pp. Repr. in Chief European Dramatists, 1916: see General Reference, Collections.
The best tr.

Tr. and adapted Lady Gregory as Mirandolina. London and N.Y., Putnam, 1924. 105 pp. Repr. in The Classic Theatre, vol. 1, 1958: see Collections.
A poor performance.

Tr. and adapted Helen Lohman. N.Y., Longmans, 1926. 100 pp.

Tr. Anthony Intreglia. Pacific, Mo., Pacific Pr., 1964. 103 pp.

————Memoirs of Goldoni Written by Himself, Forming a Complete History of His Life and Writing. Tr. John Black from the original French. London, Colburn, 1814. 2 vols. Many reprs., especially with essay by William Dean Howells, Boston, Osgood, 1877; also Boston, Houghton Mifflin [1905]; and with intro. William Drake, N.Y., Knopf, 1926.

————The Post-Inn (*L'Osteria della posta*). Tr. W. H. H. Chambers, in The Drama, vol. 5 (1903), pp. 259–83.

————The Servant of Two Masters. Tr. Edward J. Dent. Cambridge, Cambridge Univ. Pr., 1928. Repr. 1952, xvi, 86 pp.; in The Classic Theatre, vol. 1, 1958: see Collections.

Tr. adapted Frederick H. Davies for a children's theatre. London, Heinemann, 1961. xiv, 66 pp. Repr. N.Y., Theatre Arts, 1965.

————The Squabbles of Chioggia (*Le baruffe chiozzotte*). Tr. Charles W. Lemmi. The Drama (periodical), vol. 15 (1914), 346–533.
> One of the best of the Goldoni trs.

> Tr. Frederick H. Davies for a children's theatre as It Happened in Venice. London, Heinemann, 1965. xi, 87 pp.

> For the many 18th c. trs., often adaptations, of the Goldoni plays, see CBEL, vol. 2, p. 810.

On Goldoni, see H. C. Chatfield-Taylor, *Goldoni: A Biography* (London, Chatto, 1914, and N.Y., Duffield, 1913, xvii, 695 pp.), the most extensive and useful discussion. See also Joseph Spencer Kennard, *Goldoni and the Venice of His Time* (N.Y., Macmillan, 1920, xxi, 251 pp.; repr. N.Y., Benjamin Blom, 1967). For biblio. information, see Nicola Mangini, *Bibliografia goldoniana: 1908--1957* (Venezia-Roma, Istituto per la collaborazione culturale, 1961).

Gozzi, Carlo (1720–1806). The Blue Monster: A Fairy Tale in Five Acts (*Il mostro turchino*). Tr. Edward J. Dent. Cambridge, Cambridge Univ. Pr., 1951. xxii, 71 pp.

————The King Stag. See The Classic Theatre, Collections, above.

————The Love for Three Oranges. Free tr. Victor Seroff as libretto for Prokofieff's opera. N.Y., Boosey and Hawkes, [1949]. 17 pp.

————The Memoirs of Count Carlo Gozzi. Tr. John Addington Symonds. London, Nimmo, and N.Y., Scribner, 1890. 2 vols. (with some curtailing and rearrangement). Repr. as Useless Memoirs, ed., rev. and abridged by John Horne, London and N.Y., Oxford Univ. Pr., 1962. 285 pp.

————Turandot, Princess of China. Tr. Jethro Bithell from the German version of Karl Vollmoeller. London, Unwin, and N.Y., Duffield, 1913. 128 pp.
> This tr. of a tr. loses much of the spirit of the original. Other trs. of a German version by Schiller are listed in British Museum Catalogue.

> Tr. Jonathan Levy, in The Genius of the Italian Theater: see Collections, above.

Guerrazzi, Francesco Domenico (1804–1873). Beatrice Cenci, A Tale of the Sixteenth Century. Tr. Luigi Monti. N.Y., Rudd and Carleton, 1858. 2 vols. in 1. Many reprs. to N.Y., National Alumni, [1906].

> Tr. Mrs. Watts Sherman. N.Y., Mason Bros., and Philadelphia, Lippincott, as well as Boston, Crosby Nichols, 1858. 2 vols.

> Tr. C. A. Scott. London, 1858.

————Isabella Orsini, an Historical Novel of the Fifteenth Century. Tr. Luigi Monti. N.Y., Rudd and Carleton, 1859. 330 pp.

————Manfred, or The Battle of Benevento. Tr. Luigi Monti. N.Y., G. W. Carleton, 1875. x, 447 pp.

Leopardi, Giacomo (1798–1837). Essays, Dialogues, and Thoughts. Tr. Patrick Maxwell. London, Walter Scott, [1893]. xvii, 303 pp. Repr. Glasgow, 1905.
> Most extensive material in prose. New tr. would be welcome.

> Tr. James Thomson as Twelve Dialogues. London, 1893. Repr. London, Routledge, 1905. xxvi, 389 pp.

————Poems. Ed. and tr. Geoffrey L. Bickersteth in the original metres. Cambridge Univ. Pr., and N.Y., Macmillan, 1923. xii, 544 pp.
> A masterpiece of tr.: dignified, exact, musical.

> Tr. R. C. Trevelyan as Translations from Leopardi. London, Cambridge Univ. Pr. and N.Y., Macmillan, 1941. viii, 59 pp.
> Fourteen of the fifty-one poems of *Canti*, with Leopardi's "Dialogue between Tasso and his Familiar Spirit," catch the spirit of the original.

> Tr. John Heath-Stubbs. London, Lehmann, and N.Y., New Directions, 1947. 71 pp.

> Tr. verse J. H. Whitfield as *Canti*. Napoli, G. Scalabrini, 1962. 267 pp.
> A straightforward and literal tr.

> Tr. Jean Pierre Barricelli. N.Y., Las Americas Pub. Co., 1963. 159 pp., parallel texts.
> Smooth enjoyable versions.

————Poems and Prose. Trs. various, ed. Angel Flores, intro. Sergio Pacifici. Bloomington and London, Indiana Univ. Pr., 1966. 253 pp., parallel texts of the poems.

————Selected Prose and Poetry. Tr. Iris Origo and John Heath-Stubbs. London, Oxford Univ. Pr., 1966. xiii, 312 pp. Repr. N.Y., New Amer. Lib., 1967.

> Less successful are the selections of verse tr. into prose by William Fletcher Smith as *Masterpieces* (Menasha, Wis., Banta, 1939, 31 pp.) and *Lesser Masterpieces* and *To Angelo Mai* (Colorado Springs, Colo., pr. pr., 1941, 53 pp.). Other trs. of the verse should be noted: Francis Henry Cliffe, London, 1893, repr. 1903; J. M. Morrison, London, 1900; Sir Theodore Martin, London, 1904.

On Leopardi's life and character, see Iris Origo, *Leopardi: A Biography* (London and N.Y., Oxford Univ. Pr., 1935, 228 pp.), repr. rev. and enlarged as *Leopardi: A Study in Solitude* (London, H. Hamilton, 1953, xv, 305 pp.); J. H. Whitfield, *Giacomo Leopardi* (Oxford, Blackwell, 1954, 266 pp.); and Ghan Shyam Singh, *Leopardi and the Theory of Poetry* (Lexington, Univ. of Kentucky Pr., 1964, 384 pp.). For biblio., see Kenneth McKenzie and John Van Horne, "American Contributions to the Study of Leopardi," *Italica*, vol. 2 (1925), 66–68.

Liguori, Alfonso Maria de', St. (1696–1787). The Works. Tr. Rev. Robert A. Coffin. London, Burns Oates, 1854–68. 6 vols.

> Vol. 1: The Christian Virtues, 1854.
> Vol. 2: The Mysteries of the Faith: The Incarnation, 1854. Repr. retr. E. Vaughan, 1901.
> Vol. 3: The Mysteries of the Faith: The Holy Eucharist, 1855.
> Vol. 4: The Mysteries of the Faith: The Redemption, 1861. Repr. 1924.
> Vol. 5: The Eternal Truths, 1857.
> Vol. 6: The Glories of Mary, 1868.

————The Complete Works. Centenary Ed. Tr. from the Italian and ed. Rev. Eugene Grimm. N.Y., Benziger, and London, Washbourne, 22 vols., including 5 vols. of Letters. Repr. Brooklyn and St. Louis, Redemptorist Fathers, 1926–29; repr. the same, 1934.

————An Exposition and Defence of All the Points of Faith Discussed and Defined by the Sacred Council of Trent, along with a Refutation of the Errors of the Pretended Reformers and of the Objections of Paolo Sarpi. Tr. by a Catholic Clergyman. Dublin, James Duffy, 1846. 464 pp.

————The History of Heresies, and their Refutation. Tr. John T. Mullock. Dublin, James Duffy, 1847. 2 vols.

————The Hours of the Passion. Tr. Dr. Walsh, Bishop of Halifax. Baltimore, Lucas, 1859? 232 pp.

　　Tr. by a Catholic Clergyman as The Clock of the Passion. N.Y. and Montreal, Sadlier and Co., 1864. 256 pp.

————How to Converse Continually and Familiarly with God. Tr. L. X. Aubin. Boston, St. Paul Edns., 1963. 75 pp.

————Instructions and Considerations on the Religious State. Tr. J. B. Pagani. London, Richardson and Son, 1848. 180 pp.

————The Passion of Jesus Christ. Tr. anon. Baltimore, Helicon, 1965. xii, 230 pp.

————Reflections on Spiritual Subjects and on the Passion of Jesus Christ. Tr. J. M. C. London, Burns, 1849. xv, 240 pp.

　　For trs. of several shorter works, see the British Museum Catalogue, s.v. Alphonsus Maria, St., and add: *The Way of St. Alphonsus Liguori*, tr. Robert A. Coffin et al. (London, Burns Oates, 1961, xv, 367 pp.).

Loredano, Giovanni Francesco (1607–1661). Accademical Discourses upon Several Choise and Pleasant Subjects (*Bizarrerie accademiche*). Tr. John Bulteel. London, 1664.

————The Ascents of the Soul: Being Paraphrases on the Fifteen Psalms of Degrees (*I gradi dell'anima*). Tr. Hugh Hare, Baron Coleraine. London, 1681.

————Dianea (*La Dianea*). Tr. Sir Aston Cokayne. London, 1654.

————The Life of Adam (*Adamo*). Tr. J. S. London, 1659. Repr. Gainesville, Fla., Scholars' Facsimiles, 1968.

　　Tr. R. Murray as The Life of Man. London, 1779.

————The Novells (*Novelle amorose*). Tr. anon. London, 1682. 153 pp.

Manzoni, Alessandro (1785–1873).   The Betrothed (*I promessi sposi*). Tr. Charles Swan as The Betrothed Lovers. Pisa, Niccolo Capurro, 1828. 3 vols.

Tr. anon. London, Bentley, 1834. Repr. 1856.

Tr. anon. London, James Burns, 1844. 2 vols. Repr. 1876, 1889; Philadelphia, 1925.

Tr. anon. (with The Column of Infamy). London, Longmans, 1845. 3 vols.

Tr. Maurice Francis Egan. N.Y., Appleton, 1898. 582 pp.

Tr. Archibald Colquhoun. London, Dent, and N.Y., Dutton, 1951. xv, 592 pp. Repr. EL, 1956, 1961.

Tr. anon. as *I Promessi Sposi*, abridged with intro. Bergen Evans. Greenwich, Conn., Fawcett, 1962. 400 pp.

————The Column of Infamy (*La colonna infame*). Tr. anon. with The Betrothed, 1845, q.v. above.

Tr. Kenelm Foster (with Beccaria's Of Crimes and Punishments, q.v. above). N.Y., Oxford Univ. Pr., 1964, pp. 103–212.

————The Sacred Hymns and Napoleonic Ode. Tr. verse Joel Foote Bingham. London and N.Y., Oxford Univ. Pr., 1904. 230 pp.

For a biographical-critical study, see Archibald Colquhoun, *Manzoni and His Times* (London, Dent, 1954, x, 281 pp.); and for a good critical survey of Manzoni's works, see Joseph Francis De Simone, *Alessandro Manzoni: Esthetics and Literary Criticism* (N.Y., Vanni, 1946, 340 pp.). More specialized students can profit from Barbara Reynolds, *The Linguistic Writings of Alessandro Manzoni: A Textual and Chronological Reconstruction* (Cambridge, Heffer, 1950, 225 pp.).

Marana, Giovanni Paolo (1642–1693).   The Eight Volumes of Letters Writ by a Turkish Spy, Giving an Impartial Account of the Divan at Constantinople, and of the Most Remarkable Transactions of Europe from 1637 to 1682. Tr. probably W. Bradshaw. London, 1694. 8 vols. Repr. to 26th edn., 1770.
Though ostensibly written in Arabic by Muhammad the Turkish Spy and thence tr. into Italian, the work was in part written in Italian by Marana as *L'Esploratore turco e le di lui relazioni segrete alla Porta Ottomana* (Paris, 1684).

Mazzini, Giuseppe (1805–1872). The Life and Writings. Tr. unidentified. London, Smith Elder, 1864–70. 6 vols. Repr. 1890–91.

> The most extensive tr. Vols. 1, 3, 5, Autobiographical and Political Writings; vols. 2, 4, 6, Critical and Literary Writings. Recent selections have been published as *Living Thoughts of Mazzini*, ed. Ignazio Silone (N.Y., Longmans, 1939, 167 pp.); and as *Selected Writings*, ed. N. Gangulee (London, Drummond, 1945, 253 pp.).

————The Duties of Man. Tr. Mrs. E. A. Venturi. London, Chapman and Hall, 1862. xvi, 220 pp. Repr. 1875 in her Joseph Mazzini: A Memoir, and adding his Thoughts upon Democracy in Europe; repr. 1885.

*————The Duties of Man, and Other Essays. Tr. mainly Thomas Okey (reprinting his Essays, see below). EL, 1907 et seq. xxxvii, 327 pp.

> The Okey trs.: The Duties of Man. Interests and Principles. Faith and the Future. The Patriots and the Clergy. To the Italians. Thoughts on the French Revolution of 1789. Tr. Ella Noyes: To the Italian Working Class. Tr. L. Martineau: From the Council to God.

————Essays by Joseph Mazzini: Most of Them Translated for the First Time. Tr. Thomas Okey. London, Dent, and N.Y., Macmillan, 1894. xxxii, 263 pp. Repr. in the preceding item, EL, 1907 et seq.

> The best of the trs.

———— Mazzini's Letters. Tr. Alice de Rosen Jervis. London, Dent, and N.Y., Dutton, 1930. xvi, 211 pp.

————Mazzini's Letters to an English Family [the Ashursts], 1844–18[72]. Ed. E. F. Richards. London, Lane, 1920–22. 3 vols.

————Royalty and Republicanism in Italy: Or Notes and Documents Relating to the Lombard Insurrection and the Royal Way of 1848. Tr. anon. London, Charles Gilpin, 1850. xix, 237 pp.

For trs. of a number of pamphlets, see British Museum Catalogue.

For a fascinating as well as scholarly biography, see Stringfellow Barr, *Mazzini: Portrait of an Exile* (N.Y., Holt, 1935, 308 pp.). See also E. E. Y. Hales, *Mazzini and the Secret Societies: The Making of a Myth* (N.Y., P. Q. Kenedy, and London, Eyre and Spottiswoode, 1956, 226 pp.); Joseph

Rossi, *The Image of America in Mazzini's Writings* (Madison, Univ. of Wisconsin Pr., 1954, 188 pp.); Gaetano Salvemini, *Mazzini*, tr. I. M. Rawson (Stanford, Calif., Stanford Univ. Pr., 1957, 192 pp.).

Metastasio, Pietro Antonio (1698–1702).   The Works of Metastasio. Tr. verse John Hoole. London, 1767. 2 vols. Rev. enl. as Dramas and Other Poems. London, Otridge, 1800. 3 vols.

> Vol. 1: Artaxerxes. The Olympiad. Hypsipyle. Titus. Demetrius. The Dream of Scipio. Cantatas.
> Vol. 2: Achilles in Scyros. Demophoon. Adrian in Syria. Dido. Aetius. The Uninhabited Island. The Triumph of Glory.
> Vol. 3: Zenobia. Themistocles. Siroes. Regulus. Romulus and Hersilia. The Discovery of Joseph. Cantatas.
> *The Dream of Scipio* tr. repr. in *The Drama*, vol. 5, 1903: see Collections of Translations, above.

————Dido Forsaken (*Didone abandonnata*). Tr. Joseph G. Fucilla in blank verse, with rimed verse for the ariettas. Florence, Valmartina, 1952. 129 pp., parallel texts.

For the text of many adaptations of Metastasio's plays and operas for the English stage from 1731 for nearly a century, see the British Museum Catalogue. The only extensive study in English is that of Charles Burney, *Memoirs of the Life and Writings of the Abate Metastasio, in Which Are Incorporated Translations of His Principal Letters* (London, 1796, 3 vols.). For a bibliography of trs. of Metastasio's minor poems, see J. G. Fucilla, "The European and American Vogue of Metastasio's Shorter Poems," *Italica*, vol. 29 (1952), pp. 13–33.

Muratori, Ludovico Antonio (1672–1750).   A Relation of the Missions of Paraguay. Tr. anon. from the French version. London, Marmaduke, 1759. xvi, 294 pp. Repr. 1788 as The Jesuits' Travels in South America.

Nievo, Ippolito (1831–1861).   The Castle of Fratta (*Le confessioni di un ottuagenario*). Tr. Lovett F. Edwards. London, Oxford Univ. Pr., 1957, and Boston, Mass., Houghton Mifflin, 1958. 589 pp.

> The same tr. published a partial version: London, Folio Soc., 1954, 222 pp.

*Parini, Giuseppe (1729–1799).   The Day: Morning, Midday, Evening,

Night. Tr. blank verse Herbert Morris Bower. London, Routledge, 1927. 208 pp.

A remarkably good tr.

Pellico, Silvio (1789–1854). The Duties of Man. Tr. Thomas Roscoe. London, 1834. Repr. 1837.

Tr. R. A. Vain. London, 1869.

—————Esther of Engaddi: A Tragedy. Tr. anon. London, Whittaker Teacher [1836]. 84 pp.

—————Euphemia of Engaddi: A Tragedy. Tr. Mrs. E. F. Ellet. N.Y., Bancroft, 1834. 62 pp.

—————Francesca da Rimini: A Tragedy. Tr. J. G. V. P. London, 1851.

Tr. Joel Foote Bingham. Cambridge, Mass., Seaver, 1897. lvii, 89 pp. Reprs., especially 5th ed., London and N.Y., Oxford Univ. Pr., 1905.

Tr. Florence Kendrick Cooper, with My Prisons (see below).

Tr. A. O'D. Bartoleyne. London, Allen and Unwin, 1915. 83 pp.

—————The Life of the Marchesa Giulia Falletti di Barolo. Tr. Lady G. Fullerton. London, 1866.

—————My Prisons. Tr. Thomas Roscoe as My Imprisonments: Memoirs of Silvio Pellico. London, 1833, and N.Y., Harper, 1833. 214 pp. Repr. Boston, 1868; N.Y., 1886.

Tr. Florence Kendrick Cooper (with Francesca da Rimini). N.Y., National Alumni [1906]. 317 pp.

Tr. I. G. Capaldi, S.J. London and N.Y., Oxford Univ. Pr., 1963. xxiv, 199 pp.
Certainly the best of the trs. For several other 19th c. trs., see the British Museum Catalogue.

Tassoni, Alessandro (1565–1635). *La Secchia Rapita*: The Trophy Bucket. Tr. John Ozell. London, Sanger, 1710. 2 vols.

Tr. James Atkinson as La Secchia Rapita: Or the Rape of the Bucket. London, J. M. Richardson, 1825. 2 vols. in 1.
Deserves a new tr.

Verdi, Giuseppe (1813–1901).   Librettos. Tr. William Weaver. Garden City, N.Y., Doubleday, 1963. 417 pp.

Verga, Giovanni (1840–1922).   *Cavalleria Rusticana* and Other Tales of Sicilian Peasant Life. Tr. A. Strettell. London, Unwin, 1893. 189 pp.

Tr. D. H. Lawrence as *Cavalleria Rusticana* and Other Stories. London, Cape, 1928. 224 pp. Repr. N.Y., Longmans, 1928; London, 1932.

Ed. J. I. Rodale as *Cavalleria Rusticana* and Other Narratives. Emmaus, Pa., Story Classics, 1950. 173 pp.

Dramatized Eric Bentley, in The Modern Theatre, 1955, vol. 1: see Collections of Trs. Tr. Archibald Colquhoun, in Italian Regional Tales of the Nineteenth Century, 1961: see Collections.

————The House by the Medlar Tree (*I malavoglia*). Tr. M. A. Craig, with intro. William Dean Howells. N.Y., Harper, 1890. vii, 300 pp. Repr. 1891.

Tr. Eric Mosbacher. London, Weidenfeld, 1950. 247 pp.

Tr. Raymond Rosenthal. N.Y., New Amer. Lib., 1964. 272 pp.

————Little Novels of Sicily (*Novelle rusticane*). Tr. D. H. Lawrence. N.Y., Seltzer, 1925. 226 pp. Repr. Oxford, Blackwell, 1925, 191 pp.; N.Y., Grove Pr., 1953, 226 pp.

————Mastro-Don Gesualdo. Tr. M. A. Craig. London, Osgood, 1893. 2 vols.

Tr. D. H. Lawrence. N.Y., Seltzer, 1923, and London, Cape, 1925. 454 pp. Repr. London, Calder, N.Y., Grove Pr., 1955, ix, 454 pp.
The Lawrence trs. are good reading, but not always accurate.

————The She-Wolf and Other Stories. Tr. Giovanni Cecchetti. Berkeley, Univ. of California Pr., and London, Cambridge Univ. Pr., 1958. xxiv, 197 pp.

A more accurate translator than Lawrence, but does not necessarily displace him.

————Under the Shadow of Etna: Sicilian Stories. Tr. Nathan Haskell Dole. Boston, Knight, 1896. x, 178 pp.

————The Wolf-Hunt. Tr. Isaac Goldberg, in Plays of the Italian Theatre: see Collections, below. On Verga, see Thomas Goddard Bergin, *Giovanni Verga* (New Haven, Conn., Yale Univ. Pr., 1931, 135 pp.); and Olga Ragusa, *Verga's Milanese Tales* (N.Y., Vanni, 1964, 126 pp.).

Verri, Alessandro (1741–1816).   The Roman Nights (*Le notti romane al sepolcro de' Scipioni*). Tr. anon. London, Molini, 1798. 334 pp. Repr. Edinburgh, 1825.

Tr. Henry W. Hilliard as Roman Nights at the Tombs of the Scipios. Philadelphia, Pa., Ball, 1850. 208 pp.

*Vico, Giambattista (1668–1774).   The Autobiography. Tr. Max Harold Fisch and Thomas Goddard Bergin. Ithaca, N.Y., Cornell Univ. Pr., 1944. 240 pp. Repr. Ithaca, 1948; London, Oxford Univ. Pr., 1949; Ithaca, 1963. Extremely well done.

*————The New Science (*Principi di una scienza nuova*). Tr. Thomas G. Bergin and Max H. Fisch. Ithaca, N.Y., Cornell Univ. Pr., 1948. 413 pp. Repr. N.Y., Doubleday (Anchor), 1961, liii, 384 pp.; rev. Cornell Univ. Pr., 1968.
A welcome version of a most important book.

————On the Study Methods of Our Time (*De nostri temporis studiorum ratione*). Tr. Elio Gianturco. N.Y., Bobbs-Merrill, 1965. 98 pp.

On Vico, see Benedetto Croce, *The Philosophy of Vico*, tr. R. G. Collingwood (London, Latimer, and N.Y., Macmillan, 1913, xii, 317 pp., repr. N.Y., Russell, 1964); Henry P. Adams, *The Life and Writings of Vico* (London, Allen and Unwin, 1935, 236 pp.); A. Robert Caponigri, *Time and Idea: The Theory of History in Giambattista Vico* (Chicago, Regnery, and London, Routledge, 1953, 225 pp.); Alfonsina Albini Grimaldi, *The Universal Humanity of Giambattista Vico* (N.Y., Vanni, 1958, xiv, 271 pp.). For the tercentenary of Vico's birth, note *Giambattista Vico: An International Symposium*, ed. Giorgio Tagliacozzo (Baltimore, Johns Hopkins Pr., 1968, 608 pp.).

Contemporary Period

Bibliography

Luciani, Vincent. "Modern Italian Fiction in America, 1929–1954: An Annotated Bibliography of Translations." Bulletin New York Public Library, vol. 60 (1956), pp. 12–34.
A virtually exhaustive list.

Molinaro, Julius A. "American Studies and Translations of Contemporary Italian Poetry, 1945–1965: An Historical Survey and a Bibliography." Bulletin New York Public Library, vol. 72 (1968), pp. 522-58.
Full listing of poetic trs. in books and periodicals, as well as a complete bibliography of criticism of Italian poetry pub. in America.

For current bibliography, the quarterly "Bibliography of Italian Studies in America" in the periodical *Italica* (vol. 1—, 1924—) lists most current trs. from Italian which are printed in America.

Literary Studies

Bentley, Eric. In Search of Theater. N.Y., Knopf, and London, Dobson Books, 1953. 411 pp.
Contains interesting chs. on De Filippo, pp. 281–95, and Pirandello, pp. 296–314.

Collins, Joseph. Idling in Italy: Studies of Literature and Life. N.Y., Scribner, 1920. x, 316 pp.
Mainly on D'Annunzio, Papini, and the Futurists.

Columbia Dictionary of Modern European Literature [since 1870]. Ed. Horatio Smith. N.Y., Columbia Univ. Pr., 1947. xiv, 899 pp.

    Contains articles on "Italian Criticism" and "Italian Literature" by Giuseppe Prezzolini, and on 99 recent Italian authors by various scholars.

Drake, William A. Contemporary European Writers. N.Y., Day, 1928. x, 408 pp.

    Discusses Sibilla Aleramo and Pirandello.

Heiney, Donald. Three Italian Novelists: Moravia, Pavese, Vittorini. Ann Arbor, Univ. of Michigan Pr., 1968. 232 pp.

Livingston, Arthur. Essays on Modern Italian Literature. N.Y., Vanni, 1950. 197 pp.

    Essays on Papini, Pirandello, Croce, and on various general topics.

McClintock, Lander. The Age of Pirandello. Bloomington, Indiana Univ. Pr., 1951. 341 pp. Repr. N.Y., Kraus, 1968.

    The development of the Italian theatre from 1915 to 1940. Lively informal discussion.

——————The Contemporary Drama of Italy. Boston, Little, Brown, 1920. 321 pp.

    Good background material from Giacosa to Futurist writers.

Mazza, Maria Serafina, S. C. Not for Art's Sake: The Story of *Il Frontispizio*. N.Y., King's Crown Pr., 1948. 219 pp.

    History of an important periodical, its collaborators, and its policy, with full discussions of Bargellini, Giuliotti, Papini.

McLeod, Addison. Plays and Players of Modern Italy. London, Smith Elder, and Chicago, Sergel, 1912. 355 pp.

    Informative.

Pacifici, Sergio. A Guide to Contemporary Italian Literature: From Futurism to Neorealism. Preface by Thomas G. Bergin. N.Y. and Cleveland, Ohio, World Pub. Co., 1962. 352 pp.

    Most complete and satisfactory presentation to date.

——————The Modern Italian Novel from Manzoni to Svevo. Carbondale, Southern Illinois Univ. Pr., 1967. 224 pp.

Phelps, Ruth Shepard. Italian Silhouettes. N.Y., Knopf, 1924. 227 pp. Repr. Freeport, N.Y., Books for Libraries, 1969.

> Keen insights on Carducci, Pascoli, Vivanti, Gozzano, Papini, Ada Negri, Pirandello, Fucini, Guglielminetti, Di Giacomo, Panzini, Sibilla Aleramo, and Serra.

Collections

An Anthology of Italian Writers. Ed. Marguerite Caetani, selected from the review Botteghe Oscure. N.Y., New Directions, 1950, and London, Lehmann, 1951. 477 pp.

> Fourteen contributors of fiction and verse in tr., notably Bassani, Landolfi, Guglielmo Petroni, Pratolini, and Soldati.

Arrowsmith, William, ed. and tr. Six Modern Italian Novellas. N.Y., Pocket Books, 1964. xiv, 398 pp.

> Stories by Calvino, Cassola, Rea, Tobino, Tozzi, Vittorini.

Bergin, Thomas Goddard, tr. Italian Sampler: An Anthology of Italian Verse. Montreal, Mario Casalini, 1964. xvii, 227 pp.

> Verse trs. of poems by twenty-six contemporaries, notably Dell'Arco, Palazzeschi, Saba, Ungaretti, and Villaroel.

Bradshaw, Vittoria, tr. "An Anthology of Italian Post-War Poets," in Italian Quarterly, vol. 7 (fall 1964), pp. 10–64.

Contemporary Italian Poetry: An Anthology. Trs. various, ed. Carlo L. Golino. Berkeley, Univ. of California Pr., and London, Cambridge Univ. Pr., 1962. xxvi, 223 pp., parallel texts.

> Twenty-five poets from the *crepuscolari* to representatives of most recent tendencies, two fifths of them writers of the hermetic school. Satisfactory trs., can be used in classes.

Corman, Cid, ed. and tr. "Post-War Italian Poetry," in Origin, no. 9, ser. 2 (April 1963), pp. 11–62.

> Poets represented are Erba, Fabiani, Gramigna, Guidacci, Montale, Pasolini, Risi, Sala Tadini, and Volponi.

Fulton, Robert, tr. An Italian Quartet: Versions after Saba, Ungaretti, Montale, and Quasimodo. London, Allen Ross, 1966. 112 pp.

Goldberg, Isaac, tr.   Plays of the Italian Theatre: Verga, Morselli, Lopez, and Pirandello. Boston, Luce, 1921. 202 pp.
> The Wolf-hunt; Water upon Fire, and Gastone the Animal Trainer; The Sparrow; Sicilian Limes.

Guenther, Charles, tr.   Modern Italian Poets. San Francisco, Calif., Inferno Pr., 1939. 39 pp.

Italian Stories of Today.   Ed. John Lehmann, various trs. London, Faber, 1959. 256 pp.
> Stories repr., with one exception, from several British magazines, written by leading Italian authors: Arbasino, Bassani, Brancati, Calvino, Landolfi, Marotta, Moravia, Palazzeschi, Silone, Soldati, and Tobino.

Masterpieces of the Modern Italian Theatre.   Ed. R. W. Corrigan, various trs. N.Y., Collier Books, 1967. 351 pp.
> Pirandello, Six Characters, and Pleasure of Honesty; Betti, Crime on Goat Island; Eduardo De Filippo, Filumena Marturano; Fratti, The Academy, and The Return.

Miller, Peter, tr.   "Italian Poetry of the Novecento," in Folio, vol. 23 (summer 1958), pp. 11–34.

Modern European Poetry.   Tr. Willis Barnstone, et al. N.Y., Bantam, 1966. xxiii, 605 pp.
> The Italian section, pp. 269–370, ed. and tr. Sonia Raiziss and Alfredo de Palchi. Includes poems of Campana, Cardarelli, Cetaffi, Erba, Luzi, Montale, Orelli, Pasolino, Pavese, Piccolo, Quasimodo, Saba, Scotellero, Sereni, Sinisgalli, Turoldo, and Ungaretti.

Modern Italian Short Stories.   Ed. Marc Slonim. N.Y., Simon and Schuster, 1954. 429 pp.
> Thirty-four stories from Verga to the present time.

The Poem Itself: 45 Modern Poets in a New Perspective.   Ed. Stanley Burnshaw. N.Y., Holt, 1960. Italian section, pp. 270–327.
> Includes trs. from Campana, Gozzano, Montale, Quasimodo, Saba, and Ungaretti.

The Promised Land, and Other Poems: An Anthology of Four Con-

temporary Italian Poets.   Selected with intro. Sergio Pacifici. N.Y., Vanni, 1957. 156 pp.
> Montale, Quasimodo, Saba, and Ungaretti.

Rietty, Robert, tr.   Limes from Sicily, and Other Plays. Leeds, E. J. Arnold, 1967. 110 pp.
> The Pirandello play, with two others: Carlo Fruttero and Franco Lucentini, *The Memory Machine*; and Dario Niccodemi, *The Poet*.

Singh, Ghan, tr.   Contemporary Italian Verse. London, London Magazine Edns, 1968. 215 pp., paper, parallel texts.

Stories of Modern Italy from Verga, Svevo, and Pirandello to the Present.   Ed. with intro. Ben Johnson, various trs. ML, 1960. xx, 513 pp.
> Stories of twenty-two writers.

Strachan, Walter John, ed. and tr.   Modern Italian Stories. London, Eyre, and N.Y., Philosophical Lib., 1956. 304 pp.
> Includes thirty-two contemporary authors.

Trevelyan, Raleigh, ed. and tr.   Italian Short Stories/*Racconti Italiani*. Penguin, 1965. 195 pp., parallel texts.
> Works by Calvino, Cassola, Gadda, Ginzburg, Moravia, Pavese, Pratolini, and Soldati.

————Italian Writing Today. Penguin, 1967. 285 pp., parallel texts.
> Selections from thirty-four authors: novelists, critics, poets.

> For issues of periodicals devoted to modern Italian literature in tr., see *Briarcliff Quarterly*, vol. 3, no. 12 (January, 1947); *Italian Literary Digest*, vol. 1, no. 1 (April, 1947); *Mandrake* (Italian Arts Number: Poetry, Prose, Criticism), vol. 2, no. 7 (1950–51); *Perspective*, vol. 3, no. 3 (1950); *Wake*, vol. 12 (1953).

INDIVIDUAL AUTHORS

Aleramo, Sibilla (pseud. of Rina Faccio, 1879—).   A Woman at Bay (*Una donna*). Tr. Maria H. Lansdale. N.Y. and London, Putnam, 1908. 392 pp.

Alvaro, Corrado (1889–1956). The Long Night of Medea. Tr. E. Fisher Friedman, in Plays for a New Theater: Playbook 2. N.Y., New Directions, 1966. 282 pp.

————Revolt in Aspromonte (*Gente in Aspromonte*). Tr. Frances Frenaye. N.Y., New Directions, 1962. 120 pp.

Antonioni, Michelangelo (1912—). Screen Plays. Tr. Roger J. Moore. N.Y., Orion Pr., 1963. 361 pp.

Arpino, Giovanni (1927—). A Crime of Honor (*Un delitto d'onore*). Tr. Raymond Rosenthal. London, Weidenfeld, and N.Y., Braziller, 1963. 250 pp. Repr. London, Pan Books, 1965.

————The Novice (*La suora giovane*). Tr. Peter Green. London, Hodder and Stoughton, and N.Y., Braziller, 1962. 219 pp. Repr. London, Pan Books, 1964, 125 pp.

Bacchelli, Riccardo (1891—). The Devil at the Long Bridge (*Il Diavolo di Pontelungo*). Tr. Orlo Williams. London and N.Y., Longmans, 1929. xvi, 346 pp.

————The Fire of Milan (*L'incendio di Milano*). Tr. Kathleen Nott. London, Secker and Warburg, 1958. 302 pp.

————Love Town (*Città degli amanti*). Tr. Orlo Williams. London, Duckworth, 1930. 296 pp.

————The Mill on the Po (*Il mulino sul Po*). Tr. Frances Frenaye. N.Y., Pantheon, 1950. 590 pp. Repr. London, Hutchinson, 1952, 391 pp.

————Nothing New Under the Sun (*Mondo vecchio sempre nuovo*). Tr. Stuart Hood. London, Hutchinson, and N.Y., Pantheon, 1953. 518 pp.

————Son of Stalin. Tr. Kathleen Nott. London, Secker, 1956. 256 pp. Repr. as Seed of Steel, N.Y., Walker, 1963, 256 pp.

Bartolini, Luigi (1892—). Bicycle Thieves. Tr. C. J. Richards. N.Y., Macmillan, 1950. 149 pp. Repr. London, H. Hamilton, 1964.

Bassani, Giorgio (1916—). The Garden of the Finzi-Continis. Tr. Isabel Quigly. London, Faber, and N.Y., Atheneum, 1965. 294 pp.

—————The Gold-rimmed Spectacles (*Gli occhiali d'oro*). Tr. Isabel Quigly. N.Y., Atheneum, 1960. 143 pp.

—————A Prospect of Ferrara (*Cinque storie ferraresi*). Tr. Isabel Quigly. London, Faber, 1962. 220 pp.

Benelli, Sem (1875–1949). The Jester's Supper (*La cena delle beffe*). Tr. K. H. B. de Jaffa. N.Y., Ricordi, [1924–25], 67 pp.
    Libretto, with parallel texts, for an opera, with music by Umberto Giordano.

    Tr. and adapted Edward Sheldon as The Jest. N.Y., French, 1949. 100 pp. The version used by the Barrymores in their production of 1919.

—————The Love of the Three Kings. Tr. Howard Mumford Jones. Univ. of California Chronicle, Jan. 1923, pp. 383–411. Repr. in Chief Contemporary Dramatists, Third Series: see General Reference, Collections, above.

Berto, Giuseppe (1914—). Antonio in Love (*La Cosa buffa*). Tr. William Weaver. N.Y., Knopf, 1968, and London, Hodder, 1969. 303 pp.

—————The Brigand. Tr. Angus Davidson. London, Secker, and Norfolk, Conn., New Directions, 1951. 224 pp.

—————Incubus (*Male oscuro*). Tr. William Weaver. N.Y., Knopf, and London, Hodder, 1966. 389 pp.

—————The Sky Is Red. Tr. Angus Davidson. London, Secker, and N.Y., New Directions, 1948. 379 pp. Repr. N.Y., New Amer. Lib., 1952, 318 pp.

—————The Works of God and Other Stories. Tr. Angus Davidson. London, Secker, 1949, and Norfolk, Conn., New Directions, 1950. 242 pp.

Bertolini, Elio (1922—). *La Signora* (*La bellezza d'Ippolita*). Tr. Glauco Cambon. N.Y., Lion Books, 1957. 126 pp.

Betocchi, Carlo (1899—).   Poems. Tr. I. L. Solomon. N.Y., Clark and Way, 1964. 116 pp., parallel texts. Repr. N.Y., October House, 1968. 168 pp.

Betti, Ugo (1892–1953).   Three Plays: The Inquiry (*Inquisizione*), tr. David Gullette and Gino Rizzo; Goat Island (*Delitti all'isola delle capre*), tr. Gino Rizzo and David Gullette; The Gambler, tr. Barbara Kennedy. N.Y., Hill and Wang, 1966. xviii, 202 pp., paper.

————Three Plays: The Queen and the Rebels; The Burnt Flower-bed; Summertime (*Il paese delle vacanze*). Tr. Henry Reed. London, Gollancz, 1956, and N.Y., Grove Pr., 1958. 283 pp. The three plays repr. separately, London, French, 1957. The first play repr. in Three European Plays, Penguin, 1958; in The Makers of the Modern Theater, ed. Barry Ulanov, 1961; in The Modern Theatre, ed. R. W. Corrigan, 1964.

————Three Plays on Justice: Landslide (*Frana allo scalo nord*); Struggle till Dawn; The Fugitive (*La fuggitiva*). Tr. G. H. McWilliam. San Francisco, Calif., Chandler, 1964. 183 pp.

————Corruption in the Palace of Justice. Tr. Henry Reed, in The New Theatre of Europe, ed. R. W. Corrigan, vol. 1, 1962.

————Crime on Goat Island. Tr. Henry Reed. London, French, 1960. 59 pp. Repr. San Francisco, Calif., Chandler, 1961; in Masterpieces of the Modern Italian Theatre, 1967, see Collections, above.

Tr. Gino Rizzo and David Gullette, in Three Plays, above.

Bettiza, Enzo.   The Inspector. Tr. Frances Frenaye. N.Y., Stuart, 1967. 164 pp.

Bianciardi, Luciano (1922—).   It's a Hard Life (*La vita agra*). Tr. Eric Mosbacher. London, Hodder, and N.Y., Viking, 1965. 192 pp.

Bona, Gian Piero (1926—).   The Naked Soldier. Tr. Lyon Benzimira. London, Blond, 1963. 181 pp.

Bono, Elena (1921—).   The Widow of Pilata (*Morte d'Adamo*). Tr. Isabel Quigly. London, Hutchinson, 1958. 252 pp.

Borgese, Giuseppe Antonio (1882–1952). Rubè. Tr. Isaac Goldberg. N.Y., Harcourt, and London, Lane, 1923. 324 pp.
The best Italian novel written between the wars.

Borsi, Giosuè-Francesco (1888–1915). A Soldier's Confidences with God (*Colloqui*). Tr. Rev. Pasquale Maltese. N.Y., Kenedy, 1918. xxii, 362 pp.

Bracco, Roberto (1862–1943). The Hidden Spring (*La piccola fonte*). Tr. Dirce St. Cyr. Palermo, R. Bracco, 1906. 41, 34, 26, 18 leaves. Repr. in Poet Lore, vol. 18 (1907), pp. 143–86.

————Phantasms: A Drama in Four Acts (*I Fantasmi*). Tr. Dirce St. Cyr in Poet Lore, vol. 19 (1908), pp. 241–93. Repr. in Modern Continental Plays, ed. S. M. Tucker, 1929: see General Reference, Collections, above.

————A Snowy Night (*La notte di neve*). Tr. Arthur Livingston in Twenty-five Short Plays, International, ed. Frank Shay. N.Y., Appleton, 1925, pp. 249–64.
These and six other plays by Bracco are listed as performed in New York or London between 1907 and 1922 (*Cumulated Dramatic Index 1907–1949*, s.v.).

Brancati, Vitaliano (1907–1954). Antonio the Great Lover (*Il bell' Antonio*). Tr. Vladimir Kean. London, Dobson, and N.Y., Roy, 1952. 280 pp. Repr. London, Panther Books, 1959.

Buzzati, Dino (1906—). Catastrophe: The Strange Stories of Dino Buzzati. Tr. Judith Landry and Cynthia Jolly. London, Calder, 1966. 139 pp.

————Larger Than Life (*Il grande ritratto*). Tr. Henry Reed. London, Secker, 1962. 154 pp. Repr. N.Y., Walker, 1967.

————A Love Affair (*Un amore*). Tr. Joseph Green. N.Y., Farrar Straus, 1964, and London, Deutsch, 1965. 299 pp. Repr. N.Y., Dell, 1965.

————The Tartar Steppe (*Il deserto dei Tartari*). London, Secker, and N.Y., Farrar Straus, 1952. 214 pp. Repr. N.Y., 1965, paper.

Cacciatore, Vera (1911—).   The Swing and Two Stories. Tr. W. J. Strachan. London, Eyre, 1959; and Philadelphia, Lippincott (as The Swing; Three Novellas), 1961. 189 pp.
  The Swing; *The Bridge*; *Demetrio*.

Calvino, Italo (1923—).   Adam, One Afternoon, and Other Stories (from *Ultimo viene il corso*). Tr. Archibald Colquhoun and Peggy Wright. London, Collins, 1957. 190 pp.

————Baron in the Trees (*Il barone rampante*). Tr. Archibald Colquhoun. London, Collins, 1959. 255 pp., and N.Y., Random House, 1959, 217 pp.

————Cosmicomics. Tr. William Weaver. N.Y., Harcourt, 1968. 153 pp. Twelve short stories.

————Ed., Italian Fables. Tr. Louis Brigante. N.Y., Orion Pr., 1959. xi, 242 pp.

————The Nonexistent Knight and the Cloven Viscount (*Il visconte dimezzato*). Tr. Archibald Colquhoun. London, Collins, 1962. 191 pp., and N.Y., Random House, 1962, 246 pp.

————The Path to the Nest of Spiders. Tr. Archibald Colquhoun. London, Collins, 1956. 192 pp. Repr. Boston, Beacon Pr., 1957, 145 pp.

On Calvino, see J. R. Woodhouse, *Italo Calvino: A Reappraisal, and an Appreciation of the Trilogy* (Hull, Univ. of Hull, 1968, 96 pp.).

Campana, Dino (1885–1932).   Orphic Songs. Ed. and tr. I. L. Salomon. N.Y., October House, 1968. 167 pp., parallel texts.

Cannavale, Renato (1910—).   Bitter Destiny (*Ponti che crollano*). Tr. Marianne Ceconi. N.Y., Wyn, 1953. 247 pp.

Cassieri, Giuseppe (1926—).   The Bald Man (*La cocuzza*). Tr. Raymond Rosenthal. London, Secker, 1963. 243 pp.

Cassola, Carlo (1907—).   An Arid Heart. Tr. William Weaver. N.Y., Pantheon, 1964. 219 pp.

————Bebo's Girl. Tr. Marguerite Waldman. London, Collins, and N.Y., Pantheon, 1962. 249 pp.

————Fausto and Anna. Tr. Isabel Quigly. London, Collins, and N.Y., Pantheon, 1960. 318 pp.

Cecchierini, Silvano. The Transfer (*La traduzione*). Tr. Isabel Quigly. London, Harvill Pr., 1966. 159 pp., and N.Y., Braziller, 1967, 239 pp.

Chiarelli, Luigi (1884—). The Mask and the Face: A Satire. Adapted C. B. Fernald. London and N.Y., French, 1927. 78 pp. (privately printed, not for sale). Repr. N.Y., French, 1929.

Tr. Noel de Vic Beamish, in International Modern Plays. EL, 1950.

An adaptation by W. S. Maugham was produced in New York in 1933.

Cibotto, Gian Antonio (1925—). Scano Boa. Tr. Jane Grigson. London, Hodder, 1963. 127 pp.

Coccioli, Carlo (1920—). Daughter of the Town. Tr. Mary McLean. London, Heinemann, 1957. 210 pp.

————The Eye and the Heart. Tr. Bernard Frechtman from the French original. London, Heinemann, 1960. 406 pp.

————Heaven and Earth. Tr. Frances Frenaye. N.Y., Prentice-Hall, 1952. 318 pp. Repr. London, Heinemann, 1953, ix, 276 pp.

————The Little Valley of God. Tr. Campbell Nairne. London, Heinemann, 1956. vi, 232 pp., and N.Y., Simon and Schuster, 1957, 244 pp.

————Manuel the Mexican. Tr. Hans Koningsberger from the French. N.Y., Simon and Schuster, 1958. 370 pp.

————The White Stone, A Novel. Tr. Elisabeth Sutherland and Vera Bleuer from the French original. N.Y., Simon and Schuster, 1960. 271 pp.

Colizzi, Giuseppe (1925—). The Night Has Another Voice. Tr. Lyon Benzimra. London, Abelard-Schuman, 1962, and N.Y., the same, 1963. 207 pp.

Croce, Benedetto (1866–1952). "Aesthetics." Tr. R. G. Collingwood. Encyclopaedia Britannica, 14th ed., 1928. Vol. 1, pp. 263–72.

————Aesthetic as Science of Expression and General Linguistic. Tr. Douglas Ainslie. London, Macmillan, 1909. xxxi, 403 pp. Repr. 1922, with complete tr. of historical portion.
  Vol. 1 of *Filosofia dello spirito.*

————Ariosto, Shakespeare, and Corneille. Tr. Douglas Ainslie. N.Y., Holt, 1920. 422 pp., and London, Allen and Unwin, 1921, viii, 440 pp. Repr. N.Y., Russell, 1966.

————An Autobiography (*Contributo alla critica di me stesso*). Tr. R. G. Collingwood. Oxford, Clarendon Pr., 1927. 116 pp.

————The Conduct of Life (*Frammenti di etica*). Tr. Arthur Livingston. N.Y., Harcourt, 1924, and London, Harrap, 1925. xiv, 326 pp.

————Croce, the King, and the Allies: Extract from the Diary of Benedetto Croce, July, 1943—June, 1944. Tr. Sylvia Sprigge. London, Allen and Unwin, 1950. 158 pp.

————Essays on Marx and Russia. Selected and tr. Angelo A. De Gennaro. N.Y., Ungar, 1966. xvi, 129 pp.

————The Essence of Aesthetic. Tr. Douglas Ainslie. London, Heinemann, 1921. vii, 104 pp.
  First pub. as "The Breviary of Aesthetic," in *Book of the Opening of Rice Institute* (Houston, Texas, 1912, vol. 2, pp. 430–517); repr. in *Rice Institute Pamphlet*, 1915 (vol. 2, pp. 223–310); repr. ibid., (II, iv, 1961, pp. 1–88).

  Tr. Patrick Romanell as Guide to Aesthetics. Indianapolis, Ind., Bobbs-Merrill, 1965. xxxii, 88 pp.

————European Literature in the Nineteenth Century. Tr. Douglas Ainslie. London, Chapman and Hall, 1924. ix, 373 pp.

————Germany and Europe: A Spiritual Dissension. Tr. Vincent Sheean. N.Y., Random House, 1944. 83 pp.

—————Goethe. Tr. Emily Anderson, with intro. Douglas Ainslie. London, Methuen, and N.Y., Knopf, 1923. xxi, 208 pp.

—————Historical Materialism and Economics of Karl Marx. Tr. C. M. Meredith. London, Latimer, and N.Y., Macmillan, 1914. xxiii, 188 pp. Repr. N.Y., Russell, and London, Cass, 1966.
    Vol. 4 of the *Saggi filosofici*.

—————History as the Story of Liberty (*La storia come pensiero e come azione*). Tr. Sylvia Sprigge. London, Allen and Unwin, and N.Y., Norton [1941]. 314 pp. Repr. N.Y., Meridian Books, 1955, 333 pp.

—————History: Its Theory and Practice. See The Theory of History, below.

—————History of Europe in the Nineteenth Century. Tr. Henry Furst. N.Y., Harcourt [1933], and London, Allen and Unwin, 1934. 375 pp. Repr. Cambridge, Mass., Harvard Univ. Pr., 1963.
    Tr. from the 3d Italian ed. (1932).

—————A History of Italy, 1871–1915. Tr. Cecilia M. Ady. Oxford, Clarendon Pr., 1929. 333 pp. Repr. N.Y., Russell, 1963.

—————Logic as the Science of the True Concept. Tr. Douglas Ainslie. London, Macmillan, 1917. xxxiii, 606 pp.
    Vol. 2 of the *Filosofia dello spirito*.

—————My Philosophy and Other Essays on the Moral and Political Problems of Our Time. Selected by R. Libansky, tr. E. F. Carritt. London, Allen and Unwin, and N.Y., Macmillan, 1950. 240 pp.

—————The Philosophy of Giambattista Vico. See s.v. Vico, above.

—————Philosophy of the Practical, Economic and Ethic. Tr. Douglas Ainslie. London, Macmillan, 1913. ix, 591 pp. Repr. N.Y., Biblo and Tannen, 1966.
    Vol. 3 of the *Filosofia dello spirito*.

—————Philosophy, Poetry, History: An Anthology of Essays. Tr. Cecil Sprigge. London and N.Y., Oxford Univ. Pr., 1966. xxi, 1133 pp.

—————The Poetry of Dante. See s.v. Dante, above.

————Politics and Morals. Tr. Salvatore J. Castiglione. N.Y., Philosophical Lib., 1945, 204 pp., and London, Allen and Unwin, 1946, 138 pp.
   Essays collected from earlier separate publications.

————The Task of Logic. Tr. from the German in W. Windelband and Arnold Ruge, Encyclopaedia of the Philosophical Sciences, vol. 1, Logic. London, Macmillan, 1913.

————The Theory and History of Historiography. Tr. Douglas Ainslie. London, Harrap, and N.Y., Harcourt, 1921. 317 pp. Repr. N.Y., Russell, 1960.
   The title of the American eds. is *History: Its Theory and Practice*. The work is vol. 4 of the *Filosofia dello spirito*.

————What Is Living and What Is Dead of the Philosophy of Hegel. Tr. Douglas Ainslie. London, Macmillan, 1915. xviii, 217 pp.
   Tr. from 3d ed. (1912).

On Croce, see Merle E. Brown, *Neo-Idealistic Aesthetics: Croce-Gentile-Collingwood* (Detroit, Mich., Wayne State Univ. Pr., 1966, 260 pp.); A. Robert Caponigri, *History and Liberty: The Historical Writings of Benedetto Croce* (Chicago, Regnery, 1955, xi, 284 pp.); Herbert Wildon Carr, *The Philosophy of Benedetto Croce: The Problem of Art and History* (London, Macmillan, 1917, 213 pp.); Angelo A. De Gennaro, *The Philosophy of Benedetto Croce: An Introduction* (N.Y., Philosophical Lib., 1961, v, 103 pp.); Gian G. N. Orsini, *Benedetto Croce: Philosopher of Art and Literary Critic* (Carbondale, Southern Illinois Univ. Pr., 1961, x, 379 pp.), the most penetrating of the books on Croce; Calvin G. Seerveld, *Benedetto Croce's Earlier Aesthetic Theories and Literary Criticism: A Critical Philosophical Look at the Development during His Rationalistic Years* (Kampen, Holland, J. H. Kok, 1958).

D'Alessandro, Pia.   Bull's Eye (*Tiro a bersaglia*). Tr. J. R. Chanter. London, H. Hamilton, 1962. 128 pp.

D'Annunzio, Gabriele (1863–1938).   The Child of Pleasure (*Piacere*). Tr. Georgina Harding. London, Heinemann, and N.Y., George Richmond, 1898. xii, 311 pp.
   Seems to follow the French version by G. Hérelle.

*————The Daughter of Jorio: A Pastoral Tragedy. Tr. Charlotte Porter,

Pietro Isola, and Alice Henry, in Poet Lore, vol. 18 (1907), pp. 1–142. Repr. Boston, Little Brown, 1907, 208 pp.
　　Fairly literal, yet pleasing, verse tr.

*————The Dead City. Tr. Arthur Symons. London, Heinemann, 1900. 182 pp.
　　Literal; preserves well the spirit of the original.

　　Tr. Gaetano Mantellini. Chicago, Laird and Lee, 1902. 282 pp. Repr. in Eleanora Duse Series of Plays, N.Y., and London, Brentano, 1924, iv, 88 pp.

————The Dream of an Autumn Sunset. Tr. Anna Colby [Knowlton] Schenck, in Poet Lore, vol. 15 (1904), pp. 6–29. Repr. Boston, Badger, 1903; 1911.

————The Dream of a Spring Morning. Tr. the same, in Poet Lore, vol. 14 (1902), pp. 6–35. Repr. Boston, Badger, 1911.

————Episcopo and Company (*Giovanni Episcopo*). Tr. Myrta Leonora Jones. Chicago, Ill., Stone, 1896. xiii, 112 pp.

————The Flame of Life (*Fuoco*). Tr. Kassandra Vivaria. London, Heinemann, and Boston, Page, 1900. 403 pp. Repr. ML, 1932, 403 pp.

*————*Francesca da Rimini*. Tr. Arthur Symons. London, Heinemann, and N.Y., Stokes, 1902. xiv, 223 pp. Repr. in Modern Continental Plays, and in Twenty-five Modern Plays, both ed. S. Marion Tucker, 1929, and 1931; in Contemporary Drama: European Plays, III (ed. E. B. Watson and Benefield Pressey) [1933].
　　A remarkable tr.

————*Gioconda*. Tr. Arthur Symons. London, Heinemann, and N.Y., Russell, 1902. 144 pp. Repr. Chicago, Ill., Dramatic Pub. Co., 1913; in Chief Contemporary Dramatists, Second Ser., 1921; in Types of Domestic Tragedy, ed., Robert M. Smith, Prentice-Hall, 1928.

————The Honeysuckle. Tr. Cecile Sartoris and G. Enthoven. N.Y., Stokes, 1911, and London, Heinemann, 1915. 214 pp.
　　Reads easily.

————The Intruder (*L'innocente*). Tr. Arthur Hornblow. N.Y., Richmond, 1898. 331 pp. Repr. Boston, Page, 1919.

Tr. anon. as The Victim. London, Heinemann, 1915. 338 pp.

————The Maidens of the Rocks (*Le vergini delle roccie*). Tr. Annette Halliday-Antona and Giuseppe Antona. N.Y., Richmond, 1898. 296 pp. Repr. ML, 1926.

Tr. A. Hughes as The Virgins of the Rocks. London, Heinemann, 1899. 247 pp.

————Tales of My Native Town (*Le novelle della Pescara*). Tr. Gaetano Mantellini. N.Y., Doubleday, and London, E. Nash, 1920. xvii, 287 pp. (12 of the original 18 tales).

————The Triumph of Death. Tr. Arthur Hornblow. N.Y., Richmond, 1896. 412 pp. Repr. 1911, 1914, 1923, 1926.
Better than the next tr.

Tr. Georgina Harding. London, Heinemann, 1898. 316 pp.

For bibliog., see Joseph G. Fucilla and Joseph M. Carrière, *D'Annunzio Abroad: A Bibliographical Essay* (N.Y., Institute of French Studies, 1935–37, 2 vols.). On D'Annunzio, see Tom Antongini, *D'Annunzio*, tr. anon, from Italian (Boston, Little, Brown, and London, Heinemann, 1938, 591 pp.) Federico Nardelli, *Gabriel the Archangel*, tr. Arthur Livingston from Italian (N.Y., Harcourt, and London, Cassell [as *D'Annunzio: A Portrait*], 1931, 336 pp.); Anthony Rhodes, *D'Annunzio: The Poet as Superman, A Life* (N.Y., McDowell, Obolensky, 1960, 298 pp.); Frances Winwar, *Wingless Victory: A Biography of Gabriele D'Annunzio and Eleonora Duse* (N.Y., Harper, 1956, 374 pp.).

Da Verona, Guido (1881–1939). The Woman Who Invented Love. Tr. May M. Sweet. N.Y., Dutton, 1928. 336 pp.

De Benedetti, Aldo. Two Dozen Red Roses. Adapted Kenneth Horne. London, English Theatre Guild, 1950, and N.Y., Dramatists' Play Service, 1963. 91 pp.

De Bosis, Lauro (1901–1931). *Icaro.* Tr. Ruth Draper, et al. London, Oxford Univ. Pr., 1933. x, 201 pp., parallel texts.

De Cespedes, Alba (1911—). The Best of Husbands (*Dalla parte di lei*). Tr. Frances Frenaye. N.Y., Macmillan, 1932, and London, 1933. 343 pp.

————Between Then and Now (*Prima e dopo*). Tr. Isabel Quigly. London, Cape, 1959, and Boston, Houghton Mifflin, 1960. 160 pp.

————Remorse. Tr. William Weaver. N.Y., Doubleday, 1967. 397 pp.

————The Secret (*Quaderno proibito*). Tr. Isabel Quigly. London, Harvill Pr., 1957. 216 pp., and N.Y., Simon and Schuster, 1958, 249 pp.

De Filippo, Eduardo (1900—). Filumena Marturano: A Mother's a Mother. Tr. Eric Bentley, in The Genius of the Italian Theatre, 1964: see Collections. Repr. in Masterpieces of the Modern Italian Theatre, 1967: ibid. An essay by De Filippo, "Son of Pulcinella," was also tr. by Eric Bentley with the preceding in Masterpieces, etc., 1967.

————Oh, These Ghosts (*Questi fantasmi*). Tr. Marguerite Carra and Louise H. Warner. Tulane Drama Review, vol. 8, 1964, pp. 118–62.

Del Buono, Oreste. One Single Minute (*Un intero minuto*). Tr. Helen R. Lane. London, Faber, 1963. 215 pp.

Deledda, Grazia (1875–1936). After the Divorce. Tr. Maria Horner Lansdale. N.Y., Holt, 1905. 341 pp.

————Ashes: A Sardinian Story. Tr. Helen Hester Colvill. London and N.Y., John Lane, 1908. 307 pp.

————Nostalgia. Tr. Helen Hester Colvill. London, Chapman and Hall, 1905. xiii, 299 pp.

————The Woman and the Priest (*La madre*). Tr. Mary G. Steegman. London, Cape, 1922, and (as The Mother) N.Y., Macmillan, 1923. 256 pp. Repr. with intro. D. H. Lawrence, London, Cape, 1928.

De Roberto, Federico (1866–1927). The Viceroys. Tr. Archibald Colquhoun. London, MacGibbon, and N.Y., Harcourt, 1962. 627 pp.

Dessi, Giuseppe (1909—).   The Deserter. Tr. Virginia Hathaway Moriconi. N.Y., Harcourt, 1962. 110 pp.

Tr. Donata Origo. London, Harvill Pr., 1962. 159 pp.

————The House at San Silvano (*San Silvano*). Tr. Isabel Quigly. London, Harvill Pr., 1966. 159 pp.

Emanuelli, Enrico (1909—).   The Man from New York (*Uno da New York*). Tr. W. J. Strachan. London, MacDonald, 1962. 192 pp.

Fallaci, Oriana.   If the Sun Dies. Tr. Pamela Swinglehurst. N.Y., Atheneum, 1966, and London, Collins, 1967. ix, 403 pp.

————Limelighters (*Gli antipatici*). Tr. Pamela Swinglehurst. London, Joseph, 1967. xii, 244 pp.

————Penelope at War. Tr. Pamela Swinglehurst. London, Joseph, 1966. 223 pp.

————The Useless Sex. Tr. Pamela Swinglehurst. London, Joseph, and N.Y., Horizon Pr., 1964. 183 pp. Repr. London, New English Lib., 1967.

Fellini, Federico.   Juliet of the Spirits. Tr. Howard Greenfeld. N.Y., Ballantine, 1966. 318 pp.

Ferrero, Guglielmo (1871–1942).   The Greatness and Decline of Rome. Tr. Alfred E. Zimmern and H. J. Chaytor. London, Heinemann, and N.Y., Putnam, 1907–09. 5 vols.
For fourteen other books of history past and present by Ferrero, see the British Museum Catalogue.

————The Seven Vices: A Novel of History in Our Own Times (*La terza Roma*). Tr. Arthur Livingston and Elisabeth Abbott. N.Y., Harcourt, 1929. 2 vols.

Flaiano, Ennio (1910—).   The Short Cut (*Tempo di uccidere*). Tr. Stuart Hood. N.Y., Pellegrini and Cudahy, 1950. 302 pp.

Fracchia, Umberto (1889–1930).   Robino and Other Stories (*Piccola gente di città*, and two other stories). Tr. S. H. Scott. N.Y., R. O. Ballou, 1933. x, 86 pp.

Fratti, Mario (1927—).   The Academy. Tr. Raymond Rosenthal, in Masterpieces of the Modern Italian Theatre, 1967, q.v. in Collections, above. Repr. in Best Short Plays of the World Theatre 1958–1967, ed. Stanley Richards, N.Y., Crown, 1968.

————The Cage; The Suicide. Tr. Marguerite Carra and Louise Werner, in The New Theatre of Europe, ed. R. W. Corrigan, vol. 2, 1964.

————The Return. Tr. R. W. Corrigan and Mario Fratti, in Masterpieces of the Modern Italian Theatre, 1967, as above.

Gadda, Carlo Emilio (1893—).   Acquainted with Grief. Tr. William Weaver. N.Y., Braziller, 1969. 244 pp.

————"The Fire in Via Keplero." Tr. Andrew Hale and Guido Waldman from *Novelle dal Ducato in Fiamme*, in The Penguin Book of Italian Short Stories, 1969.

————That Awful Mess on Via Merulana (*Quer pasticciaccio brutto di Via Merulana*). Tr. William Weaver. N.Y., Braziller, 1965, and London, Secker, 1966. xi, 388 pp.

Gallarati-Scotti, Tommaso (1878–1966).   The Life of Antonio Fogazzaro. Tr. Mary Prichard Agnetti. London, Hodder, 1922. xii, 314 pp.

————Thy Will Be Done (*Così sia*). Tr. Valerie Petri, in The Eleonora Duse Series of Plays, ed. Oliver M. Sayler. N.Y., Brentano, 1923. 78 pp.

Gentile, Giovanni (1875–1944).   The Genesis and Structure of Society. Tr. H. S. Harris. Urbana, Univ. of Illinois Pr., 1966. 228 pp.

————The Reform of Education. Tr. Dino Bigongiari. N.Y., Harcourt, 1922. 250 pp.

————The Theory of Mind as Pure Act. Tr. from 3d ed. with intro. H. Wildon Carr. London, Macmillan, 1922. xxvii, 280 pp.

On Gentile, see Roger Wellington Holmes, *The Idealism of Giovanni Gentile* (N.Y., Macmillan, 1937, 264 pp.); Patrick Romanelli, *Gentile: The Philosophy of Giovanni Gentile: An Inquiry into Gentile's Conception of Experience* (N.Y., Vanni, [1938], 191 pp.); Merritt M. Thompson, *The Educational Philosophy of Giovanni Gentile* (Los Angeles, Univ. of Southern California Pr., 1934, 217 pp.).

Ginzburg, Natalia (1916—). Dead Yesterdays (*Tutti i nostri ieri*). Tr. Angus Davidson. London, Secker, 1956. 300 pp. Repr. (as A Light for Fools) N.Y., Dutton, 1956, 256 pp.

—————Family Sayings (*Lessico famigliare*). Tr. D. M. Low. London, Hogarth Pr., and N.Y., Dutton, 1967. 222 pp.

—————The Road to the City (and The Dry Heart: Two Novelettes) (*La strada che va in città*). Tr. Francis Frenaye. London, Hogarth Pr., 1952. 149 pp.

—————Voices in the Evening (*Le voci della sera*). Tr. D. M. Low. London, Hogarth Pr., 1963. 171 pp.

Guareschi, Giovanni (1908–1968). Comrade Don Camillo (*Il compagno di Don Camillo*). Tr. Frances Frenaye. N.Y., Farrar Straus, and London, Gollancz, 1964. 159 pp. Repr. Penguin, 1966.

—————Don Camillo and the Devil. Tr. Frances Frenaye. N.Y., Farrar Straus, and London, Gollancz, 1957. 224 pp.

—————Don Camillo and His Flock (*Don Camillo e la sua grege*). Tr. Frances Frenaye. N.Y., Pellegrini and Cudahy, 1952. 250 pp.

—————Don Camillo's Dilemma (selections from "*Corrierino delle famiglie*" in the weekly *Candido*). Tr. Frances Frenaye. N.Y., Farrar Straus, 1953. 255 pp.

—————My Home Sweet Home (selections from the same). Tr. Joseph Green. N.Y., Farrar Straus, 1966. 214 pp.

—————The House That Nino Built (selections from the same). Tr. Frances Frenaye. N.Y., Farrar Straus, 1953. 238 pp.

————A Husband in Boarding School (*Il marito in collegio*). Tr. anon. N.Y., Farrar Straus, 1967, and London, Macdonald, 1968. 229 pp.

————The Little World of Don Camillo (*Mondo piccolo di Don Camillo*). Tr. Uno Vincenzo Troubridge. N.Y., Pellegrini and Cudahy, 1950. 205 pp. Repr. N.Y., Washington Square Pr., 1967. 153 pp., paper.

La Capria, Raffaele (1922——). The Mortal Wound (*Il ferito a morte*). Tr. Marguerite Waldman. London, Gollancz, and N.Y., Farrar Straus, 1964. 191 pp.

Levi, Carlo (1902——). Christ Stopped at Eboli. Tr. Frances Frenaye. N.Y., Farrar Straus, 1947. 268 pp. Repr. London, Cassell, 1948; London, Landsborough Pubs., 1959; N.Y., Time [1964].

————Of Fear and Freedom (*Paura della libertà*). Tr. Adolphe Gourevitch. N.Y., Farrar Straus, 1950. 154 pp.

————The Linden Trees (*La doppia notte dei tigli*). Tr. Joseph M. Bernstein. N.Y., Knopf, 1962. xii, 170 pp.

————The Watch. Tr. John Farrar with Marianna Gifford. N.Y., Farrar Straus, 1951. 432 pp. Repr. London, Cassell, 1952, 296 pp.

————Words Are Stones: Impressions of Sicily. Tr. Angus Davidson. N.Y., Farrar Straus, 1958. 212 pp. Repr. London, Gollancz, 1959.

Levi, Primo. If This Is a Man. Tr. Stuart Woolf. London, Bodley Head, 1966. 205 pp.

————The Truce. Tr. Stuart Woolf. London, New English Lib., 1966. 189 pp.

Malaparte, Curzio (pseud. of Curt Erich Suckert, 1898–1957). Kaputt. Tr. Cesare Foligno. N.Y., Dutton, 1946. 407 pp. Repr. London, Redman, 1948; London, Panther Books, 1964. N.Y., Avon, 1966.

————The Skin. Tr. David Moore. London, Redman, and Boston, Mass., Houghton Mifflin, 1952. 344 pp. Repr. N.Y., New Amer. Lib., 1954; London, Panther Books, 1964.

————Those Cursed Tuscans (*Maledetti Toscani*). Tr. Rex Benedict. Athens, Ohio Univ. Pr., 1964. 236 pp.

————The Volga Rises in Europe (*Il Volga nasce in Europa*). Tr. David Moore. London, Redman, 1957. 281 pp.

Malerba, Luigi.   The Serpent (*Il serpente cannibale*). Tr. William Weaver. N.Y., Farrar Straus, 1968. 206 pp.

Maraini, Dacia (1936—).   The Age of Malaise (*L'età del benessere*). Tr. Frances Frenaye. N.Y., Grove Pr., and London, Weidenfeld (as The Age of Discontent), 1963. 203 pp.

————The Holiday (*La vacanza*). Tr. Stuart Hood. London, Weidenfeld, 1966. 176 pp.

Marinetti, Filippo Tommaso (1876–1944).   An Initial Manifesto of Futurism. London, Sackville Gallery Exhibition of Works by the Italian Futurist Painters, 1912. 36 pp.

————"Poems by Marinetti." Tr. Anne Simon, in Poet Lore, vol. 26, 1915, 707–43.

> Five poems, including "Invocation to the Avenging Sea to Liberate Me from Infamous Reality."

> Three miniature plays were tr. Mildred Cram in two articles in *Vanity Fair*, vol. 12, 1919, as follows: "Anti-Neutrality" (p. 28) and "Simultaneity" (pp. 28, 92), in her article "Are You Ready for the Futurist Theatre?" (no. 2, April, pp. 28, 92–3); "Moonlight" (p. 56), together with several like pieces by other authors, in her article "Futurist Plays: A New Art-form" (no. 3, May, pp. 56, 80).

Marotta, Giuseppe (1902–1964).   Enchanted in the Sun (*Gli alunni del sole*). Tr. Vladimir Kean. London, Dobson, 1963. 192 pp.

————San Gennaro Never Says No. Tr. Frances Frenaye. N.Y., Dutton, 1950. 255 pp.

————The Slaves of Time (*Gli alunni del tempo*). Tr. Shirley Bridges. London, Dobson, 1964. 204 pp.

————The Treasure of Naples (*L'oro di Napoli*). Tr. Frances Frenaye. N.Y.,

Dutton, 1949. 254 pp. Repr. (as Neapolitan Gold) London, Hogarth Pr., 1950. 192 pp.

Mazzetti, Lorenza (1933—).   Rage (*La rabbia*). Tr. Isabel Quigly. London, Bodley Head, and N.Y., McKay, 1965. 221 pp.

——————The Sky Falls. Tr. Marguerite Waldman. London, Bodley Head, 1962. 158 pp.

Meneghello, Luigi.   The Outlaws (*I piccoli maestri*). Tr. Raleigh Trevelyan. N.Y., Harcourt, 1967. 272 pp.

Modica, Nino.   Heart of Stone. Tr. Dennis Chamberlin. London, Redman, 1965, and N.Y., Doubleday, 1966. 318 pp.

Montale, Eugenio (1896—).   Montale Issue. Ed. Irma Brandeis. Quarterly Review of Literature, vol. 11, 1962, 219–306.

——————Poems. Tr. Edwin Morgan. Reading, Univ. School of Art, 1959. 61 pp. Selections from three vols. of his poems.

——————*Poesie*/Poems. Tr. George Kay. Edinburgh Univ. Pr., 1964. 237 pp., parallel texts.

—————— Selected Poems. Tr. Glauco Cambon, C. W. Corman, Robert Lowell, James Merrill, Mario Praz, et al., intro. Glauco Cambon. N.Y., New Directions, and Edinburgh Univ. Pr., 1966. xxiv, 161 pp.

Monterosso, Carlo.   The Salt of the Earth. Tr. Isabel Quigly. London, Faber, 1967. 191 pp., and Englewood Cliffs, N. J., Prentice-Hall, 1967. 156 pp.

Morante, Elsa (1912—).   Arturo's Island. Tr. Isabel Quigly. London, Collins, and N.Y., Knopf, 1959. 272 pp.

——————House of Liars (*Menzogna e sortilegio*). Tr. Adrienne Foulke. N.Y., Harcourt, 1951. 565 pp.

Moravia, Alberto (pseud. of Alberto Pincherle, 1907—).   Beatrice Cenci. Tr. Angus Davidson. London, Secker, 1965, and N.Y., Farrar Straus, 1966. 187 pp.

————Bitter Honeymoon and Other Stories. Tr. Bernard Wall, Baptista Gilliat Smith, and Frances Frenaye. London, Secker, 1954, and N.Y., Farrar Straus, 1956. 221 pp. Repr. Penguin, 1961.

————Command and I Will Obey You. Tr. Angus Davidson. London, Secker, 1969. 190 pp.

————The Conformist. Tr. Angus Davidson. N.Y., Farrar Straus, 1951, 376 pp., and London, Secker, 1952, 317 pp. Repr. Garden City, N.Y., Garden City Books, 1952; Penguin, 1968.

————Conjugal Love. Tr. Angus Davidson. London, Secker, 152 pp., and N.Y., Farrar Straus, 1951, 183 pp. Repr. Penguin, 1964.

————Disobedience. Tr. Angus Davidson. London, Secker, 1950. 160 pp.

————The Empty Canvas (*La noia*). Tr. Angus Davidson. London, Secker, and N.Y., Farrar Straus, 1961. 306 pp. Repr. N.Y., New Amer. Lib., 1962. Repr. Penguin, 1965.

————The Fancy Dress Party (*La mascherata*). Tr. Angus Davidson. London, Secker, 1947. 184 pp. Repr. N.Y., Farrar Straus, 1952, 299 pp.; Penguin, 1968.

————The Fetish (*L'automa*) and Other Stories. Tr. Angus Davidson. London, Secker, 1964, and N.Y., Farrar Straus, 1965. 285 pp. Repr. Penguin, 1967; N.Y., Dell, 1967.

————Five Novels: Mistaken Ambitions, Agostino, Luca, Conjugal Love, A Ghost at Noon. Intro. Charles J. Rolo. N.Y., Farrar Straus, 1955. xv, 549 pp.

————A Ghost at Noon (*Il disprezzo*). Tr. Angus Davidson. London, Secker, 1955. 223 pp., and N.Y., Farrar Straus, 1955, 247 pp. Repr. N.Y., New Amer. Lib., 1956; repr. Penguin, 1964.

————The Indifferent (*Gli indifferenti*). Tr. Aida Mastrangelo. N.Y., Dutton, 1932. 327 pp.
    This first tr. was unsuccessful.

Tr. Angus Davidson as The Time of Indifference. London, Secker, and N.Y., Farrar Straus, 1953. 303 pp.

————The Lie (*L'attenzione*). Tr. Angus Davidson. London, Secker, 1966. 350 pp., and N.Y., Farrar Straus, 1966. 334 pp. Repr. N.Y., Dell, 1967, paper.

————Man as an End: A Defense of Humanism. Tr. Bernard Wall. London, Secker, 1965, and N.Y., Farrar Straus, 1966. 254 pp.

————Mistaken Ambitions. See Wheel of Fortune, below.

————More Roman Tales. Tr. Angus Davidson. London, Secker, 1963, and N.Y., Farrar Straus, 1964. 255 pp.

————Roman Tales (*Racconti romani*). Tr. Angus Davidson. London, Secker, 1956, and N.Y., Farrar Straus, 1957. 229 pp. Repr. N.Y., New Amer. Lib., 1959. 191 pp.

————Two Adolescents. Agostino and Disobedience. Tr. Beryl de Zoete and Angus Davidson. N.Y., Farrar Straus [1950]. 268 pp. Repr. London, Secker, 1952; Penguin, 1960; N.Y., New Amer. Lib., 1962.

————Two Women (*La ciociara*). Tr. Angus Davidson. London, Secker, 1958, 356 pp., and N.Y., Farrar Straus, 1958, 339 pp. Repr. N.Y., New Amer. Lib., 1959; Penguin, 1961.

————The Wayward Wife and Other Stories (*I racconti*). Tr. Angus Davidson. London, Secker, and N.Y., Farrar Straus, 1960. 221 pp. Repr. N.Y., New Amer. Lib., 1961; Penguin, 1963; N.Y., Ace, 1968.
   Eight short stories.

————Wheel of Fortune (*Le ambizioni sbagliate*). Tr. Arthur Livingston. N.Y., Viking, 1937, and London, Cassell, 1938. 549 pp. Repr. (as Mistaken Ambitions), N.Y., New Amer. Lib., 1961.

————The Woman of Rome. Tr. Lydia Holland. London, Secker, 1949. 389 pp., and N.Y., Farrar Straus, 1949, 433 pp. Repr. N.Y., Grosset, 1950; N.Y., New Amer. Lib., 1951; Penguin, 1952; N.Y., Signet, 1966.

On Moravia, see Giuliano Dego, *Moravia* (London, Oliver and Boyd, 1966, and N.Y., Barnes and Noble, 1967, 120 pp.), which presents an excellent clarification of the major themes in the author's works.

Moretti, Ugo (1885—). Rogue Wind (*Vento caldo*). Tr. Giuseppina T. Salvadori and Bernice L. Lewis. N.Y., Prentice-Hall, 1953. 217 pp.

Morselli, Ercole Luigi (1882–1921). Gastone the Animal Trainer; Water upon Fire. Tr. Isaac Goldberg, in Plays of the Italian Theatre, 1921: see Collections. (Two plays.)

Moscardelli, Nicola (1894–1943). The Third State. Tr. Margaret Daruelly Naylor. Bristol, Poets' Pr., 1953. 31 pp. (An anthology.)

Neera (pseud. of Anna Zuccari Radius, 1846–1918). The Soul of an Artist (*Anima sola*). Tr. E. L. Murison. San Francisco, Calif., Elder, 1905. vi, 126 pp.

Negri, Ada [Garlanda] (1870–1945). Fate and Other Poems. Tr. A. M. Blomberg. Boston, Copeland and Day, 1898. 98 pp. Repr. 1907.

Ojetti, Ugo (1871–1946). As They Seemed to Me (*Cose viste*, selections from the 3 vols.). Tr. Henry Furst, intro. Gabriele D'Annunzio. N.Y., Dutton, 1927, and London, Methuen, 1928. xxvi, 252 pp. Repr. Freeport, N.Y., Books for Libraries [1968].

Ongaro, Alberto. Excelsior (*Il complice*). Tr. Giles Cremonesi. London, Bodley Head, 1967, and Chicago, Regnery, 1968. 205 pp.

Ortese, Anna Maria (1914—). The Bay Is Not Naples (*Il mare non bagna Napoli*). Tr. Frances Frenaye. London, Collins, 1955. 194 pp.

Ottieri, Ottiero (1924—). The Men at the Gate (*Donnarumma all'assalto*). Tr. I. M. Rawson. Boston, Houghton Mifflin, 1962. 244 pp.

Palazzeschi, Aldo (1885–1963). Materassi Sisters. Tr. Angus Davidson. London, Secker, 1953. 300 pp., and Garden City, N.Y., Doubleday, 1953. 316 pp.

————Perelà, the Man of Smoke (*Il codice di Perelà*). Adapted Peter M. Riccio. N.Y., Vanni, 1936. 278 pp.

————*Roma*. Tr. Mihaly Czikzentmihalyi. Chicago, Regnery, 1965. 216 pp.

Palumbo, Nino (1912—). Tomorrow Will Be Better (*Pane verde*). Tr. Isabel Quigly. London, Harvill, 1966. 253 pp.

Panzini, Alfredo (1863–1939). Wanted—A Wife (*Io cerco moglie*). Tr. Frederic Taber Cooper. N.Y., Brown, 1921. 294 pp.

Papini, Giovanni (1881–1956). *Dante Vivo*. Tr. Eleanor Hammond Broadus and Anna Benedetti. London, Lovat Dickson, 1934, and N.Y., Macmillan, 1935. xiii, 340 pp.

————The Devil. Tr. Adrienne Foulke. N.Y., Dutton, 1954, and London, Eyre and Spottiswoode (as The Devil: Notes for a Future Diabology), 1955. 159 pp.

————The Failure (*Un uomo finito*). Tr. Virginia Pope. N.Y., Harcourt [1924]. vi, 326 pp.

 Tr. Mary Prichard Agnetti as A Man—Finished. London, Hodder [1924]. vii, 320 pp.
 The first is a better tr.

————Four and Twenty Minds (*24 cervelli*). Tr. Ernest H. Wilkins. N.Y., Crowell [1922] and London, Harrap, 1923. 324 pp.
 Includes ten essays from *24 cervelli*; six from *Stroncature*; eight from *Testimonianze*.

————Gog. Tr. Mary Prichard Agnetti. N.Y., Harcourt, 1931. xiii, 300 pp.

————Labourers in the Vineyard. See Literary Studies, above.

————The Letters of Pope Celestine VI to All Mankind (*Lettere agli uomini del papa Celestino sesto*). Tr. Loretta Murnane. N.Y., Dutton, 1948. 223 pp.

————Life and Myself (*Il tragico quotidiano*, and *Il pilota cieco*). Tr. Dorothy Emmrich. N.Y., Brentano, 1930. 241 pp.

————The Memoirs of God. Tr. anon. Boston, Mass., Bell Pub. Co., 1926. 137 pp.

————Michelangelo, His Life and His Era. Tr. Loretta Murnane. N.Y., Dutton, 1952. 542 pp.

————St. Augustine. Tr. Mary Prichard Agnetti. London, Hodder, and N.Y., Harcourt, 1930. 327 pp.

————The Story of Christ (*Vita di Cristo*). Tr. Mary Prichard Agnetti. London, Hodder [1923]. xi, 453 pp. Many reprs. to 15th ed., 1924.

Tr. freely Dorothy Canfield Fisher as The Life of Christ. N.Y., Harcourt, 1923. 416 pp. Repr. 1949.

Pareto, Vilfredo (1848–1923). The Mind and Society (*Trattato di sociologia generale*). Tr. Arthur Livingston and Andrew Bongiorno. N.Y., Harcourt, and London, Cape, 1935. 4 vols. Repr. N.Y., Dover. 1963, 4 vols. in 2.

Parise, Goffredo (1929—). The Boss (*Il padrone*). Tr. William Weaver. N.Y., Knopf, 1966, and London, Cape, 1967. 246 pp.

————The Dead Boy and the Comets. Tr. Marianne Ceconi. N.Y., Farrar Straus, 1953. 240 pp.

————The Priest among the Pigeons (*Il prete bello*). Tr. Stuart Hood. London, Weidenfeld, 1955. 256 pp. Repr. as Don Gaston and the Women, N.Y., Avon, 1957, 191 pp.

Pascoli, Giovanni (1855–1912). Poems of Giovanni Pascoli. Tr. freely Evaleen Stein. New Haven, Conn., Yale Univ. Pr., 1923. 72 pp.
She states that she has tried to "suggest in some measure the charm of the Italian singer," but falls short of aim.

Tr. (selections) Arletta M. Abbott. N.Y., Vinal, 1927. 108 pp.
Trs. mostly failures.

Pasolini, Pier Paolo (1922—). The Ragazzi (*Ragazzi di vita*). Tr. Emile Capouya. N.Y., Grove Pr., 1968. 256 pp.

————A Violent Life. Tr. William Weaver. London, Cape, 1968. 320 pp.

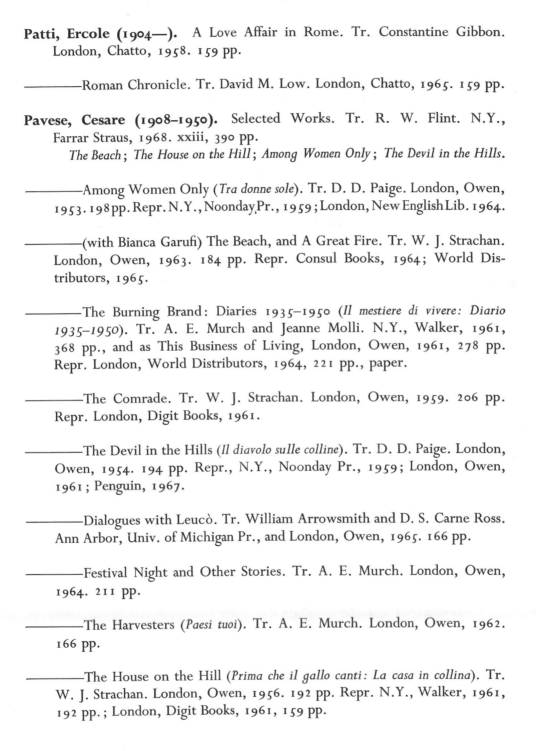

Patti, Ercole (1904—). A Love Affair in Rome. Tr. Constantine Gibbon. London, Chatto, 1958. 159 pp.

————Roman Chronicle. Tr. David M. Low. London, Chatto, 1965. 159 pp.

Pavese, Cesare (1908–1950). Selected Works. Tr. R. W. Flint. N.Y., Farrar Straus, 1968. xxiii, 390 pp.
   The Beach; *The House on the Hill*; *Among Women Only*; *The Devil in the Hills*.

————Among Women Only (*Tra donne sole*). Tr. D. D. Paige. London, Owen, 1953. 198 pp. Repr. N.Y., Noonday Pr., 1959; London, New English Lib. 1964.

————(with Bianca Garufi) The Beach, and A Great Fire. Tr. W. J. Strachan. London, Owen, 1963. 184 pp. Repr. Consul Books, 1964; World Distributors, 1965.

————The Burning Brand: Diaries 1935–1950 (*Il mestiere di vivere: Diario 1935–1950*). Tr. A. E. Murch and Jeanne Molli. N.Y., Walker, 1961, 368 pp., and as This Business of Living, London, Owen, 1961, 278 pp. Repr. London, World Distributors, 1964, 221 pp., paper.

————The Comrade. Tr. W. J. Strachan. London, Owen, 1959. 206 pp. Repr. London, Digit Books, 1961.

————The Devil in the Hills (*Il diavolo sulle colline*). Tr. D. D. Paige. London, Owen, 1954. 194 pp. Repr., N.Y., Noonday Pr., 1959; London, Owen, 1961; Penguin, 1967.

————Dialogues with Leucò. Tr. William Arrowsmith and D. S. Carne Ross. Ann Arbor, Univ. of Michigan Pr., and London, Owen, 1965. 166 pp.

————Festival Night and Other Stories. Tr. A. E. Murch. London, Owen, 1964. 211 pp.

————The Harvesters (*Paesi tuoi*). Tr. A. E. Murch. London, Owen, 1962. 166 pp.

————The House on the Hill (*Prima che il gallo canti: La casa in collina*). Tr. W. J. Strachan. London, Owen, 1956. 192 pp. Repr. N.Y., Walker, 1961, 192 pp.; London, Digit Books, 1961, 159 pp.

————The Moon and the Bonfire (*La luna e i falò*). Tr. Louise Sinclair. London, Lehmann, 1952. 189 pp. Repr. Penguin, 1963.

    Tr. Marianne Ceconi, with foreword Paolo Milano. N.Y., Farrar Straus, 1953. 220 pp. Repr. N.Y., New Amer. Lib., 1954, 144 pp.

————The Political Prisoner (*Carcere*); The Beautiful Summer. Tr. W. J. Strachan. London, Owen, 1955. 237 pp. Repr. of The Beautiful Summer, London, Digit Books, 1961, 159 pp.; of The Political Prisoner, London, Mayflower, 1966. 176 pp.

————Summer Storm and Other Stories. Tr. A. E. Murch. London, Owen, 1966. 204 pp.

On Pavese, see Gian-Paolo Biasin, *The Smile of the Gods, a Thematic Study of Cesare Pavese's Work*, tr. Yvonne Freccero (Ithaca, Cornell Univ. Pr., 1968. 368 pp.).

Pea, Enrico (1881–1963).   Moscardino. Tr. Ezra Pound. Milan, Insegno del Pesce, 1956. 81 pp.

Piovene, Guido (1907—).   Confession of a Novice (*Lettere di una novizia*). Tr. Eithne Wilkins. London, Kimber, 1950. x, 193 pp.

Pirandello, Luigi (1867–1936).

COLLECTIONS OF PLAYS

————Each in His Own Way and Two Other Plays. Tr. Arthur Livingston. N.Y., Dutton, 1923, and London, Dent, 1925. xiv, 258 pp.
Besides the title play, *The Pleasures of Honesty*; and *Naked* (*Vestire gl'ignudi*). The first play was repr. in *Naked Masks*, q.v. below; also in *Avant-Garde Drama* (N.Y., Bantam, 1969). The other two were retr. in *To Clothe the Naked*, q.v. below. *Naked* was repr. in *Chief Contemporary Dramatists*, Third Series, 1930: see General Reference, Collections, above.

————The Mountain Giants and Other Plays. Tr. Marta Abba. N.Y., Crown, 1958. ix, 277 pp.

The other plays are *The New Colony*; and *When Someone Is Somebody*. The last was repr. separately, 1963, see under individual plays, below.

———————Naked Masks. Ed. Eric Bentley. EL, 1952. 413 pp. Repr. 1957, paper. Includes *Each in His Own Way*, tr. Arthur Livingston, repr. from the collection with that title, above; a repr. of *Three Plays*, below (*Six Characters in Search of an Author*; and *Enrico IV*, both tr. Edward Storer; and, given a new title, *It Is So! If You Think So*, tr. Arthur Livingston; and *Liolà*, tr. Eric Bentley and Gerardo Guerrieri.

———————The One-Act Plays of Luigi Pirandello. Tr. Elisabeth Abbott, Arthur Livingston, and Blanche Valentine Mitchell. N.Y., Dutton, 1928. 230 pp.
Imbecile; *By the Judgment of the Court* (*La Patente*); *Our Lord of the Ship* (*La sagra del Signor del Nave*); *The Doctor's Duty*; *The Man with the Flower in His Mouth*; *At the Gate* (*All'uscita*); *The Vise*; *The House with the Column* (*L'Altro figlio*); *Sicilian Limes*; *The Jar*.

———————Pirandello's One-Act Plays. Tr. William Murray. Garden City, N.Y., Doubleday (Anchor Books), 1964. xvii, 356 pp.
The same plays, some with different titles, plus *Chee-Chee*(*Cecè*); *Bellavita*; *I'm Dreaming, But Am I?*

———————Right You Are! (If You Think So) [and other plays]. Ed. with intro., E. Martin Browne. Penguin, 1962. 247 pp.
The title play and *Henry IV* tr. Frederick May; *All for the Best*, tr. Henry Reed.

———————Three Plays: The Rules of the Game; The Life I Gave You; Lazarus. Tr. Roberty Rietty and Frederick May. Penguin, 1959. 219 pp.

———————Three Plays: Six Characters in Search of an Author; Henry IV; Right You Are! (If You Think So). Tr. Edward Storer and (the third play) Arthur Livingston. N.Y., Dutton, 1922, and London, Dent, 1923. 233 pp.
Six Characters repr. in *A Treasury of the Theatre*, ed. John Gassner, vol. 1. 1951; in *Naked Masks*, 1952, see above. *Henry IV* repr. in *Contemporary Drama*, ed. E. B. Watson and B. Pressey, 1931; in *Representative Modern Dramas*, ed. Charles H. Whitman, 1936; in *Sixteen Famous Modern Plays*, ML, 1943; in *Drama: An Introductory Anthology*, ed. Otto Reinert, 1961; in *The Makers of the Modern Theater*, ed. Barry Ulanov, 1961; in *Masters of Modern Drama*, ed. H. M. Block and R. G. Shedd, 1962; in *Modern Drama*,

ed. Anthony Caputi, 1962. *Right You Are!* repr. in *Dramas of Modernism*, ed. Montrose J. Moses, 1931, 1941; and in *Naked Masks*, 1952, see above, the title modified.

—————To Clothe the Naked, and Two Other Plays. Tr. William Murray. N.Y., Dutton, 1962. 198 pp.
  Includes *The Rules of the Game*; *The Pleasure of Honesty*.

INDIVIDUAL PLAYS

—————As You Desire Me (*Come tu me vuoi*). Tr. Samuel Putnam. N.Y., Dutton, 1931. 231 pp. Repr. in Modern Continental Dramas, ed. Harlan Hatcher, 1941.

  Tr. Marta Abba, in Twenty Best European Plays in the American Theatre, ed. John Gassner. N.Y., Crown, 1957. 733 pp.

—————Bellavita. Tr. William Murray, in Best Short Plays of the World Theatre 1958–1967: 1968, see Collections.

—————Diana and Tuda. Tr. Marta Abba. N.Y., French, 1960. 66 pp.

—————The Emperor. See Henry IV.

—————Henry IV. Tr. Edward Storer in Three Plays, above, and reprs.

  Tr. Frederick May, in Right You Are! Penguin, 1962, see above.

  Tr. Eric Bentley as The Emperor, in The Genius of the Italian Theatre, see Collections, above. Repr. in The Modern Theatre, ed. R. W. Corrigan, 1964.

—————The Jar. Tr. in The One-Act Plays of Pirandello, 1928, see above.

  Tr. William Murray, in Pirandello's One-Act Plays, 1964, see above.

  Tr. Frederick May, in Four Continental Plays, ed. John Allen. London, Heinemann, 1964. 149 pp.

—————The Man with the Flower in His Mouth. Tr. in The One-Act Plays of Pirandello, 1928, see above.

  Tr. Eric Bentley, in Tulane Drama Review, vol. 1, no. 3, 1957, 15–22.

Tr. Frederick May. Leeds, Univ. Pirandello Soc., 1959. 15 pp.

————No One Knows How. Tr. Marta Abba. N.Y., French, 1963. 73 pp.

————The Pleasure of Honesty. Tr. Arthur Livingston as The Pleasures of Honesty, in Each in His Own Way, 1923, see above.

Tr. William Murray, in To Clothe the Naked, 1962, see above. Repr. in Masterpieces of the Modern Italian Theatre: see Collections, above.

————The Rest Is Silence (*Sgombero*). Tr. Frederick May. Leeds, Pirandello Soc., 1958. 14 pp.

————Right You Are! (If You Think So). Tr. Arthur Livingston in Three Plays, 1922, see above, and reprs.

Tr. Eric Bentley as Right You Are, A Stage Version. N.Y., Columbia Univ. Pr., 1954. 165 pp.

Tr. Frederick May, in Right You Are! Penguin, 1962, see above.

————Sicilian Limes. Tr. Isaac Goldberg, in Plays of the Italian Theatre, 1921. See Collections, above.

Tr. Elisabeth Abbott, in Theatre Arts Magazine, vol. 6, 1922, 329–44. Repr. in The One-Act Plays, 1928, above.

Tr. Robert Rietty, in Limes from Sicily, and Other Plays, 1967: see Collections, above.

————Six Characters in Search of an Author. Tr. Arthur Livingston, in Three Plays, 1922, see above, and reprs.

Tr. Frederick May. London, Heinemann, 1954. xii, 70 pp.

Adapted Paul Avila Mayer, in The Modern Theatre, ed. R. W. Corrigan, 1964.

————To Find Oneself. Tr. Marta Abba. N.Y., French, 1960. 78 pp.

————Tonight We Improvise (*Questa sera si recita soggetto*). Tr. Samuel Putnam. N.Y., Dutton, 1932. 231 pp.

Tr. Marta Abba. N.Y., French, 1961. 99 pp.

————When One Is Somebody. Tr. Marta Abba. N.Y., French, 1963. 73 pp. Repr. from The Mountain Giants, etc., above.

————The Wives' Friend (*L'amica delle mogli*). Tr. Marta Abba. N.Y., French, 1960. 70 pp.

NOVELS

————The Late Mattia Pascal. Tr. Arthur Livingston. N.Y., Dutton, 1923. 321 pp.

Tr. William Weaver. N.Y., Doubleday, 1964. viii, 252 pp.

————The Old and the Young. Tr. C. K. Scott Moncrieff. N.Y., Dutton, 1933. 268 pp.

————One, None, and a Hundred Thousand. Tr. Samuel Putnam. N.Y., Dutton, 1933. 268 pp.

————The Outcast (*L'esclusa*). Tr. Leo Ongley. N.Y., Dutton, 1925. 334 pp.

————Shoot: The Notebooks of Serafino Gubbio, Cinematograph Operator (*Si gira*). Tr. C. K. Scott Moncrieff. N.Y., Dutton, 1926. 334 pp.

SHORT STORY COLLECTIONS

————Better Think Twice About It, and Twelve Other Stories. Tr. Arthur and Henrie Mayne. London, Lane, 1933, and N.Y., Dutton, 1934. 309 pp. Repr. London, 1934, as The Naked Truth, and Eleven Other Stories.
These stories are from Pirandello's series, *Novelle per un anno*. Other collections from this series follow.

————A Character in Distress. Tr. anon. London, Duckworth, 1938, and (as The Medals and Other Stories) N.Y., Dutton, 1939. 284 pp.

————The Horse in the Moon: Twelve Short Stories. Tr. Samuel Putnam. N.Y., Dutton, 1932. 238 pp.

————Short Stories. Tr. Lily Duplaix. N.Y., Simon and Schuster, 1959. 303 pp. Repr. 1960.

OTHER SHORT STORY COLLECTIONS

————The Merry-Go-Round of Love and Selected Stories. Tr. Frances Keene and Lily Duplaix. N.Y., New Amer. Lib., 1964. 320 pp.

————Short Stories. Tr. Frederick May. London and N.Y., Oxford Univ. Pr., 1964. 288 pp. Repr. 1965.

On Pirandello, see Walter Starkie, *Luigi Pirandello: 1867–1936* (3rd ed., Berkeley, Univ. of California Pr., and London, Cambridge Univ. Pr., 1965, xiii, 304 pp., earlier eds. 1926, 1937); Domenico Vittorino, *The Drama of Luigi Pirandello* (Philadelphia, Univ. of Pennsylvania Pr., 1935, 351 pp.), all the plays analyzed; "Pirandello, the Perfect Pessimist," ch. 7 in Lander McClintock, *The Age of Pirandello* (Bloomington, Indiana Univ. Pr., 1951, pp. 175–229); Oscar Büdel, *Pirandello: Studies in Modern European Thought and Literature* (N.Y., Hillary House, and London, Bowes, 1966, 126 pp.); Antonio Illiano, "Pirandello in England and the United States: A Chronological List of Criticism" (*Bulletin* of the New York Public Library, vol. 70, 1967, pp. 105–30). See also *Pirandello: A Collection of Critical Essays*, ed. Glauco Cambon (Englewood Cliffs, N.J., Prentice-Hall, 1967, 182 pp.), containing studies by Stark Young, Adriano Tilgher, Francis Fergusson, Thomas Bishop, Wylie Sypher, Giovanni Sinicropi, Ulrich Leo, A. I. de Castris, Robert Brustein, Aureliu Weiss, Luigi Squarzina and Gino Rizzo (co-authors), and William Herman.

Pirro, Ugo.   The Campfollowers (*Le soldatesse*). Tr. Archibald Colquhoun. London, Hutchinson, and N.Y., Dutton, 1958. 155 pp.

Pomilio, Mario.   The New Line (*Il nuovo corso*). Tr. Archibald Colquhoun. London, Hutchinson, and N.Y., Harper, 1961. 141 pp.

————The Witness (*Il testimone*). London, Hutchinson, 1959. 168 pp.

Praga, Marco (1862–1929).   The Closed Door. Tr. Anne Sprague MacDonald. N.Y., Brentano, 1923. iv, 88 pp.; also in The Eleonora Duse Series of Plays, ed. Oliver M. Sayler, ibid., 1923.

Pratolini, Vasco (1913—).   Bruno Santini (*La costanza della ragione*). Tr. Raymond Rosenthal. London, Chatto, and Boston, Mass., Little Brown, 1965. 313 pp.

————A Hero of To-day (*Un eroe del nostro tempo*). Tr. Eric Mosbacher. London, H. Hamilton, 1951. 250 pp. Repr. as A Hero of Our Time, N.Y., Prentice-Hall, 1951; N.Y., New Amer. Lib., 1953.

————Metello. Tr. Raymond Rosenthal. Boston, Atlantic-Little, Brown, and London, Chatto, 1968. 283 pp.

————A Tale of Poor Lovers (*Cronache di poveri amanti*). Tr. anon. London, H. Hamilton, and N.Y., Viking, 1949. 377 pp.

————A Tale of Santa Croce (*Il quartiere*). Tr. Peter and Pamela Duncan. London, Owen, 1952, 254 pp., and (as The Naked Streets), N.Y., Wyn, 1952, 217 pp.

————Two Brothers. Tr. Barbara Kennedy. N.Y., Orion Pr., 1962. 173 pp.

On Pratolini, see Frank Rosengarten, *Vasco Pratolini: The Development of a Social Novelist* (Carbondale, Southern Illinois Univ. Pr., 1965, xi, 143 pp.).

Prisco, Michele (1920—).   Heirs of the Wind. Tr. Violet N. Macdonald. London, Verschoyle, 1953. 462 pp.

Quasimodo, Salvatore (1901–1968).   The Poet and the Politician and Other Essays. Tr. Thomas G. Bergin and Sergio Pacifici. Carbondale, Southern Illinois Univ. Pr., 1964. vii, 166 pp.

————Selected Poems. Tr. Jack Bevan. Penguin, 1965. 110 pp.

————The Selected Writings. Tr. Allen Mandelbaum. N.Y., Farrar Straus, 1960. 269 pp.

————"Thirty Poems by Quasimodo." Tr. Charles Guenther. Literary Review, vol. 3, 1960, 366–82.

Rea, Domenico (1921—).   A Blush of Shame (*Una vampata di rossore*). Tr. Maureen Duffy. London, Barrie and Rockliff, 1963. 222 pp.

Rimanelli, Giose (1926—).   The Day of the Lion (*Tiro al piccione*). Tr. Ben Johnson. N.Y., Random House, 1954. 244 pp. Repr. London, Heinemann, 1956.

————Original Sin. Tr. Ben Johnson. N.Y., Random House, 1957. 179 pp. Repr. London, Heinemann, 1958; London, World Distributors, 1959.

Rocca, Guido (1928—). Indiscretion (*La ragazza imprudente*). Tr. David Moore. London, Redman, 1958. 241 pp.

Rosso di San Secondo (pseud. of Piermaria Rosso, 1887–1958). The Stairs (*La scala*). Tr. anon., in Italian Theatre Review (Rome), vol. 4, ii (1955), 31–49.

————The Unveiling. Tr. Frederic May. Leeds, Pirandello Soc., 1961. 16 pp.

Santucci, Luigi (1918—). Orfeo in Paradise. Tr. Joseph Green. N.Y., Knopf, 1969. 210 pp.

Sciascia, Leonardo (1921—). The Council of Egypt. Tr. Adrienne Foulke. N.Y., Knopf, and London, Cape, 1966. 212 pp.

————Mafia Vendetta (*Il giorno della civetta*). Tr. Archibald Colquhoun and Arthur Oliver. London, Cape, 1963, and N.Y., Knopf, 1964. 122 pp.

————A Man's Blessing (*A Ciascuno il suo*). Tr. Adrienne Foulke. N.Y., Harper, 1968, and London, Cape, 1969. 146 pp.

————Salt in the Wound. Tr. Judith Green. N.Y., Grossman-Orion, 1969. 212 pp.

Seminara, Fortunato (1903—). The Wind in the Olive Grove. Tr. Isabel Quigly. London, Lane, 1958. 192 pp.

Senesi, Mauro. His Beard Grew on Only One Cheek. Tr. not named. N.Y., Scribner, 1968. 160 pp.

————Longshadow and Nine Stories. Tr. not named. Chicago, Regnery, 1965. 180 pp.

Serao, Matilda (1856–1927). After the Pardon. Tr. anon. London, Eveleigh Nash, and N.Y., Stuyvesant, 1909. 334 pp.

——————The Ballet Dancer and On Guard (*All'erta sentinella*). Tr. anon. London, Heinemann, and N.Y., Harper, 1901. 266 pp.

——————The Conquest of Rome. Tr. Dora Knowlton Ranous. London, Heinemann, and N.Y., Harper, 1902. 317 pp. Repr. N.Y., National Alumni, 1906.

——————The Desire of Life (*Evviva la vita*). Tr. William Conninge. London, Stanley Paul, [1911]. 321 pp.

——————Fantasy, a Novel (*Fantasie*). Tr. Henry Harland and Paul Sylvester. London, Heinemann, and N.Y., U.S. Book, 1890. vii, 280 pp.

——————Farewell Love. Tr. anon. N.Y., Minerva, 1892. 278 pp.

Tr. Mrs. Henry Harland. London, Heinemann, 1894. xi, 280 pp.

——————The Harvest (*Mors tua*). Tr. William Collinge. London, E. Nash and Grayson, 1928. 314 pp.

——————In the Country of Jesus. Tr. Richard Davey. London, Heinemann, and N.Y., Dutton, 1905. xiv, 293 pp. Repr. London, 1919.

——————The Land of Cockayne. Tr. anon. London, Heinemann, and N.Y., Harper, 1901. 369 pp.

——————The Severed Head. Tr. David R. Lamb. London, Stanley Paul, [1925]. 316 pp.

——————Souls Divided (*Ella non rispose*). Tr. William Collinge. London, Stanley Paul, 1919. 298 pp.

On Serao, see the well-balanced analysis of Anthony G. Gisolfi, *The Essential Serao* (N.Y., Las Americas, 1968, xvi, 143 pp.).

Servadio, Gaia.   Don Giovanni: Notes for a New Opera. Tr. L. K. Conrad, together with Salome: Notes for a New Novel. N.Y., Farrar Straus, 1969. 168 pp.

——————Melinda (*Tanto gentile e tanto onesta*). Tr. L. K. Conrad. N.Y., Farrar Straus, 1968. 375 pp., and London, Weidenfeld, 1968, 335 pp. Repr. N.Y., Ace, 1969, paper.

Silone, Ignazio (pseud. of Secondo Tranquilli, 1900—). And He Did Hide Himself: A Play. Tr. Dorina Laracy Tranquilli. London, Cape, 1946. 118 pp. Repr. N.Y., Harper (as He Hid Himself), 1946, vi, 126 pp.

————Bread and Wine. Tr. Gwenda David and Eric Mosbacher. London, Methuen, 1936. 316 pp. Repr. N.Y., Harper, 1937, 219 pp.; London, Cape, 1939.

   Tr. Harvey Fergusson II. N.Y., Atheneum, 1962, and London, Gollancz, 1964. 331 pp. Repr. N.Y., New Amer. Lib., 1963; London, Panther, 1967.

————Emergency Exit. Tr. Darina Silone. N.Y. Harper, 1968. xv, 207 pp.

————Fontamara. Tr. Michael Wharf. N.Y., Harrison Smith and Haas, 1934. xix, 299 pp. Repr. N.Y., Random House, 1934.

   Tr. Gwenda David and Eric Mosbacher. London, Methuen, 1934. 250 pp. Repr. Penguin, 1938; London, Cape, 1948; London, Panther, 1965.

   Tr. Harvey Fergusson II, intro. Malcolm Cowley. N.Y., Atheneum, 1960. 240 pp. Repr. N.Y., Dell, 1961.

————The Fox and the Camellias. Tr. Eric Mosbacher. London, Cape, 1961. 160 pp., and N.Y., Harper, 1961, 130 pp. Repr. N.Y., Popular, 1962.

————A Handful of Blackberries. Tr. Darina Silone. N.Y., Harper, 1953. 314 pp., and London, Cape, 1954, 288 pp.

————Mr. Aristotle. Tr. Samuel Putnam. N.Y., McBride, 1935. 221 pp.

————The School for Dictators. Tr. Gwenda David and Eric Mosbacher. London, Cape, and N.Y., Harper, 1938. 336 pp.

   Tr. William Weaver, with new preface by author. London, Gollancz, 1961, and N.Y., Atheneum, 1963. viii, 244 pp.

————The Secret of Luca. Tr. Darina Silone. N.Y., Harper, 1959, 183 pp., and London, Cape, 1959, 207 pp. Repr. Garden City, N.Y., Doubleday, 1961, 157 pp.

————The Seed Beneath the Snow. Tr. Frances Frenaye. N.Y., Harper, 1942. 360 pp., and London, Cape, 1943, 384 pp.

Tr. Harvey Fergusson II. N.Y., Atheneum, 1965. 464 pp.

The original Italian was first pub. in Rome, 1945.

Soldati, Mario (1906—).   The Capri Letters. Tr. Archibald Colquhoun. London, Hamish Hamilton, 1955. 255 pp. Repr. (as Affair in Capri: The Capri Letters) N.Y., Berkeley Pub. Corp., 1957, 221 pp.; repr. London, Harborough, 1958, 205 pp.

————The Commander Comes to Dine (*Si cena col commendatore*). Tr. Gwyn Morris and Henry Furst. London, Lehmann, 1952, 223 pp., and N.Y., Knopf, 1953, 273 pp.

————The Confession. Tr. Raymond Rosenthal. London, Deutsch, 1958, 184 pp., and N.Y., Knopf, 1958, 180 pp. Repr. London, New English Lib., 1962.

————The Orange Envelope. Tr. Bernard Wall. N.Y., Harcourt, 1969. 251 pp., and London, Deutsch, 1939, 223 pp.

————The Real Silvestri. Tr. Archibald Colquhoun. London, Deutsch, 1960, and N.Y., Knopf, 1961. 188 pp.

Strati, Saverio (1924—).   Empty Hands. Tr. Peter Moule. N.Y., Abelard-Schuman, 1963. 264 pp.

————The Lights of Reggio (*Avventure in città*). Tr. Angus Davidson. London, Murray, 1965. 206 pp.

————Terrarossa (*La teda*). Tr. Elizabeth Ellman. N.Y., and London, Abelard-Schuman, 1962. 233 pp. Repr. London, Panther, 1965.

Svevo, Italo (pseud. of Ettore Schmitz, 1861–1928).   As a Man Grows Older (*Senilità*). Tr. Beryl de Zoete. N.Y. and London, Putnam, 1932. Repr. with intro. Stanislaus Joyce, Norfolk, Conn., New Directions, and London, Putnam, 1949, 267 pp. Repr. London, Secker, 1962; repr. Penguin, 1965.

————Confessions of Zeno (*La coscienza di Zeno*). Tr. Beryl de Zoete. N.Y., Knopf, and London, Putnam, 1930. 412 pp. Repr. with intro. Renato

Poggioli, N.Y. and London, 1948; repr. N.Y., Vintage Books, 1958; repr. London, with intro. Edouard Roditi, Secker, 1962; repr. Penguin, 1964.

————The Further Confessions of Zeno. Tr. Ben Johnson and P. N. Furbank. Berkeley, Univ. of California Pr., 1969. 242 pp.

————The Hoax (*Una burla riuscita*). Tr. Beryl de Zoete. London, L. and V. Woolf, 1929. 150 pp.

————A Life. Tr. Archibald Colquhoun. London, Secker, and N.Y., Knopf, 1963. 320 pp.

————The Nice Old Man and the Pretty Girl, and Other Stories. Tr. Lacy Collison-Morley. London, Hogarth Pr., 1930. 162 pp.

————Short Sentimental Journey and Other Stories. Tr. Beryl de Zoete, L. Collison Morley, and Ben Johnson. London, Secker, and Berkeley and Los Angeles, Univ. of California Pr., 1967. 319 pp.

On Svevo, see Philip Nicholas Furbank, *Italo Svevo the Man and the Writer* (Berkeley and Los Angeles, Univ. of California Pr., 1967, 232 pp.), and *Essays on Italo Svevo*, ed. Thomas F. Staley. (Tulsa, Okla., Univ. of Tulsa Pr., 1969.)

Tecchi, Bonaventura (1896—). The Egoists. Tr. Dennis Chamberlin. N.Y., Appleton-Century, 1964. 282 pp.

Terni-Cialenti, Fausta. The Levantines (*Ballata Levantina*). Tr. Isabel Quigly. London, Faber, and Boston, Mass., Houghton Mifflin, 1963. 322 pp.

Tobino, Mario (1910—). The Deserts of Libya. Tr. Archibald Colquhoun and Antonia Cowan in The Lost Legions: Three Italian War Novels. London, MacGibbon and Kee, 1967. 412 pp.
   The two other works are Renzo Biasion, *The Army of Love*; Mario Rigoni Stern, *The Sergeant in the Snow*.

————The Mad Women of Magliano: An Imaginary Journal (*Le libere donne di Magliano*). Tr. Archibald Colquhoun. London, Verschoyle, 1954. 154 pp., and N.Y., Putnam, 1954 (as Women of Magliano), 183 pp.

————The Underground (*Il clandestino*). Tr. Raymond Rosenthal. N.Y., Doubleday, 1966, and London, Heinemann, 1967. 419 pp.

Tomasi di Lampedusa, Giuseppe (1896–1957).   The Leopard (*Il gattopardo*). Tr. Archibald Colquhoun. London, Collins, 1960, 254 pp., and N.Y., Pantheon, 1960, 319 pp. Repr. N.Y., New Amer. Lib., 1961; London, Collins, 1963; N.Y., Signet, 1966; N.Y., Pocket Books, 1967.

————Two Stories and a Memory (*Racconti*). Tr. Archibald Colquhoun. London, Collins, 1962, 129 pp., and N.Y., Pantheon, 1962, 189 pp. Repr. London, Fontana Books, 1963; repr. Penguin, 1966.

Tozzi, Federigo (1883–1920).   Three Crosses. Tr. R. Capellero. N.Y., Moffat Yard, 1921. 173 pp.

Trilussa (pseud. of G. A. Salustri, 1873–1950).   Roman Satirical Poems and Their Translations in English. Tr. Grant Showerman. N.Y., Vanni, 1944. 185 pp.
    Tries to convey the spirit of the original.

Ungaretti, Giuseppe (1888—).   Life of a Man. Tr. Allen Mandelbaum. London, H. Hamilton, and N.Y., New Directions, 1958. xv, 163 pp.
    Selections from four volumes of the poetry.

    On Ungaretti, see Glauco Cambon's monograph, *Giuseppe Ungaretti* (Columbia Essays on Modern Writers, 20: N.Y. and London, Columbia Univ. Pr., 1967, 48 pp.).

Vergani, Orio (1899—).   Poor Nigger (*Io, povero negro*). Tr. W. W. Hobson. Indianapolis, Ind., Bobbs-Merrill, 1930. 306 pp.

Vittorini, Elio (1908—).   Conversation in Sicily. Tr. Wilfrid David, with intro. Ernest Hemingway. London, Lindsay Drummond, and N.Y., New Directions, 1949. 164 pp. Repr. Penguin, 1961.

————The Dark and the Light: Erica and La Garibaldina (*Erica e i suoi fratelli, La garibaldina*). Tr. Frances Keene. N.Y., New Directions, 1961. 182 pp. Repr. (with Women on the Road) 1961, see below.

————The Red Carnation. Tr. Anthony Bower. Norfolk, Conn., New Directions, 1952, and London, Weidenfeld, 1953. 244 pp. Repr. N.Y., New Amer. Lib., 1953, 157 pp.

————The Twilight of the Elephant (*Il Sempione strizza l'occhio al Freyjus*). Tr. Cinina Brescia. Norfolk, Conn., New Directions, 1951. 121 pp.

 Tr. Eric Mosbacher as Tune for an Elephant. London, Weidenfeld, 1955. 98 pp.

————Women on the Road: Three Short Novels. Tr. Frances Keene and Bernard Wall. London, Cape, 1961. 240 pp. Repr. London, New English Lib., 1965.
Reprinting the two novelettes, *Erica* and *La garibaldina*, published 1961 as *The Dark and the Light*, above.

Volpini, Flora (1908—). The Woman of Florence. Tr. David Moore. London, Redman, 1955. Repr. London, Mayflower, 1966, 348 pp.

————Yes, Madam (*Comandi Signora*). Tr. David Moore. London, Redman, 1955. 207 pp.

Volponi, Paolo. My Troubles Began (*Memoriale*). Tr. Belén Sevareid. N.Y., Grossman, 1964. 231 pp. Repr. as The Memorandum, London, Calder, 1967.

————The Worldwide Machine (*La macchina mondiale*). Tr. Belén Sevareid. N.Y., Grossman, 1967, and London, Calder, 1969. 213 pp.

Zangrandi, Ruggero (1915—). A Train to the Brenner (*La tradotta del Brennero*). Tr. Roger Wolcott-Behnke. London, Galley, 1963. 288 pp.

Zuccoli, Luciano (1870–1930). Things Greater Than He. Tr. Eloise Parkhurst. N.Y., Holt, 1926. 370 pp.

PORTUGUESE LITERATURE

WILLIAM BERRIEN,
ALFRED HOWER,
GERALD M. MOSER,
AND MARION A. ZEITLIN
REVISED BY BENJAMIN MATHER
WOODBRIDGE, JR.

Atkinson, William C. A History of Spain and Portugal. Penguin, 1960. 382 pp.
> Portuguese culture is treated as an integral part of Iberian civilization. Map, bibliography, index.

Barnes, Wilfrid John. Portugal: Gateway to Greatness. London, Stanford, 1950. xii, 188 pp.

Bell, Aubrey F. G. Portugal of the Portuguese. (Countries and People Series) N.Y., Scribner, and London, Pitman, 1915. 268 pp.
> Ch. 9 contains trs. of extracts from a number of Gil Vicente's plays.

————Portuguese Portraits. Oxford, Blackwell, 1917. 144 pp.
> Biographies of King Dinis, Nun' Alvares, Prince Henry the Navigator, Vasco da Gama, Duarte Pacheco Pereira, Afonso de Albuquerque, and Dom João de Castro.

Campbell, Roy. Portugal. London, Reinhardt, 1957, and Chicago, Ill., Regnery, 1958. 206 pp.
> Includes some verse trs. of Portuguese poetry.

Livermore, Harold V. A History of Portugal. Cambridge, Univ. Pr., 1947. 502 pp. Repr. as A New History of Portugal, 1956, xi, 365 pp.
> Essentially a political history. Illustrations, maps, bibliography.

Namora, Fernando (1919—). Mountain Doctor. Tr. Dorothy Ball. London, Kimber, 1956. 200 pp.

Nowell, Charles E. A History of Portugal. N.Y., Van Nostrand, 1952, and London, Macmillan, 1953. xii, 259 pp.
> Political and cultural history. Illustrations, maps, bibliography.

Oliveira Martins, Joaquim Pedro de.   The Golden Age of Prince Henry the Navigator. Tr. J. J. Abraham and W. E. Reynolds. London, Chapman and Hall, 1914. ix, 324 pp.
A tr. of *Os filhos de D. João I*, with additions and annotations.

————A History of Iberian Civilization. Tr. Aubrey F. G. Bell, pref. Salvador de Madariaga. London and N.Y., Oxford Univ. Pr., 1930. xix, 292 pp.
Attempts to show the unity of Iberian civilization.

Portugal and Brazil, An Introduction.   Ed. H. V. Livermore and W. J. Entwistle. Oxford, Clarendon Pr., and N.Y., Oxford Univ. Pr., 1963. 418 pp.
Various aspects of Portuguese culture, mostly by British scholars. Illustrations, bibliographies.

The Portuguese and the Tropics: Suggestions Inspired by the Portuguese Methods of Integrating Autochthonous Peoples and Cultures. Tr. Helen M. D'O. Matthew and F. De Mello Moser. Lisbon, Executive Committee for Commemoration of the Death of Prince Henry the Navigator, 1961. xi, 296 pp.

Prestage, Edgar.   "The Chivalry of Portugal." Ch. 6, in Chivalry: A Series of Studies to Illustrate Its Historical Significance and Civilizing Influence. Ed. Edgar Prestage. London, Kegan Paul, and N.Y., Knopf, 1928. 231 pp.

————The Portuguese Pioneers. London, Black, and N.Y., Macmillan, 1933. 352 pp.
An account of the Portuguese voyages of discovery to the mid-16th c.

Sérgio, António.   A Sketch of the History of Portugal. Tr. Constantino J. dos Santos. Lisbon, Seara Nova, 1928. 208 pp.

Stanislawski, Dan.   The Individuality of Portugal: A Study of Historical-Political Geography. Austin, Univ. of Texas Pr., 1959. 248 pp.

Wohlrabe, Raymond A., and Krusch, Werner.   Portugal and Her People. Philadelphia, Pa., Lippincott, and London, Lutterworth Pr. (as The Land and People of Portugal), 1965. 128 pp.

Bibliography

Bell, Aubrey F. G.   Portuguese Bibliography. London, Oxford Univ. Pr. for Hispanic Soc. of America, 1922. 381 pp.

> Continued less systematically for 1922–37 by Bell and M. A. Cilley in *Hispania*, vol. 22, 1939, 381–89, and, for scholarship since 1945, more or less triennially by Gerald M. Moser in *Hispania*, vol. 31, 1948, 163–74, and in *Modern Language Journal*, vol. 32, 1948; vol. 35, 1951; vol. 38, 1954; vol. 41, 1957; vol. 44, 1960; vol. 45, 1961; vol. 46, 1962; vol. 50, 1966. Cf. also his "Portuguese Writers of This Century" in *Hispania*, vol. 50, 1967, 947–54. Other current bibliographies of the scholarship of Portuguese literature are included in the annual *Year's Work in Modern Language Studies* (Cambridge, 1930—); and since 1957 in the annual *PMLA* Bibliography.
>
> See also Gerald M. Moser, "African Literature in the Portuguese Language" (with bibliography) in *Journal of General Education*, vol. 13, 1962, 270–304.

Estorninho, Carlos.   "Portuguese Literature in English Translation," in Portugal and Brazil: An Introduction, pp. 129–38 (see above under Background).

> Lists trs. since 1640.

Garcia Peres, D. Domingo.   *Catalogo razonado biográfico y bibliográfico de los autores portugueses que escribieron en castellano.* Madrid, Imprenta del Colegio Nacional de sordo-mudos y de ciegos, 1890. 660 pp.

> Lists more than 600 Portuguese authors who wrote solely or occasionally in Spanish.

Thomas, Henry.   "English Translations of Portuguese Books before 1640." In The Library, ser. 4, vol. 7, 1926, 1–30.

Literary Studies

Bell, Aubrey F. G.   Portuguese Literature. Oxford, Clarendon Pr., 1922. 375 pp.

> The standard work in English. Includes an intro. on the characteristics and problems of Portuguese literature, and an appendix dealing with the literature of the people and with modern Galician literature.

————Studies in Portuguese Literature. Oxford, Blackwell, 1914. xviii, 247 pp.
> Includes representative selections, many with English tr.

Da Cal, Ernesto G. "Portuguese Literature" [since 1870], in Columbia Dictionary of Modern European Literature. N.Y., Columbia Univ. Pr., 1947, pp. 638–43.
> The *Dictionary* includes 36 articles on recent Portuguese writers, principally by Professor Da Cal, also by Gerald M. Moser and Ramón Martinez-López and others.

Figueiredo, Fidelino de. Characteristics of Portuguese Literature. Tr. Constantino José dos Santos. Coimbra, Imprensa da Universidade, 1916. 43 pp.
> Lists as the most striking characteristics: the cycle of discoveries; predominance of lyricism; frequency of epic taste; scarcity of drama; absence of both the philosophical and the critical spirit; aloofness from the public; a certain mysticism of thought and sentiment.

Collections

Campbell, Roy. The Collected Poems. III. Translations. London, Bodley Head, 1960. 144 pp.
> Includes trs. of 13 Portuguese poets from the Middle Ages to the present.

Cancioneiro da Ajuda. Ed. and tr. Carolina Michaëlis de Vasconcelos into German. Halle, Niemeyer, 1904. 2 vols.
> This collection of lyrics, made about 1350, is the oldest preserved not only in Portuguese but in any language of the Iberian peninsula.

Coelho, Francisco Adolfo. Tales of Old Lusitania, from the Folk-Lore of Portugal. Tr. H. Monteiro. London, Sonnenschein, 1885. 190 pp.

Folk-Lore from the Cape Verde Islands. Ed. Elsie Clews Parsons. Memoirs of the American Folk-Lore Society, vol. 15, 1923. 2 vols.
> With the music. vol. 1, Folk-Tales in English; vol. 2, Folk-Tales in Portuguese (Storia Belh), Proverbs and Sayings, Riddles. The material was collected in 1916–17 from Portuguese mulatto immigrants.

Folk Music and Poetry of Spain and Portugal. Ed. Kurt Schindler. N.Y., Hispanic Institute, 1941. 985 selections of music, 127 pp.
  Words and music for some 60 Portuguese folk songs.

*Gallop, Rodney. Portugal: A Book of Folk-Ways. Cambridge, Univ. Pr., 1936. 291 pp. Repr. 1961.

Lusitania Illustrata: Notices on the History, Antiquities, Literature, etc., of Portugal. Tr. John Adamson. Literary Department, part 1. Newcastle-upon-Tyne, T. and J. Hodgson, 1842. 100 pp.
  Trs. of sonnets by A. Ferreira, Camões, Diogo Bernardes, Agostinho da Cruz, Violante do Céu, Bocage, and others, with biographical sketches of the authors.

Odyssey Review, vol. 3, no. 2, June 1963.
  Includes a short story by Domingos Monteiro, six poems by Alexandre O'Neill, and a play by José Régio.

Poems from the Portuguese. Tr. Aubrey F. G. Bell. Oxford, Blackwell, 1913. 131 pp., parallel texts.

The Poets and Poetry of Europe. Ed. Henry Wadsworth Longfellow. Philadelphia and Cambridge, Mass., 1845. 779 pp. Many reprs. to 1896.
  Among the Portuguese authors represented are Bernardin Ribeiro, Gil Vicente, Sá de Miranda, Camões, Diogo Bernardes, Bocage, and Almeida Garrett. The trs. are by Adamson, Bowring, Mrs. Hemans, Thomas Roscoe, and Strangford.

Portugal: An Anthology. Tr. George Young, pref. (in Portuguese) Teofilo Braga. Oxford, Clarendon Pr., 1916. 168 pp.

Portuguese Folk-Tales. Ed. Zofimo Consiglieri Pedroso, and tr. Henriqueta Monteiro. Publications of the Folk-Lore Society, London, vol. 9, 1882. 124 pp.

Portuguese Poems and Translations. Tr. Leonard S. Downes. Lisbon, no pub., 1947. 58 pp.

Portuguese Poems with Translations. Ed. J. B. Trend. Cambridge, Dolphin Book Co., 1954. 32 pp.

Selections from Contemporary Portuguese Poetry: A Bilingual Collection. Ed. Jean R. Longland, intro. Ernesto Da Cal. N.Y., Harvey House, 1965. 96 pp.

Portuguese Voyages 1498–1663. Ed. Charles D. Ley. EL, 1947. xxii, 360 pp.

> Trs. of excerpts from Vasco da Gama, Mendes Pinto, Francisco Alvares, Jeronimo Lobo, and others.

Sonnets from the Portuguese. Comp. and ed. J. Silvado Bueno. Recife, Brazil, Dutch-Alley Pr., 1933. 95 pp.
> Various poets and translators.

The Tragic History of the Sea, 1589–1622. Compiled by Bernardo Gomes de Brito. Tr. C. R. Boxer. Hakluyt Society Works, ser. 2, no. 112, 1959. 297 pp.

Early Period:
Thirteenth to Sixteenth Centuries

Many important Portuguese writers wrote in Latin or Spanish. The works of those who wrote in Latin are edited in the *Collecção das obras de auctores classicos portuguezes que escreveram em latin* (Coimbra, 1791–93, 16 vols.). Those who wrote in Spanish are listed in the Garcia Peres Catálogo, above. Some important Portuguese works are known only in a Spanish tr.: the *Amadís de Gaula*, ascribed to Vasco de Lobeira, known in the Spanish version by Garciordóñez de Montalvo (published Saragossa, 1508); *Palmeirin de Inglaterra*, by Francisco de Morais (published in a lost edition of 1544), known in a Spanish tr. (Toledo, 1547–48). The *Diana* (Valencia, 1559) was written in Spanish by a Portuguese author, Jorge de Montemayor (originally Montemôr). For English trs. of these works, see Spanish Literature.

INDIVIDUAL AUTHORS

Albuquerque, Brás (1500–1580).   The Commentaries of the Great Afonso Dalboquerque, Second Viceroy of India. Tr. Walter de Gray Birch. Hakluyt Society Works, nos. 53, 55, 62, 69,: 1875–84. Repr. N.Y., Burt Franklin, 1963.

Alvares, Francisco (c.1470–c.1540).   Narrative of the Portuguese Embassy to Abyssinia during the Years 1520–27. Tr. Lord Stanley of Alderley. Hakluyt Society Works, no. 64, 1881. 416 pp. Re-ed. (with additions from ms.) C. F. Beckingham and G. W. B. Huntingford, as The Prester John of the Indies, ibid., 2d ser., nos. 114–15, 1961.

This first modern description of Abyssinia was also abridged in an English tr. in Samuel Purchas, *Purchas his Pilgrimes* (1625).

Azurara.   See Zurara.

Barbosa, Duarte (c.1480–1521).   Account of the Countries Bordering on the Indian Ocean and Their Inhabitants. Tr. Mansel L. Dames. Hakluyt Society Works, ser. 2, nos. 44, 49, London 1918, 1921.

An earlier tr. from the Spanish version was made by H. E. J. Stanley, ibid., ser. 1, no. 35, 1866, 236 pp.

Barros, Joâo de (1496–1570).   *Decada*. in The Voyages of Cadamosto and Other Documents on Western Africa in the Second Half of the Fifteenth Century. Tr. G. R. Crone. Hakluyt Society Works, ser. 2, no. 80, 1937.

About 10 chs. of Barros' first *Decada*.

————The History of Ceylon from the Earliest Times to 1600 A.D. Tr. Donald Ferguson. Colombo, H. M. Richards, 1909. 445 pp.

Repr. from Journal of the Royal Asiatic Society, Ceylon Branch, vol. 20, no. 60, 1908. This is a tr. of portions of the monumental history of the Portuguese in Asia, entitled the *Asia*. Barros completed four Decades, and Diogo da Couto added eight more, the complete work being published by 1788. An abridged tr. into German was made by D. W. Soltau (1821, 5 vols.), but the two selections above are the only trs. into English.

Camões, Luis de (1524–1580).   The Lusiads. Tr. verse (octaves) by Sir Richard Fanshawe. London, 1655. 224 pp. Repr. ed. J. D. M. Ford, Cambridge, Mass., Harvard Univ. Pr., 1940, xxix, 307 pp. Repr. ed. Geoffrey Bullough (with Fanshawe's ms. corrections), London, Centaur Pr., 1963, and Carbondale, Southern Illinois Univ. Pr., 1964, 352 pp.

Tr. verse (heroic couplets) William John Mickle. Oxford and London, 1776. clxvii, 484 pp. Reprs. to 1877, including repr. in Chalmers' English Poets, vol. 21, 1810.

Tr. verse Thomas Moore Musgrave. London, Murray, 1826. xxi, 585 pp.

Tr. T. Livingston Mitchell. London, Boone, 1854. xxix, 310 pp.

Tr. verse J.J. Aubertin. London, Kegan Paul, 1878. 2 vols., parallel texts.

Tr. verse Sir Richard F. Burton. London, Quaritch, 1880. 2 vols.

Tr. verse (Spenserian stanzas) Robert French Duff. Lisbon and London, 1880. xlviii, 506 pp.

*Tr. verse Leonard Bacon. N.Y., Hispanic Society of America, 1950. xxxii, 435 pp.

Tr. prose William C. Atkinson. Penguin, 1952. 248 pp.

————The Lyricks (*Rhythmas*). Tr. Sir Richard F. Burton. London, Quaritch, 1884. 540 pp.

Selections from the lyrics were tr. Viscount Strangford as *Poems* (London, 1803 et seq., 159 pp.); J. J. Aubertin as *Seventy Sonnets* (London, Kegan Paul, 1881, xxiii, 253 pp., parallel texts); Richard Garnett (forty sonnets, in *Dante, Petrarch, Camoens: 124 Sonnets*, London, Lane, 1896, xii, 147 pp.); Edgar Prestage (*The Passion of Christ, Two Elegies*: Watford, 1924, 21 pp.; and *Minor Works*: London, 1924, 30 pp.); in various Collections, see above; and by Henry H. Hart in the commentary, below.

On Camões, see Aubrey F. G. Bell, *Luis de Camões* (Hispanic Notes and Monographs: London, Oxford Univ. Pr., 1923, 160 pp.); Henry H. Hart, *Luis de Camoëns and the "Epic of the Lusiads"* (Norman, Univ. of Oklahoma Pr., 1962, 335 pp.); William J. Freitas, *Camoens and his Epic: A Historic, Geographic, and Cultural Survey* (Stanford, Calif., Institute of Hispanic American and Luso-Brazilian Studies, Stanford Univ., 1962, 227 pp.).

Castanheda, Fernão Lopes de (c.1500–1559). The First Booke of the Historie of the Discouerie and Conquest of the East Indies. Tr. Nicholas

Lichfeild. London, East, 1582. 164 pp. Repr. modernized, in Robert Kerr, A General History and Collection of Voyages and Travels (Edinburgh, 1811, vol. 2, pp. 292–504).

No more of the eight books has been tr.

Castanhoso, Miguel de (d. 1565?).   The Portuguese Expedition to Abyssinia in 1541–43, as Narrated by Castanhoso, etc. Tr. R. S. Whiteway. Hakluyt Society Works, ser. 2, no. 10, 1902. pp. 3–104.

Correia, Gaspar (c.1495–c.1555).   The Three Voyages of Vasco da Gama and His Viceroyalty. Tr. H. E. J. Stanley. Hakluyt Society Works, no. 42, 1869. 430 pp. Repr. N.Y., Burt Franklin, 1963.

Part tr. of the *Lendas da India*.

Ferreira, António (1528–1569).   Ignez de Castro: A Tragedy (*A Castro*). Tr. verse Thomas Moore Musgrave. London, Murray, 1825. iv, 179 pp.

The best classical tragedy written in Portugal in the 16th c. An English adaptation written by Catherine Cockburn (later Trotter) as *Agnes de Castro*, was produced at Drury Lane in 1695, and published (London, 1696). A later adaptation by the Portuguese playwright Domingos de Reis Quita was tr. by Benjamin Thompson as *Ignez de Castro* (London, 1800); and another by Nicolau Luis was tr. John Adamson as *Dona Ignez de Castro* (London, 1808).

A comedy by Ferreira, *O Cioso*, is reported as tr. into English in 1825, but has not been located.

Galvão, António (1490–1557).   The Discoveries of the World. Tr. anon. for Richard Hakluyt. London, Bishop, 1601. 97 pp. Repr. ed. C. R. D. Bethune, Hakluyt Society Works, no. 30, 1862, 242 pp., parallel texts; repr. N.Y., Burt Franklin, 1963.

Góis, Damião de (1502–1574).   See Neo-Latin Literature, vol. 1, above.

Holanda, Francisco de (1518–1584).   Four Dialogues on Painting. Tr. Aubrey F. G. Bell. London, Oxford Univ. Pr., 1928. 110 pp.

Partial tr. of the *Tratado da pintura antiga*, containing conversations with Michelangelo and Vittoria Colonna in Rome. An English tr. of the first three dialogues is contained in Charles Holroyd, *Michael Angelo Buonarroti* (London, 1903).

Jesus, Tomé de (?1529–1582).   The Sufferings of the Son of God. Tr. Richard Welton from the French version. London, 1720–21.

Tr. anon. from the French version. London, 1753.

Tr. Mr. and Mrs. E. B. Pusey. Oxford, Parker, and London, Rivingtons, n.d. 2 vols.

Lopes, Fernão (?1380–?1460).   The Chronicles of Fernão Lopes and Gomes Eannes de Zurara, with translated extracts, by Edgar Prestage. Watford, Voss and Michael, 1928. 99 pp.
Brief extracts from the *Cronica del Rey D. Joham* (mid-15th c.).

Magalhães Gandavo, Pero de (16th c.).   The Histories of Brazil. Ed. facs. and tr. John B. Stetson, Jr. Documents and Narratives Concerning the Discovery and Conquest of Latin America, no. 5. N.Y., Cortes Society, 1922. 2 vols.

Trs. of the *Historia da provincia Sācta Cruz*, and of *Tratado da terra do Brasil.*

Mendes Pinto, Fernão (1509–1583).   The Voyages and Adventures of Fernand Mendez Pinto. Tr. Henry Cogan. London, 1653. 326 pp. Repr. 1663; 1692; (abridged) London, Unwin, 1891, 464 pp., repr. 1897; facs. repr. of 1653 tr., London, Dawsons, 1969, 318 pp.

A part tr. was published by Samuel Purchas, *Purchas his Pilgrimes*, 1625.

Orta, Garcia da (c.1495–c.1570).   Colloquies on the Simples and Drugs of India. Tr. Sir Clements Markham. London, Sotheran, 1913. 508 pp.
Also known as *ab Horto* and *du Jardin*. Much of the material of the *Coloquios* was incorporated in the Spanish work of José de Acosta, *Historia Natural y Moral de las Indias* (1590), which was tr. into English by Edward Grimston, London 1604.

Osório, Jerónimo (1506–1580).   See Neo-Latin Literature, vol. 1, above.

Pacheco Pereira, Duarte (?1465–?1533).   *Esmeraldo de Situ Orbis*. Tr. George H. T. Kimble. Hakluyt Society Works, ser. 2, no. 79, 1937. 193 pp.
This cosmography, completed 1508, remained in ms. until 1892.

Pires, Tomé (c.1468–1540). *Suma Oriental*, An Account of the East, from the Red Sea to Japan, Written in Malacca and India in 1512–1515. Ed. and tr. from ms., together with Francisco Rodrigues, Rutter [routier] of A Voyage in the Red Sea, by Armando Cortesão. Hakluyt Society Works, ser. 2, nos. 89, 90: 1944.

[Soto, Hernando de]. Virginia Richly Valued, by the Description of . . . Florida . . . out of the foure yeers continuall Trauell and Discouerie . . . of Don Ferdinando de Soto . . . Written by a Portugall gentleman of Eluas. Tr. Richard Hakluyt. London, 1609. Repr. 1611; 1688 (with additions) as A Relation of the Invasion and Conquest of Florida by the Spaniards; repr. (with additions), ed. W. B. Rye as The Discovery and Conquest of Terra Florida, Hakluyt Society, Works, no. 9, 1851, which repr. N.Y., Burt Franklin, 1963.

> Tr. Buckingham Smith in Narratives of the Career of Hernando de Soto in the Conquest of Florida as Told by a Knight of Elvas. N.Y., Bradford Club, 1866. 324 pp. Repr., ed. Edward G. Bourne, in Narratives of the Career of Hernando de Soto, N.Y., Allerton, 1904, 2 vols., repr. 1922.

> Facs. ed. and tr. James Alexander Robertson as True Relation of the Hardships Suffered by Governor de Soto and Certain Portuguese Gentlemen during the Discovery of the Province of Florida. Deland, Florida State Historical Society, 1933. 2 vols.

Usque, Samuel (fl. 1553). A Consolation for the Tribulation of Israel. Tr. (third dialogue) Gershon I. Gelbart. N.Y., Bloch Pub. Co., 1964. xi, 458 pp.

> Tr. Martin A. Cohen. Philadelphia, Jewish Pub. Co., 1965. xiii, 354 pp.

> > The Portuguese original was ostensibly pub. in Ferrara in 1553, but is now thought to have been actually pub. in Amsterdam c. 1600.

Vaz de Caminha, Pedro (early 16th c.). The Voyage of Pedro Alvares Cabral to Brazil and India [1503]. Tr. William B. Greenlee (with other documents). Hakluyt Society Works, ser. 2, no. 81, 1938. lxix, 228 pp.

Vicente, Gil (c.1465–1536?). (Eight plays). Trs. various from the original Spanish, in Early Spanish Plays, ed. Robert O'Brien. N.Y., Las Américas, 1964: see Spanish Literature, Collections.

> Vol. 1: *Cassandra the Sibyl*, tr. Rachel Benson; *The Ship of Hell* (a trilogy), tr. A. F. G. Bell, q.v. below s.v.

Vol. 2: *The Sailor's Wife* (*Auto da India*); *Serenade*; *The Three Wise Men*; *The Widower's Comedy*, all tr. Jill Booty. Repr. from Tulane Drama Review, vol. 5, no. 3, 1960, 160–86.

————Four Plays. Tr. Aubrey F. G. Bell. Cambridge, Univ. Pr., 1920. 98 pp. *The Soul's Journey* (*Auto da alma*); *Exhortation to War*; *The Carriers* (*Farsa dos Almocreves*); and *Tragicomedia pastoril da Serra da Estrella*. For other trs. of these plays, see the extracts in Bell's *Portugal of the Portuguese*, in Background, above, and in *Portugal: An Anthology*, in Collections, above.

————Lyrics. Tr. Aubrey F. G. Bell. Oxford, Blackwell, 1914. 129 pp., parallel texts. Repr. enlarged 1921, 132 pp.; repr. Watford, Voss and Michael, 1925.
The poems are taken from the plays.

————The Play of the Sibyl Cassandra. Tr. Georgiana G. King. Bryn Mawr, Pa., Bryn Mawr College, and N.Y., Longmans, 1921.

————The Ship of Hell. Tr. A. F. Gerald (pseud. of Aubrey F. G. Bell). Watford, 1929. 98 pp. Repr. in Early Spanish Plays, see first entry, above. The trilogy consisting of *Barca do Inferno*, *Barca do Purgatorio*, and *Barca da Gloria* (in Spanish). The tr. of the first play was repr. Lisbon, Agência Geral do Ultramar, 1954, 35 pp.

On the author, see Aubrey F. G. Bell, *Gil Vicente* (Hispanic Notes and Monographs, London, Oxford Univ. Pr., 1921, 70 pp.).

Zurara, Gomes Eannes de (c.1410–1474). The Chronicle of the Discovery and Conquest of Guinea. Tr. Charles Raymond Beazley and Edgar Prestage. Hakluyt Society Works, nos. 95, 100: 1896–99. Repr. N.Y., Burt Franklin, 1964.

Tr. abridged Bernard Miall as The Conquests and Discoveries of Henry the Navigator: Being the Chronicles of Azurara. London, Allen and Unwin, 1936. 253 pp.

Seventeenth and Eighteenth Centuries

INDIVIDUAL AUTHORS

Alcoforado, Marianna (1640–1723).   The Letters of a Portuguese Nun. Tr. Edgar Prestage. London, Nutt, 1893. 209 pp. Repr. 1897, 80 pp.; 1903, 75 pp.

> The first ed. reprinted the original *Lettres Portugaises* (published in French), and also the English verse tr. of 1713.

> Tr. Donald E. Ericson. N.Y., Crown, 1941. 66 pp.

Sir Roger L'Estrange was the first English tr. of the *Letters* (1678). Twelve more trs. are recorded to 1731; a tr. by W. R. Bowles was published N.Y., 1904.

The *Letters* are now thought fiction, originating in France: see Frederick C. Green, in *Modern Language Review*, vol. 21, 1926, 159–67.

Costa, Uriel da (c.1580–1640).   (Writings). Tr. Carl Gebhardt into German as *Schriften*. Bibliotheca Spinoziana, t. 2. Amsterdam, Hertzberger, 1922. 285 pp.

> The *Propostas contra a tradicão*; *Sobre a mortalidade da alma*; *Exemplar humanae vitae*.

Faria e Sousa, Manuel de (1590–1649).   The History of Portugal . . . to the Year 1640 (*Europa Portuguesa*). Tr. John Stevens (and continued to the year 1698). London, 1698. 572 pp.

————The Portuguese Asia; or, The History of the Discovery and Conquest of India by the Portuguese (*Asia Portuguesa*). Tr. John Stevens (and somewhat compressed). London, 1695. 3 vols.

Faria e Sousa wrote his histories in Spanish.

Freire de Andrada, Jacinto (1597–1657).   The Life of Dom John de Castro, the Fourth Vice-Roy of India [1545–48]. Tr. Sir Peter Wyche. London, 1664. Repr. 1693, 272 pp.; (Broadway Travellers), 1929.
The work is called grandiloquent.

Freire de Andrade, Rui (d. 1633).   Commentaries of Ruy Freyre de Andrada . . . His Exploits from 1619 [as general of the Persian Gulf]. Tr. C. R. Boxer. Broadway Travellers. London, Routledge, and N.Y., McBride, 1930. lvi, 328 pp.

Lacerda e Almeida, Francisco José Maria de (d. 1798).   The Lands of Cazembe: Lacerda's Journey to Cazembe in 1798 [in an attempted east-west crossing of southern Africa]. Tr. Captain Richard F. Burton. London, Royal Geographical Society, 1873. vii, 271 pp.

Lobo, Jerónimo (1593–1678).   A Short Relation of the River Nile. Tr. Sir Peter Wyche from ms. (a part of the work later published in French as *Voyage historique d'Abissinie*). London, 1669. 105 pp. Repr. 1673, 1798.

Tr. Samuel Johnson from the French (as an abridged version of the whole work) as A Voyage to Abyssinia. London, 1735. 396 pp.

Manrique, Frei Sebastiâo (d. 1664).   Travels . . . 1629–1643 (*Itinerário de las Missiones Orientales*). Tr. C. Eckford Luard, assisted by H. Hosten, S.J. Hakluyt Society Works, ser. 2, nos. 59, 61: 1926–27.

Melo, Francisco Manuel de (1608–1666).   The Government of a Wife. Tr. John Stevens. London, 1697. xxiii, 240 pp.

Tr. of *Carta de guia de casados*, with a letter written by Antonio de Guevara. Extracts are tr. by Edgar Prestage, in his *D. Francisco Manuel de Mello*, see below.

————Relics of Melodino. Tr. Edward Lawson from Spanish and Portuguese ms. London, Baldwin Cradock, 1815. 244 pp. Repr. 1820.
The Musas de Melodino (part 1, Spanish; part 2, Portuguese). Melo's *Auto da fidalgo aprendiz*, the only good play of the century, is not tr.

On the author, see Edgar Prestage, *D. Francisco Manuel de Mello* (Hispanic Notes and Monographs, London, Oxford Univ. Pr., 1922, 98 pp.).

Pereira de Figueiredo, Pe. António (1725–1797). A Narrative of the Earthquake and Fire of Lisbon (*Comentário Latino e Portuguez sobre o Terramoto e Incendio de Lisboa*). Tr. anon. from the Latin. London, Hawkins, 1756.

Ribeiro, João. History of Ceylon Presented by Captain John Ribeyro to the King of Portugal in 1685 (*Fatalidade Histórica da Ilha de Ceylão*). Tr. George Lee from the French version of Abbé LeGrand. Colombo, Government Pr., 1847. 247 pp.

> Tr. P. E. Pieris as Ribeiro's History of Ceilão (with other documents). Colombo, Apothecaries Co., 1909. xvii, 416 pp. Repr. 1925 as The Historic Tragedy of the Island of Ceilão, xx, 276 pp. Repr. 1948.

Semmedo, Lavaro, S.J. (1585–1658). The History of that Great and Renowned Monarchy of China. Tr. anon. London, 1655. Repr. 1670.

> Tr. from an Italian version (1643) of the first published edition of the *Relaçam*, a Spanish tr. (1642) by Faria e Sousa.

Sousa, Frei Luis de (name in religion of Manuel de Sousa Countinho, 1555–1632). The Life of Dom Bartholomew of the Martyrs [Archbishop of Braga]. Tr. Lady Herbert. London, 1880.

Nineteenth and Twentieth Centuries

INDIVIDUAL AUTHORS

Almeida Garrett, J. B. de (1799–1854). Brother Luiz de Sousa. Tr. Edgar Prestage. London, E. Mathews, 1909. 137 pp.
Perhaps the best Portuguese prose drama.

———Camoëns. Tr. Henri Faure into French. Paris, A. Quantin, 1880. xiv, 221 pp.
A poem in blank verse marking the beginning of romanticism in Portugal.

————*Romanceiro.*

Several ballads were tr. in the Longfellow anthology, see above. A few other lyrics were tr. by Bell in *Studies in Portuguese Literature*, see above.

Câmara, João da (1852–1908). The Packet-Boat. Tr. Edgar Prestage. Oxford, 1923. 21 pp.

Castelo Branco, Camilo (1825–1890). *Amor de perdición.* Tr. Blanco Suárez into Spanish. Colección Austral, 582. Buenos Aires and Mexico, Espasa-Calpe, 1946. 214 pp.

Also tr. into Italian (1883) and Swedish (1887): a perennially favorite novel of passion.

Castro, Eugénio de (1869–1944). Dona Briolanja and Other Poems. Tr. Leonard Downes. Lisbon, n. pub., 1944. 51 pp.

The outstanding symbolist poet of Portugal. Some poems were early tr. into English by Bell, in *Studies in Portuguese Literature*, see above.

Dantas, Julio (1877–1962). The Cardinals' Collation. Freely adapted H. A. Saintsbury. London, Cecil Palmer, 1926. 25 pp.

————The Fountain and the Satyr. Tr. E. W. Olmsted and F. D. Burnet, in Poet Lore, vol. 21 (1910), pp. 68–94 (a lyrical one-act verse play).

Roses All the Year Round is reported tr. in 1912, but the tr. has not been located.

Delgado, Humberto (1906–1965). The Memoirs. London, Cassel, 1964. xii, 234 pp.

Deus, João de (1830–1896). Some trs. of his lyrics in Bell, *Studies in Portuguese Literature*, and also in *Portugal: An Anthology*, see Collections above.

Diniz, Júlio (pseud. of Joaquim Guilherme Gomes Coelho, 1839–1871). Aunt Philomela. Tr. Luis Marques. Philadelphia, Pa., McKay, and London, Harrap, 1927. 55, 55 pp., parallel texts.

————The Fidalgos of Casa Mourisca. Tr. R. L. Dabney. Boston, Mass., Lothrop, 1891. 399 pp.

Eça de Queiroz, José Maria de (1845–1900). The City and the Mountains. Tr. Roy Campbell. London, Reinhardt, 1955. 217 pp. Repr. Philadelphia, Pa., Dufour, 1962; Athens, Ohio Univ. Pr., 1967.

————Dragon's Teeth (*O primo Basílio*). Tr. Mary J. Serrano. Boston, Mass., Ticknor, 1889. 516 pp.

Tr. Roy Campbell as Cousin Bazilio. London, Reinhardt, 1953. 296 pp. Repr. N.Y., Noonday Pr., 1956, 343 pp., and paper.

Often called the Portuguese *Madame Bovary*.

————The Illustrious House of Ramires. Tr. Ann Stevens. Athens, Ohio Univ. Pr., 1968. 310 pp.

————José Mathias, and A Man of Talent. Tr. Luis Marques. London, Harrap, 1947. 94 pp., parallel texts.
José Mathias is a story from the *Contos*. *A Man of Talent* is a fictional letter in *A Correspondência de Fradique Mendes*: it was apparently tr. as *Pacheco* by Edgar Prestage (Oxford, 1922, 19 pp.).

————The Maias. Tr. Patricia McGowan Pinheiro and Ann Stevens. London, Bodley Head, and N.Y., St. Martin's Pr., 1965. 633 pp.

————The Mandarin and Other Stories. Tr. Richard Franko Goldman. Athens, Ohio Univ. Pr., 1965, and London, Bodley Head, 1966. viii, 76 pp.

————Our Lady of the Pillar (*O Defunto*). Tr. Edgar Prestage. London, Constable, 1906. 88 pp. (from the *Contos*).

————Perfection. Tr. Charles Marriott. London, Selwyn & Blount, 1923. 43 pp. (a story from the *Contos*).

————The Relic. Tr. Aubrey F. G. Bell. N.Y., Knopf, 1925. 289 pp. Repr. with intro. John Garrett Underhill, 1930; repr. with intro. Francis Steegmuller, N.Y., Noonday Pr., 1954, 289 pp., and London, Reinhardt, 1954, 231 pp.

————The Sin of Father Amaro. Tr. Nan Flanagan. London, Reinhardt, 1962, and N.Y., St. Martin's Pr., 1963. 352 pp.

————The Sweet Miracle. Tr. Edgar Prestage. London, Nutt, 1904. 36 pp. Repr. 1905; Portland, Me., Mosher, 1906, 33 pp.; Oxford, 1914; Oxford and N.Y., 1916.

Tr. A. de Alberti. London, Nutt, 1913. 30 pp.

A tale from the *Contos*. A drama adaptation by Alberto d'Oliveira and Bernardo Pindela (1902) was tr. by the Sisters of Notre Dame (Edinburgh, Sands, 1910, 32 pp.), and by Henry Gaffney, with intro. Edgar Prestage (Dublin, Talbot Pr., 1928, 40 pp.).

Ferreira de Castro, José Maria (1898—).　Emigrants: A Novel. Tr. Dorothy Ball. N.Y. and London, Macmillan, 1964. 284 pp.

————Jungle: A Tale of the Amazon Rubber-Trappers (*A selva*). Tr. Charles Duff. N.Y., Viking, and London, Lovat Dickson, 1935. xi, 340 pp.

————The Mission. Tr. Ann Stevens. London, H. Hamilton, 1963. 126 pp.

Herculano de Carvalho e Aráujo, Alexandre (1810–1877).　History of the Origin and Establishment of the Inquisition in Portugal. Tr. J. C. Branner. Stanford Univ. Pub. in History, etc., vol. 1, no. 2, 1926, pp. 189–636.

A vindication of scientific history against clerical attacks, written by the foremost Portuguese historian of the 19th c. His historical fiction has been tr. into German: *Eurico o Presbytero*, tr. G. Heine as *Eurich der Priester der Gothen* (Leipzig, 1847); *Lendas e Narrativas*, same tr. and date.

Lacerda, Alberto de (1928—).　77 Poems. Tr. Alberto de Lacerda and Arthur Waley. London, Allen and Unwin, 1955. 85 pp., parallel texts.

Mello, Pedro Homem de (1904—).　Lusitanian Lyrics. Tr. Arnold G. Hawkins. Porto, Lello, 1941. 92 pp.

Monteiro, Luis de Sttau.　The Rules of the Game (*Angustia para o jantar*). Tr. Ann Stevens. London, Putnam, 1964, and N.Y., Knopf, 1965 (as A Man of Means). 188 pp.

Oliveira Martins, Joaquim Pedro de (1845–1894).　The England of Today. Tr. C. J. Willdey. (As Others See Us, vol. 1) London, Allen, 1896. 335 pp. An unfavorable report. For his historical works, see Background, above.

Paço d'Arcos, Joaquim (1908—). *La forêt de ciment: Grandeur et misère des Etats-Unis* (*A floresta de cimento*). Tr. Jean-B. Haupt into French. Paris, Nouvelles Editions Latines, 1958. 288 pp.

——————Memoirs of a Banknote. Tr. Robert Lyle. Chicago, Ill., Regnery, 1968. 180 pp.

——————Nostalgia (*Poemas imperfeitos*). Tr. verse Roy Campbell. London, Sylvan Pr., 1960. 51 pp.

Quental, Antero Tarquínio de (1842–1891). Sixty-four Sonnets. Tr. Edgar Prestage. London, Nutt, 1894. xiv, 133 pp.
    *Tr. S. Griswold Morley as Sonnets and Poems. Berkeley, Univ. of California Pr., 1922. 133 pp.

    Trs. also in Bell, and in Young, in Collections, above.

Rebêllo da Silva, Luís Augusto (1822–1871). The Last Bull-Fight at Salvaterra. Tr. Edgar Prestage. London, 1909. 15 pp.
    The best-known historical short-story in Portuguese, one of the *Contos e lendas.*

Redol, Antonio Alves (1911—). The Man with Seven Names (*A barca dos sete lemes*). Tr. Linton L. Barrett. N.Y., Knopf, 1964. 381 pp.

Ribeiro, Aquilino (1885—). When the Wolves Howl. Tr. Patricia McGowan Pinheiro. London, Cape, and N.Y., Macmillan, 1963. 288 pp.

Serpa Pinto, Alexandre Alberto de la Rocha (1846–1900). How I Crossed Africa: From the Atlantic to the Indian Ocean (*De Angola a Contra-costa*). Tr. Alfred Elwes from the ms. London, 1881. 2 vols.

Torga, Miguel (pseud. of Adolfo Rocha, 1907—). Farrusco the Blackbird, and Other Stories. Tr. Denis Brass. London, Allen and Unwin, 1950, and N.Y., Arts Inc., 1951. 93 pp.

Trindade Coelho, José Francisco de (1861–1908). *Mes Amours: contes et ballades* (*Os meus amores*). Tr. A. Savine into French. Paris, 1928.

BRAZILIAN LITERATURE

WILLIAM BERRIEN,
JOHN MORTON FEIN,
AND
BENJAMIN MATHER WOODBRIDGE, JR.
REVISED BY
BENJAMIN MATHER WOODBRIDGE, JR.

Many of the entries under Spanish American Literature, below, include material on Brazilian, especially those labeled Latin American.

Background

Armitage, John. The History of Brazil [1808–1931]. London, Smith Elder, 1836. 2 vols.
A continuation of Southey's *History of Brazil*, see below.

Azevedo, Fernando de. Brazilian Culture: An Introduction to the Study of Culture in Brazil. Tr. William Rex Crawford. N.Y., Macmillan, 1950. 562 pp.
An important historical survey by an eminent sociologist. Numerous and varied illustrations, bibliographies.

Bello, José Maria. A History of Modern Brazil. Tr. James L. Taylor. Stanford, Calif., Stanford Univ. Pr., 1966. xix, 362 pp.

Brant, Alice. The Diary of "Helena Morley." Tr. Elizabeth Bishop. N.Y., Farrar Straus, 1957, and London, Gollancz, 1958. 281 pp.
Provincial life in the late 19th century.

Brazil. Ed. Lawrence F. Hill. UN Series. Berkeley, Univ. of California Pr., 1947. 394 pp.
Chs. by many hands on various aspects of Brazilian culture. The ch. on literature is by Samuel Putnam. Bibliographies.

Brazil, Portrait of Half a Continent. Ed. Thomas Lynn Smith and Alexander Merchant. N.Y., Dryden Pr., 1951. 466 pp.
Essays by Brazilian and American scholars on social, economic, political, and cultural aspects. The essay on literature is by Earl W. Thomas. Illustrations, bibliographical references.

Calógeras, João Pandiá. A History of Brazil. Tr. Percy A. Martin. Inter-
Amer. Hist. Ser. Chapel Hill, Univ. North Carolina Pr., 1939. Repr.
N.Y., Russell, 1963, 374 pp.
> Excellent for political history, not for social and cultural aspects.

Castedo, Leopoldo. The Baroque Prevalence in Brazilian Art. N.Y., Frank,
1964. 151 pp.
> Illustrations, bibliography.

*Chase, Gilbert. A Guide to the Music of Latin America. See Spanish
American Literature.

──────Concerning Latin American Culture. Ibid.
> Includes Gilberto Freyre, "Some Aspects of the Social Development of
> Portuguese America"; Robert C. Smith, "Brazilian Art"; William
> Berrien, "Some Considerations Regarding Contemporary Latin American
> Music."

Contemporary Latin American Philosophy. Ed. Aníbal Sánchez Reulet,
tr. Willard R. Trask. Albuquerque, Univ. of New Mexico Pr., 1954. 285 pp.
> Includes selections from Farias Brito, Graça Aranha, and Jackson de
> Figueiredo.

Corrêa da Costa, Sérgio. Every Inch a King: A Biography of Dom Pedro I,
First Emperor of Brazil. Tr. Samuel Putnam. N.Y., Macmillan, 1950.
230 pp.
> Colorful biography of an impetuous prince devoted to his people.

Corrêa de Azevedo, Luiz Heitor. *A Música Brasileira e Seus Fundamentos*. [Brief
History of Music in Brazil. Tr. Elizabeth M. Tylor and Mercedes de Moura
Reis.] Music Series, no. 16. Washington, Pan American Union, 1948.
92 pp. (with music and bibliographies).

*Costa, Luiz Edmundo da. Rio in the Time of the Viceroys [1763–1808].
Tr. Dorothea H. Momsen, with intro. Hugh Gibson. Rio de Janeiro,
J. R. de Oliveira, 1936. 353 pp.
> A scholarly work attractively presented.

Crawford, William Rex. A Century of Latin American Thought. See Spanish
American Literature.

Includes a chapter on Euclydes da Cunha, Manoel Bomfim, and Gilberto Freyre.

Cruz Costa, João.   A History of Ideas in Brazil: The Development of Philosophy in Brazil and the Evolution of National History. Tr. Suzette Macedo. Berkeley, Univ. of California Pr., 1964. 427 pp.
Authoritative, scholarly treatment.

Freyre, Gilberto de Mello (1900—).   Brazil: An Interpretation. N.Y., Knopf, 1945. vi, 175, ix pp. Rev. expanded as New World in the Tropics: The Culture of Modern Brazil, N.Y., Knopf, 1959, 286 pp.
An admirable synthesis based on Freyre's works of sociological interpretation. Includes a special chapter on modern literature.

—————Indian Justice. Tr. William E. Colford, in Classic Tales from Spanish America, 1962: see Spanish American Literature, Collections.

—————The Mansions and the Shanties: The Making of Modern Brazil (*Sobrados e mucambos*). Tr. Harriet de Onís. N.Y., Knopf, 1963. 431 pp.

—————The Masters and the Slaves (*Casa grande e senzala*), A Study in the Development of Brazilian Civilization. Tr. Samuel Putnam. N.Y., Knopf, 1946, and London, Secker, 1947. xliv, 537, xliv pp. Repr. (from 2d abridged ed. of original) N.Y., Knopf, 1964, 432 pp.

Furtado, Celso.   Diagnosis of the Brazilian Crisis (*Dialética do desenvolvimento*). Tr. Suzette Macedo. Berkeley, Univ. of California Pr., 1965. xxiv, 168 pp.

—————The Economic Growth of Brazil: A Survey from Colonial to Modern Times. Tr. Ricardo W. de Aguiar and Eric C. Drysdale. Berkeley, Univ. of California Pr., 1965. 300 pp., paper.

Goodwin, Philip L.   Brazil Builds: Architecture New and Old, 1652–1942. N.Y., Museum of Modern Art, 1943. 198 pp.
Parallel texts; maps, photographs, plans.

*A Guide to the Art of Latin America.   Ed. Robert Chester Smith and Elizabeth Wilder. Latin American Ser., 21. Washington, Library of Congress, 1948. 480 pp.

Includes material published up to 1942. For subsequent pubs., see the next item.

**Handbook of Latin American Studies.   Annual volume, eds. various. Cambridge, Mass., Harvard Univ. Pr., 1936—.
Sections on Brazilian life, culture, and literature.

Hanke, Lewis.   Modern Latin America: Continent in Ferment. Vol. 2: South America. Anvil Books, 46. Princeton, N.J., Van Nostrand, 1959. 191 pp.
Compact, readable, and enlightening section on Brazil, accompanied by readings.

Haring, Clarence H.   Empire in Brazil: A New World Experiment with Monarchy. Cambridge, Mass., Harvard Univ. Pr., 1958. 182 pp.
For the general public, engagingly written by a scholar.

Jesus, Carolina Maria de.   Child of the Dark. Tr. David St. Clair. N.Y., Dutton, 1962. 190 pp.
Graphic diary by a slum dweller.

Latin America and the Enlightenment.   See Spanish American Literature. Alexander Marchant's "Aspects of the Enlightenment in Brazil" is a study of the academies, and of the ideas of educated men as shown in their libraries. Other essays touch on Brazil.

Merryman, Montgomery.   Portuguese: A Portrait of the Language of Brazil. Intro. William Rex Crawford. Rio de Janeiro, Pongetti, 1945. 229 pp.
Popular intro. to the spirit of Brazil through its language.

Mindlin, Henrique E.   Modern Architecture in Brazil. Pref. by Prof. S. Giedion. N.Y., Reinhold Pub. Corp., 1956. 256 pp.
Supplement to Goodwin, above, with stress on the contemporary.

*Nabuco, Carolina.   The Life of Joaquim Nabuco. Ed. and tr. Ronald Hilton, and Lee B. Valenti, Frances E. Coughlin, Joaquin M. Duarte, Jr. Stanford, Calif., Stanford Univ. Pr., 1950. 373 pp.
Brilliant, moving biography of a great statesman, diplomat, and writer (1849–1910) by a daughter. Tr. adds an account of the historical background, and a bibliography of Nabuco's principal works.

Oliveira Lima, Manuel de. The Evolution of Brazil Compared with That of Spanish and Anglo-Saxon America. Ed. Percy Alvin Martin. Stanford Univ., Calif., The University, 1914. 159 pp.
>Lectures by a distinguished diplomat and scholar.

Perspective of Brazil: An Atlantic Supplement. Ed. Carleton Sprague Smith. N.Y., Intercultural Pubs., 1956. 72 pp.
>From the *Atlantic Monthly*, vol. 197, 1956, 97–168. Articles by Brazilians on various aspects of culture, along with short stories and poems by contemporary authors.

Portugal and Brazil: An Introduction. Ed. H. V. Livermore and W. J. Entwistle. See Portuguese Literature.
>"Brazilian Literature" was written by Ronald Hilton.

Prado, Caio, Jr. The Colonial Background of Modern Brazil. Tr. Suzette Machado. Berkeley, Univ. of California Pr., 1969. 530 pp.

Readings in Latin American Civilization. Ed. A. Curtis Wilgus. N.Y., Barnes and Noble, 1946. 430 pp.
>Includes some twenty selections on Brazil.

Readings in Latin-American Civilization, 1492 to the Present. Ed. Benjamin Keen. Boston, Houghton, 1955. 477 pp.
>Includes selections by Brazilians and foreigners. Glossary.

Schurz, William Lytle. Brazil, the Infinite Country. N.Y., Dutton, 1961. 346 pp.
>General survey of contemporary Brazil. Maps, reading lists.

The Southern Americas: A New Chronicle. Ed. Abel Plenn. N.Y., Creative Age Pr., 1948. 455 pp.
>Includes historical and travel accounts illustrating the development of Brazil.

Slonimsky, Nicolas. Music of Latin America. N.Y., Crowell, 1945. 374 pp.
>Includes "Panorama of Latin American Music," "Brazil," and "Dictionary of Latin American Musicians, Songs and Dances, and Musical Instruments."

Southey, Robert.   History of Brazil. London, Longmans, 1810–19. 3 vols.
From the beginnings to 1808: based on elaborate documentation.

Tavares de Sá, Ernane.   The Brazilians, People of Tomorrow. N.Y., Day, and
Toronto, Longmans, 1947. 248 pp.
A sprightly interpretation by a native.

Vianna Moog, Clodomir.   Bandeirantes and Pioneers. Tr. L. L. Barrett.
N.Y., Braziller, 1964. 316 pp.
A challenging, controversial comparison.

Wagley, Charles.   An Introduction to Brazil. N.Y. and London, Columbia
Univ. Pr., 1963. xi, 322 pp. Repr. 1965, paper.
Sympathetic presentation of Brazil as a cultural unit.

Williams, Mary W.   Dom Pedro the Magnanimous, Second Emperor of
Brazil. Chapel Hill, Univ. of North Carolina Pr., 1937. 414 pp.
A standard biography based on considerable research in unpublished
material.

Bibliography

Gorham, Rex.   The Folkways of Brazil: A Bibliography. Ed. Karl Brown.
N.Y., N.Y. Public Library, 1944. 67 pp.
From the *Bulletin* of the N.Y. Public Library, vols. 47, 48, 1943–44.
Classified and annotated. Includes a section on fiction with folklore
background, and a glossary of special terms.

Griffin, William J.   "Brazilian Literature in English Translation," in Revista
Interamericana de Bibliografía, vol. 5, 1955, 21–37.
Includes many poems and stories not listed here.

Johnson, Harvey L.   "The Brazilian Mirror: Some Brazilian Writings in
English Translations." The Americas, vol. 21, 1965, 274–94

Latin American Prose in English Translation.   Ed. Claude L. Hulet. See
Spanish American Literature.
For prose, the most comprehensive guide to date.

Leavitt, Sturgis E. Hispano-American Literature in the United States: A Bibliography of Translations and Criticism (1932). See Spanish American Literature.

An Outline History of Spanish American Literature. Ed. John E. Englekirk. 3d ed. N.Y., Appleton, 1965. 252 pp.
> Appendix A, by Marion Zeitlin, is a classified bibliography of Brazilian literature for those reading only English or Spanish; it lists both critical works and translations.

Traduções de Autores Brasileiros e Livros sobre o Brasil Escritos em Idioma Estrangeiro. Rio de Janeiro, Ministério das Relaçoes Exteriores, Serviço de Documentação, Biblioteca, c.1960. 92 leaves, mimeographed.
> Useful for translations into languages other than English.

Literary Studies

Bandeira, Manuel. Brief History of Brazilian Literature (*Pensamiento de América*). Tr. and ed. Ralph Edward Dimmick. Washington, Pan American Union, 1958. 188 pp. Repr. N.Y., Charles Frank Pubs., 1964.
> Excellent introduction by a fine critic and poet. Bibliographies.

Batchelor, Courtenay Malcolm. Stories and Storytellers of Brazil. Vol. 1, Folklore. Havana, Ucar García, 1953. 226 pp.
> Includes excellent trs. Bibliography.

Coutinho, Afrânio. An Introduction to Literature in Brazil. Tr. Gregory Rabassa. N.Y., Columbia Univ. Pr., 1969. xii, 326 pp.

Driver, David Miller. The Indian in Brazilian Literature. N.Y., Hispanic Institute in the U.S., 1942. 190 pp.
> An historical survey, 17th to 20th centuries. Bibliography.

Ellison, Fred P. Brazil's New Novel: Four Northeastern Masters. Berkeley, Univ. of California Pr., 1954. 191 pp.
> Sensitive sociological and literary study of José Lins do Rego, Jorge Amado, Graciliano Ramos, and Rachel de Queiros. Bibliography.

Goldberg, Isaac. Brazilian Literature. Pref. J. D. M. Ford. N.Y., Knopf, 1922. 303 pp.
> An outline history of the literature, and essays on selected writers. Annotated bibliography of important contributions to Brazilian literary history.

Henríquez-Ureña, Pedro. Literary Currents in Hispanic America. See Spanish American Literature.
> Brazilian literature is treated as part of the whole, not as a separate unit.

Lincoln, Joseph N. Charts of Brazilian Literature. Ann Arbor, Mich., Edwards, 1947. 86 pp.
> Classified lists of authors and works by periods. Historical backgrounds sketched in. Useful for quick reference.

Loos, Dorothy Scott. The Naturalistic Novel of Brazil. N.Y., Hispanic Institute in the U.S., 1963. 163 pp.
> Native and foreign elements in the work of five major novelists.

Monegal, E. R. "The Contemporary Brazilian Novel." Daedalus, vol. 95, 1966, 986–1003.

Morais Neto, Prudente de. The Brazilian Romance. Tr. Luiz Victor LeCocq d'Oliveira. Ministry of State for Foreign Affairs of Brazil, Division of Intellectual Cooperation, Résumé no. 4. Rio de Janeiro, Imprensa Nacional, 1943. 56 pp.
> Historical survey of the novel.

Putnam, Samuel. Marvelous Journey: A Survey of Four Centuries of Brazilian Writing. N.Y., Knopf, 1948. 269 pp.
> The development of Brazilian literature in its social environment. The bibliography includes works in English, Spanish, and French.

Sayers, Raymond S. "Brazilian Literary Criticism Today." Luso-Brazilian Review, vol. 1, 1964, 66–79.

————"Brazilian Literature: 1964." Books Abroad, vol. 39, 1965, 146–50.

————"Contemporary Brazilian Criticism." Comparative Literature Studies (University of Maryland), vol. 1, 1964, 287–304.

————The Negro in Brazilian Literature. N.Y., Hispanic Institute in the U.S., 1956. 240 pp.

Thomas, Earl W. "Folklore in Brazilian Literature." In Brazil: Papers Presented in the Institute for Brazilian Studies, Vanderbilt University. Nashville, Tenn., Vanderbilt Univ. Pr., 1953, pp. 91–135.

Torres-Ríoseco, Arturo. The Epic of Latin American Literature. See Spanish American Literature.

The ch. on Brazilian literature indicates parallels with Spanish American. For further discussion of this subject, see the same author's New World Literature, listed ibid., especially the chs. "Social Poetry" and "The Parallel between Brazilian and Spanish American Literature."

Veríssimo, Érico. Brazilian Literature: An Outline. N.Y., Macmillan, 1945. 184 pp.

. .   A popular contemporary novelist tells the story of his country's literature to his American students in conversational style.

Vianna Moog, Clodomir. An Interpretation of Brazilian Literature. Tr. John Knox. Rio de Janeiro, Ministry of Foreign Relations, Cultural Division, Service of Publications, 1951. 101 pp.

A suggestive regional interpretation.

Collections

*Anthology of Contemporary Latin American Poetry.** Ed. Dudley Fitts. See Spanish American Literature.

Selections from six Brazilian poets (in the revised ed.), tr. Dudley Poore. Parallel texts.

*Brazilian Tales.** Ed. and tr. Isaac Goldberg. Boston, Four Seas, 1921, and London, Allen and Unwin, 1924. 149 pp. Repr. Boston, Mass., International Pocket Library, 1965, 96 pp.

Stories by Machado de Assis, Medeiros e Albuquerque, Coelho Netto, and Carmen Dolores.

Contistas Brasileiros: New Brazilian Short Stories. Ed. José Saldanha Coelho, and tr. Rod W. Horton. Rio de Janeiro, Revista Branca, 1957. 238 pp.

Ten authors, each represented by one tale.

Eells, Elsie Spicer. Fairy Tales from Brazil: How and Why Tales from Brazilian Folklore. N.Y., Dodd Mead, 1917. 210 pp.

——————Tales of Giants from Brazil. N.Y., Dodd Mead, 1918. 179 pp.

——————Brazilian Fairy Book. N.Y., Stokes, 1926. 193 pp.

——————Magic Tooth and Other Tales from the Amazon. Boston, Little Brown, 1927. 243 pp.
Folktales from various sources.

Flores, Angel, ed.   Fiesta in November. See Spanish American Literature. Includes a lyrical passage from Jorge Amado, "Sea of the Dead."

Folklore in Brazil. Translations into English, French, and German. Ed. Edison Carneiro. Rio de Janeiro, Ministério da Educação, Campanha de Defesa do Folclore Brasileiro, 1963. 48 pp.

*The Golden Land: An Anthology of Latin American Folklore in Literature. See Harriet de Onís, in Spanish American Literature.
"Part V: Brazil" contains trs. from Euclydes da Cunha, Affonso Arinos, Gustavo Barroso, Monteiro Lobato, José Lins do Rego, and Mario de Andrade.

*The Green Continent. See Germán Arciniegas, in Spanish American Literature.
Includes selections by Graça Aranha, Heitor Lyra, Érico Vérissimo, and Euclydes da Cunha; biobibliographical data.

An Introduction to Modern Brazilian Poetry. Verse Translations by Leonard S. Downes. São Paolo, Clube de Poesia do Brasil, 1954. 86 pp.
Fifty poets represented by one or two pieces each; photographs.

Modern Brazilian Poetry: An Anthology. Tr. and ed. John Nist, with the help of Yolanda Leite. Bloomington, Indiana Univ. Pr., 1962. 175 pp.
Twelve poets well represented; biographical notes.

Modern Brazilian Poetry Read by Professor Cassiano Nunes.   Ed. Raymond S. Sayers and Cassiano Nunes. Folklore Records Album No. FL 9914. N.Y., Folkways Records and Service Corporation, 1965.
> A pamphlet intro., with parallel Brazilian-English texts of poems read on the record.

Modern Brazilian Short Stories.   Tr. William L. Grossman. Berkeley, Univ. of California Pr., 1967. 167 pp.
> One story each by seventeen authors, including Andrade, Guimarães Rosa, Jardim, Lispector, Rachel de Queiros, and Ramos.

Odyssey Review, vol. 1, no. 1, December 1961.
> Includes a play by Antônio Callado, short stories by Dinah Silveira de Queiroz and Clarice Lispector, and a critical article by Armando Correia Pacheco.

Twelve Modern Brazilian Poets.   Ed. and tr. Eugenio Villicaña. N.Y., October House, 1969.
> The poets describe their own work in the light of the poetic manifesto of 1921.

Eighteenth and Nineteenth Centuries

INDIVIDUAL AUTHORS

Alencar, José Martiniano de (1829–1877).   Iracéma, the Honey-Lips: A Legend of Brazil. Tr. Isabel Burton. London, Bickers, 1886. 101 pp.
> Bound with Pereira da Silva, *Manuel de Moraes*: see below.

> Tr. N. Biddell as Iracema (A Legend of Ceará). Rio de Janeiro, Imprensa Inglesa, n.d. 114 pp.
>> Highly poetic tale of the encounter of white man and Indian. In the original, a classic of poetic prose.

————The Jesuit. Tr. Edgardo R. de Britto. Poet Lore, vol. 30, 1919, 475–
547.
A nationalistic drama.

Almeida, Manuel Antônio de (1831–1861). Memoirs of a Militia Sergeant.
Tr. Linton L. Barrett. UNESCO Collection of Representative Works, Latin
American Series. Washington, Pan American Union, 1959. 244 pp.
This hilarious and realistic novel of manners is a classic.

Azevedo, Aluízio (1857–1913). A Brazilian Tenement (*O Cortiço*). Tr.
Harry W. Brown. N.Y., McBride, 1926, and London, Cassell, 1928,
320 pp.
Realistic novel of slum life in Rio de Janeiro.

Bilac, Olavo (1865–1918). (Part tr. by Lillian E. Elliott of the historical
poem *O Caçador de Esmeraldas*), in Hispanic Anthology, ed. Thomas Walsh:
see Spanish Literature, Collections.

Escragnolle Taunay, Alfredo de (1843–1899). Innocencia: A Story of the
Prairie Regions of Brazil. Tr. James W. Wells. London, Chapman and Hall,
1889. 312 pp.

Tr. Henriqueta Chamberlain as Inocência. N.Y., Macmillan, 1945.
209 pp.

Machado de Assis, Joaquim Maria (1839–1908). Don Casmurro. Tr.
Helen Caldwell, intro. Waldo Frank. N.Y., Noonday Pr., 1953. 283 pp.,
and London, W. H. Allen, 1953, 240 pp. Repr. N.Y., 1960, paper;
Berkeley, Calif., 1965, paper.
Memoirs of a disenchanted lover of life. Generally acclaimed as the
masterpiece of Brazil's greatest fiction writer.

————Esau and Jacob. Tr. Helen Caldwell. Berkeley, Univ. of California Pr.,
1965, and London, Owen, 1966. xx, 287 pp.

————Philosopher or Dog? Tr. Clotilde Wilson. N.Y., Noonday Pr., 1954.
271 pp. Also (as The Heritage of Quincas Borba), London, W. H. Allen,
1954, 255 pp.
A sequel to the next entry.

————The Posthumous Memoirs of Braz Cubas. Tr. William L. Grossman. São Paulo, São Paulo Editore, 1951. 221 pp. Repr. (as Epitaph of a Small Winner) N.Y., Noonday Pr., 1952, and London, W. H. Allen, 1953; repr. N.Y., 1966, paper; Penguin, 1968.

Tr. E. Percy Ellis as Posthumous Reminiscences of Braz Cubas. Coleção de traduções de Grandes Autores Braseilores, 1. Rio de Janeiro, Ministério da Educação e Cultura, Instituto Nacional do Livro, 1955. 304 pp.

————The Psychiatrist and Other Stories. Tr. William L. Grossman and Helen Caldwell. Berkeley, Univ. of California Pr., 1963. 147 pp.

Tr. Patricia McGowan Pinheiro. London, Cape, 1963. 288 pp.

A dozen ironic tales by a master craftsman.

————What Went On at the Baroness'. Tr. Helen Caldwell. Santa Monica, Calif., Magpie Pr., 1963. Unpaged.

Two stories, "The Attendant's Confession" and "The Fortune Teller", are tr. in Isaac Goldberg, Brazilian Tales, see Collections, above.

Cf. José Bettencourt Machado, *Machado of Brazil: The Life and Times of Machado de Assis* (N.Y., Bramerica, 1953, 246 pp.), a somewhat novelized biography, with bibliography; and Donald M. Decker, "Machado de Assis: Short Story Craftsman" (*Hispanic World*, vol. 28, 1965, 76–81).

Martins Penna, Luís Carlos (1815–1848).   A Rural Justice of the Peace. Tr. Willis Knapp Jones. Poet Lore, vol. 54, 1948, 99–119.
Farcical comedy of manners.

Pereira da Silva, João Manuel (1817–1898).   Manuel de Moraes: A Chronicle of the Seventeenth Century. Tr. Sir Richard F. and Lady (Isabel) Burton. London, Bickers, 1886. 138 pp. (bound with Alencar's novel, see above).
An early historical novel.

Twentieth Century

INDIVIDUAL AUTHORS

Accioly, Breno (1921–1966). "*João Urso*". Tr. R. P. Joscelyne from the vol. of short stories with this title, in Latin American Writing Today, Penguin, 1967.

Amado, Jorge (1912—). Gabriela, Clove and Cinnamon. Tr. James L. Taylor and William L. Grossman. N.Y., Knopf, 1962, and London, Chatto, 1963. 426 pp. Repr. Greenwich, Conn., Fawcett, 1964, paper.
Urban growth and changing mores in southern Bahia.

————Home Is the Sailor (*Os velhos marinheiros*). Tr. Harriet de Onís. N.Y., Knopf, and London, Chatto, 1964. xv, 298 pp.
Lusty tale of a landlubber who successfully passed himself off as a sea captain.

————The Two Deaths of Quincas Wateryell (*A morte e a morte de Quincas Berro Dágua*). Tr. Barbara Shelby. N.Y., Knopf, 1965. 97 pp.

————The Violent Land (*Terras do Sem Fin*). Tr. Samuel Putnam. N.Y., Knopf, 1945. x, 335 pp.
Epic of the struggle for fertile land in the cacao region of Bahia.

Andrade, Mário de (1893–1945). Fräulein (*Amar, Verbo Intransitivo*). Tr. and adapted Margaret Richardson Hollingsworth. N.Y., Macaulay, 1933. 252 pp.
Satirical novel of manners in São Paulo.

————Hallucinated City (*Paulicea Desvairada*). Tr. verse Jack E. Tomlins. Nashville, Vanderbilt Univ. Pr., 1968. 152 pp., parallel texts.

Barroso, Gustavo (1888—). Mapirunga. Tr. R. B. Cunninghame Graham. London, Heinemann, 1924. 39 pp.
Tragedy in the wilds of Brazil.

Callado, Antônio.   Frankel: A Play in Three Acts. Coleção Teatro. Rio de Janeiro, Ministério da Educação e Cultura, Serviço de Documentação, 1955. 89 pp.
Psychological drama in the jungle.

Carneiro, Cecilio J. (1911—).   The Bonfire. Tr. Dudley Poore. N.Y., Farrar and Reinhart, 1944. 334 pp. Repr. London, Cassell, 1948, 297 pp.
The life of a Syrian immigrant in Brazil. The novel won honorable mention in the first Latin American Prize Novel Competition.

Cruls, Gastão (1888—).   The Mysterious Amazonia. Tr. J. T. W. Sadler. Rio de Janeiro, Valverde, 1944. 263 pp.
A popular novel incorporating Amazon folklore.

Cunha, Euclydes da (1866–1909).   Rebellion in the Backlands (Os Sertões [Campanha de Canudos]). Tr. Samuel Putnam. Chicago, Univ. Pr., 1944. 526 pp. Repr. 1957, paper. Repr. abridged as Revolt in the Backlands, London, Gollancz, 1947, 347 pp.
Report of a military campaign against religious fanatics: a classic of Brazilian literature.

Dias Gomes, Alfredo.   Journey to Bahia (O pagador de promessas). Tr. and adapted Stanley Richards. Players Magazine (Department of Speech and Drama, Univ. of Kansas), Jan. 1964. Repr. Washington, D.C., Brazilian-American Cultural Institute, 1964. 79 pp.
The martyrdom of a sincere, simple-minded countryman.

Dourado, Waldomiro Autran.   A Hidden Life (Uma vida em segredo). Tr. Edgar H. Miller, Jr. N.Y., Knopf, 1969. 150 pp.

Drummond de Andrade, Carlos (1902—).   In the Middle of the Road. Ed. and tr. John Nist. Tucson, Univ. of Arizona, 1965. 121 pp., parallel texts.
Selected poems.

Figueiredo, Guilherme.   A God Slept Here: A Play. Tr. Lloyd F. George. Coleção Teatro. Rio de Janeiro, Ministério da Educação e Cultura, Serviço de Documentação, 1957. 106 pp.

Graça Aranha, José Pereira da (1868–1931). Canaan. Tr. Mariano Joaquín Lorente, pref. Guglielmo Ferrero. Boston, Mass., Four Seas, 1920, and London, Allen and Unwin, 1921. 321 pp.
> A classic novel of ideas on the disillusion of a German immigrant.

Guimarães Rosa, João (1908—). The Devil to Pay in the Backlands (*Grande sertão: veredas*). Tr. James L. Taylor and Harriet de Onís. N.Y., Knopf, 1963. 494 pp.
> Chronicle of life in the wilds of Minas Gerais.

————Sagarana. Tr. Harriet de Onís. N.Y., Knopf, 1966. xvi, 303 pp.
> Nine stories.

————The Third Bank of the River, and Other Stories. (*Primeiras Estórias*). Tr. Barbara Shelby. N.Y., Knopf, 1968. 238 pp.
> The title story was tr. R. P. Joscelyne in Latin American Writing Today (Penguin, 1967).

Jardim, Luís (1901—). The Armadillo and the Monkey. Tr. Maria Comino. N.Y., Coward-McCann, 1942. 46 pp.
> A folktale zestfully told.

Leão, Sylvia. White Shore of Olinda. N.Y., Vanguard, 1943. 246 pp.
> Written in English: a story of fisherfolk in northeastern Brazil.

Lima, Jorge de (1893–1953). Poems. Tr. Melissa S. Hull. Rio de Janeiro, 1952. 56 pp.
> Twenty-three poems by a modernist and mystic.

Lins Do Rego, José (1901–1957). Plantation Boy. Tr. Emmi Baum. N.Y., Knopf, 1966. 530 pp.

————Pureza. Tr. Lucie Marion. London, Hutchinson, 1948. 175 pp.
> Psychological study in moral disintegration, a frequent theme in this author.

Lispector, Clarice. The Apple in the Dark (*A maçã no escuro*). Tr. Gregory Rabassa. N.Y., Knopf, 1967. 361 pp.

Monteiro Lobato, José Bento (1883–1948). Brazilian Short Stories. Tr. anon., ed. Isaac Goldberg. Little Blue Book 733. Girard, Kansas, Haldeman-Julius, 1925. 64 pp.
  Plain language and realistic subject-matter.

Queiros, Rachel de (1910—). The Three Marias. Tr. Fred P. Ellison. Texas Pan-American Series. Austin, Univ. of Texas Pr., 1963. 178 pp.
  Three girls grow up to face the world.

Ramos, Graciliano (1892–1955). Anguish. Tr. L. C. Kaplan. N.Y., Knopf, 1946. 259 pp.
  Powerful psychological novel.

————Barren Lives (*Vidas sêcas*). Tr. Ralph Edward Dimmick. Austin, Univ. of Texas Pr., 1965. xxxiv, 131 pp.

Sabino, Fernando [Tavares]. A Time to Meet: A Novel (*O encontro marcado*). Tr. John Procter. London, Souvenir Pr., 1967. 319 pp.

Setúbal, Paulo (1893–1907). Domitila, the Romance of an Emperor's Mistress (*A Marquesa de Santos*). Tr. adapted Margaret Richardson. N.Y., Coward-McCann, 1930. 324 pp.
  Historical novel about the mistress of Dom Pedro I, first Emperor of Brazil.

Suassuna, Ariano (1927—). The Rogues' Trial. Tr. Dillwyn F. Ratcliff. Berkeley, Univ. of California Pr., 1963. 107 pp.
  Delightful miracle play based on folklore themes.

Vasconcelos Maia, C. (1923—). "Sun". Tr. R. P. Joscelyne from *O Cavalo e a Rosa*, in Latin American Writing Today. Penguin, 1967.

Veríssimo, Érico (1905—). Brazilian Literature: An Outline. See Literary Studies, above.

————Consider the Lilies of the Field. Tr. Jean Neel Karnoff. N.Y., Macmillan, 1947. 371 pp.
  Not Veríssimo at his best, but immensely popular in Brazil.

————Crossroads. Tr. L. C. Kaplan. N.Y., Macmillan, 1943. 373 pp. Repr. as Crossroads and Destinies, London, Arco, 1956.
   Cinematographic technique. Infused with a cynicism rare in the author's usually mild realism.

————Mexico. Tr. Linton Barrett. Garden City, N.Y., Doubleday, 1962. 399 pp.

————Night. Tr. L. L. Barrett. N.Y., Macmillan, and London, Arco, 1956. 166 pp.
   A night of amnesia in a city.

————The Rest Is Silence. Tr. L. C. Kaplan. N.Y., Macmillan, 1946. 485 pp. Repr. London, Arco, 1956.
   Various aspects of city life.

————Time and the Wind. Tr. L. L. Barrett. N.Y., Macmillan, 1951. Repr. London, Arco, 1954, 624 pp.
   Epic historical novel of the author's native Rio Grande do Sul.

Cf. Richard A. Mazzara, "Structure and Verisimilitude in the Novels of Érico Veríssimo," *PMLA*, vol. 80, 1965, 451–58.

PROVENÇAL LITERATURE

CONSULTANT,
ALPHONSE VICTOR ROCHE

Brandin, Louis. "Provençal Language and Literature," in Encyclopaedia Britannica, 14th ed., 1929, vol. 18, pp. 637–42.

Holmes, Urban T., Jr. "Provençal Literature," in Encyclopedia of Literature. N.Y., Philosophical Lib., 1946. vol. 2, pp. 813–17.

Roche, Alphonse Victor. "Provençal Literature," in Sidney Braun, Dictionary of French Literature. N.Y., Philosophical Lib., 1958, pp. 263–68.

————"Provençal Literature," in New Catholic Encyclopedia. N.Y., McGraw-Hill, 1967, vol. 11, pp. 912–13.

Bibliography

Provençal Literature and Language, including the Local History of Southern France. Compiled Daniel C. Haskell. N.Y., N.Y. Public Library, 1925. 885 pp.
    Lists works in the New York Public Library; an important bibliography.

For an annual survey of Provençal scholarship, see *The Year's Work in Modern Language Studies*, 1930—; *PMLA*, 1957—.

Medieval Period

Anglade, Joseph. *Histoire sommaire de la littérature méridionale au moyen âge (des origines à la fin du XVᵉ siècle)*. Paris, Boccard, 1921. 274 pp.
    Scholarly and complete.

————*Les Troubadours*: *Leurs vies, leurs oeuvres, leur influence*. Paris, Colin, 1908. 328 pp.

Briffault, Robert.   The Troubadours (*Les Troubadours et le sentiment romanesque*). Tr. the author, ed. and rev. Lawrence F. Koons. Bloomington, Indiana Univ. Pr., 1965. xvi, 296 pp.
　　Includes many trs. (prose) of quotations from poets.

Chaytor, Henry John.   The Provençal Chanson de Geste. Taylorian Lecture, 1946. London, Oxford Univ. Pr., 1946. 39 pp.

————The Troubadours. Cambridge Manuals. Cambridge, Univ Pr., and N.Y., Putnam, 1912. 151 pp.

Fleming, John Arnold.   Troubadours of Provence. Glasgow, MacLellan, 1952. 150 pp.

Jeanroy, Alfred.   *La poésie lyrique des troubadours*. Paris, Didier, 1934. 2 vols. Indispensable; most up-to-date study.

Nykl, A. R.   Hispano-Arabic Poetry and Its Relations with the Old Provençal Troubadours. Baltimore, Md., J. H. Furst, 1946. xxvii, 416 pp.

Roche, A. V.   "Troubadours," in New Catholic Encyclopedia. N.Y., McGraw-Hill, 1967, vol. 14, p. 320.

Valency, Maurice.   In Praise of Love: An Introduction to the Love-Poetry of the Renaissance. N.Y., Macmillan, 1958. xii, 319 pp. Repr. 1961, paper.

Bibliography

Jeanroy, Alfred. *Bibliographie sommaire des chansonniers provençaux* (mss. et éditions). Paris, Champion, 1916. 86 pp.

Collections

Anthologie des Troubadours, XIIe–XIIIe siècles.   Ed. Alfred Jeanroy. Paris, Boccard, 1927. 183 pp.
　　Texts in French tr.

An Anthology of Medieval Lyrics.   Ed. Angel Flores, trs. various. ML, 1962.
>Forty-eight Provençal lyrics are included in tr., pp. 1–83.

The Lives of the Troubadours.   Tr. Ida Farnell from medieval Provençal in the edn. by K. A. F. Mahn. London, Nutt, 1896. ix, 288 pp.
>Many poems tr. with the biographies.

Six Vaudois Poems from the Waldensian Mss. in the University Libraries of Cambridge, Dublin, and Geneva.   Ed. with tr. and glossary by Henry John Chaytor. Cambridge, Univ. Pr., 1930. xxi, 127 pp.

Smith, Justin A.   The Troubadours at Home. N.Y., Putnam, 1899. 2 vols.
>Many trs., with rather elementary and discursive intro. to the period.

Trobador Poets: Selections from the Poems of Eight Trobadors.   Tr. Barbara Smythe. New Medieval Lib. London, Chatto, and N.Y., Duffield, 1911. xxiii, 198 pp.

Troubadour Songs. Compiled Clarence Dickinson, intro. and tr. Helen A. Dickinson. N.Y., Gray, [1920]. 14, 22 pp.

INDIVIDUAL AUTHORS

NOTE.   Many works of other writers than those listed (e.g., Arnaut Daniel) are tr. into French.

Aimeric de Peguilhan (13th c.).   The Poems. Ed. and tr. W. P. Shepard and F. M. Chambers. Evanston, Ill., Northwestern Univ. Pr., 1950. vi, 254 pp.

Bernart de Ventadorn (12th c.).   The Songs. Ed. and tr. Stephen G. Nichols, Jr., et al. Chapel Hill, Univ. of North Carolina Pr., 1962. 235 pp.

Flamenca (13th c.).   Tr. condensed William Aspenwall Bradley as The Story of Flamenca. N.Y., Harcourt, 1922. 66 pp.

>Tr. H. F. M. Prescott. London, Constable, and N.Y., R. R. Smith, 1930. 158 pp.

Tr. Merton Jerome Hubert as The Romance of Flamenca, with Provençal text ed. Marion E. Porter. Princeton, N.J., Princeton Univ. Pr., 1962. 466 pp.

Jaufre (13th c.).   Tr. Alfred Elwes from the French version by Mary Lafon as Jaufry the Knight and the Fair Brunissende. Ill. Gustave Doré. London, Addey, 1856. xi, 158 pp. Repr. with the Doré ill. as Geoffrey the Knight, London, Nelson, 1869, 215 pp. Rev. Vernon Ives from the Provençal, N.Y., Holiday House, 1935, 124 pp.

Peirol (c.1200).   Ed. and tr. S. C. Aston as Peirol, Troubadour of Auvergne. Cambridge, Univ. Pr., 1953. viii, 191 pp., parallel texts.

Raimbaut III, Comte d'Orange (c.1146–1173).   Ed. and tr. Walter T. Pattison in The Life and Works of the Troubadour Raimbaut d'Orange. Minneapolis, Univ. of Minnesota Pr., and London, Oxford Univ. Pr., 1952. xiv, 225 pp., parallel texts.

William of Poitou (1071–1127).   Poems. Tr. Thomas G. Bergin. New Haven, Conn., pr. pr., 1955. 43 pp.

Modern Period

Literary Studies

Roche, Alphonse Victor.   "Modern Provençal Literature during the Last Twenty-five Years." Books Abroad, vol. 28, 1954, 170–74.

————Provençal Regionalism: A Study of the Movement in the Revue félibréenne, Le Feu, and Other Reviews. Evanston, Ill., Northwestern Univ. Pr., 1954. 271 pp.
Acclaimed as a timely and valuable contribution to the history of French civilization.

Bibliography

Roche, Alphonse Victor.   Bibliography of Modern Provençal in the English Language 1840–1940. N.Y., N.Y. Public Library, 1946.
> Originally pub. in *Bulletin New York Public Library* 1942, pp. 379–88. Lists many reviews and trs. of short pieces.

INDIVIDUAL AUTHORS

Gras, Félix (1844–1901).   The Reds of the Midi, an Episode of the French Revolution. Tr. Catherine A. Janvier. N.Y., Appleton, 1896. 366 pp. Many reprs. to 1938.

————The Terror, a Romance of the French Revolution. Tr. the same. N.Y., Appleton, 1898. 512 pp. Repr. 1899 (6 American eds.).

————The White Terror, a Romance of the French Revolution and After. Tr. the same. N.Y., Appleton, 1899. 437 pp. Reprs. to 1912.
> These are three successive parts of *Li Rouge dóu Miejour*.

For the author, see A. V. Roche in *Columbia Dictionary of Modern European Literature*, s.v.

Mistral, Frédéric (1830–1914, Nobel Prize 1904).   Anglore: the Song of the Rhone (*Lo Pouèmo dóu Rone*). Tr. Maro Beath Jones. Claremont, Calif., Saunders Studio, 1937. 187 pp.

————Memoirs of Mistral (*Moun espelido, memòri e raconte*). Tr. Constance Elizabeth Maud, lyrics tr. Alma Strettell. London, Arnold, 1907. 336 pp.

————Mirelle, a Pastoral Epic of Provence (*Mirèio*). Tr. verse H. Chrichton. London, Macmillan, 1868. 383 pp.
> Tr. C. H. Grant as Mirèio. Avignon, J. Roumanille, 1867.

> Tr. verse Harriet Waters Preston as Mirèio: A Provençal Poem. Boston, Roberts Bros., 1872. 249 pp. Repr. London, Unwin, 1890, 186 pp. Repr. (with other selections from Mistral's poems) in C. D. Warner, Library of the World's Best Literature, vol. 25, 1898, pp. 10097–10109.

Mistral's poems are generally available in French tr. For his works, see Richard Aldington, *Introduction to Mistral* (London, Heinemann, 1956, viii, 209 pp.), a fine critical essay and scholarly study; Rob Lyle, *Mistral* (New Haven, Conn., Yale Univ. Pr., and Cambridge, Bowes, 1953, 68 pp.), a comprehensive analysis of each of Mistral's major works, with long quotations from well-selected and well-translated passages; Tudor Edwards, *The Lion of Arles, a Portrait of Mistral and His Circle* (N.Y., Fordham Univ. Pr., 1964, 215 pp.).

NOTE.   The works of other modern Provençal writers have been published in French trs.; e.g., the poems of Joseph d'Arbaud (1874–1950); the poems of Théodore Aubanel (1829–1886); the stories of Joseph Roumanille (1818–1891). For these authors, see A. V. Roche in Columbia Dictionary of Modern European Literature, *articles on each, and also his "Modern Provençal Literature and Joseph d'Arbaud,"* Books Abroad, *vol. 16, 1942, 131–34.*

RUMANIAN LITERATURE

THEODORE ANDRICA
REVISED BY VICTOR ANGELESCU
AND THOMAS A. PERRY

Basdevant, Denise. Against Tide and Tempest: The Story of Rumania (*Terres roumaines: contre vents et marées*, 1961). Tr. Florence Dunham and Jane Carroll from French. N.Y., Speller, 1965. 181 pp.

Bibescu, Princess Marthe. "Isvor," The Country of the Willows. Tr. Hamish Miles from French. London, Heinemann, and N.Y., Stokes, 1924. 244 pp.

    A fictional description of country and peasant life, somewhat romantic in style. Various members of the Bibescu family write customarily in French or English.

Contrasts in Emerging Societies: Readings in the Social and Economic History of South-eastern Europe in the Nineteenth Century. Tr. G. F. Cushing, et al., ed. Dorine Warriner. London, Athlone Pr., 1965. xx, 402 pp.

    One of the four sections relates to Rumania.

Cretzianu, Alexandre, ed. Captive Rumania: A Decade of Soviet Rule. London, Atlantic Pr., 1957. xvi, 424 pp.

    Tr. from *La Politique de paix de la Roumanie à l'égard de l'Union Soviétique* (1954).

Daicoviciu, C. *La Formation du peuple roumain et de sa langue.* Bucharest, R. P. R. Academy Publishing House, 1963.

Eliade, Pompiliu. *Histoire de l'esprit publique en Roumanie au dix-neuvième siècle. (La Roumanie au xixe siècle.)* Paris, 1905–14. 2 vols.

Fischer-Galati, Stephen. The New Rumania: From People's Democracy to Socialist Republic. Cambridge, Mass., M.I.T. Pr., 1967. 126 pp.

Forter, Norman L., and **Rostovsky, Demeter B.** The Roumanian Handbook. London, Simpkin Marshall, 1931. vi, 320 pp.

Ionescu, Ghita.   Communism in Rumania 1944–1962. London, Royal Institute of International Affairs, 1964. xvi, 378 pp.

*Iorga, Nicolae.   A History of Roumania: Land, People, Civilization. Tr. Joseph McCabe from the French of the 2d enlarged ed. (Bucharest, 1922). London, Unwin, 1925, and N.Y., Dodd, 1926. xii, 284 pp.

Latham, Peter.   Romania, a Complete Guide. London, Garnstone Pr., 1967. 245 pp.

Lindsay, Jack, and **Cornforth, Maurice.**   Rumanian Summer: A View of the Rumanian People's Republic. London, Lawrence & Wishart, 1953. 152 pp.

Mackintosh, May.   Rumania. London, Hale, 1963. 191 pp.

Roberts, Henry L.   Rumania: Political Problems of an Agrarian State. New Haven, Conn., Yale Univ. Pr., and London, Oxford Univ. Pr., 1951. xiv, 414 pp.

Romania.   Ed. Stephen Fischer-Galati. Published for Mid-European Studies Center of the Free Europe Committee. N.Y., Praeger, and London, Stevens, 1957. xv, 399 pp.

Romania: Geography, History, Economy, Culture.   Bucharest, Meridiane, 1966. 224 pp.

Roucek, Joseph S.   Contemporary Roumania and Her Problems. Stanford, Univ. Pr., and London, Oxford Univ. Pr., 1932. xxv, 422 pp.

Seton-Watson, G. H. W.   Eastern Europe between the Wars 1918–1941. Cambridge, Univ. Pr., and N.Y., Praeger, 1945. xv, 442 pp. Repr. 1946, 1956.

————The East European Revolution. London, Methuen, 1950. xv, 406 pp. Repr. 1952; Hamden, Conn., Shoe String Pr., 1963.

Seton-Watson, R. W.   The History of the Roumanians from Roman Times to the Completion of Unity. Cambridge, Univ. Pr., 1934. viii, 596 pp. Repr. Hamden, Conn., Shoe String Pr., 1963.

Tappe, E. D. "Rumania," in Central and South East Europe 1945–1948. Ed. R. R. Betts. London, Royal Institute of International Affairs, Oxford Univ. Pr., 1950. x, 227 pp.
> By one of the chief British authorities on the subject.

Bănăţeanu, Tancred, and **Focşa, M.**   The Ornament in the Rumanian Folk Art. Bucharest, Meridiane, 1962. 50 pp. ill.

Beza, Marcu.   Byzantine Art in Roumania. London, Batsford, 1940. xxi, 106 pp.

Oprescu, George.   Great Masters of Painting in the Museums of Rumania. 3d rev. ed. Bucharest, Meridiane, 1963. xxx, 116 pp. ill.

————Grigorescu. Bucharest, Meridiane, 1961. 181 pp., 86 pl. Repr. 1963.
> An important study of one of Rumania's foremost artists.

————Oriental Art in Rumania. Bucharest, Meridiane, 1963. 142 pp. ill.
> Excellent ill. and printing.

————Rumanian Sculpture. Bucharest, Foreign Languages Pub. House, 1957. 158 pp. ill.

Siegfried, W.   Theatre, Opera, Ballet in Rumania. Tr. anon. Bucharest, Foreign Languages Pub. House, 1957. 52 pp. ill.

Twentieth Century Rumanian Painting.   Tr. anon. Bucharest, Foreign Languages Pub. House, 1956. 198 pp. ill.

Literary Studies

Angelescu, Victor.   "Contemporary Rumanian Literature 1962," in Books Abroad, vol. 37 (1963), 394–96.

Beza, Marcu, and **Bibesco, Antoine.**   "Rumanian [Language and] Literature," in Encyclopaedia Britannica (14th ed., 1928).

Feraru, Leon.   The Development of Rumanian Poetry. N. Y. Institute of Rumanian Culture, Columbia Univ., 1929. vii, 122 pp.

————"The Development of the Rumanian Novel," in Romanic Review, vol. 17 (1926), 291-302. Repr. in the preceding item.

————"Rumanian Literature," in Columbia Dictionary of Modern European Literature (1947), pp. 693–94.
   The late Professor Feraru was also the author of articles in the same work on individual Rumanian authors.

Haneș, Petru V.   *Histoire de la littérature roumaine.* Tr. from the Rumanian. Paris, Leroux, 1934. xiii, 272 pp.

Isopescu, Claudiu.   "Rumanian Literature," in New International Encyclopedia (1930 ed.).

Lovinescu, Monica.   "The New Wave of Rumanian Writers." East Europe, vol. 16, xii (1967), 9–15.

Manning, Clarence A.   "Rumanian Literature," in Encyclopedia of Literature, vol. 2 (1948), pp. 818–23.

Munteanu, Basil.   *Panorama de la littérature roumaine contemporaine.* Paris, 1938. Tr. by Cargill Sprietsma as Modern Rumanian Literature. Bucharest, Curentul Pr., 1939. x, 321 pp.

Tappe, E. D., ed.   Rumanian Prose and Verse: A Selection with an Introductory Essay. London, Athlone Pr., 1956. xxvii, 195 pp.
   The introduction in English gives a useful survey.

The Theatre in the Rumanian People's Republic.   Bucharest, Meridiane, n.d.

For annual bibliography of literary scholarship, see *The Year's Work in Modern Language Studies*, 1930—; and PMLA, 1963—.

Collections

Anthologie de la littérature roumaine des origines au xxᵉ siècle.
Traductions et extraits des principaux poètes et prosateurs. Ed. Nicolae Iorga and Septime Gorceix. Paris, Delagrave, 1920. xxxi, 311 pp. (the trs. in French).

Introduction to Rumanian Literature. Ed. Jacob Steinberg. N.Y., Twayne, 1966. xiv, 441 pp.

Pub. for the Cultural Exchange Program of the United States and Rumania: a collection of trs. of short works by 24 authors, numbering 15 short stories and 9 selections from novels. The translators are unidentified, being directed by the editor of Meridiane, publisher of Bucharest.

We list eleven of these writers below: *Bogza, *Caragiale, Creangă, Camil Petrescu, *Cezar Petrescu, Popovici, Preda, *Rebreanu, Sadoveanu, Slavici, and *Stancu. The others are *Ion Agirbicianu (1882–1963); *Eugen Barba (1924—); *A. Bratescu-Voinesti (1868–1946); George Calinescu (1899–1965); *Matei I. Caragiale (1885–1936); *Barbu Delavrancea (1858–1918); *Gala Galaction (1879–1961); Fanus Neagu (1935—); *Simion Pop (1930—); *Dumitriu Radu Popescu (1933—); *Vasile Rebreanu (1934—); *I. M. Sadoveanu (1893–1964); *Alexandru Sahia (1908–1937). (*indicates a short story.)

Rouman Anthology: Or Selections of Rouman Poetry, Ancient and Modern. Ed. Henry Stanley. London, Longmans, 1856. 226 pp.

Short Stories [by contemporary Rumanian Writers]. Tr. Lazăr Marinescu, W. Staadecker, et al. Bucharest, "The Book" (vol. 1), Foreign Languages Pub. House (vol. 2), 1955–56. 2 vols. (205 pp., 472 pp.).

Vol. 1: Geo Bogza, Adrian Cernescu, Petru Dumitriu, et al.
Vol. 2: Mihai Beniuc, G. Călinescu, Eusebiu Calimar, Victor Eftimiu, V. Em. Galan, Nicolae Jianu, Aurel Mihali, Francisc Munteanu, Ferenc Pap, Titus Popovici, and Erwin Witstock.

Folk Literature

Beza, Marcu. Rumanian Proverbs Selected and Translated. London, A. H. Philpot, 1921. 63 pp., parallel texts.

Creangă, Ion. Folk Tales from Roumania. Tr. Mabel Nandris. London, Routledge, 1952, and N.Y., Roy, 1953. v, 170 pp. ill.

Doine: Or the National Songs and Legends of Romania. Ed. Eustace C. G. Murray. London, Smith Elder, 1854. 21 pp.

Six national airs for piano.

Ispirescu, Petre (1830–1887).   The Foundling Prince and Other Tales. Tr. and adapted Julia Collier Harris and Rea Ipcar. Boston, Houghton, 1917. 284 pp.

————Roumanian Fairy Tales. Tr. M. Kremnitz from the German version. N.Y., Holt, 1885. 243 pp.
> For children.

————Roumanian Folk Tales: Retold by J. B. Segall. Univ. of Maine Pubs. Orono, Maine, 1925. 105 pp.

Patterson, Robert Stewart.   Romanian Songs and Ballads. London, John Long, 1917. 125 pp.
> Excellent trs.

Roumanian Stories.   Tr. Lucy Byng. London and N.Y., John Lane, 1921. 287 pp.

*Ure, Jean, tr.   Pacala and Tandala, and Other Rumanian Folk Tales. London, Methuen, 1960, and N.Y., Watts, 1961. 194 pp.

Vacarescu, Elena.   The Bard of Dimbovitza: Roumanian Folk-Songs Collected from the Peasants. Tr. Carmen Sylva (pseud. of Queen Elizabeth of Rumania, see below) and Alma Strettell. London, Osgood [1892]. viii, 130 pp. Repr. 1897, 1908.

————Songs of the Valiant Vaivode and Other Strange Folklore. Collected and tr. Elena Vacarescu. N.Y., Scribner, 1908. xii, 238 pp.

On folk literature, see the work of the scholar Marcu Beza, *Paganism in Roumanian Folklore* (London, Dent, and N.Y., Dutton, 1928, x, 161 pp.).

INDIVIDUAL AUTHORS

Arghezi, Tudor (pseud. of Ion N. Teodorescu, 1880—).   His poetry has not been tr. into English. Cf. a study of it by Dumitriu Micu, *Tudor Arghezi*, tr. H. A. Richard [for Richard Hillard] and Michael Impey (Bucharest, Meridiane, 1965, 164 pp.).

Beza, Marcu (1885—). Doda. Tr. Lucy Byng. London, Bles, 1925. 155 pp.

————Rays of Memory. Tr. Lucy Byng. London, Dent, 1929. vi, 143 pp.

Bogza, Geo (1908—). Years of Darkness. Tr. Lazăr Marinescu. Bucharest, "The Book," 1956. 331 pp.
> See also *Short Stories*, vol. 1, 1955, above, for other tr.

Cantemir, Demetrius, Prince of Moldavia (1673–1723). See Neo-Latin Literature, in vol. 1, above.

Caragiale, Ion Luca (1852–1912). The Lost Letter and Other Plays. Tr. Frida Knight. London, Lawrence and Wishart, 1956. 181 pp.
> A classic. See *Columbia Dictionary of Modern European Literature*, art. "Caragiale" by Leon Feraru.

Ciprian, George. The Man with the Hack (A Comedy in Four Acts). Tr. V. Stoenescu. Bucharest, Meridiane, 1960. 109 pp.

Craciunas, Silviu (1914—). The Lost Footsteps. Tr. anon. N.Y., Farrar Straus, 1961. 318 pp.

Creangă, Ion (1837–1889). Recollections. Tr. Lucy Byng, pref. Marcu Beza. London, Dent, and N.Y., Dutton, 1930. 254 pp.
> *Amintiri*, and four stories from *Povesti*: a classic.

Dorian, Dorel. Should Anyone Ask You (A Play in Three Acts). Tr. Carol Kormos. Bucharest, Meridiane, 1960. 126 pp.

Dumitriu, Petru (1924—). The Boyars. Part I: The Family Jewels. Tr. Edward Hyams from French. London, Collins, and N.Y., Pantheon, 1961. 448 pp.

————The Prodigals (Part II of The Boyars). Tr. Norman Denny from French. London, Collins, 1962, and N.Y., Pantheon, 1963. 446 pp.

————Incognito. Tr. Norman Denny from French. London, Collins, and N.Y., Macmillan, 1964. 471 pp.

──────Meeting at the Last Judgment. Tr. Richard Howard from French. N.Y., Pantheon, 1962. 309 pp.

──────The Sardinian Smile. Tr. Peter Green from French. N.Y., Holt, 1968. 138 pp.

──────Stormy Petrel. Tr. Eugenia Farca from Rumanian. Bucharest, Foreign Languages Pub. House, 1966. 531 pp.

──────Westward Lies Heaven. Tr. Peter Wiles from French. London, Collins, and N.Y., Holt (as The Extreme Occident), 1966. 380 pp.

Eliade, Mircea (1907—). (Writes in French, lives in the United States.) Birth and Rebirth: The Religious Meanings of Initiation in Human Culture. Tr. Willard R. Trask. N.Y., Harper, 1958. 175 pp. Repr. London, Harvill, 1961.

──────The Forge and the Crucible (*Forgerons et alchimistes*). Tr. Stephen Corrin. N.Y., Harper, and London, Rider, 1962. 208 pp.

──────(ed. with Joseph M. Kitagawa) The History of Religions: Essays in Methodology. Chicago, Univ. of Chicago Pr., 1959. xi, 163 pp.

──────Images and Symbols: Studies in Religious Symbolism. Tr. Philip Mairet. London, Harvill, and N.Y., Sheed & Ward, 1961. 189 pp.

──────Myth and Reality. Tr. Willard R. Trask. N.Y., Harper, 1963, and London, George Allen, 1964. 204 pp.

──────The Myth of the Eternal Return. Tr. Willard R. Trask. N.Y., Pantheon, and London, Routledge, 1955. xi, 198 pp. Repr. as Cosmos and History: The Myth of the Eternal Return, N.Y., Harper, 1959, paper.

──────Myths, Dreams, and Mysteries: The Encounter between Contemporary Faiths and Archaic Realities. Tr. Philip Mairet. London, Harvill, 1960, and N.Y., Harper, 1961. 256 pp. Repr. N.Y., 1967, paper.

──────Patterns in Comparative Religion. Tr. Rosemary Sheed. London and N.Y., Sheed, 1958. 484 pp. Repr. N.Y., Meridian Books, 1963.

————The Sacred and the Profane: The Nature of Religion. Tr. Willard R. Trask. N.Y., Harcourt, 1959. 256 pp.

————Shamanism: Archaic Techniques of Ecstasy. Tr. Willard R. Trask. N.Y., Pantheon, and London, Routledge, 1964. xiii, 610 pp.

————The Two and the One (*Méphistophélès et l'androgyne*). Tr. John M. Cohen. London, Harvill Pr., 1965. 223 pp.

————Yoga: Immortality and Freedom. N.Y., Pantheon, and London, Routledge, 1958. xxii, 529 pp.

Cf. Thomas J. J. Altizer, *Mircea Eliade and the Dialectic of the Sacred* (Philadelphia, Westminster Pr., 1963, 219 pp.).

Eminescu, Mihail (1850–1889).   Poems. Tr. E. Sylvia Pankhurst and I. O, Stefanovici, with preface G. B. Shaw and intro. Nicolae Iorga. London. Kegan Paul, 1930. xxiv, 120 pp.

Tr. Dimitrie Cuclin. Bucharest, 1938. 176 pp.

Tr. P. Grimm. Cluj, 1939. 55 pp.

————Lucifer. Tr. anon. Bucharest, Meridiane, 1964. 84 pp. (in Rumanian, French, English, Spanish).

Cf. Mihai Benuic (president of the Writers' Council of Rumania), *Mihail Eminescu: A Poet of the Love of Life* (Bucharest, Grafica Nouă Unitatea, 1964), commemorating the 75th anniversary of the poet's death. Cf. D. A. Nanu, *Le Poète Eminescu et la poésie lyrique française* (Paris, 1930, 152 pp.).

Gheorghiu, Constantin Virgil (1916—).   The Death of Kyralessa. Tr. Marika Mihályi from French. Chicago, Regnery, 1968. 268 pp.

————The Twenty-fifth Hour. Tr. Rita Eldon from French. London, Heinemann, and N.Y., Knopf, 1950. 404 pp. Repr. Chicago, Regnery, 1966.

Ionescu, Eugene (1912—).   Since he was brought up in France, writes in French, and has lived only a short time in Rumania, he is listed under French Literature.

Ionescu, Take (1858–1922). Some Personal Impressions. Tr. from the French, with intro. Viscount Bryce. London, Nisbet, 1919. x, 264 pp. Repr. N.Y., Stokes, 1920, xi, 292 pp.

   Much of the book was originally published in the periodical *La Roumanie de Bucarest.*

Iorga, Nicolae (1871–1940). The Byzantine Empire. Tr. Allen H. Powles from French. London, Dent, 1907. viii, 236 pp.

————A History of Roumania. See Background, above.

————A History of Anglo-Roumanian Relations. Bucharest, Societate Anglo-Romană, 1931. 126 pp.

————My American Lectures. Collected and arranged by Norman L. Forter. Bucharest, State Printing Office, 1932. 191 pp. ill.

   Cf. his *Anthologie de la littérature roumaine*, in Collections, above. Of his numerous works in French, note *Art et littérature des Roumains: Synthèses parallèles* (Paris, 1929); *L'Art populaire en Roumanie* (Paris, 1923); *Essai de synthèse de l'histoire de l'humanité* (Paris, Gamber, 1926–28, 4 vols.); and *Histoire des Roumains et de la romanité orientale* (Bucharest, Académie Roumaine, 1937, 4 vols. in 5). Both the Britannica art. (under Jorga) and the *Columbia Dictionary of Modern Foreign Literature* art. are inadequate.

Istrati, Panait (1884–1935). Wrote mostly in French and published in Paris: notably the two tetralogies (fiction) *Les Récits d'Adrien Zograffi* (1924–26) and *La Vie d'Adrien* Zograffi (1933–35). The latter has not been tr.

————The Balkan Tavern. Tr. Anthony Thorne. London, Toulmin, 1931. 285 pp. (vol. 2 of *Les Récits*).

   Tr. Maude Valérie White as Uncle Anghel. N.Y., Knopf, 1927. 271 pp.

————The Bandits. Tr. William A. Drake. N.Y., Knopf, 1929. 286 pp. (vols. 3, 4 of *Les Récits*).

————The Bitter Orange Tree. Tr. Rosalind Zoglin. London, Stein & Gollancz, and N.Y., Vanguard, 1931. 232 pp.

————Kyra Kyralina. Tr. James Whitall, with intro. Romain Rolland. N.Y., Knopf, 1926. xi, 219 pp. (vol. 1 of *Les Récits*).

    Tr. Anthony Thorne as Kyra My Sister. London, Toulmin, 1930. 256 pp.

————Russia Unveiled (*La Russie nue*). Tr. R. J. S. Curtis. London, Allen and Unwin, 1931. 272 pp.

————The Thistles of the Baragan. Tr. Jacques LeClercq. N.Y., Vanguard, 1930. 184 pp.

Kirițescu, Alexandru.   The Magpies (A Comedy in Three Acts). Tr. V. Stoenescu. Bucharest, Meridians, 1960. 110 pp.

Luca, Remus.   *Ana Nucu* (A Novel). Tr. Sanda Stolojan. Bucharest, "The Book," 1956. 234 pp.

Mirodan, Alexandru.   The Famous 702 (A Play in Three Acts). Tr. Carol Kormos. Bucharest, Meridians, 1961. 78 pp.

Musatescu, Tudor.   Titanic-Waltz (A Comedy in Three Acts). Tr. Lazăr Marinescu. Bucharest, Meridians, 1961. 78 pp.

Neagoe, Peter (1890?—).   Writes in English.

————Americans Abroad: An Anthology (ed.). The Hague, Service Pr., 1932. xi, 475 pp.

————Easter Sun. Paris, Obelisk Pr., and N.Y., Coward-McCann, and London, Hutchinson (First Novel Series), 1934. 349 pp., 316 pp., 288 pp.

————Storm: A Book of Short Stories. Intro. Eugène Jolas. Paris, New Review Pubns, 1932. 179 pp.

————There Is My Heart. London, Dent, and N.Y., Coward-McCann, 1934. 383 pp.

————A Time to Keep. N.Y., Coward-McCann, 1949. 281 pp. (autobiographical).

————Winning a Wife, and Other Stories. N.Y., Coward-McCann, 1935. 292 pp.

Petrescu, Camil (1894–1957).   A Man amongst Men. Tr. Eugenia Farca and Dan Duțescu. Bucharest, Foreign Languages Pub. House, 1958. 2 vols. (774 pp.), ill.

————Those Poor Stout Hearts (A Play in Three Acts). Tr. V. Stoenescu. Bucharest, Meridians, 1960. 132 pp.

Petrescu, Cezar (1892–1961).   Gathering Clouds. Tr. anon. Bucharest, Foreign Languages Pub. House, 1957. 3 vols. (975 pp.).

Popovici, Titus (1930—).   The Stranger. Tr. Lazăr Marinescu. Bucharest, Foreign Languages Pub. House, 1957. 672 pp. Repr. 1962.
   An important novel illustrating postwar literary trends in Rumania.

Preda, Marin (1922—).   In a Village (A Story). Tr. Lazăr Marinescu. Bucharest, "The Book," 1956. 223 pp.

————The Morometes. Tr. N. Mișu. Bucharest, Foreign Languages Pub. House, 1957. 656 pp. ill.

Prisnea, Constantin.   Bacchus in Rumania. Tr. Dan Duțescu and Leon Levițchi. Bucharest, Meridiane, 1964. 247 pp.

Rebreanu, Liviu (1885–1894).   The Forest of the Hanged. Tr. A. V. Wise. London, Allen and Unwin, and N.Y., Duffield, 1930. 350 pp., 406 pp. Repr. London, Owen, 1967.
   A novel dealing with the First World War.

————Ion. Tr. anon. Bucharest, Meridians, 1962. 279 pp.

   Tr. Richard Hillard. UNESCO Collection. London, Owen, 1965. viii, 411 pp.

   Tr. and ed. Ralph M. Aderman. N.Y., Twayne, 1967. 442 pp.

————The Uprising. Tr. P. Grandjean and S. Hartaner. UNESCO Collection. London, Owen, and Carbondale, Southern Illinois Univ. Pr., 1964. 385 pp. Repr. London, Mayflower, 1965, paper.

Cf. Alexandru Piru, *Liviu Rebreanu*. Tr. anon. Bucharest, Meridiane, 1965. 144 pp.

Relgis, Eugen (1895—). Muted Voices. Tr. Rose Freeman-Ishill, intro. Stefan Zweig. Berkeley Heights, N.J., Oriole Pr., 1938. 200 pp. ill.
His *Cosmétapolis* was tr. into French (Bucharest and Paris, 1935). Living in Uruguay since 1947, he writes now in Spanish: e.g., *Perspectivas culturales en Sudamérica* (Montevideo, Pubs. de la Universidad, 1958). See William T. Starr and Frederick L. Stimson in *Books Abroad*, vol. 35, 1961, 123–27.

Sadoveanu, Mihail (1880–1961). Ancuţas Inn. Tr. anon. Bucharest, Meridians, 1962. 95 pp.

————Evening Tales. Tr. Eugenia Farca, Lazăr Marinescu, et al. Bucharest, Foreign Languages Pub. House, 1958. 446 pp. Repr. N.Y., Twayne, 1962, 374 pp.
An excellent anthology of his short stories.

————The Hatchet, a Short Story. Tr. Eugenia Farca. Bucharest, "The Book," 1956. 195 pp. Repr. 1962; repr. London, Allen and Unwin, and Mystic, Conn., Verry, 1965, 163 pp.

————The Mill That Came with the Floods. Tr. Eugenia Farca. Bucharest, Meridiane, 1963. 289 pp.

————Mitrea Cocor. Tr. P. M., foreword Mulk Raj Anand, intro. Jack Lindsay. London, Fore Pubns, 1953. xx, 178 pp.

————The Mud-Hut Dwellers. Tr. anon. Bucharest, Meridiane, 1962. 73 pp. Repr. N.Y., Twayne, 1964. 107 pp.

————Nicoara Poteoavă. Tr. anon. Bucharest, Meridiane, 1963. 401 pp.

————Tales of War. Tr. anon. N.Y., Twayne, 1962. 140 pp.

————Under the Sign of the Crab. Tr. anon. Bucharest, Meridiane, 1963. 326 pp.

Slavici, Ion (1848–1915).   The Lucky Mill. Tr. A. Mircea Emperle. N.Y., Duffield, 1919. 219 pp.

————Short Stories. Tr. Ana Cartianu. Bucharest, "The Book," 1955. 312 pp.

Stancu, Zaharia (1902—).   Barefoot. Tr. P. M., with intro. Jack Lindsay. London, Fore Pubs., 1951. 272 pp.

Sylva, Carmen (pseud. of Queen Elizabeth of Rumania, 1843–1916). A Roumanian Vendetta and Other Stories. Written in German with the title *Rache*, and tr. E. H.   London, R. A. Everett, 1903. 250 pp.
    For her many writings in several languages (not Rumanian), see George Bengescu, *Carmen Sylva: Bibliographie et extraits de ses oeuvres* (Bruxelles, Paul Lacomblez, 1904, 367 pp.).

Zamfirescu, Duliu (1858–1922).   Sasha. Tr. Lucy Byng. London, Philpot, 1926. 246 pp.

SPANISH LITERATURE

REMIGIO U. PANE

**Adams, Nicholson B. The Heritage of Spain: An Introduction to Its Civilization. N.Y., Holt, 1943. 331 pp. Repr. 1959, lxiv, 380 pp.
> "The main facts about Spain's history, culture, and art, with emphasis on her literature." Beautifully illustrated; excellent bibliography, especially for the literature. Best manual for student or teacher.

**Altamira, Rafael. A History of Spain from the Beginnings to the Present Day. Tr. from Spanish by Muna Lee. N.Y., Van Nostrand, and London, Macmillan, 1950. 748 pp.
> Best manual in English.

**————A History of Spanish Civilization. Tr. P. Volkov from Spanish. London, Constable, 1930. xiii, 280 pp. Repr. N.Y., Biblo and Tannen, 1968.
> Well illustrated; excellent bibliography. Standard work.

Atkinson, William C. Spain: A Brief History. London, Methuen, 1934. 200 pp.

Bevan, Bernard. History of Spanish Architecture. London, Batsford, 1938. 199 pp.
> Well illustrated and up to date.

*Borrow, George. The Bible in Spain. London, Murray, 1843. 328 pp. Many reprs., esp. EL, 1907, repr. 1931, 1947; WC, 1925.

*Brenan, Gerald. The Spanish Labyrinth. Cambridge, Cambridge Univ. Pr., and N.Y., Macmillan, 1943. 384 pp. Repr. 1960.
> An impartial work on the conditions leading to the Spanish Civil War.

Castillejo, José. Wars of Ideas in Spain: Philosophy, Politics, and Education. London, Murray, 1937. 167 pp.

Castro, Américo. The Structure of Spanish History (*España en su historia*). Tr. Edmund L. King. Princeton, Princeton Univ. Pr., and London, Oxford Univ. Pr., 1954. 689 pp.

*Chase, Gilbert.   The Music of Spain. N.Y., Norton, 1941. 375 pp.
  Good bibliography; an extensive list of phonograph records of Spanish music of all epochs.

*Dozy, Reinhart.   Spanish Islam. A History of the Moslems in Spain. Tr. F. C. Stokes. London, Chatto & Windus, 1913. xxxvi, 769 pp.
  Best treatment of the subject.

**Ellis, Havelock.   The Soul of Spain. London, Constable, and Boston, Houghton Mifflin, 1908. ix, 420 pp. Repr. 1926; repr. with intro. on Spanish Civil War, 1937, xvii, 420 pp.
  Best interpretation of the psychology of the Spanish people.

Ganivet, Ángel.   Spain: An Interpretation (*Idearium español*). Tr. J. R. Carey from the Spanish. London, Eyre & Spottiswoode, 1946. 136 pp.
  A fine analysis of Spanish character.

Mackay, John A.   The Other Spanish Christ. London, Student Christian Movement, 1932, and N.Y., Macmillan, 1933. 288 pp.
  Best work on the spiritual history of Spain.

*Madariaga, Salvador de.   Englishmen, Frenchmen, Spaniards. London, Milford, 1928. 256 pp. Repr. 1931.
  A penetrating analysis.

————Spain: A Modern History. London, Cape, 1942, and N.Y., Creative Age Pr., 1943. 509 pp. Repr. N.Y., Praeger, 1960, 736 pp., paper.
  Historical analysis of the period from the 19th c. through the Civil War.

Menéndez Pidal, Ramón.   The Spaniards in Their History. Tr. Walter Starkie. London, Hollis & Carter, and N.Y., Norton, 1950. 259 pp.

Olague, Ignacio.   This Is Spain. Tr. Walter Starkie from French. London, Cohen and West, 1954. 167 pp.

Peers, E. Allison.   Spain in Eclipse, 1937–1943. London, Methuen, 1943. 275 pp.

————The Spanish Tragedy, 1930–1936. London, Methuen, and N.Y., Oxford Univ. Pr., 1936. 247 pp.

*Post, Chandler R.   A History of Spanish Painting. Cambridge, Harvard Univ. Pr., 1930–41. 8 vols. in 12.
  The best and most thorough work on the subject.

Ramos-Oliveira, Antonio.   Politics and Men of Modern Spain (1808–1946). Tr. Teener Hall. London, Gollancz, 1946, and N.Y. Crown, 1948. 720 pp.

*Spain: A Companion to Spanish Studies.   Ed. E. Allison Peers. London, Methuen, and N.Y., Dodd Mead, 1929. 302 pp. Repr. 1930, 1938, etc., 5th ed. rev. R. F. Brown, 1956, 319 pp.
  A survey by specialists of the ethnology, history, literature, and art of Spain.

*The Texas Quarterly.   Image of Spain: A Special Issue. Austin, Univ. of Texas, Spring 1961. 284 pp.
  Excellent survey of contemporary Spanish life and letters.

*Trend, J. B.   The Civilization of Spain. Home Univ. Library. London and N.Y., Oxford Univ. Pr., 1944. 223 pp.
  Brief but accurate introduction, with critical bibliography.

Bibliography

*Fitzmaurice-Kelly, James.   Spanish Bibliography. London, Oxford, 1925. 389 pp.
  Substantially the same matter is found in the author's New History of Spanish Literature, see below.

*Foulché-Delbosc, Raymond, and Barrau-Dihigo, L.   *Manuel de l'Hispanisant.* N.Y., Putnam, 1920–25. 2 vols. Repr. N.Y., Kraus, 1959.
  Fundamental for material to 1920. Vol. 2 lists contents of all collections of Spanish texts.

O'Brien, Robert.   Spanish Plays in English Translation: An Annotated Bibliography. N.Y., Las Americas, 1963. 82 pp.

Pane, Remigio U.   English Translations from the Spanish, 1484–1943: A Bibliography. New Brunswick, N.J., Rutgers Univ. Pr., 1944. 218 pp.

Randall, Dale B. J.   The Golden Tapestry: A Critical Survey of Non-Chivalric Spanish Fiction in English Translation (1543–1657). Durham, N.C., Duke Univ. Pr., 1963. 262 pp.

Literary Studies

Adams, N. B., and Keller, J. E.   A Brief Survey of Spanish Literature. Littlefield College Outlines. Paterson, N.J., Littlefield, Adams, 1960. 196 pp.

Bell, Aubrey.   Castilian Literature. Oxford, Clarendon Pr., 1938. xiv, 261 pp. Repr. N.Y., Russell, 1968.

Boggs, Ralph S.   Outline History of Spanish Literature. London and N.Y., Oxford Univ. Pr., 1926. 551 pp.

*****Brenan, Gerald.**   The Literature of the Spanish People. London, Cambridge Univ. Pr., 1951. 496 pp. Repr. 1953; N.Y., Meridian Books, 1957, 342 pp.

Chandler, R. E., and Schwartz, K.   A New History of Spanish Literature. Baton Rouge, Louisiana State Univ. Pr., 1961. 696 pp.

Fitzmaurice-Kelly, James.   New History of Spanish Literature. London and N.Y., Oxford Univ. Pr., 1926. 521 pp.

Green, Otis H.   Spain and the Western Tradition: The Castilian Mind in Literature from "El Cid" to Calderón. Madison, Univ. of Wisconsin Pr., 1963–66. 4 vols.

******Mérimée, Ernest, and Morley, S. Griswold.**   A History of Spanish Literature. N.Y., Holt, 1930. 635 pp.

Newmark, Maxim.   Dictionary of Spanish Literature. New Students' Outline Series. Paterson, N.J., Littlefield, Adams, 1963. 352 pp.

Northup, George Tyler.   An Introduction to Spanish Literature. Chicago, Univ. Pr., 1925. 479 pp. Repr. 1936; repr. enlarged by N. B. Adams, 1960, 532 pp., repr. 1965.

Ticknor, George.   History of Spanish Literature. N.Y., Harper, 1849. 3 vols. Many reprs. to 6th ed., Boston, Houghton Mifflin, 1891, 3 vols., later reprs. to 1965.

Collections

An Anthology of Spanish Literature in English Translation.   Ed. Seymour Resnick and Jeanne Pasmantier. N.Y., Ungar, 1958. 2 vols.
> Mostly brief pieces or passages, vol. 1 from *The Cid* to Gracián; vol. 2 by 46 authors from the 18th to the 20th c.

Borrow, George.   The Zincali, or an Account of the Gipsies of Spain: With an Original Collection of Their Song and Poetry. London, Murray, 1841. 2 vols. Many reprs., esp. EL, 1914 et seq., 251 pp.
> Vol. 2 contains "Rhymes of the Gitanos" in Spanish and English.

Brown, Irving H.   Deep Song: Adventures with Gypsy Songs and Singers in Andalusia and Other Lands, with Original Translations. N.Y. and London, Harper, 1929. 355 pp.

Busk, Rachel Harriette.   Patrañas, or Spanish Stories, Legendary and Traditional. London, 1870. 376 pp.

*****Cohen, J. M.,** ed. and tr.   The Penguin Book of Spanish Verse, with Plain Prose Translations of Each Poem. Penguin, 1956. 442 pp.

Craig, K. S., tr.   Spanish Lyrics. London, Bumpus, 1929. 171 pp.

Farnell, Ida.   Spanish Prose and Poetry Old and New, with Translated Specimens. Oxford, Clarendon Pr., and N.Y., Oxford Univ. Pr., 1920. 185 pp.
> Many trs. from Juan Ruiz to Antonio Machado.

*****Flores, Angel,** ed., various trs.   An Anthology of Spanish Poetry from Garcilaso to García Lorca, in English Translations with Spanish Originals. N.Y., Anchor Books, 1961. 516 pp.
> Poets represented by several poems each are Garcilaso, Luis de León, San Juan de la Cruz, Góngora, Lope de Vega, Quevedo; and from the later periods, Bécquer, Rosalía de Castro, González Prada, García Lorca, Jiménez, and Machado; and from overseas Sor Juana Inés de la Cruz, Rubén Darío and Gabriela Mistral.

————Great Spanish Short Stories. Trs. various. N.Y., Dell, 1962. 304 pp.
Two stories from the Golden Age: *The Abencerraje*, and Cervantes'
"Curioso impertinente"; nine stories by modern authors (since 1800:)
Alarcón, Azorín, Cela, Jarnés, Miró, Pardo Bazán, Trueba, Unamuno, and
Valle-Inclán; and five stories by Spanish Americans, qq.v. below.

————Great Spanish Stories. ML, 1956. xiv, 490 pp.
Sixteen stories of the 19th and 20th c. by Alarcón, Alas, Bécquer,
Pérez de Ayala, and Pérez Galdós; and Aub, Ayala, Cela, Chacel, Dieste,
Gironella, Jarnés, Laforet, Sánchez Barbudo, Unamuno, and Valle-
Inclán.

————Spanish Drama. N.Y., Bantam, 1962. 473 pp.
Ten plays from Rueda to Lorca: Calderón, *Life Is a Dream*; Cervantes,
The Vigilant Sentinel; Rueda, *The Olives*; Ruiz de Alarcón, *The Truth
Suspected*; Tirso, *The Rogue of Seville*; Vega Carpio, *Fuente Ovejuna*;
Moratín, *When a Girl Says Yes*; Echegaray, *The Great Galeoto*; Benavente,
The Bonds of Interest; García Lorca, *Blood Wedding*. For translators, see
the individual authors, below.

————Spanish Stories/*Cuentos Españoles*. N.Y., Bantam, 1960. xii, 339 pp.,
parallel texts.
Stories by nine Spanish authors (Juan Manuel, selections from *Lazarillo*,
Cervantes, Alarcón, Pardo Bazán, Alas, Cela, Goytisolo, and Unamuno)
and by five Spanish American writers. See also collections ed. by Flores in
later periods.

Franco, Jean, ed. and tr.   Short Stories in Spanish: *Cuentos Hispánicos*. Penguin,
1966. 204 pp.
Seven of the eight authors are Spanish American; the European author is
Camilo José Cela ("La Romería").

Galloway, Clifford H., ed. and tr.   *Refranes Españoles*: The Book of Spanish
Proverbs. N.Y., Spanish-American, 1944. 223 pp.

Gems of Spanish Poetry.   Ed. F. J. Vingut. N.Y., F. J. Vingut Co., 1855.
271 pp.

The Genius of The Spanish Theater.   Ed. Robert O'Brien, various trs.
N.Y., New Amer. Lib., 1964.

Of the nine plays, five are by authors of the Golden Age: Calderón, *The Banquet of King Belshazzar*; Quiñones de Benavente, *The Drunkard*; Rojas Zorrilla, *None But the King*; Tirso de Molina, *Prudence in Woman*; Vega Carpio, *The Idiot Lady*. Four are by contemporary authors: Buero Vallejo, *The Weaver of Dreams*; Casona, *The Lady, the Dawn*; García Lorca, *The Love of Don Perlímplin*; Grau Delgado, *Mister Pygmalion*.

Hispanic Anthology.   Ed. Thomas Walsh. Hispanic Society of America. N.Y. and London, Putnam, 1920. xii, 799 pp. Repr. N.Y., Kraus, 1969.

Jones, Willis Knapp, ed. and tr.   Spanish One-Act Plays in English: A Comprehensive Anthology of Spanish Drama from the Twelfth Century to the Present. Dallas, Texas, Tardy Pub. Co., 1934. 296 pp.
> Sixteen plays from the 13th c. *Magi* to Álvarez Quintero and Arniches. The earlier period is represented by Juan del Encina, Lope de Rueda, and Alonso de la Vega, qq.v.; the Golden Age is represented by Calderón, Cervantes, Moreto y Cubaña, and Vega Carpio; Ramón de la Cruz is of the 18th c.; Bretón de los Herreros, Javier de Burgos, and Zorrilla are of the 19th.

Madariaga, Salvador de, ed. and tr.   Spanish Folk Songs. London, Constable, 1922. 58 pp.

Middlemore, Mrs. S. G. C., ed. and tr.   Spanish Legendary Tales. London, Chatto, 1885. 302 pp.

Onís, Harriet de, ed. and tr.   Spanish Stories and Tales. N.Y., Knopf, 1954. 270 pp. Repr. N.Y., Pocket Books, 1956.
> Twenty-three stories, largely tr. by the editor: 11 by Spanish writers from Juan Manuel and Cervantes to Valle-Inclán, 12 by Spanish American writers.

*Roscoe, Thomas,** ed. and tr.   The Spanish Novelists: A Series of Tales, from the Earliest Period to the Close of the Seventeenth Century. London, Bentley, 1832. 3 vols. Repr. Chandos Classics, 1880.
> From Juan Manuel to 1700, including *Lazarillo* and *Guzmán de Alfarache*, some Cervantes, Quevedo, etc.

Stevens, Capt. John, tr.   The Spanish Libertines: Or the Lives of Justina, the Country Jilt; Celestina, the Bawd of Madrid; and Estevanillo Gonzalez. London, 1707. Repr. 1709.

Tales from the Italian and Spanish. N.Y., Review of Reviews, 1920.
8 vols.
> The Spanish in vols. 5–8: vol. 5, *Don Quixote*; vol. 6, *Guzmán de Alfarache*,
> *Lazarillo*, and Quevedo's *Paul of Segovia*; vol. 7, Palacio Valdés' *Marta y*
> *María*, and Valera's *Pepita Jiménez*; vol. 8, thirty short stories by 19th and
> 20th c. authors.

**Translations from Hispanic Poets. N.Y., Hispanic Society of America,
1938. 271 pp.

*Turnbull, Eleanor L, tr. verse. Ten Centuries of Spanish Poetry: An
Anthology in English Verse with Original Texts, from the XIth Century
to the Generation of 1898. Baltimore, Johns Hopkins Pr., 1955. 452 pp.
> See also Ticknor's *History*, above, which contains many trs.

Medieval Period

Literary Studies

Keller, John E.   "Medieval Spanish Literature," in The Medieval Literature of
Western Europe: A Review of Research, Mainly 1930–1960, ed. John H.
Fisher. N.Y., Modern Language Association, 1966, pp. 329–61.

Menéndez Pidal, Ramón.   The Cid and His Spain. Tr. Harold Sunderland.
London, Murray, 1934. 494 pp.

Post Chandler R.   Medieval Spanish Allegory. Cambridge, Mass., Harvard
Univ. Pr., 1915. 331 pp.

Trend, J. B.   Alfonso the Sage and Other Spanish Essays. London, Constable,
1926. 216 pp.

Collections

***Bowring, John,** ed. and tr.   Ancient Poetry and Romances of Spain. London, Taylor and Hessey, 1824. 328 pp.

Cushing, Caleb.   Reminiscences of Spain. Boston, Carter Hendee, 1885. 2 vols. in 1.
Includes fifteen *romances* tr. by the author.

Early Spanish Plays.   Ed. Robert O'Brien, various trs. N.Y., Las Américas, 1964. 2 vols.
The Magi (13th c.); Gómez Manrique; Rodrigo Cota; and Renaissance dramatists, qq.v. below.

Gibson, James Young.   The Cid Ballads and Other Poems and Translations from the Spanish and German. London, Kegan Paul, 1887. 2 vols. Repr. 1898, 1 vol., 605 pp.

King, Georgiana C.   Heart of Spain. Cambridge, Mass., Harvard Univ. Pr., 1941. 170 pp.
Contains fifty *coplas*, six *romances*, and three poems by Luis de León.

****Lockhart, J. G.,** ed. and tr.   Ancient Spanish Ballads, Historical and Romantic. Edinburgh, Blackwood, 1823. xxvii, 209 pp. Many reprs. to 1890, London, Routledge, and N.Y., Dutton, 320 pp.

Longfellow, Henry Wadsworth, tr.   *Coplas de don Jorge Manrique.* Boston, Allen and Ticknor, 1833. 89 pp. Part repr. Oxford, Blackwell, 1919, 53 pp. Besides the *coplas*: "sonnets moral and devotional" by Lope de Vega, Aldana, Madrano, and one anon., parallel texts. The repr. has only the *coplas*.

Merwin, William S., ed. and tr.   Some Spanish Ballads. N.Y. and London, Abelard-Schuman, 1961. 127 pp., and N.Y., Anchor Books, 1961, 158 pp.

Percy, Thomas, tr.   Ancient Songs, Chiefly on Moorish Subjects. London, Oxford Univ. Pr., 1932. 56 pp.

***Rodd, Thomas,** tr.   Ancient Ballads from the Civil Wars of Granada and the Twelve Peers of France. London, Ostell, 1803. 199 pp.

————Ancient Spanish Ballads, verse tr., in his tr. of the History of Charles the Great and Orlando. London, T. Rodd and T. Boosey, 1812. 2 vols. in 1. Repr. 1821; in Mediaeval Tales, ed. Henry Morley, 1884, which repr. 1886, 1890.

> Mostly composed of *Cid* ballads, in Spanish and English, those ed. Damián López de Tortajada, *Floresta de varios romances* (1611?).

INDIVIDUAL AUTHORS

Alfonso X, El Sabio (1221–1284).   *Las Cantigas de Santa Maria*. Tr. Miguel Unamuno, in The Tragic Sense of Life (tr. 1921, q.v. below).

————*Las siete partidas*. Tr. Samuel Parsons Scott. Chicago and N.Y., Commerce Clearing House, 1931. xcvii, 1505 pp.
> Another tr., New Orleans, 1818.

Alfonso, Pedro (1062–1110).   *Disciplina clericalis*. See Medieval Latin Literature, in vol. 1, above.

Auto de los Reyes Magos.   See The Magi, below.

The Book of Apollonius (13th c.).   Tr. verse Raymond L. Grismer and Elizabeth Atkins. Minneapolis, Univ. of Minnesota Pr., 1936. xx, 113 pp.

Book of Women's Wiles and Deceits (1253).   Tr. H. C. Coote in his tr. from the Italian of Domenico Comparetti, Researches Respecting the Book of Sindibad. London, Folk-Lore Society Pubs., 9, 1882, pp. 73–164.

> Tr. J. E. Keller as Sindbad, The Philosopher: The Book of the Wiles of Women. Chapel Hill, Univ. of North Carolina Pr., 1956. 60 pp.

> The original was tr. into Spanish by the Infante Fadrique from an Arabic version of the Indic Sindibad.

El Cid Campeador (12th c.).   Tr. prose Robert Southey as The Chronicle of the Cid. London, Longmans, 1808. 468 pp. Many reprs. to N.Y., Dial, 1958, 230 pp.; N.Y., Doubleday, 1961, 288 pp.

> Tr. John Ormsby as The Poem of the Cid, in literal verse and condensed prose. London, Longmans, 1879. Repr. N.Y., Stechert, 1915; 1938, 124 pp.

Ed. and tr. Archer M. Huntington as Poem of the Cid. N.Y., Putnam, 1897–1903. 3 vols. Repr. smaller format N.Y., Hispanic Society of America, 1907–08; repr. reduced facs. of first ed., ibid., 1921; repr. offset of 2d ed., ibid., 1942, 1 vol., 513 pp.

    Vol. 1, text (from the unique ms.); vol. 2, tr.; vol. 3, notes.

Tr. R. Sheldon Rose and Leonard Bacon as The Lay of the Cid. Berkeley, Univ. of California Pr., 1919. 130 pp.

Tr. prose Merriam Sherwood as The Tale of the Warrior Lord. N.Y., Longmans, 1930. 156 pp. Repr. 1957, 173 pp.

Tr. Lesley Byrd Simpson as The Poem of the Cid. Berkeley, Univ. of California Pr., 1957. 139 pp.

*Tr. verse W. S. Merwin as Poem of the Cid from the Spanish text of R. Menéndez Pidal. London, Dent, 1959, 240 pp., and N.Y., Las Américas, 1960, 311 pp. Repr. N.Y., New Amer. Lib., 1962.

Tr. J. Gerald Markley as The Epic of the Cid. Indianapolis, Bobbs-Merrill, 1961. 132 pp.

Tr. Paul Blackburn as Poem of the Cid. N.Y., Amer. RDM Corporation, 1966. 155 pp.

Cota de Maguaque, Rodrigo (d. before 1495).   Dialogue between Love and an Old Man. Tr. Lucia Newton, in Early Spanish Plays, 1964, q.v. in Collections.

The Dance of Death (15th c.).   Tr. anon. in H. W. Longfellow, Poets and Poetry of Europe, 1845 et seq. Repr. in Literature of All Nations, ed. Julian Hawthorne, 1897.

Desclot, Bernardo (fl. 1300).   Chronicle of the Reign of King Pedro III of Aragon (etc., A.D. 1134–1285). Tr. F. L. Critchlow from Catalan. Princeton, N.J., Princeton Univ. Pr., 1928–34. 2 vols.

Díaz de Gámez, Gutierre (c.1379–c.1450).   The Unconquered Knight: A Chronicle of the Deeds of Don Pero Nino, Count of Buelna. Tr. and selected Joan Evans. London, Routledge, 1929. 232 pp.

    The original is El victorial, history of Castile at end of 14th c.

González de Clavijo, Ruy (d. 1412).   Narrative of the Embassy to the Court of Timour at Samarcand, A.D. 1403–1406. Tr. Clements R. Markham. London, Hakluyt Soc. Works no. 26, 1859. lvi, 200 pp. Repr. N.Y., Burt Franklin, 1963.

> Tr. Guy Le Strange as Embassy to Tamerlane, 1403–06. Broadway Travellers. London, Routledge, 1928. 375 pp.

Jaime I of Aragon (1208–1276).   The Chronicle of Jaime I, King of Aragon, Surnamed The Conqueror. Tr. John Forster from Catalan. London, Chapman and Hall, 1883. 2 vols.

Lull, Ramón (1235–1315).   Blanquerna: A Thirteenth Century Romance. Tr. E. Allison Peers from Catalan. London, Jerrold, 1926. 536 pp.

————The Book of the Beasts. Tr. E. Allison Peers from Catalan. London, Burns Oates, 1927. 90 pp.
One section, complete in itself, of the romance *Felix*.

————The Book of the Ordre of Chyualry. Tr. William Caxton from a French version. Westminster, Caxton, 1484. Repr. ed. Alfred T. P. Byles. EETS OS 168. London, 1926. lxvii, 143 pp.

————The Tree of Love. Tr. E. Allison Peers from Catalan. London, S.P.C.K., and N.Y., Macmillan, 1926. 127 pp.
Tr. of the latter half of the *Arbre de philosophia de amor*.

> Cf. *A Life of Ramón Lull, Written by an Unknown Hand about 1311*, tr. from Catalan by E. Allison Peers (London, Burns Oates, 1927, 86 pp.), which is the *Vida coetánia* by Tomás la Myésier, Lull's disciple.

The Magi (*Auto de los reyes magos*, c.1145).   Tr. Willis K. Jones as A Spanish Mystery Play of the 12th Century, in Poet Lore, vol. 39 (1928), 306–9. Repr. in his Spanish One-Act Plays in English, 1934, see Collections above.

> Tr. Lucia Newton in Early Spanish Plays, 1964, q.v. ibid.

Manrique, Gómez (c.1412–c.1490).   The Birth of Our Lord. Tr. Robert O'Brien in Early Spanish Plays, 1964, q.v. in Collections.

Manrique, Jorge (?1440–1479).   The *Coplas* (*Coplas por la muerte de su padre*). Tr. Henry Wadsworth Longfellow, in The *Coplas*, 1833, see Collections, above.

> Tr. Thomas Walsh, in Hispanic Anthology, 1920, see ibid. Repr. in his Catholic Anthology. N.Y., Macmillan, 1927, which repr. 1932, 1939.

**Manuel, Juan (1282–1347).   Count Lucanor, or the Fifty Pleasant Stories of Patronio. Tr. James York. Westminster, Pickering, 1868. 246 pp. Repr. 1896, 1899, and in Broadway Translations, London, Routledge, and N.Y., Dutton, 1924, xxviii, 259 pp.
> One story, "The Man Who Married an Ill-Tempered Wife," was tr. Harriet de Onís in her *Spanish Stories and Tales*: see Collections.

Martínez de Toledo, Alfonso (Arcipreste de Talavera, 1398?–1470?). Little Sermons on Sin. Tr. Lesley Byrd Simpson. Berkeley, Univ. of California Pr., and London, Cambridge Univ. Pr., 1959. 200 pp.
> The original is *El Arcipreste de Talavera o sea El Corvacho*.

Muntaner, Ramón (d. 1336).   The Chronicle of Muntaner [1208 1328]. Tr. Anna Lady Goodenough from Catalan. London, Hakluyt Soc. Works, ser. 2, nos. 47, 50: 1920–21.

Mystery of Elche (15th c. play of the Assumption).   Tr. Walter Starkie from Catalan in Eight Spanish Plays of the Golden Age, 1964: see Collections.

Rázon de Amor (12th c.).   Tr. Thomas Walsh, in Hispanic Anthology, 1920, q.v. in Collections.

Ruiz, Juan (Arcipreste de Hita, 1283?–1350).   The Book of Good Love. Tr. Elisha K. Kane, intro. John Esten Keller. N.Y., W. E. Rudge, 1933, 320 pp. Repr. Chapel Hill, Univ. of North Carolina Pr., 1968, lv. 269 pp.

Sánchez Talavera, Ferrán (15th c.).   *Dezir*. Tr. Thomas Walsh, in his Hispanic Anthology, 1920, q.v. in Collections.

Santillana, Marques de (1398–1458).   The Proverbes with the Paraphrase of D. Peter Diaz of Toledo. Tr. Barnabe Googe. London, Watkins, 1579.

Tafur, Pero (1410?–1484?).   Travels and Adventures, 1435–1439. Tr. Malcolm Letts. Broadway Travellers. London, Routledge, and N.Y., Harper, 1926. xv, 260 pp.
>The travels throughout Europe went as far as Constantinople.

The Renaissance

INDIVIDUAL AUTHORS

Casas, Bartolomé de las (1474–1566).   An Account of the First Voyages and Discoveries made by the Spaniards in America. Tr. anon. London, 1699.
>Six of the nine tracts pub. as the *Brevissima relación de la destrucción de las Indias*. The first tract was tr. several times: by M. M. S. from the French version, as *The Spanish Colonie*, 1583, 74 pp., repr. in Samuel Purchas, *Purchas his Pilgrimes*, 1625; tr. John Phillips as *The Tears of the Indians*, 1656; tr. anon, from the French as *Popery Truly Display'd*, 1689. The bishop's important history of the discoveries has not been tr.

Cisneros, Garcias, O.S.B. (d. 1510).   Book of Spiritual Exercises and a Directory for the Canonical Hours. Tr. by a Monk of St. Augustine's Monastery, Ramsgate. London, Burns and Oates, 1876. xv, 265, 50 pp.

>Tr. E. Allison Peers as Book of Exercises for the Spiritual Life. Montserrat, Monastery of Monserrat, 1929. 333 pp.

*Colombo, Cristoforo (1451–1506).   The Voyages of Christopher Columbus, Being the Journals of His First and Third, and the Letters Concerning His First and Last Voyages, to Which Is Added the Account of the Second Voyage Written by Andrés Bernaldez. Tr. Cecil Jane. London, Argonaut Pr., 1930. 347 pp.

*————Journals and Other Documents on the Life and Voyages of Columbus. Ed. Samuel E. Morison. N.Y., Heritage Pr., 1964. 417 pp.

> Many earlier collections of the letters, journals, and other documents could be noted, especially those pub. by the Hakluyt Society:

————Select Letters, with Original Documents Relating to the Discovery of the New World. Ed. and tr. R. H. Major. Hakluyt Society Works, no. 2, 1848, xv, 249 pp. Re-ed. and enlarged by the same, ibid., no. 43, 1870; much enlarged, re-ed. Cecil Jane as Select Documents Illustrating the Four Voyages of Columbus, ibid., ser. 2, nos. 65, 1929, and 70, 1932, parallel texts.

> An abridgement of the R. H. Major edn is pub. as *Four Voyages to the New World: Letters and Selected Documents* (N.Y., Corinth Books, 1961, 240 pp., parallel texts). A part of the Jane edn is pub. as *The Journal* (N.Y., C. N. Potter, 1960, and London, Anthony Blond, 1961, 227 pp.).

The Life of the Admiral Christopher Columbus by his Son Ferdinand has been tr. from the Italian (the only surviving version) by Benjamin Keen (New Brunswick, N.J., Rutgers Univ. Pr., 1959, 316 pp.).

Cortés, Hernán (1485–1547).   Letters of Cortés: The Five Letters of Relation to the Emperor Charles V, 1519–1526. Tr. Francis A. MacNutt. N.Y. and London, Putnam, 1908. 2 vols.
  Tr. abridged J. Bayard Morris as Five Letters. Broadway Travellers. London, Routledge, 1928, and N.Y., McBride, 1929. xlvii, 388 pp. Repr. ed. Sir E. Denison Ross and Eileen Power, London, Argonaut Pr., 1929.

Díaz del Castillo, Bernal (1492–1581?).   The True History of the Conquest of Mexico. Tr. Maurice Keatinge. London, Wright, 1800. viii, 514 pp. Repr. Argonaut Series, N.Y., McBride, 1927, and London, Harrap, 1928, 2 vols.; repr. N.Y., 1938, xxvii, 362 pp.

> Tr. John Ingram Lockhart. London, Hatchard, 1844. 2 vols.

> *Tr. Alfred P. Maudslay from a new edn of the Spanish ms. London, Hakluyt Society Works, ser. 2, nos. 23, 24, 25, 30, 40: 1908–16. Repr. ed. Sir E. Denison Ross and Eileen Power, Broadway Travellers, London, Routledge, and N.Y., Harper, 1928, vii, 595 pp.; N.Y., Limited Edns Club, 1942; N.Y., Farrar Straus, 1956, 478 pp.; N.Y., Grove Pr., 1958.

Tr. Albert Idell as The Bernal Diaz Chronicles: The True Story of the Conquest of Mexico. N.Y., Doubleday, 1956. 414 pp.

Encina, Juan del (c.1468–c.1530). The Courtier Turned Shepherd (*Egloga de amores*, I). Tr. Robert Lima, in Early Spanish Plays, 1964: see Collections, Medieval.

————Plácida and Vitoriano. Tr. Hugh A. Harter, ibid.

————The Shepherd Turned Courtier (*Egloga de amores*, II). Tr. Robert Lima, ibid.

————Three Shepherds. Tr. Robert Lima, ibid.

Flores, Juan de (15th c.). The Historie of Aurelio and of Isabell, Daughter of the Kinge of Scotlande. Tr. anon. in polyglot edn (French, Italian, Spanish, English). Antwerp, 1556. Repr. London, 1586, 1588, Brussels 1608.

Furió Ceriol, Federico (1532–1592). The Council and Counselors of a Prince (*El Consejo i Consejeros del Principe*). Tr. Thomas Blundeville from an Italian version as A Treatise Declaring How Many Counsells, and What Maner of Counselers a Prince . . . Ought to Have. London, Seres, [1570]. Repr. Gainesville, Fla., Scholars' Facsimiles, 1963, 140 pp.

Garcilaso de la Vega (1501?–1536). The Works of Garcilaso de la Vega, Surnamed the Prince of Castilian Poets. Tr. verse J. B. Wiffen. London, Hurst Robinson, 1823. xxii, 407 pp.

*Part tr. verse James Cleugh as Odes and Sonnets. London, Aquila Pr., 1930. 94 pp.

See anthologies also for further trs.

The standard study is Hayward Keniston, *Garcilaso de la Vega: A Critical Study of His Life and Works* (N.Y., Hispanic Society of America, 1922, 509 pp.).

Guevara, Antonio de (1480?–1545). The Golden Boke of Marcus Aurelius (*Libro llamado Relox de Principes, en el qual va encorporado el muy famoso libro de Marco Aurelio*). Tr. John Bourchier, Baron Berners from a French version.

London, 1534. Repr. 12 times to 1586; repr. ed. J. M. G. Olivares, Berlin, 1916.

Tr. Sir Thomas North from the French as The Diall of Princes. London, 1557. Repr. rev. 1568, 1582, 1619; selections ed. K. N. Colville, 1919.

————————The Familiar Epistles of Sir Anthony of Guevara. Tr. Edward Hellowes. London, 1574. Repr. 1577, 1584.

Tr. Geoffrey Fenton from French as Golden Epistles. London, 1575. Repr. 1577, 1582.

For other Elizabethan trs. of the bishop's moralist writings, see CBEL, I, 814.

López de Gómara, Francisco (1511–1560?).   Annals of the Emperor Charles V. Ed. and tr. R. B. Merriman. Oxford, Clarendon Pr., 1912. 302 pp., parallel texts.

————————The Pleasant Historie of the Conquest of the Weast India . . . by . . . Cortes. Tr. Thomas Nicholas. London, 1578. Repr. 1596; N.Y., Scholars' Facsimiles, 1940, xxi, 405 pp.; Ann Arbor, Mich., Univ. Microfilms, 1966.
Part 2 of the *Historia General de las Indias y Nuevo Mundo*, part 1 dealing with the conquest of Peru.

Martire d'Anghiera, Pietro (1455–1526).   See Neo-Latin Literature, in vol. 1, above.

Mexía, Pedro (1496?–1552?).   A Delectable Dialogue Concerning Phisicke and Phisitions (*Diálogos*). Tr. Thomas Newton, London, 1580.

————————The Foreste, or Collection of Historyes (*Silva de varia lección*). Tr. Thomas Fortescue from the French version. London, 1571. Repr. 1576.

For other early translated selections from the *Silva*, etc., see CBEL, I, 816.

————————The Historie of All the Romane Emperors. Tr. William Traheron from the Italian version. London, 1604. 890 pp. Rev. Edward Grimeston as The Imperial Historie, 1623.

Núñez Cabeza de Vaca, Álvaro (1507?–1550?). Commentaries of the Governor in a Journey through Brazil (*Comentarios*). Tr. Luis L. Dominguez, in The Conquest of La Plata, 1535–1555. London, Hakluyt Society Works, no. 81, 1889, part 2, pp. 95–262. Repr. N.Y., Burt Franklin, 1963.

————Relation (*Naufragios*). Tr. T. Buckingham Smith. Washington, pr. pr., 1851. 138 pp. Several reprs. to San Francisco, Grabhorn Pr., 1929.

Tr. Fanny R. Bandelier as The Journey of Alvar Nunez . . . from Florida to the Pacific, 1528–1536. N.Y., A. S. Barnes and Co., 1905. xxii, 231 pp. Repr. 1922; repr. Chicago, Rio Grande Pr., 1964, xi, 231 pp.

An account of the Narvaez expedition westward from Florida, pub. 1542; it was first tr. by or for Richard Hakluyt in his *Principal Navigations* (vol. 3, 1600). The account was republished in 1555 with the *Comentarios* describing the Brazil journey.

Oviedo y Valdés, Gonzalo Fernández de (1478–1557). The Natural History of the West Indies. Tr. Sterling A. Stoudemire. Chapel Hill, Univ. of North Carolina Pr., 1959. 158 pp.

The short *Natural historia de las Indias* (1526), not the large *Historia general* (1535 et seq.).

Rojas, Fernando de (c.1475–after 1537). Celestina. Tr. James Mabbe as The Spanish Bawd. London, 1631. Repr. in the Tudor Trs., ed. James Fitzmaurice-Kelly as Celestina or the Tragicke-Comedy of Calisto and Melibea, London, Nutt, 1894, xxxvi, 287 pp., which repr. N.Y., AMS Pr., 1967. Repr. ed. H. W. Allen, Library of Early Novelists, London, Routledge, 1908; repr. Broadway Trs., London, Routledge, and N.Y., Dutton, 1923, xci, 345 pp.; repr. London, Dent, 1959, 211 pp. Rev. Eric Bentley in The Classic Theatre, vol. 3, 1959: see Collections, Golden Age, below.

Tr. John Stevens in The Spanish Libertines, 1707: see Collections, above.

Tr. Lesley Byrd Simpson as The Celestina: A Novel in Dialogue. Berkeley, Univ. of California Pr., 1955. xii, 162 pp. Repr. 1959, paper.

Tr. Mack H. Singleton. Madison, Univ. of Wisconsin Pr., 1958. 314 pp.

Tr. J. M. Cohen. Penguin, 1964. 247 pp. Repr. N.Y., New York Univ. Pr., and London, Univ. of London Pr., 1966.

On the *Celestina*, see generally Stephen Gilman, *The Art of La Celestina* (Madison, Univ. of Wisconsin Pr., 1956, 261 pp.).

Rueda, Lope de (1510–1565). Cuckolds Go to Heaven (*Cornudo y contento*). Tr. Angel Flores, adapted by Joseph Liss. Poet Lore, vol. 46 (1940), 208–12.

————Eufemia. Tr. W. S. Merwin, in Tulane Drama Review, vol. 3, no. 2 (1958), 57–88.

————The Mask. Tr. Walter Starkie, in Eight Spanish Plays of the Golden Age: see Collections.

————The Olives. Tr. George Henry Lewes, in The Spanish Drama. London, Knight, 1846. 254 pp.

Tr. W. H. H. Chambers as The Seventh Farce, in The Drama, ed. Alfred Bates, vol. 6, 1903, pp. 281–86.

Tr. Willis K. Jones as The Seventh Paso, in Spanish One-Act Plays in English Translation, 1934: see Collections, above. Repr. in Anthology of Spanish Literature, vol. 1, see ibid.

Tr. Angel Flores in Spanish Drama, ed. Angel Flores, 1962: see ibid.

San Pedro, Diego de (fl. 1492).   (Arnalte and Lucenda). Tr. John Clerc from the French version as *Lamant mal tracte de samye*. London, 1543.

Tr. Claudius Holyband from the Italian version. London, 1575. 366 pp. Repr. 1583, 1591, and (appended to The Italian Schoole-maister) 1597, 1608.

Tr. verse Leonard Lawrence from the Italian version. London, 1639.

————The Castell of Love (*Cárcel de amor*). Tr. John Bourchier, Baron Berners, from the French version. London, [1540?]. Repr. [1549], [1560]; and Gainesville, Fla., Scholars' Facsimiles, 1960, 226 pp.

Sánchez de Badajos, Diego (16th c.). Theological Farce in Which Are Chiefly Discussed the Incarnation and Birth. Tr. Willis K. Jones in his Spanish One-Act Plays in English Translation, 1934: see Collections.

Torres Naharro, Bartolomé (c.1480–c.1530). The Buttery (*Comedia tinellaria*). Tr. Jill Booty, in Early Spanish Plays, 1964, q.v. in Collections.

————Hymen (*Comedia himenea*). Tr. W. H. H. Chambers in The Drama, vol. 6, 1903: see Collections.

Tr. Robert O'Brien in Early Spanish Plays, 1964: see Collections.

Valdés, Alfonso de (d. 1532).   (*Lactancio y el Arcadiano*). Tr. John E. Longhurst and R. R. MacCurdy as Alfonso de Valdés and the Sack of Rome. Albuquerque, Univ. of New Mexico Pr., 1952. 120 pp.

Early tr. anon. as *The Sacke of Rome* (London, 1590).

Valdés, Juan de (c.1500–1541).   *Alfabeto Christiano.* Tr. Benjamin B. Wiffen from the Spanish version of the Italian original. London, Spottiswoode, 1860–61. 3 vols. in 1. Repr. in *Obras antiguas de los Españoles Reformados* (in three languages), vol. 15, Madrid and London, 1865.

————The Hundred and Ten Considerations . . . Treating of Those Things Which Are Most Profitable . . . in Our Christian Profession. Tr. Nicholas Ferrar from the Italian version. Oxford, 1638. Repr. Cambridge 1646 as Divine Considerations, 437 pp.; repr. London and N.Y., John Lane, 1905.

Tr. John T. Betts from the Italian version, in Benjamin B. Wiffen, Life and Writings of Juan de Valdés. London, 1865.

————XVII Opuscules. Tr. J. T. Betts. London, Trübner, 1882. xii, 188 pp.

————Spiritual Milk, or Christian Instruction for Children. Tr. J. T. Betts from the Italian version. London, Trübner, 1882. xii, 188 pp.

For Valdés' Biblical commentaries, tr. John T. Betts in 1882 and 1883, see British Museum Catalogue.

Vicente, Gil (c.1465–1536?).   This Portuguese dramatist wrote eleven plays in Spanish: for trs. of eight of them, see his listing in Portuguese Literature, above.

Villalobos, Francisco López de (1473?–1549?).   The Medical Works (*Sumario de la medecina*). Tr. George Gaskoin. London, Churchill, 1870. 313 pp.

Vives, Juan Luis (1492–1540).   See Neo-Latin Literature, in vol. 1, above.

The Golden Age
Later Sixteenth and the Seventeenth Centuries

Literary Studies

Bourland, Caroline B.   The Short Story in Spain in the Seventeenth Century. Northampton, Mass., Smith College, 1927. 217 pp.

Chandler, Frank Wadleigh.   Romances of Roguery. Part I. The Picaresque Novel in Spain. N.Y., Columbia Univ. Pr., 1899. 483 pp. Repr. N.Y., Burt Franklin, 1961.

Pccrs, E. Allison.   Studies of the Spanish Mystics. London, Sheldon Pr., and N.Y., Macmillan, 1927–30. 2 vols.

Rennert, Hugo A.   The Spanish Pastoral Romances. 2d edn, Philadelphia, Univ. of Pennsylvania, 1912. 206 pp. Repr. N.Y., Biblo and Tannen, 1968.

Thomas, Henry.   Spanish and Portuguese Romances of Chivalry. Cambridge, Univ. Pr., 1920. 335 pp.

Collections

Alpert, Michael, tr.   Two Spanish Picaresque Novels. Penguin, 1969. 214 pp.
Lazarillo; Quevedo, *The Swindler* (*El buscón*).

The Classic Theatre.   Vol. 3, Six Spanish Plays, ed. Eric Bentley, tr. principally Roy Campbell. N.Y., Anchor Books, 1959. 516 pp.
Rojas, *Celestina*, tr. James Mabbe, rev. by ed.; the remaining plays tr. verse Roy Campbell: Calderón, *Love after Death*, and *Life Is a Dream*; Cervantes, *Numantia*; Tirso de Molina, *The Trickster of Seville*; Lope de Vega Carpio, *Fuente Ovejuna*.

L'Estrange, Roger, tr.   The Spanish Decameron: or Ten Novels Made English. London, 1687. Repr. 1720.
Five *novelas* by Cervantes, q.v.; five by Castillo Solórzano, q.v.

Masterpieces of the Spanish Golden Age. Ed. Angel Flores, trs. various. N.Y., Rinehart, 1957. xxix, 395 pp.

> *The Abencerraje*; *Lazarillo de Tormes*; Calderón, *The Great Theater of the World*; Quevedo, *Don Pablos the Sharper*; Tirso de Molina, *The Trickster of Seville*; Vega Carpio, *Fuente Ovejuna*.

Peers, E. Allison. Spanish Mysticism: A Preliminary Survey. London, Methuen, 1924. 277 pp.

> Pp. 51–272 contain trs. of writings by the mystics.

Rivers, Elias L., ed. and tr.   Renaissance and Baroque Poetry of Spain, with English Prose Trs. N.Y., Dell, 1966. 351 pp.

The Soul Afire: Revelations of the Mystics. Ed. H. A. Reinhold. N.Y., Pantheon, 1944, and London, Burns Oates (as The Spear of Gold), 1947. 386 pp.

> Brief passages from Loyola, St. John of the Cross, Lull, St. Rose of Lima, and St. Teresa.

Spanish Novelists. N.Y., Worthington, 1890, and London, n.d. (as Old Spanish Novelists). 12 vols.

> *Don Quixote*, 4 vols.; *Gil Blas*, 3 vols.; *Lazarillo*, 2 vols.; *Asmodeus*; *The Bachelor of Salamanca*; *Estevanillo González*.

Spanish Short Stories of the Sixteenth Century in Contemporary Translation. Ed. and rev. J. B. Trend. WC, 1928. 358 pp.

> *Lazarillo*; *The Abencerraje*; selections from *Guzmán de Alfarache*, *Diana*, and from Cervantes' *Don Quijote*, *Persiles*, and *Novelas*.

The Spirit of the Spanish Mystics: Anthology of Religious Prose from the Fifteenth to the Seventeenth Century. Ed. and tr. Kathleen Pond. London, Burns Oates, and N.Y., Kenedy, 1958. 170 pp.

Starkie, Walter, ed. and tr.   Eight Spanish Plays of the Golden Age. ML, 1964. xlviii, 328 pp.

> Ruiz de Alarcón, *The Gallant, the Bawd, and the Fair Lady*; Rueda, *The Mask*; Vega Carpio, *Peribañez and the Comendador*; Calderón, *The Mayor of Zalamea*; Cervantes, *Pedro the Artful Dodger*, and *The Jealous Old Man*; Tirso de Molina, *The Playboy of Seville*; and the *Mystery Play of Elche*.

Three Classic Spanish Plays. Ed. Hyman Alpern, various trs. N.Y., Washington Square Pr., 1963. 229 pp.

> Calderón, *Life Is a Dream*, tr. Denis F. McCarthy; Rojas Zorrilla, *None beneath the King*, tr. Isaac Goldberg; Vega Carpio, *The Sheep Well*, tr. J. G. Underhill.

INDIVIDUAL AUTHORS

The Abencerraje (1551 et seq.).   Tr. Bartholomew Yong as The Abindarraez and the Fair Sharifa, in his tr. of Jorge de Montemayor, Diana (q.v. below), in which the story had been inserted. London, 1598. Repr. Oxford, 1968. The story repr. separately in Spanish Short Stories of the Sixteenth Century, 1928: see Collections.

> Tr. Angel Flores from the version pub. by Antonio de Villegas in his *Inventario* (1565), who is considered its author, in Masterpieces of the Spanish Golden Age, 1957; repr. in Great Spanish Short Stories, 1962: see Collections.

> Tr. with intro. John Esten Keller, of the same version. Chapel Hill, Univ. of North Carolina Pr., 1964. 86 pp., parallel texts (the Spanish ed. by Francisco López Estrada).

Alcalá Yánez y Rivera, Gerónimo (1563–1632).   The Life and Adventures of Alonso, the Chattering Lay Brother and Servant of Many Masters (*El donado hablador: o, Alonso, mozo de muchos amos*). Tr. anon. N.Y., W. M. Christy, 1844–45. 2 vols. in 1.

Alemán, Mateo (1547–1615?).   The Rogue: Or the Life of Guzman de Alfarache. Tr. James Mabbe. London, 1622. Repr. 1623, Oxford, 1630, 1634, 1656; abridged 1655; with Celestina, 1707–08, 2 vols.; in Tudor Translations, 1924, 4 vols., q.v. in General Reference, Collections, and which repr. 1967.

> Tr. A. O'Conner from French. London, 1812. 3 vols. Repr. 1816, 1817.

> Tr. John Henry Brady. London, Longmans, 1821. 2 vols. Repr. 1823, 1881.

> Tr. Thomas Roscoe in The Spanish Novelists, 1832: see Collections, above. Repr. 1880.

> Tr. E. Lowdell. London, Vizetelly, 1883. viii, 478 pp.

For commentary, see Donald McGrady, *Mateo Alemán* (N.Y., Twayne, 1968, 190 pp.).

Amadis of Gaul.   Tr. Anthony Munday and Lazarus Pyot from the French version. London, 1619. 4 parts, 818 pp.

> Tr. Robert Southey. London, Longmans, 1803. 4 vols. Repr. Library of Old Authors, 1872.
>
> > Four parts of the 12 parts or books of the Amadis series. See R. U. Pane, *English Trs. from the Spanish*, in Bibliographies, above.

Ávila y Zúñiga, Luis de (d. 1572).   Commentaries of Don Lewes de Avila and Suniga Which Treateth of the Great Wars in Germany, Made by Charles the Fifth (*Commentario de la guerra de Alemania*). Tr. John Wilkinson. London, 1555.

Calderón de la Barca, Pedro (1600–1681).   Eight Dramas of Calderón. Tr. "freely into verse" Edward Fitzgerald. London and N.Y., Macmillan, 1906. 517 pp. Repr. N.Y., Doubleday, 1961, 440 pp.

This edn combines two earlier titles: *Six Dramas of Calderón* (London, 1853; repr. 1854 et seq. with the next item); and *The Mighty Magician, and Such Stuff as Dreams Are Made Of* (*La vida es sueño*, London, 1865). Both were combined in *The Works of Edward Fitzgerald* (London, 1902); in an edn by Hermann Oelsner (London, 1903, repr. EL, 1928); and in *Eight Dramas*, as above.

The six plays are: *The Painter of His Own Dishonor*; *Keep Your Own Secret*; *Gil Perez the Galician*; *Three Judgments at a Blow* (*Las tres justicias en una*); *The Mayor of Zalamea*; *Beware of Smooth Water*.

Tr. Denis Florence McCarthy in four installments as follows:
1. Dramas of Calderon, Tragic, Comic, and Legendary. London, Dolman, 1853. 2 vols.
   The plays are *Love after Death*; *The Scarf and the Flower*; *The Physician of His Own Honor*; *The Constant Prince*; *The Purgatory of Saint Patrick*; *The Secret in Words*.
2. Calderon's Dramas: The Wonderworking Magician; Life Is a Dream; The Purgatory of St. Patrick. London, H. S. King, 1873. xvi. 377 pp.
3. Mysteries of Corpus Christi. Dublin, J. Duffy, 1867. 352 pp.
   The plays are *Belshazzar's Feast*; *The Divine Philothea*; *The Poison and the Antidote* (but only one scene of the last).

4. Three Dramas of Calderón: Love the Greatest Enchantment; The Sorceries of Sin; The Devotion of the Cross. Dublin, W. B. Kelly, 1870. 316 pp.

A selection from these trs. has been brought together as *Six Plays*, rev. Henry W. Wells (N.Y., Las Americas, 1961, 464 pp.); the plays are *Belshazzar's Feast*; *The Constant Prince*; *The Devotion of the Cross*; *Life Is a Dream*; *Love after Death*; *The Wonderworking Magician*.

————Four Plays. Tr. Edwin Honig. N.Y., Hill and Wang, 1961. 319 pp. *Devotion to the Cross*; *The Mayor of Zalamea*; *The Phantom Lady*; *Secret Vengeance for Secret Insult*.

————(Two Plays:) The Feast of Belshazzar; Juan Rana's Duel. Tr. Willis K. Jones, in his Spanish One-Act Plays in English, 1934, q.v. in Collections, above.

————Two Comedies: The Fairy Lady, and Keep Your Own Secret. Tr. Lord Holland, in his Three Comedies Translated from the Spanish. London, 1807.

INDIVIDUAL PLAYS (*additional trs.*)

————Belshazzar's Feast. Tr. Willis Barnstone, in The Genius of the Spanish Theater, 1964, q.v. in Collections.

The McCarthy tr. was repr. in The Drama, ed. Alfred Bates, vol. 4, 1903, 251–98.

————Elvira, or the Worst Not Always True. Tr. George Digby, Earl of Bristol. London, 1667.

————The Fairy Lady (*La dama duenda*). Adapted Thomas Killigrew as The Parson's Wedding. London, 1664.

Tr. Edwin Honig as The Phantom Lady, in Four Plays: see above.

————Fortune Mends (*Mejor está que estaba*). Tr. Fanny Holcroft, in The Theatrical Recorder, vol. 2, 1806.

————From Bad to Worse (*Peor está que estaba*). Tr. Fanny Holcroft, in The Theatrical Recorder, vol. 1, 1805.

——————The Great Theatre of the World. Tr. Richard C. Trench, in The Life and Genius of Calderon. London, Macmillan, 1856. Repr. 1880; rev. John G. Underhill in Twenty Non-Royalty One-Act Classics, ed. Margaret Mayorga, N.Y., 1944.

Tr. Francis E. Sipman as The Great World Theatre. Einsiedeln, Gesellschaft der geistlichen Spiele, 1955.

Tr. Mack H. Singleton, in Masterpieces of the Golden Age, ed. Angel Flores, 1957, q.v. in Collections, above.

The adaptation by Hugo von Hofmannsthal of this play as *The Salzburg Great Theatre of the World* has been tr. from German by Vernon Watkins in *Selected Plays and Libretti* of the playwright (N.Y., Pantheon, 1963, lxiii, 562 pp.).

——————A House with Two Doors Is Difficult to Guard. Tr. Edwin Muir in Tulane Drama Review, vol. 7 (1963), 157–217.

——————Life Is a Dream. Tr. Frank Birch and J. B. Trend for the English Stage, with a stage plan and two ill. Cambridge, Heffer, 1925. 72 pp.

Tr. H. Carter. Sanderstead, the author, 1938.

Tr. William F. Stirling. Habana, La Veronica, 1942. 259 pp., parallel texts.

Tr. William E. Colford. N:Y., Barron, 1958. 101 pp.

Tr. verse Roy Campbell, in The Classic Theatre, vol. 3, 1959: see Collections, above.

Tr. Edward and Elizabeth Huberman in Angel Flores, ed., Spanish Drama, 1962, see ibid.

The McCarthy tr. was repr. in *Chief European Dramatists*, ed. Brander Matthews, 1916: see General Reference, Collections; and in *Three Classic Spanish Plays*, ed. Hyman Alpern, 1963, see Collections.

The Fitzgerald tr. (*Such Stuff as Dreams Are Made Of*) was repr. in Harvard Classics, vol. 26, 1910.

The development by Hugo von Hofmannsthal of the theme of *Life Is a Dream* resulted in the large dramatic composition called *The Tower*; it has been tr. Michael Hamburger from German in *Selected Plays and*

Libretti of Hofmannsthal (N.Y., Pantheon, 1963, lxiii, 562 pp.), and again by Alfred Schwarz in *Three Plays* by Hofmannsthal (Detroit, Wayne State Univ. Pr., 1966, 242 pp.).

————Love after Death. Tr. verse Roy Campbell, in The Classic Theatre, vol. 3, 1959: see Collections.

————The Mayor of Zalamea. Adapted Adolfo Pierra as The Nobility of the Alcalde of Zalamea. Philadelphia, 1885. 48 pp.

Tr. William E. Colford. Woodbury, N.Y., Barron, 1959. 128 pp.

Tr. Walter Starkie, in Eight Spanish Plays of the Golden Age, 1964: in Collections, above.

————The Physician of His Own Honor. Tr. Roy Campbell as The Surgeon of His Honour. Madison, Univ. of Wisconsin Pr., 1960. 82 pp.

————The Prince of Fez. Adapted Fr. P. Haenders. St. Louis, Herder, 1905. 40 pp., paper.

————The Two Lovers of Heaven. Tr. Denis F. McCarthy. Dublin, Fowler, and London, Hotten, 1870. 60 pp.

For Calderón, see R. C. Trench, *An Essay on the Life and Genius of Calderon* (London, 1880), and Alexander A. Parker, *The Allegorical Drama of Calderón* (Oxford and London, Dolphin Book Co., 1943, 232 pp.).

Castillo Solórzano, Alonso de (1584–1647?).   La Picara, or the Triumphs of Female Subtility (*La garduña de Seville y anzuelo de las bolsas*). Tr. John Davies from the French version. London, 1665. 304 pp. The three *novelas* included were separately repr. 1665 and 1712 as Three Ingenious Spanish Novels.

————The Spanish Pole-Cat, or the Adventures of Seniora Rufina. Tr. Roger L'Estrange, rev. John Ozell. London, 1717. 394 pp. Repr. 1727.

Five *novelas* by Castillo were tr. Roger L'Estrange in *The Spanish Decameron* (London, 1687; repr. 1720), together with five by Cervantes. The Castillo titles are: "The Amorous Miser"; "The Impostour Outwitted"; "The Metamorphos'd Lover"; "The Perfidious Mistress"; "The Pretended Alchymist."

Three *novelas* by Castillo were tr. "by a Lady" in *Novelas Espanolas, or Moral and Entertaining Novels* (London, 1747, 263 pp.).

Two *novelas* were tr. Thomas Roscoe in vol. 3 of his *Spanish Novelists* (London, 1832): "The Duchess of Mantua" and "The Mask."

Cervantes Saavedra, Miguel de (1547–1616). Complete Works. Ed. James Fitzmaurice-Kelly. Glasgow, Gowans and Gray, 1901–03.
    Of the projected 12 vols., only vols. 2–8 were pub.: vol. 2, *Galatea*, tr. H. Oelsner and A. B. Welford (1903); vols. 3–6, *Don Quixote*, tr. John Ormsby (1901); vols. 7–8, *Exemplary Novels*, tr. Norman Maccoll (1902).

————The Portable Cervantes. Tr. Samuel Putnam. N.Y., Viking, 1951. 863 pp. Repr. 1956, paper.
    Don Quixote, with omissions; two *Novelas* (*Riconete*; *The Man of Glass*).

————The History of . . . Don Quixote de la Mancha. Tr. Thomas Shelton. London, 1612–20. 2 vols. Reprs. to 1740; rev. John Stevens, 1700, 1706; repr. again 1895, 1896 (ed. J. Fitzmaurice-Kelly in Tudor Trs., 4 vols., which repr. 1967), 1901 (ill. Frank Brangwyn).

Tr. John Phillips. London, 1687. 616 pp.

Tr. Peter Motteux. London, 1700–3. 4 vols. in 2. Rev. John Ozell, 1719. Many reprs., esp. from 1822 (with intro. J. G. Lockhart), e.g. (Motteux version) London, Bohn, 1882 et seq.; EL, 1909 et seq., 2 vols.; (Ozell revision) ML, 1930 et seq.

Tr. Charles Jervis as The Life and Exploits, etc. London, 1742. 2 vols. Numerous reprs., probably the most popular version in the 19th c., e.g., ill. Gustave Doré 1864–67; WC, 1907; N.Y., Dodd Mead, 1929, 1962.

Tr. Tobias Smollett as The History and Adventures, etc. London, 1755. 2 vols. Many reprs. to 1858.

Tr. Mary Smirke as Don Quixote de la Mancha. London, Cadell, 1818. 4 vols. Repr. 1842, Bohn 1847, 1850?, 1862, 1877.

Other trs. Charles Henry Wilmot, 1769?; George Kelly, 1769; A. J. Duffield, 1881.

Tr. John Ormsby as The Ingenious Gentleman Don Quixote de la Mancha. London, Smith Elder, 1885. 4 vols. Repr. in Complete Works, vols. 3–6, 1901 (see above); N.Y., Knopf, 1926, 2 vols.; N.Y., Crowell, 1932;

N.Y., Limited Edns, 1933; N.Y., Grosset, 1936, 2 vols. in 1; in Great Books, 1952, vol. 29.

Tr. Robinson Smith as That Imaginative Gentleman, etc. London, Routledge, 1910. xvi, 686 pp. Repr. 1914, 1932 (Hispanic Soc. of America).

*Tr. Samuel Putnam as The Ingenious Gentleman, etc. N.Y., Viking Pr., 1949. 2 vols. Repr. (with omissions), in The Portable Cervantes, 1951 (see above), 1956; repr. London, Cassell, 1953; London, Folio Soc., 1961.

**Tr. J. M. Cohen as The Adventures of Don Quixote. Penguin, 1950. 940 pp. Repr. 1951, 1952, et seq.

Tr. abridged Walter Starkie as Don Quixote de la Mancha. N.Y., St. Martin's Pr., 1954. 593 pp. Repr. N.Y., New Amer. Lib., 1957, 432 pp. Tr. complete, ibid., 1964, 1052 pp.

The above entries are generally taken condensed from R. U. Pane, *English Translations from the Spanish, 1484–1943*: see Bibliographies, above. A whole library of commentaries on *Don Quixote* is noted in every history of Spanish literature, and reference may be made to *Cervantes across the Centuries* in the final note on Cervantes, below.

————Exemplary Novels. Part tr. (6 out of 12) James Mabbe. London, 1640. Repr. 1654, 1742, 1743, 1747, 1750, 1900 (ill. Frank Brangwyn); part repr. (3 stories) 1909, 1928 (as The Spanish Ladie and Two Other Stories).

Tr. Walter K. Kelly. London, Bohn, 1846. 440 pp. Reprs. to 1908.
The twelve *novelas*, with two other contemporary ones.

Tr. Norman Maccoll in The Complete Works, vols. 7–8, 1903: see above.

*Part tr. Harriet de Onís as Six Exemplary Novels. N.Y., Barron, 1961. 297 pp.

Many other trs. of one or more *novelas*, notably Roger L'Estrange in *The Spanish Decameron* (London, 1687; repr. 1700, 1712, 1720), five stories; Walter Pope, *Select Novels* (1694), six stories; Samuel Croxall, *A Select Collection*, 1720–21, nine novels; S.C. (1722), eight stories; Harry Bridges (1728), six stories; Robert Goadby (1741, 1742, 1766, 1767), two stories; Maria Sarah Moore (London, Cadell, 1822, 2 vols.), nine stories; Thomas Roscoe, in *The Spanish Novelists* (1832, 3 vols.), two stories; Samuel Putnam, *Three Exemplary Novels* (N.Y., Viking, 1950, 258 pp.; repr. London, Cassell, 1953, 232 pp.); Walter Starkie, *The Deceitful Marriage and Other Exemplary Novels* (N.Y., New Amer. Lib., 1963, 320 pp.); and one or more stories in most anthologies of trs.

————Galatea. Tr. Gordon W. J. Gyll. London, Bell, 1867. xvii, 349 pp. Repr. 1883, 1892.

Tr. H. Oelsner and A. B. Welford in The Complete Works, vol. 2, 1903: see above.

Earlier trs.: An Officer (Dublin, 1791); anon. (Boston, 1798); Miss Highly (London 1804); W. M. Craig (London, 1813).

————The Interludes of Cervantes. Tr. S. Griswold Morley. Princeton, N.J., Princeton Univ. Pr., and London, Oxford Univ. Pr., 1948. 233 pp., parallel texts.

Tr. Edwin Honig. N.Y., New Amer. Lib., 1964. 160 pp.

For trs. of individual interludes, see Robert O'Brien, *Spanish Plays in English Tr.*, 1963: in Bibliographies, above. We may note trs. by W. K. Jones of *The Cave of Salamanca* and the suppositious *Two Chatterboxes* (*Dos habladores*) in *Spanish One-Act Plays in English*, 1934; *The Faithful Dog*, later re-titled *The Vigilant Sentinel* in Angel Flores, ed., *Spanish Drama*, 1961; and *The Judge of the Divorce Court*, two trs. 1919 and 1939: see O'Brien; and add *Pedro the Artful Dodger*, and *The Jealous Old Man*, tr. Walter Starkie, in *Eight Spanish Plays of the Golden Age*, 1964: see Collections.

————Numantia: A Tragedy; The Commerce of Algiers; together with The Voyage to Parnassus. Tr. verse Gordon W. J. Gyll. London, Murray, 1870. v, 288 pp.
The play *The Commerce of Algiers* has not otherwise been tr. *Numantia* has had other trs. as follows:

Tr. verse James Y. Gibson. London, Kegan Paul, 1885. xviii, 127 pp.

Tr. verse Roy Campbell, in The Classic Theatre, vol. 3 (1959), 97–160.

————The Travels of Persiles and Sigismunda. Tr. M. L. from a French version. London, 1619. 399 pp.

Tr. anon. London, 1741. 2 vols. Repr. 1745.

Tr. Louisa Dorothea Stanley. London, Joseph Cundall, 1854. xvii, 477 pp.

—————The Voyage to Parnassus. Tr. verse Gordon W. J. Gyll, 1870: see Numantia, above.

Tr. tercets James Y. Gibson. London, Kegan Paul, 1883. lxxv, 387 pp.

For studies of Cervantes, see William J. Entwistle, *Cervantes* (Oxford, Clarendon Pr., 1940, 192 pp.); *Cervantes across the Centuries: A Quadri-centennial Volume*, ed. Angel Flores and M. J. Benardete (N.Y., Dryden Pr., 1947, 371 pp.); Rudolph Schevill, *Cervantes* (N.Y., Duffield, 1919, 388 pp., repr. N.Y., Ungar, 1966); Sebastian Juan Arbo, *Cervantes, The Man and His Time*, tr. Ilsa Barea (N.Y., Vanguard Pr., 1955, 261 pp.).

Cespedes y Meneses, Gonzalo de (1585?–1638). The Famous History of Auristella. Tr. anon. London, 1683 (including also a version of Paul of Segovia, by Quevedo, q.v. below).

—————Gerardo the Unfortunate Spaniard, or a Patterne for Lascivious Lovers. Tr. Leonard Digges. London, 1622. Repr. 1653.

Coello y Ochos, Antonio (1611–1652). The Adventures of Five Hours. Adapted Sir Samuel Tuke. London, 1663. Repr. 1664, rev. 1671, 1704 et seq.; ed. V. Van Thal (1671 ed. collated with 1704 ed.), London, Holden, 1927, xxxii, 155 pp.

Tr. A. E. H. Swaen in ed. of the preceding (1663, 1671 eds.). Amsterdam, Swets & Zeitlinger, 1927. liii, 260 pp.

Contreras, Alonso (1592–1641?). The Life of Captain Alonso de Contreras, 1582–1633, Written by Himself (*Memorias autobiográficas*). Tr. Catherine A. Phillips. London, Cape, and N.Y., Knopf, 1926. 288 pp.

Erauso, Catalina de (1592–1635). Spanish Military Nun. Tr. Thomas De Quincey from the French. Tait's Edinburgh Magazine, May–July, 1847. Repr. in Works of De Quincey.

Tr. James Fitzmaurice-Kelly as Nun Ensign. London, T. Fisher Unwin, 1908. xl, 303 pp.

The original is *Historia de la monja alferez Dona Catalina de Erauso, escrita por ella misma.*

*Ercilla y Zúñiga, Alonso de (1533–1594).   The Araucaniad: A Version in English Poetry of La Araucana. Tr. Charles Maxwell Lancaster and Paul Thomas Manchester. Nashville, Tenn., Vanderbilt Univ. Pr., 1945. 326 pp.

*Espinel, Vicente Martinez (1550–1624).   The History of the Life of the Squire Marcos de Obregon. Tr. Major Algernon Langton. London, J. Booth, 1816. 2 vols.

Góngora y Argote, Luis de (1561–1627).   (Poems) Tr. Edward Churton, in Gongora: An Historical and Critical Essay on the Times of Philip III and IV of Spain. London, Murray, 1862. 2 vols. (trs. of 188 of Góngora's poems).

————The Solitudes. Tr. verse by Edward Meryon Wilson. Cambridge, England, The Minority Pr., 1931. 80 pp.

Tr. Gilbert F. Cunningham. Alva, Robert Cunningham, 1964. xiii, 146 pp. Repr. Baltimore, Johns Hopkins Pr., 1968.

González, Esteban (fl. 1646).   Estevanillo Gonzales, the Most Arch and Comical of All Scoundrels. Tr. Captain John Stevens in The Spanish Libertines, 1707, see Collections, above.

Gracián, Baltasar (1601–1658).   The Art of Worldly Wisdom (*Oráculo manual y arte de Prudencia*). Tr. Joseph Jacobs. London and N.Y., Macmillan, 1892. lxxiv, 197 pp. Repr. 1904, 1943, 1960 (N.Y., Ungar).

Tr. Leslie Mannister Walton as The Oracle: A Manual of the Art of Discretion. London, Dent, 1953. 307 pp.

Tr. Lawrence C. Lockley as The Science of Success and the Art of Prudence. San Jose, Calif., Univ. of Santa Clara Pr., 1967. 93 pp.

Cf. *The Best of Gracián*, tr. Thomas G. Corvan (N.Y., Philosophical Lib., 1964, 84 pp.).

Granada, Luis de (1504–1588).   Summa of the Christian Life: Selected Texts. Tr. and adapted Jordan Aumann. St. Louis and London, Herder, 1954. 379 pp.

————A Memoriall of a Christian Life. Tr. Richard Hopkins. Rouen, 1586.

————Of Prayer and Meditation (*Libro de la oracion y consideracion*). Tr. Richard Hopkins. Paris, 1582.

Tr. Francis Meres as Granados Devotion (from a French version). London, 1598.

————The Sinners Guyde: contayning the whole regiment of a Christian Life. Tr. Francis Meres. London, 1598. 2 vols. Repr. 1614; Dublin, 1813.

For other early trs., see CBEL, I, 815.

Herrera, Fernando de (1534?–1597). (Poems tr. in Hispanic Anthology, and in Translations from Hispanic Poets, in Collections, above.)

Huarte, Juan (1530?–1591?). The Examination of Mens Wits (*Examen de ingenios*). Tr. Richard Carew (from the Italian version). London, 1594. Repr. 1596, 1604, 1616.

Hurtado de Mendoza, Antonio (1586–1644). Festivals Represented at Aranjuez. Tr. Sir Richard Fanshawe. London, 1654. Repr. 1670, 2 parts.

————To Love Only for Love Sake (*Querer por sol querer*). Tr. Sir Richard Fanshawe. London, 1670. 167 pp. Repr. 1671.

Juan de la Cruz, San (1542–1591). The Complete Works of Saint John of the Cross. Tr. E. Allison Peers. London, Burns Oates, and Westminster, Md., Newman Pr., 1953. 3d ed. rev. 3 vols. Repr. ibid., 1964, 3 vols. in 1.

Tr. Kieran Kavanaugh and Otilio Rodriguez as Collected Works. Garden City, N.Y., Doubleday, 1964, and London, Nelson, 1966. 745 pp.

————The Dark Night of the Soul. Tr. abridged Kurt F. Reinhardt., N.Y. Ungar, 1956. xxxiv, 222 pp.

————The Poems. Tr. Roy Campbell. London, Harvill Pr., 1951. 90 pp., parallel texts. Repr. Penguin, 1960, 109 pp., N.Y., Grosset, 1967.

Tr. John F. Nims. N.Y., Grove Pr., and London, Calder, 1959. 147 pp., parallel texts, paper.

Tr. Willis Barnstone. Bloomington and London, Indiana Univ. Pr., 1968. 124 pp., parallel texts.

The poems are also tr. in various anthologies: see Collections.

Lazarillo de Tormes (before 1555). Tr. David Rouland as The Pleasaunt Historie of Lazarillo de Tormes. London, 1586 (but registered for pubn in 1569). Repr. 1596, 1624, 1639; ed. J. E. V. Crofts, Oxford, Blackwell (Percy Reprs.), 1924, xv, 80 pp.; in Spanish Short Stories of the Sixteenth Century, WC, 1928.

Tr. Thomas Roscoe in The Spanish Novelists. London, 1832, vol. 1.

Tr. Sir Clements R. Markham. London, Black, 1908. xxvi, 105 pp.

Tr. Louis How from the restitution by Foulché-Dubosc of the editio princeps, intro. Charles P. Wagner. N.Y., Kennerley, 1917. xliv, 150 pp.

Tr. Mariano Joaquín Lorente. N.Y., Luce, 1924. 143 pp.

Tr. L. Rice-Oxley. Oxford, Blackwell, 1924.

Tr. anon. in The Rogues' Bookshelf. N.Y., Greenberg, 1926. xxv, 240 pp.

Tr. J. Gerald Markley. N.Y., Liberal Arts Pr., 1954. 68 pp., paper.

Tr. Mack H. Singleton, in Masterpieces of the Golden Age, 1957: see Collections.

Tr. Harriet de Onís. N.Y., Barron, 1959. 74 pp., paper.

Tr. W. S. Merwin. N.Y., Doubleday, 1962. 152 pp. Repr. Gloucester, Mass., Peter Smith, 1964.

Tr. James Parsons. N.Y., American RDM Corporation, 1966. 96 pp.

Tr. Michael Alpert, in Two Spanish Picaresque Novels, 1969: see Collections.

————The second parte. Tr. W[illiam] P[histon]. London, 1596.
An anon. sequel, sometimes included in later eds. of the tr. of the original. For a further sequel, see Juan de Luna, below.

León, Fray Luis de (1527?–1591). Lyrics of Luis de Leon. Tr. Aubrey F. G. Bell. London, Burns Oates, 1928. 149 pp.

————The Names of Christ. Tr. Edward J. Schuster. St. Louis, Herder, 1955. 315 pp.

————The Perfect Wife (La perfecta casada). Tr. Alice P. Hubbard. Denton, Texas, The College Pr. (Texas State College for Women), 1943. xxxv, 102 pp.

López de Tortajada, Damián (fl. 1610). The Flower of the Ballads of France, Together with the History of Orlando by Turpin. Tr. verse Thomas Rodd. London, 1812. Repr. 1821.

> The original is *Floresta de varios romances sacados de las historias antiguas the los Doce Pares de Francia.*

López de Úbeda, Francisco (fl. 1608). The Life of Justina, the Country Jilt (*La picara Justina*). Tr. John Stevens in The Spanish Libertines, 1707: see Collections.

Loyola, San Ignacio de (1491–1556). See Neo-Latin Literature, in vol. 1, above.

Luna, Juan de (fl. 1620). The Pursuit of the Historie of Lazarillo de Tormes. Tr. T. W. Calkley. London, 1622. Repr. 1631.

Mariana, Juan de (1536–1624). See Neo-Latin Literature, in vol. 1, above.

The Mirrour of Princely Dedes and Knighthood. For Elizabethan trs., 1578 et seq., of the parts of this romance, begun by Diego Ortúñez de Calahorra, see CBEL, vol. 1, 817.

Montemayor, Jorge de (1520–1561). The Diana of George of Montemayor. Tr. Bartholomew Yong. London, 1598. 496 pp. Repr. ed. Judith M. Kennedy, Oxford, Clarendon Pr., 1968, lxxx, 468 pp.

> The tr. includes also the continuations by Alonso Perez and Gil Polo; the tr. of the Polo continuation was ed. with the original Spanish by Raymond L. and Mildred B. Grismer as *Diana Enamorada* (Minneapolis, Burgess Pub. Co., 1959, 317 pp.). For the *Abencerraje* story inserted in the *Diana*, see that title, above.

Moreto y Cabana, Agustín (1618–1669). Entremes of Mariquita. Tr. Willis K. Jones, in Spanish One-Act Plays: see Collections.

——————Love's Victory, or the School for Pride (*El desdén con el desdén*). Tr. G. Hyde. London and Edinburgh, Hurst, 1825.

> Tr. J. Westland Marston in his Dramatic and Poetical Works. London, Chatto, 1876. 2 vols.

————Tarugo's Wiles, or the Coffee House. Adapted Thomas St. Serfe. London, 1668.

Adapted John Crowne as Sir Courtly Nice, or It Cannot Be. London, 1685. The original is *No puede ser guarder una mujer*.

For Moreto, see Ruth Lee Kennedy, *The Dramatic Art of Moreto* (Northampton, Mass., Smith College Studies in Modern Languages 13, 1932, 221 pp.).

Palmerin of England. Romances. Tr. (nine parts) Anthony Munday, 1580–97. See R. U. Pane, English Translations from the Spanish, nos. 455–66: see Bibliographies, above.

Pérez de Hita, Ginés (1544?–1619). The Civil Wars of Granada. Tr. Thomas Rodd. London, Ostell, 1803. 438 pp. (vol. 1 only, vol. 2 of the tr. remaining in ms.).

Pérez de Montalván, Juan (1602–1638). Aurora, and The Prince. Tr. Thomas Stanley. London, 1647. Repr. 1650, 1657; 1907, ed. Louise Imogen Guiney.
The originals are *La hermosa Aurora* and *Los prodigios*, two *novelas* from the collection *Sucesos y prodigios de amor*.

————The Illustrious Shepherdess; The Imperious Brother. Tr. E. P. London, 1656. 2 parts.

See also *Novelas Españolas*, 1747, for trs. "by a Lady" of "The First Lovers" and "The Year 1000"; and Thomas Roscoe, *The Spanish Novelists* (vol. 2, 1832) for trs. of "The Test of Friendship" and "The Effect of Being Undeceived."

Polo, Gaspar Gil (d. 1585). See Montemayor, above.

Quevedo y Villegas, Francisco de (1580–1645). The Choice Humourous and Satirical Works. Tr. Sir Roger L'Estrange (vol. 1), John Stevens, and Others. Edinburgh and London, 1798. 2 vols. Rev. Charles Duff, with intro. notes, and a version of The Life of the Great Rascal (*Vida del Buscón*), Broadway Trs., London, Routledge, and N.Y., Dutton, 1926, xlvii, 407 pp.

————The Comical Works. Tr. John Stevens. London, 1707. 564 pp. Repr. 1709, 1742, 1745, and in preceding item.
Contains *The Night-adventurer*; *The Life of Paul the Spanish Sharper*; *The*

Retentive Knight and His Epistles; *The Dog and the Fever*; *A Proclamation by Old Father Time*; *A Treatise of All Things Whatsoever*; *Fortune in Her Wits* (first pub. separately 1697, 131 pp.).

————The Dog and the Fever, a Perambulatory Novella. Tr. William Carlos Williams and Raquel Hélène Williams. Hamden, Conn., Shoe String Pr., 1954. 96 pp.

————Hell Reformed. Tr. E. M., Gent. London, 1641.

————The Life and Adventures of Buscon the Witty Spaniard. Tr. John Davies from the French, with A Spanish Cavalier. London, 1657. Repr. 1670.

Tr. anon. as Paul of Segovia, in Cespedes, The Famous History of Auristella, 1683: see Cespedes, above.

Tr. John Stevens as Paul the Spanish Sharper, in The Comical Works, 1707, etc., see above. Repr. separately as Pablo of Segovia the Spanish Sharper, with intro. Henry E. Watts, London, T. Fisher Unwin, 1892, xiii, 239 pp., which repr. N.Y., Knopf, 1926, and London, Unwin, 1927, vii, 272 pp.

Tr. Francisco Villamiqual y Hardín (Frank Mugglestone) as The Life and Adventures of Don Pablos the Sharper. Leicester, Minerva Co., 1928. 220 pp.

Tr. Mack H. Singleton and others as Don Pablos, in Masterpieces of the Spanish Golden Age, 1957: see Collections.

Tr. Hugh A. Harter as The Scavenger. N.Y., Las Americas, 1962. 146 pp.

Tr. Michael Alpert as The Swindler, in Two Spanish Picaresque Novels, 1969: see Collections.

————The Visions, or Hels Kingdome, and the Worlds Follies and Abuse (*Sueños*). Tr. Richard Croshawe. London, 1640. 187 [for 209] pp.

Tr. Sir Roger L'Estrange. London, 1667. 344 pp. Numerous reprs. to 19th edn, 1795; repr. with intro. J. M. Cohen, Fontwell, Centaur Pr., and Carbondale, Southern Illinois Univ. Pr., 1963, 146 pp.

Tr. William Elliott. Philadelphia, H. H. Porter, 1832. 216 pp.

The pubn *The Novels* [of Quevedo], with *Machiavel, The Marriage of Belphagor*, tr. anon., London 1671, 159 pp., actually includes, with the Italian novella, *Don Diego de noche* of Salas Barbadillo, q.v. below.

Quiñones de Benavente, Luis (1589?–1651).   The Doctor and the Sick Man. Tr. Willis K. Jones. Evanston, Ill., Row Peterson, 1931.

————The Drunkard. Tr. Willis K. Jones, in Spanish One-Act Plays, 1934: see Collections.

Tr. Barbara Rowan, Robert Lima, and Dolores Bagley, in The Genius of the Spanish Theater, 1964: see ibid.

Quintana, Francisco de (pseud. of Francisco de las Cuevas, fl. 1625). The Most Entertaining History of Hippolyto and Aminta. Tr. John Stevens. London, 1718. Repr. 1729, 1733?, 1742?

Rojas Zorrilla, Francisco de (1607–1648).   The False Friend (*La traición busca el castigo*). Tr. Sir John Vanbrugh from the French version of LeSage. London, 1702. Repr. in Vanbrugh's Plays, London 1730, vol. 2, et seq.

————None beneath the King (*Del rey abajo ninguno*). Tr. Isaac Goldberg. Little Blue Book. Girard, Kansas, Haldeman-Julius, 1924. 64 pp. Repr. in Three Classic Spanish Plays, 1963: see Collections.

Tr. Rachel Benson as None But the King, in The Genius of the Spanish Theater, 1964: see ibid.

Ruiz de Alarcón, Juan (1581?–1639).   The Gallant, the Bawd, and the Fair Lady. Tr. Walter Starkie in Eight Spanish Plays of the Golden Age, 1964: see Collections.

————The Truth Suspected (*La verdad sospechoso*). Tr. Julio del Toro and Robert V. Finney. Poet Lore, vol. 38 (1927), 475–530.

Tr. Robert C. Ryan, in Angel Flores, ed., Spanish Drama, 1962: see Collections.

Several English adaptations of Pierre Corneille's adaptation as *Le Menteur* may be noted: anon., *The Mistaken Beauty, or the Lyar*, 1671; Richard Steele, *The Lying Lover, or the Ladies Friendship*, 1704 et seq.; Samuel

Foote, *The Lyar*, 1764. The Steele play is the best known: he thought the author of the original was Lope de Vega.

Saavedra Fajardo, Diego de (1584–1648). Republica Literaria, or the Republick of Letters: Being a Vision. Tr. J. E. London, S. Austen, 1727. xxviii, 186 pp.
>Written c.1612 and rev. c.1640, the work was pub. first 1665 as written by Claudio Antonio de Cabrera, with the title *Juicia de artes y sciencias*.

————The Royal Politician Represented in One Hundred Emblems (*Idéa de un príncipe político cristiano, ó Empresas políticas*). Tr. Sir James Astry. London, 1700. 2 vols.

Salas Barbadillo, Alonso Geronimo de (1581–1635).   The Fortunate Fool. Tr. Philip Ayres. London, 1670. 380 pp. Repr. as The Lucky Idiot, 1712, 1736; Worcester, Mass., 1797.

Tr. a Person of Quality as The Lucky Idiot. London, 1760.

————The Hypocrites. Tr. John Davies from the French version by Scarron. London, 1657.
>The original is *La hija de Celestina* (1612), enlarged and pub. (1614) as *La ingeniosa Elena*.

————The Night-Adventurer, or the Day-Hater (*Don Diego de noche*). Tr. anon. in The Novels of Quevedo. London, 1671.

Tr. John Stevens in The Comical Works of Quevedo. London, 1707, q.v. under Quevedo, above.

Sandoval, Prudencio de (1553?–1620).   The Civil Wars of Spain (*Historia del Emperador Carlos V*). Tr. James Wadsworth. London, 1652.

Tr. John Stevens as The History of Charles the Vth. London, 1703. 464 pp.
>An abridged tr. of the *Historia*, which supplements Mariana.

Solís y Rivadeneyra, Antonio de (1610–1686). The History of the Conquest of Mexico by the Spaniards. Tr. Thomas Townsend. London, 1724. Repr. 1738, 1753.

————One Fool Makes Many (*Un bobo hace ciento*). Tr. Lord Holland, in his Three Comedies. London, 1807.

The Son of the Rogue, or the Politic Thief (*La desordenada codicia*). Tr. anon. from the French version. London, 1638.

The Star of Seville.   For this play, see Vega Carpio, below, once thought its author.

Teresa de Jesús, Santa (1515–1582).   The Works of . . . Saint Teresa of Jesus. Tr. anon. London, 1675. 3 parts.

> Tr. E. Allison Peers from the critical ed. by P. Silverio de Santa Teresa. London and N.Y., Sheed and Ward, 1946. 3 vols.
> Contains all the works except the letters.

————The Letters of St. Teresa: A Complete Edition. Tr. and annotated by the Benedictines of Stanbrook, with intro. Cardinal Gasquet. London, T. Baker, 1921–26. 4 vols.
> Contains more than 400 letters 1561–82.

> Tr. and ed. E. Allison Peers. London, Burns Oates, 1961. 2 vols.

————The Minor Works. Conceptions of the Love of God. Exclamations, Maxims, and Poems. Tr. the Benedictines of Stanbrook, rev. Fr. Benedict Zimmerman. London, Thomas Baker, 1913. xl, 278 pp.
> For previous separate publication of these trs., see British Museum Catalogue.

————The Book of the Foundation. Tr. John Dalton. London, 1853.

> Tr. David Lewis. London, 1871. Repr. ed. Fr. Benedict Zimmerman, London, Thomas Baker, 1913, lxxv, 489 pp.

> Tr. Sister Agnes Mason. Cambridge, Univ. Pr., 1909. xviii, 282 pp.

————The Lyf of the Mother Theresa of Iesus . . . Written by her self. Tr. W. M., S. J. London [for Antwerp], Henry Iaye, 1611. 364 pp.

> Tr. Sir Tobie Mathew as The Flaming Heart, or the Life of the Glorious S. Teresa. Antwerp, Meursius, 1642. 660 pp.

> Tr. anon. London, 1669–71. 2 parts.

Tr. John Dalton. London, 1851.

Tr. David Lewis. London, 1870. Repr. 1888; rev. Fr. Benedict Zimmerman, London, Thomas Baker, 1904, xlviii, 489 pp.; repr. 1911; repr. Westminster, Md., Newman Pr., 1962, 432 pp.

*Tr. J. M. Cohen. Penguin, 1957. 316 pp.

————The Way of Perfection and Conceptions of Divine Love. Tr. John Dalton. London, Thomas Baker, 1901. xxxiv, 329 pp.

Ed. A. R. Waller. Cloisters Lib. London, Dent, 1901. xii, 230 pp.

Tr. a Bendictine of Stanbrook. London, Baker, 1911. xxxviii, 299 pp. Repr. rev. Fr. Benedict Zimmerman, to 6th ed., London, Burns Oates, 1961, and Westminster, Md., Newman Pr., 1963.

Tr. E. Allison Peers. Garden City, N.Y., Doubleday, 1964. 280 pp.

Timoneda, Juan de (d. 1583). The Castle of Emmaus, and The Church. (Two *autos*) ed. and tr. Mildred E. Johnson. Iowa City, State Univ. of Iowa Studies in Spanish Language and Literature, 5, 1933. 80 pp.

Tirso de Molina (pseud. of Gabriel Téllez, 1583–1648). The Love-Rogue: A Poetic Drama in Three Acts.** Tr. verse Harry Kemp, with intro. and a Don Juan bibliography. N.Y., Lieber and Lewis, 1923. 229 pp.

Tr. verse Roy Campbell as The Trickster of Seville and the Guest of Stone, in Masterpieces of the Golden Age, 1957: see Collections. Repr. in The Classic Theatre, vol, 3. 1959: see ibid.

Tr. Robert O'Brien as The Rogue of Seville, in Angel Flores, ed., Spanish Drama, 1962: see ibid.

Tr. Walter Starkie as The Playboy of Seville, in Eight Spanish Plays of the Golden Age, 1964: see ibid.

The original title of this first Don Juan play was *El burlador de Sevilla*.

————Prudence in Woman. Tr. Jill Booty, in The Genius of the Spanish Theater, 1964: see Collections.

————Three Husbands Hoaxed (*Tres maridos burlados*). Tr. Ilsa Barea. Emmaus, Pa., and London, Rodale Pr., 1955. 74 pp.

Torquemada, Antonio de (16th c.).   The Spanish Mandeville of Mysteries, or the Garden of Curious Flowers (*Jardín de flores curiosas*). Tr. Lewis Lewkenor. London, 1600. Repr. 1618.

Vega, Alonso de la (d. before 1566).   Love Avenged. Tr. Willis K. Jones, in Spanish One-Act Plays, 1934: see Collections.

Vega Carpio, Lope Félix de (1562–1635).   Five Plays. Tr. Jill Booty. N.Y., Hill and Wang, 1961. 278 pp.
> *Peribañez*; *Fuente ovejuna*; *The Dog in the Manger*; *The Knight from Olmedo*; *Justice without Revenge.*

————Four Plays. Tr. John Garrett Underhill. N.Y., Scribner, 1936. xxiii, 585 pp.
> *A Certainty for a Doubt*; *The King the Greatest Alcalde*; *The Gardener's Dog*; *The Sheep Well.* The last play was repr. in *Poetic Drama*, ed. Alfred Kreymborg, N.Y., 1941; in *The Art of the Play*, ed. Alan S. Downer, N.Y., 1955; in *Three Classic Spanish Plays*, ed. Hyman Alpern, N.Y., 1963.

————*Castelvines y Monteses*. Tr. F. W. Cosens. London, Chiswick Pr., 1869. 105 pp. Repr. in New Variorum edn of Shakespeare's Romeo and Juliet, ed. H. H. Furness, Philadelphia, 1871, et seq.

————The Discovery of the New World by Christopher Columbus: A Comedy in Verse. Tr. prose Frieda Fligelman. Helena, Mont., the Tr., 1950. 62 pp.

————Father Outwitted. Tr. Fanny Holcroft, in The Theatrical Recorder. London, 1805.

————The Gardener's Dog. Tr. W. H. H. Chambers as The Dog in the Manger, in The Drama. N.Y., 1903, vol. 6.
> Also tr. in Four Plays, 1936, above; and in Five Plays (as The Dog in the Manger), 1961, above.

————The Idiot Lady. Tr. William I. Oliver, in The Genius of the Spanish Theater, 1964: see Collections.

————The King the Greatest Alcalde. Tr. John G. Underhill, in Poet Lore, vol. 29 (1918). Repr. in World Drama, ed. Barrett H. Clark, vol. 2, 1933; in Four Plays, 1936, above.

————The Outrageous Saint (*La fianza satisfecha*). Tr. Willis Barnstone, in Tulane Drama Review, vol. 7, no. 1 (1962), 58–104.

————The New Art of Writing Plays. Tr. W. T. Brewster. N.Y., Columbia Univ. Dramatic Museum, 1914. 56 pp.

————The Pastrybaker. Tr. Morits A. Jagendorf. Theatre Arts Monthly, vol. 19 (1935), 713–21.

————*Peribañez*. Tr. Eva R. Price. Redlands, Calif., Valley Pr., 1936. 112 pp.

   Tr. Jill Booty, in Five Plays, 1961, above.

   Tr. Walter Starkie in Eight Spanish Plays of the Golden Age, 1964: see Collections.

————The Rape of Helen. Tr. Willis K. Jones, in Spanish One-Act Plays, 1934: see Collections.

————The Sheep Well. Tr. John Garrett Underhill, in Four Plays, 1936, see above; and note reprs. of this play, ibid.

   Tr. Angel Flores and Muriel Kittel, in A Treasury of the Theatre, ed. John Gassner, vol. 1, 1950. Repr. in Masterpieces of the Spanish Golden Age, ed. Angel Flores, 1957; in Angel Flores, Spanish Drama, 1962: see Collections.

   Tr. verse Roy Campbell, in The Classic Theatre, ed. Eric Bentley, 1959, vol. 3.

   Tr. Jill Booty, in Five Plays, 1961, above.

   Tr. William E. Colford. Woodbury, N.Y., Barron, 1969. 192 pp., parallel texts.

————The Star of Seville. Tr. Philip M. Hayden, in Chief European Dramatists, ed., Brander Matthews, 1916: see General Reference, Collections.
   This play is no longer ascribed to Vega.

   Tr. Henry Thomas. Newton, Wales, Gregynog Pr., 1935. 108 pp. Repr. London, Oxford, Univ. Pr., 1950, 83 pp.

   Tr. Elizabeth C. Hullihen. Charlottesville, Va., Jerman Print Co., 1955. 172 pp.

For commentary, see Hugo A. Rennert, *The Spanish Stage in the Time of Lope de Vega* (N.Y., Hispanic Soc. of Amer., 1909, 635 pp.); Rudolph Schevill, *The Dramatic Art of Lope de Vega* (Berkeley, Univ. of California Pr., 1918, 340 pp.); Jack H. Parker and Arthur M. Fox, eds., *Lope de Vega Studies 1937–1962* (Toronto, Univ. of Toronto Pr., 1964, 210 pp.).

Vélez de Guevara, Luís (1579–1644). See French Literature for René LeSage's adaptation of *El Diablo cojelo* as *Le Diable boiteux*, which was tr. into English.

Villegas, Antonio de (fl. 1565). See *Abencerraje*, above, for his version of that story.

Zayas y Sotomayor, María de (1590–1650). A Shameful Revenge, and Other Stories. Tr. John Sturrock. London, Folio Soc., 1963. x, 200 pp.

Eighteenth Century

Literary Study

Pellissier, Robert E. The Neo-Classic Movement in Spain during the XVIII Century. Stanford, Calif., Stanford Univ. Pr., 1918. 187 pp.

INDIVIDUAL AUTHORS

Cruz, Ramón de la (1731–1795). Pride's Fall (*La presumida burlada*). Tr. Willis Knapp Jones in Spanish One-Act Plays: see Collections, above. Repr. in An Anthology of Spanish Literature, vol. 2, 1958: see ibid.

Feijóo, Benito Geronimo (1676–1764). For trs. of parts of his *Teatro critico universal* (1726–39), see R. U. Pane, English Translations from the Spanish: in Bibliographies, above.

Iriarte, Tomás de (1750–1791). Literary Fables. Tr. J. Belfour. London, 1804. Repr. 1806.

Tr. Richard Andrews. London, Smith Elder, 1835. 128 pp.

Tr. Robert Rockliff. London, 1851. Repr. 1854, 1866.

Tr. verse George H. Devereux. Boston, Ticknor and Fields, 1855. 145 pp.

————Music, a Didactic Poem, in five cantos. Tr. John Belfour. London, 1807. 192 pp.

Isla, José Francisco de (1703–1781). The History of the Famous Preacher Friar Gerund de Campazas: otherwise Gerund Zotes. Tr. Thomas Nugent. London, 1772. 2 vols.

Llorente, Juan Antonio (1756–1823). History of the Inquisition. Tr. anon. abridged. London, Whittaker, 1826. 583 pp. Repr. 1827.

Tr. "by an American" from an abridgement by Leonard Gallois. N.Y., G. C. Morgan, 1826. 271 pp.

Mayáns y Siscar, Gregorio (1699–1781). The Life of Cervantes. Tr. John Ozell. London, Tonson, 1738. Repr. in Jarvis' tr. of Don Quixote, 1742, et seq.

Miranda, Francisco de (c.1754–1816). The New Democracy in America: Travels in the United States 1783–84. Tr. Judson P. Wood. Norman, Univ. of Oklahoma Pr., 1963. 217 pp.

Moratín, Leandro Fernández de (1760–1828). The Baron. Tr. Fanny Holcroft, in Theatrical Review, vol. 2, no. 11. London, 1805.

————Fanny's Consent: A Comedy (*El sí de las niñas*). Tr. Anna E. Bagstad. in Poet Lore, vol. 40 (1929), 159–214.

Tr. William M. Davis as When a Girl Says Yes, in Angel Flores, ed., Spanish Drama, 1962: see Collections. Repr. in Spanish Plays of the Nineteenth Century, ed. Robert O'Brien, 1964: see ibid.

Tr. Harriet de Onís as The Maiden's Consent. Woodbury, N.Y., Barron, 1963. 128 pp.

Quintana, Manuel José (1772–1857). Lives of Celebrated Spaniards . . . the Cid Campeador. Guzman the Good. Roger de Lauria. The Prince of Viana. The Great Captain. Tr. T. R. Preston. London, Fellowes, 1833. xxvii, 355 pp.

Vol. 1 of the *Vidas de españoles celebres*. The last of these lives was tr. Joseph Russell as *Memoirs of Gonzales Hernandez de Cordova, Styled the Great Captain* (London, Churton, 1851, 227 pp.).

Ríos, Vicente Gutierrez de los (18th c.).   The Life of Cervantes. Tr. abridged by Charles Jarvis, pub. in his tr. of Don Quixote, 1801.

Torres Villaroel, Diego de (1693–1770).   The Remarkable Life of Don Diego. Tr. William C. Atkinson. London, Folio Society, 1958. 223 pp. The *Vida*, a picaresque autobiography.

Nineteenth Century

Literary Studies

*Peers, E. Allison.   A History of the Romantic Movement in Spain. Cambridge, Univ. Pr., 1940. 2 vols. Repr. abridged as The Romantic Movement in Spain: A Short History, Liverpool, Univ. of Liverpool Pr., 1968, ix, 230 pp.

Piñeyro, Enrique.   The Romantics of Spain. Tr. E. Allison Peers with intro. and biblio. Liverpool, Institute of Hispanic Studies, 1934. 256 pp.

Collections

Colford, William E., tr.   Classic Tales from Modern Spain. Woodbury, N.Y., Barron, 1964. 224 pp., and paper.
Alarcón, "The Gypsy Fortune"; Alas, "*Adiós Cordera!*"; Azorín, "The Children at the Beach"; Baroja, "Elizabide the Rover"; Bécquer, "The Kiss"; Blasco Ibañez, "Man Overboard"; Caballero, "The Two Friends"; Gómez de la Serna, "The Triangular House"; Marqueríe, "Self-Service Elevator"; Palacio Valdés, "Polyphemus"; Pardo Bazán, "The Talisman"; Pérez de Ayala, "The Substitute Professor"; Romanos, "The Shortsighted Lover"; Unamuno, "Juan Manso: A Dead Man's Tale"; Valle-Inclán, "My Sister Antonia."

Kennedy, James, ed. and tr.   Modern Poets and Poetry of Spain. London, Longmans, 1852. xl, 388 pp. Rev. London, Williams and Norgate, 1860.

Poems by Arriaza; Bretón de los Herreros; Espronceda; Heredia; Iriarte; Jovellanos; Martínez de la Rosa; Meléndez Valdés; Moratín; Saavedra.

Masterpieces of Modern Spanish Drama.   Ed. Barrett H. Clark. N.Y., Duffield, 1917. 290 pp. Repr. Cincinnati, Stewart Kidd, 1922; N.Y., Appleton, 1928.

Echegaray, *El gran Galeoto*; Guimerá, *La pecadora Daniela*; Pérez Galdós, *The Duchess of San Quentin*.

Spanish Plays of the Nineteenth Century.   Ed. Robert O'Brien, trs. various. N.Y., Las Americas, 1964.

Echegaray, *The Great Galeoto*; García Gutierrez, *The Troubadour*; Moratín, *When a Girl Says Yes*; Saavedra, *Don Alvaro*; Tamayo y Baus, *A New Drama*; Zorrilla, *Don Juan Tenorio*.

Tales from the Italian and Spanish, vol. 8, 1920: see Collections.   30 short stories by 19th and 20th c. authors.

Turrell, Charles Alfred, tr.   Contemporary Spanish Dramatists. Boston, Badger, 1919. 397 pp.

Álvarez Quintero, *The Women's Town*; Dicenta, *Juan José*; Linares Rivas, *The Claws*; Marquína, *When the Roses Bloom Again*; Pérez Galdós, *Electra*; Zamacois, *The Passing of the Magi*.

INDIVIDUAL AUTHORS

Alarcón, Pedro Antonio de (1833–1891).   Brunhilde, or the Last Act of Norma (*El final de Norma*). Tr. Mrs. Francis J. A. Darr. N.Y., Lovell, 1891. 311 pp.

————Captain Spitfire (*El capitán veneno*). Tr. anon. London, Vizetelly, 1886.

Tr. Gray Casement as Captain Venom or Poison. Cleveland, Gardner Printing Co., 1914. 103 pp.

————The Child of the Ball. Tr. Mary J. Serrano. N.Y., Cassell, 1892. 333 pp.

Tr. Robert Graves as The Infant with the Globe. N.Y., Yoseloff, 1959. 240 pp.

————"The Gypsy Fortune." Tr. William E. Colford, in Classic Tales from Modern Spain, 1964: see Collections.

————Moors and Christians, and Other Tales. Tr. Mary J. Serrano. N.Y., Cassell, 1891. 266 pp.
Ten short stories from *Historistas nacionales* and *Narraciones inverosímiles*.

————"The Nun" (*La comedadora*). Tr. Martin Nozick, in Great Spanish Short Stories, 1962: see Collections.

————"The Prophecy." Tr. Harriet de Onís, in Spanish Stories and Tales, 1954: see Collections.

————The Scandal. Tr. Philip E. Riley and Hubert James Tunney. N.Y., Knopf, 1945. 382 pp.

————The Strange Friend of Tito Gil (*El amigo de la muerte*). Tr. Mrs. Francis J. A. Darr. N.Y., Lovell, 1890. 133 pp.

Tr. "adapted from the Spanish" by Mary J. Serrano as The Friend of Death. N.Y., Cassell, 1891. 163 pp.

————"The Stub-book." Tr. Angel Flores, in Spanish Stories/*Cuentos Españoles*, 1960: see Collections.

————The Three-Cornered Hat (*El sombrero de tres picos*).

Tr. anon. in The Three-Cornered Hat and Other Spanish Stories. London, Vizetelly, 1886. 128 pp.

Tr. Francis J. Amy as The Cocked Hat. N.Y., Minerva Pub. Co., 1891. 140 pp.

Tr. Mary Springer. N.Y., Cassell, [1891]. xxxviii, 243 pp.

Tr. Lady Goodenough. London, Nutt, 1905. viii, 152 pp.

Tr. Jacob S. Fassett, Jr. N.Y., Knopf, 1918. 208 pp. Repr. 1935.

Tr. Martin Armstrong. London, Howe, 1927, and N.Y., Simon and Schuster, 1928. xiv, 129 pp. Repr. 1933; Los Angeles, Limited Edns Club, 1959, 154 pp.; in Great Spanish Stories, ML, 1956.

Tr. Lawrence M. Levin. N.Y., Bittner, 1944. 154 pp.

Tr. William H. Warden. N.Y., Vantage Pr., 1952. 59 pp.

*Tr. Harriet de Onís. N.Y., Barron, 1958. 128 pp., paper.

Tr. H. F. Turner. London, Calder, 1960. 134 pp. Repr. Chester Springs, Pa., Dufour, 1965.

Tr. Glen Wilbern. N.Y., American RDM Corporation, 1966. 95 pp.

————True to Her Oath: A Tale of Love and Misfortune (*La pródiga*). Tr. Ramiro Montblanc. N.Y., Ogilvie, 1899. v, 235 pp.

Alas, Léopoldo (1852–1901, using pseud. "Clarin"). *"Adiós Cordera!"*

Tr. Charles B. McMichael, in Short Stories from the Spanish, 1920: see Collections. Rev. in Anthology of Spanish Literature, 1958: see ibid.

Tr. William E. Colford, in Classic Tales from Modern Spain, 1964: see Collections.

————"The Cock of Socrates." Tr. M. M. Lesley, in Harriet de Onís, Spanish Stories and Tales, 1954: see ibid.

————"Doña Berta." Tr. Zenia da Silva, in Great Spanish Stories, ML, 1956.

————"The Substitute." Tr. Angel Flores, in Spanish Stories/*Cuentos Españoles*, 1960: see ibid.

Bécquer, Gustavo Adolfo (1836–1870). The Infinite Passion, Being the Celebrated Rimas and the Letters to an Unknown Woman. Tr. Young Allison. Chicago, W. M. Hill, 1924. 97 pp.
The originals: *Rimas* (1860–61); *Desde mi celda*; *Cartas literarias*.

————"The Kiss." Tr. William E. Colford, in Classic Tales from Modern Spain, 1964: see Collections.

————"El Miserere." Tr. Alice Gray Cowan, in Poet Lore, vol. 15, no. B (1904), 25–33.

————"Our Lady's Bracelet." Tr. Edward J. O'Brien, in Stratford Journal, vol. 2, no. 4 (1918), 3–10.

————The "Rimas." Tr. Jules Renard. Boston, Badger, 1908. 78 pp.

Part tr. Rupert Croft-Cooke as Rimas: Twenty Poems from the Spanish of Bécquer. Oxford, Blackwell, 1927. 33 pp.

————Romantic Legends of Spain. Tr. Cornelia Frances Bates and Katherine Lee Bates. N.Y., Crowell, 1909. xxviii, 271 pp.

————Three Tales. Tr. J. R. Carey. London, Harrap, and Philadelphia, McKay [1921]. 108 pp., parallel texts. Repr. 1946 as The Inn of the Cats and Other Stories.

Contains "Master Perez the Organist"; "How Strange!"; and "The Inn of the Cats." The first story is also tr. Martin Nozick in Angel Flores, ed., *Great Spanish Stories*, ML, 1956.

Bretón de los Herrores, Manuel (1796–1873).   One of Many. Tr. Willis K. Jones, in Spanish One-Act Plays, 1934: see Collections.

Caballero, Fernán (pseud. of Cecilia Böhl de Faber, 1796–1877).   Air Built Castles, Stories from the Spanish. Tr. Mrs. Pauli. London, Literary Society, 1887. 240 pp.

————Alvareda Family: A Novelette. Tr. Viscount Follington. London, T. C. Newby, 1872.

————Bird of Truth, and Other Fairy Tales. Tr. John H. Ingram. London, Sonnenschein, and Philadelphia, Lippincott, 1881. 241 pp. Repr. N.Y., Burt, 1920(?), as Spanish Fairy Tales.

————The Castle and the Cottage in Spain. Tr. Lady Wallace. London, Saunders and Co., 1861.

————Elia: Or Spain Fifty Years Ago. Tr. anon. N.Y., Appleton, 1868. 324 pp.

————La Gaviota: A Spanish Novel. Tr. J. Leander Starr. N.Y., Bradburn, 1964. 283 pp. Repr. Philadelphia, Peterson, 1877.

Tr. Augusta Bethell as The Sea-Gull. London, Richard Bentley, 1867. 2 vols.

Tr. Joan MacLean as The Sea Gull. Woodbury, N.Y., Barron, 1965. 160 pp., and paper.

————National Pictures (*Quadros de costumbres*). Tr. by the author of Tasso's Enchanted Ground. London, Burns Oates, 1882. 213 pp.

————Silence in Life and Forgiveness in Death. Tr. J. J. Kelly. London, T. Richardson, 1883. 105 pp.

————"The Two Friends." Tr. William E. Colford, in Classic Tales from Modern Spain, 1964: see Collections.

Castro, Adolfo de (1823–1898). The History of the Jews in Spain. Tr. Edward D. G. M. Kirwan. Cambridge, Deighton, and London, Bell, 1851. 276 pp.

————History of Religious Intolerance in Spain: Or an Examination of Some of the Causes Which Led to That Nation's Decline. Tr. Thomas Parker. London, W. and F. G. Cash, 1853. xxiv, 227 pp.

————The Spanish Protestants and Their Persecution by Philip II. Tr. Thomas Parker. London, Gilpin, and Edinburgh, Black, 1851. lxiv, 386 pp.

Castro, Rosalía de (1837–1885). Beside the River Sar (*En las orillas del Sar*). Tr. S. G. Morley. Berkeley, Univ. of California Pr., 1937. 151 pp., parallel texts.

Coloma, Luis (1851–1914). Currita, Countess of Albornoz: A Novel of Madrid Society (*Pequeneces*). Tr. Estelle Huyck Attwell. Boston, Little Brown, 1900. 450 pp.

————First Mass and Other Stories. Tr. E. M. Brookes. Philadelphia, Kilner, and London and Leamington, Art and Book Co. (as Tales from the Spanish), 1892. 150 pp.

————John Poverty. Tr. E. M. Brookes. Philadelphia, Kilner, 1911. 263 pp.

————Perez the Mouse. Adapted Lady Moreton. N.Y., Dodd, 1914. Repr. London, Lane, 1915, 39 pp.

─────────The Story of Don John of Austria (*Jeromin: Estudios historicos sobre el siglo XVI*). Tr. Lady Moreton. London and N.Y., Lane, 1912. 428 pp.

─────────A True Hidalgo (*Boy*). Tr. Harold Binns. London and Freiburg, Herder, 1911. 323 pp.

Condé, José Antonio (d. 1820). History of the Dominion of the Arabs in Spain. Tr. Mrs. Jonathan Foster. London, Bohn, 1854–55. 3 vols.

Dicenta, Joaquín (1863–1917). Juan José. Tr. Charles A. Turrell, in Contemporary Spanish Dramatists, 1919: see Collections.

Echegaray y Eizaguirre, José (1832–1916). Always Ridiculous. Tr. T. Walter Gilkyson. Poet Lore, vol. 27 (1916), 233–325. Repr. in Poet Lore Plays, 1916.

─────────The Great Galeoto. Tr. prose Hannah Lynch, in The Great Galeoto; Folly or Saintliness: Two Plays. Boston, L. Wolffe, and London, Lane, 1895. xxxvi, 195 pp. Repr. separately, Garden City, N.Y., Doubleday, 1914; repr. in Angel Flores, ed., Spanish Drama, 1962: see Collections.

Adapted C. F. Nirdlinger as The World and His Wife. N.Y., Kennerley, 1908. 215 pp. Repr. in Representative Continental Dramas, ed. M. J. Moses, 1924; made into a film play, 1920.

Tr. Caroline Sheldon. Grinnell, Iowa, Ray and Frisbie, 1912. 76 pp.

Tr. Jacob S. Fassett, Jr. Boston, Badger, 1914. 202 pp.

Tr. Eleanor Bontecou, in Masterpieces of Modern Spanish Drama, 1917; repr. in Continental Plays, ed. T. H. Dickinson, vol. 2, 1935.

Tr. Robert Wesley in Spanish Plays of the Nineteenth Century, 1964: see Collections.

─────────Folly or Saintliness. Tr. Hannah Lynch, with the preceding title, 1895, q.v.

Tr. Ruth Lansing as Madman or Saint. Poet Lore, vol. 24 (1912), 161–220. Repr. in Poet Lore Plays, 1912.

─────────The Madman Divine (*El loco Dios*). Tr. Elizabeth Howard West. Poet Lore, vol. 19 (1908), 3–86. Repr. in Poet Lore Plays, 1916.

————The Man in Black (*El hombre negro*). Tr. Ellen Watson, in Universal Anthology, vol. 27, 1899.

————Mariana. Tr. James Graham. Boston, Roberts Bros., and London, Unwin, 1895. 126 pp. Repr. Boston, Little Brown, 1915.

    Tr. Federico Sarda and Carlos D. S. Wuppermann. N.Y., Moods Pub. Co., 1909. 157 pp. Repr. Boni, 1914; Boni and Liveright, 1918.

————The Son of Don Juan. Tr. James Graham. Boston, Roberts Bros., and London, Unwin, 1895. 131 pp. Repr. Boston, Little Brown, 1911, 1918.

————The Street Singer. Tr. John G. Underhill. The Drama, vol. 7, no. 25 (1917), 62–76. Repr. in Twenty-five Short Plays, ed. Frank Shay, 1925; in The Nobel Prize Treasury, ed. Marshall McClintock, Garden City, N.Y., Doubleday, 1948.

    In *Spanish Plays in English Translation*, s.v. Echegaray, Robert O'Brien mentions trs. of other plays by this author which are not located.

Espronceda, José de (1808–1842). The Student of Salamanca. Tr. Ernest O. Lombardi. San Francisco, Cunningham Publ., 1958. 68 pp.

Ferdinand VII (1784–1833). Memoirs of Ferdinand VII, King of Naples. Tr. Michael J. Quinn. London, 1824.

Fernández Shaw, Carlos (1865–1911). A Brief Life (*La vida breve*): Lyric Drama in Two Acts and Four Tableaux. Music by Manuel de Falla. Tr. Frederick H. Martens. N.Y., Rullman, 1925. 23 pp., parallel texts.

García Gutierrez, Antonio (1813–1884). The Troubadour. Tr. Rachel Benson in Spanish Plays of the Nineteenth Century, 1964: see Collections.

Gil y Carrasco, Enrique (1815–1846). The Mystery of Bierzo Valley: A Tale of the Knights Templars (*El señor de Bembibre*). Tr. C. W. Gethen and L. Vesho Sydenham. Bournemouth, 1938.

Hartzenbush, Juan Eugenio (1806–1880). Lame Girl and Bashful Man. Tr. F. B. Wilson. N.Y., Fenno, 1902. 216 pp.

————The Lovers of Teruel: A Drama in Prose and Verse. Tr. Henry Thomas. Newtown, Wales, Gregynog Pr., 1938. 112 pp. Repr. London, Oxford Univ. Pr., 1950. 72 pp.

Javier de Burgos y Larragoiti, Francisco (1842–1902). The Bullies. Tr. Willis K. Jones in Spanish One-Act Plays, 1934. Repr. in Poet Lore, vol. 43 (1937), 339–59.

Larra, Mariano José de (1808–1837). Quitting Business (*No más mastrador*). Tr. K. C. Kaufman. Poet Lore, vol. 35 (1924), 159–209.

Palacio Valdés, Armando (1853–1938). Faith. Tr. Isabel F. Hapgood. N.Y., Cassell, 1892. 353 pp.

————The Fourth Estate. Tr. Rachel Challice. N.Y., Brentano's, and London, Grant Richards, 1901. 461 pp.

————The Froth. Tr. Clara Bell. London, Heinemann, and N.Y., U.S. Book Co., 1891. 346 pp.
   The original title: *La espuma*; the American title, *Scum*.

————The Grandee (*El maestrante*). Tr. Rachel Challice. London, Heinemann, 1894, and N.Y., Peck, 1895.

————José. Tr. Minna Caroline Smith. N.Y., Brentano's, 1901. 278 pp. Repr. 1922; repr. Translation Pub. Co., c.1931.
   *Tr. Harriet de Onís. N.Y., Barron, 1961. 189 pp.

————The Joy of Captain Ribot. Tr. Minna Caroline Smith. N.Y., Brentano's, and London, Downey, 1900. 277 pp. Repr. 1922.

————The Marquis of Peñalta: A Realistic Social Novel (*Marta y María*).
   Tr. Nathan Haskell Dole. N.Y., Crowell, 1886. 342 pp. Repr. as Marta y Maria in Tales from the Italian and Spanish, vol. 7, 1920: see Collections.

————Maximina. Tr. Nathan Haskell Dole. N.Y., Crowell, 1888. 390 pp.

————"Polyphemus." Tr. William E. Colford, in Classic Tales from Modern Spain, 1964.

————"I Puritani." Tr. Joan Coyne MacLean, in Spanish Stories and Tales, 1956.

————Sister Saint Sulpice. Tr. Nathan Haskell Dole. N.Y., Crowell, 1890. Repr. 1925, 395 pp.

————Tristan: A Novel (*Tristan: o, El pesimismo*). Tr. Jane B. Reid. Boston, Four Seas Co., 1925. 390 pp.

Pardo Bazán, Emilia (1852–1921). The Angular Stone. Tr. Mary J. Serrano. N.Y., Cassell, 1892. 288 pp.

————A Christian Woman (*La cristiana*). Tr. Mary Springer. N.Y., Cassell, 1891. 368 pp. Repr. as The Secret of the Yew Tree, or a Christian Woman, N.Y., Mershon, 1900.

————A Gallician Girl's Romance (*La gallega*). Tr. Mary J. Serrano. N.Y., Mershon, 1900. 331 pp.

————"The Heart Lover" (*Un destripador de antaño*). Tr. Edward and Elizabeth Huberman, in Great Spanish Short Stories, 1962: see Collections.

————Midsummer Madness (*Insolación*). Tr. Amparo Loring. Boston, Clark, 1907. 191 pp.

————*Morriña* (Homesickness). Tr. Mary J. Serrano. N.Y., Cassell, 1891. 331 pp.

————The Mystery of the Lost Dauphin (Louis XVII). Tr. Annabel Nord Seeger. N.Y. and London, Funk and Wagnalls, 1906. 377 pp.

————"The Pardon." Tr. anon. in An Anthology of Spanish Literature, vol. 2, 1958: see Collections, above.

————"The Revolver." Tr. Angel Flores, in Spanish Stories/*Cuentos Españoles*, 1960: see ibid.

————Russia: Its People and Its Literature. Tr. Fanny Hale Gardiner. Chicago, McClurg, 1890. 293 pp.

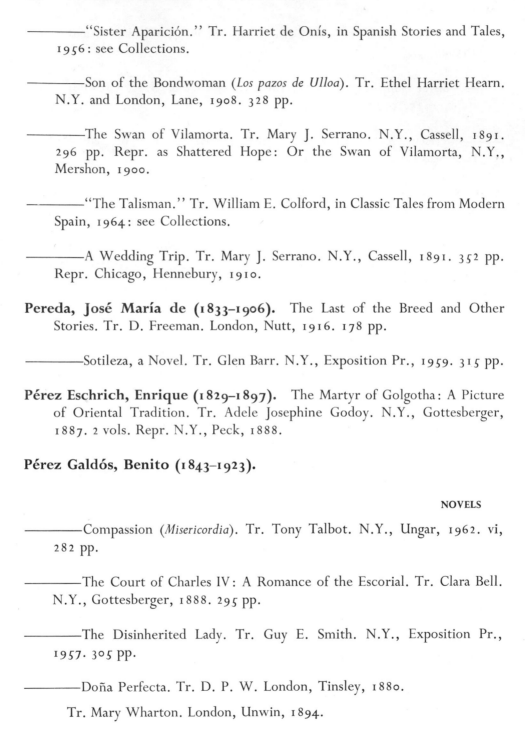

————"Sister Aparición." Tr. Harriet de Onís, in Spanish Stories and Tales, 1956: see Collections.

————Son of the Bondwoman (*Los pazos de Ulloa*). Tr. Ethel Harriet Hearn. N.Y. and London, Lane, 1908. 328 pp.

————The Swan of Vilamorta. Tr. Mary J. Serrano. N.Y., Cassell, 1891. 296 pp. Repr. as Shattered Hope: Or the Swan of Vilamorta, N.Y., Mershon, 1900.

————"The Talisman." Tr. William E. Colford, in Classic Tales from Modern Spain, 1964: see Collections.

————A Wedding Trip. Tr. Mary J. Serrano. N.Y., Cassell, 1891. 352 pp. Repr. Chicago, Hennebury, 1910.

Pereda, José María de (1833–1906). The Last of the Breed and Other Stories. Tr. D. Freeman. London, Nutt, 1916. 178 pp.

————Sotileza, a Novel. Tr. Glen Barr. N.Y., Exposition Pr., 1959. 315 pp.

Pérez Eschrich, Enrique (1829–1897). The Martyr of Golgotha: A Picture of Oriental Tradition. Tr. Adele Josephine Godoy. N.Y., Gottesberger, 1887. 2 vols. Repr. N.Y., Peck, 1888.

Pérez Galdós, Benito (1843–1923).

NOVELS

————Compassion (*Misericordia*). Tr. Tony Talbot. N.Y., Ungar, 1962. vi, 282 pp.

————The Court of Charles IV: A Romance of the Escorial. Tr. Clara Bell. N.Y., Gottesberger, 1888. 295 pp.

————The Disinherited Lady. Tr. Guy E. Smith. N.Y., Exposition Pr., 1957. 305 pp.

————Doña Perfecta. Tr. D. P. W. London, Tinsley, 1880.

Tr. Mary Wharton. London, Unwin, 1894.

Tr. Mary J. Serrano. London, Gay and Bird, 1895, and N.Y., Harper, 1896. 319 pp. Repr. N.Y., Translation Pub. Co., 1923.

Tr. Harriet de Onís. N.Y., Barron, 1960. 256 pp., paper.

————The Family of Leon Roch. Tr. Clara Bell. N.Y., Gottesberger, 1886. Repr. as Leon Roch, ibid., and London, Kegan Paul, 1888, 2 vols.

————Gloria, a Novel. Tr. Clara Bell. N.Y., Gottesberger, 1882. 2 vols. Repr. 1890, 1892.

Tr. N. Wetherhill. London, 1897.

————Marianela. Tr. Clara Bell. N.Y., Gottesberger, 1883. 264 pp. Repr. N.Y., Translation Pub. Co., 1923, 243 pp.

Tr. Helen W. Lester. Chicago, McClurg, 1892. 243 pp. Repr. 1907.

Tr. Mary Wharton. London, Digby and Long, 1893.

————Miau. Tr. J. M. Cohen. London, Methuen, 1963, and Philadelphia, Dufour, 1965. 311 pp. Repr. Penguin, 1966.

————Saragossa: A Story of Spanish Valor. Tr. Minna Caroline Smith. Boston, Little Brown, 1899. 353 pp.

————The Spendthrifts (*La de Bringas*). Tr. Gamel Woolsey. London, Weidenfeld, 1951, and N.Y., Farrar Straus, 1952. 285 pp. Repr. London, New English Lib., 1962.

————Torment. Tr. J. M. Cohen. London, Weidenfeld, 1952, and N.Y., Farrar Straus, 1953. 312 pp.

————"Torquemada in the Flames." Tr. Willard Trask, in Great Spanish Stories, ML, 1956.

————Trafalgar. Tr. Clara Bell. N.Y., Gottesberger, and London, Kegan Paul, 1884. 225 pp. Repr. 1888.

————Tristana. Tr. R. Selden Rose. Peterborough, N.H., R. R. Smith, 1961. 143 pp.

————The Duchess of San Quentin. Tr. Philip M. Hayden, in Masterpieces of Modern Spanish Drama, 1917: see Collections.

————Electra. Tr. Charles A. Turrell in Contemporary Spanish Dramatists, 1919: see Collections. Repr. in Modern Continental Plays, ed. S. Marion Tucker, 1929: see General Reference, Collections.

————The Grandfather. Tr. Elizabeth Wallace. Poet Lore, vol. 21 (1910), 161–233.

See Theodore A. Sackett, *Pérez Galdós: An Annotated Bibliography* (Albuquerque, Univ. of New Mexico Pr., 1969).

Picón, Jacinto Octavio (1852–1923).   "After the Battle"; "The Menace"; "Souls in Contrast." Tr. Charles B. McMichael, in Short Stories from the Spanish, 1920: see Collections.

Ramos Carrión, Miguel (1845–1915) and Vital Aza (1851–1912).   Zaragueta: A Comedy in Two Acts. Tr. Stephen Scatori and Roy Temple House. Poet Lore, vol. 33 (1922), 1–57.

Reinoso, Félix José (1772–1841).   Who Is the Liberator of Spain? Tr. H. Wood. London, 1846.

Saavedra, Angel de, Duke of Rivas (1791–1865).   Don Alvaro. Tr. Robert Lima in Spanish Plays of the Nineteenth Century, 1964: see Collections.

Sinués de Marco, María del Pilar (1835–1893).   Doña Uraca, Queen of Leon and Castile: An Historical Romance of the Middle Ages. Tr. Reginald Huth. Bath, Wilkinson Bros., 1890. 127 pp.

Tamayo y Baus, Manuel (1829–1898).   A New Drama. Tr. John Driscoll Fitz-Gerald and Thacher Howland Guild. N.Y., Hispanic Soc. of America, 1915. xxvi, 152 pp.

Tr. Robert O'Brien, in Spanish Plays of the Nineteenth Century, 1964.

Trueba, Antonio de (1819–1889). The Old Campeador: A Historical Romance. Tr. Henry J. Gill. London and N.Y., Longmans, 1895. 397 pp. Repr. Dublin, 1902.

————"The Portal of Heaven." Tr. Arthur B. Myrick, in Stratford Journal, vol. 6 (1920), 86–96.

————"The Thrashing." Tr. Wm. M. Davis, in Great Spanish Short Stories, 1962: see Collections.

Valera, Juan (1824–1905). Commendador Mendoza. Tr. Mary J. Serrano. N.Y., Appleton, 1893. 291 pp.

————Doña Luz. Tr. Mary J. Serrano. N.Y., Appleton, 1891. 284 pp.

————Don Braulio (*Pasarse de listo*). Tr. Clara Bell. N.Y., Appleton, 1892. 244 pp.

————Pepita Ximenes. Tr. Mary J. Serrano. N.Y., Appleton, 1886. 273 pp. Repr. 1891.

Tr. Maurice Francis Egan. N.Y., Collier [1886]. Repr. in Tales from the Italian and Spanish, vol. 7, 1920: see Collections.

Tr. Harriet de Onís. Great Neck, N.Y., Barron, 1964. 224 pp., paper.

Zorrilla y Moral, José (1817–1893). Dagger of the Goth. Tr. Willis K. Jones. Poet Lore, vol. 40 (1929), 426–42. Repr. in Spanish One-Act Plays in English, 1934.

————Don Juan Tenorio. Adapted and tr. verse Walter Owen. Buenos Aires, The translator, 1944. 241 pp.

Tr. William I. Oliver in The Theatre of Don Juan, ed. Oscar Mandel. Lincoln, Univ. of Nebraska Pr., 1963. Repr. in Spanish Plays of the Nineteenth Century, 1964: see Collections.

————Translations from the Spanish Poet José Zorrilla by Samuel Eliot. Boston, 1846. 43 pp.

Twentieth Century

Literary Studies

Balbotín, José Antonio.   Three Spanish Poets: Rosalía de Castro, Federico García Lorca, Antonio Machado. Tr. J. A. Balbotín. London, Redman, 1961. 157 pp.

Bell, A. F. G.   Contemporary Spanish Literature. Rev. ed. N.Y., Knopf, 1933. 315 pp.

Eoff, Sherman H.   The Modern Spanish Novel: Comparative Essays Examining the Philosophic Impact of Science on Fiction. N.Y., N.Y Univ. Pr., 1961. 280 pp.

Ilie, Paul.   The Surrealist Mode in Spanish Literature. Ann Arbor, Univ. of Michigan Pr., 1968. 242 pp.

Kercheville, F. M.   A Study of Tendencies in Modern and Contemporary Spanish Poetry from the Modernist Movement to the Present. Albuquerque, Univ. of New Mexico Pr., 1933. 64 pp.

Madariaga, Salvador de.   The Genius of Spain, and Other Essays on Spanish Contemporary Literature. Oxford, Clarendon Pr., 1923. 164 pp.

Salinas, Pedro.   "Spanish Literature" [since 1870], in Columbia Dictionary of Modern European Literature, 1947, q.v. in Histories of Literature, General Reference, above.
  The *Dictionary* contains numerous articles on Spanish authors.

Spanish Thought and Letters in the 20th Century.   Ed. and tr. Germán Bleiberg and E. Inman Fox. Nashville, Tenn., Vanderbilt Univ. Pr., 1966. xvi, 610 pp.
  Commemorating the centenary of the birth of Unamuno.

Young, Howard T.   The Victorious Expression: A Study of Four Contemporary Spanish Poets: Unamuno, Machado, Jiménez, and Lorca. Madison, Univ. of Wisconsin Pr., 1965. 248 pp.

Collections

And Spain Sings: Fifty Loyalist Ballads.   Adapted by American Poets, ed. M. J. Benardete and Rolfe Humphries. N.Y., Vanguard Pr., 1937. 123 pp.

Caponigri, A. Robert, ed. and tr.   Contemporary Spanish Philosophy: An Anthology. Notre Dame, Ind., and London, Univ. of Notre Dame Pr., 1967. xvi, 383 pp.
  Lengthy selections from eleven authors.

Colford, William E., ed. and tr.   Classic Tales from Modern Spain. See Nineteenth Century, Collections, above.

Flores, Angel, ed. and tr.   Spanish Writers in Exile. Sausalito, Calif., B. Porter, 1948. 114 pp.

Masterpieces of the Modern Spanish Theatre.   Trs. various, ed. R. W. Corrigan. N.Y., Collier, 1967. 384 pp.
  Benavente, *The Witches' Sabbath*; Buero Vallejo, *The Dream Weaver*; García Lorca, *The Love of Don Perlímplin and Belisa in the Garden*; Martínez Sierra, *The Cradle Song*; Sastre, *Death Thrust*.

McMichael, Charles B., ed. and tr.   Short Stories from the Spanish. N.Y., Boni and Liveright, 1920. 116 pp. Repr. Girard, Kans., Haldeman-Julius, 1923, 60 pp.
  Alas, *"Adiós Cordera!"*; Darío, "The Box," "The Death of the Empress of China," "The Veil of Queen Mab," qq.v. in Spanish American Literature, below, Nicaragua; Picón, "After the Battle," "The Menace," "Souls in Contrast."

Turnbull, Eleanor L., ed. and tr.   Contemporary Spanish Poetry: Selections from Ten Poets: With the Spanish Originals, and Personal Reminiscences of the Poets by Pedro Salinas. Baltimore, Johns Hopkins Pr., 1945. 401 pp.
  One hundred and forty-six poems from Alberti, Vicente Aleixandre, Manuel Altolaguirre, Luis Cernuda, Gerardo Diego, García Lorca, Guillén, Moreno Villa, Prados, and Salinas.

Turrell, Charles Alfred, ed. and tr.   Contemporary Spanish Dramatists: see Nineteenth Century, Collections, above.

Wells, Warre B., ed. and tr.   Great Spanish Short Stories: Representing the Work of Leading Spanish Writers of Today; Biographical Notes by J. G. Gorkin, intro. Henri Barbusse. Boston, Houghton Mifflin, and London, Eyre (as The Spanish Omnibus), 1932. 386 pp.

> Arderíus, "Night of Frost"; Baroja, "The Abyss"; Blasco Ibáñez, "Dimoni"; Díaz Fernández, "Africa at His Feet"; Espina de Serna, "The Minor Friar"; Espina García, "Luis Candelas"; Miró Ferrer, "The Schoolmaster"; Giménez Caballero, "The Lowly-Born Redeemer"; Gómez de la Serna, "The Man in the Gallery"; Jarnés, "Saint Alexis"; Pérez de Ayala, "The Assistant Professor"; Martínez Ruiz (Azorín), "The Reverse of the Tapestry"; Sénder, "The Journey"; Unamuno, "Solitude"; Valle-Inclán, "The Golden Rose." An excellent cross-section.

INDIVIDUAL AUTHORS

Acebal, Francisco (1866–1933). Face to Face (*Huellas de almas*), and Dolorosa: Two Novels of Modern Spain. Tr. Martin Hume. London, Constable, and N.Y., Dutton, 1906. 352 pp.

Alberti, Rafael (1902—). Selected Poems. Tr. Lloyd Mallan. N.Y., New Directions, 1944. 32 pp.

————Selected Poems. Tr. Ben Belitt, intro. Luis Monguió. Berkeley, Univ. of California Pr., 1966. 219 pp., parallel texts.

————Concerning the Angels. Tr. Geoffrey Connell. London, Rapp and Carroll, 1967. 65 pp.

————A Spectre Is Haunting Europe: Poems of Revolutionary Spain. Tr. Ira Jan Wallach and Angel Flores. N.Y., Critics Group, 1936. 32 pp.

Álvarez Quintero, Serafín (1871–1938) and **Joaquin (1873–1944).**   Four Comedies: Love Passes By; Don Abel Wrote a Tragedy; Peace and Quiet; Doña Clarines. Tr. Helen and Harley Granville-Barker. London, Sidgwick and Jackson, and N.Y., French, 1932. 311 pp.

> *El amor que pasa*; *La musa loca*; *La escondida senda*; *Doña Clarines*. The last play was repr. in Twentieth Century Plays, ed. F. W. Chandler, 1934.

————Four Plays: The Women Have Their Way; A Hundred Years Old; Fortunato; The Lady from Alfaqueque. Tr. Helen and Harley Granville-Barker. London, Sidgwick and Jackson, 1927, and Boston, Little Brown, 1928. 260 pp.
  Puebla de las mujeres; *El centenario*; *Fortunato*; *La consuela*.

————A Bright Morning: see A Morning of Sunshine, below.

————By the Light of the Moon: see In the Moonlight, below.

————By Their Words Ye Shall Know Them (*Hablando se entienda la gente*). Tr. John G. Underhill. The Drama, vol. 7, no. 25 (Feb. 1917), 26–39. Repr. in M. J. Moses, Representative One-Act Plays by Continental Authors, 1922; repr. 1926.

————Fortunato. Tr. also Anna S. MacDonald. N.Y., Sunwise Turn, 1918.

————The Fountain of Youth: A Poetic Drama in Four Acts (*La flor de la vida*). Tr. Samuel M. Baker. Cincinnati, Stewart Kidd, 1922. 71 pp.

————Grief: A Drama in Two Scenes (*La pena*). Tr. Ana Lee Utt. Poet Lore, vol. 41 (1930), 391–402.

————In the Moonlight (*A la luz de la luna*). Tr. Willis K. Jones, in Spanish One-Act Plays in English, 1934, q.v. in Collections.

  Tr. William D. Moore as By the Light of the Moon. Poet Lore, vol. 48 (1942), 99–110.

————Malvaloca: A Drama in Three Acts. Tr. Jacob S. Fassett, Jr. N.Y., Doubleday Page, 1916. xxviii, 151 pp. Repr. 1922; in Chief Contemporary Dramatists, Third Series, ed. T. H. Dickinson, 1930.

  Tr. Beatrice Erskine. (Performed in London, 1925.)

————A Morning of Sunshine (*Mañana de sol*). Tr. Lucretia X. Floyd. N.Y., French, 1914. 18 pp. Repr. as A Sunny Morning, in Frank Shay and Pierre Loving, Fifty Contemporary One-Act Plays, 1920; also repr. in J. P. Webber and H. H. Webster, One-Act Plays for Secondary Schools, 1923; in Thirty Famous One-Act Plays, ML, 1943; in Modern One-Act Plays, ed. F. J. Griffith, N.Y., 1950.

Tr. C. C. Castillo and E. L. Overman as A Bright Morning. Poet Lore, vol. 27 (1916), 669–79. Repr. in Continental Plays, ed. T. H. Dickinson, vol. 1, 1930.

Tr. Isaac Goldberg, in Stratford Journal, vol. 1, no. 1 (1916), 39–51.

Tr. Anna S. MacDonald. (Played in New York in 1921.)

————Papa Juan or the Centenarian. Tr. Thomas Walsh. Poet Lore, vol. 29 (1918), 253–318.

Tr. Helen and Harley Granville-Barker as A Hundred Years Old, in Four Plays, 1928, q.v. above.

————Widow's Eyes: A Comedy in One Act (*Ojos de luto*). Tr. Ana Lee Utt, in Poet Lore, vol. 40 (1929), 552–56.

————The Women's Town. Tr. C. A. Turrell, in his Contemporary Spanish Dramatists, 1919: see Collections.

Tr. Helen and Harley Granville-Barker as The Women Have Their Way, in Four Plays, 1928, q.v. above.

Arniches, Carlos (1866–1943).   The Philosophic Cobbler, or Another Year, Another Chance. Tr. Willis K. Jones, in his Spanish One-Act Plays, 1934: see Collections.

Ayala, Francisco (1906—).   "The Bewitched." Tr. Caroline Muhlenberg, in Angel Flores, Great Spanish Stories, ML, 1956, q.v. in Collections.

————Death as a Way of Life (*Muertes de perro*). Tr. Joan MacLean. N.Y., Macmillan, 1964, and London, Joseph, 1965. 218 pp.

Azorín (pseud. of José Martínez Ruíz, 1876–1967).   "The Children at the Beach." Tr. William E. Colford, in Classic Tales from Modern Spain, 1964: see Collections.

————Don Juan. Tr. Catherine Alison Phillips. London, Chapman and Dodd, 1923, and N.Y., Knopf, 1924. 144 pp.

————"The First Miracle." Tr. John M. Flores, in Great Spanish Short Stories, 1962: see Collections.

————An Hour of Spain between 1560 and 1590. Tr. Alice Raleigh. London, Routledge, 1930. 209 pp.

————"The Reverse of the Tapestry." Tr. Warre B. Wells, in Great Spanish Short Stories, 1932: see Collections.

————The Syrens, and Other Stories (*Blanco en Azul: Cuentos*). Tr. Warre B. Wells. London, Scholartis Pr., 1931. 133 pp.

Barea, Arturo (1897—). The Brocken Root. Tr. Ilsa Barea. London, Faber, and N.Y., Harcourt, 1951. 308 pp.

————The Forge. Tr. Ilsa Barea. London, Landsborough, 1958. 252 pp.

————The Track. Tr. Ilsa Barea. London, Landsborough, 1958. 254 pp.

————The Clash. Tr. Ilsa Barea. London, Landsborough, 1958. 317 pp.
    The original of these three novels is *La forja de un rebelde: La forja, La ruta, La llama.*

Baroja y Nessi, Pio (1872–1956). "The Abyss." Tr. Warre B. Wells, in Great Spanish Short Stories, 1932: see Collections.

————"The Cabbages of the Cemetery." Tr. Harriet de Onís, in Spanish Stories and Tales, 1954: see Collections.

————Caesar or Nothing. Tr. Louis How. N.Y., Knopf, 1919. 337 pp.

————The City of the Discreet (*La feria de los discretos*). Tr. Jacob S. Fassett, Jr. N.Y., Knopf, 1917. 356 pp.

————"Elizabide the Rover." Tr. William E. Colford, in Classic Tales from Modern Spain, 1964: see Collections.

————The Lord of Labraz (*El Mayorazgo de Labraz*). Tr. Aubrey F. G. Bell. N.Y. and London, Knopf, 1926. 251 pp.

————Paradox, King, a Novel. Tr. Neville Barbour. London, Wishart, 1931. 260 pp.

————The Quest. Tr. Isaac Goldberg. N.Y., Knopf, 1922. 289 pp.

La busca is the first vol. of the trilogy *Struggle for Life*. The second is *Weeds*, the third *Red Dawn*, qq.v. below.

————Red Dawn. Tr. Isaac Goldberg. N.Y., Knopf, 1924. 347 pp.

————The Restlessness of Santi Andia, and Other Writings. Tr. Anthony Kerrigan. Ann Arbor, Univ. of Michigan Pr., 1959. 415 pp. Repr. N.Y., New Amer. Lib., 1962.

————The Tree of Knowledge. Tr. Aubrey F. G. Bell. N.Y., Knopf, 1928. 329 pp.

————Weeds. Tr. Isaac Goldberg. N.Y., Knopf, 1923. 334 pp.

————Youth and Egolatry. Tr. Jacob S. Fassett Jr. and Frances L. Phillips. N.Y., Knopf, 1920. 265 pp.

Benavente, Jacinto (1866–1954). Plays. Tr. John Garrett Underhill. N.Y., Scribner, 1917–24. 4 vols.

First series: *His Widow's Husband*; *The Bonds of Interest* (*Los intereses creados*); *The Evil Doers of Good*; *The Passion Flower* (*La malquerida*). Second series: *No Smoking*; *Princess Bebé*; *The Governor's Wife*; *Autumnal Roses*. Third series: *The Prince Who Learned Everything out of Books*; *Saturday Night*; *In the Clouds*; *The Truth*. Fourth series: *The School of Princesses*; *A Lady*; *The Magic of an Hour*; *Field of Ermine*.

The Bonds of Interest tr. was repr. in *Chief Contemporary Dramatists*, second series, 1921: see General Reference, Collections; in *Representative Continental Dramas*, ed. M. J. Moses, 1924; in *Representative Modern Dramas*, ed. Charles H. Whitman, 1936; in *Spanish Drama*, ed. Angel Flores, 1962. It was rev. Hyman Alpern (N.Y., Ungar, 1967, 169 pp., parallel texts).
The Governor's Wife tr. was pub. in *Poet Lore*, vol. 29 (1918), 1–72.
His Widow's Husband was repr. separately (Boston, Baker, 1935, 52 pp.); and in *The Nobel Prize Treasury*, ed. Marshall McClintock, 1948.
The Magic of an Hour was repr. separately (Boston, Baker, 1935, 17 pp.).
The *No Smoking* tr. was pub. in *The Drama*, vol. 7, no. 25 (1917), 78–88.
The Passion Flower tr. was repr. in *Modern Continental Plays*, ed. S. Marion Tucker, 1929; in *Contemporary Drama*, ed. E. B. Watson and B. Pressey,

1931; in *Twenty Best European Plays on the American Stage*, ed. John Gassner, 1957.

The Prince Who Learned Everything out of Books was pub. in Poet Lore, vol. 29 (1918), 505–30.

Saturday Night was pub. in *Poet Lore*, vol. 29 (1918), 127–93.

The Truth was pub. separately (Boston, Baker, 1935, 19 pp.).

OTHER TRANSLATIONS

————At Close Range: A Comedy in One Act (*De cerca*). Tr. John G. Underhill. N.Y., French, 1936. 29 pp.

————Brute Force: A Comedy in Two Acts. Tr. John Garrett Underhill. N.Y., French, 1935. 55 pp.

————The Smile of Mona Lisa: A Play in One Act (*La sonrisa de Gioconda*). Tr. John Armstrong Herman. Boston, Badger, [1915]. 34 pp.

————The Witches' Sabbath. Tr. William I. Oliver, in Masterpieces of the Modern Spanish Theatre, 1967: see Collections.

For Benavente, see Walter Starkie, *Jacinto Benavente* (London and N.Y., Oxford Univ. Pr., 1924, 218 pp.).

Blasco Ibáñez, Vicente (1867–1928). "The Abandoned Boat"; "The Functionary." Tr. Isaac Goldberg, in Stratford Journal, vol. 4 (1919), 245–62.

————Alfonso XIII Unmasked: The Military Terror in Spain (*Una nación sequestrada: el terror militarista en España*). Tr. Leo Ongley. N.Y., Dutton, 1924, and London, Nash and Grayson, 1925. 121 pp.

————The Argonauts. Tr. anon. N.Y., Dutton, n.d.

————The Blood of the Arena (*Sangre y arena*). Tr. Frances Douglas. Chicago, McClurg, 1911. 385 pp.

Tr. Mrs. W. A. Gillespie as Blood and Sand. London, Simpkin Marshall, 1913. Repr. London, Nelson, 1918 (as The Matador); N.Y., Dutton, 1919. xii, 356 pp.; London, Benn, 1921; N.Y., Grosset, 1941; London, Benn, 1961.

*Tr. Frances Partridge as Blood and Sand. London, Elek, and N.Y., Ungar, 1958. viii, 320 pp. Repr. London, Mayflower, 1964, paper.

—————The Borgias, or at the Feet of Venus (*A los pies de Venus*). Tr. Arthur Livingston. N.Y., Dutton, 1930, and London, Skeffington (as At the Feet of Venus: A Tale of the Borgias), 1931. 340 pp.

—————The Bull-fight. Ed. and tr. C. D. Campbell. London, Harrap, and Philadelphia, McKay, 1919. 63, 63 pp., parallel texts.

—————The Cabin. Tr. Francis Haffkine Snow and Beatrice M. Makota. N.Y., Knopf, 1917, and London, Hurst and Blackett, 1919. 288 pp. Repr. N.Y., 1919, 1924, 1934, ML, n.d.

—————The Dead Command. Tr. Frances Douglas. N.Y., Duffield, 1919. 350 pp.

—————"Dimoni." Tr. Warre B. Wells, in Great Spanish Short Stories, 1932.

—————The Enemies of Women. Tr. Irving Brown. N.Y., Dutton, 1920. 547 pp. Repr. London, Unwin, 1922; N.Y., Burt, 1926; N.Y., Dutton, 1930.

—————The Four Horsemen of the Apocalypse. Tr. Charlotte Brewster Jordan. N.Y., Dutton, 1918. 489 pp. Repr. London, Constable, 1919; N.Y., Burt, 1926; N.Y., Dutton, 1941; London, Landsborough, 1959, 319 pp.; N.Y., Dell, 1961, 415 pp.

—————The Fruit of the Vine, A Novel (*La bodega*). Tr. Isaac Goldberg. N.Y., Dutton, 1919. 368 pp. Repr. London, Unwin, 1923.

—————The Intruder. Tr. W. A. Gillespie. N.Y., Dutton, 1928. 338 pp. Repr. London, Butterworth, 1930.

—————In the Land of Art. Tr. Frances Douglas. N.Y., Dutton, 1923. 338 pp. Repr. London, Unwin, 1924.

—————The Knight of the Virgin. Tr. Arthur Livingston. N.Y., Dutton, 1930. 305 pp. Repr. London, Butterworth, 1931.

—————The Last Lion, and Other Tales. Tr. Mariano J. Lorente. Boston, Four Seas Co., 1919. 73 pp.
  "The Last Lion"; "The Toad"; "Compassion"; "The Windfall"; "Luxury"; "Rabies."

—————Luna Benamor. Tr. Isaac Goldberg. Boston, Luce, 1919. 209 pp.
  With the novel are included the short stories of the preceding item.

—————"Man Overboard." Tr. William E. Colford, in Classic Tales from Modern Spain, 1964: see Collections.

—————Mare Nostrum (Our Sea). Tr. Charlotte Brewster Jordan. N.Y., Dutton, 1919. 518 pp. Repr., London, Constable, 1920, and N.Y., Burt, 1926.

—————The Mayflower: A Tale of the Venetian Seashore (*Flor de mayo*). Tr. Arthur Livingston. N.Y., Dutton, 1921. 256 pp. Repr. London, T. Fisher Unwin, 1922; N.Y., Burt, 1929.

—————The Mob (*La horde*). Tr. Mariano Joaquin Lorente. N.Y., Dutton, and London, Butterworth, 1927. 395 pp.

—————A Novelist's Tour of the World. Tr. Leo Ongley and Arthur Livingston. N.Y., Dutton, 1926, and London, Butterworth, 1927. 420 pp.

—————The Old Woman of the Movies, and Other Stories. Tr. anon. N.Y., Dutton, 1925. 391 pp.
  Fifteen stories from *El prestamo de la difunta*.

—————The Paradise of Women. Tr. anon. N.Y., Dutton, 1922.

—————The Phantom with Wings of Gold. Tr. Arthur Livingston. N.Y., Dutton, 1931. 280 pp.

—————The Pope of the Sea: An Historical Medley. Tr. Arthur Livingston. N.Y. Dutton, 1927. 363 pp.

—————Queen Calafia. Tr. anon. N.Y., Dutton, 1924. 332 pp. Repr. London, Butterworth, 1925; N.Y., Burt, 1929.

————Reeds and Mud. Tr. Isaac Goldberg. N.Y., Dutton, 1928, and London, Butterworth, 1929.289 pp. Repr. N.Y. 1932.

Tr. Lester Beberfall. Boston, Humphries, 1966. 194 pp.

————The Shadow of the Cathedral (*La catedral*). Tr. Mrs. W. A. Gillespie. London, Constable, 1909. Repr. with intro. W. D. Howells, N.Y., Dutton, 1919, 341 pp.

————Sonnica (*Sonnica la cortisana*). Tr. Frances Douglas. N.Y., Duffield, 1912. 331 pp.

————The Temptress (*La tierra de todos*). Tr. Leo Ongley. N.Y., Dutton, and London, Butterworth, 1923. 405 pp. Repr. N.Y., Burt, 1929.

————The Three Roses (*Arroz y tartana*). Tr. Stuart Edgar Grummon. N.Y., Dutton, 1932. 348 pp.

————The Torrent (*Entre naranjos*). Tr. Isaac Goldberg and Arthur Livingston. N.Y., Dutton, 1921. 332 pp. Repr. N.Y., Burt, 1926.

————Unknown Lands, the Story of Columbus (*En busca del Gran Kan: Cristóbal Colón*). Tr. Arthur Livingston. N.Y., Dutton, 1929, and London, Butterworth, 1931. 285 pp.

————Woman Triumphant (*La maja desnuda*). Tr. Hayward Keniston., N.Y., Dutton, 1920, and London, Constable, 1921. 322 pp. Repr. N.Y., Burt, 1929.

Tr. Frances Partridge as The Naked Lady. London, Elek, 1959. 224 pp.

Buero Vallejo, Antonio (1916—). The Weaver of Dreams. Tr. William I. Oliver, in The Genius of the Spanish Theatre, 1964; repr. as The Dream Weaver, in Masterpieces of the Modern Spanish Theatre, 1967: see Collections.

Cascales y Muños, José (1865–1933). Francisco de Zurbaran: His Epoch, His Life, and His Works. Tr. Nellie Seelye Evans. N.Y., pr. pr., 1918. xxiii, 158 pp.

Casona, Alejandro (1903—). The Lady, the Dawn. Tr. Barbara Rowan and Robert O'Brien, in The Genius of the Spanish Theater, 1964: see Collections.

Cela, Camilo José (1916—). The Family of Pascual Duarte. Tr. Anthony Kerrigan. Boston, Little Brown, and London, Weidenfeld, 1965. xx, 166 pp. Repr., N.Y., Avon Books, 1966, paper.

————The Hive. Tr. J. M. Cohen, in consultation with Arturo Barea. London, Gollancz, and N.Y., Farrar Straus, 1953. 257 pp.

————Journey to Alcarria. Tr. Frances M. Lopez Morillas. Madison, Univ. of Wisconsin Pr., 1964. 160 pp.

————"A Misunderstood Genius" (excerpt from *El Molino de viento*). Tr. John W. Kronik, in Great Spanish Short Stories, 1962: see Collections.

————Mrs. Caldwell Speaks to Her Son. Tr. J. S. Bernstein. Ithaca, N.Y., Cornell Univ. Pr., 1968. 224 pp.

————Rest Home. Tr. Herma Briffault. N.Y., Las Americas, 1961. 219 pp.

————"The Romería." Tr. Gordon Brotherston, in Short Stories in Spanish/ *Cuentos Hispánicos*, 1966: see Collections.

————"Samson García, Traveling Photographer." Tr. Angel Flores, in Spanish Stories/*Cuentos Españoles*, 1960: see Collections.

————"The Village Idiot." Tr. Beatrice P. Patt, in Angel Flores, ed., Great Spanish Stories, 1956: see Collections.

Chaves Nogales, Manuel (1897—). Heroes and Beasts of Spain (*A sangre y fuego, heroes, bestias y mártires de España*). Tr. Luis de Baeza, ed. D. C. F. Hardin. Garden City, N.Y., Doubleday Doran, 1937, and London, Heinemann, 1938. 303 pp.

————Juan Belmonte, Killer of Bulls: The Autobiography of a Matador. Tr. Leslie Charteris. London, Heinemann, and Garden City, N.Y., Doubleday, 1937. 340 pp.

Clariana, Barnardo. Rendezvous with Spain: A Poem. Tr. Dudley Fitts. N.Y., Conor Pr., 1946.

Espina de Serna, Concha (1877–1955). Mariflor (*La esfinge maragata*). Tr. Frances Douglas. N.Y., Macmillan, 1924. 425 pp.

————"The Minor Friar." Tr. Warre B. Wells, in Great Spanish Short Stories, 1932: see Collections.

————The Red Beacon (*Dulce nombre*). Tr. Frances Douglas. N.Y. and London. Appleton, 1924. 286 pp.

————The Woman and the Sea (*Agua de nieve*). Tr. Terrel Louise Tatum, N.Y., R. D. Henkle, 1934. 279 pp.

Fernández de la Reguera, Ricardo (1916—). In the Darkness of My Fury (*Cuando voy a morir*). Tr. Ilsa Barea. London, O. Wolff, 1959. 224 pp.

————Reach for the Ground (*Cuerpo a tierra*). Tr. Ilsa Barea. N.Y., Abelard-Schuman, 1965. 224 pp.

Fernández-Flórez, Wenceslao (1886?—). The Seven Pillars. Tr. Sir Peter Chalmers Mitchell. London and N.Y., Macmillan, 1934. 288 pp.

Ferrater Mora, José (1912—). Being and Death: An Outline of an Integrationist Philosophy. Tr. rev. by author. Berkeley, Univ. of California Pr., 1965. viii, 267 pp.

————Man at the Crossroads. Tr. Willard R. Trask. Boston, Beacon Pr. [1957]. 252 pp.

————Ortega y Gasset, an Outline of His Philosophy. New Haven, Conn., Yale Univ. Pr., 1957. 69 pp. Rev. 1963, 103 pp., paper.

————Philosophy Today: Conflicting Tendencies in Contemporary Thought. N.Y., Columbia Univ. Pr., 1960. x, 193 pp.

————Unamuno, a Philosophy of Tragedy. Tr. Philip Silver. Berkeley, Univ. of California Pr., 1962. 136 pp.

Fonseca, Rodolfo L.   Tower of Ivory (*Turris eburnea*). Tr. Walter Starkie. London, Cape, and N.Y., Messner, 1954. 279 pp.

García Lorca, Federico (1899–1936).

PLAYS

————From García Lorca's Theatre. Tr. Richard L. O'Connell and James Graham-Lujan. N.Y., Scribner, 1941. xxxvi, 251 pp.
  Yerma; *The Shoemaker's Prodigious Wife*; *The Love of Don Perlímplin*; *If Five Years Pass*; *Doña Rosita the Spinster*. *Yerma* rev. in *Three Tragedies*, below; *The Shoemaker's Prodigious Wife*, *The Love of Don Perlímplin*, and *Doña Rosita* were repr. in the next item. *Don Perlímplin* was also repr. in *From the Modern Repertoire*, series 1, 1951; in *The Genius of the Spanish Theater*, 1964; and in *Masterpieces of the Modern Spanish Theatre*, 1967: see Collections.

————Five Plays: Comedies and Tragedies. Tr. the same. N.Y., New Directions, 1964. vi, 246 pp. Repr. 1967, paper.
  Repr. of three of the plays in the preceding item, adding *The Billy-Club Puppets*; *The Butterfly's Evil Spell*.

————Three Tragedies. Tr. the same. N.Y., New Directions, 1947, and London, Falcon Pr., 1948. 378 pp. Repr. N.Y., 1956, 212 pp.; London, Secker, 1959, 216 pp.
  Blood Wedding; *Yerma* (rev. from the first collection); *The House of Bernarda Alba*. The first play was repr. in *Treasury of the Theatre*, ed. John Gassner (vol. 1, 1951); in *Contemporary Drama: Fifteen Plays*, ed. E. B. Watson and B. Pressey, 1959; in *Masters of Modern Drama*, ed. H. M. Block and R. G. Shedd, 1962; and in *Spanish Drama*, ed. Angel Flores, 1962. The second play was repr. in *The Makers of the Modern Theater*, ed. Barry Ulanov, 1961; and in *The Modern Theatre*, ed. R. W. Corrigan, 1964. The third play was repr. in *Contemporary Drama: 13 Plays*, ed. Stanley Clayes and David Spencer, 1962. See these titles under Collections.

————Blood Wedding was also tr. Gilbert Neiman. New Directions 1939, pp. 1–61.

————Mariana Pineda. Tr. James Graham-Lujan, in Tulane Drama Review, vol. 7, no. 2 (1962), 18–75.

————(Playlets). Tr. Tim Reynolds, in Accent, vol. 17 (1957), 131–39. *Buster Keaton's Promenade*; *Chimera*; *The Virgin, the Sailor, and the Student*.

————The Tragicomedy of Don Cristobal and Doña Rosita. Tr. William I. Oliver, in New World Writing Number 8, 1955.

POEMS

————Poems: with English Translations by Stephen Spender and J. L. Gili, selected and intro. by R. M. Nadal. London, Dolphin Bookshop, and N.Y., Oxford Univ. Pr., 1939. xxviii, 143 pp.

————Selected Poems. Tr. Lloyd Mallan. Prairie City, Ill., Press of James A. Decker, 1941. 40 pp.

————Selected Poems. Tr. J. L. Gili and Stephen Spender. London, Hogarth Pr., 1943, and N.Y., Transatlantic Arts, 1947. 56 pp.

————Selected Poems. Tr. Francisco García Lorca and Donald M. Allen. Norfolk, Conn., New Directions, 1955. 180 pp. Repr. 1961, paper.

————Selected Poems, with plain prose trs. J. L. Gili. Penguin, 1960. 144 pp.

————The Gypsy Ballads: Three Historical Ballads. Tr. Rolfe Humphries. Bloomington, Indiana Univ. Pr., 1953. 64 pp., paper.

————Lament for the Death of a Bullfighter and Other Poems. Tr. A. L. Lloyd. London, Heinemann, and N.Y., Oxford Univ. Pr., 1937. 60 pp., parallel texts. Repr. 1953; repr. Philadelphia, Dufour, 1962, 46 pp.

————The Poet in New York and Other Poems. Tr. Rolfe Humphries. N.Y., Norton, 1940. 209 pp., parallel texts.

Tr. Ben Belitt. N.Y., Grove Pr., 1955. 191 pp.

Many brief pieces have been tr. by Edwin Honig: in *New Directions*, vol. 7 (1944, pp. 359–407); in *García Lorca* (Norfolk, Conn., New Directions, 1944, 232 pp., and London, PL, Editions Poetry, 1945, 202 pp.). See also Arturo Barea, *Lorca: The Poet and His People* (tr. Ilsa Barea, London, Faber, 1944, 103 pp., repr. N.Y., Harcourt, 1949, 191 pp., and N.Y., Grove Pr.,

1958, 176 pp.); and Manuel Durán, ed., *Lorca: A Collection of Essays* (Englewood Cliffs, N.J., Prentice-Hall, 1962, 181 pp.).

Gironella, José María (1917—). "The Cathedral of Hearts." Tr. Marcel Mendelson, in Angel Flores, ed., Great Spanish Stories, ML, 1956.

—————The Cypresses Believe in God. Tr. Harriet de Onís. N.Y., Knopf, 1955. 2 vols.

—————The Million Dead. Tr. Joan MacLean. Garden City, N.Y., Doubleday, 1963. xii, 684 pp.

—————Peace after War (*Ha estallado la paz*). Tr. Joan MacLean. N.Y., Knopf, 1969. 774 pp.

—————Phantoms and Fugitives: Journeys to the Improbable. Tr. L. Broch Fontseré. N.Y., Sheed and Ward, 1964. viii, 177 pp.

—————Where the Soil Was Shallow (*Un hombre*). Tr. Anthony Kerrigan. Chicago, Regnery, 1957. 374 pp.

Gómez de la Serna, Ramón (1880–1963). "The Man in the Gallery." Tr. Warre B. Wells, in Great Spanish Short Stories, 1932: see Collections.

—————Movieland (*Cinelandia*). Tr. Angel Flores. N.Y., Macaulay, 1930. 273 pp.

—————"The Triangular House." Tr. William E. Colford, in Classic Tales from Modern Spain, 1964: see Collections.

Goytisolo, Juan (1931—). Children of Chaos (*Duelo en el paraiso*). Tr. Christine Brook-Rose. London, Macgibbon and Kee, 1958. 250 pp.

—————Fiestas. Tr. Herbert Weinstock. N.Y., Knopf, 1960, and London, Macgibbon and Kee, 1961. 246 pp.

—————"The Guard." Tr. Angel Flores, in Spanish Stories/*Cuentos Españoles*, 1960: see Collections.

————Marks of Identity. Tr. Gregory Rabassa. N.Y., Grove Pr., 1969. 352 pp.

————The Party's Over (*Fin de fiesta*). Tr. José Yglesias. London, Weidenfeld, 1966. 188 pp. Repr. London, Panther, 1968.

————Sands of Torremolinos (*La isla*). Tr. José Yglesias. London, Cape, 1962. 176 pp., and N.Y., Knopf, 1962 (as Island of Women), 210 pp.

————The Young Assassins (*Juegos de manos*). Tr. John Rust. N.Y., Knopf, 1959, and London, Macgibbon and Kee, 1960. 256 pp.

Grau, Jacinto (1877–1958). Mister Pygmalion. Tr. William P. Giuliano, in The Genius of the Spanish Theater, 1964: see Collections.

Another play, *The Prodigal Son*, tr. by John G. Underhill in the 1920s, is extant in typescript.

Guillén, Jorge (1893—). Affirmation: A Bilingual Anthology 1919–1966. Tr. Julian Palley. Norman, Univ. of Oklahoma Pr., 1968. xvi, 208 pp.

————The Poetry of Jorge Guillén: Including some Trs. by Francis Avery Pleak. Princeton, N.J., Princeton Univ. Pr., 1942. xxiv, 114 pp.

Guimerá, Angel (1847–1924). Marta of the Lowlands (*Terra baixa*). Tr. José Echegaray from Catalan into Spanish, Wallace Gillpatrick from Spanish into English. Garden City, N.Y., Doubleday, 1914. xxiii, 111 pp.

————*La Pecadora* (*Daniela*): A Play in Three Acts. Tr. Wallace Gillpatrick. N.Y., Hispanic Soc. of America, and London, Putnam, 1916. 162 pp.

Tr. John G. Underhill in Masterpieces of Modern Spanish Drama, 1917: see Collections, above.

Hortelano, Juan García. Summer Storm. Tr. Ilsa Barea. London, Weidenfeld, and N.Y., Grove Pr., 1962. 333 pp. Repr. Penguin, 1963.

Jarnés, Benjamín (1888–1950). Saint Alexis. Tr. Warre B. Wells, in Great Spanish Short Stories, 1932: see Collections.

Tr. Angel Flores, in Great Spanish Stories, 1956: see ibid.

————Vivien and Merlin. Tr. Angel Flores, in Great Spanish Short Stories, 1962: see ibid.

Jiménez, Juan Ramón (1881–1958). Fifty Spanish Poems with English Translations. Tr. John Brande Trend. Oxford, Dolphin Book Co., 1950. 100 pp., and Berkeley, Univ. of California Pr., 1951, 97 pp.

————Platero and I. Tr. William and Mary Roberts. Oxford, Dolphin Book Co., and N.Y., Duschnes, 1956. 159 pp. Repr. N.Y., New Amer. Lib., 1960, 128 pp.

Tr. Eloise Roach. Austin, Univ. of Texas Pr., 1957, and Edinburgh, Nelson, 1958. ix, 218 pp.

————Selected Writings. Tr. H. R. Hays. N.Y., Farrar Straus, 1957. 260 pp. Repr. N.Y., Grove Pr., 1958, 296 pp.

*————Three Hundred Poems, 1903 1958. Tr. Eloise Roach. Austin, Univ. of Texas Pr., 1962. 263 pp.

Laforet, Carmen (1921—). *Nada.* Tr. Inez Munoz. London, Weidenfeld, 1958. 255 pp.

Tr. Charles F. Payne as Andrea. N.Y., Vantage Pr., 1964. 229 pp.

————"The Return." Tr. Martin Nozick, in Angel Flores, Great Spanish Stories, ML, 1956.

Laszlo, Andreas. My Uncle Jacinto. Tr. Isabel Quigly. London, Cape, 1958. 117 pp., and N.Y., Harcourt, 1958, 138 pp.

León, Ricardo (1877–1943). A Son of the Hidalgos (*Casta de hidalgos*). Tr. Catalina Paez (Mrs. Seumas MacManus). N.Y., Doubleday, 1921. 296 pp.

Lera, Angel Maria de. The Horns of Fear (*Los clarines del miedo*). Tr. Ilsa Barea. London, Faber, and N.Y., Dutton, 1961. 256 pp.

————The Wedding. Tr. Stephen Kaye. N.Y., Dutton, 1962. 242 pp.

Lezama, Antonio de, and Meneses, Enrique de. Wasted Lives: A Comedy in Four Acts. Tr. Hermann Schnitzler, adapted for the English stage by Gustav Davidson. Poet Lore, vol. 41 (1930), 159–230.

Linares Rivas, Manuel (1866–1938).   The Claws (*La garra*). Tr. Charles A. Turrell in Contemporary Spanish Dramatists, 1919: see Collections.

Lorenzo de Azertis (pseud. of Lorand Orbók, 1884–1924).   Cazanova: A Play in Three Acts. Tr. Sidney Howard. N.Y., Brentano's, 1924. 84 pp.

Luca de Terna, Torcuato (1922?—).   Another Man's Wife. Tr. John Marks. London, Constable, and N.Y., Knopf, 1965. 309 pp.

————The Second Life of Captain Contreras. Tr. Barnaby Conrad. Boston, Houghton Mifflin, 1960. 216 pp.

Machado y Ruiz, Antonio (1875–1939).   Castilian Ilexes. Tr. Charles Tomlinson and Henry Gifford. London and N.Y., Oxford Univ. Pr., 1963. xvi, 45 pp.

————Eighty Poems. Tr. Willis Barnstone. N.Y., Las Americas, 1959. 209 pp., parallel texts.

————Juan de Mairena: Epigrams, Maxims, Memoranda, and Memoirs of an Apocryphal Professor. Tr. Ben Belitt. Berkeley, Univ. of California Pr., 1963. 135 pp.

————Sea of San Juan: A Contemplation. Tr. Eleanor L. Turnbull. Boston, Bruce Humphries, 1950. 89 pp.

————Selected Poems. Tr. Alice Jane McVan, in her Antonio Machado. N.Y., Hispanic Soc. of America, 1959. 249 pp.

————Zero. Ed. and tr. Eleanor L. Turnbull. Baltimore, Contemporary Poetry, Distinguished Poets Series, 1947. 37 pp., parallel texts.

Madariaga y Rojo, Salvador de (1886—).   (His works were either written in English or tr. by the author.)

————Anarchy or Hierarchy. London, Allen and Unwin, 1937. 244 pp.

————The Blowing Up of the Parthenon, or How to Lose the Cold War. London, Pall Mall Pr., 1960. 93 pp.

————Bolivar. London, Hollis and Carter, 1952. xix, 711 pp.

————A Bunch of Errors. London, Cape, 1954. 190 pp.

————Christopher Columbus (*Vida del muy magnífico señor don Cristóbal Colón*). London, Hodder and Stoughton, 1939, and N.Y., Macmillan, 1940. xi, 524 pp. Repr. London, Hollis and Carter, 1949; N.Y., Ungar, 1967.

————Democracy versus Liberty: The Faith of a Liberal Heretic. London, Pall Mall Pr., 1958. 124 pp.

————Disarmament. N.Y., Coward-McCann, 1929. xiii, 379 pp.

————Don Quixote: An Introductory Essay in Psychology (*Guía del lector del Quijote*). Tr. the author and Constance H. M. de Madariaga. Newtown, Wales, Gregynog Pr., 1934. xv, 136 pp. Repr. Oxford, Clarendon Pr., 1935, 159 pp.; rev. ibid., 1961, 185 pp.

————Elysian Fields, a Dialogue [of] Goethe, Mary Stuart, Voltaire, Napoleon, Karl Marx, and President Washington. London, Allen and Unwin [1937]. 110 pp.

————Englishmen, Frenchmen, Spaniards: An Essay in Comparative Psychology. London, Oxford Univ. Pr., 1928. xix, 256 pp. Repr. 1931.

————Essays with a Purpose. London, Hollis, 1954. viii, 191 pp.

————The Fall of the Spanish American Empire. London, Hollis, 1947, and N.Y., Macmillan, 1948. 443 pp.

————The Genius of Spain, and Other Essays on Comparative Spanish Literature. Oxford, Clarendon Pr., 1923. 164 pp.

————On Hamlet. London, Hollis, 1948. xii, 130 pp. Repr. London, Cass, 1964.

————The Heart of Jade. Tr. the author. London, Collins, 1944. 574 pp., and N.Y., Creative Age Pr., 1944, 642 pp. Repr. London, Hamilton, 1964.

—————Hernán Cortés, Conqueror of Mexico. N.Y., Macmillan, 1941, and London, Hodder, 1942. ix, 554 pp. Repr. London, 1955.

—————Latin America between the Eagle and the Bear. London, Hollis, 1962. xii, 192 pp.

—————Portrait of a Man Standing. London, Allen and Unwin, 1968. 168 pp.

—————Portrait of Europe. London, Hollis, 1952. viii, 204 pp. Repr. London, Hollis, and University, Univ. of Alabama Pr., 1967.

—————The Rise of the Spanish American Empire. London, Hollis, and N.Y., Macmillan, 1947. 408 pp.

—————The Sacred Giraffe, Being the Posthumous Works of Julio Arceval. London, Hopkinson, 1925. x, 269 pp.

—————Shelley and Calderon, and Other Essays on English and Spanish Poetry. London, Constable, 1920. vii, 198 pp.

—————Sir Bob. N.Y., Harcourt, [1930]. vii, 202 pp., ill. Lynd Ward.

—————Spain. London, Benn, and N.Y., Scribner, 1930. 507 pp.

—————Spain [a different work]. London, Cape, 1942. 509 pp.

—————Theory and Practice in International Relations. Philadelphia, Univ. of Pennsylvania Pr., 1937. 105 pp.

—————Victors, Beware! London, Cape, 1946. 304 pp.

—————War in the Blood. London, Collins, 1957. 320 pp.

—————The World's Design. London, Allen and Unwin, [1938]. xx, 291 pp.

Marañon, Gregorio (1887—). Tiberius: A Study in Resentment. Tr. Warre B. Wells. London, Hollis and Carter, and N.Y., Duell Sloane, 1956. 234 pp.

Marichalar, Antonio (1893—).   The Perils and Fortune of the Duke of Osuna. Tr. Harriet de Onís. Philadelphia and London, Lippincott, 1932. 300 pp.

Marquína, Eduardo (1879–1946).   When the Roses Bloom Again. Tr. Charles A. Turrell, in Contemporary Spanish Dramatists, 1919: see Collections.

Martín Descalzo, José Luis (1930—).   God's Frontier. Tr. Harriet de Onís. N.Y., Knopf, 1959. 243 pp.

Martín-Santos, Luis.   Time of Silence. Tr. George Leeson. N.Y., Harcourt, 1964, and London, Calder, 1965. 247 pp.

Martínez Ruíz, José.   See Azorín, above.

Martínez Sierra, Gregorio (1881–1947).   The Plays. N.Y., Dutton, and London, Chatto, 1917–23. 2 vols.

> Vol. 1, tr. John G. Underhill. Repr. 1923 as The Cradle Song and Other Plays.
>> The Cradle Song; The Lover; Love Magic; Poor John; Madam Pepita (tr. in collaboration with May Heywood Broun).
>> The Cradle Song was first pub. in Poet Lore, vol. 28 (1917), 625–79; it was repr. separately (N.Y., French, 1934, 107 pp.); it was repr. in Modern Continental Dramas, ed. Harlan Hatcher, 1941; in Sixteen Famous European Plays, ML, 1943; in Twenty Best European Plays on the American Stage, 1957; in Masterpieces of the Modern Spanish Theatre, 1967. The Lover was repr. in The Stratford Journal, vol. 5 (1919) 33–44; and in Representative One-Act Plays by Continental Authors, ed. M. J. Moses, 1923. Love Magic was pub. in The Drama, vol. 7, no. 25, 1917; as was Poor John.
> Vol. 2. Tr. Helen and Harley Granville-Barker. Repr. 1929 as The Kingdom of God and Other Plays.
>> The Kingdom of God; The Two Shepherds (Los pastores); Wife to a Famous Man (La mujer del heroe); The Romantic Young Lady (Sueño de una noche de agosto). The Two Shepherds was repr. in Plays for the College Theatre, ed. G. H. Leverton, 1932.

————Ana María (*Tu eres la paz*). Tr. Mrs. Emmons Crocker. Boston, Badger, 1921. 330 pp. (a novel).

————The Forgotten Song. Adapted George Portnoff. Boston, Meador, 1936. 2 vols. in 1 (with Portnoff's The Divine Treasure).

————Holy Night: A Miracle Play in Three Scenes (*Navidad*). Tr. Philip Hereford. N.Y., Dutton, 1928. 55 pp. Repr. London, Sheed and Ward, 1952. 40 pp.

————Idyll. Tr. Charlotte M. Lorenz in Poet Lore, vol. 37 (1926), 63–72.

————A Lily among Thorns. Tr. Helen and Harley Granville-Barker, in Chief Contemporary Dramatists, ed. T. H. Dickinson, third series, 1930: see Collections.

————Take Two from One: A Farce in Three Acts. Tr. Helen and Harley Granville-Barker. London, Sidgwick and Jackson, and N.Y., French, 1931. 89 pp.

Matute Ansejo, Ana María (1926—).   The Lost Children (*Los hijos muertos*). Tr. Joan MacLean. N.Y., Macmillan, 1965, and London, Collier-Macmillan, 1968. 538 pp.

————School of Sun (*Primera memoria*). Tr. Elaine Kerrigan. N.Y., Pantheon, 1963. 242 pp.

  Tr. James H. Mason as The Awakening. London, Hutchinson, 1963. .307 pp.

Meneses, Enrique de.   The Glittering Highway: A Play in Four Acts. Adapted Gustav Davidson, in Poet Lore, vol. 38 (1927), 317–57.

Miró, Gabriel (1879–1930).   Figures of the Passion of Our Lord. Tr. C. J. Hogarth. London, G. Chapman, 1924, and N.Y., Knopf, 1925. 309 pp.

————Our Father San Daniel, Scenes of Clerical Life. Tr. Charlotte Remfry-Kidd. London, Benn, 1930. 228 pp.

————"Señor Cuenca and His Successor." Tr. Angel Flores, in Great Spanish Short Stories, 1962: see Collections.

Ortega y Gasset, José (1883–1955).   Concord and Liberty. Tr. Helene Weyl. N.Y., Norton, 1946. 182 pp.

————The Dehumanization of Art, and Notes on the Novel. Tr. Helene Weyl. Princeton, N.J., Princeton Univ. Pr., 1948. 103 pp.

Tr. Willard R. Trask as The Dehumanization of Art and Other Writings on Art and Culture. N.Y., Doubleday, 1956. 187 pp. Repr. Gloucester, Mass., Peter Smith, 1959.

*————Invertebrate Spain. Tr. Mildred Adams. N.Y., Norton, 1937. 212 pp.

————On Love: Aspects of a Single Theme (*Estudios sobre el amor*). Tr. Toby Talbot. N.Y., Meridian Books, 1957. 204 pp. Repr. London, Cape, 1967. 160 pp., paper.

————Man and Crisis (*En torno a Galileo*). Tr. Mildred Adams. N.Y., Norton, 1958. 217 pp. Repr. London, Allen and Unwin, 1959; N.Y., 1962.

————Man and People. Tr. Willard R. Trask. N.Y., Norton, 1957, and London, Allen and Unwin, 1959. 272 pp.

————Meditations on Quijote. Tr. Evelyn Rugg and Diego Marin. N.Y., Norton, 1961. 192 pp.

————Mission of the University. Tr. Howard Lee Nostrand. Princeton, N.J., Princeton Univ. Pr., 1944. 103 pp. Repr. London, Kegan Paul, 1946, 81 pp.

————The Modern Theme (*El tema de nuestro tiempo*). Tr. James Cleugh. London, C. W. Daniel, 1931, and N.Y., Norton, 1933. 152 pp. Repr. N.Y., Harper, 1961.

————The Origin of Philosophy. Tr. Toby Talbot. N.Y., Norton, 1967. 125 pp.

————The Revolt of the Masses. Tr. anon. N.Y., Norton, and London, Allen and Unwin, 1932. 204 pp. Repr. N.Y., New Amer. Lib., 1950, 141 pp.

————Toward a Philosophy of History (*Historia como sistema*). Tr. Helene Weyl. N.Y., Norton, 1941. 273 pp.

————Velázquez. Tr. C. David Ley. N.Y., Random House, 1953. lxxxiii pp. Repr. London, Collins, 1954.

————What Is Philosophy? Tr. Mildred Adams. N.Y., Norton, 1961. 252 pp.

Oteyza, Luis de (1883—).   The White Devil. Tr. Frederick Taber Cooper. N.Y., Stokes, 1930. 310 pp.

Pérez de Ayala, Ramón (1880–1962).   "The Assistant Professor." Tr. Warre B. Wells, in Great Spanish Short Stories, 1932: see Collections.

Tr. William E. Colford as "The Substitute Professor," in Classic Tales from Modern Spain, 1964: see ibid.

————The Fox's Paw, a Novel of Spanish Life (*La pata de la raposa*). Tr. Thomas Walsh. N.Y., Dutton, 1924. 314 pp.

————Prometheus; The Fall of the House of Limón; Sunday Sunlight: Poetic Novels of Spanish Life. Tr. Alice P. Hubbard, poems tr. Grace Hazard Conkling. N.Y., Dutton, 1920. 224 pp.
"Prometheus" repr. Angel Flores, Great Spanish Stories, ML, 1956: see Collections.

————Tiger Juan. Tr. Walter Starkie. London, Cape, and N.Y., Macmillan, 1933. 320 pp.

Pérez Lugín, Alejandro (1870–1926).   The House of Troy. Tr. Mrs. Emmons Crocker. Boston, Badger, 1922. 288 pp.

————Shadows of the Sun (*Currito de la cruz*). Tr. Sidney Franklin. N.Y., Scribner, 1934. 439 pp.

Pérez de la Ossa, Huberto (1897—).   Maria Fernanda (*La santa duquesa, novela*). Tr. E. Allison Peers. London, Eyre, 1931. 241 pp. Repr. Boston, Little Brown, 1931, 362 pp.

Porras, Antonio.   Adam and Eve: A Three-Act Comedy. Tr. Willis Knapp Jones and Glenn Barr. Poet Lore, vol. 41 (1930), 1–49.

Ramón y Cajal, Santiago (1852–1934).   Precepts and Counsels on Scientific Investigation: Stimulants of the Spirit (*Reglas y consejos, investigación cientifica, los tonicos de la voluntad*). Tr. J. M. Sanchez-Perez. Mountain View, Calif., Pacific Pr. Pub. Assoc., 1951. 180 pp.

Riba Bracons, Carlos (1893—).   Poems. Tr. J. L. Gili from Catalan. Oxford, Dolphin, 1964. 71 pp., parallel texts.

Ribera y Tarragó, Julián (1858–1934).   Music in Ancient Arabia and Spain (*La música de las cántigas*). Tr. abridged Eleanor Hague and Marion Leffingwell. Stanford, Calif., Stanford Univ. Pr., 1929. 283 pp.

Robles, Antonio (pseud. Antoniorrobles, 1897—).   Merry Tales from Spain. Tr. Edward Huberman. Philadelphia, Winston, 1939. 141 pp.

——————The Refugee Centaur. Tr. Edward and Elizabeth Huberman. N.Y., Twayne, 1952. 245 pp.

——————Tales of Living Playthings. Tr. Edward Huberman. N.Y., Modern Age Books, 1938. 119 pp.

Rodoreda, Merce.   The Pigeon Girl: A Novel (*La placa del Diamant*, 1962). Tr. Eda O'Shiel from Catalan. London, Deutsch, 1967. 208 pp.

Rusiñol y Prats, Santiago (1861–1931).   The Prodigal Doll: A Comedy for Marionettes in One Act and Four Scenes (*El titella pródigo*). Tr. John G. Underhill from Catalan. The Drama, vol. 7, no. 25 (Feb., 1917), 90–116.

Salazar y Chapela, Esteban (1902—).   Naked in Piccadilly (*Perico, en Londres*). Tr. Patricia Crampton. N.Y., Abelard-Schuman, 1961. 284 pp.

*Salinas, Pedro (1891–1951).   Lost Angel and Other Poems. Tr. Eleanor L. Turnbull, preface by the author. Baltimore, Johns Hopkins Pr., 1938. 169 pp., parallel texts.

——————Reality and the Poet in Spanish Poetry. Tr. Edith Fishtine Helman. Baltimore, Johns Hopkins Pr., 1940. 165 pp.

————Truth of Two and Other Poems. Tr. Eleanor L. Turnbull. Baltimore, Johns Hopkins Pr., 1940. 289 pp., parallel texts.

Salisachs, Mercedes.   The Eyes of the Proud (*Una mujer llega al pueblo*). Tr. Delano L. Ames. London, Methuen, and N.Y., Harcourt, 1961. 302 pp. Repr. London, New English Lib. 1965.

Sánchez Ferlosio, Rafael (1927—).   The One Day of the Week (*El Jarama*). Tr. J. M. Cohen. London and N.Y., Abelard-Schuman, 1962. 383 pp.

Sánchez-Silva, José María.   The Miracle of Marcelino (*Marcelino pan y vino*). Tr. John P. Debicki. Chicago, Ill., Scepter Pr., 1963. 123 pp.

Sastre, Alfonso (1927—).   Anna Kleiber. Tr. Leonard C. Pronko, in The New Theatre of Europe, ed. R. W. Corrigan. N.Y., Dell, vol. 1, 1962, paper. Repr. in The Modern Theatre, ed. the same, N.Y., Macmillan, 1964.

————Death Thrust. Tr. Leonard C. Pronko in Masterpieces of the Modern Spanish Theatre, ed. R. W. Corrigan, 1967: see Collections, above.

Segovia, Gertrudis.   Spanish Fairy Tales. Tr. Elizabeth Vernon Quinn. N.Y., Stokes, 1918. 321 pp.

Sénder, Ramón J. (1901—).   The Affable Hangman. Tr. Florence Hall. London, Cape, 1954. 336 pp. Repr. N.Y., Las Americas, 1963.

————Before Noon: A Novel in Three Parts. Chronicle of Dawn: Tr. W. R. Trask. The Violent Griffin, The Villa Julieta: Tr. F. W. Sender. Albuquerque, Univ. of New Mexico Pr., 1957. 408 pp. Repr. London, Gollancz, 1959.
    The first part was originally published N.Y., Doubleday Doran, 1944, 201 pp.

————Counter-Attack in Spain. See The War in Spain, below.

————Dark Wedding (*Epitalamio del prieto Trinidad*). Tr. Eleanor Clark. N.Y., Doubleday Doran, 1943. 305 pp. Repr. London, Grey Walls Pr., 1948, 299 pp.

————Earmarked for Hell (*Iman*). Tr. James Cleugh. London, Wishart, 1934. 342 pp. Repr. as Pro Patria, Boston, Houghton Mifflin, 1935, 295 pp.

————"The Journey." Tr. Warre B. Wells, in Great Spanish Short Stories, 1932: see Collections.

————The King and Queen. Tr. Mary Low. N.Y., Vanguard Pr., 1948. 231 pp.

————A Man's Place. Tr. Oliver La Farge. N.Y., Duell Sloane, 1940. 280 pp.

————Mr. Witt among the Rebels (*Míster Witt en el cantón*). Tr. Sir Peter Chalmers Mitchell. London, Faber, and Boston, Houghton Mifflin, 1938. 367 pp.

————Requiem for a Spanish Peasant: A Novel. Tr. Elinor Randall. N.Y., Las Americas, 1960. 123 pp.

————Seven Red Sundays. Tr. Sir Peter Chalmers Mitchell. London, Faber, and N.Y., Liveright, 1936. 438 pp.

————The Sphere (*Proverbio de la muerte*). Tr. Felix Giovanelli. N.Y., Hellman, Williams, 1949. 264 pp. Repr. London, Grey Walls Pr., 1950, 304 pp.

————Tales of Cibola. Tr. Florence Sender et al. N.Y., Las Americas, 1964. 383 pp.

————War in Spain (*Contra-Ataque*). London, Faber, and Boston, Houghton (as Counter-Attack in Spain), 1937. 288 pp.
    For trs. of 3 playlets, pub. 1938, 1943, 1950: see Robert O'Brien, Spanish Plays in English Translation, 1963: in Bibliographies, above.

Soler, Bartolomeo (1892—).   Marcos Villari: A Novel. Tr. William Stirling. London, Francis Aldor, 1948. 242 pp.

Sotillo, Antonio, and Andréa Micho.   The Judgment of Posterity: A Comedy in One Act. Tr. John Garrett Underhill. N.Y., French, 1936. 30 pp.

Suárez Carraño, José (1914—).   The Final Hours. Tr. Anthony Kerrigan. N.Y., Knopf, 1954. 273 pp.

Tomás, Mariano (1891—).   Life and Misadventures of Miguel de Cervantes. Tr. Warre B. Wells. London, Allen and Unwin, and Boston, Houghton, 1934. 225 pp.

Unamuno, Miguel de (1865–1936).   Abel Sanchez and Other Stories. Tr. Anthony Kerrigan. Chicago, Regnery, 1956. 216 pp.

——————"Juan Manso: A Dead Man's Tale." Tr. William E. Colford, in Classic Tales from Modern Spain, 1964: see Collections, above.

——————Mist: A Tragi-Comic Novel. Tr. Warner Fite. N.Y., Knopf, 1928. 322 pp.

——————"Saint Manuel Bueno, Martyr." Tr. Harriet de Onís in Spanish Stories and Tales, 1954: see Collections.

Tr. Anthony Kerrigan, in Abel Sanchez, above, 1956. Repr. Angel Flores in Great Spanish Stories, ML, 1956.

Tr. Francisco Segovia and Jean Perez. London, Harrap, 1957. 55, 55 pp., parallel texts.

——————"Solitude." Tr. Warre B. Wells, in Great Spanish Short Stories, 1932.

——————Three Exemplary Novels and a Prologue. Tr. Angel Flores. N.Y., Boni, 1930. 227 pp. Repr. N.Y., Grove Pr., 1956.
"The Marquis of Lumbria"; "Two Mothers"; "A He Man" (*Nada menos que todo un hombre*). The first was repr. in Spanish Stories/*Cuentos Españoles*, 1960; the third was repr. as "Every Inch a Man," in Great Spanish Short Stories, 1962: see Collections.

NON-FICTION

——————The Agony of Christianity. Tr. Pierre Loving. N.Y., Payson and Clarke, 1928. 183 pp.

Tr. Kurt F. Reinhardt. N.Y., Ungar, 1960. 192 pp.

—————Essays and Soliloquies. Tr. with intro. J. E. Crawford Flitch. N.Y., Knopf, 1925. 244 pp.

Twenty essays from *Ensayos* (1916–18).

—————The Life of Don Quixote and Sancho. Tr. Homer P. Earle. N.Y., Knopf, 1927. 327 pp.

Tr. Anthony Kerrigan in Selected Works of Unamuno, vol. 3. Princeton, N.J., Princeton Univ. Pr., and London, Routledge, 1968. 589 pp. See below.

—————Perplexities and Paradoxes. Tr. Stuart Gross. N.Y., Philosophical Lib., 1945. 165 pp. Repr. 1968.

Twenty-three essays from *Ensayos* (1916–18).

—————The Tragic Sense of Life in Men and Peoples. Tr. J. E. Crawford Flitch. London and N.Y., Macmillan, 1921. xxxv, 332 pp. Repr. N.Y., Dover, 1954; London, Collins, 1962.

POEMS

—————The Christ of Velasquez. Tr. Eleanor L. Turnbull. Baltimore, Johns Hopkins Pr., and London, Oxford Univ. Pr., 1951. 132 pp.

—————Poems. Tr. Eleanor L. Turnbull. Ibid., 1952. 225 pp.

Cf. Arturo Barea, *Unamuno* (tr. Ilsa Barea, Cambridge, Bowes, and New Haven, Conn., Yale Univ. Pr., 1952, 61 pp.), an excellent study; and Julián Marías Aguilera, *Miguel de Unamuno* (tr. Frances M. López-Morillas, Cambridge, Mass., Harvard Univ. Pr., 1966, and London, Oxford Univ. Pr., 1967, xii, 224 pp.).

A new edn of *Selected Works of Miguel de Unamuno* in English is sponsored by the Bollingen Foundation, New York: vol. 3, *Our Lord Don Quixote*, includes the new tr. (see above) of *The Life of Don Quixote and Sancho* and sixteen essays on the Don Quixote theme, also tr. Anthony Kerrigan with intro. Walter Starkie.

Valle-Inclán, Ramón del (1859–1936). The Dragon's Head. Tr. May Heywood Broun. Poet Lore, vol. 29 (1918), 531–64.

————The Dream Comedy. Tr. Murray Paskin and Robert O'Brien, in La Voz, vol. 6, no. 2 (1961).

————"The Golden Rose." Tr. Warre B. Wells, in Great Spanish Short Stories, 1932: see Collections.

————The Pleasant Memoirs of the Marquis de Bradomin: Four Sonatas (*Sonatas*). Tr. May Heywood Broun and Thomas Walsh. N.Y., Harcourt, 1924. 316 pp. "Sonata of Autumn" repr. Angel Flores in Great Spanish Stories, 1956: see Collections.

————"My Sister Antonia." Tr. Harriet de Onís, in Spanish Stories and Tales, 1954: see Collections.

Tr. Anita Volland, in Great Spanish Short Stories, 1962: see ibid.

Tr. William E. Colford, in Classic Tales from Modern Spain, 1964: see ibid.

————The Tyrant, a Novel of Warm Lands (*Tirano Banderas*). Tr. Margarita Pavitt. N.Y., Holt, 1929. 295 pp.

For this writer, see Madariaga, *The Genius of Spain*, above.

Vázquez, José Andrés (1885—).   With Chains of Gold. Tr. Willis Knapp Jones. Poet Lore, vol. 34 (1923), 417–35.

Zamacois, Eduardo (1866–1955).   The Passing of the Magi. Tr. Charles Alfred Turrell, in Contemporary Spanish Dramatists, 1919: see Collections.

————Roots. Tr. Eliseo Vivas. N.Y., Viking Pr., 1929. 342 pp.

————Their Son, The Necklace. Tr. George Allan England. N.Y., Boni and Liveright, 1919. 186 pp.

Zamacois was born, lived, and died in France, and wrote in French.

SPANISH AMERICAN LITERATURE

WILLIS KNAPP JONES

NOTE.   The English translations of Spanish American writing, from William Cullen Bryant's version of Heredia's "Ode to Niagara" in U.S. Review and Literary Gazette of Boston (1827) to the present day, are too numerous to present here. My Latin American Writers in English Translation (Pan American Union, 1943) occupied 140 pages; it was extended in 1964 by Professor Claude L. Hulet's Latin American Prose in English Translation to 191 pages, and in 1965 by his Latin American Poetry in English Translation to 192 further pages. In addition, other lists of travel books, of folk lore, of articles, and of works in other classifications may need to be consulted by the inquiring student.

This present listing aims to include the work of the better known writers. It has not been possible to list many short pieces translated in periodicals, but those printed in collections of translations are noted, usually with reference to the editor of the collection rather than to the individual translator.

The life dates of many authors are uncertain. For reference I have used the Englekirk Outline History of Spanish American Literature (3rd. ed., 1965) and the Anderson-Imbert Historia de la Literatura Hispano-Americana (2nd ed., 1957).

The nature of the writing listed is indicated by an abbreviation in parentheses after the title: B. Biography or Autobiography; E. Essays; H. History; N. Novel or Novelette; O. Orations, Speeches, Addresses; P. Philosophy; S. Short Story or Stories; T. Theatrical Works; V. Verse, Poetry in general.

In listing the works of individual authors, we give books first, then shorter works.

Arciniegas, Germán. Latin America: A Cultural History. Tr. Joan MacLean. N.Y., Knopf, 1967, xxvii, 594 pp.
See also under Colombia for his other books.

Artists and Writers in the Evolution of Latin America. Ed. Edward D. Terry. University, Univ. of Alabama Pr., 1969. 204 pp.

Chapman, Charles E. Colonial and Republican Hispanic America. N.Y., Macmillan, 1938. 2 vols. in 1 (vol. 1 originally pub. 1933; vol. 2, 1937).

Chase, Gilbert. A Guide to Latin American Music. Washington, D.C., Library of Congress, 1945. xiii, 274 pp. Rev. enl. as A Guide to the Music of Latin America. Ibid., Pan American Union, 1962, xi, 411 pp.

Clark, Gerald. The Coming Explosion in Latin America. Philadelphia, Pa., McKay, 1963. 436 pp.

Concerning Latin American Culture. Ed. Charles Carroll Griffin. (Papers read at Byrdecliff, Woodstock, N.Y., 1939.) N.Y., Columbia Univ. Pr., 1940. xiv, 234 pp. Repr. 1944; N.Y., Russell, 1967.

Crawford, William Rex. A Century of Latin-American Thought. Cambridge, Mass., Harvard Univ. Pr., 1944. 320 pp. Repr. 1961.

Crow, John A. The Epic of Latin America. N.Y., Doubleday, 1946. xxiv, 756 pp.

Diffle, Baily W., and Justine, W. Latin American Civilization: Colonial Period. Harrisburg, Pa., Stackpole, 1945. 812 pp.

Fagg, John Edwin. Latin America: A General History. N.Y., Macmillan, 1963. 1070 pp.

Franco, Jean.   The Modern Culture of Latin America: Society and the Artist. London, Pall Mall Pr., 1967. 339 pp.

Frank, Waldo David.   America Hispana: A Portrait and a Prospect. N.Y. and London, Scribner, 1931. xviii, 331 pp. Repr. as America Hispana: South of Us, the Characters of the Countries and the People of Central and South America. N.Y., Garden City Pub. Co., 1940, xviii, 388 pp.

García Calderón, Francisco.   Latin America: Its Rise and Progress. Tr. Bernard Miall from French. London, Unwin, 1918. 406 pp.

Hague, Eleanor.   Latin American Music, Past and Present. Santa Ana, Calif., Fine Arts, 1943. 98 pp.

Handbook of South American Indians.   Ed. Julian H. Steward. (Bulletin 43, Bureau of Amer. Ethnology, Smithsonian Institution.) Washington, D.C., Government Printing Office, 1946–59. 7 vols.

Haring, Clarence H.   The Spanish Empire in America. N.Y., Oxford Univ. Pr., 1947. 388 pp.

Herring, Hubert C.   A History of Latin America from the Beginnings to the Present. N.Y., Knopf, 1955, and London, Cape, 1956. xx, 796, xxvi pp. Rev. 1961, 845 pp.

James, Preston E.   Latin America. N.Y., Odyssey Pr., 1942, and London, Cassell, 1943. xviii, 908 pp. Repr. N.Y., 1950; London, 1954; N.Y. and London, 1959.
  The standard geography.

Johnson, John J.   Political Changes in Latin America. Stanford, Calif., Stanford Univ. Pr., 1958. 272 pp.

Kandel, I. L., ed.   Education in the Latin American Countries. (19th Educational Yearbook of the Institute of International Education.) N.Y., Teachers College, Columbia Univ., 1942. xxviii, 410 pp.

Kelemen, Pál.   Medieval American Art. N.Y., Macmillan, 1943. 2 vols.

Kirstein, Lincoln. The Latin American Collection of the Museum of Modern Art. N.Y., Museum of Modern Art, 1943. 110 pp.

Lanning, John Tate. Academic Culture in the Spanish Colonies. London and N.Y., Oxford Univ. Pr., 1940. 149 pp.

Latin America. N.Y., Encyclopedia Americana Corporation, 1943. 126 pp.

Latin America and the Enlightenment. Ed. Arthur P. Whitaker, intro. Federico de Onís. N.Y. and London, Appleton, 1942. xiii, 130 pp.

Madariaga, Salvador de. Rise of the Spanish American Empire. London, Hollis and Carter, and N.Y., Macmillan, 1947. xix, 408 pp.

————Fall of the Spanish American Empire. London, Hollis, 1947, and N.Y., Macmillan, 1948. viii, 443 pp.

Moses, Bernard. The Intellectual Background of the Revolution in South America, 1810–1824. (Hispanic Notes and Monographs.) N.Y., Hispanic Society of America, 1926. x, 234 pp.

New World Guides to the Latin American Republics. Ed. Earl Parker Hanson. N.Y., Duell Sloan, 1943. 2 vols. Repr. 1945, 3 vols.
    Vol. 1: Mexico, Central America, and West Indies.
    Vol. 2: The Andes and West Coast Countries.
    Vol. 3: East Coast Countries.

Pendle, George. A History of Latin America. Penguin, 1963. 249 pp.

Picón Salas, Mariano. A Cultural History of Spanish America, From Conquest to Independence. Tr. Irving A. Leonard. Berkeley, Univ. of California Pr., 1962. 192 pp. Repr. 1963, paper.

Schurz, William L. This New World: The Civilization of Latin America. N.Y., Dutton, 1954, and London, George Allen, 1956. 429 pp. Repr. N.Y., 1964, paper.

Shepherd, William Robert. Latin America. N.Y., Holt, 1914. 256 pp.

Szulc, Tad.   The Winds of Revolution: Latin America Today and Tomorrow. N.Y., Praeger, 1965. 308 pp.

Wagley, Charles.   The Latin American Tradition. N.Y., Columbia Univ. Pr., 1968. viii, 242 pp.

Wilgus, A[lva] Curtis.   The Development of Hispanic America. N.Y., Farrar and Rinehart, 1941. 941 pp.

————Ed. Papers Delivered at the Annual Conference on the Caribbean, 1950—. Gainesville, Univ. of Florida Pr., 1951—.
  1950: The Caribbean at Mid-Century.
  1951: The Caribbean: Peoples, Problems, and Prospects.
  1952: The Caribbean: Contemporary Trends.
  1955: The Caribbean: Its Culture.
  et seq.

Williams, Mary Wilhelmine.   The People and Politics of Latin America. Boston, Mass., Ginn, 1930. vii, 845 pp. Reprs. to 4th ed., 1955, 950 pp.

Worcester, Donald E., and Schaeffer, W. G.   The Growth and Culture of Latin America. London and N.Y., Oxford Univ. Pr., 1956. 963 pp.

Zea, Leopoldo.   The Latin American Mind (*Dos etapas del pensamiento en Hispano-América*). Tr. James Abbott and Lowell Dunham. Norman, Univ. of Oklahoma Pr., 1963. 308 pp.

Bibliographies

Behrendt, Richard F. W.   Modern Latin America in Social Science Literature: A Selected Annotated Bibliography of Books, Pamphlets, and Periodicals in English in the Fields of Economics, Politics, and Sociology of Latin America. Albuquerque, Univ. of New Mexico Pr., 1949. 152 pp.

Bryant, Shasta M.   A Selective Bibliography of Bibliographies of Hispanic American Literature. Washington, Pan American Union, 1966. vi, 48 pp.

Cox, Edward Godfrey.   A Reference Guide to the Literature of Travel [in English]. Vol. 2, The New World. Seattle, Univ. of Washington Pr., 1938. 591 pp.

Granier, James Albert.   Latin American Belles-Lettres in English Translation: A Selective and Annotated Guide. Washington, D.C., 1942. ii, 38 pp. Repr. 1943.

Grismer, Raymond L.   A Reference Index to 12,000 Spanish American Authors: A Guide to the Literature of Spanish America. N.Y., Wilson, 1939. 150 pp.

Herring, Hubert C.   A History of Latin America, etc. See Background, above. Bibliographical section, pp. 831–45 in 2d ed.

Hulet, Claude L.   Latin American Poetry in English Translation: A Bibliography. Washington, D.C., Pan American Union, 1965. ix, 192 pp.

――――Latin American Prose in English Translation: A Bibliography. Ibid., 1964. 191 pp.
Includes several classifications omitted in this volume: e.g., philosophy, oratory, archeology, literary criticism.

Humphreys, R. A.   Latin American History: A Guide to the Literature in English. London, Royal Institute of International Affairs, and N.Y., Oxford Univ. Pr., 1958. xiii, 197 pp.

Jones, Cecil K.   A Bibliography of Latin American Bibliographies. (Library of Congress.) 2d ed. Washington, D.C., Government Printing Office, 1942. 311 pp.
Alphabetical, not classified, lists.

Jones, Willis Knapp.   "Latin America through Drama in English." Hispania, vol. 28, 1945, 220–27. Rev. repr., Washington, D.C., Pan American Union, 1950. 12 pp.

――――Latin American Writers in English Translation (Bibliographic Series, 30.) Washington, D.C., Pan American Union, 1944. 141 pp.
Containing many short items not repeated below.

Leavitt, Sturgis E.   Hispano-American Literature in the United States, A Bibliography of Translations and Criticism. Cambridge, Mass., Harvard Univ. Pr., 1932, 54 pp.
Covers the years 1827–1931.

Moses, Bernard. Spanish Colonial Literature in South America. N.Y., Hispanic Society of America, 1922. 585–650.

Pane, Remigio U. "A Selected Bibliography of Latin American Literature in English Translation." Modern Language Journal, vol. 26, 1942, 116–22. Repr. enl. as "Two Hundred Latin American Books in English Tr.," ibid. vol. 27, 1943, 593–604.

Phelan, Marion. A Bibliography of Latin American Fiction in English. Phoenix, Ariz., Latin American Area Research, 1956. 47 pp.

Shelby, Charmion. "The Cronistas and Their Contemporaries: Recent Editions of Works of the Sixteenth and Seventeenth Centuries." Hispanic American Historical Review, vol. 29, 1949, 295–317.

Steck, Francis Borgia. A Tentative Guide to Historical Materials on the Spanish Borderlands. Philadelphia, Pa., Catholic Historical Society, 1943. 106 pp.

Topete, José Manuel. A Working Bibliography of Latin American Literature. St. Augustine, Fla., W. B. Fraser, 1952. 162 pp.
    Compiled for the Inter-American Bibliographical Library Assoc.

For bibliog. of current scholarship in Spanish American literature see the annual June (formerly May) number of *PMLA*, Spanish VII, now Spanish II.

Literary Studies

Anderson Imbert, Enrique. Spanish American Literature. Tr. John V. Falconieri. Detroit, Mich., Wayne State Univ. Pr., 1963. x, 616 pp.

Coester, Alfred Lester. The Literary History of Spanish America. 2d ed. N.Y., Macmillan, 1928. 522 pp.

Contreras, Francisco. *L'esprit de l'Amérique espagnole.* Paris, Editions Nouvelle Revue Critique, 1931. 254 pp.

Davison, Ned J. The Concept of Modernism in Hispanic Criticism. Boulder, Colo., Pruett, 1966. 118 pp.

Goldberg, Isaac. Studies in Spanish American Literature. N.Y., Brentano, 1920. x, 377 pp.

Harss, Luis, and Dohmann, Barbara. Into the Mainstream: Conversations with Latin-American Writers. N.Y., Harper, 1967. 385 pp.
 Ten authors: Asturias, Borges, Carpentier, Cortázar, Fuentes, García Marquez, Guimarães Rosa, Onetti, Rulfo, and Vargas Llosa.

Henríquez Ureña, Pedro. A Concise History of Hispanic American Culture. Tr. Gilbert Chase with an additional chapter. N.Y., Praeger, 1966, and London, Pall Mall Pr., 1967. 214 pp.

————Literary Currents in Hispanic America. Cambridge, Mass., Harvard Univ. Pr., and London, Oxford Univ. Pr., 1945. 345 pp. Repr. N.Y., Russell, 1963.

Instituto Internacional de Literatura Ibero-Americana. Outline History of the Spanish American Literature. By a committee: John E. Englekirk, chairman, and Irving A. Leonard, John T. Reid, and John A. Crow. N.Y., Crofts, 1941. 170 pp. Repr. 1942; 1965, 252 pp.

Jones, Willis Knapp. Behind Spanish American Footlights. Austin, Univ. of Texas Pr., 1966. xvi, 609 pp.

Moses, Bernard. Spanish Colonial Literature in South America. N.Y., Hispanic Society of America, 1922. 661 pp.

Rosenbaum, Sidonia Carmen. Modern Women Poets of Spanish America. N.Y., Hispanic Institute, 1945. 273 pp.

Sánchez, Luis Alberto, et al. A New World Literature: A Series of Informative Critical Essays on the Literature of America South. N.Y., The Nation, 1943. 30 pp.
 Four valuable essays repr. from the periodical: The Novel (Sánchez); Modern Poetry (Alfonso Reyes); The Young Writers (Eduardo Mallea); Hispano-American World (Waldo Frank).

Spell, Jefferson Rea. Contemporary Spanish-American Fiction. Chapel Hill, Univ. of North Carolina Pr., 1944. ix, 323 pp. Repr. N.Y., Biblo and Tannen, 1968.

Stabb, Martin S. In Quest of Identity: Patterns in the Spanish American Essay of Ideas 1890–1960. Chapel Hill, Univ. of North Carolina Pr., 1967. 244 pp.

Torres Rioseco, Arturo. Aspects of Spanish American Literature. Seattle, Univ. of Washington Pr., 1963. 102 pp.

————The Epic of Latin American Literature. N.Y. and London, Oxford Univ. Pr., 1942. 279 pp. Repr. 1946.

————New World Literature: Tradition and Revolt in Latin America. Berkeley, Univ. of California Pr., 1949. 250 pp.

Collections

NOTE.   Translated articles of literary criticism of Spanish American writers are listed in the Instituto Internacional Outline History, above; in Hulet's Latin American Prose, pp. 86–102; and in the files of Américas (since 1950) of the Pan American Union. The key word at the end of each entry here will be used for cross-reference later.

Allen, John Houghton, ed. and tr.   Latin American Miscellany [prose and verse]. Randado, Texas, pr. pr., 1943. 77 pp.   Allen

————Translations. Ibid., pr. pr., 1945. 65 pp.

Arciniegas, Germán, ed.   The Green Continent: A Comprehensive View of Latin American by Its Leading Writers. Tr. Harriet de Onís and others. N.Y., Knopf, 1944. xiii, 533 pp. Repr. London, Editions Poetry, 1947, 483 pp.   Arciniegas

Blackwell, Alice Stone.   Some Spanish American Poets. N.Y., Appleton, 1929. xli, 559 pp., parallel texts. Repr. Philadelphia, Univ. of Pennsylvania Pr., and London, Oxford Univ. Pr. 1937; N.Y., Biblo and Tannen, 1968.
                                                                    Blackwell

Brewton, John E., ed.   Literature of the Americas. Chicago, Laidlaw Bros., 1950. 768 pp.   Brewton

Cardwell, Guy Adams, ed.   Readings from the Americas: An Introduction to Democratic Thought. N.Y., Ronald Pr., 1947. 982 pp.   Cardwell

Clark, Barrett H. and Maxim Lieber.   Great Short Stories of the World. N.Y., McBride, 1925. 1072 pp. Repr., London, Heinemann, 1927, 1928; Garden City, N.Y., Garden City Pub. Co., 1938.   Clark
    Four stories from Spanish American.

Cohen, J. M., ed. and tr.   Latin American Writing Today. Penguin, 1967. 267 pp.   Cohen
    Verse and prose by 32 authors, of whom 26 are Spanish American.

Colford, William E., ed. and tr.   Classic Tales from Spanish America. Great Neck, N.Y., Barron, 1962. xii, 210 pp., paper.   Colford
    21 stories by 19 authors.

Craig, G. Dundas.   The Modernist Trend in Spanish American Poetry: A Collection of Representative Poems. Berkeley, Univ. of California Pr., 1934. 347 pp., parallel texts.   Craig

Fitts, Dudley, ed.   Anthology of Contemporary Latin American Poetry. Trs. various. Norfolk, Conn., New Directions, 1942. xxi, 667 pp., parallel texts. Rev. 1947.   Fitts

Flakoll, Darwin J., and Claribel Alegría.   New Voices in Hispanic America. Boston, Mass., Beacon Pr., 1962. 226 pp.   Flakoll

Flores, Angel, ed.   Great Spanish Short Stories. N.Y., Dell, 1962. 304 pp.
              Flores GS
    Four of the authors are Spanish American: Ayala, López y Fuentes, Palma, Téllez.

————Spanish Stories/*Cuentos Españoles*. N.Y., Bantam, 1960. 339 pp., parallel texts.   Flores SS
    Four of the thirteen stories are by South American authors: Borges, Lynch, Palma, and Quiroga.

————**and Dudley Poore,** eds. and trs.   Fiesta in November: Stories from Latin America. Boston, Mass., Houghton Mifflin, 1942. 608 pp.   Flores FN
    The work of 18 authors from 11 countries.

Franco, Jean, ed. and tr. Short Stories in Spanish: *Cuentos Hispánicos.*
Penguin, 1966. 204 pp., parallel texts.   Franco
> Seven of the eight authors are Spanish American: Benedetti, Borges.
> García Márquez, Martínez Moreno, Onetti, and Rulfo.

Garnett, Richard; Vallée, Léon; and Brandl, Alois. Universal Anthology.
London, Clarke, and N.Y., Merrill and Baker, 1899–1902. 33 vols.
> Excerpts from Jorge Isaacs of Colombia (vol. 32) and José Rizal y Alonso
> of the Philippines, qq.v.

Green, Ernest S., and von Lowenfels Harriet. Mexican and South American
Poems. San Diego, Calif., Dodge and Burbeck, 1892. 398 pp., parallel
texts.   Green

Haydn, Hiram, and Cournos, John. A World of Great Stories. N.Y.,
Crown, 1947. 950 pp.   Haydn

Hays, H. R. Twelve Spanish American Poets. New Haven, Conn., Yale Univ,
Pr., and London, Oxford Univ. Pr., 1943. 336 pp.   Hays

Hispanic Poets. Ed. Thomas Walsh. N.Y., Hispanic Soc. of America, 1938.
271 pp.   Hispanic Poets
> Trs. of 1 Brazilian and 34 Spanish American poets.

Homenaje a Walt Whitman/Homage to Walt Whitman: A Collection
of Poems in Spanish, tr. Didier Tisdel Jaén. University, Univ. of Alabama
Pr., 1969, 104 pp.

Johnson, Mildred E. Swans, Cygnets, and Owl: An Anthology of Modernist
Poetry in Spanish America. Columbia, Univ. of Missouri Studies, 1956.
199 pp.   Johnson

Jones, Willis Knapp. Spanish American Literature before 1888 in Translation. N.Y., Ungar, 1966. xv, 356 pp.   Jones, Before 1888

————Spanish American Literature Since 1888. N.Y., Ungar, 1963. xxi,
469 pp.   Jones, Since 1888

————Spanish One-Act Plays in English Translation. Dallas, Texas, Tardy Pub.
Co., 1934. 296 pp.

Literature in Latin America. Washington, D.C., Pan American Union, 1950. 112 pp.

New Directions 8, 1944. "Latin-American Section," pp. 267–361.
Trs. by various hands from Argentina (Leopoldo Marechal), Chile (Eduardo Anguita, Pablo Neruda), Cuba (Afro-Cuban Poetry), Guatemala (Rafael Arévalo Martínez), Mexico (Bernardo Ortíz de Montellano), qq.v. under individual authors.

Onís, Harriet de, ed. and tr. The Golden Land: An Anthology of Latin American Folklore and Literature. N.Y., Knopf, 1948. xviii, 395 pp. Repr. 1961.   Onís, Golden Land

——————Spanish Stories and Tales. N.Y., Knopf, 1954. xiii, 270 pp.
Twelve of the twenty-three stories are Spanish American.   Onís, SS

Plays of the Southern Americas. Stanford, Calif., Stanford Univ. Dramatists' Alliance, 1942. 3 vols. in 1.   PSA

Poor, Agnes B. Pan American Poems. Boston, Gorham, 1918. 80 pp.
                                                                        Poor

Prize Stories from Latin America: Winners of the "Life en Español" Literary Contest. Garden City, N.Y., Doubleday, 1963. 398 pp. Repr. Dolphin, 1964, paper.   Prize Stories

Resnick, Seymour. Spanish-American Poetry: A Bilingual Selection. Irvington-on-Hudson, N.Y., Harvey House, 1964. 96 pp., parallel texts.   Resnick

Sánchez Reulet, Aníbal (1910—). Contemporary Latin American Philosophy. Tr. Willard Trask. Albuquerque, Univ. of New Mexico Pr., 1954. 285 pp.   Sánchez Reulet

Tales from the Italian and Spanish. N.Y., Review of Reviews, 1920. 8 vols.   Tales
Vol. 8 contains stories by eleven South American authors.

Three Spanish American Poets: Pellicer, Neruda, Andrade. Tr. Lloyd Mallan, Mary and C. V. Wicker, and Joseph Grucci. Albuquerque, N.M., Swallow and Critchlow, 1942. 73 pp.   Three SA Poets

Torres-Rioseco, Arturo.   Short Stories of Latin America. Tr. Zoila Nelken
and Rosalie Torres Rioseco. N.Y., Las Americas Pub. Co., 1963. 203 pp.
Fourteen authors and fifteen stories.   Torres

Van Doren, Carl.   Anthology of World Prose. N.Y., Reynal and Hitchcock,
1935. Repr. Halcyon House, 1939, 1582 pp.   Van Doren
Three brief selections, pp. 596–623.

Vingut, F[rancisco] J[avier].   Gems of Spanish Poetry: *Joyas de la Poesía
Española*. N.Y., F. J. Vingut and Co., 1855. 120 pp., parallel texts.
Vingut, *Joyas*
Eight Latin American poems.

Vingut, G[ertrude] F[airfield].   Selections from the Best Spanish Poets.
N.Y., Vingut, 1856.   Vingut, Selections
Ten Latin American poems.

Walsh, Thomas, ed.   The Catholic Anthology: The World's Great Catholic
Poetry. N.Y., Macmillan, 1927. ix, 552 pp. Rev. ibid., 1939, xii, 584 pp.
Walsh, Catholic

————Hispanic Anthology. N.Y., Hispanic Soc. of America, 1920. 779 pp.
Walsh

Warner, Charles Dudley, ed.   Library of the World's Best Literature. See
The Warner Library, in General Reference, Collections of Translations,
above.
The 1902 ed. (39 vols. of selections) includes excerpts from Spanish
American authors as follows: vol. 1, Alarcón (Ruiz de Alarcón) of Mexico;
vol. 8, Las Casas, historian of the discoveries; vol. 11, Díaz of Mexico;
vol. 20, Jorge Isaacs of Colombia; vol. 25, Juana de la Cruz of Mexico.
The article on Latin American literature by M. M. Ramsey (vol. 22)
gives an interesting view of that literature as of about 1900.

Williams, Blanche Colton, and Lieber, Maxim.   Great Short Stories of
All Nations. N.Y., Tudor Pub. Co., 1932. 1132 pp.   Williams
Four stories from South America.

For listed translations of Spanish American philosophy, see Hulet, Prose,
pp. 113–17.

Colonial Spanish American Literature

Background

PRE-COLUMBIAN HISTORY AND CULTURE

Arias-Larreta, Abraham. Pre-Columbian Literature: Aztec-Incan-Maya-Quiché. Indoamerican Literature 1. Los Angeles, Calif., New World Library, 1964.

————From Columbus to Bolivar: Conquest, Colonial Period, Independence. Indoamerican Literature 2. Ibid., 1965.

See also Hulet, Prose, under Bibliography, above.

Means, Philip Ainsworth. Ancient Civilizations of the Andes. N.Y., Scribner, 1931. 586 pp.

Spinden, Herbert Joseph. Ancient Civilizations of Mexico and Central America. N.Y., Amer. Museum Pr., 1922. 242 pp.

Vaillant, George C. Aztecs of Mexico. N.Y., Doubleday Doran, 1941. 540 pp.

See also Mexico, Background, and Peru, Background, below.

Literary Studies

Moses, Bernard. Spanish Colonial Literature in South America. N.Y., Hispanic Soc., 1922. 661 pp.

Wilgus, A. Curtis. Histories and Historians of Hispanic America. N.Y., Wilson, 1942.

See also under Background above: Chapman, vol. 1; Diffie; Haring; Herring; Lanning; Madariaga; Picón Salas; and under Bibliography: Hulet (Prose); Humphreys.

THE LITERATURE OF DISCOVERY

NOTE.   The successive contemporary historians are as follows:

Peter Martyr of Anghiera.   The Decades of the New World (*Decades de Orbe Novo*, 1504–30). Part tr. from the Latin, 1555. Tr. Michael Lock, 1612. Retr. Francis A. MacNutt, 1912. See vol. 1, Neo-Latin Literature, above.

Fernández de Oviedo y Valdés, Gonzalo.   *La hystoria general de las Indias* (part pub. 1535–47; pub. complete 1851–55). Not tr. For his earlier descriptive treatise, *La hystoria natural de las Indias* (1526), see under Mexico, below.

López de Gómara, Francisco.   The Pleasant Historie of the Conquest of the Weast India . . . by . . . Cortes (*La Historia de las Indias y conquista de Mexico*, 1552 et seq.). Tr. Thomas Nicholas, 1578. See under Mexico.

Las Casas, Bartolomé de, Bishop of Chiapas.   *Historia de las Indias* (c.1560, pub. 1875). Not tr.
> His *Breuissima relación de la destruyción de las Indias* (pub. 1552), denouncing the enslaving of the Indians, was in part tr. in 1583, 1656, 1689, and 1699: the last tr. included six of the nine treatises collected under this title. His writings have been studied by Francis A. MacNutt, *Las Casas, His Life, His Apostolates, and His Writings* (N.Y., Putnam, 1909, xxxviii, 472 pp.).

"Motolinía," History of the Indians of New Spain (1568).   See Benavente, under Mexico.

Fray Bernardino de Sahagún.   A General History of New Spain (1577, pub. 1829). See under Mexico.

Acosta,' José de.   The Naturall and Morall History of the East and West Indies (1590). See under Peru.

Herrera y Tordesillas, Antonio.   The General History of the Vast Continent and Islands of America, Commonly Called the West Indies (*Historia de los hechos de los Castellanos en las islas y tierra firma del mar oceano*, 1601–15). Tr. John Stevens. London, Batley, 1725–26. 6 vols.

Solís y Rivadeneyra, Antonio de.   The History of the Conquest of Mexico by the Spaniards (1684). See under Mexico.

Reports of the Discoverers, in Recent English Versions.

Columbus, Christopher (1451–1506). The Voyages, Being the Journals of His First and Third, and the Letters Concerning His First and Last Voyages, . . . [and] the Account of His Second Voyage Written by Andrés Bernáldez. Ed. and tr. Cecil Jane. London, Argonaut Pr., 1930. 347 pp.

————Select Documents Illustrating the Four Voyages. Ed. and tr. Cecil Jane. London, Hakluyt Soc., ser. 2, vols. 65, 70: 1929, 1932.

————Journals and Other Documents on the Life and Voyages of Columbus. Ed. Samuel E. Morison. N.Y., Heritage Pr., 1964. 417 pp.

Cf. also the biography written by his son:

Colón, Fernando. The History of the Life and Actions of the Admiral Christopher Columbus. Tr. anon. (from the Italian version of the lost Spanish original), in A. and J. Churchill, A Collection of Voyages and Travels. London, 1704, vol. 2, pp. 557–688. Repr. 1732, 1744, 1752.

Tr. Benjamin Keen as The Life of the Admiral Christopher Columbus. New Brunswick, N.J., Rutgers Univ. Pr., 1959. xxxii, 316 pp.

The Discoverers in Central America.

NOTE. See under Mexico, below: Alvarado, Cortés, Díaz del Castillo, Cervantes de Salazar, Grijalva, Landa, Léon Portilla, López de Gómara, Sahagún, Solís y Rivadaneyra, Vásquez de Tapia, *and* Zorita. *See also:*

Los Conquistadores: First Person Accounts of the Conquerors of Mexico. Tr. Patricia de Fuentes. N.Y., Orion Pr., 1963. xxii, 250 pp.

Spanish Discoverers of North America.

NOTE. The earlier ones (before 1700) are brought together most conveniently in English in the series Original Narratives of American History:

Spanish Explorers in the Southern United States, 1528–1543. Ed. and tr. Frederick W. Hodge and Theodore H. Lewis. N.Y., Scribner, 1907. xx, 411 pp.

Núñez Cabeza de Vaca; Hernando de Soto (from the Portuguese account); Vásquez de Coronado. [Another De Soto narrative not given here is that of Garcilaso de la Vega, *El Florida del Inca*: see under Peru.]

Spanish Explorers in the Southwest, 1542–1706. Ed. Herbert E. Bolton. N.Y., Scribner, 1916. xii, 487 pp. Repr. 1925, 1929.
> California: Cabrillo-Ferrelo; Vizcaino. New Mexico: Rodríguez; Espejo; Oñate. Texas: Bosque-Larios; Mendoza López; De León-Massanet. Arizona: Jesuits in Pimería Alta.

NOTE. *Two contemporary works on the first Spanish governor of Florida should be noted*:

Barrientos, Bartolomé. Pedro Menéndez de Avilés, Founder of Florida (*Vida y hechos*, 1567, pub. 1902). Tr. Anthony Kerrigan. Gainesville, Univ. of Florida Pr., 1965. xxviii, 161, 149 pp., parallel texts.

Solís de Merás, Gonzalo. Pedro Menéndez de Avilés . . . Memorial (1567; pub. 1893). Tr. Jeannette Thurber Connor. Deland, Florida State Historical Soc., 1923. 286 pp. Repr. Gainesville, Univ. of Florida Pr., 1964.

NOTE. *Many later travelers and historians have been tr., notably for the Quivira Soc., 12 vols., 1929–51, and for the University of Texas Pr. See also Jones*, Latin American Writers, *pp. 1–9, and Hulet*, Latin American Prose, *pp. 74–83; also Humphreys*, Latin American History. *The following may be specially noted*:

Dominguez, Fr. Francisco Atanasio. The Missions of New Mexico, 1776: A Description, with Other Contemporary Documents. Tr. Eleanor B. Adams and Fray Angélico Chávez. Albuquerque, Univ. of New Mexico Pr., 1956. xxi, 387 pp.

Freytas, Nicolás de, O.S.F. The Expedition of Don Diego Dionisio de Peñalosa to . . . Quivira in 1692. Tr. John G. Shea. N.Y., J. G. Shea, 1882. 101 pp., parallel texts. Repr. Chicago, Ill., Rio Grande Pr., 1964, vii, 101 pp.

Janssens, Augustín (1817–1894). The Life and Adventures in California of Don Augustin Janssens. Tr. William H. Ellison and Francis Price. San Marino, Calif., Huntington Library, 1953. 165 pp.

Kino, Fr. Francisco Eusebio (1644–1711). Kino's Historical Memoir of Pímeria Alta . . . 1683–1711: A Contemporary Account of the Beginnings of California, Sonora, and Arizona. Ed. and tr. Herbert E. Bolton. Berkeley, Univ. of California Pr., 1919. 2 vols. Repr. 1948, 2 vols. in 1, 708 pp.

Montoya, Juan de.   Relation of the Discovery of New Mexico [in 1602]. Tr. George P. Hammond and Agapito Rey. Albuquerque, N.M., Quivira Soc., 1938. 143 pp., parallel texts. Repr. N.Y., Arno Pr., 1967.

Pérez de Villagrá, Gaspar.   History of New Mexico. Tr. Gilberto Espinosa, intro. F. W. Hodge. Los Angeles, Calif., Quivira Soc., 1933. 308 pp.
A verse history (1610), tr. in prose.

Venegas, Fr. Miguel, S.J.   A Natural and Civil History of California (*Noticia de la California, y de su Conquista Temporal, y Espiritual*). Tr. anon. London, 1759. 2 vols.

Vizcaíno, Juan.   The Sea Diary of Father Juan Vizcaíno to Alta California (1602–03). Tr. Arthur Woodward. Los Angeles, Calif., Dawson, 1959. 27 pp.

Spanish Discoverers in Peru.

NOTE.   For the conquest, we note the principal original works in order.

Pedro Sancho de la Hoz.   An Account of the Conquest of Peru (1550). Tr. Philip A. Means. N.Y., The Cortés Soc., 1917. 208 pp.

————Report on the Distribution of the Ransom of Atahualpa. Tr. Clements R. Markham. Hakluyt Soc. Works, no. 47, 1872, part iv. Repr. N.Y., Burt Franklin, 1963.

Pedro de Cieza de León (1519–1560).   *La Crónica del Perú* (Part 1 pub. 1553; parts 2, 4 pub. 1873). Part 1 tr. John Stevens as The Seventeen Years Travel of Peter de Cieza through the Mighty Kingdom of Peru. London, 1709. Repr. 1711.

Tr. Clements R. Markham as The Travels . . . 1532–50. Hakluyt Soc. Works, no. 33, 1864. lvii, 438 pp. Repr. N.Y., Burt Franklin, 1963.

————Part 2 [The History of the Incas] tr. Clements R. Markham. Ibid., no. 68, 1883. lx, 247 pp. Repr. with preceding, 1963.

Tr. Harriet de Onís as The Incas, ed. Victor Wolfgang von Hagen. Norman, Univ. of Oklahoma Pr., 1959. lxxx, 397 pp.

The ms. was used by W. H. Prescott in *The Conquest of Peru*, but he ascribed the work to Sarmiento, q.v. below.

—————Part 4 (The Civil Wars). Tr. Clements R. Markham as follows:
Book 1, The War of Las Salinas. Hakluyt Soc. Works, ser. 2, no. 54, 1923. xxiv, 304 pp.
Book 2, The War of Chupas. Ibid., ser. 2, no. 42, 1918. xlvii, 386 pp.
Book 3, The War of Quito. Ibid., ser. 2, no. 31, 1913. xii, 212 pp.

Zárate, Agustín de.   *Historia del descubrimiento y conquista del Perú* (1555). Part tr. (books 1 to 4 out of 6) Thomas Nicholas as The Strange and Delectable History of the Discoverie and Conquest of the Provinces of Peru. London, 1581. 89 leaves. Repr. London, Penguin Pr., 1933, xlvii, 222 pp.

Tr. (books 1 to 4) J. M. Cohen as The Discovery and Conquest of Peru. Penguin, 1968.

Pizarro, Pedro (1515–1571).   History of the Discovery and Conquest of Peru (H, 1571; pub. 1837). Tr. Philip A. Means. Cortés Soc., 1921. 2 vols.

Sarmiento de Gamboa, Pedro.   History of the Incas. See under Peru, below.

Molina, Cristóbal.   The Fables and Rites of the Incas (1585). See ibid.

Garcilaso de la Vega, El Inca.   The Royal Commentaries of Peru (1609). See ibid.

Juan, Jorge, and Ulloa, Antonio de.   A Voyage to South America: Describing at Large the Spanish Cities, Towns, Provinces (*Relación histórica del viaje a la América Meridional para medir algunos grados de meridiano terrestre*, 1748). Tr. John Adams. London, 1758. 2 vols. Repr. Dublin, 1758; rev. London, 1760; repr. enl. London, 1772; repr. in John Pinkerton, A Collection of Voyages, vol. 14, 1814, pp. 313–696. Repr. abridged Irving A. Leonard, N.Y., Knopf, 1964, 246 pp.

The Spanish in Chile.

Ercilla y Zúñiga, Alonso de.   The Araucana. See under Chile, below.

Ovalle, Alonso de.   An Historical Relation of the Kingdom of Chile (1646). See ibid.

The Spanish in Eastern South America.

Andagoya, Pascual de (d. 1548).   Narrative of the Proceedings of Pedrarias Dávila in the Province of Tierra Firma. Tr. Clements R. Markham. Hakluyt Soc. Works, no. 34, 1865. xxxix, 68 pp. Repr. N.Y., Burt Franklin, 1963.

Expeditions into the Valley of the Amazon, 1539, 1540, 1630.   Collected and Tr. Clements R. Markham. Hakluyt Soc. Works, no. 24, 1859. lxiv, 190 pp. Repr. N.Y., Burt Franklin, 1963.

> Further journeys in the Amazon region were tr. Clements R. Markham, in Hakluyt Soc. Works, nos. 28, 29: 1861, 1862, repr. 1963. See also Gaspar de Carvajal, *The Discovery of the Amazon*, tr. from ms. Bertram T. Lee, ed. H. C. Heaton (N.Y., Amer. Geographical Soc., 1934, xiv, 467 pp.).

Núñez Cabeza de Vaca, Alvaro (c.1480–c.1564).   Commentaries of the Governor in a Journey through Brazil (*Comentarios*, 1555). Tr. Luis L. Dominguez, in The Conquest of La Plata, 1535–1555. Haklyut Soc. Works, no. 81, 1889: part 2, pp. 95–262. Repr. N.Y., Burt Franklin, 1963.

Sarmiento de Gamboa, Pedro (1532–1608).   Voyage to the Straits of Magellan, 1579–1580 (pub. 1768). Tr. Clements R. Markham. Hakluyt Soc. Works, no. 91, 1894. xxx, 401 pp. Repr. N.Y., Burt Franklin, 1963.

Díaz de Guzmán, Ruy (1558?–1629).   *Historia argentina del descubrimiento, población y conquista de las provincias del Río de la Plata* (1612). See under Paraguay, below.

Argentina

Background

Hudson, William Henry.   Far Away and Long Ago. London, Dent, 1918. xii, 332 pp. Many reprs., including EL, 1939 et seq., and tr. into Spanish. Autobiography dealing with his early life (1841 to 1874) on the pampas. He wrote also about Argentina: *A Crystal Age* (N, 1887); *The Naturalist in*

La Plata (1892); *Idle Days in Patagonia* (1893); *El Ombù* (S, 1902); *A Shepherd's Life* (1910).

Levene, Ricardo.   A History of Argentina. See under Individual Authors, below.

Lipp, Solomon.   Three Argentine Thinkers. N.Y., Philosophical Lib., 1969. The development of José Ingenieros, Alejandro Korn, and Francisco Romero.

Pendle, George.   Argentina. London, Royal Institute of International Affairs, 1955. 159 pp.

Rennie, Ysabel F.   The Argentine Republic. N.Y., Macmillan, 1945. xvii, 431 pp. Repr. London, Macmillan, 1949.

Romero, José Luis.   A History of Argentine Political Thought. Tr. Thomas F. McGann. Stanford, Calif., Stanford Univ. Pr., 1963. 270 pp.

Sarmiento, Domingo Faustino.   Facundo: Life in the Argentine Republic. See under Individual Authors, below.

Literary Studies

Lichtblau, Myron I.   The Argentine Novel in the Nineteenth Century. N.Y., Hispanic Institute, 1959. 225 pp.

Nichols, Madaline W.   The Gaucho, Cattle Hunter, Cavalryman, Ideal of Romance. Durham, N.C., Duke Univ. Pr., 1942. ix, 152 pp.

Collections

Tales from the Argentine.   Tr. Anita Brenner, ed. Waldo Frank. N.Y., Farrar and Rinehart, 1930. 268 pp.
   Seven stories.

Three Plays of the Argentine.   Tr. Jacob S. Fassett, Jr., ed. Edward Hale Bierstadt. N.Y., Duffield, 1920. xiii, 147 pp.

Silverio Manco, *Juan Moreira*; Luis Bayón Herrera, *Santos Vega*; Julio Sánchez-Gardel, *The Witches' Mountain*.

INDIVIDUAL AUTHORS

Anon. "The Ranch Girl's Love" (T), in Jones, Before 1888, 317–20.

Alberdi, Juan Bautista (1810–1884). The Crime of War (*El crimen de la guerra*, E, 1866). Tr. C. J. MacConnell. London, Dent, 1913. xxxii, 343 pp.

Alberti, Rafael. Selected Poems. Ed. and tr. Ben Belitt, intro. Luis Monguío. Berkeley, Univ. of California Pr., and Cambridge, Eng., Univ. Pr., 1966. 219 pp., also paper.

———— Concerning the Angels. Tr. Geoffrey Connell. London, Poetry Europe Series, 128 Baker St., 1967. 665 pp.

Álvarez, José S. ("Fray Mocho," 1858–1903). "Hunting the Condor" (S), in Andean Monthly, vol. 3 (1940), 241–44.

Anderson Imbert, Enrique. The Other Side of the Mirror (*El grimorio*). Tr. Isabel Reade, intro. J. Cary Davis. Carbondale, Southern Illinois Univ. Pr., 1967. 226 pp.

————Spanish American Literature. See Literary Studies, above.

Andrade, Olegario Victor (1839–1882). "Atlantida" (V), and "The Condor's Nest" (V), in Fitts.
Poems in Blackwell, 314–26; Jones, Before 1888, 221–24.

Arrieta, Rafael Alberto (1889—). Poems in Fitts, 466–77; Hispanic Poets, 191; Johnson, 170–75.

Ayala, Francisco (1906—). "The Bewitched" (S). Tr. Caroline Muhlenberg in Flores, GSS.

————Death as a Way of Life (*Muertes de perro*, N, 1958). Tr. Joan MacLean. N.Y., Macmillan, 1964. 218 pp.

Banchs, Enrique (1888—). Poems in Craig, 174–81; Hispanic Poets, 190; Johnson, 162–69; Jones, Since 1888, 155–56.

Bayón Herrera, Luis. Santos Vega (T, 1913). Tr. Jacob S. Fassett, Jr., in Three Plays of the Argentine. See Collections, above.

Bioy Casares, Adolfo (1914—). The Invention of Morel and Other Stories. Tr. Ruth L. C. Simms. Austin, Univ. of Texas Pr., 1964. 237 pp.
>His 1941 Buenos Aires municipal award novella, and six science fiction stories from La trama celeste (1948).

—————and Jorge Luis Borges. "The Twelve Figures of the World" (S). Tr. Donald A. Yates. Texas Quarterly, vol. 3 (1960), 127–39.

Borges, Jorge Luis (1899—). Dream Tigers (S). Tr. Mildred Boyer and Harold Morland. Austin, Univ. of Texas Pr., 1964. 95 pp.
>Short prose pieces from El hacedor, with poems written since 1953.

—————Ficciones (S). Tr. and ed. Anthony Kerrigan. N.Y., Grove Pr., 1962. 174 pp. Repr. London, Calder, 1965.

—————The Gaucho. Tr. J. R. Wilcox, photographs by René Burri. N.Y., Crown, 1968.

—————**and Margarita Guerrero.** The Imaginary Zoo. Tr. Tim Reynolds. Berkeley, Univ. of California Pr., 1969. 175 pp.

—————Labyrinths: Selected Stories. Tr. Donald A. Yates and James E. Irby, Norfolk, Conn., New Directions, 1962. 248 pp. Repr. enl. 1964, xxiii. 260 pp.
>From Ficciones and El Aleph, with some essays.

—————Other Inquisitions, 1937–1952 (E). Tr. Ruth L. C. Simms. Austin, Univ. of Texas Pr., 1964, and London, Joseph, 1965. xviii, 205 pp.

—————A Personal Anthology. Ed. and tr. Anthony Kerrigan. N.Y., Grove Pr., 1967, and London, Calder, 1968. xiii, 210 pp.

—————"Emma Zunz" (S). Tr. Donald A. Yates, in Franco, 13–25. Repr. from Labyrinths, above.

————"The Garden of Forking Paths" (S). Tr. Donald A. Yates, in Michigan Alumni Quarterly Review, May, 1958; and Jones, Since 1888, 343–54.

————"The Handwriting of God" (S). Tr. J. M. Cohen, in Cohen, 18–22.

————"The Secret Miracle" (S). Tr. Harriet de Onís, in Onís, SS, 17–23.

————"The Shape of the Sword" (S). Tr. Angel Flores, in Flores GSS, 248–53; Flores SS, 224–37.

Poems in Craig, 226–35; *Fantasy*, no. 26, 1942, 71; Fitts, 310–37; Hays, 240–65; Johnson, 182–85; Jones, Since 1888, 160–63; 16 other sources cited in Hulet, 118–19.

On Borges see Ana María Barrenechea, *Borges the Labyrinth Maker* (*La expresión de las irrealidades en la obra de Jorge Luis Borges*), tr. Robert Lima (N.Y., N.Y. Univ. Pr., 1965, 171 pp.); and Thomas R. Hart, Jr., "The Literary Criticism of Jorge Luis Borges," *Modern Language Notes*, vol. 78, 1963, 489–503.

Campo, Estanislao ("Anastasio el Pollo," 1834–1880). Faust (V). Tr. Walter Owen. Buenos Aires, Walter Owen, 1943. 104 pp.
Excerpts in Jones, Before 1888, 243–48.

Cancela, Arturo (1892—). "Life and Death of a Hero" (S). Tr. M. M. Lasley, in Onís, SS, 102–32.

Castillo, Laura del (1928—). "A Plum for Coco" (S). Tr. Jerome Rothenberg, in Prize Stories, 147–200.

Conti, Haroldo Pedro (1925—). "The Cause" (S). Tr. Jerome Rothenberg, in Prize Stories, 259–318.

Cortázar, Julio (1914—). Cronopios and Famas. Tr. Paul Blackburn. N.Y., Pantheon, 1969. 161 pp.

————The End of the Game, and Other Stories. Tr. Paul Blackburn. N.Y., Pantheon, 1967, and London, Collins, 1968. 277 pp.

————Hopscotch (*Rayuela*, N). Tr. Gregory Rabassa. N.Y., Pantheon, and London, Harvill, 1966. 564 pp. Repr. N.Y., Bantam, 1967.

————The Time of the Hero (*La ciudad y los perros*). Tr. Lysander Kemp. N.Y., Grove, 1966. 400 pp.

————The Winners (*Los Premios*, N). Tr. Elaine Kerrigan. N.Y., Pantheon, and London, Souvenir Pr., 1965. 374 pp.

————"Bestiary" (S). Tr. Jean Franco, in Cohen, 72–86.

————"The Gates of Heaven" (S), in Flakoll, 136–47.

Cruz Varela, Juan (1791–1839). "The 25th of May, 1838, in Buenos Aires" (V), in Green, 294–303; in Jones, Before 1888.

Dávalos, Juan Carlos (1887—). "The White Wind" (N), in Flores, FN; in Flores GSS, 208–22.

Denevi, Marco (1922—). Rose at Ten O'Clock (N). Tr. Donald A. Yates. N.Y., Holt, 1964. 191 pp.

————"The Secret Ceremony" (S). Tr. Harriet de Onís, in Prize Stories, 1–64.
    First prize among 3149 entries.

Echeverría, Esteban (1805–1851). "The Captive Woman" (V), in Jones, Before 1888, 224–28.

————"The Pansy" (V), in Green, 378–81; in Jones, Before 1888; in Poor.

————"The Slaughter House" (*El matadero*, S, c.1840). Tr. Angel Flores, in New Mexico Quarterly Review, vol. 12 (1942), 389–405. Repr. in Adam International Review, vol. 16 (1948), 5–13; separately, Committee on Cultural Relations with Latin America, 1942; repr. N.Y., Las Americas Pub. Co., 1959, 37 pp., parallel texts.
    Excerpts in Jones, Before 1888, 113–19.
    Argentina's first short story.

Fábregas, Elba (1922—). "Demented Stone" (V), in Flakoll, 171–74.
    Bilingual surrealism.

Gálvez, Manuel (1882–1951). Holy Wednesday (*Miércoles santo*, N, 1930). Tr. Warre B. Wells. N.Y., Appleton, and London, Lane, 1934. 169 pp.

————*Nacha Regules* (N, 1919). Tr. Leo Ongley. N.Y., Dutton, and London, Dent, 1923. 304 pp.

————"María del Rosario" (S), in Inter-America, vol. 4 (1921), 372–82.

Gerchunoff, Alberto (1884–1950). The Jewish Gauchos of the Pampas (S). Tr. Prudencio de Pereda. N.Y. and London, Abelard-Schuman, 1955–59. 169 pp.
    Excerpts: "The Owl," in Colford, 92–96; Onís, Golden Land, 210–13.

Girri, Alberto (1918—). Poem in Cohen, 141–42.

González Arrili, Bernardo (1892—). The Life of General San Martín (B). Tr. Margaret S. de Lavenás. Buenos Aires, J. Perrotti, 1940. 63 pp.

Gorostiza, Carlos (1920—). The Bridge (T, 2 acts, 1949). Tr. Louis L. Curcio. N.Y., French, 1961. 104 pp.
    First prize, Rosamond Gilder International Theatre Competition, 1960.

Guido, Beatriz (1924—). End of a Day (N, *El incendio y las vísperas*). Tr. A. D. Towers. N.Y., Scribner, 1966. 274 pp.

————The House of the Angel (N, *La caída*, 1956). Tr. Joan Coyne MacLean. N.Y., McGraw-Hill, and London, Deutsch, 1957. 172 pp.

Güiraldes, Ricardo (1886–1927). Don Segundo Sombra: Shadows on the Pampas (N). Tr. Harriet de Onís. N.Y., Farrar and Rinehart, 1935. 270 pp. Repr. Penguin, 1948; Signet, 1965; London, New Eng. Lib., 1966.
    Excerpts in Onís, Golden Land, 214–21; in Jones, Since 1888, 242–49.

————"The Old Ranch" (S). Tr. Harriet de Onís, in Onís, SS, 176–81.

————"Rosauro" (S). Tr. Anita Brenner, in Frank, 181–235.

    Cf. Giovanni Previtali, *Ricardo Güiraldes and* Don Segundo Sombra: *Life and Works* (N.Y., Hispanic Institute, 1963, 225 pp.).

Gutiérrez, Eduardo (1835–1890) and Podestà, José J. (1856–1937).
"Juan Moreira" (T). Tr. Willis K. Jones and Carlos Escudero, in Poet
Lore, vol. 51 (1945), 101–17.
> (Pantomime, 1884; play, 1886). Excerpts in Jones, Since 1888, 371–79.

Hernández, José (1834–1886).   The Gaucho Martín Fierro (*Martín Fierro*,
1872; *La vuelta de Martín Fierro*, 1879). Tr. verse (adapted) Walter Owen.
Oxford, Blackwell, 1935, and N.Y., Farrar and Rinehart, 1936. xxiv,
326 pp.

> Tr. C. E. Ward as Martín Fierro. Albany, State Univ. of N.Y. Pr., 1967.
> xvii, 507 pp. ill., parallel texts.

> Part tr. ("Fragment") Joseph Auslander, in Hispanic Notes and Mono-
> graphs, 1932, 13 pp.; excerpts in Jones, Before 1888, 233–43. See Henry
> A. Holmes, *Martín Fierro: The Argentine Gaucho Epic* (N.Y., Hispanic
> Institute, 1948, 229 pp.).

Larreta, Enrique.   See Rodríguez Larreta, Enrique.

Leguizamón, Martiniano P. (1858–1935).   Calandria: A Drama of Gaucho
Life (T, 3 acts, 1896). Tr. Orosi. N.Y., Hispanic Society of America, 1932.
65 pp.

Levene, Ricardo (1885—).   A History of Argentina (*Lecciones de la historia
argentina*, 1919). Tr. William S. Robertson. Chapel Hill, Univ. of North
Carolina Pr., 1937. 585 pp. Repr. N.Y., Russell, 1963.

López, Lucio Vicente (1848–1894).   "Holiday in Buenos Aires" (S, *La gran
aldea*, 1882), in Frank, 105–24.

Lugones, Leopoldo (1874–1938).   "Death of a Gaucho" (S, *La guerra
gaucha*), in Frank, 81–102.

————"A Good Cheese," in Inter-America, vol. 3, 1920, 160–62.

————"Boy and Shepherd Girl" (*Yzur*), in Inter-America, vol. 3, 1920,
157–60; in Colford, 79–89.

————Poems in Blackwell, 326–40; Craig, 96–111; Hispanic Poets, 185–90;
Johnson, 102–07; Jones, Since 1888, 149–54; Walsh, 664–70.

Lynch, Benito (1890–1951). "The Sorrel Colt" (S, "*El potrillo roano*," 1940), in Flores, SS, 208–23; Haydn, 922–26.

Mallea, Eduardo (1903—). All Green Shall Perish (N and SS). Tr. John B. Hughes. N.Y., Knopf, 1966. xxiii, 431 pp.
> Contains 3 novelettes: Fiesta in November (1938); All Grenn Shall Perish (*Perecerá todo verde*, 1941); Chaves (1953); and four stories: Anguish; The Lost Cause of Jacob Uber; The Heart's Reason; The Shoes.

——————The Bay of Silence (N, 1940). Tr. Stuart E. Grummon. N.Y., Knopf, 1944. 339 pp.

——————Fiesta in November (N). Tr. Alis de Sola, in Flores, FN, 11–119. Repr. London, Calder, 1969, 121 pp.

> Tr. John B. Hughes, in All Green Shall Perish: see above.

——————"By the Shores of the Sea" (S). Tr. G. R. Coulthard, in Adam International Review, vol. 17, 191, 1949, 17.

——————"Conversation" (S). Tr. Hugo Manning, in Fantasy, no. 26, 1942, 61–65; in Jones, Since 1888, 294–302.

——————"The Gay Fellow" (S). Tr. Lloyd Mallan, in American Prefaces, vol. 7, 1941–42, 106–24.

——————"The Heart's Reason" (S). Tr. Harriet de Onís, in Onís, SS, 188–208.

——————"Pillars of Society" (S), in Whit Burnett, 105 Greatest Living Authors. N.Y., Dial, 1950.

——————"The Promise" (S). Tr. Helen B. Macmillan, in New Mexico Quarterly, vol. 14, 1944, 337–39.

——————"Serena Barca" (S). Tr. Janet Brassert, in Tomorrow, vol. 2, 1943, 24–28.

Manco, Silverio. "Juan Moreira" (T, 2 acts, 1896). Tr. Jacob S. Fassett, in Three Plays of the Argentine, pp. 1–19: see Collections, Argentina, above.

Maréchal, Leopoldo. "The Centaur." Tr. Richard L. O'Connell and James Graham Luhan. New Directions 8, 1944, 294–308.

Mármol, José (1817–1871). Amalia: A Romance of the Argentine (N, 1851–55). Tr. Mary J. Serrano. N.Y., Dutton, 1919. 419 pp. Repr. 1944.
Excerpt in Jones, Before 1888, 138–42.

——————"To Rosas" (V), in Poor.

Martínez Zuviría, Gustavo ("Hugo Wast," 1883–1962). Black Valley (N, 1918). Tr. Herman and Miriam Hespelt. N.Y., Longmans, 1928. 302 pp.

——————House of the Ravens (N, 1916). Tr. Leonard Matters. London, Williams and Norgate, 1924. 319 pp.

——————Peach Blossom (N, 1911). Tr. Herman and Miriam Hespelt. N.Y. and London, Longmans, 1929. 300 pp.

——————A Stone Desert (N, 1925). Tr. Louis Imbert and Jacques LeClercq. N.Y. and London, Longmans, 1928. 302 pp.

——————Strength of Lovers (N, Lucía Miranda, 1929). Tr. Louis Imbert and Jacques LeClercq. N.Y. and London, Longmans, 1930. 315 pp.

——————"The Missing Hand" (S), in Inter-America, vol. 7, 1925, 540–61; in Jones, Since 1888, 235–42.

——————"The Thatched Roof" (S), in Inter-America, vol. 9, 1926, 416–34.

Méndez Calzada, Enrique (1898—). "Christ in Buenos Aires" (S). Tr. Edmund C. García, in Fantasy, no. 27, 1943; in Jones, Since 1888, 363–67.

——————"Criminals" (T), in Inter-America, vol. 7, 1923, 115–25.

Mitre, Bartolomé (1821–1906). The Emancipation of South America (Historia de San Martín y de la emancipación sud-americana, 1888, 3 vols.). Tr. abridged William Pilling. London, Chapman and Hall, 1893. xxviii, 409 pp.
Excerpt, "History of Belgrano," in Jones, Before 1888.

————"To Santos Vega" (V), in Jones, Before 1888, 229–33.
Poems in Blackwell, 382; Hispanic Poets, 183; Inter-America, vol. 5, 1921, 74–78, 181–95.

Molinari, Ricardo E. (1898—).   Poem in Cohen, 28–29.

Murena, H. A. (1923—).   "The Cavalry Colonel" (S). Tr. Gordon Brotherston, in Franco, 43–63.

Nale Roxlo, Conrado (1898—).   Poems in Fitts, 497–99.

Obligado, Rafael (1851–1920).   "Santos Vega" (V). Excerpts in Blackwell, 348–77; Inter-America, vol. 5, 1920, 85–94; Jones, Before 1888, 248–52.

Payró, Roberto J. (1867–1928).   "The Devil in Pago Chico" (S, *Pago chico*, 1908). Tr. Anita Brenner, in Brewton; in Frank, 157–78; in Onís, Golden Land, 193–202.

————"Laucho's Marriage" (S, 1906). Tr. Anita Brenner in Frank, 3–76; in Onís, Golden Land, 192–202.

————"The Tragic Song" (T, 1 act, 1900). Tr. Willis K. Jones and Carlos Escudero, in Poet Lore, vol. 50, 1944, 3–24.

Pico, Pedro E. (1882–1945).   "Common Clay" (T, 1 act: *Del mismo barro*, 1918). Tr. Willis K. Jones, in PSA, vol. 2.

————"You Can't Fool with Love" (T, 1 act: *No hay burlas con el amor*, 1907). Tr. Willis K. Jones and Carlos Escudero, in Poet Lore, vol. 49, 1943, 107–34.

Rodríguez Larreta, Enrique (1875–1961).   The Glory of Don Ramiro: A Life in the Times of Philip II (N: *La Gloria de don Ramiro*, 1908). Tr. L. B. Walton. N.Y., Dutton, 1924. 307 pp.
Excerpts in Jones, Since 1888, 253–57.

Rojas, Ricardo (1882–196?).   Ollantay (T, 4 acts, 1940). Excerpts in Bulletin Pan Amer. Union, vol. 74, 1940, 149–53; in Theatre Arts, vol. 24, 1940, 252–56.

————San Martín, Knight of the Andes (B, *El santo de la espada*, 1933). Tr. Herschel Brickell and Carlos Videla. N.Y., Doubleday, 1945. xiii, 370 pp.

Excerpt tr. Harriet de Onís, in Arciniegas, 270–85.

Sábato, Ernesto (1912—).   The Outsider (N, *El Tunel*, 1948). Tr. Harriet de Onís. N.Y., Knopf, 1950. 177 pp.

Sánchez Gardel, Julio (1879–1937).   "The Witches' Mountain" (T, 3 acts: 1913). Tr. Jacob S. Fassett, in Three Plays of the Argentine, pp. 77–130: see Collections, Argentina, above.

Sánchez Reulet, Aníbal (1910—).   Contemporary Latin American Philosophy (E). Tr. Willard R. Trask. Albuquerque, Univ. of New Mexico Pr., 1954. 285 pp.

————"A Philosophy and Its Consequences" (E), in Américas, vol. 7, 1953, 36–37.

Sarmiento, Domingo Faustino (1811–1888).   Facundo: Life in the Argentine Republic in the Days of the Tyrants, or Civilization and Barbarism (H, *Civilización y barbarie*, 1845). Tr. Mrs. Horace Mann. N.Y., Hurd and Houghton, 1868. xxxv, 400 pp. Repr. N.Y., Hafner, 1960; N.Y., Collier, 1961. Excerpt in Frank; in Jones, Before 1888, 119–24.

See Stuart S. Grummon, *A Sarmiento Anthology* (Princeton, N.J., Univ. Pr., and London, Oxford Univ. Pr., 1948, 336 pp.).

Storni, Alfonsina (1892–1938).   Poems in Blackwell, 386–90; Craig, 220–25; Fitts, 512–21; Hispanic Poets, 192–94; Johnson, 150–55; Jones, Since 1888, 157–60.

"Tiempo, César."   See Zeitlin, Israel.

Ugarte, Manuel (1878–1951).   The Destiny of a Continent (H, 1923). Tr. Catherine A. Phillips. N.Y., Knopf, 1925. 296 pp.

————"The Gringo" (S), in Tales.

————"The Healer" (S), in Clark, 937–42.

————————"Tiger of Macuza" (S). Tr. H. C. Schweikert, in Stratford Monthly, vol. 7, 1925, 71–76.

Venturini, Rolando. "Sunday for an Architect" (S). Tr. Isaak A. Langnas, in Prize Stories, 374–98.

Vigil, Constancio C. (1876—?). The Adventures of Hormiguita (S, *La hormiguita viajera*, 1920). Tr. Gilda Mossa. Forest Hills, N.Y., Las Americas, 1943. 49 pp.

————————The Fallow Land (E, *El erial*, 1915). Tr. Lawrence Smith. N.Y., Harper, 1946. 207 pp.

"Wast, Hugo." See Martínez Zuviría, Gustavo.

"Yunque, Alvaro" (Arístides Gandolfi Herrero, 1893—). 1 + 1 = 3 (S). Tr. Rachel Loughridge, in Univ. of Kansas City Review, vol. 10, 1943, 127–33.

Zeitlin, Israel ("César Tiempo," 1906—). Poems in Fitts, 233–40.

Bolivia

Background

Kirchoff, Herbert. Bolivia: Its People and Scenery. Tr. from Spanish (Buenos Aires, 1942). Buenos Aires, Guillermo Kraft, 1944. xvi, 105 plates on 58 leaves.

Leonard, Olen E. Bolivia: Land, People, and Institutions. Washington, D.C., Scarecrow Pr., 1952. 297 pp.

Osborne, Harold. Bolivia: A Land Divided. London, Royal Institute of International Affairs, 1954. 142 pp. Rev. 1955, 157 pp.

INDIVIDUAL AUTHORS

Arguedas, Alcides (1879–1946). "Funeral of the Indian" (S), in Jones, Since 1888, 187–90.

————*Raza de bronce* (E, *Wata Wara*, 1904). Excerpts in Arciniegas, 205–22; Onís, Golden Land, 231–37.

Céspedes, Augusto (1904—). "The Well" (S, *El Pozo*, from *Sangre de mestizos*, 1936). Tr. Mary and C. V. Wicker, in American Prefaces, vol. 7, 1941–42, 125–39.

————Tr. Harriet de Onís, in Arciniegas, 482–95; in Haydn, 882–91.

Costa du Rels, Adolfo (1891—). Bewitched Lands (N, *Tierras hechizadas*, 1940). Tr. Stuart E, Grummon. N.Y., Knopf, 1945. 203 pp.

————The King's Standard (T, 3-act). Tr. Helen A. Gaubert. N.Y., French, 1960. 72 pp.

————"La Misqui-Simi" (S). Tr. Elizabeth Wallace, in Flores FN, 458–65. Repr. in Mexican Life, vol. 25, 1949, no. 8.

————"The Two Horsemen" (S). Tr. Helen Macmillan, in New Mexico Quarterly, vol. 14, 1944, 409–24.

Díaz de Medina, Fernando. "Legend of the Aymará" (S), in Américas, vol. 5, 1953, 21–23, 42–44.

Díaz Machicado, Porfirio. "The Death of Tomas" (S), in Mexican Life, vol. 37, 8, Aug. 1961, 11–12, 64–65.

Jaimes Freyre, Ricardo (1868–1933). Poems in Blackwell, 454–62; Colford, 45–51; Craig, 85–88; Johnson, 90–93; Jones, Since 1888, 115–18; Poetry, vol. 26, 1925, 119.

More, Federico (1889—). "Interlude" (T, one-act). Tr. Audrey Alden, in F. Shay and P. Loving, Fifty Contemporary One-Act Plays. Cincinnati, Ohio, Stewart and Kidd, 1920. Repr. N.Y., Appleton, 1935; Cleveland, Ohio, World, 1946, pp., 39–44.

Otero Reiche, Raúl (1906—).   Poems in Fitts, 557–77.

Ostria Gutiérrez, Alberto.   The Tragedy of Bolivia: A People Crucified (H, *Un pueblo en la cruz*, 1950?). Tr. Eithne Golden. N.Y., Devin-Adair, 1958. 224 pp.

Pereyra, Diómedes (1897—).   The Golden Web (N). N.Y., Butterick Pub. Co., 1928. 306 pp.

————The Land of the Golden Scarabs (N, *El valle del sol*). Indianapolis, Ind., Bobbs-Merrill, 1928. 308 pp.
  First pub. in two parts as "The Land of Mystery" in Golden Book, Feb.–Mar. 1928, and "Sun Gold," ibid., July–Sept. 1928.

  These novels may have been written first in English and then translated. They exist in both Spanish and English.

Ramallo, General Mariano (1817–1865).   "Impressions at the Foot of Illimani" (V), in Jones, Before 1888, 259–63; in Poor.

Sanjinés, Jenaro (1842–1900).   "Bolivian National Anthem" (V), in Bolivia, Sept.–Oct. 1941, 26.

Chile

Background

Clissold, Stephen.   Chilean Scrap-book. London, Cresset Pr., 1952. 316 pp.

Edwards, Agustín R.   My Native Land. See under Individual Authors, below.

Literary Study

Fein, John M.   *Modernismo* in Chilean Literature: The Second Period. Durham, N.C., Duke Univ. Pr., 1965. 167 pp.

Collections

Pino-Saavedra, Yolando, ed.   Folktales of Chile. Part tr. Rockwell Gray Chicago, Ill., Univ. of Chicago Pr., 1968. 317 pp.
    Selected for tr. by the editor of the 3-volume *Cuentos Folkloricos de Chile* (1960–63).

Williams, Miller, ed. and tr.   Chile: An Anthology of New Writing. Kent, Ohio, Kent State Univ. Pr., 1968. 156 pp.

INDIVIDUAL AUTHORS

Acevedo Hernández, Antonio (1886–1962).   *"Cabrerita"* (T, one-act, 1929). Tr. W. E. Bailey, in PSA, vol. 1.

————*"Chañarcillo"* (T, one scene, 1933, rev. 1950), in Jones, Since 1888, 412–15.

————*"El Velorio"* (S), in Andean Monthly, vol. 2, Nov. 1939, 31.

Aguirre, Isidora (1909—).   "Express for Santiago" (T, one-act, *Carolina*, 1955). Tr. Stanley Richards, in Margaret G. Mayorga, ed., Best Short Plays of 1959–60. N.Y., Dodd Mead, 1961, pp. 195–214.

————"The Three Pascualas" (T, 3-act, 1957). Tr. Willis K. Jones, in Poet Lore, vol. 59, 1965, no. 4. Excerpts in Jones, Since 1888, 423–29.

Alegría, Fernando (1918—).   *Lautaro* (N, 1943). Tr. Delia Goetz. N.Y., Farrar and Rinehart, 1944. 176 pp.

————My Horse Gonzalez (N, *Caballo de copa*). Tr. Carlos Lozano. N.Y., Las Américas Pub. Co., 1964. 197 pp.

————"The Cataclysm" (S), in Américas, vol. 12, 1960, 29–30.

————"Family Life" (S). Tr. Carlos Lozano, in Odyssey Review, vol. 2, June 1962, 9–12.

————"The Lassoed Philosopher" (S), in Odyssey Review, vol. 2, June 1962, 14–24.

Anguita Linares, Eduardo (1914—). "The Definition and Destruction of the Parsonage." Tr. Lloyd Mallan. New Directions 8, 1944, 320–27.

————"Passage to the End" (V). Tr. Lloyd Mallan, in Fantasy, no. 27, 1943, 57; and Fitts, 545–48.

————"The True Countenance" (V), in Flakoll, 191–93.

Arriaza, Armando ("Hermes Nahuel," 1900—). "Pilgrimage" (S). Tr. Alis de Sola, in Flores FN, 480–87; and in Mexican Life, vol. 24, no. 11, Nov. 1948, 13–14, 45–46.

Barrios, Eduardo (1884–1963). Brother Ass (N, 1926). Tr. E. Seldon Rose and Francisco Aguilera, in Flores FN, 488–608.

————"For the Sake of a Good Reputation" (T, one-act, *Por el decoro*, 1913). Tr. Willis K. Jones in PSA, vol. 2, 1–11.

————"Papa and Mama" (T, one-act), in Poet Lore, vol. 38, 1922, 286–90.

Bello, Carlos (1815–1854). *Amores del Poeta* (T, 3 acts, 1842). Excerpt in Jones, Before 1888.

Blest Gana, Alberto (1831–1920). *Martín Rivas* (N, 1862). Tr. Mrs. Charles Whitham. London, Chapman and Hall, 1916, and N.Y., Knopf, 1918. 431 pp.

————"Camara's Fight" (S, excerpt from *Durante la reconquista*, N, 1867), in Jones, Since 1888, 250–53.

Bombal, María Luisa (1910—). The House of Mist (N, expanded by the author from *La última niebla*, 1934). N.Y., Farrar Straus, 1947. 245 pp., and London, Cassell, 1948, 184 pp.

————The Shrouded Woman (N, *La amortajada*, 1941). Tr. María Bombal. N.Y., Farrar Straus, 1948. 198 pp.

Brunet, Marta (1901—). "Francina" (S, *Reloj de sol*, 1930), in Jones, Since 1888, 289–94.

Calderón Cousiño, Adolfo. Short Diplomatic History of the Chilean-Peruvian Relations, 1819-1879 (H, *La cuestión chileno-peruana*, 1920). Santiago, Imprenta Universitaria, 1920. 255 pp.

Castro Zagal, Oscar (1910–1947). "Lucero" (S, *Huellas en la tierra*, 1940). Tr. J. L. Grucci, in American Prefaces, vol. 7, 1941–42, 167–74.

　　Tr. Harry Kurz, in Haydn, 872–77.

————"Response for García Lorca" (V), in Fitts, 519.

Coloane, Francisco (1910—). The Stowaway (N, *El último grumete de La Baquedano*, 1941). Tr. Adele Breaux. N.Y., Manyland Books, 1964. 113 pp.

Cruchaga Santa María, Ángel (1893–1964). *"La oración antes del sueño"* (V), in Henry A. Holmes, Vicente Huidobro and Creationism. N.Y., Columbia Univ. Pr., 1934, p. 42.

Díaz Casanueva, Humberto (1908—). *Requiem: con la tradución al inglés de Angel Flores.* Santiago, Ediciones del Grupo Fuego, [1958]. 57 pp., parallel texts.

Díaz Garcés, Joaquín ("Angel Pino," 1875–1921). "A Baptismal Feast in Chile" (S), in Inter-America, vol. 1, 1918, 179–83; in Amigos, vol. 1, 1942, 11–12; in Jones, Since 1888, 358–63.

————"A Parisian Bargain Day" (S), in Inter-America, vol. 1, 1917, 35–38.

Díaz Loyola, Carlos ("Pablo de Rokha," 1895—). "Allegory of Torment" (V). Tr. H. R. Hays in Fitts, 399–403.

————"The Public Prosecutor Speaking" (V). Tr. Renée Tallantyre, in Fantasy, no. 27, 1943, 40.

Donoso, José (1928—). Coronation (N). Tr. Jocasta Goodwin. N.Y., Knopf, and London, Bodley Head, 1965. 262 pp.

————This Sunday. Tr. Lorraine O'Grady Freeman. N.Y., Knopf, 1967, and London, Bodley Head, 1968. 177 pp.

————"Ana María" (S). Tr. J. M. Cohen, in Cohen, 152–66.

————"Denmaker" (S), in Flakoll, 200–10.

————"Footsteps in the Night" (S), in Américas, vol. 11, 2, Feb. 1959, 21–23; and in Mexican Life, vol. 36, 6, June 1960, 10, 51–54.

Echeverría, Alfonso (1923—). "Nausícaa" (S). Tr. Echeverría, in Prize Stories, 106–33. (3rd prize.)

Edwards, Agustín R. (1878–1941). My Native Land (V, *Mi Tierra*, 1931). Ed. and tr. A. Edwards. London, Ernest Benn, 1931. 430 pp.

Edwards Vives, Alberto (1872–1932). "Adventures of Román Calvo: The Lost Sweetheart" (S), in Andean Monthly, vol. 2, June 1939, 35.

————"Trail of D. Antonio Pérez" (S), in Inter-America, vol. 1, 1918, 85–93.

Ercilla y Zuñiga, Alonso de (1533–1594). *La Araucana* (V, 1569–89). Part tr. (16 cantos) prose George Carew as The Historie of Araucana. Ed. from ms. (c.1600) Frank Pierce. Manchester, Univ. Pr., 1964. xxi, 52 pp.

  Tr. verse P. T. Manchester and C. M. Lancaster as The Araucaniad. Nashville, Tenn., Vanderbilt Univ. Pr., 1945. 326 pp.

  Many part trs.: Canto i, tr. William Hayley and Henry Boyd, in Molina, History of Chile, 1808; Canto i, tr. Walter Owen, Buenos Aires, 1945. Canto ii, in John Bowring, Ancient Poetry and Romances of Spain, 1824. Excerpts in Henry W. Longfellow, Poets of Europe, 1845, see General Reference, Collections, above; in W. H. De Puy, University of Literature, N.Y. 1895; in A. R. Spofford, Library of Choice Literature, n.d.; in Pan American Magazine, vol. 28, 1919, 249; in World Affairs, vol. 104, 1941, 180–82; in Poet Lore, vol. 48, 1942; in Jones, Before 1888, 189–94; in Walsh, 221–26.

Galdames, Luis (1881–1941).   A History of Chile (H, *Estudio de la historia de Chile*, 1906–07). Tr. Isaac J. Cox. Chapel Hill, Univ. of North Carolina Pr., 1941. 565 pp.

Garrido Merino, Edgardo (1895—).   "The Hat That Belonged to No One" (S), in Andean Monthly, vol. 1, 1938, 38, parallel texts.

Heiremans, Luis Alberto (1928–1964).   "The Azalea" (S), in Américas, vol. 12, 2, Feb. 1960, 28–34.

————"The Ninth Man" (S). Tr. Robert Losada, in Odyssey Review, vol. 2, June 1962, 58–67.

Huidobro, Vicente (1893–1948).   Mirror of a Mage (N, *Cagliostro, Novela-film*, 1926). Tr. Warre B. Wells. Boston, Mass., Houghton Mifflin, and London, Eyre and Spottiswoode, 1931. 185 pp.

————Portrait of a Paladin (N, *Mío Cid campeador*, 1929). Tr. Warre B. Wells. N.Y., Horace Liveright, and London, Eyre and Spottiswoode, 1932. 316 pp.
Poems in Craig, 236–43; Fitts, 347–51; Jones, Since 1888, 124–26. See also Henry A. Holmes, *Vicente Huidobro and Creationism* (N.Y., Columbia Univ. Pr., 1934), which contains "Nameless Moor" (S) and "Sky Quake."

Lafourcade, Enrique (1927—).   King Ahab's Feast (N, 1962). Tr. Renate and Ray Morrison. N.Y., St. Martin's Pr., 1963. 249 pp.

————"The Destruction of the Families," in Américas, vol. 13, 8, Aug. 1961, 22–24.

Latorre, Mariano (1886–1955).   "The Buried Jar" (S), in Amigos, vol. 1, 1942, 18–30.

————"Captain Oyarzo" (S), in Arciniegas, 124–37.

————"The Old Woman of Peralillo" (S), in Onís, Golden Land, 259–79.

————"The Secret of the Pine Cone" (S), in Andean Monthly, vol. 2, Apr. 1939, 46.

————"Woman of Mystery" (S). Tr. Harry Kurz, in Haydn, 864–72.

Lihn, Enrique (1929—). Poems in Cohen, 247–50.

Lillo, Baldomero (1867–1923). The Devil's Pit and Other Stories (*Sub terra*, 1906; *Sub Sole*, 1907; and *Relatos Populares*). Tr. Esther S. Dillon and Angel Flores. Washington, D.C., Pan American Union, 1959, 152 pp.

————"The Abyss" (S), in Colcord, 36–42.

Lillo, Samuel A. (1870—?). "The Abandoned Time" (V), in Pan American Magazine, vol. 26, 1917, 70.

————"To Vasco Núñez de Balboa" (V), ibid, 69; in Poet Lore, vol. 32, 1921, 407–08; in Walsh, 699–707.

Magallanes Moure, Manuel (1878–1924). Poems in Blackwell, 298–301; Pan American Magazine, vol. 26, 1917, 71; in Poetry, vol. 26, 1925, 122; in Walsh, 689–91.

Maluenda Labarca, Rafael (1885–1964). "A Man of Erudition" (S), in Inter-America, vol. 4, Oct. 1920, 17.

————"As God Desires It" (S), in Andean Monthly, vol. 1, June 1939, 24; in Jones, Since 1888, 319–26.

————"Escape," in Flores FN, 473–79; in Mexican Life, vol. 24, 10, Oct. 1949, 11–12, 46–48.

————"*La pachacha*" (S), in New Mexico Quarterly, vol. 13, 1943, 137–43.

————"The Strength of Evidence" (S), in Andean Monthly, vol. 3, 1, March 1940; in Amigos, vol. 1 1942, 11–16.

Marín, Juan (1900—). *Orestes y yo* (T). Tr. R. P. Butrick. Tokyo, Asia America, 1940. 66 pp.

————"Parallel 53 South" (N), excerpt in Arciniegas, 449–65.

"Mistral, Gabriela" (Lucila Godoy Alcayaga, 1889–1957). Selected Poems (V). Tr. Langston Hughes. Bloomington, Indiana Univ. Pr., 1957. 119 pp.

————"Christmas at Sea" (S), in Andean Monthly, vol. 2, Dec. 1939, 40.

Poems in Blackwell, 236–79; Bulletin Pan American Union, July 1924, Jan. 1926; in Cohen, 15–17; in Craig, 194–205; in Fitts, 39–49; Hispanic Poets, 199; Jones, Since 1888, 120–24; Poet Lore, vol. 46, 1940, 339–52; Walsh, 735.

See Marcia Arce de Vázquez, *Gabriela Mistral, The Poet and Her Work*, tr. Helen Masslo Anderson (N.Y., N.Y. Univ. Pr., 1964, 158 pp., paper).

Montenegro, Ernesto (1885—). "Birds Play Hockey" (S), in Andean Monthly, vol. 1, 1939, 42–44.

————"For a Dozen Hard Eggs" (S). Tr. Bradley Premers, in Andean Monthly, vol. 3, 1940, 187–89.

Poems in Christian Science Monitor, Aug. 8, 1925; in Walsh, 740–41.

Moock, Armando (1894–1942). "Don Juan's Women" (T, one-act, "*Las amigas de Don Juan*," 1931). Tr. Willis K. Jones, in Poet Lore, vol. 46, 1940, 47–75.

————"Song Book of the Baby Jesus" (T, one-act, "*Cancionero del niño Jesús*," 1920, pub. 1937). Tr. Willis K. Jones, in Poet Lore, vol. 45, 1939, 23–53.

"Neruda, Pablo" (Neftalí Ricardo Reyes, 1904—). Selected Poems. Tr. Angel Flores. Washington, D.C., pr. pr., 1944.
     Also in New Directions 8, 1944, 333–61.

————Selected Poems. Tr. Ben Belitt. N.Y., Grove Pr., 1961. 320 pp., parallel texts. Repr. 1963, paper.

————Bestiary: A Poem. Tr. Elsa Neuberger. N.Y., Harcourt, 1965. 42 pp.

————Elementary Odes (V, *Odas elementales*, 1954). Tr. Carlos Lozano. N.Y., G. Massa, 1961. 155 pp.

————The Heights of Machu Picchu. Tr. Nathaniel Tarn. London, Cape, 1966. 47 pp., parallel texts, and N.Y., Farrar Straus, 1967, xix, 71 pp., parallel texts.

————Residence on Earth and Other Poems. Tr. Angel Flores. N.Y., New Directions, 1947. 205 pp.

   Tr. Clayton Eschleman. San Francisco, Calif., City Lights Books, 1962. n.p.

————Twenty Poems. Tr. James Wright and Robert Bly. Madison, Minn., Sixties Pr., and London, Rapp and Whiting, 1968. 111 pp., parallel texts.

————We Are Many. Tr. Alistair Reid. London, Cape, 1967. 32 pp., 2 pl.

   Poems in Adam International Review, vol. 16, 1944, 14–45; American Prefaces, vol. 7, 1941, 140–41; Books Abroad, vol. 15, 1941, 165; Cohen, 30–33; Craig, 226–35; Decision, vol. 1, 1941, 49–56; Fantasy, no. 26, 1942, 55; Fitts, 310–27; Hays, 240–65; Hispanic Poets, 198; Johnson, 182–85; Jones, Since 1888, 126–33; Poetry, vol. 62, 1953, 62; Three Spanish American Poets, 25–48.

Núñez de Pineda y Bascuñán, Francisco (1607–1682). *El cautiverio feliz* (V, 1650).
   Excerpts in Jones, Before 1888, 77–81.

Oña, Pedro de (1570–1643?). Arauco Tamed (*Arauco domado*, V. 1596). Tr. C. M. Lancaster and P. T. Manchester. Albuquerque, Univ. of New Mexico Pr., 1948. 282 pp.
   Excerpt in Jones, Before 1888.

Orrego Luco, Luis (1866–1949). "A Poor Devil" (S), in Inter-America, vol. 1, 1919, 357–62.

Ovalle, Fr. Alonso de, S.J. (1601–1651). An Historical Relation of the Kingdom of Chile. Tr. anon. in A. and J. Churchill, A Collection of Voyages. London, 1704, vol. 3, pp. 1–138. Repr. in John Pinkerton, A General Collection of Voyages, vol. 14, 1814, pp. 30–210.

Six out of the eight books, omitting the conversion of the natives. Excerpts in Jones, Before 1888, 73–77.

Palma, Martín (1821–1884).   Julia Ingrand: A Tale of Catholicism in Peru. Tr. James William Duffy. London, Stock, 1877. 3 vols.

————Mysteries of the Confessional (E, 1874). London, 1888.

Parra, Nicanor (1914—).   Anti-Poems (*Poemas y antipoemas*, 1954). Tr. Jorge Elliott. San Francisco, Calif., City Lights Books, 1960. 32 pp.

————Poems and Anti-Poems. Tr. Fernando Alegria, et al. N.Y., New Directions, 1967. ix, 149 pp., parallel texts, and London, Cape, 1968, 125 pp.

————"Soliloquy of the Individual" (V), in Flakoll, 216–22.

Three poems in Cohen, 138–40.

Pérez Rosales, Vicente (1807–1886).   "Memories of the Past" (H), in Jones, Before 1888, 141–46.

Petit Marfán, Magdalena (1904—).   *La Quintrala* (N, 1932). Tr. Lulú Vargas Vila. N.Y., Macmillan, 1942. 190 pp.

"Pino, Angel."   See Díaz Garcés, Joaquín.

Pinochet Lebrún, Tancredo.   The Gulf of Misunderstanding, or North and South America as Seen by Each Other (E, *El divorcio de las Américas, cartas de un caballero chileno en Chicago a su esposa en Santiago*, 1919). Tr. Cecilia Brennen, William Sachs, and Charles Evers. N.Y., Boni and Liveright, 1920. 275 pp.

Prado, Pedro (1886–1950).   *Alsino* (N, 1920). Excerpt tr. Robert Scott, in Jones, Since 1888, 333–37.

————Country Judge: A Novel of Chile. Tr. Lesley Byrd Simpson. Berkeley, Univ. of California Pr., and London, Cambridge Univ. Pr., 1968. 143 pp.

Poems in Blackwell, 278–86; Craig, 157–67; Inter-America, vol. 8, 1924, 123–25; Poet Lore, vol. 32, 1921, 407; Stratford Journal, vol. 4, 1919, 138.

Prieto, Jenaro (1889–1946).   The Partner (N, *El socio*, 1929). Tr. Blanca de Roig and Guy Dowler. London, Butterworth, 1931. 255 pp.

Reyes, Salvador (1899—).   "Vagabond's Christmas Eve" (S), in Andean Monthly, vol. 3, 1940, 509.

Tr. Alis de Sola in Flores FN, 466–72.

Roepke, Gabriela (1920—).   "The White Butterfly" (T, one-act, 1957). Tr. Thomas M. Patterson, in M. G. Mayorga, Best Short Plays of 1959–60. N.Y., Dodd Mead, 1961, pp. 145–64.

Rojas, Gonzalo (1917—).   "Love" (V), in Flakoll, 148–55.

Rojas Sepúlveda, Manuel (1896—).   Born Guilty (N, *Hijo de ladrón*, 1951). Tr. Frank Gaynor. London, Gollancz, and N.Y., Library Publishers, 1955. 314 pp.

————"Bandits of the Highway" (S), in Andean Monthly, vol. 2, 1939, 39.

————"The Cub" (S), in Colford, 3–14.

————"A Glass of Milk" (S). Tr. J. L. Grucci, in American Prefaces, vol. 7, 1941–42, 184–92; in Colford, 15–24.

————"Gold in the South" (S), in Américas, vol. 6, 5, May 1954, 12–15, 22–23.

"Rokha, Ninette de" (Luisa Anabalón Sanderson, "Juana Inés de la Cruz," 1894—).   Poems in Craig, 145–48.

Rozas Larraín, Carlos.   "The Black Ship" (S). Tr. Lysander Kemp, in Prize Stories, 241–58.

Sanfuentes, Salvador (1817–1860).   *El Campanario* (V, 1842). Excerpts in Jones, Before 1888, 256–59.

Santiván, Fernando (1886—). "With Horse and Whip" (S, from *La hechizada*, N, 1916), in Chile, vol. 5, 1928; and Andean Monthly, vol. 4, 1941–42.

Serrano, Miguel (1917—). The Visits of the Queen of Sheba. Tr. Frank Macshane. Bombay and N.Y., Asia Pub. House, 1960. 383 pp.

Silva, Victor Domingo (1882–1960). Poems in Blackwell, 290; Craig; Pan American Magazine, vol. 26, 1917, 71; Stratford Journal, vol. 4, 1919, 139; Walsh, 723–26.

Silva Vildósola, Carlos (1870–1942). "Señor Malvoa" (S). Tr. E. Foster Thackwell, in Andean Monthly, vol. 2, 1940, 42–47.

Subercaseaux, Benjamín (1902—). Chile: A Geographic Extravaganza (E, *Chile una loca geográfica*, 1940). Tr. Angel Flores. N.Y., Macmillan, 1943. viii, 255 pp.

————From West to East (E, *Y al oeste limita con el mar*, 1937). Tr. John G. Underhill. N.Y., Putnam, 1940. 215 pp. "The Salt Sea" from this vol. repr. in Onís SS, 260–88.

————Jeremy Button (N). Tr. Mary and Fred Del Villar. N.Y., Macmillan, 1954. 382 pp

   Tr. condensed Oliver Coburn. London, W. H. Allen, 1955. 299 pp.

Torres Rioseco, Arturo (1897—). Poems in American Prefaces, vol. 7, 1941, 158–59; and in Craig.

Vattiers, Carlos. "When a Man Is Already Married" (S, *Los héroes ya estaban casados*), in Andean Monthly, vol. 2, May 1939, 29.

Vega, Daniel de la (1892–1962?). "Abolition of Vacations" (S, *Las vacaciones escolares*), in Andean Monthly, vol. 2, July 1939, 45.

————"Gift of the Wise Men" (S), in Américas, vol. 12, 12, Dec. 1960, 20–23.

   Poems in Blackwell, 302; and Pan American Magazine, vol. 26, 1917, 67.

Vial y Ureta, Román (1833–1896). "A Popular Election" (T, one-act, 1870), in Jones, Before 1888.

Vicuña Mackenna, Benjamín (1831–1888). Francisco Moyen, or The Inquisition as It Was in South America (N). Tr. J. W. Duffy. London, Sotheran, 1869. 225 pp.

Yankas, Lautaro. "The Bogeyman" (S, *El cuco*), in Amigos, vol. 1, Apr. 1942, 10–18.

Colombia

Background

Galbraith, W. O. Colombia: A General Survey. London, Royal Institute of International Affairs, 1953. 140 pp.

Romoli, Kathleen. Colombia: Gateway to South America. N.Y., Doubleday Doran, 1941. 364 pp.

INDIVIDUAL AUTHORS

Arciniegas, Germán (1900—). Amerigo and the New World: The Life and Times of Amerigo Vespucci (H). Tr. Harriet de Onís. N.Y., Knopf, 1955. 322 pp.

————The Caribbean, Sea of the New World (H, *Biografía del Caribe*). Tr. Harriet de Onís. N.Y., Knopf, 1946. 464 pp.

————Germans in the Conquest of America, A Sixteenth Century Venture (H). Tr. Angel Flores. N.Y., Macmillan, 1943. 217 pp.

————The Knight of El Dorado: The Tale of Don Gonzalo Jiménez de Quesada and His Conquest of New Granada (H, 1942). Tr. Mildred Adams. N.Y., Viking, 1942. 201 pp.

————The State of Latin America (E, *El pueblo de América*, 1945). Tr. Harriet de Onís. N.Y., Knopf, 1952. 416 pp.

————"The Little Horse of Ráquira" (S), in Onís, Golden Land, 225–30.

Caro, José Eusebio (1817–1853).   "Words of the Last Inca" (V), in Blackwell, 414–16; in Jones, Before 1888, 206–07.

Carrasquilla, Tomás (1858–1940).   "Simon Magus" (S), in Onís, Golden Land, 146–63.

Castro Saavedra, Carlos (1924—).   "Wife America" (V), in Flakoll, 22–24.

Escobar Uribe, Jorge ("Claudio de Alas," 1886–1918).   Three poems in Poet Lore, vol. 35, 1924, 456–63.

Flórez, Julio (1867–1923).   Poems in Blackwell, 416–19; Pan American Magazine, vol. 24, 1917, 238, and vol. 26, 1918, 213; and in Walsh, 687.

García Márquez, Gabriel (1928—).   No One Writes to the Colonel, and Other Stories. Tr. J. S. Bernstein. N.Y., Harper, 1968. 170 pp.

————"The Day After Saturday" (S). Tr. Jean Franco, in Cohen, 182–202.

————"Isabel's Soliloquy: Watching the Rain in Macondo" (S). Tr. Richard Southern, in Franco, 63–81.

García Tejada, Juan Manuel (1774–1845).   "To Christ on the Cross" (V), in Walsh, Catholic Anthology, 233.

Gómez Jayme, Alfredo (1878—?).   Poems in Blackwell; Bulletin Pan American Union, July 1925; Inter-America, vol. 8, 1924, 55–64; Pan American Magazine, vol. 35, 1922, 32; Poetry, vol. 26, 1925, 127.

Gómez Restrepo, Antonio (1869–1947).   Poems in Walsh, 619–21; and Walsh, Catholic Anthology, 362.

Henao, Jesús María (1870—?) and Girardo Arrubla.   History of Colombia (H, 1911–12). Tr. J. Fred Rippy. Chapel Hill, Univ. of North Carolina Pr., 1938. 578 pp.

Isaacs, Jorge (1837–1895). María, A South American Romance (N, 1867);
Tr. Rollo Ogden. N.Y., Harper, 1890. Repr. 1918, 1925, 302 pp.
Excerpts in Garnett, Universal Anthology, vol. 32, 184; Jones, Before
1888, 157–63; Tales, vol. 8; C. D. Warner, Library of World's Best
Literature, vol. 20, 1897, 8046–56.

López, Luis Carlos (1883–1950). Poems in Decisions, vol. 1, 1941, 48.
Fantasy, no. 27, 1943, 68; Fitts, 199–206; Hispanic Poets, 212; Jones,
Since 1888, 95–98; Literary Digest, vol. 69, 1921, 34; Others, vol. 3,
1916, 48; Poetry, vol. 26, 1925, 126–27; Walsh, 711–14.

Marroquín, Lorenzo (1856–1918). Peace (N, 1907). Tr. Isaac Goldberg and
W. V. Schierbrand. N.Y., Brentano, 1920. 480 pp.

Mazas Garbayo, Gonzalo (1904—). "The Valley" (S), in Colford, 172–77.

**Osorio, Miguel Ángel ("Ricardo Arenales," "Porfirio Barba Jacob,"
1883–1942).** Poems in Jones, Since 1888, 90–92; Underwood, 71;
West Indian Review, vol. 4, May 1938, 30.

Pardo y Farelo, Enrique ("Luis Tablanca," 1883—). "Country Girl"
(S). Tr. Alida Malkus in Flores FN, 265–82; in Brewton, 689–702.

Pérez, Cecilia. "The Circus" (S), in Américas, vol. 60, 7, July 1957, 23.

————"The Dance in the Wood," ibid., 22–23.

————"The House at the End of the World", ibid., 24.

Pombo, Rafael (1833–1912). "At Niagara" (V, 1854), in Jones, Before
1888, 263–65; and Walsh, 471–83.

Poems in Blackwell, 394; Boston Transcript, Apr. 8, 1926; Bulletin Pan
American Union, Sept. 1926; Pan American Magazine, vol. 39, 1926,
10, 66; Walsh, 471–83; Walsh, Catholic Anthology, 274.

Reyes, Rafael (1851–1921). The Two Americas (H, 1914). Tr. Leopold
Grahame. N.Y., Stokes, 1941. 324 pp.

Rivera, José Eustasio (1889–1928). The Vortex (N, *La vorágine*, 1924). Tr. Earle K. James. N.Y., Putnam, 1935. 320 pp.

  Excerpts in Allen, 44–48; Arciniegas, 26–43; Jones, Since 1888, 208–17.

Samper Ortega, Daniel (1895–1943). "An Old-Fashioned Christmas in the Morning" (S), in Bulletin Pan American Union, vol. 78, 1944, 85–88.

———"A Storm in the Jungle" (S, excerpt from *Zoraya*, 1931), ibid., vol. 68, 1933.

Silva, José Asunción (1865–1896). Six poems in Georgiana G. King, A Citizen of the Twilight, José Asunción Silva. N.Y. and London, Longmans, 1921. 38 pp.

  Other poems in Blackwell, 400–04; Bulletin Pan American Union, Sept. 1926; Craig, 32–37; Hispanic Poets, 205–08; Inter-America, vol. 4, 1920, 108–16; Johnson, 70–71; Jones, Since 1888, 85–90; Others, vol. 3, 1916, 52; Pan American Magazine, vol. 41, 1928, 116; Poetry, vol. 26, 1925, 123–25; Walsh, 581–88; Walsh, Catholic Anthology, 339–40.

Téllez, Hernando (1908–1966). "Ashes for the Wind" (S, 1950). Tr. Harriet de Onís, in Onís, SS, 244–49.

———"Just Lather, That's All" (S). Tr. Donald A. Yates, in Flores GSS, 254–59; in Américas, vol. 8, 1, Jan. 1956, 21–24; in Mexican Life, vol. 36, 8, Aug. 1960, 10, 56–57.

———"Rhapsody for Guitar" (S), in Américas, vol. 10, 1, Jan. 1958, 22–24.

Uribe Pedrahita, César (1897—). "The Anaconda Hunt" (excerpt from *Toa* [The Flame Girl], N, 1933), in Jones, Since 1888, 228–32.

Valencia, Guillermo (1873–1943). Poems in Blackwell, 412–15; Bulletin Pan American Union, vol. 62, 1928; Craig, 112–25; Hispanic Poets, 209–11; Jones, Since 1888, 92–95; Pan American Magazine, vol. 26, 1918, 332–34; Poet Lore, vol. 37, 1926, 616–22; Poetry, vol. 26, 1925, 125–26; Walsh; Walsh, Catholic Anthology, 386.

Vargas Tejada, Luis (1802–1829). "My Poor Nerves" (T, two acts, *Las convulsiones*, 1828). Tr. W. E. Bailey in PSA, vol. 1, 1–19.

Zalamea, Jorge (1905—). "The Inn of Bethlehem" (T, one-act, 1941). Tr. Willis K. Jones, in PSA, vol. 2, 97–106.

Costa Rica

Background

Biesanz, J. and M. Costa Rican Life. N.Y., Columbia Univ. Pr. and London, Oxford Univ. Pr., 1944. x, 272 pp.

Jones, Chester Lloyd. Costa Rica and Civilization in the Caribbean. Madison, Wis., Univ. Studies in Social Science 23, 1935. ix, 172 pp. Repr. N.Y., Russell, 1967.
    See also Calvo, in Individual Authors, below.

INDIVIDUAL AUTHORS

Brenes Mesén, Roberto (1874–1947). "Condor's Eyes" (V), in Blackwell, 480.

Calvo, Joaquín Bernardo (1857–1915). The Republic of Costa Rica (H, *Apuntamientos geográficos, estadísticos, e históricos*, 1887). Tr. L. de T. Chicago, Ill. and N.Y., Rand McNally, 1890. 292 pp.

Cardona Pena, Alfredo (1917—). "My Aunt Esther" (V), in Flakoll, 40–42.

"Carmen Lira." See Carvajal, María Isabel.

Carvajal, María Isabel (1888–1949). "Brer Rabbit, Business Man" (S), in Onís, Golden Land, 320–24.

————"The Tales of My Aunt Panchita" (S, 1920), ibid., 317–20.

————"Uvieta" (S). Tr. Astrid Hasbrouck, in Jones, Since 1888, 310–14.

Estrada, Rafael (1901–1934).   Three poems in Fitts, 157–60.

Fernández Guardia, Ricardo (1867—?).   *Cuentos Ticos*: Short Stories of Costa Rica (S, 1901). Tr. Gray Casement. Cleveland, Ohio, Burrows Bros., 1905. Repr. 1908, 1925, 307 pp.

> Excerpts in Isaac Goldberg, *Costa Rican Tales* (Girard, Kans., Haldeman-Julius, 1925); in Inter-America, vol. 5, 1921, 25; vol. 8, 1924, 39–42; in Pan American Magazine, vol. 9, 1910, 220–33, 458–63; vol. 16, 1916, 59–62.

————History of the Discovery and Conquest of Costa Rica (H, 1905). Tr. Harry W. Van Dyke. N.Y., Crowell, 1913. xxi, 416 pp.

————"Chivalry" (S), in Clark, 897–902.

González Zeladón, Manuel (1865–1936).   "The Two Musicians" (S), in Bulletin Pan American Union, vol. 68, 1934, 201–2; and in LLA.

Varona, Esteban Antonio de.   *Orosi* (H). Tr. Mrs. Gisela Gerberich. San José, Costa Rica, Trejos, 1949. 47 pp.

Cuba

Background

Guerra y Sánchez, Ramiro (1880—).   Sugar and Society in the Caribbean: An Economic History of Cuban Agriculture (H, *Azúcar y población en las Antillas*, 1961). Tr. Marjory M. Urquidi. New Haven, Conn., Yale Univ. Pr., 1964. 218 pp.

Nelson, Lowry.   Rural Cuba. Minneapolis, Univ. of Minnesota Pr., 1950, and London, Oxford Univ. Pr., 1951. x, 285 pp.

Seers, Dudley, ed.   Cuba, the Economic and Social Revolution. Chapel Hill, Univ. of North Carolina Pr., 1964. xx, 432 pp.

Collections

Cohen, J. M., ed.   Writers in the New Cuba. Penguin, 1967. 192 pp.
Twenty-three stories, poems, etc., various trs.   Cohen, Cuba

Mallan, Lloyd, ed. and tr.   "A Little Anthology of Afro-Cuban Poetry," in New Directions 8, 1944, 267–93.

Stoddard, Florence Jackson.   As Old as the Moon: Cuban Legends: Folklore of the Antilles. N.Y., Doubleday Page, 1909. xxv, 205 pp.

INDIVIDUAL AUTHORS

Acosta, Agustín (1886—).   Two poems in West Indian Review, vol. 3, Feb. 1937, 35.

Agüero, Luis (1938—).   "Santa Rita's Holy Water" (S). Tr. J. M. Cohen, in Cohen, Cuba, 167–74.

Arcocha, Juan.   Candle in the Wind. Tr. Lenna Jones. N.Y., Lyle Stuart, 1968. 187 pp.

Arenal, Humberto (1926—).   The Sun Beats Down (N, *El Sol a plomo*). Tr. Joseph M. Bernstein. N.Y., Hill and Wang, 1959. 96 pp.

————"Mister Charles" (S). Tr. J. M. Cohen, in Cohen, Cuba, 88–98.

Arrufat, Antón (1935—).   "The Discovery" (S). Tr. J. G. Brotherston, in Cohen, Cuba, 100–14.

Baragaño, José Álvarez (1932–1962).   Poem in Cohen, Cuba, 139.

Bobadilla, Emilio ("Fra Candil," 1867–1920).   "Spring" (V), in West Indian Review, vol. 3, Jan. 1937, 35.

Borrero de Luján, Dulce María (1883—?).   Poems in Blackwell, 490–95; Bulletin Pan American Union, vol. 6, 1928, 1214–19; West Indian Review, vol. 3, Sept. 1936, 37.

Brull, Mariano (1891–1956).   Poems in Pan American Magazine, vol. 27, 1918, 40; in Walsh, 759–62.

Buesa, José Ángel (1910—).   Five poems in West Indian Review, vol. 5, Nov. 1938, 31–32.

Byrne, Bonifacio (1861–1936).   Poems in Blackwell, 498–500; and West Indian Review, vol. 4, July 1938, 27.

Cabrera Infante, Guillermo (1929—).   "At the Great 'Ecbo' " (S). Tr. J. G. Brotherston, in Cohen, 203–15.

————"A Sparrow's Nest in the Awning" (S). Tr. J. M. Cohen, in Cohen Cuba, 150–57.

Cardoso, Onelio Jorge (1914—).   "The Cat's Second Death" (S). Tr. J. G. Brotherston, in Cohen, Cuba, 37–45.

————"It's a Long Time Ago." (S). Tr. the same, in Cohen, 251–59.

Carpentier, Alejo (1904—).   "The Explosion in a Cathedral" (N, *El siglo de las luces*). Tr. John Sturrock from the French version. London, Gollancz, and Boston, Mass., Little Brown, 1963. 351 pp.

————The Kingdom of This World (N, 1949). Tr. Harriet de Onís. N.Y., Knopf, 1957. 150 pp. Repr. London, Gollancz, 1967.

————The Lost Steps (N, 1953). Tr. Harriet de Onís. N.Y., Knopf, and London, Gollancz, 1956. 278 pp. Repr. Penguin, 1968, 252 pp.
Excerpts in New World Writing, 1956, 51–66.

————"Manhunt" (S), in Noon, vol. 2, 1959, 109–180.

————"Return to the Seed" (S). Tr. Zoila Nelken, in Torres, 95–110.
Tr. Jean Franco as "Journey to the Seed," in Cohen, 53–66.

Casals, Julián del (1863–1893).   Poems in Hispanic Poets, 219; Johnson, 56–59; Jones, Since 1888, 72–74; Walsh, 564–68; Walsh, Catholic, 337; West Indian Review, vol. 2, July 1936, 24, 43–48.

Casey, Calvert (1923—).   "The Execution" (S). Tr. J. G. Brotherston in Cohen, Cuba, 12–34.

————"The Lucky Chance" (S). Tr. J. M. Cohen, ibid., 48–57.

Castellanos, Jesús (1879–1912).   "An Idyll in a Minor Key" (S), in Tales, vol. 8.

Desnoes, Edmondo (1930—).   Inconsolable Memories (*Memorias del sub-desarollo*). Tr. the author, foreword by Jack Gelber. N.Y., New Amer. Lib., 1967, and London, Deutsch, 1968. 155 pp.

Díaz Rodríguez, Jesús (1941—).   "The Cripple" (S). Tr. J. M. Cohen, in Cohen, Cuba, 159–65.

Estorino, Abelardo (1925—).   "Cain's Mangoes" (T). Tr. J. M. Cohen, in Cohen, Cuba, 115–35.

Fernández, Pablo Armando (1930—).   Poems in Cohen, 233–34; in Cohen, Cuba, 86–87.

Ferrara y Marino, Orestes (1876—?).   The Last Spanish War: Revelations in "Diplomacy" (H, *Tentativas de intervención en América*). Tr. William E. Shea. N.Y., Paisley Pr., 1937. 151 pp. Repr. N.Y., Facsimile Library Pubs., 1940.

Ferreira, López, Ramón (1921—).   "Dream with No Names" (S). Tr. Paul Blackburn, in Prize Stories, 360–73.

Floret, Eugenio (1903—).   Poems in Fantasy, no. 27, 1943, 91; Fitts, 29–36.

Gómez de Avellaneda y Arteaga, Gertrudis (1814–1873).   Belshazzar (T, 4 acts, 1858). Tr. William Freeman Burbank. London, Stevens and Brown, and San Francisco, Calif., A. M. Robertson, 1914. 64 pp.

Excerpts in Jones, Before 1888, 334–40; and Poet Lore, vol. 17, 1906, 118–38.

————Cuauhtémoc, The Last Aztec Emperor. Tr. Mrs. W. W. Blake. Mexico, Hoeck, 1898.

————Love Letters. Tr. D. Malcolm. Havana, 1957. 96 pp.

————"An Anecdote from the Life of Cortes" (S, from *Guatimozin*, N, 1846), in Onís, Golden Land, 106–15.

Poems in Blackwell, 490; Green and Lowenfels, 280–355; in Hispanic Poets, 215; Jones, Before 1888, 255–56; Poor, 388–95; Walsh, 434–36; West Indian Review, vol. 2, May 1936, 34.

González, Reynaldo (1931—). "Four in a Jeep" (S). Tr. Jean Franco, in Cohen, Cuba, 175–78.

González-Aller, Faustino. "The Yoke" (S). Tr. Isaac Langnas, in Prize Stories, 201–40.

Guevara, Ernesto "Che" (1920–1967). Che Guevara on Guerrilla Warfare. N.Y., M R Pr., 1961. 127 pp. Repr. N.Y., Praeger, 1963, 85 pp.

————The Complete Bolivian Diaries and Other Captured Documents. Ed. with intro. Daniel James. London, George Allen, 1968. 330 pp.

————Socialism and Man in Cuba, and Other Works. London, Stage 1, 1968. 68 pp., paper.

Guillén, Nicolás (1902—). *Cuba Libre* (V). Tr. Langston Hughes and Ben F. Carruthers. Los Angeles, Ward Ritchie Pr., 1949. 107 pp.

Other poems in American Prefaces, vol. 7, 1941–42, 160–61; in Decision, vol. 1, 1941, 50–57; Fantasy, no. 26, 1942, 69, and no. 27, 1943, 55; Fitts, 262–77; Hays, 218–37; Jones, Since 1888, 74–78; Nation, vol. 153, 1941, 671; Poetry, vol. 62, 1943, 69; West Indian Review, vol. 2, Sept. 1935, 41.

Heredia y Campuzano, José María (1803–1839). Selections from the Poems of Heredia. Tr. verse James Kennedy. Havana, J. M. Eleizegui, 1844. 32 pp.

> Tr. Elijah C. Hills in The Odes of Bello, Olmedo, and Heredia. N.Y., Hispanic Soc., 1920. viii, 153 pp.

———"Ode to Niagara" (V). Tr. William Cullen Bryant, in U.S. Review and Literary Gazette, vol. 1, 1827, 283–86 (the first Latin American poem pub. in English tr. in the U.S.). Repr. in Bulletin Pan American Union, vol. 73, 1939, 439–52; in Jones, Before 1888, 252–54.

> Other poems in Blackwell, 486–89; Green and Lowenfels, 668–73; Francisco González del Valle, *Poesía de Heredia traducidas a otros idiomas* (Havana, Molina, 1940); E. C. Hills, *Hispanic Studies* (Stanford Univ. Pr., 1929); James Kennedy, *Modern Poets and Poetry of Spain* (London, Longmans, 1852); *North American Review*, vol. 68, 1849, 129; Poor; Vingut, *Joyas*; Vingut, *Selections*.

Hernández Catá, Alfonso (1885–1940). "Beneath the Revolving Light," (S), in Inter-America, vol. 7, 1924, 277–97.

———"Death in the Light House" (S), in Alhambra, June 1929, 10.

———"The Servant Girl" (S, *La Galleguita*). Tr. Harry Kurz, in Haydn, 927–33.

Hernández Miyares, Enrique (1854–1914). "The Most Beautiful" (V), in Blackwell, 498; Bulletin Pan American Union, vol. 62, 1928, 146–56; Jones, Since 1888, 68–69; Poetry, vol. 26, 1925, 128; Walsh, 538.
Often called "the most beautiful sonnet of the epoch."

Jamis, Fayad (1930—). Poems in Cohen, Cuba, 58–59.

Lizaso y González, Félix (1891—). Martí, Martyr of Cuban Independence (B). Tr. Esther E. Shuler. Albuquerque, Univ. of New Mexico Pr., 1953. 260 pp.

Llopis, Rogelio (1926—). "A Horrible Man" (S). Tr. Jean Franco, in Cohen, Cuba, 140–49.

Luaces, Joaquín Lorenzo (1827–1867). "On Leaving the Coffee Plantation" (V), in Jones, Before 1888; and World Affairs, Sept. 1942.

Mañach, Jorge (1898—). Martí, Apostle of Freedom (B). Tr. Coley
Taylor, with pref. Gabriela Mistral. N.Y., Devin-Adair, 1950. Repr. Las
Americas, 1963, 363 pp.

Marré, Luis (1929—). Poems in Cohen, Cuba, 99.

Martí, José (1853–1895). The America of José Martí: Selected Writings (E).
Tr. Juan de Onís. N.Y., Noonday Pr., 1953. xiii, 335 pp.

————Martí on the U.S.A. Selected and tr. Luis A. Baralt. Carbondale,
Southern Illinois Univ. Pr., 1966. xxxi, 223 pp.

————"Love Is Repaid by Love" (T, one act: *Amor con amor se paga*). Tr.
Willis K. Jones, in Archivos de José Martí, vol. 2, 1947, 50–60.

————Tuya, Other Verses from José Martí. Tr. Charles Cecil from *Versos
sencillos*. N.Y., J. E. Richardson, 1898. 75 pp.

Other poems in Johnson, 5–55; Jones, Since 1888, 69–72.

Cf. the biography by Lizaso y González above; and Richard B. Gray, *José
Martí Cuban Patriot* (Gainesville, Univ. of Florida Pr., 1962, 307 pp.).

Martínez Moles, Manuel. "A Roof-Thatching Party in Cuba" (S), in
Amigos, vol. 1, Mar. 1942, 17–21.

Milanés y Fuentes, José Jacinto (1814–1863). Poems in North American
Review, vol. 68, 1849, 144; West Indian Review, vol. 2, May 1936, 34;
Jones, Before 1888, 268–69.

Montes de Oca, Marco Antonio (1931—). Poems in Cohen, 216–18.

Novás Calvo, Lino (1905—). "The Dark Night of Ramón Yendía" (S). Tr.
Raymond Sayers, in Onís, SS, 139–64.

Tr. Zoila Nelken, in Torres, 23–24.

Ortíz, Fernando.   Cuban Counterpoint: Tobacco and Sugar (E, 1940). Tr. Harriet de Onís. N.Y., Knopf, 1947. 312 pp.

Padilla, Heberto (1932—).   Poem (extracts) in Cohen, Cuba, 46–47.

Pedroso, Regino (1896—).   Poems in Fantasy, no. 27, 1943, 56; Fitts, 227–30; Jones, Since 1888, 78–79; Tomorrow, vol. 2, Sept. 1935, 40–43; West Indian Review, vol. 1, June 1935, 42.

Piñera, Virgilio (1912—).   The Dragée (S). Tr. J. M. Cohen, in Cohen, Cuba, 60–85.

Pita Rodríguez, Felix (1909—).   "Tobías" (S). Tr. Zoila Nelken, in Torres, 11–23.

"Plácido":   see Valdés, Gabriel de la Concepción.

Poveda, José Manuel (1888–1926).   Poems in Poetry, vol. 17, 1925, 129; Walsh, 742; West Indian Review, vol. 3 Feb. 1937, 49.

Ramon, the Rover of Cuba: The Personal Narrative of That Celebrated Pirate. Tr. anon. Boston, Lord and Holbrook, 1829. xii, 164 pp.

Ramos, José Antonio (1885–1946).   "The Traitor" (T, one act). Tr. Willis K. Jones, in PSA, vol. 2.

————"When Love Dies" (T, one act). Tr. Isaac Goldberg, in Frank Shay, Twenty-five Short Plays. N.Y., Appleton, 1925, pp. 125–46.

Retamar, Roberto Fernández (1930—).   Poems in Cohen, Cuba, 35–36.

Rigali, Rolando (1941—).   Poem ibid., 158.

Serpa, Enrique (1899—).   "Against Regulations" (S), in Colford, 180–86.

Simo, Ana María (1943—).   "A Deathly Sameness" (S). Tr. J. M. Cohen, in Cohen, Cuba, 136–38.

————"Growth of the Plant" (S). Tr. idem, ibid., 179–82.

Uhrbach, Carlos Pío (1872–1897). "Silver Rhyme" (V), in West Indian Review, vol. 3, Nov. 1936, 32.

Uhrbach, Federico (1873–1931). "Retrogression" (V), in West Indian Review, vol. 3, Nov. 1936, 33.

Valdés, Gabriel de la Concepción ("Plácido," 1809–1844). Poems in Inter-America, vol. 8, 1924, 160–68; Jones, Before 1888, 266–68; London Quarterly Review, Jan. 1848; North American Review, vol. 68, 1849, 147–60; Vingut, *Joyas*, and Selections; Walsh, 431–33; Walsh, Catholic, 256–57; West Indian Review, vol. 2, May 1936, 23–24.

Varona, Enrique José (1849–1933). Cuba vs. Spain (H, 1895). Tr. anon. N.Y., Ruben's Pr., 1895. 28 pp.

The title on the cover is Manifesto of the Cuban Revolutionary Party to the United States of America.

Villaverde, Cirilo ("Simon de la Paz," 1812–1894). The Quadroon, or Cecilia Valdés (N, *Cecilia Valdés o la Loma del ángel*, 1839–79; 1882). Tr. Mariano J. Lorente. Boston, L. C. Page, 1935. 399 pp.

Tr. Sydney G. Gest as Cecilia Valdés. N.Y., Vantage Pr., 1962. 546 pp. Excerpt in Jones, Before 1888, 127–32.

Vitiers, Cintio (1921—). "Words of the Prodigal Son" (V), in Flakoll, 106–13.

Zenea, Juan Clemente ("Adolfo de la Azucena," 1832–1871). "A Day of Slavery" (V), in West Indian Review, vol. 2, May 1936, 34.

Dominican Republic

Bosch, Juan (1909—). David, the Biography of a King. Tr. John Marks. N.Y., Hawthorn, and London, Chatto, 1966. 224 pp.

————The Unfinished Experiment. N.Y., Praeger, 1965. xvi, 239 pp.

─────"The Beautiful Soul of Don Damian" (S). Tr. Lysander Kemp, in New World Writing, vol. 14, 1958, 129–36.

─────"The Great Highway" (S). Tr. E. W. Underwood, in West Indian Review, vol. 4, 1940, 18.

─────"His Master" (S). Tr. Helen B. MacMillan, in New Mexico Quarterly, vol. 14, 1944, 339–42.

─────"Two Dollars Worth of Water" (S), in Onís, Golden Land, 302–10.

Díaz Ordóñez, Alejandro. "Arcadia" (S), in Américas, vol. 12, 6, June 1960, 24–26; and Mexican Life, vol. 36, 10, Oct. 1960, 13–16, 58–59.

─────"Columbus in Hispaniola" (S), in LLA.

─────"Father Image" (S), in Américas, vol. 11, 4, Apr. 1959, 20–21; and Mexican Life, vol. 36, 2, Feb. 1960, 10, 66.

─────"Mice" (S), in Américas, vol. 10, 7, July 1958, 24–25; and Mexican Life, vol. 35, 12, Dec. 1959, 10, 65–66.

Fiallo, Fabio (1879–1926). "The Marble Bust" (S), in Clark, 949–50.

─────"The Rivals" (S), in Inter-America, vol. 9, 1926, 481–87.

─────Poems of the Little Girl in Heaven (V). Tr. Margaret B. Hurley. Ciudad Trujillo, La Opinión, 1937. 69 pp.

Other poems in Blackwell, 502–06; Jones, Since 1888, 67–68; Poetry, vol. 26, 1925, 148; West Indian Review, vol. 2, 1936: Feb., p. 36, Mar., p. 3, Dec., p. 43; vol. 3, 1937, May, p. 21; vol. 4, 1938: Apr., p. 30, May, pp. 21, 43.

Galván, Manuel de Jesús (1834–1910). The Cross and the Sword (N, Enriquillo, 1879). Tr. Robert Graves. Bloomington, Indiana Univ. Pr., 1954. 366 pp.
Excerpt in Jones, Before 1888, 132–38.

Henríquez Ureña, Max (1885—). "A Look at Dominican Literature" (E), in Américas, vol. 12, 11, Nov. 1960, 28–30.

————"Provincial Idyll" (V), in West Indian Review, vol. 2, Jan. 1936, 35.

Henríquez Ureña, Pedro (1884–1946). *Seis ensayos en busca de nuestra expresión* (E, 1928). Excerpts in Bulletin Pan American Union, vol. 68, 1934, 206–08.
 See above, Literary Studies, for his more general works.

Nanita, Abelardo René. Trujillo: A Full-Size Portrait (B, *Trujillo de cuerpo entero*, 1939). Tr. M. A. Moore. 5th ed. Ciudad Trujillo, Editora del Caribe, 1954. 385 pp.

Ovando, Leonor de (?–1610?). "Sonnet" (V). Tr. J. C. Barden, in Bulletin Pan American Union, vol. 64, 1940, 828.

Pellerano Castro, Arturo B. (1865–1916). "Americana" (V), in West Indian Review, vol. 2, Feb. 1936, 33.

Pérez, José Joaquín (1845–1900). "Home Coming" (V), in West Indian Review, vol. 2, Feb. 1936, 33.

Quisqueya, a Panoramic Anthology of Dominican Verse. Ed. and tr. Francis Edward Townsend. Ciudad Trujillo, Editora del Caríbe, 1954. (2d ed.) 101 pp.

Sanz Lajara, J. M. *"Calamidad"* (S), in Américas, vol. 10, 11, Nov. 1958, 17–18.

————"Little Ants" (S), ibid., vol. 11, 8, Aug. 1959, 27–29.

Thaly, Daniel (1880—?). Poems in West Indian Review, vol. 2, 1935, Oct., 36–37; vol. 3, 1936–37, Oct., 48–49; Feb., 31; Apr., 33; May, 35; vol. 4, 1940, July, 36, 37.

Ureña de Henríquez, Salomé (1850–1897). Poems in Blackwell, 508–15; Inter-America, vol. 8, 1925, 387–94; West Indian Review, vol. 2, 1936, Jan., 34.

Ecuador

Background

Bloomberg, Rolf, ed. Ecuador: Andean Mosaic. Stockholm, Hugo Gebers, 1952, and Los Angeles, Calif., Knud Mogensen, 1953. 319 pp.

Linke, Lilo. Ecuador, Country of Contrasts. London, Royal Institute of International Affairs, 1954. 173 pp. Repr. 1956.

INDIVIDUAL AUTHORS

Aguilera Malta, Demetrio (1909—). Don Goyo (N, 1933). Tr. Enid E. Perkins, in Flores FN, 120–228.

————*La isla virgen* (1942). Excerpts in Jones, Since 1888, 204–08.

————Manuela (N, *La caballeresa del sol*, 1964). Tr. Willis Knapp Jones. Carbondale, Southern Illinois Univ. Pr., 1967. 304 pp.

————"The Cholo Who Hated Money" (S). Tr. Erik de Mauny, in Adam International Review, vol. 17, 1949, Apr., 193–94, May, 19.

————**and Willis K. Jones.** Blue Blood (T, 3 acts, 1946). Washington, D.C., Pan American Union, 1948. 53 pp.

Campos, José Antonio ("Jack the Ripper," 1868–1930). Twenty-two stories in Inter-America, vols. 1–5, 1918–23.

————"Ecuadorean Sketches" (S, *Cosas de mi tierra*, 1906), in Inter-America, vol. 2, 1919, 223–26; vol. 3, 1920, 235–40; vol. 6, 1924, 324–29, 361–73.

————"Guaranteed Timepieces" (S), in Andean Monthly, vol. 1, 1939, 38.

————"Mamerto's Mother-in-law" (S), in Jones, Since 1888, 355–58.

Carrera Andrade, Jorge (1903—). To the Bay Bridge (V). Tr. Eleanor L. Turnbull. Stanford, Calif., Hoover Library, 1941. 20 pp.

————Secret Country (V). Tr. Muna Lee. N.Y., Macmillan, 1946. xvi, 77 pp.

————Visitor of Mist. Tr. G. R. Coulthard and Kathleen Knott. London, Williams and Norgate, 1950. 74 pp.

Poems, in American Prefaces, vol. 7, 1941–42, 145–46; Fantasy, no. 26, 1942, 57–59; Fitts, 3–20; Hays, 140–67; Jones, Since 1888, 104–07; Poetry, vol. 59, 1942, 386; Three Spanish American Poets, 49–73; Tomorrow, vol. 2, 1943, 28; West Indian Review, vol. 4, 1937, Oct., 24.

Cuadra, José de la (1903–1941). "Valley Hunt" (S). Tr. Harry Kurz, in Haydn, 877–82.

Escudero, Gonzalo (1903—). Poems in American Prefaces, vol. 7, 1941–42; Fitts, 355–57; Poetry, vol. 26, 1925, 131.

Gallegos, Luis Gerardo (1905—). "An Old Pirate Print of Haiti" (S). Tr. E. W. Underwood, in West Indian Review, vol. 5, 1939, March, 29.

————"The Mountains of Trinidad," in Amigos, vol. 1, 1942, 43–48.

Gallegos Lara, Joaquín (1907?–1947). "The Guaraguao" (S). Tr. Erik de Mauny, in Adam International Review, vol. 17, 193–94, Apr.–May, 1949, 8–10.

Gil Gilbert, Enrique (1912—). Our Daily Bread (Nuestro pan, 1941). Tr. Dudley Poore. N.Y., Farrar and Rinehart, 1943. 246 pp.

González-Suárez, Federico (1844–1917). "Atahualpa" (S). Tr. G. R. Coulthard, in Adam International Review, vol. 17, 193–94, Apr.–May 1949, 10.

Icaza, Jorge (1902—). Huasipungo (N, 1934). Tr. anon. in International Literature (Moscow, Feb. 1936).

Tr. Mervyn Seville. London, Dobson, 1962. 171 pp.

Tr. Bernard M. Dulsey as The Villagers. Carbondale, Southern Illinois Univ. Pr., 1964. xv, 223 pp.

Excerpts in Jones, Since 1888, 190–98.

————"The Cave of the Devil" (S). Tr. C. A. Hutchinson, in Tomorrow, vol. 3, 8, Apr. 1944, 28–31; and Mexican Life, vol. 21, 1, Jan. 1945, 21–22, 87–90.

————"A Tomb for the Corpse" (S). Tr. C. A. Hutchinson, in Kenyon Review, vol. 3, 1943, 346–56.

Mera, Juan León de (1832–1894).   Cumandá (N, 1879). Excerpts in Jones, Before 1888, 163–68.

Montalvo, Juan (1832–1888).   "An Ecuadorean View" (E), in Américas, vol. 3, 4, Apr. 1951, 44–45.

————"Urcu Sacha" (E, Language of the New World), and "What Is Our Country Like" (E), in Adam International Review, vol. 17, 193–94, Apr.–May, 1949, 20–21.

————"On Pichincha" (V) and "Unlimited Power" (E), in Jones, Before 1888, 153–57.

Olmedo, José Joaquin de (1780–1847).   "The Tree" (V), in Blackwell, 464; and Hills.

————"To General Flores" (V), in Jones, Before 1888, 213–18, and Poor.

Ortiz, Adalberto (1914—).   "The News" (V), in Flakoll, 82–84.

Rendón, Victor (1859–1940).   "The Lottery Ticket" (T, one act, 1924). Tr. Willis K. Jones, in PSA, vol. 2.

Salazar Tamariz, Hugo (1923—).   "The Roots" (V), in Flakoll, 4–10.

Silva, Medardo Ángel (1900–1920).   Poems, in Fantasy, no. 26, 1942, 55; and Jones, Since 1888, 103–04.

Zaldumbide, Gonzalo (1885—).   "The Return" (S). Tr. G. R. Coulthard, in Adam International Review, vol. 17, 193–94, Apr.–May 1949, 27.

Guatemala

Background

Jones, Chester Lloyd.   Guatemala, Past and Present. Minneapolis, Univ. of Minnesota Pr., 1940. xii, 420 pp. Repr. N.Y., Russell, 1966.

Kelsey, Vera, and Osborne, Lilly de Jongh.   Four Keys to Guatemala. N.Y. and London, Funk and Wagnalls, 1939. xiv, 332 pp.

Wagley, Charles.   The Social and Religious Life of a Guatemalan Village. Menasha, Wis., Amer. Anthropological Assn, Memoir 71, 1949. 150 pp.

INDIVIDUAL AUTHORS

The Annals of the Cakchiquels.   Ed. and tr. Daniel G. Brinton from Cakchique. Philadelphia, Pa., Library of Aboriginal American Literature 6, 1885. 234 pp.

> Tr. Adrian Recinos and Delia Goetz from Cakchique (with Title of the Lords of Totonicapan). Norman, Univ. of Oklahoma Pr., 1953. ix, 217 pp. (The Annals at pp. 43–159).

Arévalo, Juan José (1904—).   The Shark and the Sardines (E). Tr. June Cobb and Raúl Osegueda. N.Y., Lyle Stuart, 1961. 256 pp.

Arévalo Martínez, Rafael (1884—).   "The Man Who Resembled a Horse" (S). Tr. William G. and William Carlos Williams, in New Directions 8, 1944, 308–18; and Jones, Since 1888, 280–85.

————"Our Lady of the Afflicted" (S, *Nuestra Señora de los locos*) and "The Panther Man" (S, *Las fieras del trópico*). Tr. Victor Clark, in Living Age, vol. 231, 1924, 800–06, 1005–11, 1046–52.

> Poems in Blackwell, 474–76; Fitts, 485; Inter-America, vol. 1, 1917, 76; Johnson, 176–77; Jones, Since 1888, 285; Living Age, vol. 231, 1924, 801, 1005; Others, vol. 3, 1916, 35–42; Walsh, 731–34.

Asturias, Miguel Ángel (1899—).   The Cyclone: A Novel (*Viento fuerte*, 1950). Tr. Darwin Flakoll and Claribel Alegria. London, Owen, 1967. 238 pp.

> Tr. Gregory Rabassa as Strong Wind. N.Y., Delacorte Pr., 1969. 242 pp.

————*Mulata* (N, *Mulata de tal*, 1963). Tr. Gregory Rabassa. N.Y., Delacorte-Seymour Lawrence, and London, Owen (as The Mulatta and Mr. Fly: A Novel), 1967. vi, 304 pp.

————The President (*El señor presidente*, N, 1946). Tr. Frances Partridge. London, Chatto, 1963, and N.Y., Atheneum (as *El señor presidente*), 1964. 287 pp.

————"The Indians Came Down from Mexico" (V), in Fitts, 523.

————"Legend of the Tattooed Girl" (S). Tr. H. R. Hays, in View, vol. 3, 3, Oct. 1943, 89–90.

> Tr. Adam F. Flecker, in Eugène Jolas, Transition Workshop. N.Y., Vanguard Pr., 1949, pp. 33–37.

Cardoza y Aragón, Luis (1902—).   "Ballad of Federico García Lorca" (V), in Fitts, 523.

Drago-Bracco, Adolfo (1894—).   "Colombine Wants Flowers" (T, one act, 1923). Tr. Willis K. Jones, in Poet Lore, vol. 55, 1950, 144–62.

Gómez Carillo, Enrique (1873–1927).   Among the Ruins (H, *Campos de batalla y campos de ruinas*, 1915). Tr. Florence Simmons. London, Heinemann, 1915. 346 pp.

————In the Heart of the Tragedy (H, 1916). Tr. anon. London and N.Y., Hodder and Stoughton, 1917. 153 pp.

González, Otto Raúl (1921—).   "To the Scavenger" (V), in Flakoll, 80–81.

Monteros, Augusto (1922—).   "First Lady" (S), in Flakoll, 66–76.

Popul Vuh: The Sacred Book of the Ancient Quiché Maya.   Tr. Delia Goetz and Sylvanus J. Morley from the Spanish version by Adrián Recinos.

Norman, Univ. of Oklahoma Pr., 1950, and London, Hodge, 1951. 286 pp. Repr. Los Angeles, Limited Edns Club, 1954, 251 pp.
   Excerpts in Jones, Before 1888, 23–29.

"The Princess Xuchil" (S).   Tr. L. E. Elliott, in Pan American Magazine, vol. 37, 1924, 401–02.

"Rabinal Achí: An Ancient Play of the Quiché Indians of Guatemala" (T).   Tr. Eleanor Wolff, in Mesa, vol. 1, 1945, 4–18.
   Excerpts in Jones, Before 1888, 287–92.

Samayoa Chinchilla, Carlos (1898—).   The Emerald Lizard: Tales and Legends of Guatemala (*Madre Milpa, Cuatro suertes*, etc.). Tr. Joan C. MacLean and Harriet de Onís. Indian Hills, Colo., Falcon's Wing Pr., 1957. 274 pp.

————"The Birth of the Corn" (S), in Onís, Golden Land, 310–13.

The Shepherds' Play of the Prodigal Son (T).   Tr. George C. Barker. Berkeley, Univ. of California Pr., and London, Cambridge Univ. Pr., 1953. 167 pp.

Title of the Lords of Totonicapan.   Tr. Delia Goetz from a Spanish version of the Quiché original (with Annals of the Cakchiquels, q.v. above). Norman, Univ. of Oklahoma Pr., 1953, pp. 161–96.

Wyld Ospina, Carlos (1881–195?).   "The Honor of His House" (S, *La Tierra de los Nahuayacas*). Tr. Joan C. MacLean, in Onís, SS, 87–93.

————"The Woman Tona" (S). Tr. E. W. Underwood, in West Indian Review, vol. 6, Feb.–Mar. 1940, 27.

Honduras

Background

Stokes, William Sylvane. Honduras: An Area Study in Government. Madison, Univ. of Wisconsin Pr., 1950. xii, 351 pp.

INDIVIDUAL AUTHORS

Carías Reyes, Marcos (1905—). "Vignettes of Country Life" (S), in Bulletin Pan American Union, vol. 78, 1944, 94–95.

Díaz Lozano, Argentina (1909—). Enriqueta and I (B, *Peregrinaje*). Tr. Harriet de Onís. N.Y., Farrar and Rinehart, and London, Dennis Dobson, 1945. 217 pp.

————*Mayapán*. Tr. Lydia Wright. Indian Hills, Colo., Falcon's Wing Pr., 1955. 247 pp.

Gillén Zelaya, Alfonso (1888—). Poems, in Others, vol. 3, 1916, 46–47; in Pan American Magazine, vol. 27, 1917–18, 47, 206; Walsh, 151.

Molina, Juan Ramón (1875–1908). Autobiography (V). Tr. J. W. Chaney, in Colorado Springs, Colorado College Language Series, vol. 2, 1921. 35 pp.

Morazán, Francisco (1799–1842). Memorias del general Morazán (H). Excerpts in Jones, Before 1888, 101–03.

Turcios, Froylán (1877–1943). *El vampiro* (N, 1912). Excerpts in Jones, Since 1888, 314–19.

————"Blue Eyes" (V), in Jones, Since 1888, 61–62.

————"The Parricide" (S), in Inter-America, vol. 1, 1917, 12–13.

Valle, Rafael Heliodoro (1891—). "Thirsting Amphora" (V), in Fitts, 483.

Mexico

Background

Alcaraz, Ramón.   The Other Side (H). See Individual Authors, below.

Aragón, Ann.   Mexico, Its Social Evolution (E). See ibid.

Bernal, Ignacio.   Mexico Before Cortez: Art, History, and Legend. Tr. Willis Barnstone. Garden City, N.Y., Doubleday, 1963. 135 pp., paper.

Brenner, Anita.   Idols behind Altars. N.Y., Payson and Clark, 1929. 359 pp.

The Broken Spears: An Aztec Account of the Conquest of Mexico.   See León-Portilla, below, in Individual Authors.

Calderón de la Barca, Frances Erskine.   Life in Mexico during a Residence of Two Years in That Country. Boston, Little Brown, and London, Chapman and Hall, 1843. xii, 436 pp. Repr. London, 1852; Mexico, 1910; EL, 1913 et seq.

Chevalier, François.   Land and Society in Colonial Mexico: The Great Hacienda. Tr. Alvin Eustis and Lesley Byrd Simpson. Berkeley, Univ. of California Pr., and Cambridge, Eng., Univ. Pr., 1964. 334 pp.

Duran, Diego.   The Aztecs: The History of the Indies of New Spain (*Historia de las Indias*). Tr. Doris Hayden and Fernando Horcasitos. London, Cassell, and N.Y., Orion Pr., 1964. xxxi, 381 pp.

Helm, Mackinley.   Modern Mexican Painters. N.Y., Harper, 1941. xxi, 205 pp.

Morley, Sylvanus G.   The Ancient Maya. Palo Alto, Calif. Stanford Univ. Pr., 1946. xxxii, 520 pp.

Myers, B. S.   Mexican Painting in Our Time. London and N.Y., Oxford Univ. Pr., 1957. 283 pp., 124 plates.

Parkes, Henry B.   A History of Mexico. Boston, Mass., Houghton Mifflin, 1938, and London, Methuen, 1939. xii, 432 pp. Rev. 1950, xii, 446 pp.

Ramos, Samuel.   Profiles of Man and Culture in Mexico. Tr. Peter G. Earle. Austin, Univ. of Texas Pr., 1962. 198 pp.

Reyes, Alfonso.   Mexico in a Nutshell. See Individual Authors, below.

Rivera, Diego (1886—?).   Portrait of Mexico (paintings, with text by Bertram D. Wolfe). N.Y., Covici-Friede, and London, George Allen, 1937. 211 pp., 249 plates.

Simpson, Lesley B.   Many Mexicos. N.Y., Putnam, 1941. xiii, 336 pp. Repr. 1946; Berkeley, Univ. of California Pr., 1952.

Spinden, Herbert J.   Ancient Civilizations of Mexico and Central America. N.Y., American Museum Pr., 1928. 242 pp.

Toor, Frances.   A Treasury of Mexican Folkways. N.Y., Crown, 1947. xxxii, 566 pp.

Von Hagen, Victor W.   The Aztec: Man and Tribe. N.Y., New Amer. Lib., 1958. 222 pp., paper.

————The World of the Maya. Ibid., 1960. 224 pp., paper.

Literary Studies

Brushwood, John S.   The Romantic Novel in Mexico. Columbia, Univ. of Missouri Pr., 1954. 98 pp.

————Mexico in Its Novel: A Nation's Search for Identity. Austin and London, Univ. of Texas Pr., 1966. xii, 292 pp.

González Peña, Carlos.   History of Mexican Literature. See Individual Authors, below.

León-Portilla, Miguel.   Pre-Columbian Literature of Mexico. See Individual Authors.

Martínez, José Luis, ed.   The Modern Mexican Essay. Tr. H. W. Hilborn. Toronto, Ont., Univ. of Toronto Pr., 1965. 524 pp.

Read, John L.   The Mexican Historical Novel, 1826–1910. N.Y., Instituto de las Españas, 1939. 337 pp.

Romanell, Patrick.   The Making of the Mexican Mind. Reno, Univ. of Nevada Pr., 1952. ix, 213 pp.

Sommers, Joseph.   After the Storm: Landmarks of the Modern Mexican Novel. Albuquerque, Univ. of New Mexico Pr., 1968. xii, 208 pp.

Collections

Cranfill, Thomas M. ed.   The Muse in Mexico: A Mid-Century Miscellany. Tr. George D. Schade, et al. Austin, Univ. of Texas Pr., 1959. xi, 117 pp. (prose and verse).

"The Eye of Mexico."   Trs. of prose and verse by 17 contemporary authors. Evergreen Review, vol. 2, no. 7, 1959, 22–167.

Fuentes, Patricia, ed. and tr.   The Conquistadors. N.Y., Orion Pr., 1963. xxii, 250 pp.
    First person accounts of the conquest.

Goldberg, Isaac.   Mexican Poetry. Girard, Kans., Haldeman-Julius, 1925. 64 pp., paper.

Paz, Octavio.   Anthology of Mexican Poetry. Tr. Samuel Beckett. Bloomington, Indiana Univ. Pr., 1958. 213 pp.

Starr, Frederick.   Readings from Modern Mexican Authors. Chicago, Ill., Open Court, 1904. vii, 420 pp.

Underwood, Edna W.   Anthology of Mexican Poets from the Earliest Times to the Present Day. Portland, Maine, Mosher, 1932. xxxiii, 332 pp.

INDIVIDUAL AUTHORS

Abreu Gómez, Ermilo (1894—). "Who's Crazy" (S), in Américas, vol. 12, 2, Feb. 1955, 24–26.

Acevedo Escobedo, Antonio (1909—). "Fire in the Rain" (S). Tr. Langston Hughes, in Rocky Mountain Review, vol. 2, 1938, 8.

Acuña, Manuel (1849–1873). Poems in Blackwell, 154–56; Green, 66–175; Inter-America, vol. 1, 1918, 126–28; Jones, Before 1888, 276–79; Stratford Journal, vol. 3, 1918, 118; Underwood, 291–98; West Indian Review, vol. 2, 1936, May, 34.

Alcaraz, Ramón. The Other Side (H, *Apuntas para la historia de la guerra entre México y los Estados Unidos*, 1848). Tr. Albert C. Ramsey. N.Y. and London, Wiley, 1850. 458 pp.

Almada, Bartolomé Eligio. The Diary of Don Bartolomé Almada of Álamos. Tr. Carlota Miles. Tucson, Arizona Silhouettes, 1962. 197 pp.

Altamirano, Ignacio Manuel (1834–1893). Christmas in the Mountains (S, 1871). Tr. Harvey L. Johnson. Gainesville, Univ. of Florida Pr., 1961. 68 pp.
Excerpts in Underwood, 253–59.

———El Zarco the Bandit (N, 1894). Tr. Mary Allt. N.Y., Duchnes, and London, Folio Soc., 1957. 160 pp.
Excerpts in Jones, Before 1888, 176–80.

———"To Atroyac" (V), in Underwood, 253.

Altolaguirre, Manuel. "My Brother Luis" (S). Tr. Stephen Spender, in Mexican Life, vol. 13, Dec. 1937, 18.

Amor, Guadalupe (1920—). "My Mother's Bedroom" (S). Tr. Donald Demarest, in Evergreen Review, vol. 2, 1959, 121–26.

———"The Small Drawing Room," in Mexican Life, vol. 36, 9, Sept. 1960, 15–17, 48.

Aragón, Ann.   Mexico, Its Social Evolution (E). Tr. G. Sentinón. Mexico, J. Ballesca, 1900–04.

Arreola, Juan José (1918—).   *Confabulario* and Other Inventions (S). Tr. George D. Schade. Austin, Univ. of Texas Pr., 1964. 264 pp.

——————Nine Sketches. Tr. Lysander Kemp, in Evergreen Review, vol. 2, 1959, 134–38.

——————"A Christian Gentleman" (S). Tr. Merilu Pease, in Portfolio (Mexico, 1951), 19–27.

——————"The Parable of the Barter" (S). Tr. J. A. Langnas, in Odyssey, vol. 2, 1962, 99–102.

——————"The Prodigious Milligram," in Flakoll, 99–105.

——————"The Rhinoceros." Tr. Irene Nicholson, in New World Writing, vol. 14, 1958, 123–24.

Azuela, Mariano (1873–1952).   Marcela (N, *Mala yerba*, 1909). Tr. Anita Brenner, foreword Waldo Frank. N.Y., Farrar and Rinehart, 1932. 244 pp.

——————Two Novels of Mexico: The Flies and the Bosses (N, 1918, 1917). Tr. Lesley Byrd Simpson. Berkeley, Univ. of California Pr., 1956. 194 pp. Repr. 1961, paper.

——————Two Novels of the Mexican Revolution (N: *Los de abajo*, 1915; *Tribulaciones de una familia decente*, 1919). Tr. Beatrice Berler and Frances Kellam Hendricks. San Antonio, Texas, Trinity Univ. Pr., 1963. 267 pp.

——————The Underdogs (N, *Los de abajo*, 1915). Tr. Enrique Monguía, Jr. N.Y., Brentano, 1929. 224 pp. Repr. Signet, 1963, paper.
   Excerpts in Jones, Since 1888, 257–70.

Barreto, Larry.   "At Oaxtepec" (S), in Mexican Life, vol. 25, 10, Oct. 1949, 10.

——————"Tepozotlán," in Mexican Life, vol. 25, 11, Nov. 1949, 10.

Benavente, Fray Toribio de ("Motolinía," ?–1568). Motilinía's History of the Indians of New Spain (H). Tr. Francis B. Steck. Washington, D.C., Academy of American Franciscan History, 1951. 358 pp.

   Excerpts in Jones, Before 1888, 41–49.

Benítez, Fernando (1910—). The Century after Cortes (H, *Los primeros Mexicanos: la vida criollo en el siglo XVI*). Tr. Joan MacLean. Chicago, Ill., Univ. of Chicago Pr., and London, Univ. of London Pr., 1965. 296 pp.

————In the Footsteps of Cortés (*La ruta de Hernan Cortés*, 1950). Tr. F. Benítez. N.Y., Pantheon Books, 1952. 256 pp.

Bernal, Rafael. "Natural Causes" (S), in Colford, 155–69.

Blanco, Jorge J. "Morning of a Dictator" (S), in Mexican Life, vol. 11, 7, July 1935, 31–35.

Blasio, José Luis (1842–1923). Maximilian, Emperor of Mexico: Memoirs of His Private Secretary (B, *Maximiliano íntimo*, Paris, 1905). Tr. Robert H. Murray. New Haven, Conn., Yale Univ. Pr., 1934. 235 pp.

Bonifaz Nuño, Rubén (1923—). "The Flower" (V), in Flakoll, 60–63.

Cabada, Juan de la (1903—). "In the Drizzle" (S), in Mexican Life, vol. 35, 3, Mar. 1959, 13–14.

————"Maria-the-Voice," ibid., vol. 35, 11, Nov. 1959, 11–12, 54–62.

————"A Sailor in Campeche," ibid., vol. 10, 4, Apr. 1934, 15–16, 45–47.

Cabrera, Rafael (1884—?). Poems in Blackwell, 130–37; Goldberg, 62–64; Pan American Magazine, vol. 26, 1918, 256; Stratford Journal, vol. 5, 1919, 59–66.

Calderón, Fernando (1809–1845). Poems in Green, 222–51; and Underwood, 233.

Camarillo y Roa de Pereyra, María Enriqueta (1875—?). Poems in Goldberg, 61; Hispanic Poets, 235; Underwood, 111–16.

Campo, Enrique del.   Eleven short stories in Mexican Life, vol. 3, 1927, to vol. 14, 1940.

Campobello, Nellie ("Francisca," 1909—).   Four poems in Fitts, 213–20.

Campos, Rubén M. (1876–1943).   "Tropic Nocturne" (V), in Underwood, 105–06.

Carballido, Emilio (1925—).   The Norther (*El Norte*). Tr. Margaret Sayers Peden. Austin, Univ. of Texas Pr., 1968. 101 pp. ill.

————"The Empty Coffin" (S), in Mexican Life, vol. 35, 10, Oct. 1959, 11–12, 60–62.

Carleton Millán, Verna.   47 stories in Mexican Life, vols. 24, 1949 to 30, 1954.

Carvajal, Luis de (el Mozo, 1567?–1596).   The Enlightened: The Writings. Ed. and tr. Seymour B. Liebman, pref. Allen Nevins. Coral Gables, Fla., Univ. of Miami Pr., 1967. 157 pp.

Castellanos, Rosario (1925—).   The Nine Guardians (N, *Balun-Canan*, 1957). Tr. Irene Nicholson. London, Faber, 1959, and N.Y., Vanguard, 1960. 272 pp.

————"The Foreign Woman" (V). Tr. J. M. Cohen, in Cohen, 103–05.

Cervantes de Salazar, Francisco (1515?–1575?).   Life in the Imperial and Royal City of Mexico . . . as Described in the Dialogues for the Study of the Latin Language (E, 1554). Tr. Minnie Lee Barrett Shepard, intro. Carlos Eduardo Castañeda. Austin, Univ. of Texas Pr., 1953. 113 pp.

Chas de Chruz, Israel.   "The Job" (S). Tr. Anita Brenner, in Menorah Journal, vol. 18, 1930, 159–63.
From *El Asesino de sí mismo y otros cuentos* (1929).

Cháves, Carlos (1899—).   Toward a New Music (E). Tr. Herbert Weinstock. N.Y., Norton, 1937. 180 pp.

Chumacero, Alí (1918—). "Epitaph for a Virgin" (V). Tr. J. M. Cohen, in Cohen, 106.

Cirerol Sansorses, Manuel. "The Dwarf King of Usmal" (S), in Américas, vol. 12, 8, Aug. 1960, 23–25.

Clavijero, Francisco Javier (1731–1789). The History of Lower California (H, *Storia della California*). Tr. Sarah E. Lake and A. A. Gray. Stanford, Calif., Stanford Univ. Pr., and London, Oxford Univ. Pr., 1937. xxvii, 437 pp.

————The History of Mexico, Collected from Spanish and Mexican Historians (H). Tr. Charles Cullen from Italian original (1780–81). London, Robinson, 1787. 2 vols. Repr. 1789; Richmond, Va., Pritchard, 1806; London, 1807; Philadelphia, Pa., Dobson, 1817, repr. 1832.

Colín, Eduardo (1880–1945). "After the Rain" (V), in Underwood, 120.

Cortés, Hernando (1485–1547). The Despatches (*Cartas de relación*, 1519–26). Tr. George Folsom. N.Y. and London, Wiley and Putnam, 1843. xii, 431 pp.

Four letters; the fifth [actually the sixth, the first being lost], on the Honduras expedition, remained in manuscript until 1848. It was first pub. in English, tr. Don Pascual de Gayangos, in Hakluyt Society Works, no. 40, 1868, xvi, 156 pp.; repr. N.Y., Burt Franklin, 1963.

Tr. Francis A. MacNutt as Letters of Cortes: Five Letters of Relation. N.Y. and London, Putnam, 1908. 2 vols. Repr. Glendale, Calif., Clark, 1941.

Tr. abridged J. Bayard Morris as Five Letters. (Broadway Travellers) London, Routledge, 1928, and (Argonaut Series) N.Y., McBride, 1929. xlvii, 388 pp. Repr. N.Y., Norton, 1962, paper.

Excerpts in Jones, Before 1888, 33–38.

Cosío Villegas, Daniel (1900—). American Extremes (E, *Extremos de América*, 1949). Tr. Américo Paredes. Austin, Univ. of Texas Pr., 1964. 227 pp.

————The United States versus Porfirio Díaz (E). Tr. Nettie Lee Benson. Lincoln, Univ. of Nebraska Pr., 1963. 259 pp.

Cruz, Sor Juana Inés de la.   See Juana Inés de la Cruz.

Cuenca, Agustín F. (1850–1884).   Poems in Blackwell, 162–64; Goldberg, 17–18; Pan American Magazine, vol. 18, 1914, 29; Poor; Underwood, 308.

Delgado, Rafael (1853–1914).   Calandria (N, 1891). Excerpts in Starr, 395.

—————"The Deserter" (S). Tr. H. C. Schweikert, in Golden Book, vol. 3, 1927, 689–92.

—————"The Little Grouse" (S). Tr. Robert Cleland, in Mexican Life, vol. 32, 8, Aug. 1956, 33–34, 78.

—————"In the Mountains" (V), in Underwood, 138.

Díaz Covarrubias, Juan (1837–1859).   Poems in Underwood, 260–61.

Díaz del Castillo, Bernal (1495?–1584).   The True History of the Conquest of Mexico, by One of the Conquerors (1568). Tr. Maurice Keatinge. London, J. Wright, 1800. viii, 514 pp. Repr. Salem, Mass., 1803; (Argonaut Series) N.Y., McBride, 1927, and London, Harrap, 1928, 2 vols., repr. N.Y. 1938.

Tr. John G. Lockhart as The Memoirs of the Conquistador. London, Hatchard, 1844. 2 vols.

Tr. Alfred Percival Maudslay from ms. Hakluyt Soc. Works, ser. 2, nos. 23, 24, 25, 30, 40 (5 vols.), 1908–16. Repr. (Broadway Travellers) London, Routledge, and N.Y., Dutton, 1928, vii, 595 pp.; N.Y., Limited Edns Club, 1942; N.Y., Farrar Straus, 1956, and 1965; N.Y., Noonday Pr., 1965, paper.

Tr. Albert Idell. Garden City, N.Y., Doubleday, 1956. 414 pp.

Tr. J. M. Cohen. Penguin, 1965. 412 pp.

Excerpts in Jones, Before 1888, 39–42.

Díaz Mirón, Salvador (1853–1928).   Poems in Blackwell, 118–20; Goldberg, 18; Hispanic Poets, 222; Jones, Since 1888, 31–34; Mexican Life, vol. 3, 6, June 1927, 35; Pan American Magazine, vols. 27, 1919, 60, and 31, 1920,

190; Poetry, vol. 26, 1928, 133; Stratford Journal, vol. 3, 1918, 73; Underwood, 35–39; Walsh, 335–37.

Durán y Casahonda, J. M. "The General's Promise. A Revolutionary Episode" (S), in Mexican Life, vol. 4, 4, Apr. 1928, 19–20, 52–55.

Elizondo, José F. (1880–1943). "The Man Who Craved to Be Everything" (S), in Mexican Life, vol. 10, 8, Aug. 1934, 17–18.

————"Poor Jeremías" (S), ibid., vol. 10, 6, June 1934, 21, 50–51.

————"The Portera" (S), ibid., vol. 10, 5, May 1934, 17–18.

Estrada, Genaro (1887–1937). Poems in Bulletin Pan American Union, vol. 68, 219–221; Fitts, 434–38; Underwood, 22, 141, 302.

Farías de Issasi, Teresa (1878—?). "The Sentence of Death" (T, one act). Tr. Lilian Saunders, in Frank Shay, Twenty-five Short Plays. N.Y., Appleton, 1925, 273–81.

Fernández de Lizardi, José Joaquín (1776–1827). The Itching Parrot (N, *El periquillo sarniento*, 1816–30). Tr. abridged Katherine Anne Porter. Garden City, N.Y., Doubleday, 1942. xlii, 290 pp.
    Excerpts in The Americas (Franciscan), vol. 1, 1944, 47–49; and Jones, Before 1888, 103–08.

————"Epitaph to the Liberty of America" (V), in Underwood, 227.

Ferretis, Jorge (1902—). "The Failure" (S). Tr. Harry Kurz, in Haydn, 898–912.

————"The Man Who Dreamt of Pigs" (S), in Mexican Life, vol. 13, 12, Dec. 1937, 13–14, 69–72.

Fierro Blanco, Antonio de (pseud. of Walter Nordhoff, 1858–1937). The Journey of the Flame (N). Tr. Walter de Steiguer. Boston, Mass., Houghton Mifflin, 1933. xviii, 395 pp. Repr. 1955.

————Rico, Bandit and Dictator. Ibid., 1934, 195 pp., and London, Faber, 1935, 258 pp.

Flores, Manuel María (1840–1885).   Poems in Blackwell, 136–40; Goldberg, 14–16; and Underwood, 272–74.

Frías, José Dolores (1891–1936).   "Sonata of Beethoven" (V), in Underwood, 143.

Frías y Soto, Heriberto (1870–1925).   "Flower of Victory: A Mixtecan Legend" (S), in Mexican Life, vol. 6, 4, Apr. 1930, 17–18.
Nine other Indian legends in the same vol. 6.

Fuentes, Carlos (1929—).   Aura (N). Tr. Lysander Kemp. N.Y., Farrar, Straus, 1965. 74 pp. Repr. in Cohen, 107–37.

————A Change of Skin (N). Tr. Sam Hileman. N.Y., Farrar, Straus, and London, Cape, 1968. 462 pp.

————The Death of Artemio Cruz (N). Tr. Sam Hileman. N.Y., Farrar, Straus, and London, Collins, 1964. 306 pp. Repr. London, Panther, 1969.

————The Good Conscience (N, *Los nuevos, I: Las buenas conciencias*, 1959). Tr. Sam Hileman. N.Y., Oblensky, 1960. 148 pp.

————Where the Air Is Clear (N, *La región más transparente*, 1958). Tr. Sam Hileman. N.Y., Oblensky, 1960. 376 pp.

————"The Lifeline" (S). Tr. Lysander Kemp, in Evergreen Review, vol. 2, 1959, 75–84.

Gamboa, Federico (1864–1939).   *Suprema Ley* (N, 1896). Excerpts in Starr, 408.

Gamboa, José Joaquín (1879–1931).   The Knight, Death and the Devil (T, 3 acts, 1931). Tr. Theodore Apstein. Austin, Univ. of Texas, M.A. thesis (unpublished), 1937.

————"An Old Yarn" (T, one act: *Cuento viejo*, 1930). Tr. Willis K. Jones, in PSA, vol. 2.

García Icazbalceta, Joaquín (1824–1894).   See M. G. Martínez, Don Joaquín García Icazbalceta: His Place in Mexican Historiography. Washington, D.C., Catholic Univ. of America Pr., 1947. x, 127 pp.

Garro, Elena. Recollections of Things to Come. Tr. Ruth L. C. Simms. Austin, Univ. of Texas Pr., 1969. 289 pp.

————"A Solid House" (T, one act). Tr. Lysander Kemp, in Evergreen Review, vol. 2, 1959, 62–74.

————"The Tiztla Robbery" (S), in Américas, vol. 11, 7, July 1959, 21–25; and in Mexican Life, vol. 35, 9, Sept. 1959, 20–22, 52–53.

González Martínez, Enrique (1871–1952). Poems in Blackwell, 104–15; Bulletin Pan American Union, Mar. 1927; Craig, 146–53; Fitts; Hispanic Poets, 233–34; Johnson, 114–25; Jones, Since 1888, 40–43; Pan American Magazine, vol. 27, 1918, 36–39, 158; Poetry, vol. 26, 1925, 134; Underwood, 30–56, 110–14; Walsh, 640; Walsh, Catholic, 91–92.

González Obregón, Luis (1865–1938). The Streets of Mexico (S, 1924). Tr. Blanche C. Wagner. San Francisco, Calif., George Fields, 1937. 200 pp. The 12 stories repr. separately in Mexican Life, vols. 22–24, 1946–49.

González Peña, Carlos (1885–1955). History of Mexican Literature (H, 1928; 3d ed., 1945). Tr. Gusta Nance and Florence J. Dunston, intro. Ángel Flores. Dallas, Texas, Southern Methodist Univ., 1943. xii, 424 pp. Repr. Mexico, 1945; Dallas, 1968.

González Rojo, Enrique (1899–1939). Poems in American Prefaces, vol. 7, 1942; New Mexico Quarterly, Aug. 1941; and Underwood, 98–101.

Gorostiza, Celestino (1904—). "The Yap" (S), in Mexican Life, vol. 6, 5, May 1930, 13–14, 49–51.

Gorostiza, José (1901—). Poems in Fitts, 23–26; Underwood, 168–72.

Grijalva, Juan de (1580–1638). The Discovery of New Spain in 1518 (H). Tr. Henry R. Wagner. Berkeley, Calif., Cortés Society, 1942. 308 pp.

Gutiérrez Najéra, Manuel ("El duque Job," 1859–1895). "Rip-Rip" (S). Tr. Annie and Hensley Woodbridge, in Mexican Life, vol. 35, 1, Jan. 1959, 15–16; and in Lieber, 943–48.

Poems and "Lenten Sermon of Duque Job" in Jones, Since 1888, 34–40;

Blackwell, 2–33; Goldberg, 20–32; Hispanic Poets, 223–27; Johnson, 44–49; Poet Lore, vol. 30, 1919, 82–93; Stratford Journal, vol. 3, 1918, 73; Underwood, 3–33; Walsh, 551–58; Walsh, Catholic, 326–27; West Indian Review, vol. 5, 9, Sept. 1939, 25.

Guzmán, Martín Luis (1887—). The Eagle and the Serpent (1928). Tr. Harriet de Onís. N.Y., Knopf, 1930. 359 pp. Repr. Garden City, N.Y., Doubleday, and Gloucester, Mass., Peter Smith, 1965, 376 pp.
   Excerpts in Arciniegas, 510–22; Jones, Since 1888, 270–75.

————Memoirs of Pancho Villa (H, 1938–40, 4 vols.). Tr. Virginia H. Taylor. Austin, Univ. of Texas Pr., 1965. xii, 512 pp.

————"Death of David Berlanga" (S), in Mexican Life, vol. 3, 9, Sept. 1927, 19–20, 60.

————"The Gaucho's Last Job: From the Life of Francisco Villa" (S). Ibid., vol. 4, 7, July 1928, 15–16.

————"The Sleep of Compadre Urbina." Ibid., vol. 3, 11–12, Nov.–Dec. 1927, 23, 68–70.

Hoffman, F. C. ("R. H. Torres," 1911—). "The Brothers Jiménez" (S), in Mexican Life, vol. 13, 3, Mar. 1937, 15–17, 46–51.

Icaza, Francisco Asís de (1863–1925). Poems in Blackwell, 128; Hispanic Poets, 228; Modern Verse (Oct. 1941); Pan American Magazine, vol. 32, 1929, 208; Underwood, 88–92; West Indian Review, vol. 6, 5, May 1940, 28.

Jiménez Rueda, Julio (1896–1959). "The Unforeseen" (T, one act, 1923). Tr. Gino di Solemni, in Poet Lore, vol. 35, 1924, 1–24.

"John Very Bad" (S). Tr. Paul Bowles, in View, vol. 2, May 1945, 20. (Nahuatl literature.)

Juana Inés de la Cruz (Juana Inez de Asbaje y Ramírez de Santillana, 1648–1695). The Pathless Grave: Sonnets. Tr. Pauline Cook. Prairie City, Ill., Decker Pr., 1950. 80 pp.

————The Tenth Muse. Tr. Fanchon Royer. Paterson, N.J., St. Anthony Guild Pr., 1952. 179 pp.

Songs from plays: from *Empeños de la casa*, in Bulletin Pan American Union, vol. 76, 1943, 195–98; "Salutations" and "Phoenix" from a play, in Underwood, 222–23; "Loa" from *Divine Narcissus*, in Jones, Before 1888, 300–08.

Poems in Blackwell; Fantasy, no. 26, 1942, 43–44; Hills, 110; Hispanic Poets, 220; Jones, Before 1888, 207–10; Library of the World's Best Literature (1896), vol. 25, 9956–60; Underwood, 219–23; Walsh, 357–62; Walsh, Catholic, 214–16.

Krueger, Hilde. Malinche, or Farewell to Myths (H). Tr. H. Krueger. N.Y., Arrowhead Pr., 1948. 103 pp.

Landa, Diego de (1524–1579). Yucatán before and after the Conquest (H, *Relación de las cosas de Yucatán*). Tr. William Gates. Baltimore, Md., Maya Soc. Pubns 20, 1937. xv, 162 pp.

Tr. Alfred M. Tozzer. Cambridge, Mass., Peabody Museum of American Archaeology, Papers, vol. 18, 1941. xiii, 394 pp.

(León Portilla, Miguel). The Broken Spears: The Aztec Account of the Conquest of Mexico (*Visión de los vencidos*: Spanish tr. of the Aztec original). Tr. Lysander Kemp. Boston, Mass., Beacon Pr., 1962. xxxi, 168 pp.

————The Pre-Columbian Literature of Mexico. Tr. Grace Lobanov and the author. Norman, Univ. of Oklahoma Pr., 1969. 191 pp.

López, Rafael (1875–1943). Poems in Hemisferio (Mexico), 111, Aug. 1944, 27; Pan American Magazine, vol. 27, 1918, 46; Underwood, 74; and West Indian Review, vol. 6, 8, Aug. 1940, 35.

López de Gómara, Francisco (1510–1560). The Pleasant Historie of the Conquest of the Weast India, now called New Spayne (*Crónica de la conquista de la Nueva España*, 1552). London, Bynneman, 1578. Repr. 1596; N.Y., Scholars' Facsimiles, 1940, 405 pp.
    The second half of *La historia de las Indias*, written by Cortés' secretary.

Tr. Lesley Byrd Simpson as The Life of the Conqueror of Mexico. Berkeley, Univ. of California Pr., 1964. xxvi, 425 pp.

López-Portilla y Rojas, José (1850–1923). *La parcela* (N, 1898). Excerpts ("Amalia's Jewels" and "The Colonel's Arm") in Inter-America, vol. 2, 1919, 365–69; and in Starr, 313–33.

López Velarde, Ramón (1888–1921). Symbolist poems in Anthology of Mexican Poetry (see Octavio Paz, Collections, above), 172–87; Decisions, vol. 1, 1941, 52; Fantasy, no. 27, 1943, 78; Hays, 24–47; Jones, Since 1888, 45–48; Poetry, vol. 58, 1940, 16–17, and vol. 62, 1943, 71; and Underwood, 66–69.

López y Fuentes, Gregorio (1897—). *El Indio* (N, 1935). Tr. Anita Brenner. Indianapolis, Ind., Bobbs-Merrill, 1937. 256 pp. Repr. N.Y., Ungar, 1961, ill. Diego Rivera.

————"A Letter to God" (S), in Colford, 149–52; Flores GSS, 244–47; Jones, Since 1888, 285–89; Mexican Life, vol. 22, 11, Nov. 1944, 15–16; Tomorrow, vol. 3, 8, Apr. 1944, 21–22.

Eight other stories tr. in Mexican Life, vol. 19–28, 1943–52.

Magaña, Sergio (1924—). *"La mujer sentada"* (S). Tr. Patricia Petrocilli and Emma Gutiérrez Suárez, in Portfolio (Mexico, 1951), 47–59.

Magdaleno, Mauricio (1906—). Sunburst (N, *El resplandor*, 1937). Tr. Anita Brenner. N.Y., Viking Pr., 1944. 290 pp.

Maples Arce, Manuel (1898—). *Metropólis* (V). Tr. John Dos Passos. N.Y., pr. pr., 1930.

Poems in Fantasy, no. 26, 1941, 67–68; and Underwood, 159–63.

"María Enriqueta": see Camarillo y Roa, María.

Marqués Campos, Dr. Alfredo. I Wouldn't Dare (N, *Yo no haría eso*). Tr. Juan Berlier. N.Y., Vantage Pr., 1965. 229 pp.

Martínez, Conchita. Six stories from *Álbum onomástico* (1897) in Mexican Life, vols. 10–12, 1934–36.

Martínez Cáceres, Arturo. In Memoriam: Mexican Short Stories. Tr. D. O. Chambers. N.Y., Vantage Pr., 1967. 117 pp.

Mediz Bolio, Antonio (1884—?).   The Land of the Pheasant and the Deer (N, 1922, 1934). Tr. Enid E. Perkins. Mexico, Cultura, 1935. 155 pp.

————"The Theatrical World" (V), in Underwood, 132–34.

Mendoza, Andrés.   "Pedro de la Panza Leaves Mescaltepec" (S), in Mexican Life, vol. 17, 6, June 1941, 15–16.
Three other stories about Pedro in Mexico tr. ibid., July–Sept. 1941.

Menéndez, Miguel Ángel (1905—).   Nayar (N), in Flores FN. Repr. separately, N.Y., Farrar and Rinehart, 1942, 277 pp.
Excerpts in Mexican Life, vol. 24, 6, June 1948, 23–24, 46–47, and vol. 24, 8, Aug. 1948, 19–20, 58–63.

Mojarro, Tomás (1934—).   "The Harp" (S). Tr. Lysander Kemp, in Prize Stories, 134–46.

Molina Solís, Juan Francisco (1850–1932).   El Conde de Peñalva (N, 1896). Excerpts, "The Horrors of 1648 in Yucatán," in Starr, 108.

Mondragón Aguirre, Magdalena (1913—).   Some Day the Dream (N, Yo como pobre). Tr. Samuel Putnam. N.Y., Dial Pr., 1947. 240 pp.

Montaño Parra, Raúl.   "The Hungry Wolf of Texcoco" (S), in Mexican Life, vol. 27, 7, July 1951, 23–24.

Monterde, Francisco (1894—).   She Who Returned to Life (T, 3 acts, 1923). Tr. Louis G. Zelson, in Poet Lore, vol. 55, 1950, 291–335.

————"The Highwayman" (S, Un salteador). Tr. R. M. Duncan, in New Mexico Quarterly, vol. 12, 1942, 415–17.

————"Road to Taxco" (S). Tr. E. W. Underwood, in West Indian Review, vol. 6, 9, Sept. 1940, 35; and in Underwood, 131.

"Motolinía":   See Benavente, above.

Munagorri, J. F. de.   "Patharra's Recuperation" (S), in Mexican Life, vol. 7, 5, May 1931, 11.

Muñoz, Rafael M. (1899—).   Tales of the Mexican Revolution (S, *El feroz cabecillo*, 1926). Tr. anon., in Mexican Life: Nov., Dec., 1929; Jan., Feb., Sept., 1930; Oct., 1931.

————"Hell Dogs" (H, *¡ Vamos con Pancho Villa!*, 1932). Tr. anon., in Liberty Magazine, Oct. 28, Nov. 4–25, 1933.

Murillo, Gerardo ("Dr. Atl," 1875–1936).   "The Cantinero" (S), in Mexican Life, vol. 9, 11, Nov. 1933, 10.

————"The Wake" (S), ibid., Dec. 1933, 13–14.
From *Cuentos de todos colores* (1933).

Muro, Amado.   "¡Ay, Chihuahua!" (S), in Américas, vol. 9, 3, Mar. 1957, 22–24.

————"My Father and Pancho Villa" (H), ibid., vol. 10, 4, Apr. 1958, 34–35, and Mexican Life, vol. 34, 7, July 1958, 19–20.

————"My Grandfather's Brave Songs," in Mexican Life, vol. 37, 10, Oct. 1961, 11–12, 58–59.

————"Sunday in Little Chihuahua," in Américas, vol. 7, 11, Nov. 1955, 21–26; and in Mexican Life, vol. 32, 2, Feb., 1956, 21–22, 49–53.

Nandino, Elías (1903—).   Two poems in Mexican Life, vol. 9, 7, July 1933, 16.

Navarro, Francisco (1902—).   "The City" (T, one act, part 1 of a trilogy, 1935). Tr. Willis K. Jones, in Poet Lore, vol. 54, 1948, 72–82.

Nervo, Amado (1870–1919).   Confessions of a Modern Poet (B, *La amada inmóvil*, 1920). Tr. Dorothy Kress. Boston, Mass., Bruce Humphries, 1935. 50 pp.

————Plenitude (E, 1918). Tr. William F. Rice. Los Angeles, Calif., J. R. Miller, 1928. 153 pp.

Tr. Alfonso Teja Zabre. Mexico City, 1938.

————"Leah and Rachel" (S). Tr. Willis K. Jones, in Stratford Journal, vol. 6, 1919, 7–12; in Inter-America, vol. 2, 1919, 343–45; in Jones, Since 1888, 337–43.

Fifty or more poems tr. in Jones, Since 1888, 43–45; Blackwell, 34–67; Bulletin Pan American Union; Craig, 76–87; Goldberg; Inter-America; Johnson, 94–101; Pan American Magazine; Underwood, 59–69; Walsh, 626–34; Walsh, Catholic, 370–71.

Noriega Hope, Carlos (1896–1934). "The Bewitched Goat" (S), in Mexican Life, vol. 4, 9, Sept. 1928, 19.

Novo, Salvador (1904—). "Eight Column Banner Spread" (T, 3 acts, *A ocho columnas*, 1956). Tr. Willis K. Jones, in Poet Lore, vol. 60, 1966.

————*Nuevo Amor* (V, 1933). Tr. Edna W. Underwood. Portland, Maine, Mosher, 1935. 26 leaves.

Other poems tr. in American Prefaces, vol. 7, 1941–42; Fantasy, no. 26, 1942, 58; Fitts, 87–90; Mexican Life, vol. 4, 7, July 1928, 16; Underwood, 189–95; West Indian Review, vol. 1, 4, Apr. 1935, 37, and vol. 4, 5, May 1938, 43.

Orozco, José Clemente (1883–1949). An Autobiography (B). Tr. Robert C. Stephenson. Austin, Univ. of Texas Pr., 1962. 171 pp.

Orozco Rosales, Efren. *El mensajero del sol* (T). Mexico, Secretaría de gubernación, 1941. 64 pp., parallel texts.

Ortíz de Montellano, Bernardo (1899–1949). "Salome's Head" (T). Tr. Lloyd Mallan, in New Directions, vol. 8, 1944, 328–32.

Poems in Fitts, 327; Underwood, 164–66.

Othón, Manuel José (1858–1906). Poems in Blackwell; Christian Science Monitor, May 22, 1926; Goldberg, 23; Stratford Journal, vol. 11, 1918, 74; Underwood, 40–41; Walsh, 549; West Indian Review, vol. 6, 10, Oct. 1939, 28–29.

Outo Alabarco, Arturo (1930—). "Coyote 13" (S). Tr. Harriet de Onís, in Onís, SS.

Owen, Gilberto (1908–1952). Two poems in Underwood, 211–12.

Pacheco, José Emilio (1939—). Poem in Cohen, 260.

Pagaza, Joaquín Arcadio (1839–1918). Poems in Hispanic Poets, 221; Underwood; Walsh; Walsh, Catholic; West Indian Review, vol. 6, 5, May 1940, 28; Woman's Journal, June 25, 1910.

Parra, Manuel de la (1878–1930). Two poems in Underwood, 95–98.

Parra, Porfirio (1856–1912). *Pacotillas* (N). Excerpts in Starr, 361.

Passion Play at Tzintzuntzan (T, *Las pasiones*, 16th c.) Tr. Frances Toor, in Mexican Folkways, vol. 1, 1925, 21.

Los Pastores. Ed. and tr. M. R. Cole. American Folk-lore Soc., Memoirs, vol. 9, 1907; also Boston, Mass., Houghton Mifflin, 1907, xxxi, 234 pp.

————Version by Griego family, Santa Fe. Recorded and tr. Mary R. Van Stone, Cleveland, Gates Pr., 1933.

————*Coloquios de los Pastores.* Compiled and tr. Aurora Lucero-White; music by Alejandro Flores. Library of Congress, 1940; and Santa Fe, N.M., Santa Fe Press, 1940, 51 pp.

See also under Guatemala, Shepherds' Play of Prodigal Son.

Payno, Manuel (1810–1894). The Devil's Stick-pin (N, *El fistol del diablo*, 1845–46). Excerpt in Jones, Before 1888, 109–13.

Paz, Octavio (1914—). Selected Poems. Tr. Muriel Rukeyser. Bloomington, Indiana Univ. Pr., 1963. 171 pp., parallel texts.

————The Labyrinth of Solitude: Life and Thought in Mexico (E). Tr. Lysander Kemp. N.Y., Grove Pr., 1962. 212 pp.

————Sun Stone (V, *Piedra de sol*, 1957). Tr. Muriel Rukeyser. N.Y., New Directions, 1963. 47 pp.; and Bloomington, Indiana Univ. Pr., 1963, 171 pp., parallel texts.

Tr. Peter Miller. Toronto, Ont., Contact Pr., n.d.

————"The Blue Bouquet" (S). Tr. Lysander Kemp, in Evergreen Review, vol. 18, 1961, 99–101.

————"Eve's Dream" (V), in Flakoll, 185–190.

————"Hymn among the Ruins" (V), in Cohen, 87–89; Cranfill; Jones, Since 1888, 50–52.

————"Night Stroll" and "A Poet." Tr. Gloria Mendelsohn, in New World Writing, vol. 14, 1958, 137–38.

————"*Todos Santos, Día de Muertos.*" Tr. Lysander Kemp, in Evergreen Review, vol. 2, 1959, 22–37.

Other poems tr. in Cohen, 89–96; Fantasy, no. 27, 1943, 76; Fitts; Horizon (London, Dec. 1949).

Pellicer, Carlos (1899—). Poems, in Three Spanish American Poets; Cohen, 49–52; Fitts, 317–20; Mexican Life, vol. 7, 4, Apr. 1931, 15; Underwood, 150–57; and West Indian Review, vol. 2, 10, Oct. 1935, 56.

Peón Contreras, José (1843–1907). Gil González de Ávila (T, one act), in Jones, Before 1888, 325–31.

————*Hasta el cielo* (T, three acts, 1876). Excerpt in Starr, 245.

————"Canticles" (V), in Underwood, 280.

Peza, Juan de Dios (1852–1910). "Meditation" (V), in Las Novedades (Mexico), Feb. 25, 1917.

————"Mexico and Spain" (V), in Green, 252–58.

Piña, Roberto. "Close-up of Gallardo" (S), in Mexican Life, vol. 9, 8, Aug. 1933, 13.

Popul Vuh (H). Tr. Leah Brenner. Mexico, Graphic Arts Pubs., 1943.

Tr. Delia Goetz and Sylvanus G. Morley. Norman, Univ. of Oklahoma Pr., 1950. 268 pp. Repr. 1952, 1957, Los Angeles, Calif., Limited Edns Club, 1954, 251 pp.
Excerpts in Jones, Before 1888, 23–29.

Prieto, Guillermo (1818–1897). "An Old Man's Love" (V), in Underwood, 237.

Quintanillo, Luis ("Kyn Taniya," 1900—). "Storm" and "4861" (V), in Mexican Life, vol. 4, 1928, 16–20.

Rabasa, Emilio (1856–1930). *Sancho Polo* (N). Excerpts in Starr, 375.

Ramírez, Ignacio (1818–1908). "My portrait" V, in Underwood, 239.

Ramírez, José Fernando (1804–1871). Mexico during the War with the United States (H). Tr. Elliot B. Scherr. Columbia, Univ. of Missouri Pr., 1950. 165 pp.

Rebolledo, Efrén (1877–1929). "Hail, Lindbergh" (V), in Springfield (Mass.) Republican, Jan., 17, 1928.

Two poems in Underwood, 93–95.

Revueltas, José (1914—). The Stone Knife (N, *El luto humano*, 1943). Tr. H. R. Hays. N.Y., Reynal, 1947. 183 pp.

Reyes, Alfonso (1889–1959). Mexico in a Nutshell (E). Tr. Charles Ramsdell. Berkeley, Univ. of California Pr., 1964. vi, 145 pp.

————The Position of America and Other Essays. Tr. Harriet de Onís, foreword Federico de Onís. N.Y., Knopf, 1950. 184 pp.

————Selected Essays. Tr. Charles Ramsdell, foreword Arturo Torres-Rioseco. Berkeley, Univ. of California Pr., and London, Cambridge Univ. Pr., 1964. vi, 145 pp.

————"Eclogue of the Blind" (T). Tr. Ray Moloney, in Jones, Since 1888, 54–61.

Poems in Fitts, 45; Pan American Magazine, vol. 32, 1928, 208; Underwood, 76–80; West Indian Review, vol. 1, 1934, 49.

Riva Palacio, Vicente ("Rosa Espina," 1832–1896). His Excellency Rules (N). Tr. M. A. de Vitis. N.Y., Doubleday Doran, 1934.

Poems in Underwood, 243–50.

Roa Bárcena, José María (1827–1908). "Combats in the Air," in Starr, 262.

————"Founding of Mexico City" (V), in Underwood, 240.

Robles Soler, Antonio Joaquín ("Antoniorrobles," 1898—). The Refugee Centaur (N, *El refugiado centauro Flores*, 1931). Tr. Edward and Elizabeth Huberman. N.Y., Twayne, 1952. 245 pp.

Rojas González, Francisco (1905–1951). "Guadalupe's Gold Tooth" (S), in Mexican Life, vol. 14, 6, June 1938, 13–14.

————"Lancaster's Kid," ibid.

————"The Mysterious Alkaloid," in Inter-America, vol. 2, 1918, 288–301.

————"Watch Out for Me," in Mexican Life, vol. 13, 11, Nov. 1937, 11–12. From *Sed, pequeñas novelas*, 1937.

Romero, José Rubén (1890–1952). The Futile Life of Pito Pérez (N, 1938). Tr. Joan Coyne, in Flores FN, 303–67.

Rosas Moreno, José (1838–1888). Poems. Tr. William Cullen Bryant, in Laurel Leaves. Boston, 1876. Repr. in Poetical Works, N.Y., Appleton, 1883.

Other poems in Goldberg, 13; Underwood, 264; Walsh, 513–18.

Ruiz de Alarcón, Juan (1581?–1639). The Lying Lover or the Ladies' Friendship (T, 3 acts). Adapted Sir Richard Steele. London, Lintot, 1704. 64 pp. Repr. in Steele's Works, etc.

————The Truth Suspected. Tr. Julio del Toro and Robert V. Finney, in Poet Lore, vol. 30, 1927, 475–530.

Tr. Robert C. Ryan, in Angel Flores, ed., Spanish Drama. N.Y., Bantam, 1962, 135–89.

————"To Vesuvius" (V), in Underwood, 217, and West Indian Review, vol. 6, 5, May 1940, 27.

Rulfo, Juan (1918—).   The Burning Plain and Other Stories. Tr. George D. Schade. Austin, Univ. of Texas Pr., 1967. xv, 175 pp. ill.

————Pedro Páramo (N, 1955). Tr. Lysander Kemp. N.Y., Grove Pr., and London, Calder, 1959. 123 pp.
    Excerpt in Evergreen Review, vol. 2, 7, Winter 1959, 45–58.

————"Anacleto Morones" (S). Tr. Ann West, in Chelsea, vol. 6, 1960, 47–59.

————"Because We Are So Poor" (S). Tr. Lysander Kemp, in Flores GSS, 300–04.

————"The Miraculous Child." Tr. Irene Nicholson, in Encounter, vol. 5, 3, Sept. 1955, 13–19.

————"Talpa," in Flakoll, 32–39; and in Mexican Life, vol. 33, 1, Jan. 1957, 11–12, 62–66.

————"Tell Them Not to Kill Me." Tr. Lysander Kemp, in New World Writing, vol. 14, 1959, 116–22.

————"They Gave Us the Land" (S). Tr. Jean Franco, in Cohen, 174–78.

Other stories tr. in Mexican Life, Nov. 1956, Jan. and Mar., 1958.

Saavedra y Bessey, Rafael N.   "La Chinita" (T, two scenes). Tr. Lilian Saunders, in Poet Lore, vol. 37, 1926, 107–19.

Sabines, Jaime (1926—).   Poems in Cohen, 179–81.

Sáenz Azcorra, Franz.   "The Mestiza" and "The Prostitute" (S), in West Indian Review, vol. 1, Apr. 1935.

————"The Path," ibid., vol. 2, 10, Oct. 1935, 57.

Sahagún, Fray Bernardino de (d. 1590).   History of Ancient Mexico. Tr. Fanny Bandelier from the Spanish version. Nashville, Tenn., Fisk Univ. Pr., 1932. Vol. 1 only, 315 pp.
    Excerpts in Jones, Before 1888, 53–56.

Tr. Arthur Anderson and Charles Dibble from the original Aztec as Florentine Codex: General History of the Things of New Spain. Salt Lake City, Univ. of Utah Pr. for School of American Research, Santa Fe, N.M., 1951–63. 11 books in 10 vols.

Salazar Mallén, Rubén (1905—).   "Foam" (S), in Mexican Life, vol. 8, 8, Aug. 1930, 11–12, 66–68.

Sánchez Mármol, Manuel (1839–1916).   Antón Pérez (N). Excerpts in Starr, 336.

Sánchez Villaseñor, José.   Ortega y Gasset, Existentialist: A Critical Study of His Thoughts and Sources (*Pensamiento y trayectoria de José Ortega y Gasset*). Tr. Joseph Small. Chicago, Ill., Regnery, 1949. 272 pp.

Santa Anna, General Antonio López de (1795–1876).   The Mexican Side of the Texas Revolution (H, 1836). Tr. Carlos E. Castañeda. Dallas, Texas, P. L. Turner, 1928. 391 pp.

Sanz Lajara, J. M.   "Calamidad" (S), in Mexican Life, vol. 35, 10, Oct. 1959, 10, 65–66.

————"Little Ants," ibid., vol. 36, 5, May 1960, 10, 62–66.

Serra, Padre Junípero (1713–1784).   Writings. Ed. and tr. Antonine Tibesar. Washington, D.C., Academy of American Franciscan History, 1956–57. 4 vols.
Letters and reports of his missions. See Francisco Palou, *Life of Fray Junípero Serra*, tr. Maynard J. Geiger (ibid., 1955, 547 pp.).

Sierra, Justo (1848–1912).   "The Story of Starei: A Legend of Yellow Fever" (H), in Starr, 276–87.

Poems in Blackwell, 142; Springfield (Mass.) Republican, June 20, 1909; Underwood, 288; Woman's Journal, Oct. 12, 1912.

Sigüenza y Góngora, Carlos de (1645–1700).   The Mercurio Volante of don Carlos de Sigüenza . . . the First Expedition of don Diego de Vargas to New Mexico in 1692. Tr. Irving A. Leonard. Los Angeles, Calif., Quivira Soc., 1932. 89 pp. facs., 136 pp.

————The Misadventures of Alonso Ramírez [with English pirates]. Tr. Edwin H. Pleasants. Mexico, [Imprenta Mexicana], 1962. 105 pp.

> Excerpts in Jones, Before 1888, 86–90. The fame of the book as the first "almost novel" [1690] of Mexico is now denied by Rojas Garcidueñas (in *Anales del Instituto de Investigaciones Estéticas*, vol. 31, 1962, 57–78), since its author did not intend it as an adventure novel.

> Cf. Irving A. Leonard, *Don Carlos de Sigüenza, A Mexican Savant of the Seventeenth Century* (Univ. of California Pr., 1929, x, 287 pp.).

Solana, Rafael (1915—). Two sonnets. Tr. Lloyd Mallan, in Poet Lore, vol. 51, 1945, 75.

Solís y Rivadeneyra, Antonio de (1601–1686). History of the Conquest of Mexico by the Spaniards (H, 1684). Tr. Thomas Townsend. London, T. Woodward, 1724. Repr. Dublin, 1727; rev. Nathaniel Hooke, London, 1738, 2 vols.; London, 1753.

Song of Quetzalcoatl. Tr. J. H. Cornyn. Yellow Springs, Ohio, Antioch Pr., 1931. 207 pp.

> Excerpts in Mexican Folkways, vol. 4, 1928, 75, parallel texts; in Pan American Magazine, vol. 49, 1930, 124–31.

Souto Alabarce, Arturo. "Coyote 13" (S), in Onís, SS, 233–37.

Souza, Antonio. "Pascualina: A Playlet" (T), in Américas, vol. 9, 12, Dec. 1957, 22–25.

Spota, Luis (1925—). Almost Paradise (1956). Tr. Ray and Renate Morrison. Garden City, N.Y., Doubleday, 1963. 391 pp.

————The Enemy Blood. Tr. Robert Molloy. Garden City, N.Y., Doubleday, and London, Muller, 1961. 308 pp. Repr. Penguin, 1967, 251 pp.

————The Time of Wrath. Tr. Robert Molloy. Ibid., 1962. 472 pp.

————The Wounds of Hunger (*Más cornadas da el hambre*). Tr. R. Barnaby Conrad. Boston, Mass., Houghton Mifflin, and N.Y., New Amer. Lib., 1957. 233 pp.

Suárez Carraño, José.   The Final Hours (N). Tr. Anthony Kerrigan. N.Y., Knopf, 1954. 273 pp. Repr. New Amer. Lib., 1955.

————"Evening in Madrid" (S), in New World Writing, vol. 3, 1953, 32–47.

Tablada, José Juan (1871–1945).   Six Poems. Tr. Warren Carrier in Entre Nosotros, vol. 4, 1942, 14.

Other poems in Goldberg, 59–61; Pan American Magazine, vol. 27, 1918, 332; Underwood, 77–83; Walsh; West Indian Review, vol. 6, 12, Dec. 1939, 15.

Taracena, Alfonso (1899—).   "Extravagant Characters" (S), in Mexican Life, vol. 6, 10, Oct. 1930, 11–12.

————"The Volcano Goblin," ibid., Nov. 1930, 10–68.

Teja Zabre, Alfonso (1888–1962).   Guide to the History of Mexico: A Modern Interpretation (H). Tr. P. M. del Campo. Mexico, Press of the Ministry of Foreign Affairs, 1935. 375 pp.

Terrazas, Francisco de (1525?–1600?).   "Sonnet to a Beautiful But Heartless Coquette" (V), in Jones, Before 1888, 188; Underwood, 215; West Indian Review, vol. 6, 5, May 1940, 27.

Torres Bodet, Jaime (1902—).   Selected Poems. Ed. and tr. Sonja Karson. Bloomington, Indiana Univ. Pr., 1964. 155 pp., parallel texts.
Poems from a dozen of his volumes, from Fervor (1918) to Sin Tregua (1957).

Other surrealistic and neo-symbolist poems in American Prefaces, vol. 7, 1941–42, 166; Blackwell, 164–67; Fitts, 93–102; Hispanic Poets, 236–38; Johnson, 188–89; Jones, Since 1888, 48–50; Mexican Life, vol. 3, 6, June 1927, 20; 9, Sept. 1927, 30; vol. 7, 5, Aug. 1931, 27; Underwood, 173–77.

————"A Close-up of Mr. Lehar" (S), in Mexican Life, vol. 6, 12, Dec. 1930, 17.

————"Death of Proserpina" (Proserpina rescatada, 1931), ibid., vol. 7, 1, Jan. 1931.

————"Margaret" (*Margareta de Niebla*, 1927), ibid., vol. 6, 1, Jan. 1930.

See Sonja Karson, *Jaime Torres Bodet: A Poet in a Changing World* (Saratoga Springs, N.Y., Skidmore College, 1963, 155 pp.).

Torri, Julio (1889—).   Essays and Poems (1917). Tr. Dorothy Kress. N.Y., Institute of French Studies, 1938. 33 pp.

————"The Hero" (S). Tr. Donald Demorest, in New World Writing, vol. 14, 1958, 139–40.

"The Tostones" (T).   Tr. Frederick Starr, in Journal of American Folk-lore, vol. 15, 1902, 73–83.

Turrente Rozas, Lorenzo.   "*Vida de 'El Perro'* " (S). Tr. Lloyd Mallan, in American Prefaces, vol. 7, 1941–42.

Urbina, Luis Gonzaga (1867–1934).   Poems in Blackwell, 68–98; Goldberg, 33–44; Inter-America, vol. 5, 1922, 285–97; Pan American Magazine, vol. 27, 1918, 105; Poetry, vol. 26, 1925, 132; Stratford Journal, vol. 1, 1916, 63–76; Underwood, 83–87; Walsh.

Usigli, Rodolfo (1905—).   Another Springtime (T, one act, 1938). Tr. Wayne Wolfe. N.Y., French, 1961. 73 pp.
    Second prize, International Theatre Celebration.

————Crown of Shadows (T, 3 acts, 1943). Tr. W. F. Sterling. London, Wingate, 1940. 100 pp.
    Act 3 also tr. in Jones, Since 1888, 440–46.

————"Nocturne" (V), in Underwood, 198.

Valenzuela, Jesús E. (1856–1911).   Poems in Blackwell, 122; Goldberg, 21–22; Stratford Journal, vol. 3, 1918, 76; Underwood, 102.

Vasconcelos, José (1882–1959).   A Mexican Ulysses: The Autobiography of José Vasconcelos. Tr. W. Rex Crawford. Bloomington, Indiana Univ. Pr., 1963. 288 pp., paper.
    An abridgement of a 4-vol. work.

Vásquez de Tapia, Bernardino (16th c.). *Relación del Conquistador.* Tr. John Houghton Allen, in Allen. Repr. in New Mexico Quarterly vol. 33, 1963, 139-47.

Villaseñor Ángeles, Eduardo. "Chinese Coffee Shop" (T, one act, 1926). Tr. Howard S. Phillips, in Mexican Life, vol. 3, 9, Sept. 1927, 23–24.

Villaurrutia, Xavier (1903–1950). "The Hour Has Come" (T, one act, 1934). Tr. Edna Lue Ferness, in Odyssey Review, vol. 2, 1962, 88–98.

————"What Are You Thinking About?" (T, one act). Tr. Gregory Rabassa, ibid., 68–87.

Tr. Lysander Kemp, in New World Writing, vol. 14, 1959.

Poems in American Prefaces, vol. 7, 1941–42, 164–65; Fantasy, no. 27, 1943, 89; Fitts, 365–67; Mexican Life, vol. 7, 12, Dec. 1931, 30; Modern Verse, Oct. 1941; Underwood, 180–84.

Yáñez, Agustín (1904—). The Edge of the Storm (N, *Al filo del agua*, 1947). Tr. Ethel Brinton. Austin, Univ. of Texas Pr., 1963. 332 pp.

————The Lean Lands (*Las tierras flacas*). Tr. Ethel Brinton. Austin, Univ. of Texas Pr., 1969. ix, 328 pp. ill.

Zavala, Silvino Arturo (1909—). New Viewpoints on the Spanish Colonization of America (H). Tr. Joan Coyne. Ann Arbor, Univ. of Michigan Microfilms, 1962. 118 pp.

Zayas Enríquez, Rafael de (1848–1932). "Spring Song" (V), in Underwood, 283.

————"When Is a Coward Not a Coward?" (S), in Tales, vol. 8.

Zea, Leopoldo (1912—). The Latin American Mind (E). See General Background, above.

Zorita, Alonso de (1511?–1585). Life and Labor in Ancient Mexico: A Brief and Summary Relation of the Lords of New Spain (H, *Breve y sumaria relación*, etc., 1570?). Tr. Benjamin Keen. New Brunswick, N.J., Rutgers Univ. Pr., 1963. 328 pp.

Nicaragua

INDIVIDUAL AUTHORS

Argüello, Lino (1890–1935).   Poems in Fitts, 463; Jones, Since 1888, 66–67.

Argüello Barreto, Santiago (1872–1942).   Poems in Blackwell, 202–04; Boston Herald, July 22, 1917; and Jones, Since 1888, 64–66.

Calderón Ramirez, Salvador (1869—?).   Stories for Carmencita (S). Tr. Aloysius C. Gahan. Brooklyn, N.Y., Daily Eagle Pr., 1914. 174 pp.

Cardenal, Granada (1925—).   "With Walker in Nicaragua" (V), in Flakoll, 25–31, parallel texts.

"Darío, Rubén" (Felix Rubén García Sarmiento, 1867–1916).   Eleven Poems of Rubén Darío. Tr. Thomas Walsh and Salomon de la Salva. N.Y. and London, Putnam, 1916. ix, 49 pp.

————*Prosas profanas* and Other Poems. Tr. Charles B. McMichael. N.Y., Nicholas L. Brown, 1922. 60 pp.

————Selected Poems of Rubén Darío. Tr. Lysander Kemp, prologue by Octavio Paz. Austin, Univ. of Texas Pr., 1965. 149 pp.

Other poems tr. in Blackwell, 182–201; Colford, 127–37; Craig, 38–75; Goldberg; Hispanic Poets, 240–50; Inter-America, vol. 1, 1917, 1–12; Jones, Since 1888, 21–30; Pan American Magazine, vol. 30, 1915, 20; vol. 41, 1941, 25; Poetry, vol. 26, 1925, 135–37; Poor; Walsh, 596–613; Walsh, Catholic, 347–51; West Indian Review, vol. 11, 7, July 1936, 24.

————"The Deaf Satyr" (S), in Clark.

————"Death of the Empress of China" (S), in McMichael, above; in Colford, 129–37.

————"Impressions of Santiago" (E), in Andean Monthly, vol. 4, 1941, 84–88.

————"My Visit to Nicaragua" (E), in Bulletin Pan American Union, vol. 68, 1934, 222–24.

————"Prologue," in Allen, 1943, 36–37.

————"The Ruby" (S), in Inter-America, vol. 1, 1921, 106–07; (with 4 poems) in Jones, Since 1888, 21–30.

————"Seascape." Tr. W. G. Umphrey, in Fantasy, no. 26, 1942, 44.

————"Veil of Queen Mab," in McMichael, above.

For critical study, see Arturo Torres Rioseco, *Rubén Darío, casticismo y americanismo* (Cambridge, Mass., Harvard Univ. Pr., 1921, 253 pp.).

The Guëguënce: A Comedy Ballet in the Nahuatl-Spanish Dialect of Nicaragua (T). Ed. and tr. Daniel G. Brinton. Philadelphia, Pa., Brinton, 1883. 94 pp., parallel texts.

Maldonado, Pedro (1704–1748). "Simon the Cyrenean" (V). Tr. Oswald Tenny, in Pan American Magazine, vol. 27, 1918, 156.

Mejía Sánchez, Ernesto (1923—). "The Recluse" (V, 1953), in Flakoll, 156–57.

Ordóñez Argüello, Alberto (1914—). "Song" (V, *Cancion de Neztahual-coyotl*), in Flakoll, 43–46, parallel texts.

Pasos, Joaquín (1915–1947). "Elegy of the Bird" (V), in Flakoll, 64–65.

Selva, Salomón de la (1893—). "Elegy" (V). Tr. Donald Walsh, in Fitts, 527.

Panama

Background

Biesanz, J. and M.   The People of Panama. N.Y., Columbia Univ. Pr., and London, Oxford Univ. Pr., 1955. x, 272 pp.

Collection

Moore, Evelyn, Ed. and tr.   Sancocho: Stories and Sketches of Panama. Panama, Pan American Pub. Co., 1938. 194 pp.

INDIVIDUAL AUTHORS

Andreve, Guillermo ("Mario Marín Mirones," 1879–1940).   "Mountain Idyll" (S), "The Adventures of a Chomba," and "Manolo's Little Drinks," in Evelyn Moore (see preceding item), 12–18.

Arjona Q., Julio (1897—).   "Far Away" (V), in West Indian Review, vol. 3, 8, Aug. 1937, 34.

————"*La Junta*" (S), in Moore (see above), 126–29.

Bárcena, Lucas (1906—).   "Chola Facunda" and "The Will of Don Julian" (S), in Moore, 126–29.

Blas Tejeira, Gil.   "The Phonograph" (S), in Américas, vol. 8, 7, July 1956, 26–27; and in Mexican Life, vol. 333, 5, May 1957, 10, 49–50.

Cajar Escala, José A. (1915—).   "The Village Pilgrimage" (S), in Bulletin Pan American Union, vol. 80, 1946, 163–64.

Carrasco, M. Francisco (1899—).   "Voices" (S), in Moore, 130–37.

Castillero Reyes, Ernesto de Jesús (1889—).   "The Technique of the Tamborito" (S), in Moore, 81–86.

Castillo, Moisés (1899—). "Counterpoint," "Miracle of Ciriaco," and "The Witch's Wake" (S), in Moore, 138–43.

Crespo, Elida L. C. de.   "Maruja," "Seña Paula," and "Village Siesta" (S), in Moore, 111–19.

Herrera, Darío (1870–1914).   "Violets" (S), in West Indian Review, vol. 3, 6, June 1937, 21.

Huerte, José (1900—).   "Alma Campesina," "Dead of a Toothache," "The Little Lapdog of Yvonne," and "A Well-planned Insult," in Moore, 61–65.

Lewis, Samuel (1871–1939).   "Crossing the Isthmus in 1853," "The Legend of La Campana," and "The Ransomed Indian Maid," in Moore, 37–44.

McKay, Santiago ("Fray Rodrigo," 1898—).   "The Cross of the Escortines," "Piruli and Longolón," and "Sal si puedes," in Moore, 49–52.

Méndez Pereira, Octavio (1887–1954).   "Christmas Eve in Aguadulce" (S), in Moore, 87–89.

Miró, Ricardo (1883–1940).   Poems in West Indian Review, vol. 3, 6, June 1937, 34–35.

Ponce Aguilera, Salomón (1868–1945).   "The Recruits" (S, De la gleba), in Moore, 56–60.

Rojas Sucre, Graciela (1904—).   "On Account of the Piñata" (S, Terruñadas de lo chico), in Moore, 90–101.

Ros Zenet, José Guillermo (1930—).   "Poem of Contemporary Days and Love" (V), in Flakoll, 77–79.

"Sinán, Rogelio" (Bernardo Domínguez Alba, 1904—).   "A la crilla de las estatuas maduras" (S). Tr. Joan Coyne, in Flores FN, 409–20.

————"They Came to the River" (S), in Mexican Life, vol. 25, 2, Feb. 1949, 11–12, 60–66.

Valdés, Nacho (1902—). "Carnival in Santiago" (V), and six more poems, in Moore, 159–62.

————"Prayer" (V), in West Indian Review, vol. 3, 8, Aug. 1937, 34.

Paraguay

Background

Pendle, George. Paraguay, a Riverside Nation. London, Royal Institute of International Affairs, 1954. 115 pp. Repr. 1956.

Warren, Harris Gaylord. Paraguay, an Informal History. Norman, Univ. of Oklahoma Pr., 1949. xii, 393 pp.

INDIVIDUAL AUTHORS

Arditi, Nessim. "The Legend of the Lace" (S), in Américas, vol. 12, 7, July 1960, 14–16.

Campos Cervera, Herib (1905–1953). "A Handful of Earth" (V), in Jones, Since 1888, 140–42.

Díaz de Guzmán, Ruy (1558?–1629). *Historia argentina del descubrimiento, población y conquista de las provincias del Río de la Plata* (1612). Excerpts in Jones, Before 1888, 71–73.

Fariña Núñez, Eloy (1885–1925). "The Serpent" (V), in Jones, Since 1888, 137–38.

González, Natalicio (1897—). "The Bull of Taruma" (S), in Américas, vol. 7, 9, Sept. 1955, 27–29; and in Mexican Life, vol. 32, 6, June 1956, 22, 51.

Guanes, Alejandro (1872–1925). "The Hour of Tears" (V), in Jones, Since 1888, 128–34.

————"Your Soul" (V), in Blackwell, 468.

Molinas Rolón, Guillermo (1892–1947). "Spring" (V), in Jones, Since 1888, 139–40.

Odena, Ernesto León. "The Death of Añá: A Guarani Legend" (S), in Inter-America, vol. 6, 1922, 124–27.

O'Leary, Juan Emiliano (1879—?). "The Savage" (V), in Jones, Since 1888, 135–37.

Pane, Ignacio A. (d. 1919). "The Paraguayan Women" (V), in Blackwell, 470–72.

Pla, Josefina (1907—). "Triptych of Rebirth in Shadow" and "Forever" (V), in Jones, Since 1888, 143–46.

Rivarola Matto, José María (1917—). "The Fate of Chipi González" (T, 3 acts). Tr. Willis K. Jones, in Poet Lore, vol. 60, 1965, 99–146.

Roa Bastos, Augusto (1917—). Son of Man (N, 1960). Tr. Rachel Caffyn. London, Gollancz, 1965. 256 pp.

Excerpts tr. David W. Foster in Books Abroad, vol. 37, 1963, 16–20.

————"The Dog and His Shadow" (S), in Américas, vol. 7, 6, June 1955, 22–25.

————"The Excavation," in Flakoll, 85–90.

————"Triptych from the Four Elements" (V), in Jones, Since 1888, 146–48.

Rodríguez Alcalá, Teresa Lamas Carísimo de (1889—?). "Paraguayan Household Traditions" (S), in Inter-America, vol. 6, 1922, 3–17.

————"Py-Chay," ibid., vol. 8, 1925, 236–40.

Romero, Elvio (1927—).   "The Guitar of the People" (V), in Jones, Since 1888, 148–49.

Sánchez Quell, Horacio (1907—).   "Praise of Seccarello St." (V). Tr. Dudley Fitts, in Fitts, 149.

Peru

Background

Arthaud, Claude, and Hébert-Stevens, François.   The Andes: Roof of America. Tr. Eric E. Smith from French. London, Thames and Hudson, 1956. xxv, 189 pp. ill.

Cossío del Pomar, Felipe.   Peruvian Colonial Art: The Cuzco School of Painting (E, *Pintura colonial: escuela cuzqueña*, 1928). Tr. Genaro Arbaiza. Mexico, Editorial Libros de México, 1964. 197 pp.

Means, Philip Ainsworth.   Ancient Civilizations of the Andes. N.Y., Scribner, 1931. 586 pp.

————Fall of the Inca Empire and the Spanish Rule in Peru: 1530–1780. N.Y. and London, Scribner, 1932. 351 pp.

Von Hagen, Victor W.   Realm of the Incas. N.Y., New Amer. Lib., 1957. 231 pp. ill., paper.

Literary Study

Aldrich, Earl Maurice.   The Modern Short Story in Peru. Madison and London, Univ. of Wisconsin Pr., 1966. ix, 212 pp.

INDIVIDUAL AUTHORS

Abril de Virero, Xavier (1905—).   Poems in Decision, vol. 1, May 1941, 52; Fitts, 373–79; West Indian Review, vol. 4, 10, Oct. 1937, 26.

Acosta, José de (1539–1616).   The Naturall and Morall Historie of the East and West Indies. Tr. Edward Grimston. London, 1604. Repr. ed. Clements R. Markham, Hakluyt Soc. Works, nos. 60–61, 1879, which repr. N.Y., Burt Franklin, 1963.
  Excerpts in Jones, Before 1888, 81–86.

Alegría, Ciro (1909—).   Ayaymama (N). Excerpt in Onís, Golden Land, 254–58.

————Broad and Alien Is the World (N, 1941). Tr. Harriet de Onís. N.Y., Farrar and Rinehart, 1941. 434 pp. Repr. Philadelphia, Pa., Dufour Eds., 1962.

————The Golden Serpent (N, 1935). Tr. Harriet de Onís. N.Y., Farrar and Rinehart, 1943. 242 pp. Repr. N.Y., New Amer. Lib., 1963, 190 pp.; repr. N.Y., Signet, 1965.

————*Los perros hambrientos* (N. 1939). Excerpt, "The Hungry Dogs," in Arciniegas, 45–51.
  Excerpt, "A Small Place in the World," in Jones, Since 1888, 199–204.

————"The Stone and the Cross" (S), in Américas, vol. 10, 9, Sept. 1958, 26–29.

————"The Wanderer" (S). Tr. Sarah Corwin, in New Mexico Quarterly, vol. 13, 1943, 443–48.

Arguedas, José Maria (1913—).   The Singing Mountaineers: Songs and Tales of the Quechua People (V). Collected by J. M. Arguedas et al., Tr. Ruth Stephan. Austin, Univ. of Texas Pr., 1957, and London, Nelson, 1958. 203 pp.

Belaúnde, Victor Andrés (1883—).   Bolívar and the Political Thought of the Spanish American Revolution. Baltimore, Md., Johns Hopkins Pr., 1938. 451 pp.

Bustamante y Ballivián, Enrique (1884–1936).   Poems in Fantasy, no. 28, 1943; in Fitts, 125.

Chocano, José Santos (1875–1934).   Spirit of the Andes (V). Tr. Edna W. Underwood. Portland, Maine, Mosher, 1955. xvi, 43 pp.

> Poems in Blackwell, 206–24; Books Abroad, vol. 5, 1931, 365–66, and vol. 9, 1933, 252; Bulletin Pan Amer. Union, vol. 27, 1918, 42; Craig, 131–32; Johnson, 108–11; Jones, Since 1888, 108–12; Mexican Life, vol. 11, 9, Sept. 1935, 31; Pan American Magazine, vol. 21, 1915, 21; vol. 28, 1919, 156; vol. 34, 1922, 23; Poetry, vol. 26, 1925, 139–42; Walsh, 672–78.

Cieza de León, Pedro de (1519–1560).   *La Crónica del Perú*: see Literature of Discovery, above.

"Concolorcorvo" (Calixto Bustamente Carlos Inca) or Alonso Carrió de la Vandera (1715–1780?).   *El Lazarillo*: A Guide for Inexperienced Travelers Between Buenos Aires and Lima, 1773 (*Lazarillo de ciegos caminantes*). Tr. Walter D. Kline. Bloomington, Indiana Univ. Pr., 1965. 315 pp.

> Excerpt in Jones, Before 1888, 90–95.

Eguren, José María (1882–1942).   Poems in Fitts, 453–58; Walsh, Catholic, 438.

García Calderón, Francisco (1883–1953).   Latin America: Its Rise and Progress (E, *Les Démocraties latines de l'Amérique*, 1912). Tr. Bernard Miall. London, T. Fisher Unwin, and N.Y., Scribner, 1913. 406 pp.

García Calderón, Ventura (1886–1959).   The White Llama (N, *La venganza del condor*, 1924). Tr. Richard Phibbs. London, Golden Cockerel Pr., 1938. 123 pp.

——————"Ancestral Sin" (S), in Clark, 912–17.

——————"Legend of Pygmalion," in Haydn, 912–14.

——————"The Pin," in Onís, Golden Land, 249–52.

Garcilaso de la Vega (1539–1616).   The Florida of the Inca. Tr. Bernard
Shipp from a French version as History of the Conquest of Florida, in his
History of Hernando de Soto and Florida. Philadelphia, Pa., Collins Printer,
1881, pp. 229–487.

> Tr. John Grier Verner and Jeannette Johnson Verner as The Florida of
> the Inca: A History of the Adelantado Hernando de Soto. Austin, Univ.
> of Texas Pr., 1951. 655 pp.

————The Royal Commentaries of Peru, in two parts. Tr. Sir Paul Rycaut
[with omissions]. London, 1688. 1019 pp.

> Tr. Harold V. Livermore (parts 1 and 2), with intro. Arnold Toynbee.
> Austin, Univ. of Texas Pr., 1966. 2 vols.
>
> Tr. (part 1) Clements R. Markham as The Royal Commentaries of the
> Incas. Hakluyt Soc. Works 41, 45: 1869–71. Repr. N.Y., Burt Franklin,
> 1963.
>
> Tr. (part 1) Maria Jolas from a French version. N.Y., Orion Pr., 1961.
> xlviii, 432 pp.
>
> Excerpts in Jones, Before 1888, 65–70.
>
> Part 1 relates the history of the Incas, part 2 the conquest.

González de Acuña, Antonio, Bishop of Caracas 1676–1682.   "Life of
St. Rose of Lima" (B, *Rosa Mística, Vida y muerte de Santa Rosa de S. María
Virgen*, 1664). Tr. Frederick W. Faber from French, in The Lives of St.
Rose of Lima, the Blessed Columba of Rieti, and of St. Juliana Falconieri.
London, Derby, 1847, pp. 1–195.

> An abridgement in Spanish of Leonardus Hansen, O.P., *Vita B. Rosae*
> (Rome, 1664). The Faber volume is one of 42 unnumbered volumes ed.
> by him under the title *The Saints and Servants of God* (1847–56).

González Prada, Manuel (1848–1918).   Poems in Flores, Anthology of
Spanish Poetry, 195–203; Hispanic Poets, 251; Johnson, 42–43; Jones,
Since 1888, 107–08.

López Albújar, Enrique (1872—?).   "Adultery" (S). Tr. Harry Kurz, in
Haydn, 919–22.

————"The Target" (S), in Andean Monthly, Sept.–Nov., 1940.

————"Ushanam Jampi" (S), in Onís, Golden Land, 238–47.

Matto de Turner, Clorinda (1854–1909).   Birds without a Nest (N, 1889). Tr. J. G. Hadson. London, Thynne, 1904. 236 pp.

Excerpts in Jones, Before 1888, 168–71.

Méndez Dorich, Rafael (1903—).   Poems in Fitts, 393–98.

Meneses, Profirio (1915—).   "The Little Dark Man" (S, 1945), in Flakoll, 11–21.

Molina, Cristóbal (d. 1585).   The Fables and Rites of the Incas. Tr. Clements R. Markham. Hakluyt Soc. Works, no. 48, 1873. xx, 220 pp. Repr. N.Y., Burt Franklin, 1963.

Monforte y Vera, Antonio (18th c.).   "The Love Elf" (T, one act, c.1725). Tr. in Jones, Before 1888, 308–16.

Moro, César ("César Quíspez Asín," 1906—).   Poems in Fitts, 381–86.

"Nine Tales and Legends."   Tr. Kate and Ángel Flores, in Ruth G. Stephan, Singing Mountaineers: Songs and Tales of the Quechua People. Austin, Univ. of Texas Pr., 1957, pp. 93–169.

Ollanta: An Ancient Ynca Drama (T, Ollantay, 1780?).   Tr. Clements R. Markham from Quechua. London, Trübner, 1871. 128 pp. Repr. in C. R. Markham, The Incas of Peru, London, Dent, and N.Y., Dutton, 1910, pp. 323–407.

Excerpts in Hills, Hispanic Studies, 48; Jones, Before 1888, 297–300; Pan American Magazine, vol. 33, 1921, 281–90.

Oquendo de Amat, Carlos (1904–1936).   Surrealistic poems in Fitts, 323–26.

Palma, Ricardo (1833–1919).   The Knight of the Cape and Thirty-seven Other Selections from the Tradiciones Peruanas. Tr. Harriet de Onís, foreword by José Rollín de la Torre Bueno y Thorne. N.Y., Knopf, 1945. 246 pp.

At least twenty translated stories from the Tradiciones Peruanas (1852–1911, 10 vols.) have appeared in magazines and anthologies: Allen,

56–58; Andean Monthly, Sept. 1938, and Nov. 1938; Brewton, 736–41; Cardwell, 557–61; Colford, 54–56; Flores GSS, 107–13; Flores SS, 106–15; Inter-America, vol. 1, 280–84; 3, 135–43; 5, 251–56; 7, 295–302; 7, 278–83; Jones, Before 1888, 172–76; LLA, 84; Onís, Golden Land, 135–45; Onís, SS, 209-13.

Poems in Blackwell, 228; Bulletin Pan American Union, vol. 62, 1938, 1214–19; Walsh, 469.

Peruvian Tales Related in One Thousand and One Hours by One of the Select Virgins of Cuzco to the Ynca of Peru (S). Tr. Samuel Humphreys from French. Dublin, G. Risk, 1734. 3 vols. Reprs. to London, 1817.

Supposed an *Arabian Nights* in Quechua, now known to be a French fabrication by Thomas Simon Guellette (1683–1766).

Polar, Juan Manuel (1863—?). "Don Quijote in Yankeeland" (N), in Inter-America, 1920–21: vol. 4, 97–105, 171–184, 243–55, 310–21; vol. 5, 44–46.

Salazar Bondy, Sebastián (1924—). "I'm Sentimental" (V), in Flakoll, 178–84.

————"The Suitcase" (T). Tr. Gregory Rabassa, in Odyssey Review, vol. 1, 1962, 191–205.

Sarmiento de Gamboa, Pedro (1532–1608). History of the Incas (H, pub. 1769). Tr. Clements R. Markham. Hakluyt Soc. Works, ser. 2, no. 22, 1907. xxii, 395 pp.

————Narrative of the Voyage to the Straits of Magellan, 1579–80. Tr. the same. Ibid., ser. 1, no. 91, 1894. xxx, 401 pp. Repr. N.Y. Burt Franklin, 1963.

Segura, Manuel Ascensio (1805–1871). "Sergeant Canuto" (T, one act, 1839). Tr. Willis K. Jones, in PSA, vol. 2, 25–46.

Valdelomar, Abraham (1888–1919). Our Children of the Sun (S, *Los hijos del sol*, 1921). Tr. Merritt Moore Thompson. Carbondale, Southern Illinois Univ. Pr., 1968. 94 pp.

————"The Good Knight Carmelo" (S), in Flores FN, 448–57; in Mexican Life, vol. 24, 12, Dec. 1948, 66–71.

Vallejo, César Abraham (1892–1938). Twenty Poems. Tr. John Knoepfle, et al. Madison, Wis., Sixties Pr., 1963. 63 pp., parallel texts.

Seven poems in Fitts, 405–27; six in West Indian Review, vol. 5, 7, July 1939, 28–32; four in Cohen, 23–27; two in Jones, Since 1888, 112–15.

Varela, Blanca (1926—). "Port Supe" (V), in Flakoll, 13.

————"A Summer's Day" (S), in Américas, vol. 40, 10, Oct. 1959, 26–28.

Vargas Llosa, Mario (1938—). The Time of the Hero (N, *La ciudad de los perros*, originally *Los impostores*, 1963). Tr. Lysander Kemp. N.Y., Grove Pr., 1966, and London, Cape, 1967. 409 pp.

Velarde, Hector (1899—). "Bull Fight in Chicago" (S), in Américas, vol. 6, 9, Sept. 1954, 25–26.

————"Father's Day" (S), in Colford, 69–76.

————"Peter the Tourist" (S), in Amigos, vol. 1, 1942, 39–43.

————"Take Back Your Wheel" (S), in Américas, vol. 9, 9, Sept. 1953, 16–17.

Philippines

Background

Kroeber, A. L. Peoples of the Philippines. N.Y., American Museum of Natural History, Handbook series, 8, 1943. 244 pp.

Zayde, Gregorio F. Philippine History and Civilization. Manila, Philippine Associated Publishers, 1939. xvi, 755 pp. (bibliog., pp. 727–39).

Bibliography

Blair, Emma Helen, and Robertson, James A. The Philippine Islands, 1493–1898. Vol. 53, Bibliography. Cleveland, Ohio, Arthur H. Clark, 1908. 433 pp.

Houston, Charles O., Jr. Philippine Bibliography: An Annotated Preliminary Bibliography of Philippine Bibliographies (Since 1900). Manila, Univ. of Manila, 1960. 69, 21 pp.

Selected Bibliography of the Philippines. Prepared by Philippine Studies Program, University of Chicago. New Haven, Conn., Human Relations Area Files, 1956. vi, 138 pp.

Collection

Casper, Leonard. New Writing from the Philippines: A Critique and Anthology. Syracuse, N.Y., Syracuse Univ. Pr., 1966. xv, 411 pp.

INDIVIDUAL AUTHORS

Arguila, Manuel Estebanillo (1911—). How My Brother Leon Brought Home a Wife, and Other Stories. Manila, Philippine Book Guild, 1940.

Laya, Juan C., and Ramirez, Emiliano. Tales Our Fathers Told. Manila, I. Wika Pub. Co., 1948. viii, 182 pp. (Philippine Folklore Series).

Povedano, Diego Lope. The Povedano Manuscript of 1578. Tr. Rebecca P. Ignacio. Chicago, Ill., Philippine Studies Program, Univ. of Chicago Department of Anthropology, 1957. 72 pp.

Reyes, Severino (1861—?). The Martyrs of the Country: Blooy (T). Tr. J. Gálvez. Manila, 19—.

————Menda (T). Tr. P. Reyes, rev. William Barrett. Manila, 19—.

————Not Wounded (*Walang Sugat*, 1898). Tr. N. M. Reyes and J. A. D. Gush, music F. Toletino. Manila, 1898.

Rizal y Mercado, José (1861–1896).   The Eagle Flight (N, *Noli me tangere*, 1886). Tr. anon. from Tagalog. N.Y., McClure, Phillips, 1900. xiv, 256 pp. Repr. 1901.

> Tr. abridged Frank E. Gannett as Friars and Filipinos. N.Y., St. James Pr., 1900. xvi, 276 pp.

> Tr. Charles Derbyshire as The Social Cancer. Manila, Philippine Education Co., and N.Y., World Book Co., 1912. lvii, 502 pp.

> Tr. F. Basa and C. M. Mellen. Manila, Oriental Commercial Co. 1933.

> Tr. León M. Guerrero as The Lost Eden. Bloomington, Indiana Univ. Pr., 1961. 406 pp. Repr. with intro. J. A. Michener, N.Y., Greenwood Books, 1968.

>> Dramatized by A. Vidal, "Meeting in the Town Hall" (T) and "Souls in Torment" (T), in J. Edades, Short Plays from the Philippines, Manila, 1940.

————Letter to the Young Women of Malolos (E), in Tagalog, Spanish, and English. Manila, Bureau of Printing, 1932.

> Tr. Charles Derbyshire as Mariang Markeling. Manila, 1916.

> Tr. F. Basa and C. M. Mellen with preceding entry.

> Tr. as "A Filipino Picnic" in Tales from the Spanish, vol. 8.

————The Reign of Green (N, *El filibusterismo*, 1891). Tr. Charles Derbyshire. Manila, Philippine Education Co., 1912. xii, 367 pp.

> Tr. León M. Guerrero as The Subversive. Bloomington, Indiana Univ. Pr., 1962. 299 pp.

————Rizal's Political Writings: Nation Building, Race Differences, Basic Principles of Good Government. Ed. Austin Craig. Manila, Oriental Commercial Co., 1938. 445 pp.

————*El Último Adiós.* Tr. Godofredo Jacinto, in José P. Bantug, *Rizal:
Scholar and Scientist.* Manila, Bureau of Health, 1946. 38 pp.

See Austin Craig, *Rizal's Life and Minor Writings* (Manila, Philippine Education Co., 1927, xiii, 339 pp.); and his *Lineage, Life, and Labors of José Rizal,
Philippine Patriot* (ibid., 1913, xv, 287 pp.).

Puerto Rico

Literary Study

Babín, María Teresa. "Literary Letter from Puerto Rico," in Books
Abroad, vol. 32, 1958, 255–56.

INDIVIDUAL AUTHORS

Blanco, Tomás (1900—). The Child's Gift: A Twelfth Night Tale (S).
Tr. Harriet de Onís. San Juan, Pan American Book Co., 1954. Parallel
texts.
    Excerpt in Américas, vol. 7, 12, Dec. 1955, 22–25.

Cajigas, Luis Germán. "The Chapel" (S), in Mexican Life, vol. 32, 10,
Oct. 1956, 10.

————"Don Alejo" (S), ibid., vol. 32, 9, Sept. 1956, 10.

Cedilla, Carmen Alicia (1908—). Poems in Fitts, 503–06; Poetry, vol. 62,
1943, 65.

Coll y Toste, Cayetano (1850—?). "The Pirate's Treasure" (S, from
Leyendas puertorriqueñas, 1924), in Colford, 189–203.

Díaz Alfaro, Abelardo (1917—). "Santa Cló Comes to La Cuchilla" (S),
in Colford, 206–10.

Flores, Ángel (1900—). "The Playboy of Spain" (S), in Mexican Life, vol. 9, 1, Jan. 1933, 25–26, 62.

Gautier Benítez, José (1851–1880). "Puerto Rico" (V), in Blackwell, 516–20; in West Indian Review, vol. 4, 8, Aug. 1938, 28.

González, José Luis (1926—). "There's A Little Negro at the Bottom of the Caño" (S). Tr. Paul Blackburn, in New World Writing, vol. 14, 1958, 125–28.

Labarthe, Pedro Juan (1909—). Mary Smith (N). Tr. the author. N.Y., Whittier Books, 1958. 311 pp.

————"The Broken Urn" (V). Tr. Marshall Nunn, in West Indian Review, vol. 6, 7, July 1940, 37.

Laguerre, Enrique A. (1906—). The Labyrinth (N, 1959). Tr. William Rose. N.Y., Las Americas Pub. Co., 1960. 275 pp.

Lee de Muñoz Marín, Muna (Muna Lee, 1895—). "Symphony in White" (V), in Walsh, 769–71.

Llorens Torres, Luis (1878–1944). Poems in Jones, Since 1888, 78–80; Poetry, vol. 26, 1925, 146; West Indian Review, vol. 4, 11, Nov. 1937, 35; and vol. 5, 3, Mar. 1938, 20; and vol. 6, 4, Apr. 1939, 30.

Marqués, René (1919—). "Give Us This Day" (S). Tr. Catherine Randolph, in Flakoll, 158–70.

————"The House of the Setting Sun" (T, 3 acts, *Purificación en la calle de Cristo*, 1958). Tr. Willis K. Jones, in Poet Lore, vol. 59, 1965, 99–131. Excerpt in Jones, Since 1888, 459–64.

Mier, Calixto H. de. "Puerto Rican Sketches" (S), in Américas, vol. 8, 6, June 1956, 22–24.

Palés Matos, Luis (1898–1952). Poems in American Prefaces, vol. 7, 1941–42, 155–56; Fitts, 185–97; Jones, Since 1888, 80–82; Poetry, vol. 26, 1925, 145–46, and vol. 62, 1943, 79; Walsh, Catholic; West Indian Review, vol. 6, 4, Apr. 1940, 39.

Tapia y Rivera, Alejandro (1826–1882).   Enardo and Rosael, an Allegorical Novel (part of *Azucena*, N, 1872). Tr. Alejandro Tapia, Jr., et al. N.Y., Philosophical Lib., 1952. 56 pp.

El Salvador

Background

Osborne, Lilly de Jongh.   Four Keys to El Salvador. N.Y., Funk and Wagnalls, 1956. 221 pp.

INDIVIDUAL AUTHORS

Ambrogi, Arturo (1878–1936).   "The Shade of the Wild Fig Tree" (S), in Literature in Latin America. Pan American Union, 1950, 50–51.

Arévalo, Adrián M. (1870—?).   "The Earrings" (S, from *El 63, episodios nacionales*, 1916), in Inter-America, vol. 1, 1918, 76–77.

García-Escobar, Rafael.   Poems. Tr. Paula L. Sage. St. Louis, 1922. (Not located.)
  The collected poems were later published as *Rosas de América* (1929).

Gavidia, Francisco (1863–1955).   "The Return of the Hero" (S), in Amigos, vol. 1, 1942, 56–61.

González y Contreras, Gilberto (1904—).   Two poems in Fitts, 176–77.

Guerra, Dora (1925—).   "Tidings of Your Death" (V), in Flakoll, 130–35.

"Lars, Claudia" (Carmen Brannon Beers de Samoya Chinchilla, 1899—).
  Poems in Fitts, 178–81; Jones, Since 1888, 62–64.

Lindo, Hugo (1917—). "Sleeping in the Salt" (V), in Flakoll, 194–96.

Ramírez Peña, Abraham. "The Sad Reality" (S), in Inter-America, vol. 4, 1921, 383–84.

Salazar Arrué, Salvador (1899—). "The Pot of Gold" (S), in Onís, Golden Land, 314–17.

Uruguay

Background

Fitzgibbon, Russell H. Uruguay: Portrait of a Democracy. London, George Allen, and New Brunswick, N.J., Rutgers Univ. Pr., 1954. 301 pp.

Hudson, W. H. The Purple Land That England Lost. London, Sampson Low, 1885. 2 vols. Many reprs. as The Purple Land, to Penguin, 1935.

Pendle, George. Uruguay. London, Royal Institute of International Affairs, and N.Y., Oxford Univ. Pr., 1957. 159 pp.

INDIVIDUAL AUTHORS

Acevedo Díaz, Eduardo (1851–1924). "The Prairie Fire" (excerpt from Soledad, N, 1894), in Jones, Since 1888, 233–35.

Agustini, Delmira (1886–1914). Five poems in Johnson, 140–49.

Amorím, Enrique (1900–1960). The Horse and His Shadow (N, 1941). Tr. Richard O'Connell and James G. Lujan. N.Y., Scribner, 1943. 252 pp.

————"Metamorphosis" (S). Tr. H. B. Macmillan, in Tomorrow, vol. 4, 3, Nov. 1944, 65–67.

————"The Photographs," in Mexican Life, vol. 19, 7, July 1943, 11–12.

Benedetti, Mario (1920—). "The Budget" (S). Tr. Gerald Brown, in Franco, 27–41.

————"Gloria's Saturday" (S), in Flakoll, 121–27.

————"The Iriartes" (S). Tr. Jean Franco, in Cohen, 143–49.

Bernárdez, Manuel (1867—?). "Paid in Full" (S), in Onís, Golden Land, 179–92.

Figueira, Gastón (1905—). Three Songs of Gastón Figueira. Montevideo, 1940.

————Two Songs of Gastón Figueira. Montevideo, 1942.

Other poems in Bulletin Pan American Union, vol. 77, 1943, 198; Jones, Since 1888, 179–84; Poet Lore, vol. 47, 1941, 65–75, and vol. 51, 1945, 75; Poetry, vol. 62, 1943, 83; West Indian Review, vol. 4, 8, Aug. 1939, 29, and vol. 6, 3, Mar. 1940, 36–40.

Gunther, Ernesto. "The Duel" (S), in Américas, vol. 8, 9, Sept. 1956, 31–32.

Herrera y Reissig, Julio (1875–1910). Poems in Blackwell, 444–45; Bulletin Pan American Union, vol. 78, 1944, 102–03; Craig, 126–29; Decision, vol. 1, 1941, 46; Johnson, 112–13; Jones, Since 1888, 167–70; Poetry, vol. 26, 1925, 145–50; Walsh, 683–86; Walsh, Catholic, 396.

Ibáñez, Roberto (1907—). "Elegy for the Drowned Men Who Return" (V), in Fitts, 541.

Ibarbourou, Juana de (1895—). "A Good Death" (S), in Américas, vol. 1, 2, Feb. 1959, 22–24.

————"Military Police," in Amigos, vol. 1, Jan. 1942, 35–36.

Poems in Blackwell, 448–49; Bulletin Pan American Union, July 1925, and Feb. 1928; Fitts, 479–93; Hispanic Poets, 261–64; Inter-America, vol. 5,

1921, 107; Johnson, 156–61; Jones, Since 1888, 170–78; Poetry, vol. 26, 1925, 151–52.

Magariños Cervantes, Alejandro (1825–1893). "Glory" (V), in Green, 314–23.

Martínez Moreno, Carlos (1917—). "The Aborigines" (S). Tr. David Rubin, in Prize Stories, 65–105 (second prize).

———"The Pigeon" (S). Tr. Giovanni Pontieri, in Franco, 135–65.

Morosoli, Juan José (1899—). "Professional Mourner" (S). Tr. Willis K. Jones, in New Mexico Quarterly, vol. 15, 1945, 276–79.

Nieto, Asdrúbal. "Padre José, Cowboy Priest," in Amigos, vol. 1, 4, Apr. 1942, 19–22.

Onetti, Juan Carlos (1909—). The Shipyard. Tr. Rachel Caffyn. N.Y., Scribner, 1968. 190 pp.

———"Dreaded Hell" (S). Tr. Jean Franco, in Cohen, 34–48.

———"Jacob and the Other" (S). Tr. Izaak A. Langnas, in Prize Stories, 319–59.

———"Welcome, Bob" (S). Tr. Donald L. Shaw, in Franco, 83–101.

Oribe, Emilio (1893—). "Music" (V), in Hispanic Poets, 258.

Peña Martín, Cecilio. "The Denied Tear" (T). Tr. Morris R. Steinberg, in Poetry and Drama Magazine, vol. 2, 1959, 4–15, parallel texts.

Pérez Petit, Victor (1871–1946). "Moonlight Sonata" (T, one act, *Claro de Luna*, 1906). Tr. Willis K. Jones and Carlos Escudero, in Poet Lore, vol. 51, 1945, 353–67.

Quiroga, Carlos Buenaventura (1890—). "An Inca Legend" and "Llastay's Response" (S), in Inter-America, vol. 8, 1925, 467–73.

Quiroga, Horacio (1878–1937).   South American Jungle Tales (*Cuentos de la selva*, 1918). Tr. Arthur Livingston. N.Y., Duffield, 1922, and London, Methuen, 1923. 163 pp. Repr. N.Y., Dodd Mead, 1940, 1950.

————"The Contract Workers" (S), in Colford, 108–17.

————"The Fatherland." Tr. Howard Young, in Onís, SS, 131–41.

————"The Flamingos' Stockings" and "The Son," in Jones, Since 1888, 302–09.

————"The Fugitives," in Flores FN, 398–408; and in Mexican Life, vol. 25, 6, June 1949, 11–12, 60–68.

————"The Return of the Anaconda," in Frank, 239–69.

————"The Roof," in Flores, SS, 178–205.

————"The Son." Tr. Rachel Loughridge, in New Mexico Quarterly, vol. 16, 1946, 14–18.

————"Three Letters . . . and a Footnote." Tr. Harry Kurz, in Haydn, 934–37.

Reyles, Carlos (1868–1938).   Castanets (N, *El embrujo de Sevilla*, 1922). Tr. Jacques LeClercq. N.Y., Longmans, 1929. 297 pp.

Rodó, José Enrique (1872–1917).   Ariel (P, 1900). Tr. F. J. Stimson. Boston, Mass., Houghton Mifflin, 1922. xxii, 150 pp.

Excerpts in Allen, 66–70; Jones, Since 1888, 326–30; Van Doren, 618–23.

————The Motives of Proteus (P, 1909). Tr. Angel Flores, intro. Havelock Ellis. N.Y., Brentano, 1928, and London, Allen, 1929. xxvi, 378 pp.

————"Bolívar" (V), in Bulletin Pan American Union, vol. 64, 1930, 1390–1406.

————"Christ on Horseback" (S), in Alhambra, June 1929, 12.

————"Dialogues between Bronze and Marbles," in Inter-America, vol. 1, 1918, 197–201.

————"Montalvo," in Arciniegas, 355–65.

————"A Uruguayan's View," in Américas, vol. 3, 4, Apr. 1951, 42–44.

Sánchez, Florencio (1875–1910).   Representative Plays of Florencio Sánchez. Tr. Willis Knapp Jones. Washington, D.C., Pan American Union, 1961. 326 pp.
  Eleven plays from Obras (1902–09).

————"The Foreign Girl" (T, La gringa, 1904). Tr. Alfred Coester, in PSA, vol. 1, 1–46.
  Excerpt in Jones, Since 1888, 380–92.

————"Midsummer Day Parents" (T), in PSA, vol. 2.

————"Los Muertos." Tr. F. B. Luquiens, in Yale Review, vol. 17, 1928, 551–52.

Shroeder, Agustina (1917—).   Mother of Fair Love (N). Tr. Virginia Kirtland. Milwaukee, Wis., Bruce Pub. Co., 1957. 195 pp.

Silva Valdés, Fernán (1887—).   "A Devilish Night" (S), in Américas, vol. 8, 8, Aug. 1956, 19–22.

————"The Gaucho Troubadour" (V), in Jones, Since 1888, 176–79.

Other poems in Bulletin Pan American Union, vol. 68; Hispanic Poets, 256; Poet Lore, vol. 47, 1941.

Vasseur, Alvaro Armando ("Américo Llano," 1878—?).   "The Corsair" (V), in Mexican Life, vol. 10, 1, Jan. 1934, 12.

Viana, Javier de (1868–1926).   "Guri" (S), in Onís, Golden Land, 163–78.

————"The Horse Breaker" (S), in Colford, 97–105.

Vilarino, Idea (1920—).   "To Pass By" (V), in Flakoll, 175–77.

Zorrilla de San Martín, José (1855–1931). *Tabaré* (V, 1886, rev. 1918). Tr. R. W. Huntington. Buenos Aires, 1934. 174 pp.

Tr. Walter Owen. Washington, D.C., Pan American Union, 1956. 366 pp.

Excerpts in Jones, Before 1888, 279–83.

Other poems in Blackwell, 444; Bulletin Pan American Union, Jan. 1926; and Poor.

Zum Felde, Alberto (1888—). "Contemporary Uruguayan Poetry," in Inter-America, vol. 9, 1925, 62–84.

————"José Enrique Rodo: His Place among the Thinkers of America," in Inter-America, vol. 7, 1924, 261–74.

Venezuela

Background

Morón, Guillermo. History of Venezuela. Tr. John Street. London, Allen and Unwin, 1964. 268 pp.

Literary Study

Ratcliff, Dillwyn F. Venezuelan Prose Fiction. N.Y., Instituto de las Españas, 1933. 286 pp.

INDIVIDUAL AUTHORS

Bello, Andrés (1781–1865). Poems in Blackwell, 438–40; Jones, Before 1888, 210–13; Walsh, 389–94.

Blanco, Andrés Eloy (1897–1955). "The Glory of Mamporal" (S). Tr. Miriam Blanco Fombona, in Life and Letters Today, vol. 54, 1947, 150–56.

Blanco Fombona, Rufino (1874–1944).   The Man of Gold (N, 1916). Tr. Isaac Goldberg. N.Y., Brentano, 1920. 319 pp.
   Excerpts, "Redeemers of the Fatherland," in Jones, Since 1888, 276–80.

————"Creole Democracy" (S), in Clark, 918–22; also in Isaac Goldberg, Studies in Spanish American Literature (N.Y., 1920).

   Poems in Blackwell, 428–36; Bulletin Pan American Union, July 1925; Hispanic Poets, 263; Inter-America, vol. 7, 1924, 534–39; Pan American Magazine, vol. 26, 1918, 108; Poetry, vol. 26, 1925, 153–54.

Bolívar, Simón (1783–1830).   Selected Writings. Compiled Vicente Lecuna, ed. Harold A. Bierck, tr. Lewis Bertrand. N.Y., Colonial Pr., 1951 (2d ed.). lii, xiii, 822 pp.

————Carta de Jamaica: The Jamaica Letter: Lettre à un habitant de la Jamaïque. Caracas, Ediciones del Ministerio de Educación, 1965. 112 pp. trilingual.
   The Jamaica Letter, together with The Oath, are tr. in Jones, Before 1888, 95–100.

————Project of the Constitution for the Republic of Bolivia, with an Address of the Liberator. Tr. anon. London, W. Wilson, 1826. 40 pp.

————Speech at the Installation of the Congress of Venezuela. Tr. anon. Angostura, A. Roderick, 1819. 26 pp.

   Tr. anon. London, G. Young, 1819. 31 pp.

   Tr. Francisco Javier Yánes. Washington, D.C., B. S. Adams, 1919. 39 pp.

   Cf. V. A. Belaúnde, *Bolívar and the Political Thought of the Spanish American Revolution* (Baltimore, Md., Johns Hopkins Pr., and London, Oxford Univ. Pr., 1938, xxiv, 451 pp.); Salvador de Madariaga, *Bolívar* (London, Hollis and Carter, 1952, xix, 711 pp.) and Felipe Larrázabal and Carraciolo Parra-Pérez, below. Cf. also *Bibliography of the Liberator Simón Bolívar* (Pan American Union, Columbus Memorial Library, Bibliographic Series 1, rev. 1933, pp. 32–35).

Fabbiani Ruiz, José (1911—).   *"Agua Salada (Guaritoto)"* (S). Tr. E. W. Underwood, in West Indian Review, vol. 6, 4, Apr. 1940, 23–26.

————"The Day the President Died" (S). Tr. Lloyd Mallan, in Tomorrow, vol. 11, 7, Mar. 1943, 7–10; and in Mexican Life, vol. 19, 6, June 1943, 11–12, 57–60.

Fombona-Pachano, Jacinto (1901–1951). Poems in American Prefaces, vol. 7, 1941–42, 151; Fantasy, no. 26, 1942, 69–70, and no. 27, 1943, 69; Fitts, 269–76; Jones, Since 1888, 100–03; West Indian Review, vol. 5, 4, Apr. 1939, 31.

Gallegos, Rómulo (1884—). *Doña Bárbara* (N, 1929). Tr. Robert Malloy. N.Y., Cape and Smith, 1931. 440 pp. Repr. Gloucester, Mass., Peter Smith, 1948.
   Excerpts in Jones, Since 1888, 217–27.

————"A Man of Character" (S). Tr. Joan MacLean, in Onís, SS, 240–47.

————"Peace in the Mountain," in New World Writing, vol. 14, 1958, 143–48.

————"Poor Nigger," in Arciniegas, 467–80; and in Onís, Golden Land, 280–91.

————"The Spectre of La Barqueraña," in Life and Letters Today, vol. 54, 1947, 134–45.

Gramcko, Ida (1925—). "Dream" (V), in Flakoll, 197–99.

Larrazábal, Felipe. The Life of Simón Bolívar, Liberator of Colombia and Peru, Father and Founder of Bolivia (H). Tr. anon. N.Y., American News Co., 1866. vol. 1, viii, 410 pp. (no more published).

López Contreras, Eleázar (1883—?). Synopsis of the Military Life of Sucre (B, 1930). Tr. Kate Brown Shroeter. N.Y., Bolivarian Society of the U.S., 1942. 64 pp.

Lozano, Abigaíl (1821–1866). Poems in Green, 342–49; and in Poor.

Marquez Salas, Antonio (1919—). "Like God" (S), in Flakoll, 47–59.

Mata, Andrés A. ("Adán Marset," 1870–1931). "Soul and Landscape" (V), in Pan American Magazine, vol. 41, 1928, 154; and in Poetry, vol. 26, 1925, 154.

Meneses, Guillermo (1911—). "Moon" (S), in West Indian Review, vol. 5, May–June 1939 [from *Tres cuentos venezolanos*, 1938].

—————The Sloop "Isabel" Arrived This Evening (N, 1934), in Flores FN, 283–302.

Nogales, Rafael de (1879—?). Four Years beneath the Crescent (B, 1924). Tr. Muna Lee. N.Y., Scribner, 1926. 416 pp.

Otero Silva, Miguel (1908—). Poems in Fantasy, no. 26 (1942), 54; Fitts, 283–86; The Nation, vol. 153, Dec. 27, 1941, 671; West Indian Review, vol. 5, 4, Apr. 1939, 31.

Padrón, Julián (1910–1954). "Summer Fires" (excerpt from *La Guaricha*, N, 1934), in Bulletin Pan American Union, vol. 78, 1944, 104–05; in Mexican Life, vol. 20, 12, Dec. 1944, 15–16; in LLA, 94–96.

Parra-Pérez, Caracciolo (1888—). Bolívar: A Contribution to the Study of the Political Ideas (H). Tr. N. A. N. Cleven. Paris, Excelsior, 1929, and Pittsburgh, Pa., Pittsburgh Printing Co., 1930. 198 pp.

Parra Sanojo, Ana Teresa ("Teresa de la Parra," 1895–1936). Mamá Blanca's Souvenirs (B, Paris 1929). Tr. Harriet de Onís. Washington, D.C., Pan American Union, 1959. xix, 129 pp.

Excerpts in Bulletin Pan American Union, vol. 68, 1934, 234–36.

Picón-Salas, Mariano (1901–1965). "The Back Yard and the Geography of the Air" (S, *Viaje al amanecer*, 1943), in Onís, Golden Land, 298–302.

—————A Cultural History of Spanish America: From Conquest to Independence (H, *De la conquista a la independencia*, 1944). Tr. Irving A. Leonard. Berkeley, Univ. of California Pr., 1962. 192 pp. Repr. 1963, paper.

—————The Ignoble Savage (E, *Los malos salvajes*). Tr. Herbert Weinstock. N.Y., Knopf, 1965. xiv, 167 pp.

Pimentel Coronel, Ramón (1872?–1909). "Jesus" (V), in Walsh, 648–51 ; Walsh, Catholic, 377–80.

Prato, Luis Felipe. Windstorm: A Novel of the Venezuelan Andes. Tr. Hugh Jencks. N.Y., Las Americas Pub. Co., 1961. 221 pp.

Sola, Otto d' (1912—). Two poems in Fitts, 297–300.

Tejara, Victorino. "The Santagram" (S), in Américas, vol. 8, 12, Dec. 1956, 24–25.

Uslar Pietri, Arturo (1906—). The Red Lances (N, 1931). Tr. Harriet de Onís. N.Y., Knopf, 1963. 233 pp.

————"Ignis fatuus" (S), in Onís, Golden Land, 292–97.

————"Rain" (S), in Cardwell, 598–610; in Flores FN, 435–47; in Mexican Life, vol. 25, 1, Jan. 1949, 58–66.

————"The Voice" (S), in Colford, 118–26.

Venegas Filardo, Pascual (1911—). "Journey into Endless Night" (V), in West Indian Review, vol. 5, 4, Apr. 1939, 29.

INDEX OF TRANSLATED AUTHORS
AND ANONYMOUS WORKS

ITALICIZED PAGE NUMBERS INDICATE THE MAIN ENTRY